EIGHTH EDITION

ADVERTISING

ITS ROLE IN MODERN MARKETING

THE DRYDEN PRESS SERIES IN MARKETING

Assael
Marketing: Principles and Strategy
Second Edition

Bateson
Managing Services Marketing:
Text and Readings
Second Edition

Blackwell, Blackwell, and Talarzyk
Contemporary Cases in Consumer
Behavior
Fourth Edition

Boone and Kurtz
Contemporary Marketing
Seventh Edition

Churchill
Basic Marketing Research
Second Edition

Churchill
Marketing Research: Methodological
Foundations
Fifth Edition

Czinkota and Ronkainen
International Marketing
Third Edition

Czinkota and Ronkainen
International Marketing Strategy:
Environmental Assessment and
Entry Strategies

Dickson
Marketing Management

Krugman, Reid, Dunn, and Barban
Advertising: Its Role in Modern
Marketing
Eighth Edition

Engel, Blackwell, and Miniard
Consumer Behavior
Seventh Edition

Futrell
Sales Management
Third Edition

Ghosh
Retail Management
Second Edition

Hassan and Blackwell
Global Marketing: Managerial
Dimensions and Cases

Hutt and Speh
Business Marketing Management:
A Strategic View of Industrial and
Organization Markets
Fourth Edition

Ingram and LaForge
Sales Management:
Analysis and Decision Making
Second Edition

Kurtz and Boone
Marketing
Third Edition

Murphy and Cunningham
Advertising and Marketing
Communications Management:
Cases and Applications

Oberhaus, Ratliffe, and Stauble
Professional Selling:
A Relationship Process

Park and Zaltman
Marketing Management

Patti and Frazer
Advertising: A Decision-Making
Approach

Rachman
Marketing Today
Third Edition

Rogers, Gamans, and Grassi
Retailing: New Perspectives
Second Edition

Rosenbloom
Marketing Channels:
A Management View
Fourth Edition

Schellinck and Maddox
Marketing Research:
A Computer-Assisted Approach

Schnaars
MICROSIM
Marketing simulation available for
IBM PC and Apple

Sellars
Role Playing: The Principles of
Selling
Second Edition

Shimp
Promotion Management and
Marketing Communications
Third Edition

Sisodia and Mentzer
Marketing Decision Systems:
Transformation Through Information
Technology

Talarzyk
Cases and Exercises in Marketing

Terpstra and Sarathy
International Marketing
Sixth Edition

Tootelian and Gaedeke
Cases and Classics in Marketing
Management

Weitz and Wensley
Readings in Strategic Marketing
Analysis, Planning, and
Implementation

Zikmund
Exploring Marketing Research
Fifth Edition

EIGHTH EDITION

ADVERTISING
ITS ROLE IN MODERN MARKETING

DEAN M. KRUGMAN
THE UNIVERSITY OF GEORGIA

LEONARD N. REID
THE UNIVERSITY OF GEORGIA

S. WATSON DUNN
Professor Emeritus
UNIVERSITY OF MISSOURI–COLUMBIA

ARNOLD M. BARBAN
THE UNIVERSITY OF ALABAMA

THE DRYDEN PRESS
Harcourt Brace College Publishers

Fort Worth   Philadelphia   San Diego   New York   Orlando   Austin   San Antonio
Toronto   Montreal   London   Sydney   Tokyo

Publisher   Liz Widdicombe
Acquisitions Editor   Lyn Keeney Hastert
Developmental Editor   R. Paul Stewart
Project Editor   Jim Patterson
Production Manager   Alison Howell
Designer   Brian Salisbury
Photo Permissions Editor   Sandra Lord
Literary Permissions Editor   Sheila Shutter
Copy Editor   Dee Salisbury
Indexer   Sylvia Coates
Compositor   Monotype
Text Type   Times Roman
Cover Image   Illustration copyright © 1993 Rick Smith

Address for Editorial Correspondence
The Dryden Press, 301 Commerce Street, Suite 3700, Fort Worth, TX 76102

Address for Orders
The Dryden Press, 6277 Sea Harbor Drive, Orlando, FL 32887
1-800-782-4479, or 1-800-433-0001 (in Florida)

ISBN: 0-03-076752-0

Library of Congress Catalogue Number. 92-83855

Printed in the United States of America

3 4 5 6 7 8 9 0 1 2   032   9 8 7 6 5 4 3 2 1

The Dryden Press
Harcourt Brace College Publishers

To our wives and children,
for their generous understanding
of the time demand involved
in writing and editing this book.

Dean M. Krugman (Ph.D., M.S., University of Illinois; B.S., Southern Illinois University) is a Professor in the Department of Advertising and Public Relations at The University of Georgia. He also holds a joint appointment in the Marketing Department. Before coming to Georgia he was an Associate Professor in the Advertising Department at Michigan State University and an Assistant Professor of Marketing at Illinois State University. He has also served as Director of Graduate Studies in the College of Journalism and Mass Communication at The University of Georgia.

Dr. Krugman received awards for superior teaching and was cited as an outstanding teacher at UGA in 1989 and 1993. In 1991, graduate students in the college presented him with a separate award for his contribution to the instructional program. He also serves on the annual Freedom Forum faculty for teachers in advertising held at the University of North Carolina. In this capacity, he helps train new university teachers. He is widely published in a number of scholarly journals, including *Journal of Advertising, Journal of Advertising Research, Journal of Broadcasting and Electronic Media, Journalism Quarterly, Current Issues and Research in Advertising,* and the *Journal of the American Medical Association.* He is a member of the editorial board of the *Journal of Advertising* and the *Journal of the Broadcasting and Electronic Media.*

Dr. Krugman is also an active industry consultant in the area of advertising management and research. He has served on the staff of Ross Advertising as a management and research consultant. He regularly conducts seminars and research projects for a number of major U.S. corporations.

Leonard N. Reid (Ph.D., M.S., University of Illinois; B.S., Virginia Commonwealth University) is Professor of Advertising and Head of the Department of Advertising and Public Relations at The University of Georgia. Dr. Reid is past editor of the *Journal of Advertising* and a member of the editorial review boards of *Current Issues and Research in Advertising* and the *Journal of Advertising.* His research has appeared in the leading marketing and advertising journals, including the *Journal of Advertising, Journal of Advertising Research, Journal of Business Research, Journal of Marketing, Journal of Consumer Research, Current Issues and Research in Advertising, Communication Research, Journal of Communication, Journalism Quarterly, Journal of Broadcasting and the Electronic Media, Journal of Public Policy and Marketing,* and *Industrial Marketing Management.*

Dr. Reid has served as consultant to major advertising agencies and advertisers, including Henderson Advertising, Inc., BBDO/Atlanta, Caterpillar Tractor Company, Standard Telephone Company, Major League Baseball, Brown-Forman Corporation, Hickson Corporation, Sylvan Learning Centers, and RJR-McDonald/Canada. Dr. Reid has held faculty positions at the University of Illinois, Arizona State University, and Michigan State University. At Michigan State, he received the Teacher-Scholar Award for excellence in teaching, and at the University of Georgia he received a certificate for superior teaching.

In 1993, Dr. Reid received the Outstanding Contribution to Research Award, given by the American Academy of Advertising to individuals who have made sustained and systematic contributions to advertising research.

S. Watson Dunn (Ph.D., University of Illinois; M.B.A. and A.B., Harvard University), Professor Emeritus of Marketing, University of Missouri-Columbia, was dean of the College of Business and Public Administration and Professor of Marketing and Advertising at that university. He also taught at the University of Illinois at

Urbana-Champaign, where he was head of the Department of Advertising, and at the Universities of Wisconsin, Pittsburgh, and Western Ontario. He has been a Fulbright Lecturer in France; Gannett Distinguished Visiting Professor, University of Florida; Newhouse Distinguished Visiting Professor, Syracuse University; Visiting Professor, University of Hawaii; and Distinguished Visiting Professor, George Washington University. In 1988 he was named Distinguished Advertising Educator by the American Advertising Federation.

Dr. Dunn has given invited lectures in many countries around the world. He has supervised research in Egypt, France, and England as well as in the United States. He has served as consultant for Marsteller Inc., Burson-Marsteller, Leo Burnett Company, Young & Rubicam, Southwestern Bell, Pacific Telephone and Telegraph, and the U.S. Army.

He is a Fellow and former president of the American Academy of Advertising; also former president of the Madison (Wisconsin) and Central Illinois chapters of the American Marketing Association. He has written or edited five books in addition to the earlier editions of this book, and many articles in trade and professional magazines. He is listed in *Who's Who in America, Who's Who in the Midwest,* and *Who's Who in Advertising.* Dr. Dunn has served on the Advisory Board of Smithsonian Institution's Center for Advertising History, the Advisory Board for Sticknell Advertising Internship, and the Council of Judges of the Advertising Hall of Fame.

Arnold M. Barban (Ph.D., M.B.A., B.B.A., The University of Texas at Austin) is Professor of Advertising in the Department of Advertising and Public Relations, The University of Alabama. He has been a member of the Alabama faculty since 1987, and currently is Chair of the department. Previously, he was Professor of Advertising, and Research Professor in the Institute of Communications Research, at the University of Illinois at Urbana-Champaign (1964–83). He served as Head of the Department of Advertising from 1977 to 1983. From 1983 to 1987 he was the Jesse H. Jones Centennial Professor of Communication at The University of Texas at Austin.

Dr. Barban has co-authored five books in the field of advertising, including *Advertising Media: Strategy & Tactics* (Brown & Benchmark, 1992), *Advertising Media Sourcebook,* third edition (NTC Business Books, 1989), *Essentials of Media Planning,* third edition (NTC Business Books, 1993), and previous editions of Advertising: Its Role in Modern Marketing (Dryden Press). His published research deals primarily with the areas of consumer behavior and advertising media, and has appeared in such journals as *Journal of Marketing Research, Journal of Business, Journalism Quarterly, Journal of Applied Psychology,* and *Journal of Advertising.*

He served as President of the American Academy of Advertising in 1981–82 and was selected by that organization in 1986 as a Fellow. Dr. Barban is on the editorial review boards of the *Journal of Current Issues and Research in Advertising* and the *Journal of Advertising.* He is listed in *American Men and Women of Science (Social and Behavioral Sciences)* and *Who's Who in America.* He served four years as a member of the Council of Judges of the Advertising Hall of Fame. Dr. Barban has been a consultant to many advertisers, advertising agencies, and media organizations, as well as the Department of Defense.

PREFACE

Few, if any fields of business are as sensitive to environmental change as advertising. When practicing advertising, advertisers and their representatives must constantly watch and quickly react to myriad shifting conditions, including changes in consumer taste and customs, competitive marketing strategies, the introduction of new media and information technologies, and constantly shifting regulatory rules and guidelines.

Our objective in this eighth edition of *Advertising: Its Role in Modern Marketing* is to provide students with up-to-date and relevant information on the ever-changing world of advertising. The text, and the product of the four authors' years of teaching experience, is written to provide students—whether they be communication majors, business majors, or liberal arts students—with a foundation for understanding the enduring features of advertising theory and practice and to introduce them to the most contemporary advertising concepts and practices. The primary goal of the 8th edition, like each edition before it, is simple, yet powerful—to blend traditional thought on advertising with modern innovation.

Several significant changes and innovations are offered in this edition.

Significant Changes and Improvements

The text has undergone a substantial reorganization. This edition is organized around the Advertising Planning model shown in Chapter 1 and at the beginning of each chapter. This provides an organizational framework to guide students through the text. Part 1 sets the stage for advertising activities by describing the nature of advertising's environments. Part 2 details the strategic components of planning an advertising campaign. This section is followed by an appendix containing a sample media plan. Accordingly, Part Three looks at tactical issues in campaign planning. After exploring creative tactics, a real-life advertising campaign demonstrates how all aspects of advertising are coordinated. Part Four addresses topics of special interest and wide-reaching implications such as sales promotions, public relations, retail, and business-to-business advertising.

Previously strategic planning research and effectiveness research were set in different chapters. In this edition, the two topics have been combined into a single chapter. This brings the book down to 21 chapters which helps reach the goal of a more realistic amount of material to cover in a single semester or quarter.

Advertising research findings have been updated and additional behavioral science theory has been integrated in Chapters 8, 9, 10, and 11.

Descriptions of the new media and their role in advertising planning have been incorporated into Chapter 12.

Updated materials on voluntary and legal controls and their application to advertising appear in Chapters 3, 4, and 5.

Globalizing the text, international issues and examples are cited in most all chapters. Chapter 21 recaps these issues with a detailed look at the current state of global advertising planning and strategies.

New Features/ Innovations

Special sections titled Future Trends have been added to chapters throughout the book where applicable. These trends reflect what is on the horizon for advertising planners and strategists.

"Ad Insights," which are special sections in every chapter, show pertinent examples of advertising at work. These insights range from short case histories and success stories to important areas of advertising intelligence.

The case history of Chicago's Shedd Aquarium ties together the media planning found in Part 2. The award winning Longhorn Steaks case history brings to life many of the principles discussed in Parts 2 and 3. The case won "overall best of show" for creativity at the national ADDY awards. These two subjects were chosen because they reflect many of the most up-to-date advertising practices.

Special treatment of how advertising falls into integrated marketing communications planning is found in Chapter 7. The Sales Promotion portion of Chapter 19 has been expanded greatly. Both of these additions are geared to show advertising's crucial role in marketing communication.

Ancillaries

The text is accompanied by an expanded package of materials developed to assist instructors in their teaching:

Instructor's Manual by Roxanne Hovland, University of Tennessee

Completely updated, the Instructor's Manual provides chapter-by-chapter hints and suggestions in the form of lecture notes on text material, transparencies, and answers to questions posed by the authors. Additionally, there are supplementary exercises and assignments.

Test Bank by James Pokrywczynski, Marquette University

Perfect for quizzes and examinations, the test bank provides over 2,000 questions to test students' retention of material and ability to critically analyze the material presented in the text. The test bank is also available in computerized formats (IBM 3.5″, IBM 5.25″, and Macintosh) in the EXAMASTER II testing program.

Full-Color Transparency Acetates

Expanded to include 125 of the figures, tables, and illustrations from the book, the acetates provide instructors with a tool to pin-point critical information in the text. Notes about each transparency are integrated into the lecture notes in the Instructor's Manual.

Videos

A greatly expanded package, Dryden now presents eight video tapes including award winning television ads, current issues, advertising ethics, and an inside look at the development of advertising campaigns, including the television advertising campaign for the Longhorn Steak House in the book. An audio tape of the Longhorn Steak House's radio spots is also available. The Longhorn video and audio material are a perfect complement to the case in the text.

Acknowledgments

To evolve into its present state, the authors of *Advertising: Its Role in Modern Marketing* have had the privilege of receiving comments, criticisms, suggestions, and support from our numerous colleagues, peers, and students. From the early days at the University of Wisconsin and the University of Illinois to our present homes at the University of Georgia, and the University of Alabama we have learned much about advertising, marketing, and communication from Jan Leblanc Wicks, Bruce Vanden Bergh, Larry Soley, Jerry Lynn, Jim Looney, Nugent Wedding, Kim Rotzoll, Charles Frazer, Tom Russell, Jim Haefner, Karen King, Peggy Kreshel, Glen Nowak, Spencer Tinkham, Charles Patti, Joe Dominick, Pat Doherty, Keith Johnson, Carol Pardun, Denise DeLorme, Young Sook-Moon, Eric Haley, Kevin Keenan, Subir

Sengupta, Ron Lane, Charles Sandage, Neil Borden, Stephen Greyser, and Ed Cundiff.

We extend a special word of thanks to our professional counterparts in the advertising industry. Namely, *Advertising Age* for its permission to use the many statistics it provides each year; to John J. "Jack" Hanrahan, Media Director, and Stephen Gorski at Leo Burnett U.S.A., and to Ron Scharbo and Chrissy Cousins of Scharbo and Company, and George McKerrow, Jr., of Longhorn Steaks, Inc.

Acknowledgment is due to the following professors who reviewed the text in preparation for this edition: Earl R. Andrésen of the University of Oklahoma, Bonnie Drewniany of the University of South Carolina, Joel Geske of the Iowa State University, William F. Grazer of Towson State University, and Art Jacobson of Florida International University. In particular, we would like to thank Peggy Kreshel of the University of Georgia, who co-authored the history section of Chapter One with Leonard Reid. Professor Kreshel is an advertising historian, and we believe her contribution is significant. Herbert Rotfeld of Auburn University deserves special recognition because of his willingness to share his expertise on advertising regulation.

Lastly, we would like to thank the good people at the Dryden Press with whom we have worked closely to create this edition: Lyn Keeney Hastert, Senior Acquisitions Editor; Lisé Webb Johnson, Senior Marketing Manager; R. Paul Stewart, Developmental Editor; Jim Patterson, Project Editor; Brian Salisbury, Senior Designer; and Alison Howell, Production Manager. At the University of Georgia, we would especially like to thank Joyce B. Burton, departmental secretary, who processed much of the information contained in this edition.

Dean M. Krugman
Leonard N. Reid
S. Watson Dunn
Arnold M. Barban

October 1993

BRIEF TABLE OF CONTENTS

PART 1   Environment of Advertising   1

CHAPTER 1   Background and Evolution   3
CHAPTER 2   Marketing and Advertising Communication   37
CHAPTER 3   Social and Ethical Issues   69
CHAPTER 4   Economic Issues   103
CHAPTER 5   Regulatory Issues   127
CHAPTER 6   Organizational Structure   163

PART 2   Advertising Campaign Planning: Strategy   197

CHAPTER 7   Overview of Campaign Planning   199
CHAPTER 8   The Research Process   213
CHAPTER 9   Advertising Objectives   235
CHAPTER 10   The Budgeting Process   259
CHAPTER 11   Message Strategy   273
CHAPTER 12   Media   309
APPENDIX TO PART 2: A Sample Media Plan – Shedd Aquarium   334

PART 3   Advertising Campaign Planning: Tactics   359

CHAPTER 13   Message Tactics: Print Advertising   361
CHAPTER 14   Electronic Message Tactics   377
CHAPTER 15   Message Production   403
CHAPTER 16   Media: Newspapers and Magazines   423
CHAPTER 17   Media: Television and Radio   457
CHAPTER 18   Media: Direct Mail, Out-of-Home, and Other Media   489
APPENDIX TO PART 3: Advertising Campaign – Longhorn Steaks   520

PART 4   Special Purpose Advertising   529

CHAPTER 19   Sales Promotion and Public Relations   531
CHAPTER 20   Retail and Business-to-Business Advertising   549
CHAPTER 21   Global Advertising   569

Appendix: Sources of Information about Advertising   596

Glossary   599

Index   605

TABLE OF CONTENTS

PART 1   Environment of Advertising   1

CHAPTER 1   Background and Evolution   3
Advertising as an Economic and Social Force   5
How Advertising Works   6
The Planning of Advertising   8
Environmental Conditions and Advertising   9
Some Important Definitions   11
    Marketing   11
    Communication   11
    Advertising   12
    Sales Promotion   12
    Publicity   12
    Public Relations   12
    Personal Selling   12
Methods of Classifying Advertising   13
    Ad Audiences   13
    Types of Advertisers   14
    Media   14
    Functions   14
The Scope and Structure of Advertising Worldwide   16
    Advertising Organizations   17
The Evolution of Modern Advertising   19
    Origins of Advertising   19
    Urbanization and the Rise of Mass Production   19
    The Era of the Wholesaler   21
    The Growth of Retail Advertising   21
    Origins of the Advertising Agency   21
The Emergence of National Advertising   23
    Case Study: National Biscuit Company   23
    New Levels of Competition   25
Advertising in the Early Twentieth Century   25
    Ad Insights: The League of Advertising Women of New York   26
Advertising in the 1920s   27
The Depression Years   28
    Ad Insights: Advertising Is Tested Beyond Its Strength   29
World War II Advertising   30
The Postwar Years   32
Summary   33

CHAPTER 2   Marketing and Advertising Communication   37
Marketing Defined   38
The Marketing Concept   38
The Marketing Plan   40
    Identifying Marketing Opportunities   41
    Setting Marketing Objectives   42
    Determining Marketing Strategy   43
Advertising in the Promotion Mix   43

Ad Insights: Steps to a Sale 45
Promotion Strategies 46
Ad Insights: Advertising: One Part of Sports Marketing's Promotion Mix 47
Advertising Planning Decisions 47
The Communication Concept 48
Ad Insights: The Power of Effective Advertising Planning 50
The Communication Planning Environment 50
Communication Defined 52
Signs 52
Field of Experience 53
Meaning 54
Elements of the Communication Process 54
Source and Encoding 54
The Message 56
The Media 57
Receivers and Decoding 58
Feedback 58
Noise 58
Advertising's Communication Setting 60
Advertising's Communicative Functions 62
Summary 64

CHAPTER 3   Social and Ethical Issues 69
Ad Insights: "United Colors of Benetton" Campaign 70
How Critics Look at Advertising 70
Scholars as Critics and Defenders of Advertising 71
The General Public as Critics 72
Advertising Ethics 73
Deception in Advertising 75
Puffery 76
Watchdogs 77
Comparative Advertising 77
Subliminal Advertising 78
Bad Taste in Advertising 78
Ad Insights: Irritating TV Commercials 79
Controversial Products 80
Ad Insights: The Industry Viewpoint 81
Advertising and Children 83
Advertising and Stereotypes 84
Women 84
Ad Insights: The Sexism Watch 85
Hispanics 86
The Elderly 86
Ad Insights: She's Come a Long Way 87
African Americans 87
Ad Insights: Lessons Learned 88
The Challenge to Advertisers 89
Political Advertising 89
The Grounds for Criticism 89
Advertising Financing 90
A Look Ahead 91
Advertising and Raising Expectations 91
Advertising's Influence on the Media 91

Ad Insights: Reflecting Social Change   92
Charges of Undue Control   93
Built-in Checks against Undue Influence   93
Advertising and Freedom of Speech   93
The Advertising Council   95
Summary   97

CHAPTER 4   Economic Issues   103
The Economists' View of Advertising   103
From 1890 to 1940   104
Modern Economists   104
Ad Insights: Neil H. Borden   105
Advertising: Information or Persuasion?   105
Advertising and Prices   109
Two Views   110
Retail versus National   110
Advertising and Added Value   111
Advertising and Consumer Choice   113
Ad Insights: Another View of Added Value and Advertising Brand Equity   114
Advertising and Industry Concentration   114
Advertising's Influence on the Business Cycle   116
Ad Insights: Effective Advertising and PR Are Important, Even in a Slow Economy   118
Advertising and Aggregate Consumption   118
Advertising as Media Subsidy   119
Rolling Stone: A Case of Media Economics   119
Future Trends: Reducing Waste and Improving Economic Efficiency   122
The Duration Effects of Advertising   122
Summary   123

CHAPTER 5   Regulatory Issues   127
Advertising Regulation   127
Ad Insights: The Privileged Status of Political Advertising   128
Areas of Advertising Control   129
Regulation by the Federal Government   129
Ad Insights: The Future of Consumerism   130
Food and Drug Administration   133
Bureau of Alcohol, Tobacco and Firearms   133
Federal Communications Commission   133
Ad Insights: Tobacco Marketers Claim Ruling Spares Them from Changing Ads   134
Patent Office   136
Library of Congress   137
Postal Service   137
Other Federal Controls   137
Federal Trade Commission   137
Deceptive Advertising   139
Burden of Proof   139
Powers and Remedies   140
Affirmative Disclosures and Corrective Advertising   142
Advertising Substantiation   144
Children: A Special Market Segment   144
State and Municipal Regulation   145
Self-Regulation by the Advertising Industry   145

The NAD/NARB   146
Media Clearance   150
Ad Insights: ABC Seeks to Relax Advertising Guidelines   152
Individual Advertisers and Agencies   154
Advertising Associations   154
Trade Associations   154
The Advertising Press   156
Future Trends: Advertising Under Siege   157
Summary   157

CHAPTER 6   Organizational Structure   163
Advertisers   163
National Advertisers   163
Ad Insights: Evaluating Agency Performance   166
Ad Insights: Clients Jump Ship Quickly   169
Ad Insights: Getting the Best from an Advertising Agency   171
Local (Retail) Advertisers   172
Advertising Agencies   174
What Advertising Agencies Do for Their Clients   175
Functions of the Modern Agency   176
Ad Insights: Account Planning: The 13 Myths   180
Agency Compensation   180
Handling Competing Accounts   183
Media   183
Media Advertising Department   186
Media Representatives   190
Related Advertising Organizations   191
Specialized Services   191
Production Services   191
Art Studios   191
Research Companies   192
Future Trends: Martin Mayer Returns   193
Summary   194

PART 2   Advertising Campaign Planning: Strategy   197

CHAPTER 7   Overview of Campaign Planning   199
What Is an Advertising Campaign?   199
The Marketing Mix: Basis for Campaign Plans   200
Product   201
Price   202
Channels of Distribution (Place)   203
Promotion   203
Integrated Marketing Communications   204
Ad Insights: Kellogg's Coordinated Effort   206
The Planning of Advertising   206
Strategic Research Inputs   207
The Setting of Objectives   208
The Advertising Budget   208
Message and Media Strategy   209
The Plan in Action   209

Measuring the Effectiveness of Advertising   209
Adjustments to the Campaign   209
Summary   210

CHAPTER 8   The Research Process   213

The Research Process   213
Information Needs   214
Secondary Sources   215
Primary Sources   215
Data as Input   215
Strategic Research   215
Consumer Research   216
Product Research   217
Market Analysis   218
Measuring Advertising Effectiveness   219
Ad Insights: Sources for Strategic Research   220
Competitive Situation   218
Some Barriers to Testing   221
Classification Schemes for Measuring Effectiveness   221
Ad Insights: Communication Effectiveness Measures   222
Future Trends: Anthropologists in Advertising   230
Future Trends: Electronics
Summary   231

CHAPTER 9   Advertising Objectives   235

Advertising Objectives   235
The Function of Advertising Objectives   236
Ad Insights: The Basics of Writing an Advertising Objective   237
Understanding Advertising: Key Inputs to Objective Setting   237
Target Markets   238
Ad Insights: Target Marketing and Objective Setting   239
The Advantages of Targeting   239
Basis for the Targeting Decision   240
Types of Targeting Strategies   240
Defining Target Markets   241
Understanding How Advertising Works   248
How Advertising Can Work to Facilitate Marketing Goals   248
Ad Insights: Objective Setting and Target Marketing at Work   251
Specific Advertising Objectives   251
Different Buying Processes   252

CHAPTER 10   The Budgeting Process   259

Determining the Advertising Budget   259
The Budgeting Process   260
Advertising as an Expense and as an Investment   260
Budgeting Methods   262
Objective and Task   264
Percent of Sales   264
Unit of Sale   265
Competitive Spending   265
Quantitative/Experimental   265
Affordable and Arbitrary Methods   266

Budgeting Influences   267

Future Trends: Advertising Promotion Gap to Narrow by 1996

Summary   267

CHAPTER 11   Message Strategy   273

Message Strategy Defined   274

Message Strategy as Differentiated from Tactics   274

Determining the Message Idea   274

Ad Insights: Two Moments of Creation   275

Ad Insights: The "Big Idea"   276

The Copy Platform: The Creative Blueprint   279

Message Tactics: Elements of Ad Execution   282

Types of Message Strategies   282

Classic Creative Approaches   282

Burnett's Inherent Drama   282

Ad Insights: Heroes: Advertising's Creative Greats   286

Reeves's Unique Selling Proposition   288

Ogilvy's Brand Image   289

Bernbach's Execution Emphasis   290

Trout and Reis's Positioning   290

FCB's Message Matrix   291

Creative Style of the 1980s   292

Creative Objectives   292

Long-Range versus Short-Range Objectives   293

Hierarchy of Creative Objectives   293

General versus Specific Objectives   293

Ad Insights: That's Entertainment: Creative Coverage for Second-Tier Brands   294

Judging Message Ideas and Executions   297

Ad Insights: Creativity: Do You Have It?   298

Creativity and Message Strategy   298

Ad Insights: Kenneth Roman on How to Manage Ideas   299

Identifying Symbols   301

Trademarks, Brand Names, and Trade Names   301

Licensed Names   302

Trade Characters   303

Slogans   303

Obtaining and Retaining Protection for Identifying Symbols   304

Guidelines for Using Identifying Symbols   305

Summary   305

CHAPTER 12   Media   309

Media Trends   310

Changes in Market Structure   310

Increase in Complexity of Media   311

Increase in Total Advertising Volume   312

Changes in Buying and Selling Methods   312

Availability of Product and Media Usage Data   315

Growth of New Media Technology   316

Media Planning as Part of Marketing Strategy   318

Developing the Media Plan   319

Setting Media Objectives   319

Defining the Target Market   321

Ad Insights: A Day in the Life of the Assistant Media Planner   322

Selecting Media and Allocating the Budget   323
Choosing Media Vehicles and Units   325
Scheduling   325
   Ad Insights: Toward Even Better Media Comparisons   326
Use of Media Models   328
Summary   331
   Future Trends: General Media Strategy   332
Appendix to Part 2: A Sample Media Plan – Shedd Aquarium   334

PART 3   Advertising Campaign Planning: Tactics   359

CHAPTER 13   361
Coordinating the Major Elements   361
Attracting Attention through Headlines   362
   Types of Headlines   363
   Subheads   365
Body Copy   365
   Ad Insights: Checklist for Writing Effective Headlines   366
   Ad Insights: Guidelines for Writing Body Copy   367
Functions of a Layout   368
   How the Layout is Prepared   368
   Qualities of an Effective Layout   369
Illustrations   371
   Classifying Illustrations   372
   Illustration Techniques and Color   373
   Ad Insights: Del Monte's Effective Use of Print   374
Summary   374

CHAPTER 14   Electronic Message Tactics   377
Structure of Commercials   377
The Audience and Commercials   378
Radio Commercials   378
   Types of Radio Commercials   379
   Creating Effective Radio Commercials   381
Television Commercials   382
   Television Storyboards   383
   Types of Television Commercials   384
   Ad Insights: The Trouble with Celebrity Endorsers   389
   Ad Insights: The Match Game: Linking Celebrities and Brands   390
   Television Presentation Techniques   392
   Ad Insights: Animation: Its Stands Out on TV, and It Really Sells   393
   Creating Effective Television Commercials   394
   Ad Insights: Update: The 15-Second Commercial   395
   Ad Insights: McCollum/Spielman on Humor in Commercials   398
   Use of Color   398
   Ad Insights: Consumers' Love-Hate Relationship with Commercials   399
Summary   400

CHAPTER 15   Message Production   403
Decision Making in Advertising Production   403
   The Creation and Production Processes   404

Producing Messages for the Print Media   405
    Using Technology to Create the Message   405
    Selecting the Type   406
    Specifying Type   407
    Ad Insights: Some Tips on Type   408
    Reproducing the Illustrations   408
    Printing the Advertisement   410
    Ad Insights: Digital Stripping Creates Special Photos for Budweiser   411
    Duplicating the Advertisement   412
Producing Messages for the Electronic Media   412
Producing the Television Commercial   413
    Film or Videotape   414
    Choosing Cast and Set   414
    Using Modern Technology   415
    Ad Insights: Computer Graphics Enliven Car Ads   416
    Editing the Commercial   416
    Duplicating the Original   418
    Control over Quality and Cost   418
Producing the Radio Commercial   418
    Live versus Recording   419
    Ad Insights: The Cat's Meow of Radio Advertising   420
    Duplicating the Original   420
Summary   420

CHAPTER 16   Media: Newspapers and Magazines   423
Newspapers   423
    Advantages of Newspaper Advertising   425
    Ad Insights: A Profile of USA Today   426
    Limitations of Newspaper Advertising   430
    Readership Patterns   431
    Types of Advertising   431
    Newspaper Sizes and Shapes   432
    Ad Insights: Classified Advertising: A History . . . A Tradition . . . A Future   434
    Rate Structure   436
    Rate Comparisons   438
    Factors to Consider in Buying Newspaper Space   438
    Newspaper Supplements   440
Magazines   442
    Types of Magazines   443
    Advantages of Magazine Advertising   444
    Ad Insights: Some Marketing Success Stories   446
    Limitations of Magazine Advertising   448
    Kinds of Advertisers   448
    Circulation and Readership Patterns   449
    Magazine Sizes and Shapes   450
    Ad Insights: Some Guidelines to Effective Magazine Advertisements   451
    Rate Structure   452
    Methods of Comparison   452
Summary   452
    Future Trends: Newspapers and Magazines   453

CHAPTER 17   Media: Television and Radio   457
Television   457
    Types of Advertising   458

Advantages of Television Advertising 460

Limitations of Television Advertising 461

Ad Insights: Study Shows Advertising Executives Think Network TV Still Works, but Consider Cable and Radio More Efficient 462

Kinds of Users 464

How Television Is Used 465

Measuring Broadcasting Audiences 466

Audience Trends 470

Rate Structure 472

Cost Comparisons 473

Radio 473

Types of Advertising 474

Types of Stations 474

Advantages of Radio Advertising 475

Limitations of Radio Advertising 477

Kinds of Users 478

Programming Trends 479

Audience Measurements and Trends 479

Ad Insights: Radio: Bridging the Programming-Technology Gap 480

Rate Structure 482

Summary 484

Future Trends: Television and Radio 485

CHAPTER 18 Media: Direct Mail, Out-of-Home, and Other Media 489

Direct Mail 489

Related Concepts 490

Types of Direct Mail 490

Advantages of Direct Mail 492

Limitations of Direct Mail 493

Buying Direct Mail 493

Preparation of Direct Mail 496

Outdoor Advertising 496

Types of Outdoor Advertising 496

Advantages of Outdoor Media 498

Ad Insights: Case History on the Use of Outdoor Advertising 499

Limitations of Outdoor Media 500

Kinds of Users 500

How Outdoor Advertising Is Bought 500

Transit Advertising 501

Types of Transit Advertising 502

Advantages of Transit Advertising 504

How Transit Advertising Is Bought 504

Ad Insights: Case History on the Use of Transit Advertising 505

Other Media 506

Directory Advertising 506

Specialty Advertising 509

In-Store Media 510

Ad Insight: Two Cases Histories on the Use of Specialty Advertising 511

Miscellaneous Media 514

Summary 516

Future Trends: Direct Mail, Out-of-Home, and Other Media 517

Appendix to Part 3: A Sample Advertising Campaign – Longhorn Steaks 520

PART 4   Special Purpose Advertising   529

CHAPTER 19   Sales Promotion and Public Relations   531
Sales Promotion   531
  Differences between Advertising and Sales Promotion   532
  Consumer Promotions   532
  Trade Sales Promotion   538
Public Relations   540
  Differences between Advertising and Public Relations   540
  Size and Organization of Public Relations   541
  Activities and Planning   542
  General Public Relations Techniques   542
  Institutional Advertising as a Public Relations Technique   543
Summary   544
  Ad Insights: Food for Thought   545

CHAPTER 20   Retail and Business-to-Business Advertising   549
Retail versus National Advertising   549
Developments in Retailing   550
Promotional, Semipromotional, and Nonpromotional Stores   551
  Ad Insights: Trends in Retail Stores   552
  The Retailer's Media Mix   554
  Assistance to the Retail Advertiser   556
  Cooperative Advertising   556
  Business-to-Business Advertising   558
  Ad Insights: Characteristics of the Business Market   560
  Business Advertising Objectives   560
  Organizing for Business Advertising   561
  The Business-to-Business Media Mix   562
  The Business Advertisement   564
Summary   566

CHAPTER 21   Global Advertising   569
What Is Global Advertising?   570
Why Has Global Advertising Grown?   573
  Rise of the Multinational Corporation   573
  Increase in Global Brands   573
  Increase in Global Media   573
  New Trade Agreements   574
  Increased Trade in Goods and Services   574
  Worldwide Improvement in Living Standards   574
  Political Changes   574
  Improvements in Communication and Transportation   574
The International Language of Advertising   575
Organization of Global Advertising   575
Regulation of Global Advertising   577
  Ad Insights: International Advertising Association Head   578
Global Planning and Strategy   578
  Ad Insights: Guidelines for Transferring Advertising Strategy to a Foreign Market   580
  Marketing Mix   581
  Creative Strategy   581
  Research   584
  Media Strategy   586

Political and Economic Considerations   589
Global Advertising and Public Policy   590
   Ad Insights: Creative Strategy for US Air   592
Future of Global Advertising   593
Summary   593

Appendix: Sources of Information about Advertising   596

Glossary   599

Index   605

PART I

Environment of Advertising

Environmental Considerations: Social/Cultural, Competition, Economic, Regulatory

↓

Advertising Organizations: Advertisers, Agencies, Media, Suppliers

↓

Marketing Communication Considerations: Marketing Planning

↓

Strategic Research Inputs

↓

Objective Setting: Target Market, Buyer Behavior

↓

Determining the Advertising Budget

↓

Message Strategy ↔ **Media Strategy**

↓ ↓

Message Tactics ↔ **Media Tactics**

↓

Final Budget

↓

Plan in Action Run Campaign

↓

Impact

↓

Feedback **Measure Advertising Effectiveness** Feedback

LEARNING OBJECTIVES

In your study of this chapter, you will have an opportunity to:

- Learn how advertising is viewed by public figures, practitioners and scholars.
- Consider the impact of environment on advertising.
- Place advertising in the broader context of marketing and communication.
- Identify the organization of the advertising industry.
- Trace the evolution of modern advertising.
- Identify major events and forces in the history of modern advertising.

Chapter 1

Background and Evolution

CHAPTER TOPICS

ADVERTISING AS AN ECONOMIC AND SOCIAL FORCE

HOW ADVERTISING WORKS

THE PLANNING OF ADVERTISING

ENVIRONMENTAL CONDITIONS AND ADVERTISING

SOME IMPORTANT DEFINITIONS
Marketing
Communication
Advertising
Sales Promotion
Publicity
Public Relations
Personal Selling

METHODS OF CLASSIFYING ADVERTISING
Ad Audiences
Types of Advertisers
Media
Functions

THE SCOPE AND STRUCTURE OF ADVERTISING WORLDWIDE
Advertising Organizations

THE EVOLUTION OF MODERN ADVERTISING
Origins of Advertising
Urbanization and the Rise of Mass Production
The Era of the Wholesaler
The Growth of Retail Advertising
Origins of the Advertising Agency

THE EMERGENCE OF NATIONAL ADVERTISING
Case Study: National Biscuit Company
New Levels of Competition

ADVERTISING IN THE EARLY TWENTIETH CENTURY

ADVERTISING IN THE 1920S

THE DEPRESSION YEARS

WORLD WAR II ADVERTISING

THE POSTWAR YEARS

Few elements in our daily lives are as pervasive as advertising. Whatever we do, wherever we go, we are almost certain to encounter advertising in at least one of its many forms. As we drive our cars, we hear radio commercials and see billboards. Commercials reach us between and within programming while we watch our favorite TV programs. When we pick up a magazine or newspaper at home or in a physician's office, we are exposed not only to stories and features but also to advertisements. Every day the mail brings brochures and flyers as well as bills and letters. Even at the beach planes fly overhead pulling advertising banners, and scoreboard panels at stadiums rotate to display multiple advertising messages. According to industry estimates, the average American is exposed to between 300 and 1,500 advertisements and commercials a day; of these only 80 are consciously noted, and only 12 result in some form of response.[1]

Because advertising is such a ubiquitous part of everyday life, we are tempted to think we understand it—how it works, how it affects people, how it is created. Most people have definite ideas about advertising because, unlike other business activities, it calls attention to itself. People who would not try to speak authoritatively about statistics or even about marketing, the field of which advertising is a part, are quick to voice opinions about advertising. These opinions are typically based on feelings about a particular advertisement, slogan, product, or sponsor rather than on an understanding of advertising's larger, institutional role.[2] People tend to attribute the success of a particular product to advertising alone. They overlook the importance of less obvious influences—such as the quality of the product or the services behind it. This kind of thinking leads the critics of advertising to exaggerate its effectiveness and the defenders of advertising to oversimplify how it works.

In practice, advertising is a complicated field consisting of much more than the advertisements and commercials that are seen, read, or heard. The process of advertising decision making is like an iceberg. Only the finished ads and commercials are visible to consumers, but as shown in Figure 1.1, an overwhelming series of marketing and advertising planning decisions take place before those ads appear.

Even business executives, many of whom invest large sums of money in advertising, may misunderstand and misuse it. Despite a lack of training or advertising skills, they often plan advertising campaigns themselves or exert undue influence on hired advertising professionals. The effective use of advertising requires a thorough understanding of how and when it should be used.

This first chapter will provide an overview—what advertising is, how it works, its environmental constraints, and how it has evolved as an instrument of marketing. The book itself is designed to take you below the surface of the aforementioned iceberg—to expose you to the many managerial decisions that go into advertising planning and to explain how those decisions are influenced by factors beyond the advertiser's control. Later in this chapter, you will be introduced to the planning model around which the chapters in this textbook are organized. The model should serve as a unifying device to help you better understand the practice of advertising.

FIGURE 1.1

The Advertising Strategy and Planning Process

Ads and commercials seen by consumers are like only the tip of an iceberg, emerging from situations, objectives, and strategies developed by marketing and advertising planners.

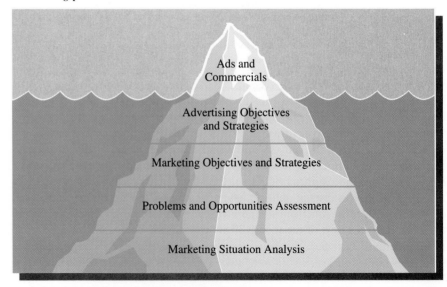

Advertising as an Economic and Social Force

The growth of advertising as an economic and a social force, even if adjusted for inflation or population growth, is one of the most remarkable developments in modern American history.[3] Leo Bogart, a leading advertising researcher, describes advertising as one of modern society's most visible aspects, with values that are interwoven with the whole fabric of American society.[4] The historian Stephen Fox calls advertising one of the dominant forces in the twentieth century. In his view, "Among the pillars of our popular culture, advertising stands with TV, sports, pop music, and the print media as unavoidable features of modern life."[5] Others, including former British Prime Minister Sir Winston Churchill and former U.S. political leader Adlai S. Stevenson, consider advertising a creator of a better standard of living, a stimulant to a healthy economy, and a catalyst for product development and improvement. Leo Burnett, one of advertising's creative greats, voiced a similar opinion in a speech, a part which is excerpted in the ad in Figure 1.2.

Analytical perspectives on the institutional role of advertising have been offered by a number of prominent scholars. Five differing views are summarized in Figure 1.3. Together they make a significant contribution to our understanding of the

FIGURE 1.2

Leo Burnett's View of Advertising

Burnett, one of advertising's greatest creative thinkers, founded the Leo Burnett agency during the Great Depression. Burnett and his agency helped found the "Chicago School of Advertising."

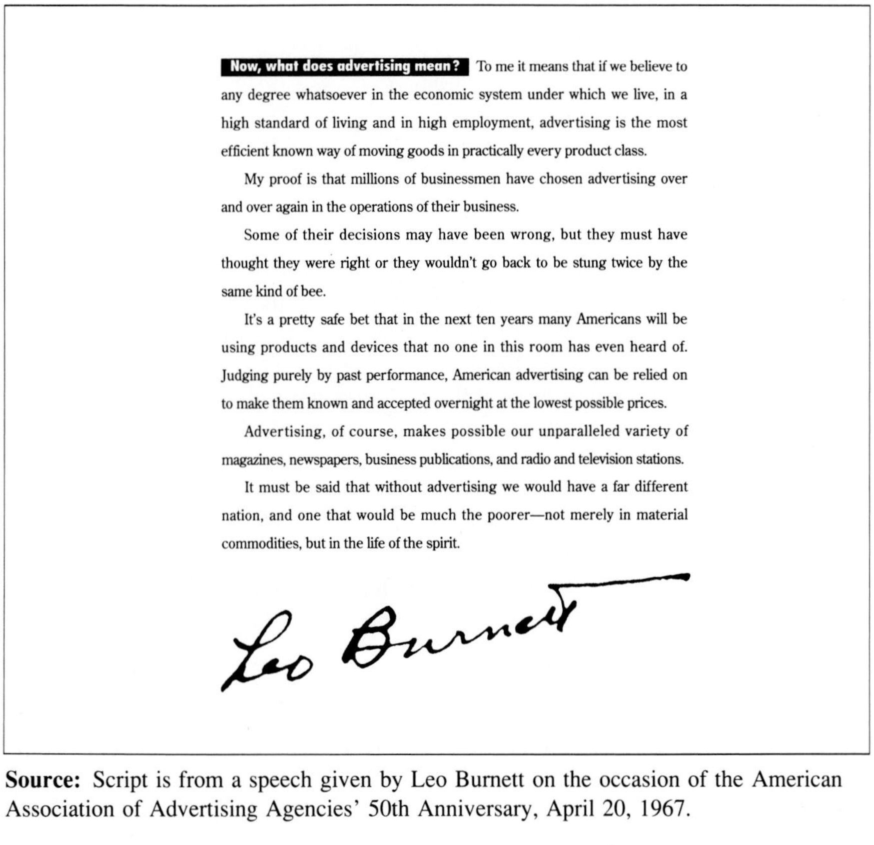

Now, what does advertising mean? To me it means that if we believe to any degree whatsoever in the economic system under which we live, in a high standard of living and in high employment, advertising is the most efficient known way of moving goods in practically every product class.

My proof is that millions of businessmen have chosen advertising over and over again in the operations of their business.

Some of their decisions may have been wrong, but they must have thought they were right or they wouldn't go back to be stung twice by the same kind of bee.

It's a pretty safe bet that in the next ten years many Americans will be using products and devices that no one in this room has even heard of. Judging purely by past performance, American advertising can be relied on to make them known and accepted overnight at the lowest possible prices.

Advertising, of course, makes possible our unparalleled variety of magazines, newspapers, business publications, and radio and television stations.

It must be said that without advertising we would have a far different nation, and one that would be much the poorer—not merely in material commodities, but in the life of the spirit.

Leo Burnett

Source: Script is from a speech given by Leo Burnett on the occasion of the American Association of Advertising Agencies' 50th Anniversary, April 20, 1967.

FIGURE 1.3

Five Views on the Institutional Role of Advertising

Theorist	Function
James Carey, Communication Scholar	Views advertising as a provider of market information, with the nature of that information, and its potential effects, influenced by self-interested sources, whose purpose is to sell their goods and services.
Vincent Norris, Mass Media Economist	Views national (producer) advertising as a means of avoiding price competition by seizing control of market power from distributors—that is, by utilizing advertising directed at consumers to stimulate demand.
David Potter, Historian	Views advertising as training people to act as consumers in an abundant economy (supply exceeds demand), but as an institution that lacks social responsibility to counter its social control of public values and media effects.
Charles Sandage, Advertising Scholar	Views advertising as contributing through information and persuasion to the maintenance of abundance by helping people make informed decisions.
Michael Schudson, Sociologist	Views advertising as an expression of capitalism—it is a part of our establishment and a reflection of social values and beliefs—that overwhelms competing values with its ubiquity and the comfort of its agreed-upon themes.

Source: Kim B. Rotzoll and James E. Haefner, *Advertising in Contemporary Society: Perspectives toward Understanding* (Cincinnati, OH: South-Western, 1986), 64–65, with the permission of South-Western Publishing Co. Copyright 1986 by South-Western Publishing Co. All rights reserved.

marketplace. Despite the social and economic importance ascribed to advertising by public figures and scholars, practitioners do not agree on its scope, nature, and function in the marketing process. Some consider it a profession, others a craft. Some refer to the science of advertising, others to the art of advertising. In 1916, John Kennedy, a brash Canadian Mountie turned copywriter, called it "salesmanship in print."[6] To former agency head William Marsteller, advertising is a form of communication that must be coordinated with other marketing activities to affect sales. To David Ogilvy, one of advertising's creative giants, it is part of the complex product/service symbol—the brand image.[7]

Advertising as it is practiced is both an art and a science. As an instrument of marketing, it sometimes completes a sale, but most often it only contributes to the final sale. It does the work of marketing at the same time that it affects and is affected by the economic and social order of the marketplace.

How Advertising Works

Scholars and practitioners of advertising have long searched for an adequate theoretical explanation of how advertising works. However, the complexity and dynamic nature of advertising have complicatd that search. With all we know today about how advertising works, one unified theory has not yet emerged.

It is clear what advertising is supposed to do: persuade consumers to take the action desired by the advertiser. It is just as clear that advertising is rarely able to accomplish its persuasive task as planned. As a consequence, the warning sounded by Martin Mayer in *Madison Avenue, U.S.A.* in 1958 still has merit today: "Only the very brave or the very ignorant . . . can say exactly what advertising does in the marketplace."[8]

In the simplistic view, advertising is thought to affect behavior in a cause-effect relationship.

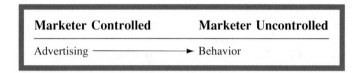

The assumption is, if money is spent on advertising, sales will follow.

Research evidence and many campaign failures, however, teil us that the effect of advertising on behavior is usually mediated by factors internal and external to consumers. The marketer controls some of the factors—product, price, distribution, and other forms of promotion. These interact with advertising to affect behavior. The marketer does not control environmental conditions or the consumer's internal state, and these uncontrollable factors often dictate the success or failure of advertising campaigns.

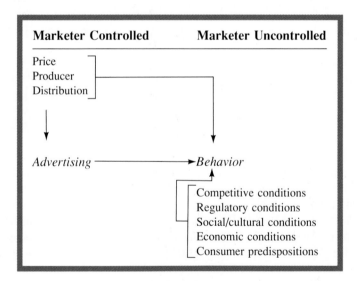

Experience has taught advertising scholars and practitioners that marketers control advertising decisions, but consumers control how they respond to the product of those decisions—the advertising campaign.

For advertising to perform its work, a sequence of communication events must occur—advertising must move "the predisposed" consumer from awareness of the product to purchase behavior. In modern advertising terms, this sequence of events is known as the **hierarchy of effects,** and effective advertising is designed to influence how information presented by advertising is hierarchically processed.

One popular model of information processing is presented in Figure 1.4. Generally, the presumption is that ad exposure leads to attention, which in turn results in three

---

FIGURE 1.4

How Advertising Information Is Processed by Consumers: From Exposure to Behavior

---

exposure to an advertisement
attention to and **perception** of the advertisement
comprehension of the advertisement
degree of **agreement** with the advertisement
retention in memory of the advertisement
ability to **retrieve** the advertisement from memory
decision making based on the advertisement in relation to other options
action taken on basis of the decision

Source: William J. McGuire, "Some Internal Psychological Factors Influencing Consumer Choice," *Journal of Consumer Research* 4 (March 1976): 302–319.

---

kinds of processing reactions among people—what they learn, how they feel, and what they do.

Although there is no agreement on the exact sequence of these communication events, most believe that effective advertising must have at least four types of communicative power: stopping power, locking power, feeling power, and moving power. Stopping power refers to the ad's ability to attract attention; locking power to its ability to produce memorability; feeling power to its ability to create positive evaluations; and moving power to its ability to cause some form of purchase-related behavior.

Unfortunately for advertisers, a direct causal relationship between what people know, how they feel, and what they do has not been established. An advertisement might attract a person's attention; at another time, the person might even be able to recognize or recall something that the ad said about the product. However, the ability to recognize or recall may have very little to do with how people feel about a product and even less to do with how they act in the marketplace. The situation is complicated even further by the fact that people's reactions to an ad may be completely separate from their reactions to the product featured in the ad.

In the final analysis, we know that people process advertising in a hierarchical fashion and that an effective ad must have the four types of power to move people through the "effects" hierarchy. We also know that just because a particular ad has locking power does not mean that it has feeling power, let alone moving power. Research has proven again and again that a person may remember an ad but not necessarily what was advertised. Other research has shown that a person's memory for an ad is not necessarily related to the ad's persuasibility, as measured by either attitude change or purchase behavior.

A widely accepted belief about advertising is that marketers use advertising because it works, albeit they are not exactly sure how it works. John Wanamaker, a Philadelphia retail merchant, is often credited with a statement that still rings true today: "I know that half of my advertising is working; I just don't know which half."

The Planning of Advertising

The planning of a successful advertising campaign requires a number of elements organized in a logical sequence. A campaign, as will be further dealt with in Chapters 2 and 7, is a scheduled and integrative advertising effort consisting of a series of ads and commercials with a unified message, delivered with sufficient repetition and coverage to targeted audiences, coordinated with other promotion tools, and directed to meeting predetermined marketing and advertising objectives.

Figure 1.5 presents the elements involved in advertising campaign planning and the order in which they usually occur. The basic advertising planning elements include strategic research, which considers environmental conditions and marketing planning, objective setting, budgeting, message and media considerations, and measuring the campaign's effectiveness. As previously mentioned, this textbook is organized around the planning model, and in later chapters we will deal with each planning element in detail.

Following is a discussion of the first section of the planning model—environmental considerations. More information about social/cultural, competitive, economic, and regulatory considerations will be presented in Chapters 3 through 5. In the following chapter, the concepts of marketing planning and communication are introduced, and in Chapter 6, the organizations that are involved in advertising planning are discussed.

Environmental Conditions and Advertising

Most people associate the word *environment* with ecology, but to advertisers **environment** means the conditions under which advertising must work. These environmental conditions, as noted earlier, substantially influence the planning of advertising and its ultimate success or failure.

Environmental factors affect advertising not only as a function of business but also as an institution in our society. The environment nurtures advertising at times but constricts and changes it at others.

On the practical level, advertising planners collect information, formulate objectives, and decide how much to spend, based on their assessment of environmental conditions. From these decisions, creative and media strategies are developed; and from these strategies, ads are produced and media time and space are purchased.

Environmental conditions have caused advertising to develop in certain ways as an institution. Our advertising system is the direct result of the "free enterprise" environment. As advertising has evolved from the environment, it has in turn interacted with and changed our environment.

The environmental structure of advertising consists of four major environments— social/cultural, competitive, regulatory, and economic. Each has unique features, but the four should be viewed as interactive rather than separate. Just as they influence and are influenced by advertising, they influence and are influenced by one another.

The social/cultural environment consists of shared beliefs, customs, values, patterns of social interaction, lifestyles, morals, ethics, and other socially defined ideas, objects, and behaviors. Sometimes people are shocked by advertising because it violates accepted standards—occasionally so shocked that they resolve not to buy the advertised product. As a general rule, most advertisers try to reflect social/ cultural standards. Occasionally they try to be a little ahead of the standards but not so far ahead that the influence of the advertising message is blunted. This is in keeping with the view of advertising as capitalist realism: advertising is not a shaper of values; it confronts us with values with which we already agree.[9]

The competitive environment consists of organizations that are competing to satisfy consumer wants and needs. Advertising, designed to influence **consumer behavior,** is in turn influenced by competitive advertising and other marketing efforts. In the marketplace, advertising effectiveness is affected by how much or how little the competition is spending, the nature of competitive messages, and where those messages are placed. To plan effective advertising, advertisers must

FIGURE 1.5

An Advertising Planning Model

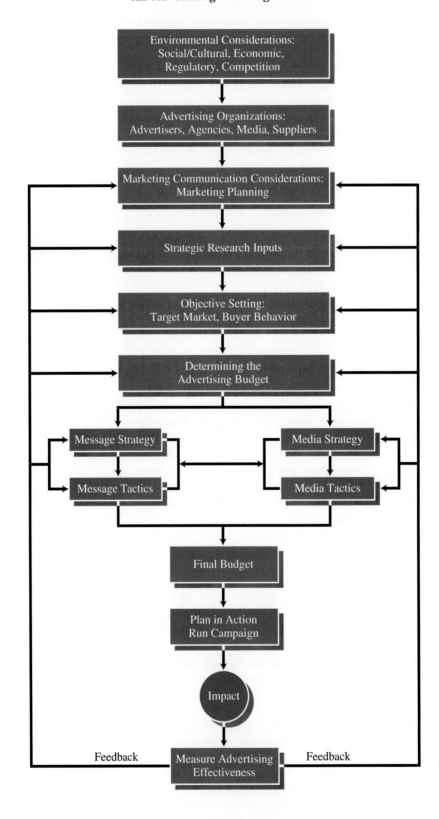

monitor the competitive environment, which consists of product strategies, distribution strategies, pricing strategies, and promotion strategies.

The regulatory environment consists of regulations and laws requiring advertisers to operate under fair competitive conditions and in the best interest of the consumer. It is an ever-changing web of regulations, some imposed by the advertising industry itself (self-regulation), others by various governmental agencies and media organizations. If regulatory conditions (which vary by product and industry) are not met, advertisers are subject to fines, public embarrassment, negative publicity, civil suits, and loss of business.

The economic environment consists of business fluctuations that affect spending, savings, income, investment, and other components of market supply and demand. Advertising, as we know it, is a product of our system of capitalism. It is affected greatly by the economic cycle of recession, depression, recovery, and prosperity. Historically, the first two stages of the cycle have adversely affected advertising: advertising budgets are cut and advertising people lose their jobs. The other two stages have meant good times for advertising: dollars are invested in advertising and more work is available for advertising professionals. No advertiser can afford to ignore economic conditions, for the planning of advertising is tied directly to economic cycles.

Some Important Definitions

To arrive at an understanding of what advertising is, we must place advertising within the broader context of marketing and communication. Advertising is an instrument of marketing communication, as will be discussed in Chapter 2. As such, it must work in harmony with the other elements of marketing planning and with the principles of communication, which constitute the marketing communication environment. A brief look at marketing and communication is offered here along with the definitions of advertising and related terms.

Marketing

In early U.S. history, marketing was given scant attention because the main objective of business and agriculture was to produce the scarce goods and services needed by society. As productivity increased and production caught up with demand, more emphasis was placed on the marketing activities of selling and promoting. In today's marketplace, **marketing** is consumer-oriented; that is, it is planned and implemented to facilitate exchange between the buyer and seller on the basis of identified consumer wants and needs.

Note that the emphasis in modern marketing is on buyer-seller exchange and consumer satisfaction. To induce consumers to engage in exchange, marketers develop a **marketing mix**—a combination of decisions about products, prices, distribution channels, and promotions. Advertising is an essential part of the promotion element of the marketing mix, which includes sales promotion, public relations, and personal selling.

Communication

Advertising's most basic function is to communicate. Consequently, **communication** is an important tool (along with entertainment features, sales promotion, public relations, and personal selling) for communicating facts and images about products, services, and ideas.

Communication is a complex process. Whether advertising communication succeeds in accomplishing its marketing task depends on the nature of the message, the choice of media, how the intended audience is predisposed to respond, and many other factors. Like the marketing mix, advertising works best when it is carefully coordinated with other forms of marketing communication. These include both controllable forms, such as public relations, and uncontrollable forms, such as word of mouth, a type of face-to-face communication.

Advertising

Advertising is paid, nonpersonal communication through various mass media by business firms, nonprofit organizations, and individuals who are in some way identified in the message and who hope to inform or persuade members of a particular audience. Certain key words (*paid, nonpersonal, mass media, identified,* and *persaude*) distinguish advertising from other forms of communication. The definition includes nonprofit as well as profit-seeking organizations. This definition approaches advertising primarily from the standpoint of advertisers, who presumably have defined their target audiences and determined the effect they hope to achieve through persuasive yet truthful ads in the media.

Sales Promotion

Promotion and sales promotion are terms that create much confusion in the advertising and marketing fields. In the broad sense, **promotion** may include such functions as advertising, personal selling, and free publicity in the editorial columns of a newspaper. More often, the terms sales promotion and promotion are reserved for activities that supplement advertising and personal selling: exhibitions, displays, demonstrations, contests, premium offers, cents-off deals, coupons, and the like. For our purposes, **sales promotion** includes all the forms of communication (other than advertising, personal selling, publicity, or public relations) that call attention to the promotional idea or reinforce the advertising message.

Publicity

Many companies supplement their advertising with publicity. Like advertising, **publicity** is nonpersonal, is exposed in the mass media, and is used for persuasion. Two important differences exist, however. Publicity is not paid for at established rates, and the sponsor is not identified. Usually, publicity appears—unidentified as such—in the editorial or news columns of print media, or in the noncommercial portion of radio or television programs. The source is usually news releases.

Public Relations

Public relations is a broader term than publicity and is sometimes confused with publicity, sales promotion, and even advertising. It has been defined in many ways, but most practitioners agree that **public relations** involves the many practices used to build goodwill and rapport with various publics—employees, stockholders, dealers, government officials, and citizens. Public relations may use advertising, publicity, or any other communication tools that might be appropriate. Some firms refer to their public relations operation as "public affairs" to reflect the broadening of this function to include communicating with government officials, politicians, editors, and labor unions, among others. Government officials tend to prefer the term public affairs rather than public relations.

Personal Selling

Personal selling is the original form of promotion. It is a presentation on a person-to-person basis involving immediate and interactive contact between two or more people. It may be face-to-face or machine-assisted. Unlike advertising, personal selling is a direct form of promotion that can be tailored to fit the demands of the selling situation. Customer reactions can be judged immediately, customers can be led to take action, and sales personnel can provide immediate feedback on customers. The three basic forms of personal selling are telephone selling, over-the-counter selling, and field selling.

Methods of Classifying Advertising

Advertising can be classified according to audiences, types of advertisers, mass media, and functions.

Ad Audiences

The two basic advertising audiences are consumers and businesses. Consumer advertising is directed at audiences who purchase the product for its own sake and for end-use consumption. They do not resell or reuse the product in some manufacturing or production process. Business-to-business advertising, on the other hand, is directed at process users, resellers, and professionals. When directed to process users (manufacturers), it is called **industrial advertising.** When directed to farmers, it is **agricultural advertising.** When directed to resellers (wholesalers or distributors), it is **trade advertising.** When directed to service groups or individuals (such as physicians, dentists, and architects), it is called **professional advertising.**

Such diverse companies as Exxon, Dow Chemical, and IBM use consumer advertising and most forms of business-to-business advertising to reach different audiences for their products and services. Two advertisements from an AT&T campaign aimed at both audiences are shown in Figure 1.6.

Advertising audiences may also be seen as *mass* or *class*. The chances are that Ivory Soap advertising, for example, will address a large, heterogeneous audience—a mass audience. In contrast, advertising for an expensive perfumed soap will

FIGURE 1.6

**AT&T Advertisements Designed to Reach Two Different Audiences:
Consumers and Businesses**

FIGURE 1.7

National and Retail Ads for Game Boy

The national ad is designed to sell the brand wherever it is sold. The retail ad is designed to sell the brand at Target.

probably be directed to a class audience, defined on the basis of variables such as income, occupation, or lifestyle.

Types of Advertisers

Most consumer advertising is done by two major types of advertisers: **national** and **local** (retail). When Maytag Company urges us via magazines, television, and radio to buy a refrigerator, this is national advertising—also called general advertising. But if an appliance dealer urges us to buy the refrigerator at his or her store, this is local advertising—also called retail advertising. Examples are reproduced in Figure 1.7. Advertising of both types for the same product may appear in a single edition of a newspaper. In most cases, the general advertiser pays higher rates for a given unit of space or time than the retail advertiser.

The national advertiser tries to persuade people to buy the firm's brand wherever they may find it. The local advertiser is eager to persuade them to purchase locally. The national advertiser emphasizes the product; the retail advertiser emphasizes the store.

The national advertiser need not cover the entire country with advertising. Some advertisers, such as General Electric and General Motors, do. But others, like Lone Star Breweries, advertise only in areas of the United States where they distribute their product. Exxon is a national advertiser, but it often advertises regionally because its heaviest gasoline distribution is in the eastern United States.

Media

Advertising can be classified on the basis of the **medium** used to deliver the message. Established mass media include daily newspapers, network TV, consumer magazines, and direct mail. Among the newer media are cable television, highly specialized magazines, videocassettes, and computer disks.

Functions

Many people look at advertising in terms of what it is expected to do. The three main functional classifications are product or institutional (nonproduct), primary or selective, and direct action or indirect action.

Product or Institutional (Nonproduct) Advertising

When Ford Motor Company runs an ad describing the virtues of a new automobile, the company is using product advertising. But an ad describing Ford's progress in designing cars that use less fuel or are less polluting is considered institutional advertising. Miller Brewing Company ads representing both types are shown in Figure 1.8.

Institutional advertising, often called nonproduct advertising or corporate advertising, sells the company rather than an individual product. Some institutional advertising is part of a firm's public relations effort to counter public criticism. Other institutional advertising is designed to promote noncontroversial causes, such as prevention of forest fires or avoidance of excessive drinking, or socioeconomic issues associated with a particular firm or industry.

Primary or Selective Advertising

Primary advertising promotes demand for generic products or services, those that carry a brand as well as those that are unbranded. Selective advertising promotes demand for a particular brand or line of related brands. For example, the demand for a motorcycle as a means of transportation is primary; demand for a Honda motorcycle is selective. Primary advertising is often used by associations, such as the American Dairy Association and the Beef Industry Council, to build demand for products produced by their members or to enhance the image of the industry.

Selective advertising is used by individual firms, usually to stimulate demand for a particular brand after primary demand has been established. It may be used also

FIGURE 1.8

Product and Nonproduct Advertisements for the Same Advertiser
(Note the Social Message That Is Placed in the Product Ad)

Advertisements Created to Build Primary and Selective Demand

The U.S. Council for Energy Awareness ad is designed to build primary demand for nuclear energy.

The Roundup Grass and Weed Killer ad is designed to build brand demand within the product category.

to maintain a brand position after primary demand stabilizes. In Figure 1.9, the U.S. Council for Energy Awareness Council ad is an example of primary advertising; the Roundup Grass and Weed Killer ad is an example of selective advertising.

Direct- or Indirect-Action Advertising

When the local K mart features its weekly specials, it is using direct-action advertising to spur immediate sales. When Sears features a closeout of patio furniture in a sales flyer, it also is using direct-action advertising. But when J.C. Penney points out in a headline, "I'd move mountains for her, but today I'll start with one extraordinary stone," it is using an indirect approach to persuade people to consider its jewelry department. Direct advertising might be called the "hard sell," indirect advertising the "soft sell." The difference is easily seen in the two battery ads in Figure 1.10.

The Scope and Structure of Advertising Worldwide

Commodore Thompson, founder of the J. Walter Thompson advertising agency, in 1916 exclaimed to a lunch companion, "Congratulate me! I just sold the business to the Resor boys. They don't know it, but the advertising agency business has seen its better days!"[10] He was very wrong.

The number of people who are influenced by advertising or the extent to which it influences society's values cannot be determined exactly. The figures available are estimates based on government and industry data, not on audited accountings of advertising dollars.[11] These estimates of domestic and worldwide advertising expenditures and employees, however, give us an approximation of advertising's size and scope.

Today, advertising is more than a 132 billion dollar business in the United States alone. Worldwide advertising expenditures are estimated to be more than $294 billion. Long a U.S. dominated enterprise, the advertising business now is a worldwide enterprise. In 1991, Tokyo replaced New York as the ad capital of the world (as measured by ad expenditures), but New York regained the edge in 1992.

The exact number of people employed worldwide in advertising is not known. In 1992, the top 500 U.S. advertising agencies employed 139,984 people in 2,994 worldwide offices. Of those people, 70,016 were employed in 1,216 domestic offices and 63,968 were employed in 1,778 non-U.S. offices. However, many others work throughout the world for foreign-based agencies, clients, media, and other advertising suppliers.

Advertising *Organizations*

The structure of advertising consists primarily of five interacting organizations. These organizations, which are discussed in greater detail in Chapter 6, are depicted in Figure 1.11.

Advertisers

At the center of the world of advertising are the advertisers. Advertisers provide the final resources that support the advertising industry. An advertiser is distinguished from a nonadvertiser by the time and space that is purchased in the mass media to deliver both commercial and noncommercial messages. An advertiser may use any

FIGURE 1.10

Rayovac's Hard-Sell Advertising Approach
Versus Duracell's Soft-Sell Approach

FIGURE 1.11

The Structure of the Advertising Industry: The Five Major Organizations

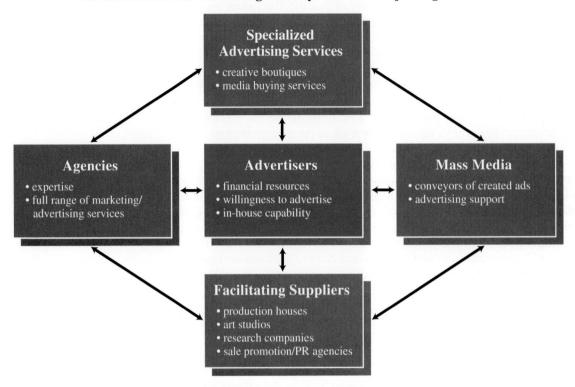

Specialized Advertising Services
• creative boutiques
• media buying services

Agencies
• expertise
• full range of marketing/advertising services

Advertisers
• financial resources
• willingness to advertise
• in-house capability

Mass Media
• conveyors of created ads
• advertising support

Facilitating Suppliers
• production houses
• art studios
• research companies
• sale promotion/PR agencies

← = possible paths of organizational interaction.

combination of the four other organizations to plan, create, and place advertising. For example, one advertiser may rely totally on a full-service advertising agency to handle the advertising function; another may perform many advertising functions with an in-house agency and use specialized advertising services and suppliers to handle others. An in-house agency is a special structure that is controlled by the advertiser, and exists to perform most, if not all, of the functions of an external advertising agency.

Advertising Agencies

Ad agencies are independent of advertisers, and are typically organizations that provide multiple marketing and advertising services, including such services as product development, research, production, and sales promotion in addition to creative and media planning. To agencies, advertisers are clients. In some cases, agencies are full partners in all aspects of clients' marketing and advertising planning; in other cases, agencies are limited to involvement in creative and media decisions.

Specialized Advertising Services

Not all advertisers use advertising agencies. Two alternatives to full-service agencies are provided by creative boutiques and media buying services. Rather than offering a host of services, creative boutiques specialize in the creation of advertising, while media buying services specialize in media planning and placement. An advertiser may select on an "à la carte" basis to use either one or both types of services.

Creative boutiques and media buying services have not grown as once expected. At one point, some predicted that they would seriously challenge the place of full-service agencies in advertising planning. Today, however, most agencies will agree to provide "à la carte" services to an interested client.

Mass Media

Ads created and produced by either in-house agencies, full-service agencies, or specialized advertising services are delivered to targeted consumers through the mass media. Most media not only deliver ads, they provide creative and research services. Some media, such as outdoor advertising, are totally supported by advertising revenue; others, such as television and newspapers, are partially supported.

Facilitating Suppliers

Services provided by production houses, art studios, research companies, sales promotion agencies, and public relations agencies, among others, are often used by the other four advertising organizations to facilitate the advertising process. For example, production houses are used by advertisers and agencies to produce some or all commercials and ads; art studios are used to produce finished artwork. Research companies supply information on markets, messages, and media on a subscription or on a project basis to media, advertising, and agencies; and sales promotion and public relations agencies are contracted to coordinate these services with advertising planning.

A more complete picture of the size and structure of the advertising business will be presented in later chapters. We now turn to how advertising evolved as such a global economic and social force.

The Evolution of Modern Advertising

Present-day advertising practices can best be understood by seeing how they were put into place. The purpose of advertising has always been to promote goods, services, and ideas; but the techniques, the media, and the institutions have changed.

While one could suggest that early forms of advertising existed in ancient, premarket societies, those early "advertising" efforts bear little resemblance to the institution of advertising as it exists today. The development of modern American advertising began during the period in history typically identified as the industrial revolution. Credit for the growth of advertising that took place over the next 150 years goes partly to advertising leaders who saw and took advantage of emerging opportunities. Environmental forces, however, were responsible for the opportunities themselves. Principal among these forces were the completion of a communication and transportation infrastructure, which made possible a revolution in production and distribution practices; the development of modern business acceptance of advertising as a strategic marketing tool; the emergence of advertising agencies as specialists in "demand stimulation"; and the evolution of mass media, which made communication with national audiences possible. An outline of the major environmental forces behind the growth of advertising in America is provided in Figure 1.12.

Origins of Advertising

During the first half of the nineteenth century, the United States remained primarily a land of farms, villages, and small enterprises. Individuals satisfied their needs with goods and services that were provided locally. The home and the workplace were one and the same. The latter half of the century, however, was marked by urbanization and business expansion. In 1870 more than half of the working population

Urbanization and the Rise of Mass Production

FIGURE 1.12

Environmental Forces behind the Growth of Advertising as a Communication and Marketing Tool

- **Acceptance of the Free-Market Philosophy** Despite a fluctuating cycle of government control over business, Americans have generally been willing to let the market rather than the government decide on allocation of resources and the rewarding of workers.
- **Technological Developments** Innovations in technology made mass production, mass communication, and mass marketing possible.
- **Growth in Productivity per Worker** As technology improved, each worker produced more goods and services for each hour of work. Advertising became a major force in stimulating demand for this growing output.
- **Increase in Disposable Income** As the United States and other countries prospered, a lower percentage of each worker's income was needed to buy the basic necessities of food, clothing, and shelter. People had more disposable income, and advertisers were eager to suggest ways to spend it.
- **Growth of the Middle Class** The prosperous middle class, increasing as a percentage of the population, became a larger and larger advertising audience.
- **Growth of Transportation** This made central and highly efficient manufacturing areas (for example, Detroit for automobiles) and regional distribution points feasible.
- **Increase in Education** A literate, better-educated . populace is eager to live better and looks to advertising as an important method of communication for information.

- **Decline of Personal Selling** Advertising has been summoned to take over many of the jobs formerly done by personal selling. Through mass communication, advertisements can reach people at a fraction of the cost of a personal message. This has been especially true at the retail level, where self-service supermarkets have become a dominant factor.
- **Growth of Specialized Advertising Organizations** Advertising agencies helped institutionalize and professionalize the advertising industry and thus helped convince business of the usefulness of advertising services.
- **Growth in Use of Research** Improvement in research methods and growth in acceptance of research by marketing executives have made advertising more productive and hence more desirable.
- **Growth of Brands and Variety of Merchandise** Advertising has become a major competitive tool for brands and types of goods and services.
- **Growth of Large-Scale Manufacturing and Servicing** After World War II, companies merged into large-scale manufacturing, servicing, and retailing groups. These enlarged firms needed expanded advertising to reach their widely dispersed markets.
- **Remoteness of the Manufacturer from the Consumer** As manufacturers were separated from the ultimate consumer by wholesalers or franchisees, they looked to advertising to bridge this gap.
- **Growth and Acceptance of Consumer Credit** The growth of credit cards has increased the sales potential that can be stimulated by advertising.

---

was comprised of farmers and farm laborers. By 1900 they were outnumbered by industrial wage earners. When the United States entered World War I in 1917, the percentage of the workforce involved in agriculture had dropped below 30 percent. The United States had become an urban nation.

In this short period, the modern business enterprise developed. This development was made possible, in part, by the completion of the transportation and communication infrastructure in the United States. Railroads not only moved mail and passengers with speed and regularity but also provided manufacturers, for the first time, with dependable, precisely scheduled, all-weather transportation of raw materials and finished goods. Correspondingly, the telephone and the telegraph, which were essential to the efficient operation of the railroads, made possible almost-instantaneous communication to most parts of the nation. Urbanization brought people together in communities that provided the stable and predictable workforce essential to industry.

Technological innovations replaced much hand labor with machinery, and productivity increased significantly. The industrial revolution, thus, made labor and capital much more productive and provided goods for sale at reasonable prices to an increasingly prosperous national market.

The Era of the Wholesaler

The tremendous increase in production capacity meant that goods had to be transported to distant markets. During the 1850s a wholesaling system emerged in the eastern urban centers, such as New York, Baltimore, and Philadelphia. Storekeepers from other parts of the nation traveled to the east coast to get their stock. Later, the development of the railroad and the telegraph allowed wholesaling operations to move west. Soon, eastern centers were in competition with new distribution centers in cities, such as Chicago, Cincinnati, St. Louis, and Omaha. "By the late 1860s," business historian Alfred D. Chandler writes, "the full-line, full-service wholesaler had taken over the distribution of the traditional consumer goods."[12]

This was an era of aggressive salesmanship. Drummers solicited new business, took orders, and sent valuable information on demand back to the **wholesalers** they represented. Drummers assisted storekeepers in maintaining inventory and improving merchandise displays. By the 1870s most wholesalers, thus, had become **jobbers,** creating extensive buying networks to purchase directly from manufacturers, as well as extensive marketing organizations to sell to rural general stores and an increasing number of specialized retailers.

The Growth of Retail Advertising

The first mass retailers were the department stores that developed in the 1860s and 1870s in large urban markets, such as New York, Philadelphia, Chicago, and Boston. Typified by Macy's, Marshall Field's, Wanamaker's, and Filene's, these stores almost universally adopted a one-price, high-volume, high-turnover strategy in an effort to assure profits. This strategy, coupled with the greater proximity to consumers, led department stores to rely much more heavily on advertising than had earlier retailers.

Advertising efforts by these retailers contributed considerable impetus to the growth of advertising in general and of advertising agencies. In many instances, a large retailer became an advertising agency's major **client.** For example, using advertising and shrewd merchandising, John Wanamaker built the country's largest men's retail clothing establishment, Wanamaker's, in Philadelphia. Wanamaker's opened in 1869 and became one of the first clients of N. W. Ayer & Son, one of the earliest advertising agencies. Advertising practitioner/historian Frank Presbrey wrote of Wanamaker's contribution to advertising:

> In this Wanamaker store in Philadelphia originated large-scale advertising, the advertising that went into page and large expenditures, produced a huge volume of business and demonstrated for the director's table of American business that advertising was a force worthy of the attention of big minds.[13]

Origins of the Advertising Agency

Volney Palmer is considered by most advertising historians to be the first advertising agent in the United States. He began by soliciting advertising for a variety of newspapers and, in 1841, established himself as an "agent" in Philadelphia. He opened a branch office in Boston in 1845 and one in New York in 1849. Initially, Palmer demanded a 25 percent commission from newspapers for all advertising he placed, but as competition from other agents increased, his commissions began to decrease.

While Palmer had been primarily concerned with newspapers, George P. Rowell was interested in all media and wanted to improve the service provided by agencies. He anticipated the needs of advertisers, bought space in large quantities, and resold it to advertisers in smaller lots at a profit. Rowell was the first agent to guarantee payment to publishers for their space, instead of asking them to wait until he had been paid by the advertisers. As a result, publishers were happy to sell him space at reduced rates and let him act as a middleman.

Another of Rowell's major contributions was the compilation of the *American Newspaper Directory* in 1869. This directory not only gave a description of 5,411 U.S. newspapers, but also included the circulation figures. In 1888 Rowell founded the first major magazine in the United States devoted to advertising, *Printers' Ink.*

Most scholars agree that early advertising agencies played a vital role in developing advertising and promoting growth in all areas of American business. Certainly, the agency facilitated the purchase and sale of advertising space. However, as historian Ralph Hower noted, in a larger sense, "the agency's chief service in this early period was to promote the general use of advertising, and thus to aid in discovering cheaper and more effective ways of marketing goods."[14]

While urbanization altered the way manufacturers could distribute goods, it also altered the manner in which they could distribute messages. Concentrated markets were simultaneously concentrated audiences. Mass media, such as the daily mass-circulation newspaper and mass-circulation magazines (made possible, in part, by rail transportation), provided a way to get messages to those audiences. As the media environment became more complex, advertising agents began to sell space in magazines as well as in newspapers, bidding for accounts principally on the basis of their "list" of newspapers, magazines, and periodicals.

Until the 1880s, the chief service of advertising agents remained space buying. Although agents would sometimes assist clients in "polishing" their copy, the writing of advertising **copy** was still not considered the proper work or responsibility of an agency. Clients, it was believed, were better qualified to write their own ads.

FIGURE 1.13

A 1908 Advertisement That Is Typical of Claude Hopkin's Long-Copy, Reason-Why Technique

How to Bake Beans

We have no secrets, madam. We are going to tell how you—if you had the facilities—could bake Pork and Beans exactly as good as Van Camp's.

Get the choicest of Michigan beans, picked over by hand. Get only the whitest, the plumpest, the fullest-grown. Have them all of one size.

You will need to pay from six to eight times what some beans would cost, but they're worth it.

Soak the beans over night, then parboil them.

Now comes the impossible. The beans must be baked in live steam, and you lack it. That steam must be superheated to 245 degrees.

Dry heat won't do. You can't supply enough dry heat without burning the beans to a crisp.

Then the beans must be baked in small parcels — we bake in the cans. That's so the full heat of the oven can attack every particle. Otherwise the beans will not be digestible. They will ferment and form gas, as do your home-baked beans now.

Bake the tomato sauce with the beans — bake it into them. That's how we get our delicious blend. When the beans are baked until they are mealy, surround the can with cold water. That stops the baking instantly, and sets the blend and savor.

Then you will have beans that are wholly digestible. All beans will be baked alike, yet not a skin will be broken. The beans will be nutty because they are whole.

Then the tomato sauce — that's impossible for you. It must be made from whole, vine-ripened tomatoes, picked when the juice fairly sparkles.

When you buy the sauce, you rarely know what you are getting. If it is made from tomatoes picked green, it lacks zest. If made of scraps from a canning factory, it lacks richness.

Some tomato sauce is sold ready-made for exactly one-fifth what we spend to make ours.

Our point is this: It isn't your fault that home-baked beans are mushy and broken — crisped on the top and half-baked in the middle. That they are neither nutty nor mealy — nor even digestible. That they always ferment and form gas. It is simply your lack of facilities.

Van Camp's
PORK AND BEANS

The best way is to let us cook them for you. We have all the facilities. Let us furnish the meals—fresh and savory—ready for instant serving.

Think how unwise it is to bake your own beans when you can get Van Camp's. Here is Nature's choicest food — 84 per cent nutriment. More food value than meat at a third the cost. A food you should serve at least three times a week. Think what you are missing, and what your people are missing when you spoil such a dish as that.

Leave the choice to your people. Ask them which beans they want. And be glad of their choice. For, if they like Van Camp's, see the bother you save. And see what you save on your meat bills.

Three sizes: 10, 15 and 20 cents per can.

The Van Camp Packing Company, *Established 1861* **Indianapolis, Ind.**

Advertising agencies, competing for accounts, began to realize that a poorly written advertisement reflected negatively on the agency. As a result, by 1900 most agencies had expanded their service to include copywriting. Albert D. Lasker, with the help of two great writers—John E. Kennedy and Claude C. Hopkins—built the Lord & Thomas agency around the function of copywriting. Hopkins was one of advertising's great copywriters. An astute student of human nature, he decided early in his career that people like to buy; moreover, he found that they wanted reasons for buying—preferably selfish reasons. Hopkins is the father of a simple, direct advertising style commonly referred to as reason-why copy, illustrated in Figure 1.13.

The Emergence of National Advertising

The business community gradually began to realize that its continued prosperity involved not only the production and distribution of goods but also the creation of a buying public. One of the first steps taken to control what has been called the *crisis in control of consumption* was the emergence of the modern industrial enterprise, a single firm which integrated the processes of mass production and mass distribution.[15] These firms were willing to invest effort not only in producing their products but in selling them as well. Thus, manufacturers began to appropriate part of the selling job formerly left to retailers. They did so in part because the existing marketers were unable to sell and distribute goods in the volume being produced. Manufacturers also realized that, as long as they produced undifferentiated products, they were at the mercy of wholesalers who forced them to compete on the basis of price. In order to regain market power, these manufacturers began to package their products, distinguish them through branding, and advertise those products directly to the consumer.

Late in the nineteenth century, corporate mergers approached the dimensions of a mania. The National Biscuit Company was the result of an 1898 merger of three companies—New York Biscuit, American Biscuit and Manufacturing, and the United States Baking Company. The newly formed company immediately made a number of changes in its internal management strategies to ensure its success. To differentiate its product, the company took its biscuits "out of the cracker barrel"; gave them a distinctive shape; developed a brand name, Uneeda, and a trademark, the boy in the slicker; and packaged the cracker in a unique, airtight package. Knowing that it had a product consumers wanted, the company turned to advertising to inform consumers of the product's existence.[16]

The advertising agency chosen by the National Biscuit Company was N. W. Ayer & Son, then one of the largest agencies in the United States. The campaign, launched in 1899, was the first million-dollar advertising campaign. Advertising was placed in magazines, newspapers, and streetcars, as well as on posters and painted signs. Slogans such as "You know Uneeda Biscuit" and "Lest you forget, we say it yet, Uneeda Biscuit" became familiar household phrases. The boy in the slicker, symbolizing the virtues of the stay-fresh inner seal, became a commonly recognized character. (He appears in an early Uneeda ad reproduced as Figure 1.14.) Within a year Uneeda crackers were selling at a rate of 10 million boxes a month.

The implications for the advertising industry were as important as the success of the campaign itself. Branding and packaging provided consumers with the "unprecedented guarantee that the experience of a particular product was repeatable."[17] The success of the Uneeda campaign proved that national advertising, trademarks, and consumer packaging could be used to attain control of a market. Mass consumption patterns apparently could be stimulated and controlled. The success of the campaign, as such, suggested the important role that advertising could

Case Study: National Biscuit Company

FIGURE 1.14

Uneeda's Famous "Boy in a Slicker" Symbolizing the Stay-Fresh Inner Seal

play in a company's marketing efforts and encouraged the acceptance of advertising as a business strategy.

The experience of the National Biscuit Company also illustrates the changing nature of the relationship between advertising agencies and their clients. Hower described this relationship in his history of the Ayer agency:

> [Ayer] set a precedent in the field by placing at the disposal of an advertiser the expanding facilities of the modern advertising agency. And here, as never before, an advertising agency amply proved its ability to plan and execute advertising as an integral part of a general selling campaign. The Ayer agency and the National Biscuit Company worked in such close cooperation that one cannot say which made the greater contribution. This much is beyond question: N. W. Ayer . . . gave counsel at every step, helped to coordinate the advertising efforts of the company's own sales force and its retailers, and contributed the name around which the campaign centered.[18]

The association with the National Biscuit Company led Ayer to adopt a "no competing accounts" policy that would eventually become standard practice throughout the advertising industry. By 1920 Ayer had developed a well-organzied publicity bureau, largely as a result of its public relations work for National Biscuit Company and Standard Oil. This rather dramatic expansion of agency services occurred at a time when agency involvement in client advertising was typically limited primarily to space buying and copywriting. Ayer thus raised the issue of what constituted "essential" agency service, an issue that continues to be a point of debate in the advertising and business communities.

As the nineteenth century drew to a close, then, several patterns in business activity were discernible. Many businesses became internally bureaucratic; that is, they developed internal management hierarchies. They also became externally oligopolistic, so that an industry was often dominated by a few large firms. Competition within oligopolistic industries was not at all the same as when small manufacturing units competed through middlemen. Competition now was carried out at every stage of the production and distribution process. It was most obvious in marketing, where advertising became one manner of competing. By the turn of the century, advertising was becoming an increasingly prevalent business strategy, as well as a highly visible cultural phenomenon.

New Levels of Competition

Advertising in the Early Twentieth Century

During the first two decades of the twentieth century, advertising continued its phenomenal growth. Advertising practitioners undertook a number of activities aimed at transforming their "trade" into a "profession." (For a brief discussion of early efforts undertaken by advertising women to professionalize the field, see the Ad Insight entitled "The League of Advertising Women of New York.") Among these activities were the following:

- Formation of local advertising clubs, such as the Agate Club (1894) in Chicago, the Advertising Club of New York (1906), and the League of Advertising Women of New York (1912)
- Formation of national associations, such as the Associated Advertising Clubs of the World (1905), the Association of National Advertisers (1910), and the **American Association of Advertising Agencies** (1912)
- Founding of a number of trade publications, such as *Printers' Ink* (1888), *Judicious Advertising* (1903), and *Advertising and Selling* (1909)
- Establishment of academic programs in the field of advertising in universities
- Internal attempts to gain ethical control of the field, characterized by the truth-in-advertising movement, the development of the Printers' Ink Statute (1911), and the formation of the National Vigilance Committee (1912), which would later become the **Better Business Bureau**

Attempts to achieve professional stature were also responsible for efforts to make advertising "scientific" through an association with the emerging social science of psychology. Harlow Gale conducted the first study in advertising psychology at the University of Minnesota as early as 1895; however, Walter Dill Scott of Northwestern University was the first to suggest in 1901 that psychology could furnish a stable foundation for a theory of advertising.

As the advertising industry became interested in applying scientific principles to consumption, a number of market **feedback** technologies arose. The analysis of keyed coupon responses, known as **inquiry testing,** was the mainstay of direct-response advertising. As such, it has long been a part of advertising industry practice.

The League of Advertising Women of New York: The Professionalization of Women in Advertising

The contributions that women made to the development of advertising have been largely ignored, despite the involvement of women in advertising from its earliest days. The successful League of Advertising Women of New York was the first of many efforts to create a community of professional advertising women.

The Advertising Club of New York was established in 1906, and several organizations of advertising men began meeting regularly in New York City in the ensuing years. None of these clubs admitted women to membership or allowed them to attend meetings. This discrimination provided the impetus for the formation of the League of Advertising Women of New York in 1912.

The League (later, the Advertising Women of New York [AWNY], a club that remains active today) was founded in the spring of that year at the instigation of J. George Frederick, at the time a contributing editor to *Printers' Ink,* and Christine Frederick, a consulting editor of *The Ladies Home Journal.* Christine Frederick later became a well-known advocate and leader of the home economics movement.

According to accounts in the trade press, approximately forty prominent women in advertising attended the first meeting. Officers were appointed and a committee was established to draft a constitution. That document outlined the purpose of the organization:

> The objects of this organization shall be to enable women doing constructive work in advertising to cooperate for the purpose of mutual advancement; to further the study of advertising in its various branches; and to emphasize the work that women are doing and are especially qualified to do in the many-sided business of advertising.

In pursuance of these objectives, the League participated in a wide variety of activities. Regular meetings featured prominent speakers, not only from advertising and business, but also from fields such as law, entertainment, and politics. Female "notables," such as Amelia Earhart and Mary Pickford, were also frequent speakers. Other speakers represented "causes" in which the League was involved (for example, suffrage, child and infant labor laws, the repeal of the eight-hour work day).

Social events were also an important part of the club's activities. Although sometimes held for the sole purpose of bringing members together, more frequently these events (which ranged from bridge parties to an annual formal ball) were efforts to raise funds for a number of League activities.

The League undertook a number of educational efforts for members, women in advertising who were not members, and consumers. Offering evening advertising classes "open to all women who wished to study the subject," the League each year provided a scholarship to a local university for the two women who had achieved the highest scores in that class. In attempting to educate consumers about advertising, the League sponsored a weekly radio program, organized a speaker's bureau, and in later years, held consumer clinics to discuss topics of concern to consumers and advertisers.

The commitment to the "mutual advancement" of advertising women is clearly evident in the League's involvement in assisting advertising women in other cities to organize. By 1916, women's advertising clubs had been formed in Boston, New York, Dayton, Denver, Los Angeles, and Philadelphia. When the Associated Advertising Clubs of the World held its convention in Philadelphia in 1916, one hundred advertising women from various parts of the country held a meeting of their own "to deal with problems of particular interest to them." This group later (1922) became the Federation of Women's Advertising Clubs of the World.

John Caples, who was to become famous as a copywriter, researcher, and author of advertising books, developed a number of copy principles based on the results of inquiry testing, using ads such as the one in Figure 1.15. He wrote this ad, one of the most successful and most widely quoted advertisements of all time, in 1925.

Beginning about 1910, a number of new types of research appeared: information on sales, information on wholesale and retail establishments, information on media

FIGURE 1.15

One of the Most Successful and Most Widely Quoted
Advertisements of All Time

audiences, and more general surveys of consumers. This research was undertaken by members of the media, such as the Chicago Tribune Company and Curtis Publishing Company; by corporations, such as U.S. Rubber and Swift and Company; by independent research organizations, such as the Business Bourse, Eastman Research Bureau, and the Market Research Company; by academic institutions, such as the Harvard Graduate School of Business Administration; and by advertising agencies.

N. W. Ayer & Son in 1879 conducted what is considered to be the first formal research project, although research did not become a part of Ayer's work until considerably later. J. Walter Thompson established the first research department in an advertising agency in 1915. In 1920, John B. Watson, a famous psychologist, joined the firm in an effort to promote the science of behaviorism in business and advertising practice.

Advertising in the 1920s

The industry's drive to achieve professional stature was aided greatly by the effort of the Committee on Public Information during World War I. The industry's perceptions of its role in that war were described later by a practitioner:

> Advertising did not win the war, but it did its bit so effectively that when the war was over advertising and its manifold mediums had the recognition of all governments as a prime essential in any large undertaking in which the active support of all the people must be obtained for success.[19]

The momentum that developed escalated in the general optimism of the age. The romantic rise of business and an increasing number of commercial rags-to-riches stories added to the perceptions of advertising's capabilities. For the first time, marketing, including advertising and selling, was not only respectable, but was considered equal in importance to production. The high-pressure salesman and the high-pressure advertising man were the heroes of the 1920s. Both contributed to the growth of mass markets needed to support the country's mass-production facilities.

During the 1920s the public thus adopted an almost evangelical view of business. Advertising, now increasingly seen to be an integral component of business activity, was able to capitalize on the positive environment. In the public view, advertising accomplished astonishing feats, and as a result was allowed its excesses. Verbal hyperbole and even blatant dishonesty were of seemingly little concern to a public caught up in jazz, speculation, flapper dresses, and the "latest model." Whatever was good for business was good for prosperity, and prosperity was good for the nation. Looking back at the era, one writer summarized: "Advertising would never again have it so plush; the public so uncritically accepting, the economy so robust, the government so approving, the trade at its zenith, high tide and green grass."[20]

The Depression Years

Given the prosperity of the twenties, it is not surprising that the reality of the Great Depression was slow to sink into public consciousness. The seriousness of the crisis was persistently denied by the business and financial communities. However, economic realities soon belied these denials. Banks closed, then businesses. Those businesses that were able to survive laid off workers or drastically cut wages. When businesses withered, new ones were not undertaken. Advertising agencies faced their first major crisis.

Many clients, experiencing steady declines in sales, saw the slashing of advertising budgets as a relatively painless way to cut costs. Advertisers also began to question the value of advertising and to scrutinize agency service. They clamored not only for more effective advertising from their agencies, but also for services beyond the essentials of copy, art, media, and research. Manufacturers were seeking someone that could help all the time—during depression and prosperity, even if no advertising was placed. As the depression continued, this increasing restlessness was reflected in intensified account shifting and high agency turnover.

Diminished advertising volume left many agencies struggling for survival, and out of necessity the advertising industry became intensely competitive. Agencies offered more and more collateral services in an effort to retain increasingly anxious clients. A writer in *Advertising and Selling*, an industry trade publication, described the expansion of agency service:

> Agencies established research departments. . . . They developed artists and made their services available for the designing of packages and the styling of goods as well as for the illustrations of advertisements. They studied selling, conducted sales meetings, dramatized selling talks, drilled salesmen, and originated sales strategies. They planned, designed, decorated and landscaped shops, factories, offices, salesrooms, and rede-signed old products and created new ones. They dressed windows, invented publicity stunts and staged conventions.[21]

To overcome the sales resistance of consumers, advertising practitioners turned more and more to research. Psychologists and researchers like A. C. Nielsen, George Gallup, Arch Crossley, and Daniel Starch developed research organizations to probe the minds of consumers and find answers to questions about their purchasing and media habits.

In these desperate times, advertising agencies were also pressured by clients to create advertisements that fell far short of the self-imposed guidelines they had established for themselves in the early years of the twentieth century. (For examples

Advertising Is Tested Beyond Its Strength: The Great Depression

"Old magazines provide a fascinating window onto our social history," writes historian Richard W. Pollay, "and it is the advertisements that comprise the most interesting pages, displaying behaviors, styles, and roles for diverse objects of culture."[1]

During the economic crisis of the depression, advertisers pulled out all the stops in trying to increase consumer spending. Although advertising practitioners had developed self-regulatory codes much earlier in the century, these codes were flagrantly disregarded by manufacturers during the prolonged market depression of the 1930s, and it seems, were easily abandoned by nervous practitioners.

In 1938, the president of the AAAA summarized the advertising of the era:

> Distress was so widespread, and a mood of panic was created. People were easily alarmed. Copy-writers took advantage of it. They appealed to all sorts of fears, of

loss of health, of waning beauty, of failure in life and love. If you did not use a certain toothpaste, you might fall a prey to pyorrhea; if you did not eat a certain food, you might be missing vitamins indispensable to health; if certain cosmetics were not used, marriage might be wrecked.[2]

As an act of self-preservation, agencies were driven by the demands of clients they could not afford to lose. As a result, the advertising industry found itself in the unenviable position of producing advertisements that handicapped its efforts to be recognized as a profession.

[1] Richard W. Pollay, "The Subsiding Sizzle: A Descriptive History of Print Advertising, 1900–1980," *Journal of Marketing* 49 (Summer 1985): 24.
[2] John Benson, "Trends in Consumer Advertising," *Journal of Marketing* 3 (July 1938): 21.

of depression-era ads, see the Ad Insight entitled, "Advertising Is Tested beyond Its Strength.") And John Benson, writing retrospectively as president of the AAAA, noted:

> Hard times have brought increased competition. The manufacturer has gotten nervous. He has put upon advertising a strain that is greater than it can bear. And his advertising, as a result, has assumed the grotesque attitudes and grimaces of a man tested beyond his strength.[22]

The depression brought about a searching examination of the economic system that had allowed such a debacle to occur. Could it be that the great capitalist machine didn't work after all? Professional critics as well as the public looked for scapegoats, and one of the favorite targets was advertising. The attacks on advertising in the 1930s were dramatically different from previous ones; they were more bitter and far-reaching. The critics struck at the very concept of advertising rather than merely at its excesses or at the products it promoted.

The indications of public disapproval were numerous. Muckraking books, such as *100,000,000 Guinea Pigs* and *Eat, Drink, and Be Wary,* portrayed advertising as an unscrupulous exploiter of the consumer. The rising tide of public resentment of advertising excesses led to a reemergence of the consumer movement. In response to the movement, Consumers' Research and Consumers Union were formed to provide unbiased information for consumers.

Some of the opposition to advertising crystallized in the form of restrictive laws. A much-modified version of the original federal **Food, Drug, and Cosmetics Act** was passed in 1938. The **Wheeler-Lea Amendment** to the Federal Trade Commission Act (1938) granted the **Federal Trade Commission** added power to curb false advertising, which was designated an "unfair or deceptive act or practice in commerce."

The years following the depression were perplexing times for the advertising industry. Clearly, as one practitioner noted, advertising appeared to have fallen upon evil days; still perhaps it was a phase of maturation.[23] Hower summarized those years:

> Faced with acute operating difficulties because of the total business situation, subjected to public ridicule and to sharp attacks by reformers, harassed by bitter competition within the industry and by rapid change in business generally, and threatened with legislative action of a drastic nature, every phase of advertising was forced to undergo readjustment. It emerged considerably deflated, both in the eyes of the consuming public and in the opinion of the firms that used it. And yet, it emerged a more effective and essential mechanism than ever in our social and economic life.[24]

World War II Advertising

World War II presented a dilemma for advertisers. Some manufacturers, like those of cosmetics, tobacco, and other items unaffected by the demands of war, could continue their normal advertising campaigns. Others knew they would have products to sell, although they didn't know how many. Still others, like the manufacturers of automobiles and farm implements, converted their plants to the production of war goods and had nothing to sell. Regardless of their situation, manufacturers feared the public would forget them if they didn't advertise, but were at a loss as to the kind of advertising to use.

What kind of advertising did we see during World War II? In many cases, manufacturers turned to institutional advertising or developed patriotic themes. Manufacturers, anxious to suggest their contribution to the war effort, capitalized on wartime tie-ins. While such tie-ins were sometimes legitimate (see Figure 1.16 for a GM ad which incorporated a patriotic theme), in many cases the connections were, at best, strained. This "brag" advertising in which a company boasted of its own achievements often bordered on the ludicrous.[25] Historian James Playsted Wood cites some examples:

> Manufacturers of bolts and nuts used full magazine pages depicting bombers and fighter planes in action to show what their nuts and bolts were doing. Soft drink manufacturers ran copy which read as though the fighting troops owed all their energy and courage to drinking their beverages. . . . One manufacturer of air-conditioning equipment proclaimed that he had helped sink torpedoed Japanese ships because the periscope lens of American submarines had been ground and polished in an air-conditioned shop.[26]

FIGURE 1.16

World War II Advertisement with a Patriotic Theme

Another type of advertising during the war was "advocacy" advertising run by the government on behalf of the war effort. Unlike Britain, where the government bought and paid for advertising supporting war efforts, the United States used little paid advertising. Instead, most of the government advertising was the work of the War Advertising Council, a group composed of representatives of advertisers, advertising agencies, and media, which would later become the **Advertising Council** (discussed in Chapter 3). The council planned, executed, and placed national campaigns in support of war bonds; recruitment; conservation of scarce resources such as paper, rubber, fat, and scrap metal; and greater use of V-mail. As one historian noted, "Government had but to mention a wish and advertising was for it."[27] By 1944, the War Advertising Council had developed more than ninety war-theme campaigns. It is estimated that in total, over a billion dollars worth of space and time was given to these campaigns.

Advertising had taken seriously its responsibility of morale building. Just as they had following World War I, advertisers perceived great success in their war efforts:

> In 1945, ad men would look back and proudly claim to have bested every competitor in its own special contribution to the war effort—providing more cultural unity than the radio, more human insight than fiction, more empathy and understanding than comics, more comprehension of issues than the movies.[28]

The Postwar Years

The growth of postwar advertising was accelerated dramatically by the rise of television. Radio, which had first risen to national prominence in the late 1920s, lost its dominance as a national medium. It had to change its format, moving from network programming to specialized programming, and became primarily a local medium.

Some business leaders and economists predicted that both business activity and advertising expenditures would drop as America shifted to a peacetime economy in the 1940s. Despite recessions during the late 1940s and the 1950s, no dramatic drop in economic activity occurred. Expenditures rose consistently as business leaders turned to advertising as an essential ingredient in maintaining high-level consumption and introducing new products.

In the years following the war, clients once again came to expect more services from their agencies—publicity, merchandising, product development, and so on. Many small agencies were forced to merge in order to provide these services and remain competitive. Advertising in the 1950s has been described as safe, dull, and lacking in flair or distinction. Some blamed this "creative drought" on the increased emphasis on market and copy research. Others saw it as a reflection of a lack of creativity in product design. Agencies were being asked to market more and more products that were essentially alike:

> Whether you are talking products, advertising ideas, layout treatments, package design, or what have you, we are in the greatest era of monkey-see, monkey-do the world has ever known.[29]

In many ways, the 1960s were a reversal of the trends of the 1950s. Emphasis shifted from large agencies to small and from research and science to creativity based on "art, inspiration, and intuition."[30] It was the decade of creative "giants." Through the creative efforts of the Leo Burnett agency, Tony the tiger, the Pillsbury dough boy, Charlie the tuna, and the Marlboro man became household friends. David Ogilvy demonstrated the power of brand image in successful campaigns for Hathaway shirts, Schweppes, and Rolls Royce. And William Bernbach introduced the American public to a small German car—the Volkswagen, with a campaign that gained one of the highest readerships ever. (See Figure 1.17 for a VW ad that is classic Bernbach.)

In contrast to the 1950s, then, the 1960s were years of creative revolution. In the 1970s, the revolution subsided. Historian Stephen Fox summarizes the decade:

> In style, back to hard sell, science, and research—an emphasis . . . on the product instead of the ad. In organization, a shift from the creative departments to management, from little boutiques to bigness and mergers, from vivid personalities to corporate anonymity. In sum, a fast trip in a time machine back to the 1950s.[31]

During the postwar period, particularly in recent years as trade barriers in Eastern Europe, Russia, and China have began to topple, advertisers, the agencies that handle the accounts, and media have moved abroad to take advantage of foreign markets. One industry observer recently wrote that, "Advertising, like its media cousin, is making the world a global village." As mentioned earlier, in 1991, for the first time, Tokyo replaced New York's Madison Avenue as the world's advertising capital.[32]

Many of the forces that have changed and will continue to change the world of advertising are of fairly recent origin and are discussed later in the textbook. Certainly, the dynamics of the media environment will be a major factor in the coming years. The proliferation of new and nontraditional media, such as cable television, videocassettes, and interactive view-data systems, as well as the nontraditional use of traditional media, such as the Airport Channel, allow advertisers to reach smaller, more selective audiences. Advances in data-base creation and management make it

FIGURE 1.17

Bernbach and the VW Bug— a Combination of Humor, Single-Point Sales Emphasis, Dramatic Layout, and Honesty

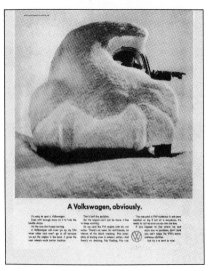

A Volkswagen, obviously.

possible for advertisers to target *individuals* with their promotional efforts. Multimedia "deals" have transformed the media-buying function. The success of advertising and marketing strategies will be assessed using an ever-expanding number of feedback technologies. Social, economic, and legislative factors, as yet uncertain, will further establish the milieu in which advertising will operate.

What can be expected of advertising in the decades to come? One thing is certain. Advertising, as an institution, has exhibited a phenomenal resiliency over the past 150 years. In that time, its work has been defined and subsequently redefined in light of changing problems and priorities. Institutional relationships have been formed and transformed in response to changing demands. In the long run, the permanence of any institution depends upon its capacity to adapt. Advertising, most certainly, has that capacity.

Summary

Most people, including many business people, have strong, widely varying, and sometimes erroneous views about advertising. Whether accurate or inaccurate, their views most likely have developed from exposure to particular advertisements. They do not reflect a true understanding of the decisions behind the ads and commercials or of advertising's institutional role in modern society.

Advertising is sometimes considered an art and sometimes a science. It is "paid, nonpersonal communication through various mass media by business firms, nonprofit organizations, and individuals who are in some way identified in the advertising message and who hope to inform or persuade members of a particular audience."

To be understood, advertising must be placed in the broader context of marketing and communication. It is a communication tool utilized by marketers to help bring about buyer-seller exchange. Advertising differs from other forms of marketing communication—sales promotion, publicity, public relations, and personal selling—but it coordinates with these forms to accomplish marketing objectives.

Advertising can be categorized in many ways—by audience, by type of advertising, by media, and by function. Although scholars and practitioners have been only partially successful in discovering how advertising works, we know that its direct influence on behavior is always mediated by the environmental structure in which it operates and by characteristics internal to targeted consumers. Its environmental structure is composed of four environments—the social/cultural environment, the regulatory environment, the competitive environment, and the economic environment.

As measured by media billings and number of employees, advertising is a large, worldwide industry. Foreign advertising spending is expected to grow at a faster rate than domestic expenditures.

As an institution, advertising experienced its greatest growth during the late 1800s and early 1900s. Industrial expansion, mass merchandising, urban concentration, and advances in transportation and communication at the end of the Civil War led to the packaging and branding of products, which in turn led to the development of advertising as we know it today.

During these years, agencies went from being brokers of media space to becoming providers of a wide variety of advertising services, including copywriting, media placement, and research. Advertising practitioners formed associations and recruited academics to make the business of advertising more professional and scientific. New media, with the capacity to more efficiently deliver advertising messages, were introduced.

Advertising prospered in the 1920s, suffered through the depression and World War II, flourished again in the postwar years as television emerged as a national advertising medium, and continues to adapt in the uncertain economic climate of the 1990s.

Questions for Discussion

1. How can advertising be classified? Why is it so difficult to define?
2. What are advertising's environments? How do they affect advertising campaign planning?
3. Collect from current magazines and newspapers examples of the best in modern advertising. Why do you believe the ads you selected are good?
4. Name and explain four functions of advertising. How do the functions relate to other marketing communication forms?
5. What is the relationship between advertising and branding?
6. Explain the relationship among the major advertising organizations. Why does the advertising business revolve around the advertiser?
7. Why did advertising develop rapidly in the United States during the late 1800s and early 1900s?
8. Which media are available to advertisers today that were not available a century ago? What influence has the development of new media had on the growth of advertising?
9. How has advertising influenced the growth of mass production in an area such as the automobile industry?
10. Why does the nature of advertising change when a country is engaged in a major war?

Notes

1. Steuart Henderson Britt, Stephen C. Adams, and Allan S. Miller, "How Many Advertising Exposures per Day," *Journal of Advertising Research* 12 (December 1972): 3–9.
2. Charles H. Sandage and John D. Leckenby, "Student Attitudes toward Advertising: Institution vs. Instrument," *Journal of Advertising* 9 (Summer 1980): 29–32, 44; also Charles H. Sandage, "Some Institutional Aspects of Advertising," *Journal of Advertising* 1 (1973): 6–9.
3. Leo Bogart, *Strategy in Advertising: Matching Media and Messages to Markets and Motivations,* 2d ed. (Chicago: Crain Books, 1984), 1.
4. Stephen Fox, *The Mirror Makers: A History of American Advertising and Its Creators* (New York: William Morrow and Company, Fall 1984).
5. Ibid., 7.
6. Sidney R. Bernstein, "What Is Advertising?" *Advertising Age,* April 30, 1980, 32.
7. David Ogilvy, *Confessions of an Advertising Man* (New York: Atheneum, 1963), 87–91.
8. Cited in Philip Kotler, *Marketing Management: Analysis, Planning, and Control,* 4th ed. (Englewood Cliffs, NJ: Prentice-Hall, 1980), 498.
9. Michael Schudson, *Advertising, the Uneasy Persuasion* (New York: Basic Books, 1984).
10. Bogart, *Strategy in Advertising,* 1.
11. Estimates taken from *Advertising Age* (March 25, 1991, and January 6, 1991).
12. Alfred D. Chandler, Jr., *The Visible Hand: The Managerial Revolution in American Business* (Cambridge, MA: Harvard University Press, 1977), 218–219.
13. Frank Presbrey, *The History and Development of Advertising* (Garden City, NY: Doubleday, Doran and Co., Inc., 1929), 300.
14. Ralph P. Hower, *The History of An Advertising Agency,* rev. ed. (Cambridge, MA: Harvard University Press, 1949), 19.
15. James R. Beniger, *The Control Revolution* (Cambridge, MA: Harvard University Press, 1986), 345–389.
16. National Biscuit Company, Annual Report (January 3, 1902), quoted in Alfred D. Chandler, Jr., *The Visible Hand: The Managerial Revolution in American Business* (Cambridge, MA: Harvard University Press, 1977), 33.
17. Daniel J. Boorstin, *The Americans: The Democratic Experience* (New York: Random House, 1973), 447.
18. Hower, *The History of an Advertising Agency,* 94.
19. Presbrey, *The History and Development of Advertising,* 566.
20. Stephen Fox, *The Mirror Makers* (New York: William Morrow, 1984), 79.
21. Lee H. Bristol, "Management Takes a Square Look at Agency Practice," *Advertising and Selling,* November 24, 1932, 13.
22. John Benson, "The True Function of Advertising," *Advertising and Selling,* July 4, 1935, 29.

[23] H. A. Batten, "An Advertising Man Looks at Advertising," *Atlanta Monthly,* July 1932, 55.

[24] Hower, *The History of an Advertising Agency,* 152.

[25] Raymond Rubicam, "What We Saw, Read, and Heard: Advertising," in *While You Were Gone: A Report on Wartime Life in the United States,* Jack Goodman, ed., (New York: Simon and Schuster, 1946), 439.

[26] James Playsted Wood, *The Story of Advertising* (New York: the Ronald Press Company, 1958), 443.

[27] Wood, *The Story of Advertising,* 447.

[28] Frank W. Fox, *Madison Avenue Goes to War* (Provo, Utah: Brigham Young University Press, 1957), 11.

[29] Sigurd Larmon writing in *Advertising Age,* December 17, 1956, quoted in Fox, *The Mirror Makers,* 180.

[30] Fox, *The Mirror Makers,* 218.

[31] Fox, *The Mirror Makers,* 314.

[32] R. Craig Endicott, "Tokyo Supplants N.Y. as Ad Capital," *Advertising Age,* April 13, 1992, S–1.

Suggested Readings

Bogart, Leo. *Strategy in Advertising: Matching Media and Messages to Markets and Motivations.* 2d ed. Chicago: Crain Books, 1984.

Borden, Neil H. *The Economic Effects of Advertising.* Homewood, IL: Irwin, 1942, Chapter 2.

Fox, Stephen. *The Mirror Makers.* New York: William Morrow, 1984.

Fox, Stephen, Richard Wightman, and T. J. Jackson Lears, eds. *The Culture of Consumption.* New York: Pantheon Books, 1983.

Goodrum, Charles, and Helen Dalrymple. *Advertising in America: The First 200 Years.* New York: Harry N. Abrams, Inc., 1990.

Gunther, John. *Taken at the Flood: The Story of Albert D. Lasker.* New York: Harper & Row, 1960.

Hower, Ralph M. *The History of An Advertising Agency.* Rev. ed. Cambridge, MA: Harvard University Press, 1949.

Leiss, William, Stephen Kline, and Sut Jhally. *Social Communication in Advertising.* 2d ed., New York: Routledge, 1990.

Marchand, Roland. *Advertising the American Dream.* Berkeley, CA: University of California Press, 1985.

Pope, Daniel. *The Making of Modern Advertising.* New York: Basic Books, 1983.

Presbrey, Frank S. *The History and Development of Advertising.* Garden City, NY: Doubleday, Doran and Company, Inc., 1929.

Roswell, George. *Forty Years as an Advertising Agent.* New York: Printers' Ink, 1906.

Rotzoll, Kim B., and James E. Haefner. *Advertising in Contemporary Society.* 2d ed., Cincinnati, OH: South-Western, 1990.

Rowsome, Frank. *They Laughed When I Sat Down: An Informal History of Advertising in Words and Pictures.* New York: McGraw-Hill, 1959.

Schudson, Michael. *Advertising, the Uneasy Persuasion.* New York: Basic Books, 1984.

Strasser, Susan. *Satisfaction Guaranteed: The Making of the American Mass Market.* New York: Pantheon Books, 1989.

Tedlow, Richard S. *New and Improved: the Story of Mass Marketing in America.* New York: Basic Books, Inc., 1990.

Environmental Considerations: Social/Cultural, Competition, Economic, Regulatory

Advertising Organizations: Advertisers, Agencies, Media, Suppliers

Marketing Communication Considerations: Marketing Planning

Strategic Research Inputs

Objective Setting: Target Market, Buyer Behavior

Determining the Advertising Budget

Message Strategy

Media Strategy

Message Tactics

Media Tactics

Final Budget

Plan in Action Run Campaign

Impact

Feedback

Feedback

Measure Advertising Effectiveness

LEARNING OBJECTIVES

In your study of this chapter, you will have an opportunity to:

• See how marketing, communication, and advertising are related

• Gain an overview of the marketing concept and the elements of marketing planning.

• Examine the role of advertising in promotion strategy.

• Understand the nature of communication and the elements of the communication process.

• Look at advertising as a form of mass communication.

• Consider the barriers to advertising communication.

• Identify the communicative functions of advertising.

Chapter **2**

Marketing and Advertising Communication

CHAPTER TOPICS

MARKETING DEFINED

THE MARKETING CONCEPT

THE MARKETING PLAN
  Identifying Marketing Opportunities
  Setting Marketing Objectives
  Determining Marketing Strategy

ADVERTISING IN THE PROMOTION MIX
  Promotion Strategies
  Advertising Planning Decisions

THE COMMUNICATION CONCEPT
  The Communication Planning Environment
  Communication Defined
  Signs
  Field of Experience
  Meaning

ELEMENTS OF THE COMMUNICATION PROCESS
  Source and Encoding
  The Message
  The Media
  Receivers and Decoding
  Feedback
  Noise

ADVERTISING'S COMMUNICATION SETTING

ADVERTISING'S COMMUNICATIVE FUNCTIONS

To understand how advertising works, one must first be knowledgeable in the two related fields of which advertising is a part—marketing and communication. Concepts from both fields form the base from which advertising is planned, and, as shown in the advertising planning model presented in Chapter 1, are central to effective advertising decision making.

Marketing and communication are interrelated in both theory and practice. According to the noted historian, Otis Pease, advertising influences society in two ways: (1) as an instrument of marketing communication and (2) as a form of social communication. As an instrument of marketing, it works to sell products, services, or ideas through persuasion; as a form of social communication, it offers "messages about society, perhaps about life as some of us ordinarily live it or would like to live it."[1]

We all easily recognize advertising's role as an instrument of marketing. What we may not see is how, as social communication, advertising helps us to construct and understand our social world. It reflects or counters how we dress or should

37

dress; it mirrors or contradicts our values and actions; and it bestows status on, or takes status away from, products and the people who consume them.[2] In either form—as marketing communication or as social communication—buyer-seller interaction is involved, and communication, whether purposeful, accidental, or incidental, is necessary for interaction to occur.

In this chapter, a more detailed look at the two interrelated fields is presented. Building on the brief background on marketing and communication in Chapter 1, we first look at marketing concepts and the role of advertising in marketing and then at communication concepts and advertising as a form of communication.

Marketing Defined

In 1985, the American Marketing Association (AMA) defined **marketing** as the "process of planning and executing the conception, pricing, promotion, and distribution of ideas, goods, and services to create exchanges that satisfy individual and organizational objectives."[3]

Although there are many definitions of marketing, the AMA definition incorporates widely accepted principles of modern marketing:

- The marketing of a product, service, or idea is guided by the ability of what is produced and marketed to satisfy consumer wants and needs.
- Consumers are willing to give something of value (for example, money) to organizations in exchange for their production.
- The marketing elements of product, price, distribution, and promotion are employed to facilitate consumer satisfaction and organizational well-being (that is, profits or donations).
- Marketing theory and techniques are applicable to both profit-seeking and nonprofit organizations.

As a human activity, marketing is based on four related conditions:

- *Human Needs and Wants*   All humans have needs and wants. Needs are few and arise out of biological conditions. Wants are many and result from social learning.
- *Objects*   Objects, in the form of products, services, places, activities, persons, organizations, or ideas, exist to satisfy human needs and wants. All objects have both physical and subjective qualities.
- *Exchange*   Exchange is the process through which two or more parties satisfy their needs and wants. Exchange occurs when each party has objects of mutual value; each party is capable of communication and delivery; and each party is free to reject or accept the objects involved in exchange.
- *Markets*   Markets consist of actual or potential buyers, who are willing and able to engage in exchange.[4]

The Marketing Concept

Much of what is known about marketing and how consumers react to marketing forces comes into focus in the **marketing concept.** As reflected in the AMA's definition of modern marketing, the marketing concept "holds that the key to achieving organizational goals consists in determining the needs and wants of target markets and delivering the desired satisfactions more effectively and efficiently than competitors."

In practice, the marketing concept means:

• The identification of actual or potential customer demand.
• The development and marketing of products, services, or ideas to satisfy identified customer demand.
• The communication of the want-satisfying qualities of products, services, or ideas to targeted customers.
• Making products, services, or ideas to reflect costs, competition, and the customer's ability to buy.
• The provision of services to ensure customer satisfaction after exchange.[5]

Advertising, as will be emphasized in the rest of this chapter, is a form of mass communication that functions to facilitate exchange by communicating the want-satisfying qualities of marketed products, services, and ideas to identified target markets. An advertisement that communicates the marketing concept is reproduced as Figure 2.1.

As a business philosophy, the marketing concept is a relatively recent phenomenon. Even though it was adopted by some organizations prior to 1950, official credence was given to the marketing concept in 1952 when General Electric publicly stated in its annual report that its management philosophy started with "what the consumer wants in a given product, and what price he [or she] is willing to pay, and where and when it will be wanted."[6]

There is a clear distinction between the marketing concept and the selling concept. According to marketing scholar Theodore Levitt, "Selling focuses on the needs of the seller; marketing on the needs of the buyer. Selling is preoccupied with the seller's need to convert his product into cash; marketing with the idea of satisfying

FIGURE 2.1

An Advertisement That Communicates the Marketing Concept

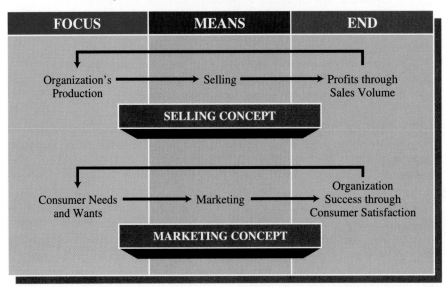

FIGURE 2.2

A Comparison of the Selling and Marketing Concepts

Source: Philip Kotler, *Marketing Management: Analysis, Planning, Implementation and Control,* 4th Edition, © 1980, p. 32. Adapted by permission of Prentice-Hall, Inc., Englewood Cliffs, N.J.

the needs of the customer by means of the product and the whole cluster of things associated with creating, delivering, and finally consuming it."[7] The philosophical distinction between the two concepts is illustrated in Figure 2.2.

Not all organizations adhere to the ideals of the marketing concept, although the concept is widely acknowledged by both profit-seeking and nonprofit organizations. Some, still, are selling oriented, and others pay lip service to the concept but do not actually practice it. It is likely that larger organizations are more consumer oriented than smaller organizations, and consumer-goods companies are more consumer oriented than industrial-goods companies. In the final analysis, adherence to the marketing concept is a managerial decision. If adopted and practiced, the concept guides all organizational marketing efforts.

The Marketing Plan

Basic to putting the marketing concept into practice and coordinating marketing with other business activities is the **marketing plan.** Few sophisticated organizations would attempt to make operating decisions without a marketing plan—usually covering a period of at least a year and often longer. Formulating such a plan typically involves the collection and analysis of secondary and primary information, the setting of marketing objectives based on this information, and the development of a marketing strategy that is most likely to accomplish the defined marketing objectives. Each step in marketing planning is covered in greater detail in Chapters 7 and 8. Here they will be described briefly to illustrate the role of advertising in marketing planning. The components of a marketing plan are presented in Figure 2.3.

The first step in marketing planning is the situation analysis. Knowing where the organization has been, where it is, and where it is going is critical to long-run market success. The situation analysis provides such information based on strategic research (see Chapter 8). It is carried out sequentially and utilizes internal and external secondary and primary data sources. Typically a situation analysis covers the following areas:

1. Organizational strengths, weaknesses, resources, and objectives
2. Product/service characteristics and features
3. Competitive activities and characteristics, including advertising efforts
4. Trade and distribution factors
5. Actual and potential buyer segments, characteristics, and behavior
6. Past organizational experiences with communication elements, including advertising efforts
7. Environmental conditions and factors.[8]

From the situation analysis, a set of marketing opportunities is identified. A **marketing opportunity,** as defined by Philip Kotler, is "an attractive arena of relevant marketing action in which a company is likely to enjoy a differential advantage."[9] There are two types of opportunities—environmental opportunities and organizational opportunities. Environmental opportunities are infinite because of unsatisfied consumer wants and needs. Improvements in technologies, changes in social values and activities, and the restructuring of governmental regulations are among the countless environmental conditions that may arise as opportunities.

Not all organizations can take advantage of environmental opportunities, however. Even if they are identified, an organization may not have the financial, technological, or personnel resources needed to gain a competitive advantage. For example, a small manufacturer that discovers an untapped market segment may be unable to take advantage of the discovery because its financial resources are insufficient to enter and develop the market. An advertising agency with a great chance to win a large account may be unable to enter the competition for the client because it lacks personnel with the necessary skills and expertise to satisfy the client's long-run needs. As these examples vividly point out, an environmental opportunity becomes

Identifying Marketing Opportunities

FIGURE 2.3

Basic Components of the Marketing Plan

1. **Situation Analysis: consumer, market, and competitive trends**
   Where have we been? Where are we now? Where are we going?
2. **Marketing Opportunities: internal and external**
   Is there a competitive advantage?
3. **Marketing Objectives: sales, volume, penetration**
   What do we want to achieve?
4. **Marketing Strategy: target markets and marketing mix elements**
   How can we get where we want to go?
   How best can we achieve our objectives?

Source: Adapted excerpt from *Contemporary Marketing,* 7th ed., by Louis E. Boone and David L. Kurtz, copyright © 1992 by The Dryden Press, adapted with permission from the publisher.

FIGURE 2.4

Steps in the Marketing Planning Process

Organizational Resources
Production
Marketing
Financial
Technological
Human

Environmental Factors
Competitive
Regulatory
Economic
Social/Cultural

Situation Analysis

Marketing Opportunities

Marketing Objectives

Marketing Strategy

Target Market

Marketing Mix

Source: Adapted Figure 3–2 from *Marketing,* by David L. Kurtz and Louis E. Boone, p. 65, copyright © 1987 by The Dryden Press, adapted with permission from the publisher.

an organizational opportunity only when the resources are available for the organization to act upon it. Some of the major organizational and environmental factors that have an impact on marketing opportunity analysis are listed in Figure 2.4, which shows the steps in the market planning process.

Once marketing opportunities have been identified, the second and third steps of marketing planning are executed: setting marketing objectives and determining marketing strategy.

Setting Marketing Objectives

Marketing objectives are statements of what the organization wants to achieve through its marketing efforts. They are conceived and stated in terms of profit, sales, and market share for profit-seeking organizations and in terms of contributions, participation, and conversion for nonprofit organizations. In either case, marketing objectives are established with respect to specific target markets, geographic locations, and time periods. As a planning device, marketing objectives guide the determination of marketing strategy, including advertising objectives. The emphasis in setting marketing objectives is on sales, whereas the emphasis in setting advertising objectives is on communicating a message that may contribute to sales. The distinction between the two can be illustrated as follows (for Rosebud Cosmetic Cream Company):

- *Marketing Objective*   to increase Rosebud's **market share** from 8 percent to 10 percent in one year.
- *Advertising [Communication] Objective*   to increase from 15 percent to

20 percent in one year the number of target consumers who believe that Rosebud Cream will keep skin soft for a longer time than competitors'.

The job of advertising is to communicate a sales message (in this case, "soft skin longevity") that will help the company achieve its marketing objective (to increase market share from 8 percent to 10 percent).

Marketing strategy, the third step in marketing planning, involves two stages: (1) identification of the **target market** and (2) establishment of the **marketing mix.** The determination of marketing strategy follows from the organization's marketing opportunity set and is formulated on the basis of marketing objectives.

Determining Marketing Strategy

The Target Market

The target market is an actual or potential group of people to whom the organization wishes to appeal. Target markets can be segmented and defined in many ways— by demographic differences, by psychological characteristics, by behavioral tendencies, or by marketing-factor sensitivities. The **market segmentation** decision is critical to advertising planning because it directs subsequent media and message strategies.

The Marketing Mix

The marketing mix combines four marketer-controlled decisions:

1. Product strategy, which involves decisions about such things as quality, branding, styles, packaging, options, services, and warranties.
2. Price strategy, which involves decisions about such things as credit, discounts, allowances, payment periods, and price lists.
3. Distribution strategy, which involves decisions about such things as wholesalers, retailers, transportation, distribution centers, and geographic coverage.
4. Promotion strategy, which involves decisions about four communication options—advertising, sales promotion, personal selling, and public relations.

Because the marketing mix is under the control of the marketer, it can be manipulated in many combinations. The mix elements are so interrelated that a decision about one will affect the decision about another (see Figure 2.5). The key is to coordinate all four decisions in a way that most effectively leads to the attainment of the marketing objectives.

Advertising in the Promotion Mix

The promotion mix is the decision point where advertising enters the process of marketing planning. Like the marketing mix, of which it is a part, the promotion mix involves the proper blending and coordination of four elements—advertising, sales promotion, personal selling, and public relations. Whether they are employed together or separately, the job of the four marketer-controlled communication tools is to influence consumer decisions.

Each form of promotion has its advantages and disadvantages (see Figure 2.6). Advertising reaches mass audiences and can create awareness very quickly. It gives the marketer control over message content and delivery, and it can be directed to

FIGURE 2.5

Elements of the Marketing Mix

Source: From *Contemporary Marketing,* 7th ed., by Louis E. Boone and David L. Kurtz, p. 21, copyright © 1992 by The Dryden Press, reprinted by permission of the publisher.

FIGURE 2.6

Comparison of the Four Elements of the Promotion Mix

	Advertising	Personal Selling	Sales Promotion	Public Relations
Advantages	• Reaches a large group of potential consumers for a relatively low price per exposure • Allows strict control over the final message • Can be adapted to either mass audiences or specific audience segments • Can be successfully used to create instant product awareness	• Permits measurement of effectiveness • Elicits a more immediate response • Allows tailoring of the message to fit the customer	• Produces a more immediate consumer response • Attracts attention and creates product awareness	• Is effective in creating a positive attitude toward a product or company • Can enhance credibility of the product or company
Disadvantages	• Does not permit totally accurate measurement of results • Usually cannot close sales • Is nonpersonal in nature	• Relies almost exclusively upon the ability of the salesperson • Involves high cost per contact	• Is nonpersonal in nature • Is difficult to differentiate from competitive efforts	• May not permit accurate measurement of effect on sales • Involves much effort directed toward nonmarketing-oriented goals

Source: Table 16.2 from *Contemporary Marketing,* 7th ed., by David L. Kurtz and Louis E. Boone, p. 534, copyright © 1992 by The Dryden Press, reprinted by permission of the publisher.

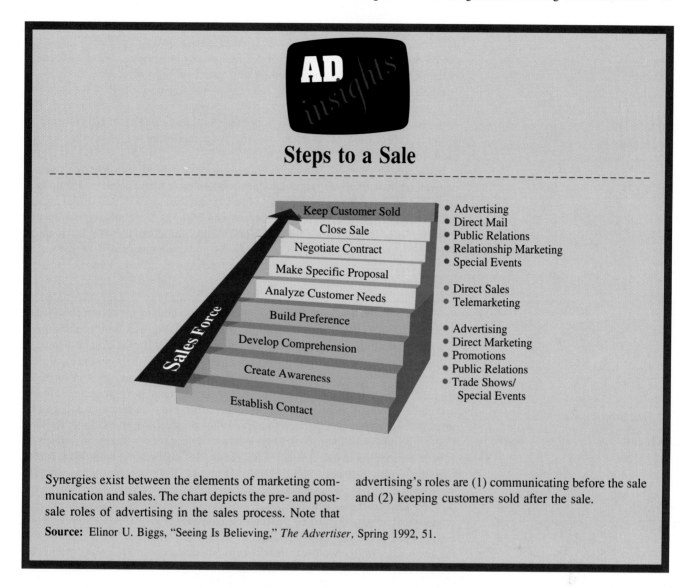

Synergies exist between the elements of marketing communication and sales. The chart depicts the pre- and post-sale roles of advertising in the sales process. Note that advertising's roles are (1) communicating before the sale and (2) keeping customers sold after the sale.

Source: Elinor U. Biggs, "Seeing Is Believing," *The Advertiser,* Spring 1992, 51.

specific audiences as well as mass audiences. On the downside, advertising has three major disadvantages. First, advertising results are difficult to measure, because advertising usually works in concert with other marketer-controlled promotion tools in an uncontrollable market environment. Second, in most cases advertising cannot close the sale, because there usually is considerable time and space between advertising exposure and purchase behavior. Finally, it is an impersonal form of communication that is audience controlled; advertising seeks people out in most cases, and they can decide whether they want to read, see, or listen. The synergies that exist between advertising and other elements of promotion are depicted in the Ad Insight entitled "Steps to a Sale."

In practice, the role of advertising in the promotion mix is determined by the marketing situation. In some situations, advertising will have a dominant role in the marketer's promotion mix. In other situations, it will have a less dominant role and may even be subordinate to other promotion elements. How advertising and sales promotions are typically employed over the life cycle of a product provides a good example of the varying emphasis that the marketer gives to advertising in the promotion mix.

Most marketers believe that every product, service, or idea has a life cycle. Although the length of every **product life cycle (PLC)** varies, there are four distinct stages. The introduction stage is the period of slow growth as the product or service is introduced in the market. The growth stage is the period of rapid market growth and consumer acceptance. The maturity stage is the slowdown period of growth as the product or service reaches the peak of consumer acceptance. The decline stage is the period when sales continue their downward spiral to zero.

Expenditures for both advertising and sales promotion may be high in the introductory stage, as the marketer attempts to build awareness and consumer trial. The emphasis on both promotion tools is needed because the marketer typically enters a highly competitive environment, where many marketers are competing for the same consumer dollars and attention.

In the growth stage, advertising and sales promotion expenditures may be reversed, depending on whether the product is a market share leader, is well differentiated, or is an imitative "me-too" product. For market leaders and well-differentiated products, advertising expenditures may remain high, as the marketer attempts to maintain identity and differentiation. For "me-too" products in the growth stage, advertising expenditures may be lower, as the imitator attempts to take advantage of competitive advertising, whereas sales promotion expenditures may remain high to induce trial and brand switching.

In the maturity stage, spending may be similar to the growth stage, depending on the degree of brand loyalty. If brand loyalty is high, advertising may be emphasized to maintain brand image. If brand loyalty is low, advertising may be de-emphasized, and sales promotion may be emphasized in an effort to attract and hold buyers.

Both advertising and sales promotion spending are reduced in the product's decline stage. Advertising may be phased out completely, while some expenditures may be allocated to trade-level sales promotion (distributors or retailers) to reduce inventory.

Another example of the varying role of advertising in the promotion mix can be seen in the sales dollars allocated to advertising spending. As an example, Kellogg Company and Ford Motor Company were two of the nation's largest advertisers in 1991.[10] Kellogg spent just over $577 million in U.S. advertising, while Ford Motor Company spent just over $676 million. However, Kellogg spent approximately 17 percent of its U.S. sales on advertising, while Ford spent around 1 percent. Based on these advertising-as-percent-of-sales figures for the two large advertisers, it is obvious that advertising played a greater role in Kellogg's 1990 promotional efforts than in Ford's. But why did they differ in advertising emphasis? To a great extent, the answer lies in the two firms' choice of promotion strategy—how the promotion elements were put together to achieve marketing objectives. The Ad Insight entitled "Advertising: One Part of Sports Marketing's Promotion Mix" illustrates how U.S. companies spent 23.5 billion on various promotional options in 1990.

▌**P**romotional Strategies

When determining the optimal promotion mix, the marketer has two strategic options—a pull promotion strategy or a push promotion strategy. In a **pull strategy,** the focus is on pulling the product or service through the distribution channel by stimulating demand at the end-user level, that is, the targeted consumer. Advertising plays a dominant role in the pull strategy because its job is to "presell" the consumer. The pull strategy forces retailers and wholesalers to stock goods or services by motivating consumers to ask for them. As depicted in Figure 2.7, the job of advertising in the pull strategy is to affect consumer demand, which in turn is to affect channel demand.

In a **push strategy,** the focus is on pushing the good or service through the distribution channel by convincing wholesalers and retailers to handle the marketer's goods or services. Advertising typically plays a less dominant role in the push strategy because its job is to supplement the primary selling tool—personal selling. In contrast to its role in pull strategy (see Figure 2.7), the job of advertising in the push strategy is to affect channel demand, which in turn gets the product or service into the hands of the consumer.

Advertising: One Part of Sports Marketing's Promotion Mix

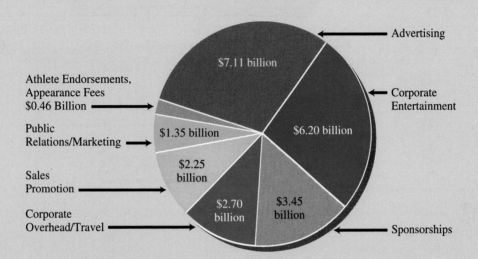

Athlete Endorsements, Appearance Fees $0.46 Billion

Public Relations/Marketing

Sales Promotion

Corporate Overhead/Travel

$7.11 billion — Advertising

$1.35 billion

$2.25 billion

$2.70 billion

$3.45 billion

$6.20 billion — Corporate Entertainment

Sponsorships

Marketers spent more to entertain corporate clients and employees at mega-events, including the World Series and the Masters, than they did on the actual sponsorships themselves.

Corporate America spent an astounding $6.2 billion on tickets, hotel rooms, and open bars at major sporting events last year.

Source: Melissa Turner, "Sponsorship Fee Just Gets a Firm Inside the Door," *Atlanta Journal,* Wednesday, October 2, 1991, E1.

The difference between push and pull promotional strategies is in the degree of emphasis placed on any of the four promotion elements. Nearly all marketers, including both Kellogg and Ford, employ all four promotion elements in their marketing efforts, but in different combinations. Kellogg allocates more of its sales dollars to consumer advertising than Ford, because advertising plays a major role in the selling of Kellogg brands. The major job of consumer advertising in Ford's promotion mix is to make customers aware of, or have a positive attitude toward, Ford products and services, and to get them into the dealer's showroom. Once they are there, the salesperson's job is to close the deal. The question facing most marketers is not what promotion element to use, but which one to emphasize in the promotional effort. That question is answered, of course, by the ability of each element to contribute to the ultimate attainment of the marketing objectives.

If advertising is employed, regardless of whether in a dominant or a subordinate role, these three decisions must be made:

1. Advertising objectives must be set and money must be allocated for the advertising effort.

Advertising Planning Decisions

FIGURE 2.7

A Comparison of Push and Pull Promotion Strategies

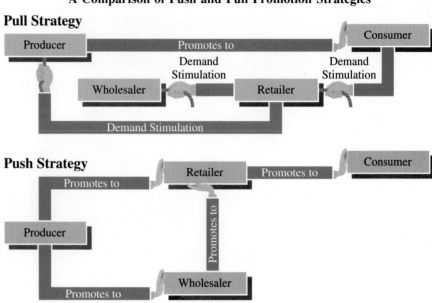

2. Copy decisions must be made about what the advertising is to communicate to the target market and how it is to be communicated.
3. Media must be selected that most efficiently and effectively deliver the advertising message to the defined target market.

The first decision establishes how marketers want targeted consumers to respond to advertising messages and how money is going to be budgeted to accomplish the advertising objectives. The second decision involves the determination of advertising message content and the manner in which it is going to be presented to targeted consumers. The third decision focuses on the means of most effectively delivering the message in its selected form via the mass media. The end result of the three decisions is an advertising campaign—that is, a scheduled and integrative advertising effort, consisting of a series of advertisements and commercials with a unified message, delivered with sufficient repetition and coverage to targeted consumers, coordinated with other promotion tools, and directed to meeting the predetermined advertising objectives.

As illustrated in Figure 2.8, advertising decisions are driven by the marketing plan and are applicable to any advertising situation, marketing organization, or time period. Advertising is planned and carried out in the same, systematic manner whether it is for an industrial marketer or a consumer package goods marketer; for a large, national retailer or a small, locally owned men's clothing store; for a profit-seeking organization or a nonprofit organization. Only the decisional conditions change—the type of advertiser, the nature of the marketing situation, the cultural or economic environment. The decisions of advertising planning remain the same. A case study of advertising planning is described in the Ad Insight entitled "The Power of Advertising Planning: A Marketing Success Story."

The Communication Concept

In formulating advertising plans, the marketer must draw heavily on what is known about communication. As we have seen, advertising is a special form of marketing communication that marketers use to facilitate interaction.

Like the marketing concept, the communication concept focuses on the needs and wants of the consumer. In the case of communication, the message is the object of consumption. One useful way of thinking about communication is the 5-W approach illustrated in Figure 2.9. In advertising terms, (1) *who* is the sponsoring advertiser and/or agent, (2) *what* is the advertisement or commercial, (3) *whom* is the target market, (4) *which medium* is the media type (for example, TV versus print) and vehicle (for example, ABC versus NBC), and (5) *what effect* is how targeted consumers respond to advertisements and commercials. However, advertising communication is not as simple as the 5-W approach implies. Many factors, both controllable and uncontrollable, make effective advertising communication a complex and unpredictable process.

FIGURE 2.8

Advertising Planning and Decision Making: An Extension of Marketing Planning

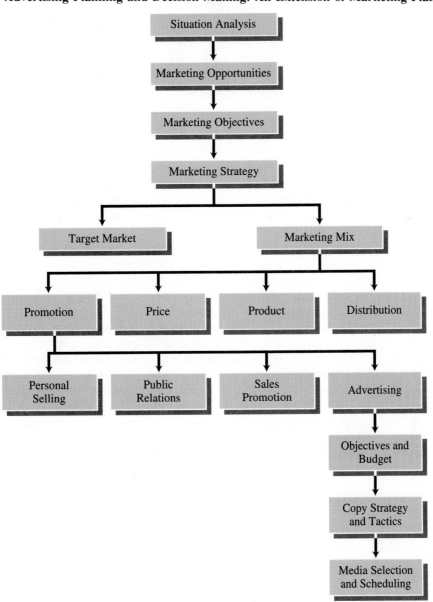

The Power of Effective Advertising Planning:
A Marketing Success Story

How magazines—and a non-stop campaign—made Absolut number one.

In 1980, Absolut was a tiny vodka brand selling about 12,000 cases a year. And it came in a strangely-shaped bottle with a painted-on label. "Who wants a Swedish vodka?" people asked. About then, an art director at TBWA, while thinking about their new client's small ad budget, went home and took a hot bath.

That's when the idea happened. He envisioned the Absolut bottle with a halo (done slightly tongue-in-cheek) and the first of the two-word headlines that would become this campaign's signature. That initial ad, "Absolut Perfection," appeared during 1980 in a short list of selected magazines.

Richard Lewis, Senior Vice President/Management Supervisor at TBWA recalls, "We weren't just selling another vodka. We wanted to make this a fashionable product . . . like perfume." Magazines were the perfect showcase. "When people pay good money to buy a magazine, they *read* it," says Lewis. "With magazines, they

have time to appreciate and savor our ads."

Absolut vodka was dedicated to building the brand. Each year, this advertiser consistently added more funds to the advertising budget. More and more new ads—each one true on the original strategy—were created to keep the campaign fresh.

By 1986, Absolut broke through the "one million case" barrier. The line extensions Absolut Peppar and Absolut Citron added to the brand's momentum. The president of Carillon Importers, Michel Roux, convinced celebrity artists such as Andy Warhol to paint ads. Occasional "spectaculars" were produced—ads that entertained readers with musical tunes, floating snow flakes, even a workable jigsaw puzzle. The brand's production budget alone began to dwarf the *media* budgets of some competitors.

Absolut Results. In 1990, Absolut vodka sold 2.7 million cases and as the #1 imported vodka claimed an amazing 58 percent of the category. Michel Roux sums it up: "We could not have had this success without the magazine medium."

Source: Impact Databank—1990.

The Communication Planning Environment

The nature of advertising communication planning is shown in Figure 2.10. Like marketing planning, effective advertising communication planning begins with a careful analysis of the impact of environmental factors. These factors were discussed in Chapter 1, but an additional comment must be made about the competitive

FIGURE 2.9

The 5-W Approach to Communication

The communicator must choose among alternatives at each stage of the 5-W process.

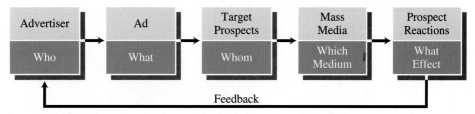

environment because of its explicit importance in advertising communication planning.

The competitive environment consists of marketing communication efforts that compete either directly or indirectly for targeted consumers' limited attention. Knowing what competitors are saying, how they are saying it, and when and where they are saying it gives the advertiser a better shot at breaking through the media clutter and turning consumers' attention from other products and services that are competing for their dollars and minds. In marketing terms, share-of-dollars relates to market share, measured in terms of percentage of sales within a competitive category (a share ranges from 0 to 100 percent). Share-of-mind relates to "share-of-voice," measured in terms of some communication response, such as top-of-mind awareness, brand recall, and brand attitude, or in terms of advertising expenditures within a competitive category.

Analysis of environmental factors leads to the determination of the advertising communication object, the formulation of advertising communication objectives, and the proper blending of the elements of advertising communication—source, message, media, and audience. The communication object is the idea or thought that is to be communicated. The communication object is a crucial decision in advertising campaign planning, for it represents shared thought between the advertiser and its defined target audience. Figure 2.11 presents an example of a Heinekin ad that attempts to break through the many competing voices of beer advertising by poking fun at typical campaign messages.

FIGURE 2.10

Diagram of Advertising Communication Planning

Environmental Factors	Communicator-Defined Factors	Communication Effects
Regulatory Environment Social/Cultural Environment Economic Environment Competitive/ Marketing Environment	Communication Object (Idea) Communication Objectives → Source Media Message Audience → Effects	Awareness Comprehension Liking Preference Trial Purchase Committed Purchase

Feedback

FIGURE 2.11

**A Heineken Advertisement That Attempts to Break through the Clutter
of Competing Messages by Parodying Other Campaigns**

Communication Defined

As a human activity, communication is the commonness of thought between the sender and the receiver. It is a process in which participants are active in a communicative relationship, meaning that communication—whether advertising or some other form of communication—is something one does *with* another person, not something one does *to* another person.[11] The result of communication is meaning, an outcome that is achieved only when there is the sharing of thought between the sender and the receiver.

As we will discuss in a few pages, advertising is a special form of communication called **mass communication.** It involves a process whereby a message is delivered via technical means to a large number of individuals at approximately the same time. Mass communication is indirect in that the sender, the advertiser, and the receiver (the individual of the target audience) are not present in time and space; and it is one-way, in that feedback from receiver to sender is not immediate.

To understand advertising as a form of communication requires an understanding of three basic communication concepts: **signs, field of experience,** and **meaning.**

Signs

The working tools of the communicator are called signs. Signs are visual, verbal, or audio elements that "stand separate and alone between the participants in the communication relationship—the elements that stand for something in the mind of one participant and, if accepted, will come to stand for something in the mind of the other."[12] Signs can stand in literal association with an object; that is, a word equates with a physical object, or, in subjective association, the same physical object has individual-specific interpretations.

An advertisement, regardless of the medium in which it appears, is a collection of signs—words, pictures, and sounds. As communicators, advertising people work as sign manipulators: their job is to select signs based on their personal experiences and research results, which will then be interpreted by the consumer as desired by the advertiser. In some cases, ad-manipulated signs are structured to reduce subjective interpretation. In other cases, they are purposefully left unstructured to facilitate subjective interpretation.

FIGURE 2.12

Signs, Communication Objects, and Interpretation: Ad-Manipulated Signs and Fields of Experience of a Message

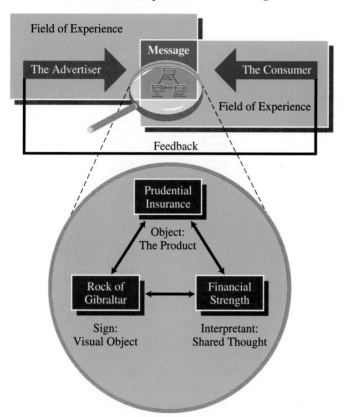

Source: Adapted from Michael R. Solomon, *Consumer Behavior* (Boston: Allgrad Bacon, 1992) 59.

An example of how ad-manipulated signs are related to a communication object and consumer interpretation of that object is provided in Figure 2.12. The communication object is the brand advertised; the signs are those elements selected to represent the intended meanings of the communication object; and the interpretant is the meaning derived from exposure to the advertisement. [13]

In advertising, sign manipulation must be a controlled undertaking, for effective communication, as we stated earlier, occurs only when consumer interpretation is consistent with what the advertiser attempted to communicate. Even though advertising may be a form of artistic expression, it is not art for its own sake. Rather, it is creativity designed to accomplish predetermined marketing and advertising objectives. [14]

A field of experience, also known as the perceptual field, is the total of a person's life experiences, and advertisers manipulate signs based on their knowledge of the consumer's field of experience. The more overlap in the field of experience between the advertiser and the consumer, the greater and more accurate is the sharing of thought—that is, more communication occurs. In advertising, for example, clients and agency people talk about GRPs. They understand each other because of common fields of experience. To you—at least for now—the letters GRP mean very little. By contrast, the letters PC probably have much meaning for you. Figure 2.12 graphically depicts the field of experience concept.

Field of Experience

FIGURE 2.13

Elements of the Commuication Process

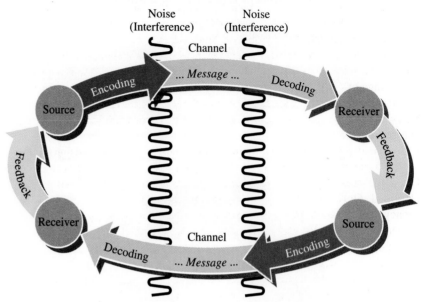

Source: Joseph R. Dominick, *The Dynamics of Mass Communication* (New York: Random House, 1990), 6.

Meaning

As discussed above, meaning is not transmitted in communication: signs are manipulated in ad messages to produce shared thought. Meaning results only when signs are shared by advertisers and consumers—that is, when they both interpret the message to mean the same thing. Communication often breaks down because signs in advertisements do not have the same meaning for advertiser and consumer; that is, their fields of experience do not overlap. Further, the meaning of signs changes as a person's field of experience changes, meaning that advertisers are always aiming their messages at moving targets.

Elements of the Communication Process

Figure 2.13 diagrams the eight elements of the communication process: The *source* and *receiver* are the principal participants in the communication process; *message* and *channel* are the objects employed by the participants to communicate; *encoding, decoding,* and *feedback* are functions of the process; and *noise* is the element that can inhibit effective communication. Each of the eight elements has a fundamental role in understanding advertising as communication.

Source and Encoding

The source—also known as the communicator, sender, or encoder—initiates the process of communication by having an idea or thought to share with another person, a small group of people, or a large group of people (a mass audience). To bring about communication, the source must transform the idea of thought into a message. The transformation of an idea or thought is called **encoding,** an event that involves sign manipulation.

Communication sources can be classified into two basic types: mass communicators and interpersonal communicators. Each works in distinct communication settings.

Mass Communicators

These types of communicators are usually professionals who work in organizational settings. They are newspaper reporters, news anchors, magazine writers, sportscasters, radio announcers, movie directors, entertainers, and advertising practitioners.

In the advertising business, they staff the advertising departments of advertisers, advertising agencies, TV production studios, and graphic arts companies. Most advertisements are the result of a team effort, although sometimes an advertisement will be the work of one person. The team typically consists of individuals with a wide range of creative talents, whose work is coordinated and unified by managers and account personnel. These specialists—copywriters, artists, musicians, photographers, cinematographers—are brought together to produce effective advertisements and commercials.

Source identification in advertising is a special case. The advertising communicator has a great deal of flexibility in identifying the source of advertising messages. Often the creator of an advertisement—the advertising agency—is not actually identified. Only when an agency is promoting itself to prospective clients is the agency named as the source. Often not even the client is named; only the brand name is identified. According to William Wilkie, a consumer behaviorist, an advertising communicator has four options in source identification:

1. Identify the company or brand as the source, especially if the advertiser or its product has a strong and positive reputation.
2. Associate the company or brand with a "catchy" slogan or theme.
3. Associate the company or brand with a media seal of approval (*Good Housekeeping* magazine) or an independent testing organization (Underwriters' Laboratory).
4. Use a spokesperson—expert, celebrity, or ordinary person. [15]

Whichever option is selected, the key is to attribute the advertisement to the source with the most credibility. Generally speaking, the more credible the identified source, the more persuasive the advertising will be. Figure 2.14 is an example of an advertisement with source credibility.

Person-to-Person Communicators

Obviously consumers do not live in isolation from one another. Instead, they are connected through social structure, which means that ad content is interpreted, modified, and passed on within this social structure. [16] Figure 2.15 presents a model of how individuals are socially connected.

Advertising is sometimes planned to take advantage of person-to-person sources. Researchers who examined a number of advertising studies concluded that "advertising campaigns accompanied by much word-of-mouth activity are much more likely to produce persisting attitudinal effects than campaigns accompanied by little or no word-of-mouth activity." [17] A diffusion theory expert, Everett Rogers, has pointed out that a diffusion strategy (a combination of interpersonal and mass communication) is more effective in selling both commercial products like toothpaste and noncommercial concepts like higher education. [18] We know from years of diffusion research that the mass media have their greatest impact during the awareness and interest steps of the adoption process. Interpersonal sources—friends, family, teachers, salespeople—are more influential during the evaluation, trial, and adoption stages.

If this process is employed, a diffusion strategy is planned on the basis of the two-step flow hypothesis. In the first step, advertising is directed to readers, listeners, and viewers in the mass media. Quite often the targets are opinion leaders, that is, people with special knowledge and expertise who are mass-media attentive and who are sometimes sought out by others for advice. In the second step, people already exposed to the advertising discuss what they have heard, seen, or read with other

An Advertisement With Source Credibility

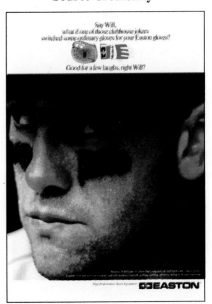

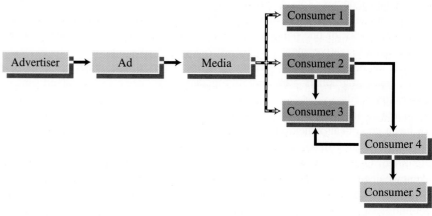

FIGURE 2.15

A Mass Communication Model in Which Consumers Are Socially Connected

Ad Content is not interpreted by isolated individuals; instead, ad content is interpreted, modified, and passed on through interpersonal communication.

⊏━▷ mass communicated

━━▶ person-to-person communicated

people, who in turn discuss the information conveyed by the advertising-influenced interpersonal source with still other people.

Whether or not advertising is planned to influence person-to-person communication, it has a carryover effect on interpersonal communication. People talk about advertising. This carryover effect sometimes can last long after the advertising has ended. For example, some people still associate Dr Pepper with "being a pepper," although that campaign ended many years ago. The interpersonal carryover effect of advertising is one of the major reasons why advertising spending should be viewed as an investment, not simply an expenditure.

▮ *T*he Message

The heart of communication, especially advertising communication, is the message. It is the physical object that results from the source's encoding of an idea or thought. In advertising, evidence suggests that the quality of the message is more important than either the medium that carries it or the amount of money behind it.[19]

Every advertisement or commercial is composed of two aspects: what is said and how it is said. As we will discuss in Chapter 11, the first is called creative strategy and the second is called creative tactics. Research has shown that both what is said in advertising and how it is said make a big difference in effectiveness.

In its most basic form, the advertising message has three properties: message appeal, message structure, and message codes.[20] Message appeal involves the supplication of what is said in an advertisement as a means of requesting a favorable response from the receiver to the advertiser's idea or thought. In advertising, message appeal is sometimes called theme, idea, unique selling proposition (USP), or image. Two basic types of appeals are used: rational and emotional. Rational appeals are directed toward the receiver's logic and self-interest. They focus on attributes, such as quality, performance, economy, value, and price. Emotional appeals, in contrast, are directed toward the receiver's feelings and focus on emotions, such as fear, joy, pride, vanity, and love. Message structure involves the organization of the appeal in an advertisement, such as message-sidedness, order of presentation, and conclusion drawing. Sometimes message structure is referred to as method of presentation. Message codes involve the verbal and nonverbal sign systems employed to encode an idea or thought. As mentioned earlier, verbal codes are words; nonverbal codes are voice qualities, vocalizations, visual imagery, and music. The way these properties are put together determines the eventual effectiveness of what the advertiser is trying to say.

In early advertising, the emphasis was on words, and until the 1930s words continued to be seen as more important than pictures in communicating advertising ideas. Albert Lasker commented in the 1930s that only three things of major importance had ever happened in the history of the advertising business: the original N. W. Ayer contract, the discovery of copy as the most important element in advertising, and the injection of sex in advertising.[21]

Today, however, advertisers have a better understanding of how pictures and words work together. As a consequence, Lasker's idea of copy has been expanded to refer not only to words but also to pictures. Recent research evidence suggests that pictures play a significant role in determining how advertising-presented information is processed and attitudes formed. One study, for example, found that visual content in a beer advertisement was just as capable of affecting brand attitudes as was verbal content.[22] And, while the jury is still out on the question of whether verbal or visual content is superior, it is perfectly clear that words, pictures, and sounds are all important in advertising communication, although the exact combinations of employed codes are dependent on the advertising situation. As a general rule, advertisers who appeal to logic depend more on the verbal than on the visual.

The Media

The channel conveys the encoded message to the receiver. In advertising, the message is delivered by the mass media, which are selected on the basis of their ability to reach a predefined target market, of which the media audience is a part, on a cost-efficient and timely basis. Media vehicles, as will be covered in greater detail later, can enhance or hinder successful communication because of their specific contextual features. A jewelry ad in *True Romance* provides quite a different media environment than the same ad in *Cosmopolitan*.

Print media can be classified by type of medium: newspapers, magazines, and so on. Each type can be further subclassified on the basis of frequency of issue (for example, weekly or monthly), area of interest (for example, women's sports), and area of coverage (city, state, or national). Broadcast media are often categorized on the basis of such classifications as power (wattage), frequency (AM versus FM or VHF versus UHF), the community covered (metropolitan, rural), and ownership (network, independent). These classifications allow advertisers to select the media combinations that will best deliver the advertising message to target audiences.

Not surprisingly, different advertisers use many different combinations of media, as dictated by their particular marketing situation. A marketer of a mass-marketed product such as toothpaste, for example, might use television because of its ability to deliver a large, national audience. In contrast, a marketer of a specialty product such as custom-made men's dress shirts might use either direct mail because of its ability to pinpoint potential buyers or men's fashion magazines because of their ability to deliver to upscale male readers. Even competitors with similar objectives will employ different media combinations. For example, a regional oil company may put most of its advertising dollars in newspapers and local TV, whereas a competitor may spend all of its dollars on outdoor and radio advertising.

In no other area of communication does the advertising practitioner find as much information as in mass media audiences. Companies that supply audience research on a continuous and specialized basis are a major industry. Yet, despite the wealth of audience information, advertisers are handicapped by gaps in the research. We have substantial information on how many people read, subscribe to, or watch and listen to media. What we do not have is much information about actual ad exposure once the ad is placed within the media. Audience research tells us that members of our target market are in the media audience. Based on this information, we presume that exposure and processing of ads will result. In essence, we guess about the size and quality of the actual advertising audience, and we will continue to guess until research closes the gap.

Receivers and Decoding

Receivers, defined individually, collectively, or institutionally, are the target of the source's message. As consumer behaviorist William Wilkie has noted, "receivers are the people who actually determine whether or not a communication mission succeeds" as planned by the source.[23] Communication occurs when receivers decode (interpret) messages into a form that has meaning for them. Because receivers are active, not passive, participants in the process, predicting communication success is a risky business that has spawned two related fields of research: audience behavior and consumer behavior.

We know from research that interpretation, the decoding activity, is influenced by all of the life experiences that the receiver takes to the message exposure situation. Sometimes receivers are the logical, highly cognitive decoders described in the dominant model of consumer information processing (CIP). At other times, they are hedonistic, driven not by logic or rationality, but by emotions in the pursuit of "fun, fantasies, feelings, and experiences."[24] Each of these driving forces is a part of the social and psychological components that determine a receiver's degree of persuasibility. To be persuasive, the advertiser needs to take into account such things as product needs, levels of interest, prior beliefs and attitudes, brand loyalties, social relationships, personality traits, and situational characteristics when creating advertising messages and selecting media schedules. In the end, even though receivers may be precisely defined and targeted, their interpretative and subsequent behaviors cannot be controlled, nor easily predicted.

Feedback

Feedback tells the source how much was actually communicated. In effect, it reverses the communication flow so that the receiver becomes the encoder and the source becomes the receiver. Feedback can be immediate, as in face-to-face interpersonal communication, or delayed, as in advertising.

Techniques for measuring audience feedback, though far from perfect, are essential in advertising planning. If used properly, audience feedback allows advertisers to alter subsequent ads and commercials into more effective messages. Feedback techniques and the way their findings are used will be treated in more detail in later chapters. Feedback results, though essential, are inexact at best, especially when attempts are made to relate advertising directly to market behaviors such as sales. Although the introduction of scanners has improved our ability to link advertising with sales, we are still unable to account for all the environmental, competitive, and marketer-controlled factors that might influence sales, unless we conduct precisely designed and executed market experiments. Results are more accurate when intermediate communication responses, such as awareness or attitude change, are used as the criteria to judge advertising effectiveness.

Noise

Noise is anything that interferes with the encoding and decoding of messages between source and receiver.

Classifications of Noise

In general, noise falls into three classifications:[25]

1. Environmental noise is interference that is external to the message exchange between source and receiver. For example, the drowning out of your television set by a neighbor's barking dog is environmental noise.

2. Mechanical noise is interference that is caused by machine-assisted problems in communication. Poor color reproduction in the latest issue of your favorite photography magazine is an example of mechanical noise.

3. Psychological noise, also called semantic noise, is interference that is caused by source encoding or receiver decoding mistakes or problems. For example, the incorrect use of signs in a TV commercial is psychological noise, as is thinking about your upcoming biology exam while watching TV.

Barriers to Advertising Communication

Even though all three types of noise can be present in any communication situation, advertising in particular must work to overcome the barriers to communication caused by mechanical and psychological noise. According to William Wilkie's analysis, there are five potential pitfalls, or gaps, in the advertising communication process (see Figure 2.16).[26] The first two are source encoding problems, which result when the advertiser selects a message strategy that is off-base with campaign goals or when the actual ads and commercials are incongruent with the message strategy. The third is a mechanical problem. It occurs when the message is not delivered by the selected media as planned. The fourth and fifth are receiver decoding problems. These result from the way the receiver attends and processes advertising-presented information.

Of the five communication pitfalls, the greatest barrier is the receiver. In the course of normal business affairs, advertisers must expect to encounter consumer defensiveness and indifference.

As we have learned from research and experience, advertising seeks people out. Rarely do people seek out advertising. And whether advertising finds them or they

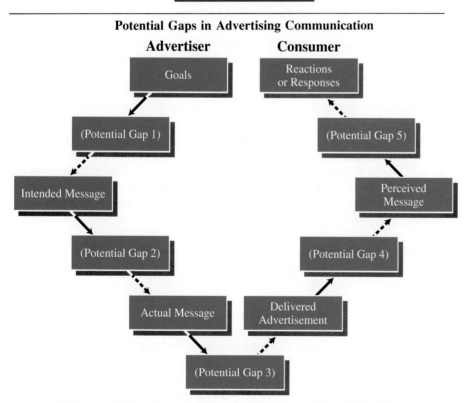

FIGURE 2.16

Potential Gaps in Advertising Communication

Source: William L. Wilkie, *Consumer Behavior* (New York: Wiley, 1986), 242.

find advertising, they know what advertising is trying to do: it is trying to persuade them to think, feel, or act in a certain way. In psychological terms, people enter the advertising communication process with their perceptual defenses up. They know it's "just advertising" and they can easily choose to avoid it, tune it out altogether, or distort its intended meaning. To overcome perceptual barriers, advertising must be designed and placed to grab the audience's attention, to reduce miscomprehension, and to facilitate memory.

In actual practice, communication barriers—environmental, mechanical, or psychological—cannot be entirely eliminated. However, they can be anticipated and planned for, especially psychological noise. Encoding and decoding problems can be reduced if advertisers make message and media decisions on the basis of research that allows them to take the consumer's perspective.

Advertising's Communication Setting

Communication takes place in three common settings: the interpersonal setting, the machine-assisted interpersonal setting, and the mass communication setting.[27] All three settings share the eight elements of the communication process; however, each has unique properties that differentiate the nature of communication. These differences are outlined in Figure 2.17, which was developed by mass communication scholar Joseph Dominick.

Advertising, even though it is sometimes designed to influence interpersonal communication, works in a mass communication setting. In mass communication terms, it can be described as follows:

1. Advertising is the product of a group of individuals who typically act with predetermined roles in an organizational setting. These individuals—advertising people—create, produce, and place ads with knowledge of audiences only as anonymous, summary statistics.

2. Advertising is a multistage encoding process, whereby a single ad is the product of a series of steps. For example, a script written by a copywriter, accompanied by a **storyboard** illustrated by an artist, is sent to a production studio where the two are transformed into a commercial, which is dubbed and mailed to the networks and/or local market TV stations for insertion in scheduled programming.

3. Advertising is mediated by one or more machines, which are imposed between source and audience. To place an ad in *USA Today,* for instance, involves computers, printing machines, and satellite transmission.

4. Advertising is public communication, which most of the time is seen, read, or heard not only by the intended audience but also by unintended audiences. As a result, advertising dollars are wasted in reaching unwanted people, who will more likely be offended or disturbed by specific advertising messages than will intended audience members.

5. Advertising decoding, like encoding, is a multistage process, whereby audience members receive ads through mechanical devices and then must mentally process them.

6. Advertising audiences are large, heterogeneous, geographically dispersed, and self-selected. As a result, the audience, no matter how well defined and understood, is in control of the communication process. Audiences can decide to attend or not attend ads, and the advertiser can do very little about it, other than say, "Don't touch that dial!"

7. Advertising's direction is overwhelmingly one-way. Feedback is minimal, delayed, and most often delivered by a third party—a research supplier.

FIGURE 2.17

Properties of Three Settings of Communication

		Setting		
		Interpersonal (face-to-face)	**Machine-Assisted Interpersonal (telephone)**	**Mass Media**
	Source	Single person; has knowledge of receiver	Single person or group; great deal of knowledge or no knowledge of receiver	Organizations; little knowledge of receivers
	Encoding	Single stage	Single or multiple stage	Multiple stages
	Message	Private or public; cheap; hard to terminate; altered to fit receivers	Private or public; low to moderate expense; relatively easy to terminate; can be altered to fit receivers in some situations	Public; expensive; easily terminated; same message to everybody
	Channel	Potential for many; no machines interposed	Restricted to one or two; at least one machine interposed	Restricted to one or two; usually more than one machine interposed
	Decoding	Single stage	Single or multiple stage	Multiple stages
Element	*Receiver*	One or a relatively small number; in physical presence of source; selected by source	One person or a small or large group; within or outside of physical presence of source; selected by source or self-defined	Large numbers; out of physical presence of source; self-selected
	Feedback	Plentiful; immediate	Somewhat limited; immediate or delayed	Highly limited; delayed; third party delivered
	Noise	Semantic; environmental	Semantic; environmental; mechanical	Semantic; environmental; mechanical

Source: Joseph R. Dominick, *The Dynamics of Mass Communication* (New York: Random House, 1990), 19.

Advertising's chances of communicating as intended are seriously diminished by environmental, mechanical, and psychological noise factors. Ads are usually attended in the presence of other activities; machines often fail; and people are more than aware of advertising's persuasive intent, even if some of its messages are more information than persuasion.

Advertising's Communicative Functions

As a unique form of mass communication, advertising performs four basic communicative functions: precipitation, persuasion, reinforcement, and reminder. The functions are summarized in Figure 2.18.

Advertising functions in its first two roles to move consumers from a state of indecision to some type of purchase behavior. In its precipitation role, advertising works to intensify existing wants and needs and to create awareness and knowledge. It is in this form that advertising is most informative. Informative advertising is most often used in national advertising in the early stages of the product life cycle, when the product is being introduced to the market.

As persuasion, advertising works not simply to intensify wants and needs or to create awareness and knowledge, but also to intensify emotions and feelings and to build preference. Persuasive advertising is most often used in the growth and maturity stages of the product life cycle, when the market situation is very competitive and consumers are aware of and knowledgeable about product offerings.

The other two functions—reinforcement and reminder—occur after purchase behavior. As reinforcement, advertising works to legitimize the consumer's purchase decision. Most often, reinforcement advertising is used to reaffirm infrequent purchases of such products as insurance policies, automobiles, computer systems, or telecommunication services.

In its reminder function, advertising works to trigger habitual purchase behaviors. As a general rule, reminder advertising is used in the maturity and decline stages of the product life cycle for frequently purchased items such as consumer packaged goods. Advertisements with different communicative functions are shown in Figure 2.19. The Stouffer Hotel and the RCA ads are designed to supply the consumer

FIGURE 2.18

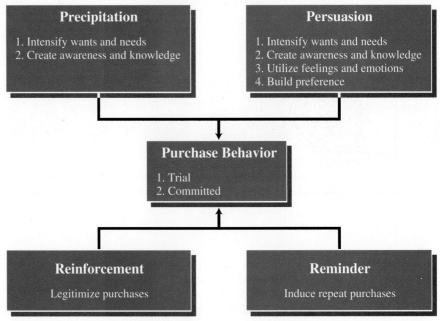

The Communicative Functions of Advertising and Their Relation to Purchase Behavior

Precipitation
1. Intensify wants and needs
2. Create awareness and knowledge

Persuasion
1. Intensify wants and needs
2. Create awareness and knowledge
3. Utilize feelings and emotions
4. Build preference

Purchase Behavior
1. Trial
2. Committed

Reinforcement
Legitimize purchases

Reminder
Induce repeat purchases

Source: Jagdish N. Sheth, "Measurement of Advertising Effectiveness: Some Theoretical Considerations," *Journal of Advertising* 3, no. 1 (1974): 8–11. Reprinted with permission.

FIGURE 2.19

Four Advertisements with Different Communicative Functions

All the excitement of Chicago is at our doorstep.

Chicago's newest luxury hotel is located right between The Loop and The Magnificent Mile. So you'll be just steps from business centers, superb shopping, and dazzling nightlife.

We'll greet you with luxurious rooms, private Club Floors,

excellent restaurants, a complete health club, and personal service that will unobtrusively cater to your every need. Including complimentary morning coffee and newspaper delivered to your door with wake-up calls.

See why Stouffer Hotels and Resorts is rated as one of the top luxury hotel chains by the nation's most prestigious consumer report.

In Chicago, you can depend on our good name. Call your travel agent or 1•800•HOTELS•1

STOUFFER
HOTELS & RESORTS

The complete Home Theatre kit

Presenting the first theatre that comes in a box. Or boxes. It's the RCA Home Theatre.™ Put it in your living room and get a big picture with big sound. Connect a laser disc player and VCR to it as easy as tying your shoe. There's SRS (•)' [Sound Retrieval System] which surrounds you with sound without ever connecting stereo speakers, a universal remote that

simply controls everything, and storage that holds it all. And you can add and subtract components as you wish. Like we say, it's your very own theatre. The one you can visit in your boxer shorts. Or curlers. Or pj's. You get the idea. To see how it all comes together, please stop by your nearby RCA dealer today. And just remember to ask for the theatre you can take home with you.

RCA
Changing Entertainment. Again.™

WE'RE THE OLD MASTERS OF FINANCIAL SECURITY.

GET MET. IT PAYS.
❖ **MetLife**®

Fresh, Pure & Natural. The Only Beer With The Genuine Taste Of The King Of Beers.

with information in the hope that the information will precipitate consumption behavior. The MetLife ad is designed not only to tell prospects about MetLife, but to reaffirm how intelligent current policy holders are to protect themselves with MetLife insurance. The Budweiser ad is designed to remind Bud drinkers to keep drinking the brand, and to remind other beer drinkers of the availability of Bud.

For advertising to perform any of its communicative functions, a sequence of communication events must occur. In modern advertising terms, the sequence of events is known as the **hierarchy of effects,** which is a major component of advertising campaign planning. Although researchers do not agree on the exact sequence of events, they agree that the hierarchy of effects consists of three parts: (1) learning (awareness and comprehension), (2) feeling (liking and preference), and (3) behavior (trial and commitment). Research suggests that each is dependent on the consumer's degree of involvement in the purchase situation.

1. The learning hierarchy [also known as learn-feel-do] works when the consumer is genuinely interested in the advertised product, mass media are used to promote the product, and the difference between competing brands of the product is clear.
2. The dissonance-attribution hierarchy [also known as do-feel-learn] works when the product is important, alternative choices are not clear, and personal selling is more important than mass media in disseminating information.
3. The low-involvement learning hierarchy [also known as learn-do-feel] works when differences between competing brands are minimal, the product is not very important to the buyer, and when repeated mass media messages are needed to keep the brand fresh in the consumer's mind.[28]

Summary

A necessary framework for understanding how advertising works and for choosing whether to use advertising in relation to other marketing communication tools is provided by the interrelated fields of marketing and communication. Advertising is an instrument of marketing and a form of mass communication.

Marketing involves all activities that direct the flow of products, services, or ideas from firms to consumers. In most modern profit-seeking and nonprofit organizations, marketing is guided by the marketing concept. Decisions are made on the basis of consumer wants and needs and marketing activities and elements are integrated to facilitate exchange between organizations and consumers.

Translating the marketing concept into a marketing plan involves the completion of a situation analysis, the determination of marketing objectives, and the development of a marketing strategy. Identification of the target market and the formulation of a marketing mix are the two decisions of marketing strategy. The marketing mix consists of four elements—product, distribution, price, and promotion.

Advertising is one element of the promotion mix in a marketing plan. How it is utilized, in either a push or pull promotional strategy, is determined on the basis of the marketing situation. Advertising planning involves three basic decisions: (1) the setting of communication objectives and the allocation of money to achieve those objectives, (2) the determination of a message strategy and executional tactics, and (3) the selection and scheduling of mass media. In any marketing situation, advertising functions as a special form of mass communication.

Communication is the complex process by which meanings are shared by sender and receiver. Only when the field of experience of both sender and receiver overlap is a message communicated properly. Successful communication is the product of the proper blending of signs to bring about meaning.

All communication events—including advertising—share eight process elements: source, encoding, message, media, decoding, receiver, feedback, and noise. In advertising communication planning, decisions must be made about the identified source of ads and commercials, about the content (message appeals, message structure, and message codes), about the targeted audiences, about mass media choices and scheduling, and about measuring delayed audience feedback.

At each step in the communication process, the communicator is faced with environmental, mechanical, and psychological noise that may distort or block out the message. Advertising in particular is subject to psychological noise. Effective advertising planning seeks to minimize communication barriers through audience research and the proper utilization of message and media properties.

In general, advertising has four communicative functions: precipitation, persuasion, reinforcement, and reminder. The first two functions, precipitation and persuasion, precede trial or committed types of purchase behavior. The latter two functions, reinforcement and reminder advertising, follow purchase behavior. Most advertising planners believe that advertising effects normally follow a hierarchy from mere awareness of the message to purchase behavior.

Questions for Discussion

1. What are the principal differences between marketing and advertising planning?

2. To what extent is communication theory related to marketing planning?

3. Distinguish between marketing and advertising objectives. How is advertising used by marketers in the promotion mix to achieve marketing objectives?

4. Select print ads that illustrate an attempt to achieve various steps in the hierarchy of effects. Identify each ad's communicative function.

5. How are signs selected for encoding an advertising message? Select one advertisement that seems to encode the message well and one that seems to encode poorly.

6. Distinguish between advertising and personal selling as forms of marketing communication.

7. What are the potential barriers to successful advertising communication?

Notes

1. Otis A. Pease, "Teaching Americans to Consume: A Re-appraisal of Advertising as a Social Force," in *Advertising and the Public,* ed. Kim B. Rotzoll (Urbana, IL: University of Illinois Press, 1980), 1–15.

2. William Leiss, Stephen Kline, and Sut Jhally, *Social Communication in Advertising: Persons, Products and Images of Well-Being* (New York: Methuen, 1986), 3. David Glen Mick, "Consumer Research and Semiotics: Exploring the Morphology of Signs, Symbols, and Significance," *Journal of Consumer Research* 13 (September 1986): 196–213.

3. "AMA Board Approves New Marketing Definition," *The Marketing News,* March 1, 1985, 1.

4. Philip Kotler, *Marketing Management: Analysis, Planning and Control,* 4th ed. (Englewood Cliffs, NJ: Prentice-Hall, 1980).

5. Joseph P. Guiltinan and Gordon W. Paul, *Marketing Management* (New York: McGraw-Hill, 1982), 3–4.

6. Annual Report, General Electric, 1952, 21.

[7] Theodore Levitt, "Marketing Myopia," *Harvard Business Review* 38 (July–August 1960): 45–46.

[8] Michael Ray, *Advertising and Communication Management* (Englewood Cliffs, NJ: Prentice-Hall, 1982), 89–90.

[9] Kotler, *Marketing Management,* 81.

[10] "The Advertising Fact Book: Special Report," *Advertising Age,* January 4, 1993, 16.

[11] James Carey, "A Cultural Approach to Communication," *Communication,* 2 (1975), 1–22; Grant McCracken, "Advertising: Meaning or Information?", in *Advances in Consumer Reports,* 14; Paul Anderson and Melanie Wallendorf, eds. (Provo, UT: Association for Consumer Research, 1987), 121–124.

[12] Michael R. Solomon, *Consumer Behavior* (Boston: Allyn and Bacon, 1992), 58–59.

[13] Wilbur Schramm, *Men, Messages and Media: A Look at Human Communication* (New York: Harper & Row, 1973), 60.

[14] Leonard N. Reid and Herbert J. Rotfeld, "Toward an Associative Model of Advertising Creativity," *Journal of Advertising,* 4 (Fall 1976): 128–134.

[15] William L. Wilkie, *Consumer Behavior* (New York: Wiley, 1986), 250.

[16] Karl-Erik Warneryd and Kjell Nowak, *Mass Communication and Advertising* (Stockholm: The Economic Research Institute, 1967), 17.

[17] Alan Sawyer and Scott Ward, *Carry-Over Effects in Advertising Communication* (Cambridge, MA: Marketing Science Institute, 1976), 80.

[18] See Everett Rogers, "Communication and Development: The Passing of the Dominant Paradigm," *Communication Research,* 3 (April 1976): 213–240.

[19] See Michael Pearce, Scott M. Cunningham, and Avon Miller, *Appraising the Economic and Social Effects of Advertising* (Cambridge, MA: Marketing Science Institute, 1971): 2.68–2.69.

[20] Terence A. Shimp, *Promotion Management and Marketing Communications,* 2d ed. (Fort Worth, TX: Dryden Press, 1990), 148–180.

[21] James Webb Young, *The Diary of an Adman* (Chicago: Advertising Publications, 1944), 101.

[22] John R. Rossiter and Larry Percy, "Attitude Change through Visual Imagery in Advertising," *Journal of Advertising* 9 (1980): 15.

[23] Wilkie, *Consumer Behavior,* 251.

[24] Solomon, *Consumer Behavior,* 15–16.

[25] Joseph R. Dominick, *The Dynamics of Mass Communication,* 3d ed. (New York: Random House, 1990), 18–19.

[26] See Wilkie, *Consumer Behavior,* 241–245.

[27] See Dominick, *The Dynamics of Mass Communication,* 10–19.

[28] Ray, *Advertising and Communication Management,* 184–188.

Suggested Readings

Aaker, David A., Rajeev Batra, and John G. Myers. *Advertising Management.* 4th ed. Englewood Cliffs, NJ: Prentice-Hall, 1992.

Assael, Henry. *Marketing Principles and Strategy.* Fort Worth, TX: Dryden Press, 1990.

Barry, Thomas E. "The Development of the Hierarchy of Effects: An Historical Perspective." *Current Issues and Research in Advertising* 10 (1987).

Boone, Louis E., and David L. Kurtz. *Contemporary Marketing.* 7th ed. Hinsdale, IL: Dryden Press, 1989.

Dominick, Joseph R. *The Dynamics of Mass Communication.* 3rd ed. New York: Random House, 1990.

Gardner, Burleigh. *A Conceptual Framework for Advertising.* Chicago: Crain Books, 1982.

Leiss, William, Stephen Kline, and Sut Jhally. *Social Communication in Advertising: Persons, Products and Images of Well-Being.* New York: Methuen, 1986.

Mayer, Martin. *Whatever Happened to Madison Avenue? Advertising in the 1990s.* Boston: Little, Brown and Company, 1991

Lodish, Leonard M. *The Advertising and Promotion Challenge.* New York: Oxford University Press, 1986.

Peter, J. Paul and Jerry C. Olson. *Consumer Behavior and Marketing Strategy.* 2d ed. Homewood, IL: Irwin, 1990.

Ray, Michael. *Advertising and Communication Management.* Englewood Cliffs, NJ: Prentice-Hall, 1982.

Rossiter, John R. and Larry Percy, *Advertising and Promotion Management,* New York: McGraw-Hill, 1987.

Shimp, Terence A. *Promotion Management and Marketing Communications.* 2d ed. Fort Worth, TX: Dryden Press, 1990.

Solomon, Michael R., *Consumer Behavior,* Boston: Allyn and Bacon, 1992.

Wilkie, William L. *Consumer Behavior.* New York: Wiley, 1986.

Environmental Considerations: Social/Cultural, Competition, Economic, Regulatory

Advertising Organizations: Advertisers, Agencies, Media, Suppliers

Marketing Communication Considerations: Marketing Planning

Strategic Research Inputs

Objective Setting: Target Market, Buyer Behavior

Determining the Advertising Budget

Message Strategy

Media Strategy

Message Tactics

Media Tactics

Final Budget

Plan in Action Run Campaign

Impact

Measure Advertising Effectiveness

Feedback   Feedback

LEARNING OBJECTIVES

In your study of this chapter, you will have an opportunity to:

• Learn what critics, defenders, and the public think of advertising.
• Explore the ethical dimensions of the practice of advertising.
• Examine the major social issues of advertising.

Chapter **3**

Social and Ethical Issues

CHAPTER TOPICS

HOW CRITICS LOOK AT ADVERTISING
    Scholars as Critics and Defenders of Advertising
    The General Public as Critics
ADVERTISING ETHICS
DECEPTION IN ADVERTISING
    Puffery
    Watchdogs
COMPARATIVE ADVERTISING
SUBLIMINAL ADVERTISING
BAD TASTE IN ADVERTISING
    Controversial Products
ADVERTISING AND CHILDREN
ADVERTISING AND STEREOTYPES
    Women
    Hispanics
    The Elderly
    African Americans
    The Challenge to Advertisers

POLITICAL ADVERTISING
    The Grounds for Criticism
    Advertising Financing
    A Look Ahead
ADVERTISING AND RAISING EXPECTATIONS
ADVERTISING'S INFLUENCE ON THE MEDIA
    Charges of Undue Control
    Built-in Checks against Undue Influence
ADVERTISING AND FREEDOM OF SPEECH
THE ADVERTISING COUNCIL

Advertising is subject to constant social, economic, and regulatory pressures. These pressures, as mentioned in Chapter 1, shape advertising and are sometimes shaped by advertising.

As depicted in the advertising planning model, and as discussed in the previous chapters, the socioeconomic environment must be considered and planned for when advertising is used. However, this environment has two dimensions that must be recognized. Advertising planners are not only responsible for the financial well-being of firms, they are also responsible for the quality of life of consumers. Both spheres of responsibility are strategically important aspects of managerial planning, and advertisers must ask not only how socioeconomic pressures influence the planning of individual campaigns but also how advertising influences the social fabric of which it is a part. One example of an advertiser's response to social conditions is provided in the Ad Insight entitled "United Colors of Benetton." As you can see, the effort has proven quite controversial. In fact, the comparison has caused friction between the chain's retailers and the parent company. Since 1988, Benetton has been losing both stores and customers in the United States, and one retailer has sued claiming the ads helped put the store out of business.

"United Colors of Benetton" Campaign: Designed to Raise Awareness of Social Problems

Images of a dying AIDS patient; a swarm of refugees clambering aboard a ship; the corpse of a Mafia hit victim; an Indian couple waist-deep in flood waters; emigrants hoisting themselves into a container car; and a burning product of terrorism are all ads from the controversial "United Colors of Benetton" campaign.

Critics charge that Benetton is guilty of making a concerted effort to present shocking images to gain attention rather than create product advertising. Benetton executives counter that the campaign's purpose is to raise the public's awareness of social problems—and Benetton's attention to them.

Source: Gary Levin, "Benetton Brouhaha," *Advertising Age* (February 17, 1992): 62.

In this first of three chapters, we will examine the social and ethical issues that confront individual advertising planners and, in fact, the very institution of advertising. The two following chapters will deal with the economic and regulatory issues. Competitive pressures, touched on in Chapter 2, will be dealt with again in Chapter 7 on advertising campaign planning.

As you read this chapter and the next, keep one thing in mind—the exact social and economic effects of advertising are not known. We know that the effects are inescapable and profound, because of the character of advertising—it is pervasive, repetitive, heavily researched, and professionally prepared.[1] However, neither its critics nor its defenders can precisely identify the socioeconomic consequences of advertising—whether positive or negative—among the many overlapping forces in modern society. An extensive body of scholarship provides empirical glimpses and enlightened reasoning about advertising's social and economic effects; yet, we must be careful not to generalize too much about advertising's socioeconomic dimensions. Whatever its effects—good or bad—advertising is a social and economic force that is a necessary part of American capitalism.[2]

How Critics Look at Advertising

Most criticism of advertising has focused on its social effects. To understand this criticism, the necessary first step is to understand what about advertising is being criticized. As shown in Figure 3.1, most criticism falls into one of four categories: the product advertised, the content of advertising, the amount of advertising, and the impact of advertising on human action.

Most of advertising's support has focused on its economic functions.[3] This is not particularly surprising because advertising is most often appraised by how much it contributes to firm profitability or how much market efficiency it produces rather than how it benefits or harms society.

As a social force, advertising has long been criticized because of its potential to adversely affect the way we think or behave. Prominent humanities and social science scholars have criticized advertising for "playing on emotions, simplifying real human situations into stereotypes, exploiting anxieties, and employing techniques of intensive persuasion that amount to manipulation."[4]

As seen by its critics, advertising has mostly negative social effects because it shapes the way society is—materialistic, cynical, irrational, selfish, socially competitive, sexually preoccupied, and powerless.[5]

To counter these criticisms, advertising's defenders have argued that advertisements must work in harmony with society by reflecting existing and readily understood social symbols and values. As seen by its defenders, advertising acts as a mirror that merely reflects the society of which it is a part.

Two proponent advertising executives have described the reflective nature of advertising in the following ways. In 1962, David Ogilvy said,

> I believe it (advertising) is nothing more than a tool of salesmanship, which follows mores but never leads them. The public is bored by most advertisements, and has acquired a genius for ignoring it.[6]

Fifteen years later, in 1977, Carl Ally commented on the relationship of advertising to society and agencies to advertisers:

> Advertising doesn't manipulate society. Society manipulates advertising. Advertising responds to social trends. Agencies respond to advertisers. Its that simple.[7]

*S*cholars as Critics and Defenders of Advertising

FIGURE 3.1

Criticism of Advertising as a Social Force

Most of the criticism of advertising falls into one of four categories: the products advertised, the content of the advertising, the amount of advertising, and the influence of advertising on human behavior.

Product Advertised

- Tobacco products
- Alcoholic beverages
- Condoms and other sexually related products
- Medical products and services
- Personal care and hygiene products

Advertising Exposure

- Repetitious
- Intrusive

Advertising Content

- Silly/insulting
- Insulting portrayals/situations
- Poor taste
- Falsity/exaggeration
- Negative stereotypes
- Insensitive argumentation
- Sexual suggestiveness
- Negative appeals
- Noninformative/manipulative suggestions

Influences on Human Behavior

- Causes people to buy things they otherwise would not
- Promotes materialistic values and lifestyles
- Lower values and moral standards
- Exploits susceptible segments of society, such as the poor, the elderly, the immature, the mentally ill, and the young

From the perspective of Ogilvy and Ally, as well as many others, advertising has neither positive nor social effects in and of itself. Criticisms of advertising, as its defenders see it, are again really criticisms of the American capitalist system. According to historian Stephen Fox, author of *The Mirror Makers*, many saw the young American republic as beyond social redemption in the early 1780s, decades before the development of national advertising.[8]

Because of the recursive nature of the two arguments—advertising as a cause or advertising as an effect—and the inability of research to establish causality, the longstanding debate on whether advertising shapes or reflects society is probably unresolvable. However, as pointed out by the advertising historian Richard W. Pollay, "Even if advertising merely reflects the values of the culture and society of which it is a part, it has become an important enough reflection of ourselves that it must be regarded as a significant factor in reinforcing and strengthening the life it portrays."[9] The lesson for all of us, no matter where we fall on the issue, is not whether advertising shapes or is shaped by society. The issue is—to what degree does advertising exert its recursive influence, for it most surely functions in society as both a cause and an effect.

The General Public As Critics

The question of how the general public feels about advertising has been studied for more than 50 years by public opinion pollsters and survey researchers.[10] From the 1920s through the 1950s Americans were basically satisfied with the advertising they saw, although there was some discontent. The studies conducted during the 1960s and 1970s found a growing disenchantment with advertising among the general public. In almost every instance when an earlier study was replicated, the replication found more negative attitudes. One study compared the attitudes toward advertising of a 1976 sample of *Consumer Reports* subscribers with a 1970 sample and found that 1976 subscribers liked advertising less than the 1970 subscribers.[11] A replication of Raymond Bauer and Stephen Greyser's classic study, *Advertising in America*, found that Americans' attitudes toward advertising were slightly more negative in 1974 than in 1964.[12] Figure 3.2 is an example of an ad from the American Association of Advertising Agencies' campaign to improve the public's view of advertising. This ad makes the case against subliminal advertising, a topic which will be discussed later in this chapter.

Although feelings about advertising have grown less favorable over time, variations can be observed among and within groups, such as college students, businesspersons, magazine subscribers, and the general population.[13] Highly educated people are more critical of advertising than less educated people. Low-income people are less satisfied with magazine and television advertising than middle-income people. Businesspersons are not as negative about advertising as college students.[14]

Attitudes toward advertising are also multidimensional. People differentiate between advertising's social and economic dimensions and between advertising as an institution and the instruments of the institution—advertisements. The research shows that the general public is more critical of advertising's social than economic dimensions, which is consistent with the scholarly critics, and more critical of the instruments of advertising than the broader institutions.[15]

Even people's personal and general attitudes toward advertising's social and economic dimensions have been shown to differ. People tend to believe that other people are more susceptible to the social effects of advertising than they themselves. On the other hand, they feel that other people tend to benefit more from advertising's economic effects.[16] Common negative beliefs about the social dimensions of advertising are listed in Figure 3.3.

When people complain about advertising, they tend to complain about particular ads, classifying those they dislike as either "annoying" or "offensive." When ads are classified as annoying, it is usually because they (1) contradict personal experience with the advertised product, (2) inflate product importance by utilizing unrealis-

FIGURE 3.2

**An Advertisement from American Association of Advertising Agencies
Designed to Improve the Image of Advertising**

**PEOPLE HAVE BEEN TRYING TO FIND THE
BREASTS IN THESE ICE CUBES SINCE 1957.**

The advertising industry is sometimes charged with sneaking seductive little pictures into ads.
 Supposedly, these pictures can get you to buy a product without your even seeing them.
 Consider the photograph above. According to some people, there's a pair of female breasts hidden in the patterns of light refracted by the ice cubes.
 Well, if you really searched you probably *could* see the breasts. For that matter, you could also see Millard Fillmore, a stuffed pork chop and a 1946 Dodge.
 The point is that so-called "subliminal advertising" simply doesn't exist. Overactive imaginations, however, most certainly do.
 So if anyone claims to see breasts in that drink up there, they aren't in the ice cubes.
 They're in the eye of the beholder.

ADVERTISING
ANOTHER WORD FOR FREEDOM OF CHOICE.
American Association of Advertising Agencies

Source: Reproduced with permission of the American Association of Advertising Agencies.

tic or disturbing methods of presentation, (3) talk down to the audience, or (4) use undue repetitions. "Offensive" ads tend to exhibit bad taste in message content or the advertised product is considered offensive itself.[17]

Advertising Ethics

A century ago business ethics were much different from today. The same is true of advertising. Advertisements such as those in Figure 3.4 were not unusual in the post-Civil War period. There was very little concern for ethical practices before the beginning of the twentieth century. By the 1930s, most of advertising's ethical codes had taken shape, however.[18]

In modern advertising, the two operating ethical systems are (1) an external system based on mandated, institutional codes, guidelines, formal regulations, and organizational procedures and (2) a personal system that commonly relies on human judgment of what is right and wrong. The first system is composed of formal bodies, such as governmental and industry regulatory guidelines, media advertising policies, and agency clearing practices. The second system is composed of individual decisions, which are made on the basis of the ethical assessment of the immediate and long-run effects of individual actions. The major ethical questions facing advertising practitioners on a day-to-day basis are these:

FIGURE 3.3

Common Negative Beliefs about the Social Dimensions of Advertising

- Advertising is not essential.
- Most advertising insults the intelligence of the average consumer.
- Advertising often persuades people to buy things they shouldn't buy.
- In general, advertisements present a false picture of the product advertised.
- In their advertising, companies should be required to tell consumers about the limitations or bad points of their products as well as about the advantages and good points.
- Advertising causes people to buy things they really don't need.
- Most product advertising is not truthful.
- Advertising is an unreliable source of information about the quality and performance of products.
- Television commercials take undue advantage of children.
- Advertising appeals to people's emotions rather than appealing to their intelligence.
- Advertising does not give people enough information about the product being advertised.
- A legal limit should be placed on the amount of money a company can spend on advertising.
- Whenever an advertising claim has been ruled false or misleading, the company involved should be required to advertise this fact until consumers are informed about it.
- Advertising leads to a waste of natural resources by creating desires for unnecessary goods.
- Today's standards of advertising are lower compared with ten years ago.

Source: Darrel D. Muehling, "An investigation of Factors Underlying Attitude-toward-Advertising-in-General," *Journal of Advertising* (Spring 1987): 35. Reprinted with permission.

Who should, and should not, be advertised to?

What should, and should not, be advertised?

What should, and should not, be the content of the advertising message?

What should, and should not, be the symbolic tone or actual character of the advertising message?

What should, and should not, be the relationship between clients, agencies, and the mass media?

What should, and should not, be advertising's business obligations versus its societal obligations? [19]

Researchers have identified two major categories of ethical problems that advertising practitioners encounter in their work: (1) the content of advertising messages and (2) agency/client relationships. [20] According to one survey, the most difficult ethical problem confronting advertising agency executives is treating clients in a fair and equitable manner. The second most difficult problem is "creating honest, nonmisleading, socially desirable advertisements," followed by handling clients whose products are unhealthy, unneeded, useless, or unethical; treating suppliers and the media fairly; treating employees and management fairly; and treating other agencies fairly. [21] As a group, advertising agency practitioners see themselves as just

FIGURE 3.4

Patent Medicine Ads from the 19th Century

as ethical as their clients, who represent business in general, and on an individual basis, even more ethical than their agency peers.[22]

Advertising practitioners today are aware of ethical issues and have institutional standards and procedures in place to deal with unethical practices. Business success is built on long-term considerations (repeat purchases), and most individual advertising practitioners and their agencies operate in an ethical manner, knowing that actions taken in the short-run for personal or organizational gain might cost them more down the road—perhaps their jobs and their business.

Deception in Advertising

Practitioners and regulators of advertising generally agree that advertising should be honest and not misleading. As a general rule, instances of deliberate and purposeful deception in advertising are rare, although they do occur. Legally, the definition of what constitutes deceptive advertising has evolved over years of litigation. An advertisement can be judged deceptive if it is perceived to have the "tendency or capacity to deceive." In practical terms this means that an ad may not contain any falsehoods, yet may be judged deceptive because it produces an impression that is deceptive. More will be said about deceptive advertising and its regulation in Chapter 5.

FIGURE 3.5

Advertisements with "Puffed" Claims

The ad for Jolly Rancher is an exaggerated spoof that no one would literally interpret as true. The point of the ad is to communicate "great taste" in a dynamic manner. The ad for Upper Deck makes a subjective claim about the brand's quality, linking its cards to attributes associated with baseball.

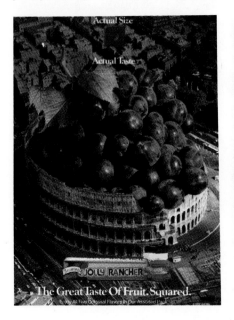

P*uffery*

Puffery, sometimes called the "permissible lie," is generally allowed in advertising. **Puffery** is defined as "advertising or other sales presentations which praise the item to be sold with subjective opinions, superlatives, or exaggerations, vaguely and generally stating no specific facts."[23] According to Aaker, Batra, and Myers, there are two forms of puffery: (1) subjective statements of opinion about a product's quality such as "best or greatest" and (2) exaggerated spoofs that are obviously not true.[24] Examples of both types are presented in Figure 3.5.

Because regulators do not usually investigate "puffed" claims, the question of puffery might be an ethical issue rather than a legal issue. However, one expert in advertising regulations, Ivan Preston, has argued that the Federal Trade Commission (FTC) should consider puffery in advertising to be deceptive and illegal. Preston contends that puffery is "soft-core deception":

> Puffery affects people's purchasing decisions by burdening them with untrue beliefs, but our regulators say it does no such thing except to the out-of-step individual who acts unreasonably and therefore deserves no protection. Puffery deceives, and regulations which have made it legal are thoroughly unjustified. There are many varieties of puffery, and they account for a huge proportion of the claims made by sellers and advertisers in the marketplace.[25]

Unfortunately, whether puffed claims (for example, "best," "premier," "king") actually affect consumer choice or conduct remains an unresolved question.[26] In the absence of concrete research evidence to the contrary, it is likely that regulators will continue to permit puffery as long as the claims cannot be objectively disproved or proven to influence consumer behavior.

Any untruth in advertising does a disservice to honest advertisers who want only to communicate the real benefits of their products. Fortunately, there is a built-in brake on untruthfulness that is sometimes overlooked; advertising in print puts the statement on record, inviting scrutiny that tends to keep dishonest people from the regular use of advertising. Other watchdogs include vigilant government and business sectors (controls that we will deal with in greater detail in Chapter 5) and the increasingly educated consumer public.

Watchdogs

Comparative Advertising

The appearance of comparative claims in advertising has increased since the early 1970s when the FTC revised its policies and encouraged advertisers to name competing brands as an alternative to the Brand X euphemism. Comparative advertising is the practice in which advertisers implicitly or explicitly compare their product categories or brands with competitive offerings, usually claiming superiority for the advertised brand. It can appear misleading especially in cases where the comparison is vague or unverifiable.

The three distinct categories of comparative advertising are: (1) ads that compare implicitly or explicitly two or more brands, (2) ads that explicitly name and/or show two or more competing brands, and (3) ads that imply a comparison with a hypothetical Brand X or "other leading brands." The ads in Figure 3.6 explicitly name or show competing brands.

The research on the communication effectiveness of comparative claims has been inconclusive. In the majority of cases, comparative advertising has not been found to be more effective than noncomparative advertising.[27] The studies that have found

FIGURE 3.6

Examples of Comparative Advertisements for Two Different Product Categories

differences tend to show that the effectiveness is influenced by a number of factors, including ad theme, market position of the advertiser, and claim substantiation. Based on the research findings, it can be concluded that comparative advertising:

- may be more suitable for convenience goods than for durables, certain services, or other high-involvement products.
- may be more effective for promoting new brands that have distinct features relative to competitive offerings.
- may be more effective if comparative claims are made to appear credible.
- may be appropriate for established brands with static sales if noncomparative claims have been ineffective—consumers perceive comparative claims as more interesting.
- may be more effective in the print media than the broadcast media.
- may be more informative than noncomparative advertising.[28]

The last finding is of particular importance because it supports the original intent of the FTC order, which encouraged comparative advertising in order to provide consumers with more information.

Subliminal Advertising

FIGURE 3.7

An ad for Seagram's That Takes Advantage of the Subliminal Advertising Controversy

FIND THE HIDDEN REFRESHMENT IN SEAGRAM'S GIN. IT'S AS EASY AS 1, 2, 3.

Subliminal advertising uses stimuli that operate below the threshold of consciousness but that can be perceived subconsciously. It is believed to influence people's behavior without their being aware that any communication has taken place. There are three types of subliminal stimulation: (1) stimuli that are presented at a rapid speed in visuals, such as movies and commercials, (2) accelerated speech in low-volume auditory messages, and (3) stimuli, such as words and sexual images, that are embedded in printed matter.[29] According to Wilson Bryan Key, author of *Subliminal Seduction, Media Sexploitation*, and *The Clam Plate Orgy*, subliminal techniques are used extensively in ads and commercials and have the power to cause people to buy the advertised products.

Although public awareness of subliminal techniques has increased over the past two decades, scientific support for the practical effectiveness of subliminal advertising is limited and contradictory.[30] Psychologist William Moore has summed up:

> While subliminal perception is a bona fide phenomenon, the effects obtained are subtle and obtaining them typically requires a carefully structured context. Subliminal stimuli are usually so weak that the recipient is not just unaware of the stimulus but is also oblivious to the fact that he/she is being stimulated. As a result, the potential effects of subliminal stimuli are easily nullified by other ongoing stimulation in the same sensory channel or by attention being focused on another modality. These factors pose serious difficulties for any possible marketing application.[31]

As shown in Figure 3.7, Seagrams has cleverly used the subliminal controversy to its advantage by featuring identified embeds.

Bad Taste in Advertising

Some people are offended by products and services themselves, others by the manner of advertising presentation. An interesting example of how viewer irritation is linked to the content of prime-time television commercials is presented in the Ad Insight entitled "Irritating TV Commercials."

Ads and commercials are generally seen as offensive or in bad taste when (1) the story is silly; (2) sexual stimuli are utilized; (3) the same ads or commercials

Irritating TV Commercials

Television commercials irritate viewers for a variety of reasons, most of which are linked to content characteristics of commercials and the nature of the product advertised. A study of 524 prime-time commercials found that viewer irritation levels are higher when:

- a sensitive product is featured, and that product's use or effect is explicitly depicted (hemorrhoid or feminine hygiene products).
- the portrayed situation is phony, unbelievable, contrived, or overdramatized.
- a person is "put down" because of appearance, knowledge, or sophistication.
- an important relationship between parent and child or between friends is threatened.
- physical discomfort is graphically portrayed.
- tension is created by an argument, an antagonistic character, or an unpleasant activity.

- an unattractive or unsympathetic character is featured.
- a sexually suggestive scene is depicted.
- the commercial is poorly cast or produced.

Viewer irritation levels were found to be lower when:

- casting and story line combined to produce believable, sympathetic scenes and characters.
- music, story line, words, phrases, and characters are used to create warm, positive, and happy moods.
- an appropriate, credible spokesperson is featured.
- the story line is amusing.
- the content is informative.

Advertisers should do whatever they can to reduce the displeasure and impatience caused by irritating commercials—irritating commercials work in spite of irritation, not because of it.

Source: David A. Aaker and Donald E. Buzzone, "Causes of Irritation in Advertising." *Journal of Marketing* 49 (Spring 1985): 45–57.

are repeated ad infinitum, ad nauseam; and (4) the advertised products or services are unpleasant. One survey has shown that TV commercials for panty hose, designer jeans, bras and girdles, laxatives, and feminine hygiene products are among the most "distasteful" on television.[32]

Of the techniques seen as objectional, sexual suggestiveness and nudity have been studied most extensively. Several content analyses have shown that, while the proportion of sexual content has not increased over the past three decades, the sexual content has become more provocative and suggestive: the public is seeing more eroticism and nudity in ads and commercials.[33]

Increases in sexual suggestiveness and nudity in advertising do not mean that "sexy" ads and commercials are more effective, however. A number of studies have shown that sexual content is attention getting, but that such content does not translate into better comprehension, attitude change, or purchase intention and that responses vary by the recipient's gender.[34]

Based on that research, there seems to be a clear consensus that "sexy" advertising—whether functional, fantasy, or symbolic in nature—works best when it is appropriate to the advertised product (perfumes, designer jeans, and so on) and targeted at the right audience. In such instances, it is less likely to be seen as offensive or in bad taste. Figure 3.8 is an example of the effective use of sexually relevant stimuli in an ad.

FIGURE 3.8

An Example of the Effective Use of Sexually Relevant Stimuli

The advertising industry cannot be expected to avoid every product or presentation technique that someone may consider in bad taste or offensive, or even crusade for the elevation of the public's taste. But society can expect advertisers to abide by the accepted rules of decency and taste of the audiences they expect their ads to reach. No other product categories have stirred more public controversy than tobacco, alcohol, and condoms. Advertisers of these products are part of a national debate over how, and even if, these products should be advertised.

Controversial Products

Tobacco and Alcohol

Whether tobacco and alcohol should receive the same promotional rights accorded other legally manufactured products is a question of significant financial importance for advertisers, agencies, and the media. Tobacco and alcohol manufactures are large advertisers, and the reduction or outright elimination of advertising expenditures for these products would most certainly have a negative impact on advertising-derived income.

As you might expect, there are two sides to the controversy, both with compelling reasons for or against the advertising of tobacco and alcohol.[35] The financial interests of the advertising industry, the critics argue, are of little public concern. What is important, they counter, is the regulation of inherently manipulative advertising for products that are detrimental to the public's health—both at the individual and collective levels. As they see it, tobacco and alcohol advertising persuades people, particularly the young and socially-vulnerable, to start smoking and drinking; causes existing smokers and drinkers to smoke and drink more often; keeps potential quitters from quitting the habits; and influences ex-smokers and ex-drinkers to resume smoking and drinking. These effects, the critics contend, are not only detrimental to the health of the individual consumer, but are also harmful to the health of others—advertising leads to tobacco and alcohol-related illness, injury, death, and social costs. To remedy these conditions, critics have proposed that tobacco and alcohol

The Industry Viewpoint: Don't Blame Advertising for Teenage Drinking

Teen drinking has been in the news a lot. And brewers, who have long worked to reduce underage consumption, welcome the attention. In fact, statistics are improving.

A 1990 survey by the National Institute on Drug Abuse reported that 57 percent of high school seniors said they'd had a drink in the last month, down from 72 percent in 1980. And the number of fatalities involving drivers aged 15–19 and alcohol declined in the '80s by 39 percent. Increased education and awareness will help push these statistics down even further.

Surgeon General Antonia Novello suggests advertising is a primary contributor to underage drinking and wants the industry to withdraw much of its advertising. Advertising doesn't cause the problem, so restricting it won't solve it.

Novello's boss seems to agree. Health Secretary Louis Sullivan's 1990 report to Congress states, "Research has yet to document a strong relationship between alcohol advertising and alcohol consumption." His findings are echoed by James C. Miller, former chairman of the Federal Trade Commission, and D.E. Strickland, who noted in a major study that alcohol beverage advertising on TV "has virtually no effect on the level of consumption among teen-agers." And, while beer advertising expenditures have gone up and up over the last decade, per capita consumption of alcohol has declined significantly.

Why do teens drink? In a Roper poll, 70 percent of teens surveyed said schoolmates' and friends' drinking habits had the most influence on them, followed by parents' drinking habits (48 percent); only 2 percent cited advertising as a factor.

Novello's own research last June revealed that "teenagers claim not to be too influenced by alcohol advertising."

Parents, friends, and schools have far more impact on youth behavior than advertising. That's why the beer industry is spending millions to support effective educational programs for use by parents, schools and communities. We are working on real solutions to these difficult problems. It's easy to use ads as a target to blame for many complex problems facing our society. But it's also the wrong target.

Source: James C. Sanders, "Don't Blame Advertising for Teen-Age Drinking," *USA Today*, Monday, December 9, 1991, 12A.

advertising be eliminated entirely or that its content (for example, elimination of image-based ads) and media placement (for example, prohibited from vehicles with vulnerable audiences) be further restricted.

Supporters offer a number of counterarguments against banning or restricting tobacco and alcohol ads, noting that no conclusive evidence exists that shows tobacco and alcohol advertising increases aggregate consumption of either product and that previous bans have been ineffective (see Ad Insight entitled "The Industry Viewpoint: Don't Blame Advertising for Teenage Drinking"). Some argue that advertising effects for the two products are limited to brand competition; that is, ads promote brand switching and brand loyalties among existing smokers and drinkers but do not cause others to start either habit. Others argue that a total ban would not only be a violation of the First Amendment rights of tobacco and alcohol advertisers but would also eliminate an intra-industry incentive to develop safer products and to engage in message strategies that communicate the detrimental consequences of tobacco and alcohol consumption. The ads in Figure 3.9 provide examples of how two large alcohol manufacturers have prosocially reacted to the controversy—both ads encourage the responsible consumption of alcohol.

FIGURE 3.9

Advertisements Sponsored by Manufacturers of a Controversial Product

The ads are designed to educate the public and to promote responsible consumption.

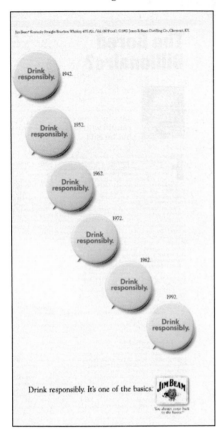

Whether tobacco or alcohol ads will be banned or further restricted is an unresolved issue at this point. Restrictions on tobacco and alcohol products, both government and industry-imposed, are not new. Cigarette commercials were eliminated from television and radio in 1971, and trade association policies prohibit the use of some presentation techniques (for example, celebrity endorsers, models depicted in unsafe use situations, and so on). One thing is sure, however, the controversy is not likely to go away in the foreseeable future, and, as most advertisers know, it is in their best interest to act in a socially responsible manner.

Condoms

Condoms, another controversial product, are considered offensive, not harmful. The issue is over condom advertising. Should the product be advertised at all and, if so, in which media? Unlike the tobacco and alcohol categories, where government has been centrally involved in regulation, condom advertising has been restricted by media policies. In the past, individual media vehicles and media associations have prohibited condom advertising on the grounds of offensiveness and taste.

Today, some of the prohibitions have broken down, primarily because of the argument that the public needs information that will help protect people from sexually transmitted diseases, including AIDS. Magazines have been more receptive to condom ads than broadcast media, although the National Association of Broadcasters has encouraged the acceptance of condom advertising. An example of a tasteful condom magazine ad is featured in Figure 3.10.

Advertising and Children

Many people believe that children are especially vulnerable to the appeals of advertising and that any advertising directed to them should be strictly regulated. They contend that advertising unfairly manipulates children because children (1) do not understand the selling intent of ads and (2) lack sufficient cognitive abilities to defend themselves against persuasive advertising appeals.

A number of organizations have issued guidelines for children's advertising. The organizations include the Federal Trade Commission, the National Association of Broadcasters, the Federal Communications Commission, and the Council of the Better Business Bureaus. In 1978 the FTC instituted rule-making procedures in response to a petition from Action for Children's Television (ACT) and other consumer interest groups. Conflicting evidence was presented on children's cognitive abilities, the nature of parent-child interactions, the effects of sugared products, and First Amendment rights. In the end, the commission terminated the proceedings on the basis that regulations would be ineffective.

Findings from the studies on children and advertising indicate that:

- Children of all ages have a considerable degree of exposure to advertising. They are not merely exposed to advertising targeted at themselves but also to advertising targeted at adults.
- Television commercials receive less attention than programs. Attention appears to decline with the age of the child. Younger children's attention to commercials is more likely to be determined by perceptual and affective factors while older children's attention is more likely to be determined by conceptual factors.
- Preschool-aged children are capable of distinguishing commercials from programs. However, they use superficial perceptual and affective aspects to make this distinction. It is not clear at what age children develop a conceptual understanding of commercials, although this understanding increases with the age of the child.
- Separators that distinguish between commercials and programs do not seem to be effective, although they appear to have no dysfunctional effects.
- The effectiveness of host-selling is questionable at best. In fact, nonhost commercials may perform better by capitalizing on the novelty of the nonhost.
- Young children (preschool-age) are not able to discern the intent of commercials. While studies using verbal responses have generally supported this finding, some studies using nonverbal responses have yielded conflicting results.
- The use of disclaimers is common in children's advertising. However, many of these disclaimers are not understood by young children and are therefore ineffective.
- Children's ability to discriminate among human, animated, and puppet characters increases with age.
- Parental education, family interaction, and peer integration generally aid children's understanding of commercials.
- Attitudes toward advertising in general become less positive with the age of the child. Older children are more cynical about advertising. Children of well-educated parents have stronger attitudinal and cognitive defenses toward advertising.
- Advertising has a moderate impact on children's attitudes toward the advertised product. Multiple but varied exposures are required to influence children's preferences and choice behaviors.
- There is no definitive evidence revealing harmful or dysfunctional effects of premium advertising or host-selling with regard to children's attitudes toward advertised products.

FIGURE 3.10

A Tasteful and Creative Approach to a Controversial—but Socially Important—Product

- The content of commercials does impact on children's preferences and choices, as revealed by studies of food advertising to children. Decreasing the commercials for nonnutritional products (sweets, snacks, and so on) and increasing public service announcements relating to nutrition are likely to be beneficial for children.
- Advertising encourages children to request products from their parents. For a variety of reasons, children's requests decline as age increases. While parental control of children's viewing habits curbs requests, an increase in parent-child interaction tends to facilitate these requests.
- Parental yielding to children's requests is generally high. Parental yielding is likely to increase with the age of the child and depends on the product advertised. Parents with higher education and a better understanding of advertising claims are less likely to yield to children's requests.
- Most studies point to the fact that the family plays a very important mediating role in the socialization of children. The family can facilitate learning in children directly by teaching consumer skills and indirectly by providing a family environment that encourages learning.
- Advertising targeted at adults may influence children's perceptions of the adult world and thus their preferences and choices as adults.[36]

In spite of these findings, we have little conclusive research on the effects of advertising on children. We know that advertising has effects; we know that some of the effects are bad and some are good, and we know that children are a special group that should be protected. The question remains, how much protection from advertising do children need?

Advertising and Stereotypes

Advertising has been accused repeatedly of creating and perpetuating stereotypes—especially of women, the elderly, and minorities. In the past, the National Organization for Women (NOW) has identified ads most insulting to women and urged its members to protest both to the advertisers and to the agencies responsible for the offending ads. Another women's group, Women Against Pornography, has issued Plastic Pig awards for ads considered pornographic and demeaning to women. The NAACP and other related groups have organized protests and boycotts against advertisers insensitive to racial issues. In response, researchers have attempted to scientifically address stereotyping accusations through analyses of advertising content.

Women

Portrayals of women in advertising became a concern in the 1960s. Criticism of advertising content most often centered on: depictions of women as sex objects, portrayals that were unrealistic and limited, themes of dependence on men, underrepresentation of working women, and depictions as "happy housewives" or incompetents.[37]

A study of 2,000 magazine ads published between 1960 and 1979 revealed the following about portrayals of women in advertising:

- Ads consistently pictured women as younger than men. The age distribution of women depicted in the ads was much younger than the female readership for the studied magazines.
- Women were more likely to be portrayed modeling fashions and cosmetics or doing housework; men were more frequently shown on the job or engaged in outdoor recreation.

The Sexism Watch: Johnnie Walker Properly Responds

Madison Avenue's stock in trade is sensitivity to popular values. Yet lapses into sexual stereotypes still pop up 20 years after the feminist movement exploded into the national consciousness.

Truth to tell, Madison Avenue lacks an effective sexism patrol. The National Advertising Review Board, a self-regulatory group, has not issued guidelines on the use of women in ads since 1978, when feminist watchfulness hit a peak. Few agencies have rules or procedures to spot sexism in ads, and top managements remain mostly male. Then, too, though crude sex stereotypes no longer sell, sexually alluring images still do. "By the early 1980s, women in ads were out of the kitchen and becoming nuclear scientists who commuted by helicopter," says

advertising critic Barbara Lippert. "But with the fitness boom, we're now seeing parts of the body formerly reserved for soft porn." A new TV ad for Reebok shows a high-heeled woman in a black minidress straddling a motorcycle. Shirtless men are being used to sell everything from laundry detergent to jeans.

At its smartest, Madison Avenue cannily plays against stereotypes. A recent whisky ad featuring two svelte women jogging on the beach carried the tag line, "He loves my mind. And he drinks Johnnie Walker." When critics protested, the company shot another version, this time with two men running along the shore. The tag line: "She loves my cooking. And she drinks Johnnie Walker."

Source: *U.S. News & World Report,* March 27, 1989, 12.

• Men and women were usually portrayed in different occupations, with one exception—more women were shown as managers than was actually true in the U.S. workforce during the years studied.
• Ads showed men and women using different products.[38]

Another study compared sex role stereotyping in three countries—the United States, Australia, and Mexico.[39] Sex role stereotypes were found in the advertising of all three countries. Male voices were used in **voice-overs** more often than female voices, women were portrayed as younger more often than men, and men were more likely to be portrayed in independent roles whereas women were portrayed in roles relative to others. Australian advertising contained less sex role stereotyping than U.S. or Mexican advertising; Mexican advertising was slightly more stereotypical than U.S. advertising.

Sensitive to the criticism that advertising conveys negative and traditional stereo-types of various social groups, many advertisers have turned the tables (see Ad Insight entitled "The Sexism Watch: Johnnie Walker Properly Responds"). Models are now often portrayed in positive characterizations in nontraditional roles. Two such advertisements are shown in Figure 3.11. The Ad Insight entitled "She's Come a Long Way" chronicles advertising's progress in the portrayal of women.

Hispanics

A more recent stereotyping issue is the depiction of Hispanics in advertising. Unfortu-nately, the amount of research on the issue is very limited.

One study of the portrayal of Hispanics in "Anglo" media found few depictions of Hispanic models in magazine ads, although Hispanics comprised almost 10 percent of the readership of the magazines studied. In the case of Hispanic media, Hispanic models were more likely to be depicted as white-collar, middle-class workers than the stereotyped mustachioed "bandito" character.[40]

Another study compared the portrayal of Hispanics and African Americans in prime-time TV commercials. Hispanics appeared in substantially fewer commercials than blacks, and primarily in background roles.[41] The results of both studies suggest that Hispanics are underrepresented in advertising content and that advertisers must become more sensitive to depictions of this population group.

The Elderly

A discrepancy between population and ad portrayal proportions was also found in the few studies on the depiction of the elderly in advertising. For example, a study of the elderly in TV commercials found only 7 percent of the commercials studied contained elderly models, although the population of people over 65 years of age was 12 percent. When portrayed, the elderly were typically cast as advisors, and not feeble, confused, or funny. Elderly women, although they outnumbered men in the population, were portrayed less often than men in advisory roles.[42] However, the overall evidence on the stereotyping of the elderly in advertising is conflicting, which suggests that we must be careful not to overgeneralize about the issue.[43] The

FIGURE 3.11

Advertisements That Effectively Counter Traditional Stereotypes

She's Come a Long Way

Since women are the nation's top consumers, advertising has always made them the center of its world. Ads portrayed proper female aspirations: to be a desirable companion, a competent cleaner, a loving mother. The women in ads found fulfillment in the supermarket aisles—and in Maidenform bras. But as millions began to venture beyond the home in the 1970s, the images had to change. Madison Avenue's women developed minds of their own. Consider the female Honda buyer, who thinks like a man. Or Charlie, reaching out to touch someone. Even romance mirrors complex modern reality: the cute young thing in the new Johnnie Walker ad seems to be a divorced mother.

Source: *Time,* Special Issue, Women: The Road Ahead, Fall 1990, 58–59.

Ad Insight entitled "Lesson Learned" offers some guidelines for advertising to this age group.

Since the mid-1960s, advertisers have faced the issue of integrated advertising. Their original dilemma—whether real or imagined—was trying to satisfy African-American consumers with more representative portrayals, while not alienating white consumers.[44] Three of the more recent studies suggest that, at least in the areas of magazine and television advertising, advertisers have made progress.

A study of African Americans in magazine ads between 1950 and 1982 found that they have gained equal status with whites in nonstereotyped portrayals, even

African Americans

Lessons Learned: Advertising to Over-50s

Advertisers have been slow to reach out to mature consumers—and some that have tried have made costly mistakes. Going for the Golden Agers can be tricky business, for the terrain is fraught with contradictions. Stressing age in ads can be a turnoff, so can leaving older people out of ads.

A study by Grey Advertising found that the older people were offended by not seeing themselves or their lifestyles in ads. According to George Moschis, director of the Center of Mature Consumer Studies at Georgia State University, one-third of people over 55 have deliberately not bought products because they did not like the way age was portrayed in ads.

With billions of future dollars at stake—even whole consumer markets—here are some lessons that advertisers are learning about advertising to mature consumers:

1. *Don't separate them from other age groups*   Mature consumers resent feeling separated—don't single them out as being totally different.
2. *Show the solution, not the problem*   Feature how products improve life.
3. *Subtract 15 years*   Mature people think of themselves as being 15 years younger than they actually are. Show them as active and attractive people.
4. *Don't mention age*   Mentioning age will alienate both older and younger consumers.
5. *Span Generations*   Portray mature consumers as individuals, yet related to everyone else.
6. *Watch that punch line*   Be careful not to make the elderly the butt of some joke.
7. *Laugh with them, not at them*   Humor has its place, but done only with taste and sincerity.
8. *Don't generalize*   Identify people by stage of life, not by age of life. All older people are not the same.

Advertisers who don't learn these lessons will find themselves not only out of touch, but maybe out of business in the years ahead. As the population ages, and takes its buying power with it, that is where the beef will be.

Source: Melinda Beck, "Going for the Gold," *Newsweek,* April 23, 1990, 74–76.

though they have not gained equality in real life.[45] Another study of magazine advertising found that the presence of African-American models in business-to-business ads has increased since the mid-1960s and that the increase has been greater in trade journals than in consumer magazines.[46] A study of African Americans in TV commercials found that the presence of black models has increased over time and that commercials now tend to be more racially integrated.[47]

All things considered, the research on stereotyping—including those studies cited here as examples—has produced mixed findings on the issue. Some stereotyping clearly exists in modern advertising, despite social criticisms and the attempts by advertisers to be more sensitive and less demeaning to both genders, to minorities, and to the elderly in their advertising.

The Challenge to Advertisers

Most sophisticated advertisers understand that it is both dangerous and irresponsible to deviate too far from reality in portraying people in their ads. For practical reasons, they know that there is danger in alienating a large number of consumers, who may then boycott offenders or even cause public ridicule of their advertising practices. They also know that they have a responsibility to society because advertising influences societal standards and values, although we do not know precisely how. The issue is a tough one, and advertisers will continually be faced with the problem of how realistically to portray people in ads while at the same time appealing to people's desires to aspire.

Political Advertising

Although political candidates have used advertising for at least a century, it was during the presidential election of 1952 that political advertising came under heavy fire from critics.[48] In that election, television **spot announcements** represented a major part of the promotional efforts to elect Dwight D. Eisenhower. An unprecedented $1.5 million was spent on airtime. Today, advertising is a major, although highly controversial, feature of American politics. Even business advertisers may tie in to politics during election years, as the Delta ad in Figure 3.12 illustrates. Delta used the major political party symbols to communicate how its service pleases all parties.

Political advertising is frequently criticized on three basic grounds:

The Grounds for Criticism

- The content: deception or misleading statements, bad taste, negativism, and unfair charges about opponents and issues
- The brevity of ads and spots: a tendency to simplify complex issues
- The high costs of time and space: discouraging financially poor but able candidates from seeking elected offices

The content of political advertising is not presently subject to the same controls as the content of product advertising. Various proposals for regulating the content of political ads and commercials have been offered. Some suggest that the nation's media should exercise more control in what goes on the air or what is printed; others suggest that the FTC or some other regulatory agency should be the watchdog of political advertising. Still others point out that political advertising is not commercial speech per se. It is protected by more First Amendment rights and, under existing laws, control of content would be considered a curtailment of freedom of expression. A related charge is that political advertising puts too much emphasis on candidate imagery, negative appeals, and too little on the discussion of the issues.

Some critics, politicians, and advertising professionals have advocated requiring political spots to be five minutes or more in length. How, they ask, can foreign policy or economic issues by fully dealt with in 30- or 60-second commercials? Defenders of the status quo point out that long before politicians used advertising,

FIGURE 3.12

**An Advertisement That Uses Political Symbols to Communicate
the Airline's Nonpartisan Service**

they oversimplifed complicated issues and probably will continue to do so regardless of time requirements.

Advertising Financing

The problem of advertising financing has been dealt with by Congress. Following the Watergate revelations, Congress placed limits on individual and organizational contributions; established spending limits for presidential, senatorial, and congressional elections; provided matching funds for qualified candidates; and required under penalty of law that candidates receiving contributions of more than $1,000 disclose the names of their contributors and campaign expenses.[49]

Despite these efforts to regulate political expenditures, heavy advertising spending by political candidates, political parties, and independent political action groups raises the question of how expenditures affect election outcomes. Some argue that massive spending is tantamount to election success. Others argue that spending has little effect on voter behavior. The studies on the issue are far from conclusive, but evidence suggests that promotional spending does influence the outcome of some elections, although it is not the only influence.[50] The studies show also that awareness, knowledge, and salience of conditions and issues can be affected by political advertising.

A *Look Ahead*

Without a change in regulatory policies, political advertising is here to stay. Under existing political conditions, it does not seem reasonable to restrict politicians' access to skilled communicators, including advertising specialists. Equalizing the advertising spending of incumbents and challengers and restricting the contribution influence of Political Action Committees (PACs) would seem more reasonable.

A nationwide survey of advertising agencies has shown that many of the nation's most respected agencies have become progressively more reluctant to accept political candidates as clients.[51] As a result, more and more independent political consultants are directing political advertising campaigns. The author of the study noted that a return to old-style political advertising practices might in the long run prove more beneficial to the democratic process as well as to politicians than the involvement of political consultants. Only time will tell.

Advertising and Raising Expectations

Critics would have us believe that advertisers, through modern research techniques, have unlimited manipulative power. Advertising is accused of causing people to worry about bad breath, body odor, lack of self-confidence, and many other ills. The charge is true, at least in part. Advertising does have the power to awaken latent desire, conscious or unconscious. For example, an exploratory research report has shown that when women compare themselves with idealized advertising images, their comparison standards for attractiveness are raised and they become less satisfied with how they look.[52] No research has shown, however, that advertising manipulates people into acting against their will—advertising tends to work when people are predisposed to products featured in ads. Persuasion and manipulation are not the same; and persuasion is a legitimate form of human interaction, utilized not only by advertisers but also by individuals and social institutions. As noted in Chapter 2, being persuasive is more difficult when your audience knows your intent—and people know the intent of advertising.

Although advertising may raise people's economic aspirations or accentuate their worries about social or physical shortcomings, it does offer solutions. The teenager with pimples may feel more confident at the next party after using an advertised acne medication. That the product will not transform the user from a wallflower to the life of the party is no reason to condemn the advertising. In assessing the argument that advertising creates insecurity, we must balance the relative value of assuaging people's fears against advertising's tendency to accentuate latent fears.

As noted earlier, advertising generally follows rather than leads social trends. Over the years, Bain de Soleil has reacted to fears about the connection between sunbathing and skin cancer by lightening the tan on the model in its ads (see Ad Insight entitled "Reflecting Social Change").

Advertising's Influence on the Media

Advertisers and their agencies complain about perceived bias in news stories, television programs, or editorials. Some of them attempt to pressure editors or

Reflecting Social Change: Bain de Soleil Model Lightens Up

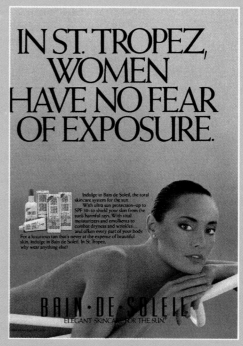

When model Kriss Ziemer first appeared in Bain de Soleil print ads [in the late 1970s], she sported one of the deepest, darkest tans to ever catch the reader's eye. How times have changed.

In 1988, Ziemer appeared in Bain de Soleil ads with a tan that was shades lighter and toured the country to promote safe sunning. Why has her tan got lighter and lighter over the years? Why has Bain de Soleil decided to promote safer tans, not darker tans?

The reason: fear of skin cancer and wrinkles. After years of warnings, the message of dermatologists has finally got through to both sunbathers and advertisers—sunbathers are concerned about sun-damaged skin and advertisers are concerned about reflecting sunbathers' concerns.

Source: Kim Painter, "To Dermatologists' Delight, Tans Fade from Favor," *USA Today*, May 2, 1988, 5D.

programmers into modifying their policies or views. Some buy their own advertising space or time to present counter viewpoints, and others keep a low profile to avoid calling more attention to the news items in question.

Advertisers may, from time to time, be interested in any of the following: the omission or "burying" of an embarrassing news story, the coloring of a news story involving them, extra publicity favorable to them, or the shading of editorial opinion to agree with their opinions. In recent years, a number of groups have charged advertisers with pressuring the media. For example, journalists, health officials, and public health researchers have charged that the tobacco industry's advertising dollars have precluded the media's willingness to convey the health hazards of smoking;

American business writers and editors have charged that advertising pressure is a growing threat to the journalistic integrity of newpapers; and editors of farm journals have experienced the withdrawal of ads because of unfavorable product publicity.[53]

The charge that advertisers exercise undue control over media is based largely on the media's dependence on advertising for their support. The average daily newspaper receives the majority of its revenue from advertising (roughly one-third of this from classified and the rest from local display and national advertising). Most television and radio stations and their networks depend entirely on advertising for support. However, if we include total revenue for broadcast industry support (for example, set sales and service, fees for cable television, and so on) we find that advertisers supply less than half of all total broadcast support.

Charges of Undue Control

Some reason exists to believe that small, financially insecure newspapers or broadcast stations are more likely to be influenced by outside pressure than the large, financially stable ones. There is little reason to believe that large, prestigious papers, magazines, or television networks are overly cautious in including controversial matters or that they cater particularly to advertisers, as charged by critics. Neither are they overly critical of business, as charged by some advertisers. The self-interest of the media encourages them to avoid both these extremes.

Special problems arise when we examine the role of one of our largest advertisers—the U.S. government. Each year the federal government spends millions in advertising, much of it to promote campaigns that at least some would call controversial (armed forces recruiting and selling booklets published by the Government Information Service, for example). This does not include the millions of dollars of "free" advertising for public service campaigns contributed by the Advertising Council and the media. Obviously the government is in a position to exert more power over media (for example, through license renewal in the case of broadcast media) than even the largest corporations could. Moreover, government advertising has so far not been subject to the same controls by the FTC and other government agencies as similar advertising by private corporations would be.[54]

Fortunately, there are certain built-in checks against advertisers exerting too much influence on the media. Perhaps the strongest check is the self-interest of media executives. They cannot afford to ignore news of interest to readers, listeners, or viewers and expect to retain public confidence. As they build confidence and goodwill, they can expand their audience and thus make the medium more valuable to advertisers. Avoidance of controversy also makes for a dull newspaper, newscast, or television series. Space and time buyers are mainly interested in audience coverage and few can afford to ignore a medium that covers a market they want to reach, whether or not they happen to agree with a particular editorial or with the way in which a particular industry is portrayed.

Built-in Checks against Undue Influence

We suspect that the media are probably much less "kept" than most people think. He who pays the piper does not necessarily call the tune.[55]

Advertising and Freedom of Speech

More and more individuals, organizations of all kinds, and corporations are turning to advertising to promote their points of view. In several labor disputes, unions have used advertising space and time to tell the public why the workers thought a strike was necessary. Management, in turn, has used advertising to tell its side of the story. Ordinary citizens and governmental bodies have used advertising to communicate their stories, in their own words, and without fear of having the

FIGURE 3.13

**Advertisement Sponsored by the National Cable Television Association
Expressing Its Viewpoint on a Political Issue**

message cut or edited. In Figure 3.13, an ad sponsored by the National Cable Television Association conveys the Association's opinion about proposed changes in television regulatory policies.

As long as these parties operate within the editorial standards established by the media, they all have the freedom to buy space and time to tell the public their stories; the public is then free to read or ignore messages, to believe or disbelieve. The meaning of this in today's society has been summed up in this way:

> The use of advertising space (and time) expands and modernizes the concept of free speech. But it is essential that . . . advertisers not be denied access to the media. Otherwise those who control the press will be able to control aspects of what is made available to the public.[56]

Some have argued that the expanding freedom of speech in advertising has altered the balance in the marketplace of ideas through the power of the purse. In their view, parties are free to express their views as long as they have the money to pay for the time and space.

In 1976, the Supreme Court reaffirmed the right of all opposing views to purchase advertising and in 1977 decided that, in some situations, commercial speech was entitled to First Amendment rights. Today, restrictions that deprive the consumer of information are considered unconstitutional. Lawyers, medical professionals, prescription drug manufacturers, abortion services, and contraceptive manufacturers are allowed to advertise as long as the ads are not deceptive or anticompetitive.

The Advertising Council

To promote the social, economic, and moral good, the advertising industry acts through the Advertising Council. Organized during World War II as the War Advertising Council, the industry-sponsored organization was nearly disbanded at the close of the war, but some of the executives involved came to its rescue and saw to its continuation. Today, the Advertising Council is a vital part of the industry's effort to address and attack some of society's major problems.

The **Advertising Council** produces public service messages, covering a wide range of social topics, that are disseminated in time and space donated by the mass media. Public service advertising is one form of noncommercial advertising, a form of advertising that was covered in Chapter 1. Its most distinguishing feature from commercial advertising is that it deals with public welfare issues and promotes the nonfinancial interests of sponsors.

Public service advertising can take two forms: (1) it can involve paid advertising messages sponsored by an individual advertiser or advertiser-sponsored association or (2) it can involve donated mass media messages, such as those produced and delivered by the Advertising Council. Sometimes nonpaid public service messages are termed public service announcements rather than advertising. In our view, the distinction is noteworthy because a public service ad refers to a message that is paid for, while a public service announcement refers to one that is donated. Examples of the two forms of public service advertising are presented in Figure 3.14.

FIGURE 3.14

Examples of Public Service Advertising

These advertisements on education were created by the ad industry's Advertising Council. The ATV campaign was unique in that four competing companies and their ad agencies cooperated in its development and execution. The agencies were Dailey & Associates, BJK&E, HDM, and Chiat/Day.

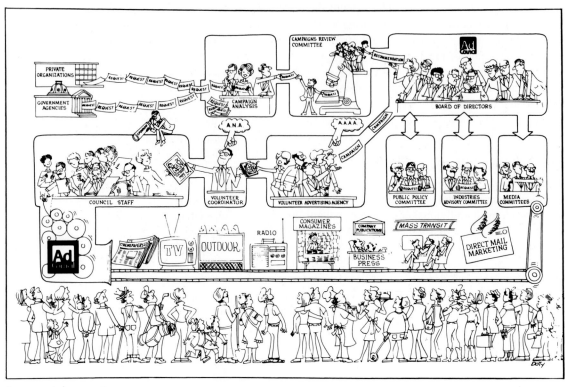

FIGURE 3.15

The Advertising Council's Organization and Operations: A "Blueprint"

Source: Courtesy of The Advertising Council, Inc.

As it exists today, the Advertising Council may plan and execute an advertising campaign designed to solve or help solve any of the nation's serious problems. Its organizational structure is shown graphically in Figure 3.15. All proposed campaigns (except those strictly in the public interest) must be approved by a three-fourths vote of the council's Public Policy Committee.

A board of directors representing advertisers, agencies, and media supervises the council's operation and plans its policies. Its main support comes from the American Association of Advertising Agencies, the Association of National Advertisers, the Newspaper Advertising Bureau, the Magazine Publishers Association, the American Business Press, the National Association of Broadcasters, the Radio Advertising Bureau, the Transit Advertising Association, and the Outdoor Advertising Association of America. Its operating budget depends entirely on contributions from advertising firms and the media. Each campaign is created by a voluntary advertising agency that donates its personnel and facilities, charging only for its out-of-pocket costs.

Typical print advertisements prepared by one of the council's volunteer agencies are shown in Figure 3.16. In one long-running and well-known campaign, "McGruff, The Crime Dog" has worked to change feelings of apathy, fear, and inevitability to an individual sense of responsibility and action toward crime prevention. In another famous campaign, "Smokey the Bear" has fought forest fires since 1942. Other campaigns created by the Advertising Council have dealt with child abuse, environmental pollution, energy conservation, drug abuse, United Way fund drives, U.S. Savings Bonds, the United Negro College Fund, and religion.

Despite its contributions to the public good, the council has run into some problems. One of its frustrations is having to turn down many worthwhile national campaigns because of limited media availabilities. The council recognizes that the

FIGURE 3.16

Advertising Council TV Commercial and Print Ad for the Program on Crime Prevention and Its Famous Smokey the Bear Campaign

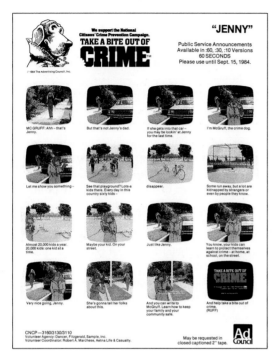

media cannot provide unlimited time and space (placement of public service ads is determined by the media) and consequently must make hard choices among the many possible campaign topics. Another problem is the enforcement of quality standards when dealing with volunteer agencies. The council has tried to spread its influence by enlisting more local organizations and business firms in public service campaign planning, offering to provide expertise where needed. In the end, the council, the dean of public service advertising, must rely on two basic qualities that must be supplied by the advertising and related industries—volunteerism and professionalism.

Summary

Social and ethical issues form an important part of the environment in which advertising operates. Perhaps the most important of these issues is that of possible deception in advertising, which forms the rationale for much control of advertising content by government organizations and industry.

Some advertising is considered offensive, but exact standards are difficult to determine because judgments about matters of taste are subjective. In particular, advertising for tobacco, alcohol, and condoms are considered offensive. Certain types of advertising may have harmful effects on children, but children are more perceptive and selective than some critics seem to realize. Advertising may also at times perpetuate undesirable stereotypes, although there has been improvement in this area and advertisers seem to be more stereotype-sensitive.

Outcomes in close political elections are sometimes influenced by advertising, especially if a well-financed incumbent is running for reelection. Little evidence exists that advertising creates social values; there is more reason to suspect that advertising itself is merely a reflection of everyday life, sometimes running a little ahead of social trends, but most of the time a few steps behind.

Advertising uses both persuasion and selected facts to convince people to buy things they want but don't really need. There is nothing diabolic in this unless we believe that it is immoral to want something we don't need. The rise of comparative advertising has brought up certain ethical questions, but at the same time it provides a competitive weapon. Advertising sometimes creates a certain sense of insecurity in its attempts to sell goods and services, but it can do this only when the seeds of anxiety are already present in people.

Advertising appears to have minor influence on what appears in the media, mainly because the self-interest of editors, programmers, agencies, and advertisers mitigates against such censorship. Other watchdogs include the trade magazines, consumer groups, and competing advertisers looking for evidence of undue pressure.

The advertising industry sponsors and supports the Advertising Council. Ad Council ads are produced free-of-charge by industry agencies and media placement is donated by the media. The function of the council is to promote the social, economic, and moral good.

Questions for Discussion

1. What are the two most important social or ethical problems facing the advertising industry today?
2. What guidelines would you suggest to an advertiser or agency trying to write a truthful but persuasive advertisement?
3. What measures would make comparative advertising more helpful to consumers?
4. What should be the public policy regarding advertising by candidates for political office? Should television be considered apart from other media?
5. Under what conditions might advertising tend to influence the news content or editorial policy of an advertising medium, directly or indirectly?
6. How is the Advertising Council related to the advertising industry? Why is it concerned with problems of society?
7. Why will some advertising always be considered in bad taste? Discuss the implications of message, media, audience, and product.
8. What role does "sex" play in creating ads? How does the public respond to sexually oriented portrayals?

Notes

1 Richard W. Pollay, "The Distorted Mirror: Reflections on the Unintended Consequences of Advertising," *Journal of Marketing* 50 (April 1986): 21.
2 Stephen Fox, *The Mirror Makers* (New York: William Morrow, 1984), 381.
3 Pollay, "The Distorted Mirror," 1986, 19.
4 Cited in ibid., 21.
5 Ibid., 18.
6 Fox, *The Mirror Makers*, 1984, 329.
7 Ibid.
8 Ibid., 381
9 Russell W. Belk and Richard W. Pollay, "Images of Ourselves: The Good Life in Twentieth Century Advertising," *Journal of Consumer Research* 11 (March 1985): 887–897.
10 Eric Zanot, "Public Attitudes toward Advertising," in *Advertising in a New Age*, ed. H. Keith Hunt. (Provo, UT: American Academy of Advertising, 1981), 142–146.
11 R. D. Anderson, J. L. Engledow, and H. Becker, "How Consumer Reports Subscribers See Advertising," *Journal of Advertising Research* 18 (December 1978): 29–34.
12 Raymond A. Bauer and Stephen A. Greyser, *Advertising in America: The Consumer View* (Boston: Harvard University Press, 1968), 176; Rena Bartos and Theodore Dunn, *Advertising and Consumers* (New York: American Association of Advertising Agencies, 1974), 44.
13 See Leonard N. Reid and Lawrence C. Soley, "Generalized and Personalized Attitudes toward Advertising's Social and Economic Effects," *Journal of

Advertising 11 (Fall 1982): 3–7.

[14] Anderson, Engledow, and Becker, "How Consumer Reports Subscribers," 1978; Bauer and Greyser, *Advertising in America*, 1968; Lawrence C. Soley and Leonard N. Reid, "Satisfaction with the Informational Value of Magazine and Television Advertising," *Journal of Advertising* 12 (Fall 1983): 27–31; Thomas P. Haller, "What Students Think of Advertising," *Journal of Advertising Research* 14 (February 1974): 33–38.

[15] Charles H. Sandage and John D. Leckenby, "Student Attitudes toward Advertising: Institution vs. Instrument," *Journal of Advertising* 9 (Summer 1980): 29–32; Darrel D. Meuhling, "An Investigation of Factors Underlying Attitude-toward-Advertising-in-General," *Journal of Advertising* 16 (Spring 1987): 32–40.

[16] Reid and Soley, "Generalized and Personalized Attitudes," 6–7.

[17] Bauer and Greyser, *Advertising in America,* 217–223.

[18] Otis A. Pease, "Advertising, Its Ethics and Its Critics," in *Frontiers of Advertising Theory and Research*, ed. Hugh W. Sargent (Palo Alto, CA: Pacific Books, 1972), 19–28.

[19] Kim B. Rotzoll, James E. Haefner, and Charles H. Sandage, *Advertising in Contemporary Society* (Cincinnati: South-Western Publishing Co., 1986), 147.

[20] Shelby D. Hunt and Lawrence B. Chonko, "Ethical Problems of Advertising Agency Executives," *Journal of Advertising* 16 (Winter 1987): 16–24; Kim B. Rotzoll and Clifford G. Christians, "Advertising Agency Practitioners' Perceptions of Ethical Decisions," *Journalism Quarterly* 57 (Autumn 1980): 425–431.

[21] Hunt and Chonko, "Ethical Problems," 23.

[22] Dean M. Krugman and O. C. Ferrell, "The Organizational Ethics of Advertising: Corporate and Agency Views," *Journal of Advertising* 10 (Winter 1981): 21–30, 48.

[23] Ivan L. Preston, *The Great American Blow-Up* (Madison: University of Wisconsin Press, 1975), 4.

[24] David A. Aaker, Rajeev Batra, and John G. Myers, *Advertising Management*, 4th ed. (Englewood Cliffs, NJ: Prentice-Hall, 1992), 536.

[25] Preston, *The Great American Blow-Up*, 4.

[26] See Michael A. Kamins and Lawrence J. Marks, "Advertising Puffery: The Impact of Using Two-Sided Claims on Product Attitude and Purchase," *Journal of Advertising* 16 (Winter 1987): 6–15; Bruce G. Vanden Bergh and Leonard N. Reid, "Puffery and Magazine Ad Readership," *Journal of Marketing* (Spring 1980): 78–81.

[27] George E. Belch, "An Examination of Comparative and Noncomparative Television Commercials: The Effects of Claim Variation and Repetition on Cognitive Response and Message Acceptance," *Journal of Marketing Research* 18 (August 1984): 334.

[28] Robert E. Harmon, Nabil Y. Razzouk, and Bruce L. Stern, "The Information Content of Comparative Magazine Advertisements," *Journal of Advertising* 12 (Winter 1984): 10–19; Terence A. Shimp, *Promotion Management and Marketing Communications*, 3d ed. (Ft. Worth, TX: Dryden Press, 1993): 154–155.

[29] Timothy E. Moore, "Subliminal Advertising: What You See Is What You Get," *Journal of Marketing* 46 (Spring 1982): 37–47.

[30] Myron Gable, Henry T. Wilkins, Lynn Harris, and Robert Feinberg, "An Evaluation of Subliminally Embedded Sexual Stimuli in Graphics," *Journal of Advertising* 16 (Spring 1987): 26–31; Eric J. Zanot, J. David Pincus, and E. Joseph Lamp, "Public Perceptions of Subliminal Advertising," *Journal of Advertising* 12 (Spring 1983): 39–45.

[31] Moore, "Subliminal Advertising," 46.

[32] "Poll Suggests TV Advertisers Can't Ignore Matters of Taste," *The Wall Street Journal*, July 23, 1981, 23.

[33] Lawrence C. Soley and Gary Kurzbard, "Sex in Advertising: A Comparison of 1964 and 1984 Magazine Advertisements," *Journal of Advertising* 15 (Fall 1986): 46–54, 64; Lawrence C. Soley and Leonard N. Reid, "Taking It Off: Are Models in Magazine Ads Wearing Less?" *Journalism Quarterly* 65 (Winter 1989): 960–966.

[34] See ibid; also Leonard N. Reid and Lawrence C. Soley, "Decorative Models and the Readership of Magazine Ads," *Journal of Advertising Research* 23 (August/September 1983): 27–32.

[35] See Aaker, Batra, and Myers, *Advertising Management,* 1992, 560–561; Robert McAuliffe, "The FTC and the Effectiveness of Cigarette Advertising Regulations," *Journal of*

Public Policy and Marketing 7 (1988): 49–64; Cheryl R. Makowsky and Paul C. Whitfield, "Advertising and Alcohol Sales: A Legal Impact Study," *Journal of Studies on Alcohol* 52 (1991): 555–567; Camila P. Schuster and Christine P. Powell, "Comparison of Cigarette and Alcohol Controversies," *Journal of Advertising* 16 (Spring 1987): 26–33.

36 P.S. Rajeev and Subbash C. Lonial, "Advertising to Children: Findings and Implications," *Current Issues and Research in Advertising* 12 (1990): 231–274.

37 Jill Hicks Ferguson, Peggy J. Kreshel, and Spencer F. Tinkham, "In the Pages of *MS:* Sex Portrayals of Women in Advertising," *Journal of Advertising* 19 (1990): 40–51.

38 Paula England and Teresa Gardner, "Sex Differentiation in Magazine Advertisements," *Current Issues and Research In Advertising* 6 (1983): 253–268.

39 Mary C. Gilly, "Sex Roles in Advertising: A Comparison of Television Advertisements in Australia, Mexico, and the United States," *Journal of Marketing* 52 (April 1988): 75–85.

40 Helen Czepiec and J. Steven Kelly, "Analyzing Hispanic Roles in Advertising," *Current Issues and Research In Advertising* 6 (1983): 233–236.

41 Robert E. Wilkes and Humberto Valencia, "Hispanics and Blacks in Television Commercials," *Journal of Advertising* 18 (1989): 19–25.

42 Linda E. Swayne and Alan J. Greco, "The Portrayal of Older Americans in Television Commercials," *Journal of Advertising* 16 (Spring 1987): 47–54.

43 Subbash C. Lonial and P.S. Raju, "The Decision Process and Media-Related Interactions of the Elderly: A Synthesis or Findings," *Current Issues and Research in Advertising* 13 (1991): 277–312.

44 Tommy E. Whittler, "The Effects of Actors' Role in Commercial Advertising: Review and Extension," *Journal of Advertising* 20 (1991): 54–60.

45 Ronald Humphrey and Howard Schuman, "The Portrayal of Blacks in Magazine Advertisements; 1950–1982,"

Public Opinion Quarterly 48 (1984): 551–563.

46 Thomas H. Stevenson, "A Contest Analysis of the Portrayal of Blacks in Trade Publications," *Journal of Current Issues and Research in Advertising* 14 (Spring 1992): 67–74.

47 Wilkes and Valencia, "Hispanics and Blacks in Television Commercials," 1989, 199.

48 Ronald J. Faber, "Advances in Political Advertising Research: A Progression From If to When," *Journal of Current Issues and Research in Advertising* 14 (Fall 1992): 1–18.

49 Lawrence C. Soley and Leonard N. Reid, "Promotional Expenditures in U.S. Congressional Elections," *Journal of Marketing and Public Policy* 1 (1982): 147.

50 Faber, "Advances in Political Advertising Research," 1992.

51 David B. Hill, "Political Campaigns and Madison Avenue: A Wavering Partnership," *Journal of Advertising* 13 (Fall 1984): 21–26, 58.

52 Marsha L. Richins, "Social Comparison and the Idealized Images of Advertising," *Journal of Consumer Research* 18 (June 1991): 71–83.

53 "Advertiser Pressure Business Journalists Say," *Atlanta Journal*, May, 1992, D2; Robert G. Hays and Ann E. Reisner, "Farm Journalists and Advertiser Influence: Issues on Ethical Standing," *Journalism Quarterly* 68 (Spring/ Summer, 1991), 172–178; William L. Weis and Chauncey Burke, "Media Content and Tobacco Advertising: An Unhealthy Addiction," *Journal of Communication* 36 (Autumn 1986): 59–69.

54 James J. Mullen and Thomas A. Bowers, "Government Advertising: A Runaway Engine," *Journal of Advertising* 8 (Winter 1979): 39–42.

55 Lawrence C. Soley and Robert Craig, "Advertising Pressure on Newspapers," *Journal of Advertising* 21 (December 1992): 1–10.

56 Kim B. Rotzoll, James E. Haefner, and Charles H. Sandage, *Advertising in Contemporary Society* (Columbus, OH: Grid, 1978), 138.

Suggested Readings

Atwan, Robert, Donald McQuade, and John W. Wright. *Edsels, Luckies, and Frigidaires: Advertising the American Way.* New York: Dell, 1979.

Barnouw, Erik. *The Sponsor: Notes on a Modern Potentate.* New York: Oxford University Press, 1979.

Berman, Ronald. *Advertising and Social*

Change. Beverly Hills, CA: Sage Publications, 1981.

Goffman, Erving. *Gender Advertisements.* New York: Harper and Row, 1979.

Hovland, Roxanne, and Gary Wilcox. *Advertising in Society.* Chicago: NTC Business Books, 1988.

Leiss, William, Stephen Kline, and Sut Jhally. *Social Communication in Advertising: Persons, Products, and Images of Well-Being.* New York: Methuen, 1986.

McNeal, James U. *Children as Consumers: Insights and Implications.* Lexington, MA: Lexington Books, 1987.

Preston, Ivan L. *The Great American Blow-Up: Puffery in Advertising and Selling.* Madison, WI: The University of Wisconsin Press, 1975.

Rotzoll, Kim B. *Advertising and the Public.* Urbana, IL: Department of Advertising, University of Illinois, 1980.

Rotzoll, Kim B., James E. Haefner, and Charles H. Sandage. *Advertising in Contemporary Society: Perspectives toward Understanding,* 2d ed., Cincinnati, OH: South-Western, 1990.

Schudson, Michael. *Advertising, the Uneasy Persuasion.* New York: Basic Books, 1984.

Spero, Robert. *The Duping of the American Voter: Dishonesty and Deception in Presidential Television Advertising.* New York: Lippincott and Crowell, 1980.

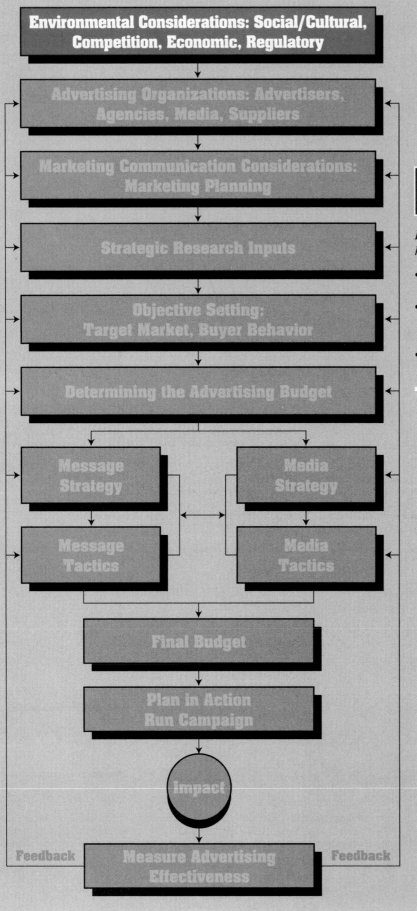

Chapter **4**

Economic Issues

CHAPTER TOPICS

THE ECONOMISTS' VIEW OF ADVERTISING
1890 to 1940
Modern Economists

ADVERTISING: INFORMATION OR PERSUASION?

ADVERTISING AND PRICES
Two Views
Retail versus National

ADVERTISING AND ADDED VALUE
Brand Equity

ADVERTISING AND CONSUMER CHOICE

ADVERTISING AND INDUSTRY CONCENTRATION

ADVERTISING'S INFLUENCE ON THE BUSINESS
CYCLE

ADVERTISING AND AGGREGATE CONSUMPTION

ADVERTISING AS MEDIA SUBSIDY
Rolling Stone: *A Case of Media Economics*

THE DURATION EFFECTS OF ADVERTISING

Advertising is an integral part of our economic system. Although advertising practitioners and economists often disagree on what exact effect advertising has on the economy, it is recognized that advertising performs an economic function for advertisers, influences the economics of households and individuals, and affects the operation of the market economy.[1]

In this chapter, we first look at what economists think of advertising—if they think about it at all. We then examine the major economic issues of advertising. As we noted in the first two chapters, these issues are especially important to advertising practitioners, for economic and competitive conditions must be considered in advertising campaign planning. Economic factors, such as market concentration and business cycles, can greatly determine the success or failure of the best advertising campaign, and while they cannot be controlled, they can be planned for, as depicted in our planning model.

Many of the following economic issues transcend the practical interests of individual advertisers. However, they all impact the institution of advertising itself and have implications for your understanding of the perplexing and complex world of economics.

The Economists' View of Advertising

Economists have generally had difficulty fitting advertising into their theories. Some have ignored its effects. Some have given it minimal attention, and a few—mainly those with a strong interest in marketing—have studied it somewhat more extensively.

From 1890 to 1940

Alfred Marshal, often called the father of neoclassical economics, referred to advertising only once in his *Principles of Economics.* In the book, published in nine editions from 1890 to 1920, Marshal dealt mainly with perfect competition, which assumes that consumers have perfect information regarding homogeneous products and can make rational choices among them.

Some economists in the early 1900s abandoned the notion of perfect competition and called for a more realistic appraisal of the marketplace. Most of these, too, were uncomfortable with advertising. Edward Chamberlin, one of the neoclassical pioneers, saw advertising as costs incurred in order to alter the shape of the demand curve for a product and reasoned (correctly) that the effect of advertising was to move the demand curve to the right. Influential British economist John Maynard Keynes devoted minimal attention to advertising in his writings. The most comprehensive study of the relationship between advertising and economics was made by Neil H. Borden, a Harvard marketing professor (see the Ad Insight entitled "Neil B. Borden: Founding Father of the Economics of Advertising"). His findings, based primarily on a series of studies conducted in the 1930s, were published in the oft-cited book, *The Economic Effects of Advertising.*

Two scholars who surveyed how economists treated advertising from 1890 to 1940 concluded that:

1. There was a shift away from overall emphasis on the positive effects of advertising toward an emphasis on advertising's negative effects.
2. There was an increase in the total number of advertising issues considered.
3. Conclusions were drawn primarily from descriptions of personal experiences or observations, although primary or secondary research findings were intermittently used.[2]

Modern Economists

British economist Nicholas Kaldor, a critic of advertising, looks on advertising as a "subsidy" (hidden support) by senders of persuasive messages to the mass media rather than something for which consumers are willing to pay. Kaldor thinks this subsidy results in incomplete market information and, even worse, causes bias in news and editorial comment in the mass media. In his view, any economic benefits derived from advertising are therefore incidental and cost consumers too much.[3]

Other less critical economists think that advertising helps competition. One of them pointed out that prices for eyeglasses are about 25 to 40 percent higher in states where eyeglass advertising is prohibited and that advertised toys have lower markups and lower prices than unadvertised ones.[4] According to Mark S. Albion and Paul W. Farris, highly advertised brands may be priced by retailers to yield lower gross profit margins than unadvertised or less advertised brands for two reasons:

1. Advertised brands have a higher rate of turnover, and inventory cost per unit sold should be lower.
2. Highly advertised brands have long been used by retailers as loss leaders or traffic builders.[5]

Both sides of the advertising question are represented in Figure 4.1, which lists both positive and negative economic effects attributed to advertising.

As should be apparent, generalizations about the economic effects of advertising on the economy remain controversial and conflicting. A summary of the literature on advertising and economics has warned that questions about advertising's economic effects might best be phrased as: "Under what conditions does advertising produce what particular effects?"[6]

Neil H. Borden: Founding Father of the Economics of Advertising

Neil H. Borden (1895–1980)
Former Professor of Advertising
Harvard Graduate School of Business Administration

He wasn't an agency founder, creative director, chief executive, or media mogul. But for thousands who worked in advertising, Harvard professor Neil H. Borden had an unparalleled impact on their understanding and practice of advertising.

After graduating from the University of Colorado in 1919, "Pete" Borden earned his MBA at Harvard Business School (HBS) in 1922, commencing a lifelong association with the school. By the time he retired in 1962, his 35-year career of teaching and research had made monumental contributions to both advertising education and advertising management. Borden's writings on the subject remain the underpinning of marketing management teaching and practice.

During his career as a professor, researcher, and consultant to advertising organizations, Borden was an indefatigable advocate of improving advertising education and research, constantly urging executives and academics to probe advertising's relationship to business success.

Professor Borden died in 1980. His legacy lives on in his writing and ideas, and in the notable careers of those still-active executives to whom he imparted wisdom.

In the long history of advertising education, he is one of a handful of greats and the one with the greatest impact on managerial practice in advertising.

In March 1992, he was inducted posthumously into the AAF Advertising Hall of Fame.

Source: "Three for the Ages," *American Advertising,* Spring 1992, 10–11.

Advertising: Information or Persuasion?

A long-standing question is whether advertising is a form of information or a form of persuasion.[7] Advertising's critics concede that consumers are eager to find out

FIGURE 4.1

Positive and Negative Economic Effects Attributed to Advertising

Positive Effects	Negative Effects
1. Effects on the economy: Encourages economic growth, investment, jobs Maintains competition Informs consumers and enhances competition 2. Effects on industry: Widens markets for new products Competition between firms grows 3. Effects on company: Provides increasing returns-to- sales Reduces marketing risk and uncertainty 4. Effects on consumers: Provides free information Serves as a tool for quality control Increases, maintains, or stabilizes demand Provides incentive to raise living standards	1. Effects on the economy: Wasteful, drains resources Leads to monopoly Creates nonprice competition 2. Effects on industry: Creates entry barriers Competition between firms cancels 3. Effects on company: Raises costs and prices Results in excess profits 4. Effects on consumers: Waste, misleading information Differentiates products by magnifying small differences

Source: Kent M. Lancaster and Duke O. Yaguchi, "How Economists Have Treated Advertising: 1890–1940," *Journal of Advertising History* 7 (October 1983): 14.

about weekly specials at local supermarkets and about the features and functions of new products and services. These critics usually approve of advertising as a source of market information, but object when it tries to persuade. Informative advertising is generally seen as objective in nature and directed toward reasoned consumer decision making. Persuasive advertising, in contrast, is seen as being subjective in nature and directed toward the manipulation of unsuspecting consumers.

Vincent Norris noted in his work on the economic effects of advertising:

> The question whether advertising is information that enables the market to function more efficiently, or a form of persuasion that creates market power and thus inhibits the functioning of the market, is central to most other questions about advertising's economic effects.[8]

Different answers to the question have been provided by two schools of economic thought: the advertising-equals-market-power school and the advertising-equals-information school.

Alfred Marshal was the first to deal with the question of whether advertising is information or persuasion, distinguishing between what he labeled "constructive" and "combative" advertising.[9] Marshal viewed constructive advertising as that which functions to inform consumers of the opportunity to purchase, and combative advertising as that which functions to draw customers from competitors. In modern economic terminology, constructive advertising is associated with the advertising-equals-information school and combative advertising with the advertising-equals-market-power school.

The market power school sees most advertising as a threat to market efficiency, arguing that it is a form of persuasion that makes markets anticompetitive by creating artificial product differentiations and raising barriers to market entry. The information school, in contrast, sees advertising as a facilitator of market efficiency, arguing that it is a fundamental form of market information that diminishes market power by stimulating competition and reducing consumer search costs. Figure 4.2 shows how each school interprets the major economic effects of advertising.

From the early 1900s through the 1960s, the market power school was the prevailing perspective on advertising's economic effects.[10] In the 1970s, however, the information school emerged as an alternative perspective. Its emergence has resulted in a shift of economic opinion about advertising from anticompetitive to procompetitive:

> Advertising was once seen primarily as a threat to competition and a tool for distorting consumer choices. Now it is more commonly seen as a subtle but highly effective adjunct to competition, tending to bring more vigorous rivalry, lower prices, improved products and more informed consumer choices.[11]

One reason the shift occurred is that theoretical and empirical challenges to the belief that information and persuasion could be separated in advertising content developed among some economists and marketing scholars. Brenda Dervin, a communication theorist, has pointed out that information is a "construction"—an idea that people form in their minds through communication.[12] Marketing theorist Shelby Hunt posed a syllogism to dramatize the nebulous nature of the information-persuasion separation:

> If informational advertising is okay (as most critics concede); and
> If much informational advertising is very persuasive (as no person
>   knowledgeable about advertising would dispute); and
> If the purpose of all advertising is to persuade (as not even critics of
>   advertising would deny); then
> All persuasive advertising *cannot* be *not* okay.[13]

On the basis of his analytical assessment of the information-persuasion dichotomy, Hunt concluded that the information-persuasion dichotomy is false and that information is receiver-specific, whether deliberately sought out or the result of incidental exposure. However, this argument does not mean that object stimulus properties in ads cannot be disinguished from subjective interpretation. A series of studies, although flawed by problems of definition and the lack of receiver-specific interpretation, has rated the informativeness of ads and commercials by counting the presence of information cues. Some of the more commonly counted information cues are: price/value, quality, performance, components/content, availability, special offers, taste, packaging, guarantees/warranties, safety, nutrition, independent research, company-sponsored research, and new ideas.[14] An example of an ad with specific information cues is presented in Figure 4.3.

Economist David N. Laband has theorized that persuasive techniques are utilized by advertisers to convey information, but what "persuades" consumers to act is the "information received."[15] It is his view that "persuasive" techniques merely enhance the efficiency of information transfer. To make his point, Laband provided the example reproduced here as Figure 4.4, an advertisement that many, including those who rate ad informativeness based on the presence of cues, would undoubtedly find informationless. It contains no verbal information other than brand name, producer, and type of product.

FIGURE 4.2

Two Schools of Thought on the Role of Advertising in the Economy

Advertising = Market Power		Advertising = Market Competition
Advertising affects consumer preferences and tastes, changes product attributes, and differentiates the product from competitive offerings.	*Advertising*	Advertising informs consumers about product attributes and does not change the way they value these attributes.
Consumers become brand loyal and less price sensitive, and perceive fewer substitutes for advertised brands.	*Consumer Buying Behavior*	Consumers become more price sensitive and buy best "value." Only the relationship between price and quality affects elasticity for a given product.
Potential entrants must overcome established brand loyalty and spend relatively more on advertising.	*Barriers to Entry*	Advertising makes entry possible for new brands because it can communicate product attributes to consumers.
Firms are insulated from market competition and potential rivals; concentration increases, leaving firms with more discretionary power.	*Industry Structure and Market Power*	Consumers can compare competitive offerings easily and competitive rivalry is increased. Efficient firms remain, and as the inefficient leave, new entrants appear; the effect on concentration is ambiguous.
Firms can charge higher prices and are not as likely to compete on quality or price dimensions. Innovation may be reduced.	*Market Conduct*	More informed consumers put pressure on firms to lower prices and improve quality. Innovation is facilitated via new entrants.
High prices and excessive profits accrue to advertisers and give them even more incentive to advertise their products. Output is restricted compared to conditions of perfect competition.	*Market Performance*	Industry prices are decreased. The effect on profits due to increased competition and an increase in efficiency is ambiguous.

Source: From Mark S. Albion, *Advertising's Hidden Effects: Manufacturer's Advertising and Retail Pricing* (Dover, MA: Auburn House, 1983), 18. Reprinted with permission.

FIGURE 4.3

An Advertisement with Specific and Objectively Defined Information Cues

A number of content-analytic studies have found these and similar cues in print ads and radio and TV commercials. Note that power, efficiency, finances, and safety lend themselves to objective measurement; however, quality, luxury, and comfort are subject to more individual-specific interpretation.

Advertisements for Calvin Klein's "Obsession" perfume transmit an informational message to the effect that use of the product will increase the user's attractiveness to members of the opposite sex. Calvin Klein could have taken out magazine ad space in typeset that transmitted that message content. Instead, he included a small picture of the perfume bottle along with a large, sexually suggestive photograph of a semi-clad woman surrounded by attentive, semi-clad men, with no wording. The informational content of the message conveyed is the same; it is the method of transfer that differentiates the two advertisements.[16]

FIGURE 4.4

An Example of Visual Content Used as Transfer Technique to Convey that Using "Obsession" Will Increase Attractiveness to the Opposite Sex

Taken together, the theoretical arguments and the research evidence suggest that advertising contributes useful information to the marketplace. However, consumers determine whether advertising content is perceived as information.

Advertising and Prices

Advertising's effect on the price that consumers pay for goods and services has long puzzled economists as well as consumers, though price is often featured in ads (see Figure 4.5). Even business people, who sometimes invest large sums of money in advertising, are not sure whether advertising raises or lowers prices. A study of 2,700 subscribers of the *Harvard Business Review* (mainly executives) found that only 35 percent thought that "advertising generally results in lower prices."[17] A study of European business executives found that 58 percent agreed with the same statement asked in the American study.[18] But, what does the research say about advertising and prices? How is advertising related to costs?

FIGURE 4.5

**An Effective Use of Price in an Advertisement
for Honda's Nighthawk Motorcycle**

Two Views

Economists who belong to the information school of thought generally believe that advertising contributes to production and distribution cost efficiencies. Although advertising is an expense, like shipping or labor, they contend that advertising leads to lower prices for two reasons. First, it allows firms that advertise to more quickly achieve economies of scale in production and distribution than firms that do not advertise. Secondly, it reduces consumer search costs.

Assuming that the "real price" of a product includes search costs as well as the retail price itself, one economist has suggested that

> advertising could reduce consumer costs even if the cost of advertising were simply added to the retail price. The effect would be to substitute a more efficient form of information-gathering (advertising) for a less efficient form (consumer search).[19]

This contention is demonstrated graphically by the American Association of Advertising Agencies in the advertisement shown in Figure 4.6.

Other economists, who believe in the market power school, counter that advertising is simply a cost and that advertisers must recoup advertising costs by raising prices. In essence, they contend that "somebody must pay" for advertising and the somebody who must pay is the consumer.[20]

Retail versus National

Which group of economists is right? Based on the empirical evidence, the answer seems to depend on whether advertising is retail or national.

In the case of retail advertising, cost savings from advertising's effect on production and distribution costs seem to be passed on to consumers in the form of lower prices. An impressive number of studies have shown that advertising reduces retail prices by intensifying competition.[21] By comparing markets with and without advertising, the studies have found that advertising leads to lower prices for a variety of products and services, including eyeglasses, eye care, prescription drugs, gasoline, and professional services.

Though the evidence is far from conclusive, national advertising apparently does not have the same market impact on consumer prices. An extensive review of the economics literature has led to the conclusion that national advertising probably raises the prices of goods and services.[22] One study, for example, compared the price above cost of 28 national advertisers and 21 retail advertisers. The study found high prices were strongly and positively correlated with national advertisers, but weakly and negatively correlated with retail advertisers.[23] However, others have analyzed the economics literature on advertising and concluded that national advertising (manufacturer) can be associated with both high and low consumer price levels.[24]

In the final analysis, what can be said about advertising's effect on the prices of goods and services is that, at the retail level, it tends to lower consumer prices. At the national level, advertising and lower consumer prices may be unrelated. As researchers say, "the data are still out."

Advertising and Added Value

There is sufficient reason to believe that advertising adds value to brands through psychological utility—by calling attention to attributes, functions, or characterizations that people would otherwise be unaware of, or by enhancing people's perception of subjective, want-satisfying qualities of products. A product is a physical thing, but a brand exists in the minds of people. Therefore, "many of the harshest critics of advertising, as well as some of its practitioners, fail to understand the fundamental

FIGURE 4.6

A Lesson in the Economics of Advertising Sponsored by the American Association of Advertising Agencies

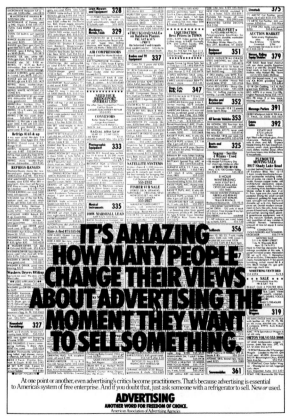

Source: Reproduced with permission of the American Association of Advertising Agencies.

truth that advertising is not always about what a product 'does,' but rather about what a brand 'means.' "[25]

A report sponsored by the American Association of Advertising Agencies, in fact, has argued that the consumer's perception of a branded product is as significant as the product's physical characteristics. As stated in the report:

> This mingling of the tangible (malt, hops, barley) with the "elusive" (positioning, brand image, perceptions) is a challenge to all managers. . . . Today, the conceptual nature of added value is no longer limited to product categories like beer, fast food, perfume, or Scotch whiskey. On the contrary, conceptual value added—the perceptions of a product's unique, singular fit into a consumer's personal system of wants, needs, and values—is increasingly becoming the single most powerful discriminator in every product category.[26]

As part of a marketer's communication mix, advertising is used to communicate about the want-satisfying qualities of brands. Its function is to affect psychological utility by communicating about such things as brand personality (for example, status product), user personality (for example, innovator), and consumption context (for example, special occasion).

To some observers, the "added value" derived from advertising seems wasteful. However, it merely represents the value people place on satisfying their wants. Some people find an imported coffee more satisfying than a domestic brand. Some want to be fashion setters, and so they are more willing to pay a premium for clothing labels. Others are not content to write with any pen, but must have that special instrument. Examples of ads that convey these added values of brands are shown in Figure 4.7. Parker associates its pens with Shakespeare and classic prose; Perry Ellis communicates that buyers show "fashion sense" with the Perry Ellis label; and First Colony Coffee & Tea Company positions itself with the best of good living. An interesting view is offered in the Ad Insight entitled "Another View of Added Value and Advertising."

FIGURE 4.7

Advertisements That Convey the Added Value of Brand Consumption

The gist of all three ads is that the consumer's psychosocial well-being will be enhanced through consumption.

But how much are people willing to pay for physically similar brands? The answer, of course, will vary by product category, but we do know that people will pay more for brands. Consider an example based on the Nielsen Food Index.

In one year, consumers purchased 48 million pounds of tea bags at a total price of $125,100,000. Minor brands accounted for $24,300,000 at an average price of $2.28 a pound; major advertised brands accounted for $100,800,000, or 37,330,000 pounds at an average price of $2.70 a pound. This difference of 42 cents a pound divided by $2.28 (the average price paid for minor brands) results in a figure of 18.4 percent as the added value consumers were willing to pay for nationally advertised brands of tea.

We can also express this added value in dollars. If 37,300,000 pounds of advertised brands of tea bags were sold at a price differential of 42 cents a pound, the dollar equivalent of the added consumer value of advertised brands of tea bags was $15,666,000 a year. This is a good example, because consumers have a choice between unadvertised and advertised brands of tea at food stores. In many food chains, the store's brand is promoted much more heavily than the nationally advertised ones.

We also see added value in the concept of brand equity. **Brand equity** is the value that a brand can add to a physical product independent of other production and marketing activities.[27] As we have suggested, brands have meanings for people beyond their physical and functional properties, and the simple addition of a brand name, such as Nike, Sony, or Ralph Lauren, to unnamed products will add value not only for people as consumers but also for people as, say, business executives. Equity is built and maintained by years of advertising support, and the financial community has demonstrated its willingness to invest in companies that have brand equity. In today's marketplace, it can be said that:

> Brands add value. Brands are assets. Advertising builds value. Promotion builds volume.[28]

The ad in Figure 4.8 makes the case for advertising in building and maintaining brands.

The Story of How Advertising Builds Brands Sponsored by the American Association of Advertising Agencies

Brand Equity

Advertising and Consumer Choice

Critics claim that advertising has been used by powerful manufacturers to narrow consumer choice to a few well-advertised brands. Advertising's defenders counter that advertising has actually expanded consumer choice through product innovations and improvements in product quality. As seen by advertising management experts David Aaker, Rajeev Batra, and John Myer, advertising encourages the development of new products and the improvement of existing products by providing an economical means of communicating with people. They note that large investments in research and development and production facilities are required to develop and improve products, and while there are other means of market communication, advertising is one of the most efficient forms.[29]

It is commonly accepted that advertising alone cannot achieve market penetration for manufacturers' products unless those products have differential advantages to consumers. In some product categories, advertising may help to limit consumer choices by building brand preferences, which in turn may drive some small competitors from the marketplace. In other categories, it may stimulate product innovation and enhance the ability of small manufacturers to compete against large, entrenched manufacturers. The problem for both critics and defenders of advertising is that economists do not know how to distinguish whether the product advantages that firms offer are real or cosmetic innovations.[30]

Another View of Added Value and Advertising

In the following comment, "Value-added Ads: The Problem, Not the Solution," Professor Lawrence Wortzel, makes the point that the role of advertising is to communicate about value—value that is built into products.

It's common knowledge that consumers perceive brands as more and more similar. Some advertising agencies would have us believe that the right response is so-called value-added advertising—increasing the *perceived* value of a brand through advertising. But this is a deception

that consumers are likely to see through even if brand owners do not.

Agencies peddling value-added advertising operate on the premise that consumers base their brand choices on brand symbology. They claim that endowing a brand with a symbolic meaning makes it more valuable in the consumer's eyes. According to this reasoning, for instance, consumers will choose a brand of baby powder when it conveys an image of "nurturing parent," select a brand of cola when it is tied to a group identification, buy a brand of running shoe for its ability to communicate fitness or go into debt for an automobile because it communicates affluence.

When Honda introduced the Acura Legend, many said it would not be successful because consumers perceived Japanese cars as low-priced econoboxes. Honda made a success of this $30,000 automobile, but not because advertising created a car people valued at $30,000.

Honda created a Legend worth $30,000 by building value into the car. When consumers spend $30,000 for an automobile, they want much more than to make a statement. They also want at least $30,000 worth of car to drive. The Acura Legend is a success because of value created by product design, comfort, quality and performance, not advertising. Advertising's role, correctly, has been to communicate the value already built into the car.

Cadillac, on the other hand, tried to create value through advertising, and failed miserably. General Motors thought advertising would add enough value to a downsized automobile, which was not significantly

Source: Lawrence H. Wortzel, "Value-added Ads: The Problem, Not the Solution," *Advertising Age* (November 6, 1989): 36.

To a proponent of the information school of advertising, the cumulative evidence indicates that advertising has widened consumers' choice by increasing the variety of goods and services marketed and by making more information available about marketed goods and services. In this view, "advertising tends to increase consumer information, improve product quality, expand the scope of available choices, and encourage a better fit between consumer preferences and consumer purchases."[31]

Advertising and Industry Concentration

Critics often point out that very large advertisers are those with the strongest market positions. They point to companies such as Campbell's, which holds a

different from an Oldsmobile or Buick, to justify a considerably higher price. GM was wrong, and Cadillac sales plummeted.

Advertising can actually add value only in one specific situation: where consumers' egos are highly involved and they are buying the product primarily for its symbolic value—and then only provided it really is a worthwhile product. The Polo logo and the Rolex name may add value to shirts and watches, but each is attached to a well-designed, well-made product. Opportunities for such value-added advertising, however, are limited. As brands purchased primarily for their symbolic value become ubiquitous, they lose their cachet. As Yogi Berra might put it, the Izod logo became so popular no one wore it any more. Moreover, product features and performance—functional rather than symbolic considerations—guide most of the ego-involving purchases consumers make.

According to Peter Georgescu (as quoted in *The New York Times,* May 22, 1989), the image premise is based on the assumption that advertising works best when it can make a connection between a brand and a consumer's deeply held feelings. In other words, consumers must be ego-involved. Implicit also are assumptions that consumers are ego-involved with almost everything they buy, that every purchase activates deep feelings and that their brand choices are inexorably conditioned by their feelings.

Paradoxically, symbolic advertising works best where consumers are uninvolved—for such products as package goods, where they know the choice doesn't matter. But advertising does *not* make one package-goods brand intrinsically more valuable than another, nor does it tap deep feelings. Here advertising works well because consumers perceive no meaningful differences in performance among brands. It works simply by implanting in the consumer's mind some small—even frivolous or whimsical—association or reason to choose a particular brand on the next purchase occasion. Because the choice really doesn't matter that much, the consumer can afford to be capricious.

Consumers' lack of involvement with such purchases limits as well as enhances advertising's role. Sales promotion, habit, vicarious or personal experience with one brand or another, various point-of-purchase stimuli and simply the vagaries of the moment can all influence the consumer's brand choice on any particular purchase occasion. Once again, each of these factors can influence because the choice simply doesn't matter that much to the consumer. Advertising for package goods works best, in fact, where there is little price difference among competing brands. Here, other things being equal, advertising can tip the balance in favor of one brand.

The strength of package-goods advertising lies in its ability to communicate images and to associate them with brands, but these images do not add enough value to command a higher price for one brand.

The lessons are clear. If you want to add value to a product in which performance is important, invest in the product rather than just in advertising. Assign advertising its proper role—the role it can play best—communicating the honest value built into a product.

disproportionate share of the concentrated-canned-soup market; they note that the ready-to-eat cereal market is dominated by four large advertisers and that the soap and detergent market is dominated by three large advertisers. Economists like John Kenneth Galbraith and Paul Samuelson contend that advertising leads to industry concentration, an anticompetitive market condition, because:

1. Economies of scale in advertising enable big advertisers to push small advertisers out of markets.
2. Large capital requirements for advertising and cultivated brand loyalty discourage other companies from entering established markets.[32]

But do heavy spending advertisers create such brand loyalty that potential competitors find it cost prohibitive to enter established markets? Do large advertisers drive out small competitors by achieving economies of scale? Is market share dominance the result of advertising spending, or are large advertising expenditures the result of market dominance?

Some studies have shown little or no relationship between advertising and concentration, while others have found positive correlations between the two market variables. A few researchers have interpreted positive correlations to mean that larger firms advertise more, not that advertising allows large firms to grow at the expense of small competitors. Others have interpreted the evidence to mean that heavy advertising spending leads to concentration. An analysis of the relationship between level of advertising and level of industry concentration concluded that advertising may be more of an effect than a cause of industry concentration.[33]

The lack of clear-cut answers on the relationship are the result of how economists have treated measures such as advertising-to-sales ratios and of how "competition" and industrial concentration have been defined. For example, brands within companies compete with each other as well as with other national, regional, and store brands. Yet, most analyses have focused on industry- or firm-level data rather than on brand data.

In view of the mixed findings and the methodological shortcomings of the research, the case against advertising as a causal factor in industry concentration is shaky at best:

> There are probably specific industries and situations when advertising can lead to higher levels of concentration, but a sweeping statement that advertising always develops concentration may not be possible at this time.[34]

Examples of how competitors have differentially addressed the problem of industry concentration are provided in the ads depicted in Figure 4.9. When monopoly charges were leveled against the oil industry, Union Oil countered the charges by featuring the 72 logos of oil marketers. In contrast, a number of communication-related organizations sponsored an ad to warn the public about dangers of "concentration" posed by the seven regional Bells.

Advertising's Influence on the Business Cycle

The influence of advertising on the business cycle has long been debated. Critics contend that advertising accentuates an economic downturn or uses money that could be better spent in some other way. Proponents of advertising counter that advertising may bolster consumer confidence in bad times or fuel economic prosperity.

As noted by Albion and Farris, "theoretically advertising could be used to mitigate the ups and downs of the business cycle. In practice, however, because most firms keep advertising as a fixed percentage of sales, advertising is procyclical—it exaggerates the business cycle."[35] Advertisers tend to increase their advertising expenditures when sales are good and decrease them when sales are slow.[36]

There is some evidence that the tendency of advertisers to cut budgets in the face of economic downturns may be lessening.[37] McGraw-Hill's Laboratory of Advertising Performance found in a study of 468 companies that those that did not cut advertising during the 1974–1975 recession reported higher earnings growth than those that did cut spending back. Companies that did not reduce advertising averaged 12 percent higher sales than those that reduced spending in the two recession years. By 1978, companies that had not cut their 1974–1975 spending had sales 132 percent above 1973 levels, while those that did cut back experienced increases of only 79 percent. The basic argument for advertising in a recession is made in the ads depicted in Figure 4.10 and in the Ad Insight entitled "Effective Advertising and PR Are Important, Even in a Slow Economy."

FIGURE 4.9

Advertising Used to Answer and to Make Accusations about Concentration Effects

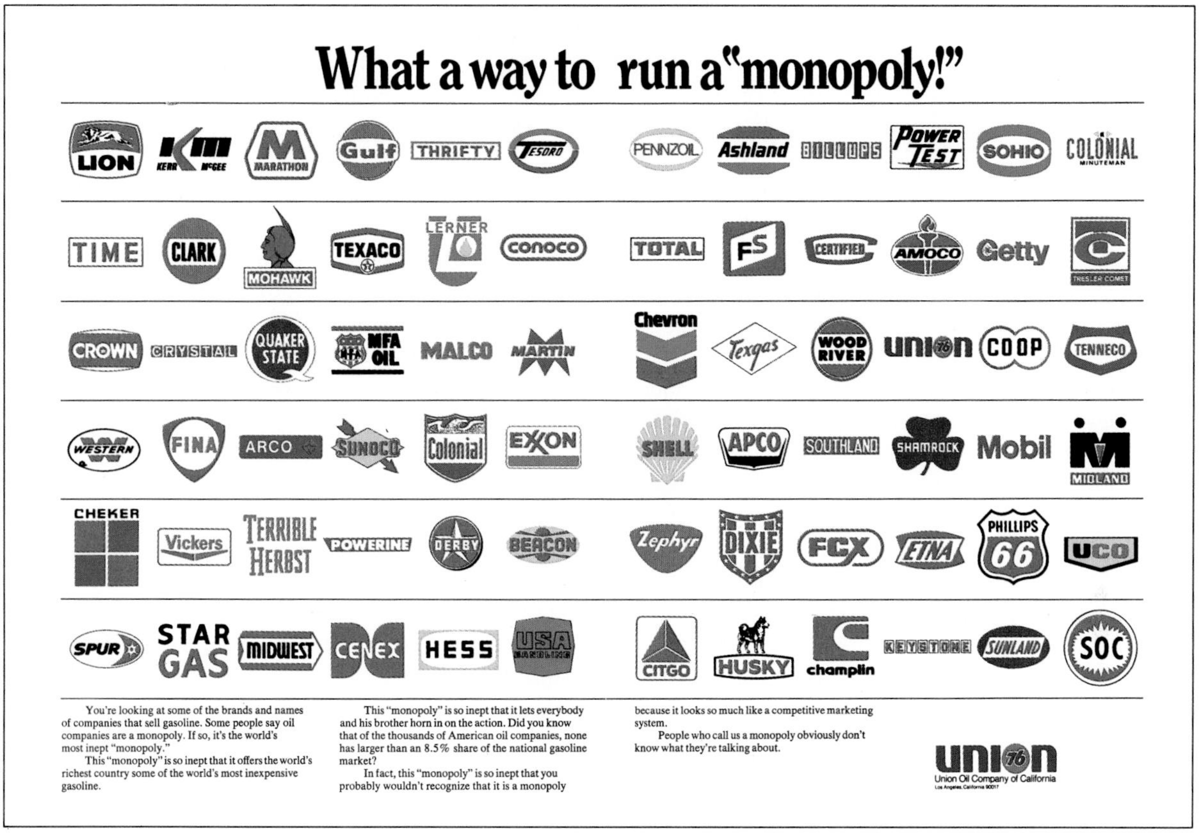
What a way to run a "monopoly!"
LION
KERR McGEE
MARATHON
Gulf
THRIFTY
TESORO
PENNZOIL
Ashland
BILLUPS
POWER TEST
SOHIO
COLONIAL MINUTEMAN
TIME
CLARK
MOHAWK
TEXACO
LERNER
conoco
TOTAL
FS
CERTIFIED
AMOCO
Getty
TRESLER COMET
CROWN
CRYSTAL
QUAKER STATE
MFA OIL
MALCO
MARTIN
Chevron
Texgas
WOOD RIVER
union
COOP
TENNECO
WESTERN
FINA
ARCO
SUNOCO
Colonial
EXXON
SHELL
APCO
SOUTHLAND
SHAMROCK
Mobil
MIDLAND
CHEKER
Vickers
TERRIBLE HERBST
POWERINE
DERBY
BEACON
Zephyr
DIXIE
FCX
ETNA
PHILLIPS 66
UCO
SPUR
STAR GAS
MIDWEST
CENEX
HESS
USA GASOLINE
CITGO
HUSKY
champlin
KEYSTONE
SUNLAND
SOC
You're looking at some of the brands and names of companies that sell gasoline. Some people say oil companies are a monopoly. If so, it's the world's most inept "monopoly."
This "monopoly" is so inept that it offers the world's richest country some of the world's most inexpensive gasoline.
This "monopoly" is so inept that it lets everybody and his brother horn in on the action. Did you know that of the thousands of American oil companies, none has larger than an 8.5% share of the national gasoline market?
In fact, this "monopoly" is so inept that you probably wouldn't recognize that it is a monopoly because it looks so much like a competitive marketing system.
People who call us a monopoly obviously don't know what they're talking about.
union 76
Union Oil Company of California
Los Angeles, California 90017

MONOPOLY IS COMPETITION.
BIG BROTHER IS ALIVE AND WELL.
In the world envisioned in George Orwell's *1984*, "war is peace," "freedom is slavery," and "ignorance is strength."
Now, in true Big Brother fashion, the seven regional Bell telephone companies are trying to foist a 1992 version of double speak on the American public – "monopoly is competition."
The $80 billion Bell monopolies are no longer satisfied controlling the telephone wires that go into our homes. They want to own and control the news, entertainment, medical, financial and sports information services that flow over these wires.
But as George Orwell would warn us, whoever controls the telephone wires may well control access to American minds.
The only way to keep Big Brother at bay is to separate control of the telephone pipeline from the information that flows through it.
That's why, until recently, the Bells were barred from providing information services over their monopoly-controlled wires.
But the Bells spent the past seven years and millions of dollars getting this ban lifted. Now they want Congress to vote against HR 3515 and S 2112. These bills would delay Bell entry into the information services business in their own regions until the Bells no longer hold a monopoly over local phone service.
The Bells' response to HR 3515 and S 2112? More double speak.
DOUBLE SPEAK: The Bells claim their entry into the information services business will be good for competition.
PLAIN SPEAK: This is absurd. How can a monopoly be good for competition? The truth is, the Bells will use their position as a monopoly to drive competitors out of business. How? They will make it difficult–if not impossible–for competitors to use Bell wires to enter your home. They could even undercut competitors' prices by inflating local phone bills to finance the cost of their own new information services. In short, they will do everything they can to ensure that there is only one supplier of information services–them. And that will let the Bells dictate exactly what information you receive.
DOUBLE SPEAK: The Bells claim they are regulated and could not abuse their monopoly position.
PLAIN SPEAK: There are not enough regulators in the world to control the monopolistic practices of the Bells. Just look at the record–every single one of the seven Bell companies has already abused its position as a regulated monopoly. Every single one. There's no reason to believe they won't in the future.
DOUBLE SPEAK: The Bells claim they will usher in a new era of information services.
PLAIN SPEAK: This is nonsense. There is already a thriving information services industry–no thanks to the Bells. Hundreds of companies now provide millions of people with valuable information over telephones, faxes and computer modems.
DOUBLE SPEAK: The Bells claim consumers are on their side.
PLAIN SPEAK: A few well-meaning groups have been persuaded into believing the Bells should be allowed to provide information services. However, America's largest consumer group, the Consumer Federation of America, and state public utility consumer advocates are against Bell entry.
DOUBLE SPEAK: The Bells claim HR 3515 and S 2112 are too restrictive.
PLAIN SPEAK: Both HR 3515 and S 2112 let the Bells do whatever they want in up to 6/7 of the country. The only restriction is where they remain an entrenched monopoly–in their own regions–and this restriction would die when competition begins to emerge.
Keep Big Brother at bay. Urge your U.S. Representative to support HR 3515 and your U.S. Senator to support S 2112.
Then call **1-800-547-7482** to learn what else you can do.
Don't baby the Bells.
Keep competition alive.

AD insights

Effective Advertising and PR Are Important, Even in a Slow Economy

In times of a slowing economy, many companies feel the temptation to reduce or cancel advertising and public relations programs, when in fact, that may be the last thing they should do.

In exploring the question of whether companies should remain aggressive during recession years, the American Business Press has sponsored several studies over the years dealing with "Advertising in Recession Years."

Through the studies, it's been found that many industries have documented the long-term benefits of maintaining advertising and promotion budgets during slow economic times. For example, in a study of one modern recession period, companies were placed in four categories:

1. Companies which did not cut advertising expenditures
2. Companies which cut advertising during the recession year
3. Companies which cut advertising following the recession year
4. Companies which cut advertising expenditures during both years

The studies showed that companies which did not cut advertising during the recession experienced higher sales and net income during those two years and the two years following than those companies which cut in either or both recession years.

However, despite improvements in budgeting practices, "the evidence to date with respect to the whole economy is that advertising has a negative though small impact in reducing the extremes of the business cycle."[38] As established before World War II, advertising tends to be procyclical—heavily used during the economic peaks and reduced during the valleys.

Advertising and Aggregate Consumption

A question related to advertising and business cycles is whether advertising causes aggregate consumption or is caused by consumption. The issue was popularized by John Kenneth Galbraith in the mid-1960s in *The New Industrial State*.[39] Galbraith labeled advertising the "high priest of materialism" and condemned it for diverting income from savings to consumption.

Most of the evidence would seem to indicate that advertising is the result rather than the cause of consumption, a finding that not unexpectedly is consistent with advertising's relationship to the business cycle. Of the attempts to assess the effects of total advertising expenditures on aggregate consumption in specific markets, such as cigarettes and alcoholic beverages, only a few studies have found modest changes in total market sales, as opposed to market shares.[40] A study that specifically addressed the Galbraithian argument found that disposable income led to consumption, which in turn led to increased advertising spending.[41]

Here again, Albion and Farris furnish a conclusion:

FIGURE 4.10

Two Ads That Make an Argument for Advertising During a Recession

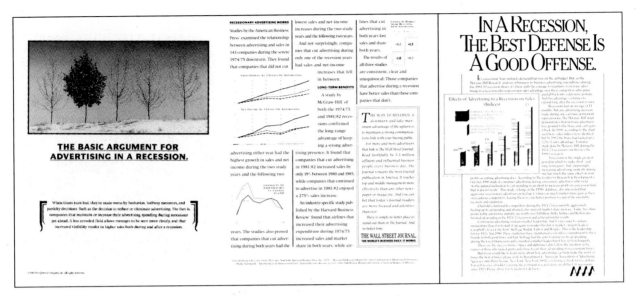

Because of difficulties in separating the impact of advertising on aggregate consumption from the many other social, economic, and political influences, our ability to make meaningful generalizations is greatly limited.[42]

It is more likely that changes in population, shifts in lifestyles, introductions of new technologies, and fluctuations in personal income have a greater impact on aggregate consumption than does advertising.

Advertising as Media Subsidy

A common misconception is that advertisers buy time and space in **media vehicles;** however, what advertisers actually buy are the audiences delivered by the media. As illustrated in Figure 4.11, time and space are simply surrogate indicators of audiences defined in terms of size (for example, circulations) or demographic segmentation. In an economic sense, audiences buy media content and advertisers buy audiences.

The revenues derived from audience consumption of media content and advertiser consumption of media-delivered audiences pay media bills. In the United States, there are four categories of mass media support: (1) media supported by audiences, for example, records and books; (2) media supported by advertisers, for example, TV and radio; (3) media supported by both audiences and advertisers, for example, magazines and newspapers; and (4) media supported by private or governmental organizations, for example, PBS and corporate publications. The importance of advertising revenue to *Rolling Stone* magazine provides a case example.[43]

"Never trust anyone over 30" was *Rolling Stone*'s anthem when it first appeared in the 1960s. During those early years, the *Stone* was a monthly publication with 24 pages of black and white pictures. Today, it is published biweekly and is filled with more than 100 pages of color and award-winning material.

On the road to success, the *Stone* encountered a serious problem—over time, the *Stone*'s readership changed from young, nonaffluent readers who professed anti-

Rolling Stone: *A Case of Media Economics*

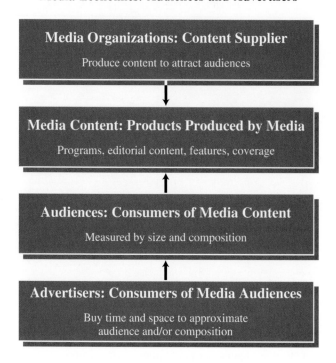

FIGURE 4.11

Media Economics: Audiences and Advertisers

Media Organizations: Content Supplier
Produce content to attract audiences

Media Content: Products Produced by Media
Programs, editorial content, features, coverage

Audiences: Consumers of Media Content
Measured by size and composition

Advertisers: Consumers of Media Audiences
Buy time and space to approximate
audience and/or composition

establishment ideals to affluent middle-aged professionals who were part of the establishment. Many of *Rolling Stone*'s current readers have never heard the sixties motto, and those who have read the magazine since its birth are now over 40. However, even as the *Stone*'s readership matured, advertisers continued to see the magazine as a cult publication targeted to people with sandals, long hair, and little income.

To correct its image problem, *Rolling Stone* turned to advertising. The result was an advertising campaign designed to reposition the magazine to potential advertisers by communicating the fact that the *Stone* had changed with the times and so had its readership. Ads such as those shown in Figure 4.12 were placed in publications targeted to potential advertisers and their agencies.

The ads directly attacked the image issue by playing on the words *perception* and *reality*. The story was always the same—the *real Rolling Stone* reader was a financially successful participant in the American dream, not the old hippie still going nowhere in life. Accompanying statistics informed advertisers about the *Stone*'s well-educated, successful readers with incomes of $30,000+ a year.

A quick perusal of today's *Stone* will convince you that the strategy worked. Advertising for electronics, shoes, grooming products, alcoholic beverages, automobiles, and other high-price products fill the pages of each issue. The lesson—content attracts audiences and audiences attract advertising dollars.

In the case of newspapers and magazines with support provided by both advertisers and audiences, it has been widely presumed that advertising revenues subsidize consumer prices. As summarized by Wilbur Schramm in his book, *Men, Messages and Media:*

> Between 60 and 75 percent of the cost of a newspaper or magazine is likely to come from advertising; the subscription price that you and I pay typically covers less than one-third of the total cost of producing and delivering the journal or periodical to us.[44]

FIGURE 4.12

Rolling Stone: **A Case of Media Economics**

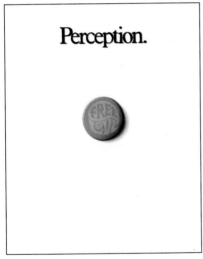

However, research studies have suggested that advertising subsidy is a myth, at least in the case of magazines.

Vincent Norris tested his observation that "some magazines ... exist without advertising support, but their prices per page of editorial content are in some cases lower than those of magazines which carry a large amount of advertising."[45] He found that the amount of advertising space in magazines had no effect on prices. The results of a later study corroborated Norris's findings, leading the researchers to conclude that advertising revenues are unrelated to the price per copy or price per editorial page of magazines, contrary to what is widely believed. Consumers pay for the editorial matter in magazines, just as they pay for other products. There is no "subsidy" from advertising for the editorial product.[46]

Because advertising subsidy is mythical in magazines does not mean that advertising is unimportant to the economic viability of the medium. Consumers seek out and use the information provided in magazine ads, and advertising does increase the number of editorial pages in magazines.[47] Without advertising's contributions in these two areas, readers might be less likely to purchase certain magazines.

Future Trends

Reducing Waste and Improving Economic Efficiency

The advertising industry has always been plagued by a certain amount of economic waste. One source of waste has been the tendency to overestimate the power of advertising; another has been the tendency to spend dollars on advertising as a reaction to competitive spending.

In the future, how you spend advertising dollars will be more important than how much you spend. Slow growth in many industries and the increased use of sales promotion will mean that advertisers must learn to produce more effective advertising campaigns rather than increase the number of ads. In *How Much is Enough?*, former ad executive John Philip Jones argues that "the best way to improve ad effectiveness is to reduce the huge amount of waste that occurs in most advertising." Jones recommends that future advertisers must follow

three guidelines if advertising is to contribute to brand growth:

1. Future advertisers must be improved by evaluating more precisely the effectiveness of previous campaigns, including the trade-off between advertising and sales promotion.
2. Future advertisers must improve the strategic foundations of campaign planning, targeting their efforts as tightly as possible to build and maintain market share.
3. Future advertisers must learn more about the field of advertising, especially about how creative ideas are produced, how advertising influences sales relative to other forms of selling, and how people respond to advertising in different media.

Source: John Philip Jones, *How Much Is Enough? Getting the Most From Your Advertising Dollar* (New York: Lexington Books, 1992).

The Duration Effects of Advertising

To determine the relation of advertising to competition, a number of studies have looked at the duration effects of advertising. In practical terms, duration effects are how long advertising expenditures continue to produce sales after the advertising has stopped.

The research findings have been strongly contradictory. Some of the studies have shown that the cumulative effects of advertising on sales last only a few months rather than years; others have found long duration effects. The issue remains largely unresolved, although sufficient reason exists to believe that advertising's communication effects carry over months and, in some cases, even years after the advertising has ended.

As you will see in Chapter 10 on advertising budgeting, the question of duration effects is related to the issue of whether advertising expenditures should be treated as an investment or as costs. Looked at from the investment point of view, it can be argued that advertising contributes to the maintenance of long-term consumer goodwill and to the production of future sales. Three factors seem to affect advertising's carryover effects:

1. *message reception and impact* Information search and processing is activated when people selectively purchase goods. Thus, how they react to advertising

is situationally defined. For example, a person interested in safety may very well remember all of those safety-oriented Volvo ads when considering the purchase of a new automobile.

2. *interpersonal influence* People talk about advertising and as a consequence are affected by advertising-related information that is passed on by others. For example, neighbors and friends share ad-conveyed information about things ranging from vacation deals to local sales.

3. *brand loyalty* People are brand loyal and advertising reinforces and legitimizes their loyalty. Therefore, they tend to attend and remember ads for "their brands," and to avoid or counterargue against competing brands.

Summary

Economists and other analysts have traditionally devoted much less attention to advertising than other methods of competition. As a consequence, less evidence exists about the economic effects of advertising than about many other economic issues.

Questions about the effects have been answered differently by two divergent schools of economic thought: the advertising-equals-market-power school and the advertising-equals-information school. The former has generally viewed advertising as a negative, anticompetitive market force because of its persuasive nature. The latter has countered with the view that advertising is procompetitive because it provides useful market information. Presently the information school interpretation seems to be the more realistic of the two, particularly because the information-persuasion dichotomy of the market power school has been called into question.

Advertising's effect on price depends partly on whether the advertising is national or retail. In the case of national advertising, the evidence generally suggests that advertising does not lead to lower prices. However, there is strong evidence that advertising at the retail level is related to lower consumer prices.

Advertising shows some ability to moderate gyrations of the business cycle. Companies that do not cut advertising during recessions tend to experience less sales decrease than competitors who do.

Advertising can add psychological value to a product even though the product remains physically unchanged. The value of a product resides in people's minds, not in the physical or functional qualities of the product. Although many companies who have a disproportionate share of a particular market are also big advertisers, it is not possible to attribute the concentration or erection of barriers to entry to advertising.

Advertising does not appear to narrow the range of product or service choices available to consumers. Instead it tends to encourage product innovation and entry of new products or services when these offer some real advantage to consumers.

In view of the cumulative theoretical and empirical analyses, it would seem that many questions and answers about advertising's economic effects remain unresolved and inconclusive.

1. Why have so many economists ignored advertising or given it only minor attention?
2. To what extent do you think that advertising has helped decrease the price of products or services?
3. To what extent might our standard of living have suffered during the past 100 years if advertising had been prohibited?
4. Economist Jules Backman has said, "The expenditures for advertising do not

Questions
for Discussion

represent a net cost to the economy, however that cost is measured." Do you agree? Why or why not?

5. Should the government encourage increased advertising during a recession or depression? If so, what form should such encouragement take?

6. Does an advertised product have more value than an unadvertised one with the same physical characteristics? What is value to the consumer? To the business community?

7. How do the proponents of advertising-equals-information versus advertising-equals-market-power handle the notion of information and persuasion?

Notes

1. David Aaker, Rajeev Batra, and John G. Myer, *Advertising Management,* 4th ed., (Englewood Cliffs, NJ: Prentice-Hall, 1992), 561.

2. Kent M. Lancaster and Duke O. Yaguchi, "How Economists Have Treated Advertising: 1890–1940," *Journal of Advertising History* 7 (October 1983): 14–29.

3. See Kim B. Rotzoll, James E. Haefner, and Charles H. Sandage, *Advertising in Contemporary Society* (Columbus, OH: Grid, 1976), 98–100, for a discussion of Kaldor.

4. Campbell R. McConnell, *Economics,* 9th ed. (New York: McGraw-Hill, 1987), 5–7.

5. See Mark S. Albion and Paul W. Farris, *The Effect of Manufacturer Advertising on Retail Pricing* (Cambridge, MA: Marketing Science Institute, 1981), 3.

6. Mark S. Albion and Paul W. Farris, *The Advertising Controversy: Evidence on the Economic Effects of Advertising* (Boston: Auburn House, 1981), x.

7. Vincent P. Norris, "The Economic Effects of Advertising: A Review of the Literature," *Current Issues and Research in Advertising* 7, No. 2 (1984): 46; Karen Whitehill King, Leonard N. Reid, Spencer F. Tinkham, and James Pokrywczynski, "The Perceived Informativeness of National and Retail Advertising," *Current Issues and Research in Advertising* 10 (1987): 173.

8. Norris, "The Economic Effects of Advertising," 46.

9. Alfred Marshal, *Industry and Trade* (London: MacMillan, 1919), 304–307.

10. John E. Calfee, "Advertising & Marketing Performance: An Interpretative Survey of the Literature," Special Report, National Association of Broadcasters, i–ii.

11. Ibid., i.

12. Brenda Dervin, "Mass Communicating: Changing Conceptions of the Audience," in *Public Communication Campaigns,* eds., Ronald E. Rice and William H. Paisley (Beverly Hills, CA: Sage, 1981), 71–87.

13. Shelby D. Hunt, "Information vs. Persuasive Advertising: An Appraisal," *Journal of Advertising* 5 (Summer 1976): 7–8.

14. Albion and Farris, *The Advertising Controversy,* 39–40.

15. David N. Laband, "The Durability of Informational Signals and the Content of Advertising," *Journal of Advertising* 18 (Spring 1989): 13–18.

16. Ibid., 18.

17. Stephen A. Greyser and Bonnie B. Reece, "Businessmen Look Hard at Advertising," *Harvard Business Review,* May–June 1971, 18–26.

18. S. Watson Dunn and David A. Yorke, "European Businessmen Look Hard at Advertising," *Columbia Journal of World Business* 9 (Winter 1974): 56.

19. Calfee, "Advertising & Marketing Performance," 19.

20. Albion and Farris, *The Advertising Controversy,* 154.

21. Calfee, "Advertising & Marketing Performance," 19.

22. Norris, "The Economic Effects of Advertising," 49.

23. Kenneth Boyer, "Informative and Goodwill Advertising," *Review of Economics and Statistics* 56 (November 1974): 541–548.

24. Albion and Farris, *The Advertising Controversy,* 169–170.

25. Bernard Ryan, Jr., *It Works! How Investment Spending in Advertising Pays Off* (New York: American Association of Advertising Agencies, 1991), 40.

26. Committee on the Value of Advertising, *The Value Side of Productivity: A Key to Competitive Survival in the 1990s* (New York: American Association of Advertising Agencies, 1990), 21.

27. Aaker, Batra, and Myers, *Advertising Management,* 562.

28. Committee on the Value of Advertising, *The Value Side of Productivity,* 41.

29. Aaker, Batra, and Myers, *Advertising Management,* 564.

30. Albion and Farris, *The Advertising Controversy,* Chapter 3.

31. Calfee, "Advertising & Marketing

Performance," ii–iii.

[32] Albion and Farris, *The Advertising Controversy,* 60.

[33] Ibid., Chapter 3.

[34] Kim B. Rotzoll and James E. Haefner, *Advertising in Contemporary Society: Perspectives Toward Understanding* (Cincinnati, OH: South-Western, 1986), 79.

[35] Albion and Farris, *The Advertising Controversy,* 82.

[36] See Neil H. Borden, *The Economic Effects of Advertising* (Homewood, IL: Irwin, 1942), 714–736; Julian L. Simon, *Issues in the Economics of Advertising* (Urbana, IL: University of Illinois Press, 1970), 67–74.

[37] "Study Supports Recession Ads," *Advertising Age* (April 24, 1980): 4.

[38] Aaker, Batra, and Myers, *Advertising Management,* 564.

[39] John Kenneth Galbraith, *The New Industrial State,* 5th ed. (Boston: Houghton Mifflin, 1967), 128.

[40] Calfee, "Advertising & Marketing Performance," 23.

[41] Rebecca Colwell Quarles and Leo W. Jeffres, "Advertising and National Consumption: A Path Analytic Re-Examination of the Galbraithian Argument," *Journal of Advertising* 12 (Summer 1983): 4–13, 33.

[42] Albion and Farris, *The Advertising Controversy,* 84.

[43] Adopted from Louis E. Boone and David L. Kurtz, *Contemporary Marketing,* 6th ed. (Hinsdale, IL: Dryden Press, 1989), 581.

[44] Wilbur Schramm, *Men, Messages, and Media* (New York: Harper & Row, 1973), 147.

[45] Vincent Norris, "Consumer Magazines and the Mythical Advertising Subsidy," *Journalism Quarterly* 59 (Summer 1982): 205–211, 239.

[46] Lawrence C. Soley and R. Krishnan, "Does Advertising Subsidize Consumer Magazine Prices?," *Journal of Advertising* 16 (Summer 1987): 8.

[47] Ibid.

Suggested Readings

Aaker, David A., Rajeev Batra, and John G. Myers. *Advertising Management,* 4th ed. Englewood Cliffs, NJ: Prentice-Hall, 1992, Chapter 17.

Albion, Mark S. *Advertising's Hidden Effects.* Boston: Auburn House, 1982.

Albion, Mark S., and Paul W. Farris. *The Advertising Controversy: Evidence on the Economic Effects of Advertising.* Boston: Auburn House, 1981.

Bauer, Raymond A., and Stephen A. Greyser. *Advertising in America: The Consumer View.* Boston: Harvard Business School, 1968.

Calfee, John E. "Advertising & Marketing Performance: An Interpretive Survey of the Literature." Special Report, National Association of Broadcasters, 1988.

Hovland, Roxanne, and Gary Wilcox. *Advertising in Society.* Chicago: NTC Business Books, 1988.

Jones, John Philip. *How Much Is Enough? Getting the Most From Your Advertising Dollar.* New York: Lexington Books, 1992.

Jones, John Philip. *What's in a Name? Advertising and the Concept of Brands.* Lexington, MA: Heath, 1986.

Lancaster, Kent M., and Duke O. Yaguchi. "How Economists Have Treated Advertising: 1890–1940." *Journal of Advertising History* 7 (October 1983): 14–29.

Norris, Vincent. "The Economic Effects of Advertising: A Review of the Literature." *Current Issues and Research in Advertising* 7, No. 2 (1984): 39–134.

Rotzoll, Kim B., James E. Haefner, and Charles H. Sandage. *Advertising in Contemporary Society,* 2d ed. Cincinnati, OH: South-Western, 1990.

Ryan, Jr., Bernard. *It Works! How Investment Spending in Advertising Pays Off.* New York: American Association of Advertising Agencies, 1991.

Steiner, Robert. "A Dual Stage Approach to the Effects of Brand Advertising on Competition and Price." In *Marketing and the Public Interest,* edited by John F. Cady, 127–150. Cambridge, MA: Marketing Science Institute, Report No. 78–105, 1978.

Environmental Considerations: Social/Cultural, Competition, Economic, Regulatory

↓

Advertising Organizations: Advertisers, Agencies, Media, Suppliers

↓

Marketing Communication Considerations: Marketing Planning

↓

Strategic Research Inputs

↓

Objective Setting: Target Market, Buyer Behavior

↓

Determining the Advertising Budget

Message Strategy → Media Strategy

Message Tactics ← → Media Tactics

Final Budget

↓

Plan in Action Run Campaign

↓

Impact

↓

Measure Advertising Effectiveness

Feedback   Feedback

LEARNING OBJECTIVES

In your study of this chapter, you will have an opportunity to:

- Compare government regulation of advertising and industry self-regulation.
- Learn how advertising regulation has changed over the past several decades.
- Examine the major mechanisms of government control.
- Understand the special role of the Federal Trade Commission and its regulatory activities.
- Examine the forms of advertising self-regulation.

Chapter 5

Regulatory Issues

CHAPTER TOPICS

ADVERTISING REGULATION

AREAS OF ADVERTISING CONTROL

REGULATION BY THE FEDERAL GOVERNMENT
 Food and Drug Administration
 Bureau of Alcohol, Tobacco and Firearms
 Federal Communications Commission
 Patent Office
 Library of Congress
 Postal Service
 Other Federal Controls

FEDERAL TRADE COMMISSION
 Deceptive Advertising
 Burden of Proof

 Powers and Remedies
 Affirmative Disclosures and Corrective Advertising
 Advertising Substantiation
 Children: A Special Market Segment

STATE AND MUNICIPAL REGULATION

SELF-REGULATION BY THE ADVERTISING
 INDUSTRY
 The NAD/NARB
 Media Clearance
 Individual Advertisers and Agencies
 Advertising Associations
 Trade Associations
 The Advertising Press

Unlike other environmental forces discussed in Chapters 3 and 4, regulation deals with direct and pragmatic influences that set limits on what, where and how products can be advertised and what advertisers can or cannot say about products in their ads. At the most basic level, control over advertising is exercised by the combined efforts of government regulation and industry self-regulation. Government control is exercised at federal, state, and municipal levels. Self-regulatory control is exercised by individual advertisers, advertiser-sponsored groups, trade associations, and advertising media. Most mechanisms of advertising regulation are designed to protect both competition and consumers from false and misleading advertising.

Advertisers often feel that advertising controls go too far. Consumerists often express the belief that they do not go far enough. Limits exist on what government and self-regulation can control, as the Ad Insights discussion of political advertising makes clear. In general, however, the mere existence (or threat) of governmental activity is a powerful force. Fear of what government authorities can or might do motivates the advertising industry to monitor its own practices and individual advertisers to cooperate with self-regulation efforts.

Advertising Regulation

In the late 1960s advertising regulation entered a unique period of activism. In the 1970s government involvement, consumer activism, and self-regulation all increased

The Privileged Status of Political Advertising

Political messages give advertising a bad name.

The public's outrage over the tactics and techniques of political messages—a biennial occurrence—stems from its belief that those messages are advertising (which they aren't) and that they're constrained by the same rules as advertising (which they aren't).

Advertising, or what the Supreme Court calls "commercial speech," is protected only when it is a truthful message for a lawful product. "Political speech" enjoys full protection under any circumstances. It can lie outrightly as long as there is no "malice" intended.

Thus, unlike a product commercial, a political message cannot be turned down by a station that believes it to be false, misleading or in bad taste. Someone deliberately misled by a political message has no recourse to the Federal Trade Commission or even the Council of Better Business Bureaus, as would be the case were it a real advertisement. An injured competitor can't sue under the Lanham Act or any other act available to victims of false advertising.

Clearly advertising and poltical messages are two totally different animals. But because the latter uses the lengths, the formats and the techniques of the former,

the public thinks they're all the same thing. And since they've learned that one type can lie to them with impunity, they will inevitably begin to doubt the credibility of it all.

The media consultants don't have to make their messages look like product advertising. They don't have to use dramatizations, jingles, animation and other formats developed for selling consumer products or services and considered by many as unsuitable for such grave endeavors as seeking public office. Nor do they have to use 15- to 30-second lengths, considered by many more to be inadequate for dealing with the complex issues about which voters seek enlightenment. Unlike advertising people, media consultants can purchase program lengths of five minutes or more for less than the cost of some 30-second spots. Their diligent attempts to resemble product advertising might suggest a strategy of "innocence by association."

I've never suggested that political messages—or any kind of speech—be banned. And as long as it's all right with the Supreme Court, it's all right with me if they lie. I simply wish they would stop impersonating advertising while doing so.

Source: John O'Toole, "Regulate Political Ads? They Give Us Bad Image," *Advertising Age*, November 28, 1988, 17. Reprinted with permission from *Advertising Age*. Copyright 1988 Crain Communications Inc. All rights reserved.

at a greater rate. The basic tenor of regulatory concerns was altered during this period; consumers were no longer presumed to be able to defend themselves against business abuses or market power or to perceive the most basic of potential deceptions.

During this period the **Federal Trade Commission (FTC),** the government's most powerful advertising control, held hearings on the techniques of modern advertising "to consider advertising addressed to children; to determine whether television advertising may unfairly exploit desires, fears, and anxieties; to determine whether technical aspects of the preparation and production of TV commericals may facilitate deception; and to consider consumers' physical, emotional, and psychological responses to advertising as they affect the standards by which advertising is judged."[1] The hearings, which began in 1971, lasted almost the entire decade. That same year, the National Advertising Review Board began operations. It represents the industry's most ambitious effort to regulate itself.

During the activitist 1970s, the concept of *caveat venditor*, "let the seller beware," seemed to guide business regulations. The concept of *caveat emptor*, "let the buyer beware," which earlier guided regulations, was a rule of law based on the assumption that consumers are capable of looking out for their own best interests. In contrast, caveat venditor is not a rule of law but a perspective applied in business regulation.

The dominant regulatory perspective taken in the 1970s was that manufacturers or their advertising agents are in the best position to know the truth of advertised claims and are therefore liable if claims do not hold up to scrutiny.[2]

Under Ronald Reagan, president of the United States from 1981 to 1989, the basic laws did not change, but the regulatory perspective did. Regulation was not viewed as the remedy for inequities in the marketplace. The regulatory perspective became deregulation, the avoidance of government-directed regulation, based on the presumption that the marketplace will regulate itself.[3]

These changes over the past three decades provide a major lesson in advertising regulation: with every change in political leadership, changes occur in regulatory perspectives. One group of elected or appointed officials may see market forces alone as the most efficient mechanism to prevent unfair and deceptive advertising practices. The next may favor imposed regulations. An interesting viewpoint on consumerism over the three decades of advertising regulation is offered in the Ad Insight entitled "The Future of Consumerism." Even though regulatory perspectives change with the "political winds," the forces of consumerism remained active in the regulatory arena.

Areas of Advertising Control

To understand today's complex web of advertising regulations, we must first identify some of the areas for which government and self-regulatory controls have been designed and implemented.

- *Content of advertising.* Controls may involve what is seen, said, or heard in ads. They concern, among other things, deception, taste, omission of information, right of privacy of individuals, copyright infringement, and trademark identification.
- *Type of product advertised.* Controls may prohibit or restrict the advertising of certain products. Examples are the 1971 broadcast ban on cigarette advertising, as well as government and self-regulatory restrictions on alcohol and tobacco products.
- *Fairness.* Controls have as their goal the protection of "special" consumers, such as children and the elderly.
- *Barriers to competition.* Controls may be concerned with practices that hinder competition, such as antitrust violations in advertising and industry organizations.

Each of these areas will be covered as we review the major aspects of government and self-regulation.

Regulation by the Federal Government

The federal government has long been engaged in advertising regulation. The major federal laws that have significantly influenced the course and nature of government controls are described in Figure 5.1. The federal agency with the broadest jurisdiction is the Federal Trade Commission. Its programs and policies on advertising set the standards that other governmental regulators follow. For example, the Federal Communications Commission refers deceptive TV commericals to the FTC. Agencies and branches of the federal government that are involved in the regulation of specific product areas are listed in Table 5.1. They will be discussed in this section, followed by a separate section on the Federal Trade Commission.

The Future of Consumerism

E. Scott Maynes, *Professor, Department of Consumer Economics and Housing, Cornell University*

Consumerism? (1) The voicing of consumer discontent and the furtherance of corrective actions (Maynes); also (2) a social movement seeking to augment the rights and power of buyers vs. those of sellers (Kotler).

A word about its nature. It is *"low-intensity,"* commanding widespread but nonintense support. Think of your own economic situation. What comes first? Everything, anything connected with your job or profession: a producer interest. Only after this producer interest is attended to do you pay attention to your consumer problems.

Whence consumerism? Each of us from our own experience in 1990 can confirm the very same instances of consumer discontent that existed in 1972: poor quality, poor service, dishonored promises, unsafe products, polluting products, deceptive advertising, and fraud. A moment's reflection also reveals the difficulty we have in dealing with our consumer problems: each is transient, nonrepeating, and, in seeking correction, we are amateurs facing professionals.

Consumerism plays a vital role in contemporary market economies. It is an avenue for communicating errors. Like business losses, it sends messages to sellers who serve poorly: shape up or go broke. It is no accident that Eastern European economies lacked consumerism.

WILL CONSUMERISM LAST?

It will be with us forever. Why so? Because the basic causes giving rise to consumer discontent defy permanent solution. The causes are: (1) consumer grievances—those listed above and more; (2) information problems—the inability of consumers to assess quality and to understand complex products/services, the as-yet-unrecognized near zero-correlation between price and quality in local markets, and, of course, deception and fraud; (3) the underrepresentation of consumers; (4) unsafe products and (5) environmental concerns.

How do these sources of consumer discontent get transformed into *"a social movement seeking to augment the rights and power of buyers?"* It starts with millions of instances of consumer frustration, be it the just-purchased VCR that won't work, the doubling of one's auto insurance premium, a repair that didn't *"fix it,"* frustrations that find voice in such phrases as *"There ought to be a law,"* or *"Those SOB's!!"*

These mutterings are picked up and voiced as outrage by consumer advocates (Ralph Nader; Steve Brobeck). Knowingly, they feed the media, understanding such essentials as *"beats,"* deadlines, the need for *"fresh"* copy, conflict, heroes, villains, clarity and simplicity. In turn, a phalanx of politicians and their staffs, eager to be viewed as pro-consumer, respond to these now-unpublicized consumer issues. The media and the politicians are not the only supporters of unorganized consumers. Almost unnoticed, new consumer organizations have come into being in the last 20 years as older organizations have become more powerful.

THE INSTITUTIONALIZATION OF CONSUMERISM

Many in the 1970s and '80s viewed consumerism as activism directed mainly at Federal intervention on behalf of consumers. People holding this view were quick to conclude that consumerism had subsided during the 1980s. They were far off the mark. Look at the accompanying table. While government organizations shrank from

Source: *At Home with Consumers,* Direct Selling Education Foundation, Vol. 11, No. 1, April 1990, pps. 6–7.

The Growth of Consumer Organizations

Type of Organization	1960	1970	1980	1990	1980 1970	1990 1980 (Percent)	1990 1970
Not-For-Profit							
Consumers Reports: (Subscribers)[1]	0.8M	2.0M	2.9M	4.5M	145%	155%	225%
Consumer Federation of American (Staff)[2]	founded 1964	3	5	8	167%	160%	267%
Nader Network (Public Citizen, etc.)[3]	NA	2M	3M	7M	50%	233%	350%
American Association of Retired Persons (Members)[4]	0.3M	1.6M	11.7M	32.2M	731%	275%	2013%
American Council on Consumer Interests (ACCI)[5]	1,266	NA	2,152	1,680	NA	78%	NA
Government							
Federal Trade Commission (Staff)[6]	782	1,316	1,573	950	120%	860%	72%
Food and Drug Administration (Staff)[7]	1,678	4,252	8,089	7,877	190%	97%	185%
Office of Consumer Affairs (Staff)[8]	founded 1964	18	52	22	288%	42%	122%
Corporate							
Society of Consumer Affairs in Business (Members)[9]	0	founded 1971	980	2,148	NM*	219%	NM*

*NM = Not Meaningful

[1] *Source: Annual Buying Guides*, "Statement of Ownership, Management and Circulation."
[2] Telephone Conversation, Stephen Brobeck, Executive Director, February 26, 1990.
[3] Estimates based on review of a sample of annual reports of organizations in the Nadar Network including national and state based organizations: Telephone Conversation, John Richard, Center for Responsive Law.
[4] Telephone Conversation, Michael Whybrew, Marketing Specialist, February 27, 1990. AARP's magazine, *Modern Maturity* has the world's largest circulation, 22.4 M. In 1990.
[5] *Source:* 1960, Henry Harap; 1980 and 1990, Helga Meyer, Administrative Assistant, ACCI, March 19, 1990.
[6] *Source:* William V. Rosano, Assistant Director For Operations, FTC, March 6, 1990.
[7] Telephone Conversation, Robert McLeod, Chief, Budget Formulation Branch.
[8] Telephone Conversation, Bonnie Jansen, Director of Public Affairs, February 26, 1990.
[9] Telephone Conversation, Louis Garcia, Executive Director, February 20, 1990.

1980 to 1990, non-government consumer organizations increased their size several times over! Equally important are factors the table doesn't show: the increasing professionalism of these organizations, the stabilization and broadening of their sources of financial support, the increasing breadth of their interests and activities.

FIGURE 5.1

Major Laws Affecting Regulation of Advertising

Federal Trade Commission Act (1914)—created federal authority to regulate unfair and deceptive acts and practices in commerce. Act contained no provisions regarding the regulation of advertising; however, the agency started dealing with advertising cases in 1915. In 1931, the Supreme Court ruled that the FTC could regulate advertising if proof was shown that deception would harm competition.

Wheeler Lea Amendments (1938)—gave the FTC power to focus on deceptive acts and practices themselves, not on harm to competition. The change gave the agency the power to protect the public as well as the competition.

Lanham Act (1947)—provided protection for trademarks. Individual advertisers were allowed to sue competitors for deceptive ad claims, an action not provided for in the FTC Act.

Magnuson-Moss Warranty Act/FTC Trade Improvements Act (1975)—authorized promulgation of trade rule specifying unfair or deceptive acts and practices and sanctioned penalties for violations.

FTC Improvements Act (1980)—prohibited FTC from using unfairness as a basis for trade rules.

TABLE 5.1

Major Federal Agencies Involved in Regulation of Advertising

Agency	Function
Federal Trade Commission	Regulates commerce between states; controls unfair business practices of advertisers and agencies; takes action on false and deceptive advertising; most important agency in regulation of advertising and promotion
Food and Drug Administration	Regulatory division of the Department of Health and Human Services; controls labeling of food, drugs, cosmetics, medical devices, and potentially hazardous consumer products, as well as advertising of prescription drugs
Federal Communications Commission	Regulates broadcast media advertising indirectly through the power to grant or withhold broadcasting licenses
Postal Service	Regulates material that goes through the mails, primarily in areas of obscenity, lottery, and fraud
Bureau of Alcohol, Tobacco and Firearms	Part of the Treasury Department; enforces a code that limits advertising of liquor
Department of Agriculture	Responsible for policing seed, meat, and insecticide advertising
Securities and Exchange Commission	Regulates advertising of securities
Patent Office	Regulates registration of trademarks
Library of Congress	Controls protection of copyrights

The Food and Drug Administration (FDA) regulates a special kind of advertising, pharmaceutical advertising, that is, advertising directed at medical practitioners for drugs and other products sold only by prescription. Pharmaceutical advertising is recognized as the medical professional's predominant source of information about prescription drugs. FDA regulations attempt to make certain that ad claims are accurate and complete. The FDA requires that certain content be included in every ad, such as contra-indications, warnings, and side effects.

The FDA also monitors medical journal advertising for possible deception and has powers and programs to halt or correct deceptive practices. In some areas, the FDA has greater authority than the FTC. For example, the agency can seize drugs and food on charges of deceptive advertising.

Food and Drug Administration

The Bureau of Alcohol, Tobacco and Firearms (BATF) is a division of the Treasury Department that oversees guidelines for the advertising and promotion of alcoholic beverages. The first guidelines were written concurrent with the repeal of Prohibition and were revised once, 50 years later.

Special attention in recent years has focused on how BATF guidelines have exempted liquor products from the type of strict regulation enforced by other governmental authorities. For example, all shampoos, cosmetics, and food products must list ingredients on labels under directives from the FDA, but liquor products are exempt from this FDA rule. Active sports figures cannot be used in alcohol ads, but the rules do not apply to retired athletes.

The BATF also oversees label guidelines such as the distinction between "nonalcoholic" or "alcohol-free" designations that may be used in advertising and on labels, with brewed products falling in both categories.

Bureau of Alcohol, Tobacco and Firearms

The Federal Communications Commission (FCC) has great potential for influencing advertising content, even though the agency does not have any direct power over advertisers, advertising agencies, print media, or broadcast networks. The FCC grants operating licenses to television and radio stations and periodically reviews each station's service to "the public interest, convenience, and necessity." Stations are thus encouraged to make certain they do not broadcast advertising or programming content that may violate FCC standards. However, most content-related rules have been terminated and virtually all FCC regulations directed at advertising have been dropped.[4]

The FCC still oversees the 1971 ban on cigarette advertising passed by Congress, but the agency itself no longer bans any products from TV or radio (see the Ad Insight entitled "Tobacco Marketers Claim Ruling Spares Them from Changing Ads" for recent activity on this regulatory issue). Restrictions against carrying hard liquor ads were self-imposed by most (but not all) television stations, not imposed by the FCC (see the following section on self-regulation), and stricter guidelines on alcohol commericals are imposed by many states. The Fairness Doctrine that once required carrying of opposing points of view for opinion ads also has been dropped, along with directives against over-commercialization that limited the quantity of broadcast advertising content per hour. Some uncertain restrictions on obscenity remain, but broadcasters see them as more of a concern for program directors than for advertisers. The only remaining advertising restrictions are on the broadcast of information on commercially run lotteries, and this is a problem only with rare local sales efforts. State-run lotteries have been specifically exempted by Congress.

A negative side effect of the dropping of restrictions on the quantity of commercials per hour has beeen the proliferation of what some call program-length commercials. Advertisers produce these programs and purchase the time for their broadcast. Since the FCC restrictions were eliminated, stations increasingly schedule **infomercials**, 30-minute or hour-long sales efforts designed to be viewed as regular programs.[5]

Federal Communications Commission

Tobacco Marketers Claim Ruling Spares Them from Changing Ads

Tobacco marketers breathed a collective sigh of relief yesterday. They won't have to make any changes in their advertising, they declared, because even though a Supreme Court decision opened the way for liability lawsuits against them, it simultaneously shut the door on most actions against their ads

But before the tobacco industry gets too comfortable, a word of caution: Legal experts said that under the ruling, certain kinds of ads are vulnerable to liability lawsuits by smokers who become ill.

Ads that can be interpreted as making implied health claims could be on dangerous ground. Pitches for low-tar and low-nicotine smokes, like American Brand's Carlton and Philip Morris's Merit, may be particularly exposed; a recent Carlton ad pictures packs of Carlton above packs of Marlboro, Camel and others, with the line, "10 packs of Carlton have less tar than one pack of these brands."

Also on potentially shaky footing, though to a lesser extent, are cigarettes with aggressively healthy-sounding slogans: Lorillard uses "Alive with Pleasure" for its Newport brand, for example, and Philip Morris boasts that its Superslims brand emits "70 percent less smoke from the lit end."

"If I were a cigarette company, those are the types of ads I would most quickly re-examine," says Matthew Myers, counsel to the Coalition on Smoking or Health, a coalition of several anti-smoking groups. Adds Laurence H. Tribe, the Harvard Law School professor who

Source: From *The Wall Street Journal*, Friday, June 26, 1992, B6.

These formats have been criticized as lending infomercials a credibility advantage that goes to the heart of numerous audience comprehension–miscomprehension–deception issues.[6]

As an example, the program "Consumer Challenge" is produced by the makers of MDR fitness tablets, who buy the half-hour period to run the show. On one typical episode, the program investigated its own product: "MDR fitness tablets: New product or consumer rip-off?" The program's answer to that question is easily guessed.

FCC regulations require all stations to clearly identify these programs as paid advertising, though cable networks such as Lifetime or Black Entertainment Network are exempt from such restrictions.[7] And many stations apparently are ignorant of

argued the latest case on behalf of the plaintiff: "Any claim that says or implies that because of the composition of the tobacco or the nature of the filter, the buyer need not beware, would be vulnerable."

The complex ruling handed down Wednesday holds that smokers may sue cigarette companies for allegedly distorting the health dangers of tobacco. Of course, most cigarette ads steer clear of making direct health claims altogether, which is why ads for low-tar and low-nicotine smokes, which often use those allegedly healthy attributes as selling points, may be most at risk.

But the ruling bars suits brought simply because cigarette ads picture healthy, robust people; suits can't claim such ads are intended to "neutralize" the federally mandated health warnings on cigarette packages. The ruling stems from a 1983 case brought against three tobacco companies by a New Jersey woman, Rose Cipollone, who died of lung cancer a year later.

Tobacco companies cite the ruling's protection of glamorous cigarette ads as a major reason why they won't need to change their marketing. It will have "no impact at all," contends a spokesman for American Brands, even though that company makes the low-tar, low-nicotine brand Carlton, sold with the slogan "Carlton is lowest."

Adds Steven Parrish, vice president and general counsel for Philip Morris, "If anything, the decision would give us additional protection with respect to advertising activities. I don't see any changes in the way we approach our advertising."

Indeed, the ruling doesn't appear to affect some of the most controversial campaigns at all. Smoking Joe Camel, the Marlboro Man, and the Kool Penguin, among others, are all lambasted by critics for allegedly appealing to children, but none make outright health claims.

The court's decision "removes the broad-scale attack on cigarette advertising," concedes Michael Pertschuk, co-director of the Advocacy Institute, an antismoking group based in Washington.

But the Supreme Court also gave states wide berth to impose marketing restrictions on cigarette companies. States can't require additional warnings in ads, but they could demand that cigarette makers include package inserts detailing smoking's health risks. They also could require cigarette marketers to set up toll-free numbers to disperse health information.

But instead of pursuing a new wave of false-advertising lawsuits, anti-tobacco forces are expected to focus on getting hold of tobacco firms' internal documents to learn "what the tobacco companies knew—and whether there was a scheme either to deceive or mislead," says Mr. Myers of the Coalition on Smoking or Health. The Supreme Court has clearly opened the way for that pursuit, and the approach may be applied to other kinds of companies, as well.

the requirements.[8] Sometimes the stations might ignore their obligations until faced with legal action from a disgruntled consumer.

Neilson vs. *Harriscope*, a case involving a disgruntled consumer, ended by settlement between the parties in 1990. For example, the depositions in the case revealed that channel 22 in Los Angeles, California, ran virtually all paid commercial broadcasting throughout its schedule. In addition to infomercials, the other news-like programs that were the bulk of the schedule all required the guests to pay a fee to appear. Despite regulations to the contrary, the station did not label the infomercials as such; nor did the news programs carry any notice that the guests paid a fee for the interview. In her depositions, Mrs. Neilson commented that she believed the sales people because of their repeated appearances on channel 22 "news" programs, and thus she invested $100,000. As it later developed, the tax shelters were a fraud and the persons who took her money eventually went to jail. She sued the station to recover her investment. After Mrs. Neilson sued the station, it began to broadcast notices that the guests paid to be on the investment interview programs and that the host was paid a fee for asking the questions. The legal action encouraged honesty on the part of the station; they now go to great lengths to make certain all programs are *clearly* identified as sponsored advertising.

For years, critics of children-oriented advertising practices have appealed to various government agencies to deal with cartoon programs, such as G.I. Joe, MASK, Teen-Aged Mutant Ninja Turtles, and Transformers. These critics assert that these programs are, as a practical matter, acting as nothing more than 30-minute commercials for lines of toys based on each program's line of characters. However, none of the programs fit the definition of advertising in Chapter 1: the programs are purchased by the network or stations for broadcast rather than the product manufacturer buying the time as with "Consumer Challenge." In some cases, the programs are based on toys, sometimes toys are based on pre-existing programs, and, in some instances (for example, Teen-Aged Mutant Ninja Turtles), both show and toys are based on characters in comic books. It is hard to discern where to draw the line on these programs, which all must gather an audience on their own merits, and the criticisms have not spawned any government action.

However, the Congress and the FTC have shown a strong interest in the consumer deceptions inherent in the 30-minute sales programs that are disguised as news. Congress has held hearings on the problem, with intense analysis of business practices and potential consumer reactions, and the FTC has started several actions against programs for their potential to deceive consumers.[9]

Patent Office

The **Lanham Act** of 1947 was passed to provide protection against trademark infringement by competitors. The Patent Office handles registration of trademarks, which include "any word, name, symbol, or device, or any combination thereof, adopted and used by a manufacturer or merchant to identify goods and distinguish them from those manufactured or sold by others." In addition to slogans, three main types of identification marks are included: (1) brand names, (2) corporate or store names, and (3) identifying symbols for brands or companies. Under the Lanham Act, the mark need not be physically affixed to the product. The act protects service marks, used to distinguish services rather than products; certification marks, used by persons other than the owner to certify geographical origin, grade, or quality; and collective marks, used to indicate membership in an organization or society.

Section 43(a) of the Lanham Act [15 U.S.C. sec 1125(a) (1988)] also grants a business's direct and indirect competitors a cause of action against a party using a "false description or presentation" (which includes misleading advertising). The action may be brought by a party who "is or is likely to be damaged by" it. Some judgments have run into millions of dollars and the threat of such competitor lawsuits might be an additional factor (similar to the existence of the threat of direct government actions) engendering firms to be certain that their claims are not deceptive. This statute encourages advertisers to police one another for potential deceptive practices instead of "letting it ride" to the consumer's detriment or filing complaints with the FTC, which would increase taxpayer costs to act on behalf of competitors.

Technically, this is not an actual "regulation" because no government agency sets guidelines or directly takes actions to restrict advertising content. On the other hand, it is a law, applied by the courts, that enables competitors to sue each other for deceptive advertising, and past decisions have interpreted the law in a fashion that is parallel to the programs and guidelines of federal regulatory agencies such as the FTC. In other words, the law imposes similar requirements on advertisers as on government regulators, with the added enforcement mechanism of potential lawsuits by competitors.

In theory, this right (or threat) for competitors to seek legal action against one another discourages deceptive advertising, holding both advertisers *and their agencies* financially liable. (And, as will be seen shortly in the discussion of the FTC, that agency only works to stop potential consumer deceptions, but does not issue fines or punishments for deceptive advertising.) Whether it is a powerful enough force that, in practice, actually halts advertising deceptions is disputed in some legal literature. Some see it as a limitation on an advertiser's free-speech rights,[10] while another concluded that "either because the wrongdoers have no competitors or because all actors in a field are similarly unscrupulous, private litigation is an ineffective regulatory force and can be expected to remain so."[11]

Library of Congress

The Library of Congress enforces the copyright laws as set forth in the U.S. Code. These laws give authors and other creators a monopoly on their creations for a certain period of time. The Copyright Act of 1978 provides for copyright protection during the creator's lifetime plus 50 years.

One authority on advertising law recommends that advertisers copyright their ads. They qualify for the easiest kind of copyright notice; all that is required is the symbol and the name of the advertiser. Even an abbreviation of the name is acceptable in the copyright notice if it is spelled out elsewhere in the ad. Despite the commonly held belief, publication of an ad in a periodical does not necessarily provide copyright protection. It protects only against direct quotation, not against paraphrasing.[12]

Postal Service

The United States Postal Service controls mailed advertising, mainly in the areas of obscenity, lottery, and fraud. The service may act against advertising that is not legally obscene but that may offend those who receive it. Anyone receiving a pandering ad can ask that no more mail be delivered from that sender. An ad is pandering if, in the opinion of the recipient, it is "erotically arousing or sexually provocative." Post office officials may also control mail that promotes a lottery.

The controls over fraud are somewhat more specific and easier to enforce than are those over obscenity and lottery. In the past, action has been taken against dubious medical cures, home-study courses, and questionable get-rich-quick schemes.

Other Federal Controls

Control over advertising practices is directly or indirectly exercised by a number of other federal authorities, including the Securities and Exchange Commission (securities), the Environmental Protection Agency (pesticides), the Federal Energy Regulatory Commission (public utilities), and the Department of Transportation (airline advertising).

Federal Trade Commission

The FTC is the most important government authority involved in advertising regulation, although it was not originally intended to serve in that capacity. Rather, it was initially empowered as an enforcement agency for antitrust laws. Created by the Federal Trade Commission Act of 1914, the agency's initial charge was to restrain potentially monopolistic practices and unfair methods of competition. Its ability to regulate advertising was established by the **Wheeler-Lea Amendments** of 1938, wherein Section 5 of the FTC act stated that the agency could take action against all unfair or deceptive acts or practices, regardless of whether or not the advertising could be shown to directly harm competition.

However, recognition of the FTC as an active and powerful force in advertising regulation is fairly recent. In the late 1960s two independent groups, a Ralph Nader research group and an American Bar Association committee, presented resounding condemnations of the FTC. Both said that the agency conveyed an impression of working for consumers while actually doing next to nothing. They recommended that the agency be dissolved. President Nixon appointed Casper Weinberger to serve as chair of the commission, and, for his brief six months in that office, he started some massive internal reorganizations. He was replaced by the chair of the American Bar Association committee, Miles Kirkpatrick, who had written a dissent from the original document. He had expressed a belief that the agency could, with proper leadership, become an effective regulator for consumer protection.

The present organization of the FTC is shown in Figure 5.2. The period during which it was headed by Weinberger and Kirkpatrick generally marks its beginning as a strong and effective force for advertising regulation. The size and nature of

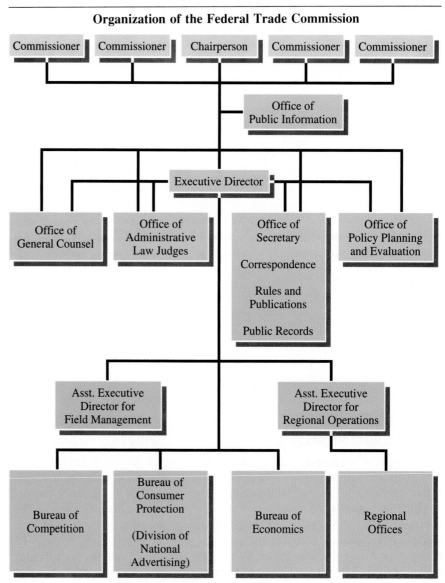

FIGURE 5.2

Organization of the Federal Trade Commission

Source: "Your Federal Trade Commission: What It Is and What It Does" (Washington, DC: Federal Trade Commission, Government Printing Office, 1977).

active cases increased. Innovative remedies were tried. Television networks were encouraged to drop restrictions on comparative advertising. Trade associations such as the American Medical Association were pressured to eliminate prohibitions on untruthful advertising. Rules and programs were instituted that gained such widespread support that they have survived the deregulatory mood of the 1980s.[13] Today many states have "Baby FTC" acts that say, in effect, that the state is empowered to act against advertisers in a manner following the standards set by the FTC.

Though deception has never been explicitly defined by Congress, it has been defined over the decades by court cases and legal interpretations. While the legal definition is framed in terms of the impression that an ad makes on consumers, the FTC is not required to use consumer research in deciding if an ad is deceptive, although it sometimes does.[14]

Deceptive Advertising

Quite simply, an ad can be considered deceptive if it communicates—by statement, implication, or omission—product values or benefits that are at variance with the facts. The FTC need not show that anyone actually believed the claims. Actual deception or harm to the public need not occur. The FTC need not prove the advertiser intended to make the claims; what the advertiser intended to convey is irrelevant. A claim may be ruled deceptive even if it is literally or technically true.[15]

From these broad statements, all specific rules or guidelines from past cases become obvious, as shown in the following examples:

- Ambiguous statements that readily lend themselves to both truthful and misleading interpretations are deceptive.
- An ad is deceptive if it fails to disclose important facts when such omissions would deceive a substantial segment of the public.
- Celebrities or expert endorsers must have made honest comparisons between the product and its competitors; if the endorsement is one of personal usage, they must be bona fide users of the product.

In 1983 the FTC introduced an alternative concept to the "tendency or capacity to deceive" called the "likeliness to deceive." Although the alternative concept represents a difference in terminology and FTC perspective, the established law regarding deceptive advertising remains unaltered.

Under today's FTC interpretation, an ad would be considered deceptive if a claim—objective, subjective, implied, or unique—is likely to mislead the typical consumer acting on a reasonable basis to that individual's detriment. (This means an average consumer, not the foolish or feeble-minded.)

The burden of proof that advertising is deceptive falls on the FTC. The agency must first determine that ad claims are conveyed to consumers, either expressly or implied, following advertising exposure. Then it must prove that the claims conveyed are deceptive in that they falsely depict the advertised product. The relevant evidence is that something false was communicated to the public. Evidence of other sorts, such as whether consumers believed what was claimed, whether they relied on the claims, or whether they were actually deceived or damaged by the claims, is not required by law.[16]

Burden of Proof

The FTC's interpretation of deception is more effective than longstanding state criminal laws on advertising deception. Most of these state laws are based on a model statute first proposed in 1911 by a former industry trade magazine, *Printer's Ink*. Unlike the original model, however, most state statutes are part of criminal laws. They attempt to prevent advertising deception by providing a strong deterrent. The idea is that, faced with possible criminal punishments, advertisers will avoid being deceptive.[17]

As part of a state's criminal code, these laws make it a misdemeanor to be responsible for false and misleading advertising. With advertisers facing criminal penalties ranging from fines to imprisonment, the burden of proof is much stronger in state deceptive advertising cases than with the FTC. The commission need only prove a potential for consumer deception. The state's attorney general who enforces the criminal laws must prove criminal intent.

Obviously, proving intent to deceive is a difficult task. Even proving that something false is communicated creates disputes over just what an ad says and whether or not the product delivers as promised.[18] With the added factor of advertiser intent, a state's attorney faces a nearly impossible task in attempting to convince a jury beyond a reasonable doubt.

The FTC, on the other hand, has only to focus on the advertising, not on the advertiser's intent. The commission does not aim to punish wrongdoers but simply stop "unfair and deceptive acts and practices." No advertisers have been fined or sent to jail by the FTC for disseminating deceptive advertising. They are merely directed to stop running the advertising and not to run similar advertising in the future.

Powers and Remedies

The FTC has two basic remedies for deceptive advertising:

- *Consent order* This is a short-cut settlement after a formal complaint has been issued.
- *Litigated cease and desist order* This is an FTC directive that is legally enforceable, but appealable to the courts.

The two remedies direct the advertiser to quit making false claims, but they can include directions for the nature and content of future advertising.

After a question is raised about an advertising claim, if it appears that the advertising might be deceptive, the FTC staff conducts an investigation. Ordinarily, complaints come from the commission itself, the public, or competitors. Commission staff members monitor the media for questionable advertising and can initiate inquiries if claims appear to be deceptive. Most cases, however, originate when the FTC's national office or one of its regional offices receives a letter of complaint. These letters can come from consumers, but more frequently a competitor raises initial questions.

Following the issuance of a complaint, the commission offers the advertiser the option of signing a consent order, by which the advertiser agrees to discontinue the advertising. The advertiser can bargain over the exact terms of the consent order, but swift agreement saves both parties time and litigation costs. Once signed, the agreement is binding on the future advertising claims made by the advertiser. Consent orders may include detailed directives for types of claims that can be made in subsequent advertising, types of additional information that must be included in advertising, or affirmative disclosures of product information.

If the advertiser and the FTC are unable to agree on a consent order, the case follows the commission's internal legal procedures. A trial is held before an administrative law judge, a commission employee who can dismiss the case or recommend a cease and desist order. Regardless of whether the decision at this level favors the FTC staff or the advertiser, it can be appealed to the full commission for a final administrative decision. The full commission can then vote to issue an order against the advertiser, who can then appeal the decision to the Federal Court of Appeals and, ultimately, to the U.S. Supreme Court, if the highest court decides to hear the appeal. Once appeals have ended, or immediately if appeals are not sought, the order becomes binding on future advertising. The procedure from the initial complaint to an appeal to the highest court is diagrammed in Figure 5.3.

The major difference between consent decrees and cease and desist orders is that consent decrees are entered by bargaining and negotiation, whereas a cease and

FIGURE 5.3

How a Deceptive Advertising Case Proceeds through the FTC and the Courts

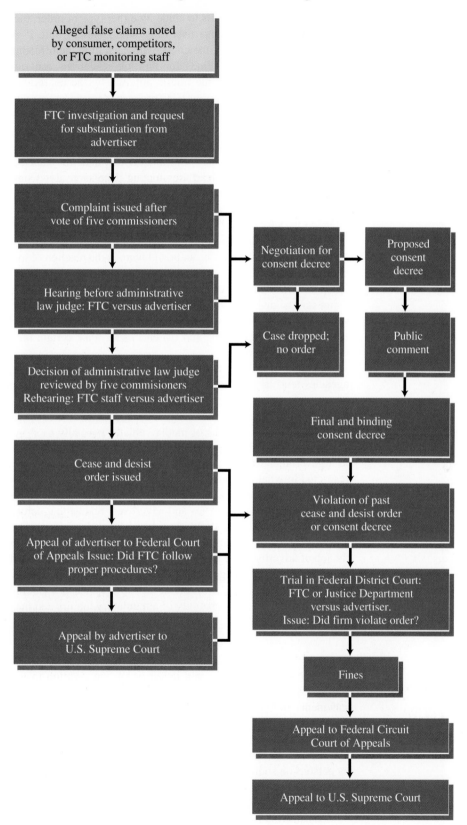

Source: Herbert J. Rotfeld, Auburn University, 1992.

desist order is the result of an adversarial process that can be appealed through the federal appellate courts. Anything that might be included in one order may be included in the other. Once finalized, both have the same impact on future advertising claims.

If the advertiser later fails to abide by either type of order, the FTC or the Justice Department can sue the advertiser in Federal District Court. If guilty, the advertiser is fined "per violation" by the court, with each time the offending ads run counting as additional violations. Fines for multiple violations can run into hundreds of thousands of dollars. But the fine is imposed by the courts, not the FTC, and the punishment is for violating an FTC order, not for deceptive advertising.

For the initial FTC finding, no one is "punished." The advertiser, as previously noted, is simply told to stop the ad claims and never make them again. This limitation of power is criticized by consumer activists, who contend that the FTC remedies encourage advertisers to run questionable ads until they are caught. On the other hand, ads that might mislead are stopped. The same ads would be left alone for lack of evidence if the commission had to prove beyond a reasonable doubt that people believed the ads, that they were harmed, and that such outcomes were intended by advertisers.[19]

Another indication that the FTC deception approach is effective, beyond simply the large numbers of cases brought and won, is the reaction of individual advertising agencies. As the FTC's programs became more active in the 1970s, advertising agencies instituted their own internal processes to make certain that proposed advertising campaigns were within the law. In general, agency clearance activities are of two types: (1) legal analysis to make certain that governmental authorities will not later find ads objectionable and (2) checks to make certain the ads are acceptable to selected media vehicles.

Of course, not all advertising agencies have the same clearance procedures. Larger agencies tend to have in-house lawyers and paralegals. Smaller agencies tend to have people assigned to make judgment calls, often lawyers on retainer. The strictness and degree of clearance formality depends on the size of the agency, the size of the accounts, and the types of media vehicles normally used by the agency.[20]

They instituted these procedures to avoid the costs and distractions of responding to a government inquiry, or even worse, being told that in the future they will be restricted in what they might say or do in future ads. While no one is punished by an FTC order in the legal meaning of "punishment"—that is, no one is sent to jail or fined—advertising agencies and advertisers realize that defending a government action is not without its costs. At a basic level, lawyers charge for their services and an FTC action can involve many costly hours of work by attorneys. In addition, the job of advertising people is to create advertising. However, when a request from the FTC or some other government or self-regulatory authority is received, people must be pulled off jobs to respond. At the very least, a careful agency clearance process minimizes the probability of a regulatory inquiry and makes initial response to one that much easier.

Affirmative Disclosures and Corrective Advertising

Consent decrees and cease and desist orders, in addition to telling advertisers to stop specific practices found, may also require that future advertising include specific statements if failure to do so would be deceptive. Orders for future affirmative disclosures, in general, direct the advertiser to offset future claims in one area with additional information.[21] For example, in a consent order for Morton Salt Company's Lite Salt, future advertising was required to contain the statement, "Not to be used by persons on sodium- or potassium-restricted diets." Firestone Tire advertising that referred to a product as a "safe tire" had to include a statement about the conditions under which Firestone tires were safer than other tires.

Many affirmative disclosure orders simply require that if one type of claim is made, an additional statement must be present to make certain that the ad is not deceptive. For the most part, an advertiser might avoid such directives by simply switching to other claims that do not trigger the need for disclosure. The problem arises when deceptive claims have been made for so long or have become so strongly associated with a brand name that any future advertising would trigger the false associations formed from the earlier deceptive ads.

To handle this problem, in the early 1970s the FTC started to require advertisers to spend money on **corrective advertising**. The corrected information had to be incorporated in future ads even if it were irrelevant to the new campaign. For example, in one early case Profile Bread was required to state in corrective ads that the bread was not significantly lower in calories than other breads. Ocean Spray had to state in corrective ads that its cranberry juice did not contain more vitamins and minerals than tomato or orange juice. A corrective advertisement from Listerine is reproduced as Figure 5.4.

FIGURE 5.4

An Example of Corrective Advertising

Although the company did not think its original commercial was misleading, the FTC required it to specify that Listerine could not cure colds or sore throats.

Source: Warner–Lambert Company.

Uncertainty still exists as to whether the FTC actually has the power to force corrective advertising actions on unwilling advertisers. Corrective advertising has, in almost all cases, been part of consent orders, and only one case was appealed. That case, for Warner-Lambert's Listerine, argued on appeal that the FTC did not have the power to order Warner-Lambert to spend $10 million over a two-year period stating that "Listerine will not help prevent colds or lessen their severity." The Court of Appeals did not accept Warner-Lambert's argument, and the Supreme Court declined to hear the case, leaving the legal precedent tied to that single type of case in that single appellate jurisdiction. Today, it is unknown if the high court would agree that the FTC has the power to force such orders on unwilling advertisers.

Regardless of the technical legal status of corrective advertising, for several years advertisers have tacitly accepted it as established under powers to require affirmative disclosures. Thus, while the actual legal power may be in question, many advertisers have acknowledged and abided by the remedy of corrective advertising.

Advertising Substantiation

The problem with the case-by-case remedies provided by consent decrees and cease and desist orders, of which corrective advertising is a part, is that they work after the fact. Questionable ad claims can be made for many years before regulatory action is taken. Using the power of trade regulation rules, the FTC has tried on occasion to set industry-wide standards to head off potential problems before they occur. The most notable of the trade regulation rules, the Advertising Substantiation Program initiated in 1971, requires that advertisers in product categories involving health and safety (for example, tires, cosmetics, or drugs) have on hand before the start of advertising a "reasonable basis" for making the claims. The substantiation must be placed on file at the FTC where any consumer group or competitor could review it. [22]

The logic for the substantiation program is quite simple: the advertiser is in the best position to ascertain claim accuracy and, desiring to promote the product, should make certain that it delivers what is promised. Up until 1984, if a complaint was filed against an advertiser for inadequate substantiation, the advertiser's defense could only use substantiation tests and data compiled before the start of the advertising campaign.

James Miller III, President Reagan's first appointee as FTC chair, expressed doubts about the substantiation program at his Senate confirmation hearings, stating his belief that it discouraged advertisers from making additional claims. To his surprise, numerous business groups very strongly supported the program. With some procedural changes, the substantiation program was reaffirmed and the procedures for enforcement streamlined in 1984. A significant change is that advertisers are now allowed to provide substantiation data that are collected after the start of the commission's inquiry. An advertiser can now make claims based on simple confidence they believe are probably true, but not be forced to provide supporting data on product tests until it is requested by the commission.

One study has examined a sample of magazine ads for two products under the program—ads that appeared before the program began and others several years after the program was in place. Many advertisers avoided the Advertising Substantiation Program requirements by making vague claims that would not require data support (they said nothing of substance). Those that did make substantive claims, however, tended to provide greater and clearer statements, resulting in consumers provided with better information overall. [23]

Children: A Special Market Segment

For the past two decades, the FTC has been especially concerned about deception and unfairness in television advertising to children. Children are a special segment of the population because of their lack of consumer experience and undeveloped cognitive abilities. [24] In 1978, the FTC considered a controversial rule banning television advertising to the youngest children (under eight years of age) and a ban on ads for sugared products to children. After extensive hearings in which volumes of research evidence were presented, the ban proposal was dropped. An interesting side effect of the FTC's decision is that research on the effects of TV advertising on children dropped off in the 1980s, probably because it seemed likely that any findings would not have much influence on future commission decisions.

State and Municipal Regulation

Many states have enacted laws regulating lotteries, cosmetics, securities, **bait-and-switch advertising**, and advertising by special groups, such as pharmacists and lawyers. Enforcement of the laws is hampered by limited personnel and operating budgets of most state enforcement agencies.

When the FTC was bringing fewer cases under the deregulatory mood of the 1980s, state attorneys general gradually increased their involvement by regulating potential consumer harms from national advertising. Toward the end of the decade, involvement was increasing at a dramatic rate: individual states aggressively pursued national advertising campaigns; ad hoc groups of states pursued a variety of claims involving the environment and nutritional claims. In 1989, acting through the National Association of Attorneys General (NAAG), all states collectively adopted guidelines to regulate airline and car rental advertising.

Most state actions have resulted in voluntary agreements between the states and the advertisers, with the advertisers agreeing to stop the challenged campaign and to pay the state's costs in pursuing the case. In some instances, the litigation continues.

Supposedly, this increased interest on the part of states is to fill a vacuum left by FTC inactivity. However, with the divergent agendas of the federal and state regulators, there are currently some turf wars over which body has the preeminent right to regulate interstate advertising. Regardless of the ensuing procedural struggles, state activity is expected to increase in the future and will be a growing factor in planning concerns for advertisers.[25]

Some municipal authorities have moved into the area of advertising control. Large cities, notably New York, have a commissioner of consumer affairs who is responsible for protecting the public against deceptive trade practices. Other cities have passed ordinances that regulate, among other things, the design, placement, and volume of outdoor advertising.

Self-Regulation by the Advertising Industry

The business sector has long exerted control over its own advertising, a control motivated by (1) fear of more stringent governmental regulations; (2) an interest in enhancing advertising effectiveness by discouraging misleading and deceptive practices; and, in some instances, (3) a general concern for public welfare. These self-regulatory activities have been praised by those who believe that advertising has a responsibility to clean its own house. Others have raised questions about advertising's ability to regulate itself: Does self-regulation conflict with the individual rights of each advertiser? Does it encourage frivolous complaints? Can advertisers be truly objective in regulating themselves without government looking over their shoulders? Does it violate antitrust laws?

In spite of the skepticism, self-regulation has proven to be an important and influential form of advertising control. Today, self-regulatory control is exercised by advertisers, agencies, trade associations, and advertising media, working alone or as part of some industry group such as the National Advertising Review Board. Self-regulatory and governmental mechanisms sometimes complement each other, but some aspects of self-regulation make it different from government control:

- Self-regulation is quicker, cheaper, and more flexible than government regulation.
- Self-regulation is based on voluntary compliance and industry cooperation; it is not imposed by law.
- Self-regulation often focuses on standards, such as taste, industry welfare, and other interests that are beyond legal standards.
- Self-regulation reduces adverse publicity, thereby promoting industry credibility and enhancing advertising effectiveness.[26]

The NAD/NARB

The advertising industry's most ambitious effort at self-regulation is a two-level system: the National Advertising Division (NAD) of the nationwide Council of Better Business Bureaus and the **National Advertising Review Board (NARB).** The NAD is operated by a permanent professional staff, whereas the NARB consists of 50 appointed members—30 advertisers, 10 agency people, and 10 public members. The NAD/NARB began operations in 1971 to ward off the increasingly strong programs of the FTC.

Complaints from consumers, competitors, and the local **Better Business Bureaus** first go to the Council of Better Business Bureau's National Advertising Division. The NAD then asks the advertiser for substantiation of the claims in question. The advertiser may withdraw the advertising, modify it, or attempt to show the NAD that the claims are substantiated. If the NAD concludes that the advertiser-supplied substantiation does not support the claims, the advertiser may then withdraw the advertising, modify it, or appeal to a full National Advertising Review Board panel.[27]

An appeal is considered by a five-member panel of three advertisers, one agency person, and one public representative. If the panel upholds the NAD staff decision, the advertiser is again asked to withdraw or change the advertising in question. If an advertiser ever does refuse to accept the NARB's decision, two steps could be taken: the NARB would publicly identify the advertiser, the complaint, and the panel's findings; and the case would be referred to the appropriate government agency, in most cases the FTC. Since no specific penalty is imposed, the system avoids the danger of antitrust violations.

The self-regulation procedure of the National Advertising Division and the National Advertising Review Board is summarized in Figure 5.5. As a regulator, the NAD/NARB has been a very efficient and active body. Although a few firms have decided to ignore lower level NAD recommendations, no advertiser has ever failed to go along with a final NARB panel decision, and few advertisers have decided against participating in an NAD inquiry. In fact, cooperation has been so high that only 59 full NARB panels met from when the NAD was formed in 1971 through mid-1992 to handle appeals from several thousand NAD decisions. One advertisement that was cited as misleading but later cleared after minor changes is shown in Figure 5.6.

Advertiser cooperation is essential, because the NAD/NARB's only real power is the business' fear of the FTC and other government regulations. Advertisers recognize that an FTC complaint would certainly be more lengthy to resolve, more costly, and would potentially entail a burden on future advertising claims.

Guidelines and parameters of NAD/NARB decisions are outlined in Table 5.2. The NAD/NARB has focused on questions of deception and not taste, style, or stereotyping. However, the NAD/NARB has made special efforts to look beyond deceptive advertising issues and study some of the more important areas of regulation. Consultative panels have been organized for such subjects as product safety, women in advertising, and comparative advertising. A special Children's Advertising Unit has been organized.

FIGURE 5.5

The Self-Regulation Procedure of the National Advertising Division and the National Advertising Review Board

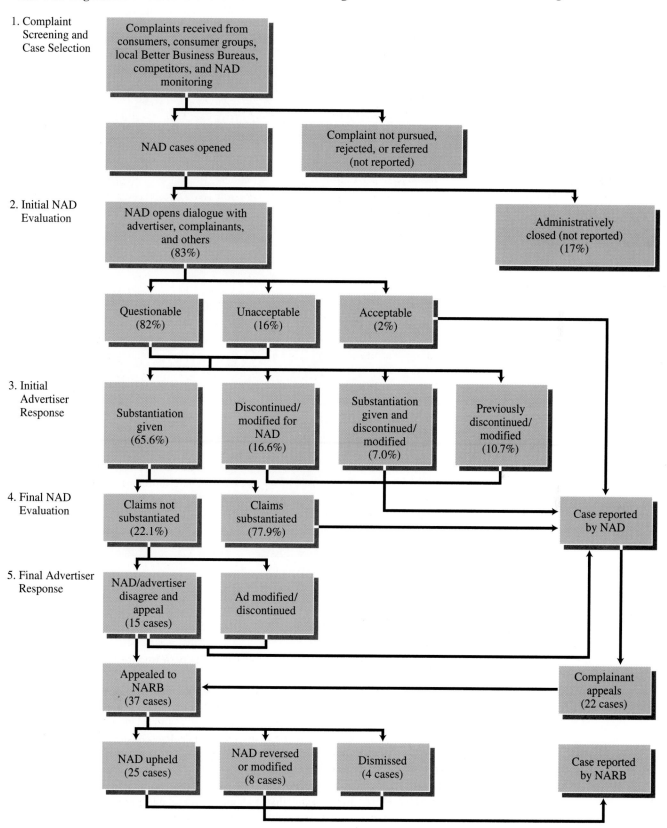

1. Complaint Screening and Case Selection

Complaints received from consumers, consumer groups, local Better Business Bureaus, competitors, and NAD monitoring

NAD cases opened

Complaint not pursued, rejected, or referred (not reported)

2. Initial NAD Evaluation

NAD opens dialogue with advertiser, complainants, and others (83%)

Administratively closed (not reported) (17%)

Questionable (82%)

Unacceptable (16%)

Acceptable (2%)

3. Initial Advertiser Response

Substantiation given (65.6%)

Discontinued/ modified for NAD (16.6%)

Substantiation given and discontinued/ modified (7.0%)

Previously discontinued/ modified (10.7%)

4. Final NAD Evaluation

Claims not substantiated (22.1%)

Claims substantiated (77.9%)

Case reported by NAD

5. Final Advertiser Response

NAD/advertiser disagree and appeal (15 cases)

Ad modified/ discontinued

Appealed to NARB (37 cases)

Complainant appeals (22 cases)

NAD upheld (25 cases)

NAD reversed or modified (8 cases)

Dismissed (4 cases)

Case reported by NARB

Source: Reprinted with permission from the *Journal of Advertising* 13, no. 2 (1985): 64.

FIGURE 5.6

**Advertisement Cited as Misleading by the NAD/NARB
but Later Cleared after Minor Changes**

Source: Courtesy of Dunlop Sports Company.

A comprehensive assessment of NAD/NARD performance has concluded that:

1. The NAD/NARB is not and never really was intended to be a clearinghouse for large numbers of consumer advertising complaints. It has a small staff and a small budget.
2. It is inner directed and industry directed rather than consumer directed. Few consumers are even aware of its existence.
3. It seems to be avoiding rather than generating controversy.
4. It uses considerable amounts of judgment in selecting and evaluating cases. Although its charter states that it should develop standards, it decided that an exhaustive code would be impractical, needlessly restrictive, and self-defeating.[28]

TABLE 5.2

Guidelines and Parameters of NAD/NARB Decisions

Problem Area	Guiding Panel Decisions	Guidelines and Parameters Set
Standard of truth and accuracy	Krackel, Fifth Avenue, Ultra Ban 5000, Sugar Association, Hardee's, Schick, Fram, Alpo*	−standard not exclusively the "literalness" of the ad −broad and flexible understanding of concept of truth and accuracy −impression more important than intent −perceived point of view of reader/viewer in target audience −FTC approval of copy not an adequate defense
Proportion of audience deceived	Bold, Fram, Alpo, National Car Rental	−no clear guidelines; panels contradictory
Dangling comparatives	Bold, Beneficial Finance, Spalding, Acushnet	−no clear guidelines; panel findings contradictory −panels have recommended that such comparisons be avoided
Problems of semantics and misuse of words	Chuck Wagon, Hardee's, Carte Blanche, Bethlehem Steel, Zenith, National Car Rental	−problems often particular to each case −misuse and imprecise use of words deemed misleading
Puffery	General Motors, Krackel, Fifth Avenue, Fram, Chicken of the Sea	−expansive statements allowed if not taken seriously by reader/viewer −expansive statements allowed if not an integral or active selling point −exaggeration deemed misleading if used in area subject to measurement −consumer "leveling" of exaggeration not an adequate defense
Omission of relevant information	Volkswagen, Alpo	−ad deemed misleading through omission of relevant information
Testimonials	American Oil	−not misleading to use celebrities as spokespersons or presenters −no cases involving celebrity claiming use or expertise
Misuse of research and survey data	Nytol, Schick, Carte Blanche*	−research data must be adequate to support ad claims −adequacy of research design behind data also a factor −research data presented out of context deemed misleading
Comparative advertising	Schick, Carte Blanche, Remington, No-Nonsense, Behold, Ban Roll-On, plus Consultive Panel*	−panels favor comparative advertising with certain qualifications −user must have clear and conclusive proof of superiority −user must not imply overall superiority on basis of superiority of single product feature −claims must be provable under conditions of general use −use comparable grades of competitors' products −demonstrations to be fair and benefits not exaggerated

Source: Eric J. Zanot, "A Review of Eight Years of NARB Casework: Guidelines and Parameters of Deceptive Advertising," *Journal of Advertising* 9 (No. 4, 1980): 25. Reprinted with permission.

* A number of other panel decisions have implicitly involved this area.

One of the oldest forms of self-regulation is media clearance. No U.S. mass media vehicle—TV station, magazine, radio station, newspaper, or outdoor company—has to accept advertising it does not wish to carry. (The sole exception is political radio or television ads placed by candidates.) The media clearance process involves the prescreening of ads to determine acceptability. It is carried out at two levels: by media associations and by individual media vehicles.

Media Associations

At one time, standards set by various media organizations were seen as an important factor in consumer protection. In recent years, however, media association codes have become a minor, or even irrelevant, part of advertising regulation. They do, however, give a basis for understanding core perspectives of various vehicles. Many managers assert they still follow now-defunct code guidelines.

The two best examples of media codes that have influenced business practices are the Comic (Book) Code Authority and the radio and television codes administered by the National Association of Broadcasters.

Comic (Book) Code Authority   In the mid-1950s, public concern of potential harm to children by comic books engendered congressional hearings that threatened possible government suppression of the medium. In response, comic book companies agreed to abide by a code of good practice for all aspects of their publications, including advertising. Each book was submitted to the Comics Code Authority and, if approved, would be permitted to carry the seal of good practice on the cover. The distributors agreed that they would not carry issues that did not have the seal.

Long after the focus of public attention had drifted away from comics in favor of the more intrusive television medium, nonadvertising materials in the May 1971 issue of *The Amazing Spider-Man* failed to meet the Code Authority's requirements. Despite the absence of the seal (and since it was the best-selling title from the company that published the majority of the most popular comic magazines at that time), it was still carried by distributors who feared repercussions on other money-making titles.

The seal has since become irrelevant for distribution; many comic books found on store racks today are not even submitted to the authority, although some comic book publishers still proudly point to the code as evidence of strong and effective consumer protection. In fact, many comic book readers are adults and many publications are beyond the understanding of young children. While comic book fans still criticize the restrictions, they feel the presence of the code diffuses any possible additional regulatory threats. Today, the code exists merely as a cautionary note for those publishers whose products are aimed at children.[29]

National Association of Broadcasters   Until 1982, the National Association of Broadcasters' Radio Code and Television Code were major influences on broadcast advertising practices. The code prohibited the advertising of certain products (such as hard liquor) and presentation approaches that were in bad taste (for example, using live models in underwear commericials). Less than two-thirds of all TV and radio stations followed the voluntary codes, but they were the basis for advertising acceptance decisions at all three major networks and the larger radio and TV stations. In total, code-abiding broadcasters accounted for nearly 80 percent of the viewing and listening audiences. An advertiser wishing to reach broadcast audiences, faced with the choice of abiding by the NAB codes or incurring the expense and possible public relations headaches of making sets of ads for both code and noncode stations, generally produced code-sanctioned ads.

However, the U.S. Justice Department sued the NAB under the antitrust laws, claiming that the code sections recommending limits on the number of commercials per hour artificially increased demand for time, limited its supply, and thus raised its price. When the U.S. District Court for the District of Columbia indicated initial agreement in 1982, the NAB suspended all code activities. This included reviewing commercials for questions of taste and claim substantiation that were not part of the original complaint.

Media Vehicle Acceptance

Media association codes still tend to have some influence on advertising. The NAB code guidelines, for example, have been found to affect individual station and network clearance procedures,[30] although claims of adherence probably exceed actual practice. American Advertising Federation statements and U.S. Postal Service Guidelines have the capacity to indirectly influence magazine clearance, though their actual impact would appear minimal.[31] On the whole, however, the management of each media vehicle—broadcast station, magazine, newspaper, or network—is responsible for setting and implementing clearance guidelines.

Television   When the NAB dropped the Code Authority and its procedures, the three major TV networks immediately revised their clearance procedures and incorporated many of the NAB standards.[32] There were changes, however. For example, underwear commercials now feature live models and some perfume and cologne spots border on being pornographic. Today, network guidelines are the industry standard, carrying an influence akin to that previously exerted by the NAB and influencing both individual broadcasters and cable operators.[33]

Unfortunately, in 1988 all three networks made extensive cuts in their clearance departments. Just what impact the cuts have had on actual advertising acceptance decisions remains uncertain, but the cuts alone were seen as bad for the public image of TV self-regulation and have been repeatedly criticized in the advertising and broadcasting trade press.[34] As revealed in the accompanying Ad Insight, one network, ABC, has proposed once again to relax its advertising guidelines even further.

Newspapers and Magazines   Although newspapers and magazines have never established media association codes of advertising standards, individual publishers exercise vehicle clearance policies.

Many newspapers, in fact, have become famous for their refusal to accept questionable advertising. *The New York Times*, for example, for more than 50 years has had a strict set of standards administered by its own Advertising Acceptability Department. Both *The Chicago Tribune* and *The Detroit News* have a board that reviews all advertising.

A recent survey of newspaper clearance practices asked publishers to identify the single most common reason for rejecting advertising. For most newspaper respondents, this was "misleading advertising," with the majority of publications concerned with protecting their readers from potentially deceptive advertising.[35]

Among the most stringent magazine clearance guidelines are those applied by *Boy's Life* and *Modern Maturity*. *Modern Maturity* expressly excludes ads that lump older persons into one category—especially ads characterizing the elderly as sick, feeble, infirm, deaf, or confused. The *Boy's Life* clearance document runs more than 25 pages and prohibits firearms, tobacco, and alcohol ads. It discusses or limits ads for medical products, games, jewelry, movies ("G" ratings only), boats, LP gas, and taxidermy, to name a few.[36]

Most magazines have a clearance-acceptance policy of some type, but their guidelines tend to be unwritten, informal, and implemented on a case-by-case basis. In one research study, fewer than a third of the magazines surveyed had a formal written policy and only a fraction of those had a detailed statement of acceptable products and ad formats.[37]

ABC Seeks to Relax Advertising Guidelines

The ABC television network wants to relax its rules of what advertisers can put in commercials, shelving some decades-old prohibitions like those that prevented actors from posing as doctors to pitch products.

ABC also is proposing to change the procedure that disgruntled advertisers must follow when they want to challenge competitors' comparative claims.

The revisions, which have been in circulation for a month for comment from the ad industry, come against a background of shrunken ad revenue for the Big Three networks because of the recession and increased competition for viewers from cable and syndicated television.

Advertisers whose commercials have been rejected by the networks often have been able to find an audience for them on local TV stations or cable networks.

But ABC said that the proposed changes weren't motivated by hopes for attracting more ad revenues to the network.

Harvey Dzodin, who heads the commercial clearance division at ABC, said the new guidelines would replace outdated rules. He said advertisers generally must provide far more documentation than they once did for their ad claims, and viewers have grown more sophisticated about viewing commercials.

He said most of the proposed changes simply codify exceptions that the network has been making informally in the old rules for months.

The old rules, for instance, generally prohibited use of "before" and "after" photos in diet plan commercials. But Dzodin said ABC has allowed such shots in commercials for Ultra SlimFast featuring dieter Tom Lasorda, the baseball manager, and the new guidelines would explicitly permit it if documentation is provided.

Another proposed rule change would allow beer commercials in which someone can be heard drinking beer off camera. Dzodin said the network had allowed that in a recent ad featuring Australian actor Paul Hogan for Foster's. The network's prohibition of on-camera beer drinking would remain in force.

But other changes such as the doctor endorsement proposal would reverse rules first adopted as long ago as the 1950s.

The so-called "white-coat" prohibition against having doctors or actors posing as doctors or other medical pro-

fessionals endorse products in commercials was put in place to head off wild unsubstantiated health claims.

But Dzodin said the level of documentation now required by both the networks and the government and a more savvy viewing audience has rendered that prohibition obsolete.

Richard Pollet, general counsel for J. Walter Thompson USA, which creates ads for the pain reliever Nuprin, said greater government regulation of ads for medicine has reduced chances for misleading commercial claims.

"Clearly a loosening was warranted in that kind of area," he said. "The net that was cast was too wide." Other proposed changes from ABC that Dzodin said simply codified current practices included:

- Allowing celebrities to pitch products used outside their professions in children's ads, such as allowing a basketball star to endorse video games.
- Permitting characters to take pills on camera in certain instances.
- Eliminating a requirement for a disclaimer on ads for fortune-telling or astrological services provided that no claim is made that the predictions have any scientific base.

ABC also proposed changes in the procedure for advertising challenges. The network previously investigated such claims itself but proposes now to investigate only after the advertiser and the challenger try to work out the differences themselves.

Pollet said the new procedure would waste time, as an advertiser could blunt a challenge by either being slow or ambiguous in replying to a complaint.

"By the time you go back and forth, the spot that could do some damage has been on the air for a couple of weeks," he said.

He said the proposal also could encourage litigation between the advertiser and challenger, and he said he hoped the change would be dropped.

Dzodin said the new challenge procedure has generated the most debate of all the proposed changes. But he said the proposals aren't "etched in stone" and that the network will reexamine the challenge proposal.

Source: Skip Wollenberg, *Marketing News*, (October 14, 1991):6.

For most magazines, the publisher decides and applies guidelines for ad acceptance, although a few magazines have a special advertising acceptance committee. As shown in Figure 5.7, the publisher or another clearance-responsible officer tends to focus on either the product advertised or the ad's presentation style. Clearance decisions seem to turn on three basic concerns: (1) audience interests, what readers will like (dislike) or what might harm them; (2) the magazine's image, a desire to maintain a certain editorial image; and (3) the publisher's or clearance officer's personal philosophy of morality or taste. The six cells in the Figure 5.7 matrix represent clearance issues:

- *Audience-presentation* concerns are about content inappropriate for the magazine's readers.
- *Image-presentation* concerns aim to maintain a certain specific appearance throughout the magazine.
- *Publisher-presentation* concerns are directed to styles, appeals, or portrayals that the publisher or clearance officer finds offensive.
- *Product-audience* concerns deal with potentially fraudulent or misleading ads.
- *Product-image* concerns are recognition that ad content reflects the overall image of the magazine.
- *Product-publisher* concerns represent idiosyncratic reactions to products advertised, such as alcohol and tobacco products.

Interestingly, some magazines have a policy of accepting all advertising, based on First Amendment considerations. An advertiser might be discouraged from placing an ad, but would not be refused unless there were legal problems involved, such as potential mail fraud.[38]

Direct Mail   Direct mail is self-policed by the Direct Mail Marketing Association (DMMA). Control is exercised by the DMMA through its Guidelines of Ethical Business Practices, which specifies how products are to be advertised. Compliance with guidelines is maintained by the threat of expulsion from the association.

Outdoor Advertising   Self-regulation of outdoor advertising occurs primarily through the Outdoor Advertising Association of America (OAAA), whose members control more than 85 percent of all standardized poster and painted billboard structures. Like other media associations, the OAAA had adopted a code of acceptable

---

FIGURE 5.7

An Analysis of Magazine Advertising Clearance Issues

		Source of Concern		
		Audience	**Image**	**Publisher**
Object of Concern	**Presentation Style**	Avoidance of Offensive Material	Standards of Magazine Image	Personal Ideology
	Product	Consumer Protection	Consistency of Image	Ban on Specific Products

Source: Herbert J. Rotfeld and Patrick R. Parsons, "Self-Regulation and Magazine Advertising," *Journal of Advertising* 18 (Winter 1989): 33–40.

practices. The association is particularly concerned with such problems as zoning, design, placement, and the construction and maintenance of billboards, not advertising content.

Individual Advertisers and Agencies

Advertising agencies, as well as their clients, are legally responsible for deceptive and fraudulent ad claims. Agencies exercise control over the advertising they produce by clearing ads with internal monitoring mechanisms—a legal staff or outside legal counsel. Most large advertisers also review their ads on a case-by-case basis. For example, Procter & Gamble has its copy section and legal section review all facts about a product's performance. The company works with its agencies to develop accurate copy. Lever Brothers follows a similar procedure. At General Foods, all claims must be approved by an advertising policy committee.

Advertising Associations

Acting as groups, advertisers and agencies also exert control over advertising. Among the many national and local advertising associations, the three most prominent are the American Advertising Federation (AAF), the American Association of Advertising Agencies (AAAA), and the Association of National Advertisers (ANA). All three organizations were involved with the founding of the NAD/NARB discussed earlier, as well as have their own codes of ethics and good practices.

The AAF is a federation of advertisers, agencies, media, and local advertising clubs in the United States and Canada. Because of its local ad club affiliations, the association takes an active role in influencing local advertising practices. In 1984, the AAF approved the advertising code in Figure 5.8. The code reflects the AAF's concern for truth in advertising and for compliance with laws.

A survey of professionals at various levels of advertising organizations who were asked about their ethical practices and the AAF principles found that:

1. Advertising agency executives perceive their own agency's advertising to substantially and consistently conform to the eight AAF principles.
2. Advertising agency executives perceive the advertising industry as a whole to be significantly less in conformity with AAF principles and, hence, less ethical.
3. At agencies where top management actively promotes high ethical standards, conformity with the AAF principles increases.

The authors of the survey concluded that since professionals perceive the industry to have lower standards than their own agencies, much more than the development of ethical codes is need to deter unethical behavior.[39]

The AAAA exercises control through its ability to refuse membership to agencies not considered ethically qualified. Through its Standard of Practice and its Creative Code, the association requires that member agencies not engage in such practices as "false and misleading statements, improper testimonials, or statements or pictures offensive to public decency." The code is reproduced in Figure 5.9.

The ANA, an association of large national advertisers, operates a committee on the Improvement of Advertising Content. The committee is run in conjunction with AAAA and focuses on the objectionable depiction of taste and opinion in ads, not on false and deceptive advertising.

Trade Associations

Self-regulation by trade associations involves agreement by companies in the same industry to abide by certain standards of advertising practice. For example, the Toy Manufacturers Association, the Motion Picture Association of America (MPAA), the U.S. Brewers Association, the Wine Institute, and the Pharmaceutical Manufacturers Association all have published advertising codes. Many trade association codes are

FIGURE 5.8

Advertising Principles Adopted by the American Advertising Federation for Enforcement by Its Members

Advertising Principles of American Business

1. **Truth**—advertising shall reveal the truth, and shall reveal significant facts, the omission of which would mislead the public.
2. **Substantiation**—advertising claims shall be substantiated by evidence in possession of the advertiser and the advertising agency prior to making such claims.
3. **Comparisons**—advertising shall refrain from making false, misleading, or unsubstantiated statements or claims about a competitor or his products or services.
4. **Bait Advertising**—advertising shall not offer products or services for sale unless such offer constitutes a bona fide effort to sell the advertised products or services and is not a device to switch consumers to other goods or services, usually higher priced.
5. **Guarantees and Warranties**—advertising of guarantees and warranties shall be explicit, with sufficient information to apprise consumers of their principal terms and limitations or, when space or time restrictions preclude such disclosures, the advertisement shall clearly reveal where the full text of the guarantee or warranty can be examined before purchase.
6. **Price Claims**—advertising shall avoid price claims which are false or misleading, or savings claims which do not offer provable savings.
7. **Testimonials**—advertising containing testimonials shall be limited to those of competent witnesses who are reflecting a real and honest opinion or experience.
8. **Taste and Decency**—advertising shall be free of statements, illustrations, or implications which are offensive to good taste or public decency.

Source: Courtesy of the American Advertising Federation, 1984.

strongly influenced by the FTC. The commission, after a conference with industry representatives, will issue Federal Practice Rules for specific industries and also provide restatements of technical regulations in lay language.

Some trade association codes go beyond federal or state requirements. The Distilled Spirits Association prohibits broadcast liquor advertising, ads in publications with Sunday datelines, and outdoor ads near military bases. The Motion Picture Association mandates that commercials for movies be prescreened to determine whether they comply with the MPAA's rating system (G, PG, PG–13, R, NC–17, and X).

However, not all trade associations are active in self-regulation. One study of 446 trade associations found that self-regulation of advertising was carried out by only 25 percent of the associations.[40] Even those that are active face the antitrust danger, as discovered by the National Association of Broadcasters when charged with antitrust violations in 1982.

The Creative Code of the American Association of Advertising Agencies

CREATIVE CODE

American Association of Advertising Agencies

The members of the American Association of Advertising Agencies recognize:

1. That advertising bears a dual responsibility in the American economic system and way of life.

To the public it is a primary way of knowing about the goods and services which are the products of American free enterprise, goods and services which can be freely chosen to suit the desires and needs of the individual. The public is entitled to expect that advertising will be reliable in content and honest in presentation.

To the advertiser it is a primary way of persuading people to buy his goods or services, within the framework of a highly competitive economic system. He is entitled to regard advertising as a dynamic means of building his business and his profits.

2. That advertising enjoys a particularly intimate relationship to the American family. It enters the home as an integral part of television and radio programs, to speak to the individual and often to the entire family. It shares the pages of favorite newspapers and magazines. It presents itself to travelers and to readers of the daily mails. In all these forms, it bears a special responsibility to respect the tastes and self-interest of the public.

3. That advertising is directed to sizable groups or to the public at large, which is made up of many interests and many tastes. As is the case with all public enterprises, ranging from sports to education and even to religion, it is almost impossible to speak without finding someone in disagreement. Nonetheless, advertising people recognize their obligation to operate within the traditional American limitations: to serve the interests of the majority and to respect the rights of the minority.

Therefore we, the members of the American Association of Advertising Agencies, in addition to supporting and obeying the laws and legal regulations pertaining to advertising, undertake to extend and broaden the application of high ethical standards. Specifically, we will not knowingly produce advertising which contains:

a. False or misleading statements or exaggerations, visual or verbal.

b. Testimonials which do not reflect the real choice of a competent witness.

c. Price claims which are misleading.

d. Comparisons which unfairly disparage a competitive product or service.

e. Claims insufficiently supported, or which distort the true meaning or practicable application of statements made by professional or scientific authority.

f. Statements, suggestions or pictures offensive to public decency.

We recognize that there are areas which are subject to honestly different interpretations and judgment. Taste is subjective and may even vary from time to time as well as from individual to individual. Frequency of seeing or hearing advertising messages will necessarily vary greatly from person to person.

However, we agree not to recommend to an advertiser and to discourage the use of advertising which is in poor or questionable taste or which is deliberately irritating through content, presentation or excessive repetition.

Clear and willful violations of this Code shall be referred to the Board of Directors of the American Association of Advertising Agencies for appropriate action, including possible annulment of membership as provided in Article IV, Section 5, of the Constitution and By-Laws.

Conscientious adherence to the letter and the spirit of this Code will strengthen advertising and the free enterprise system of which it is part.   *Adopted April 26, 1962*

Endorsed by

Advertising Association of the West, Advertising Federation of America, Agricultural Publishers Association, Associated Business Publications, Association of Industrial Advertisers, Association of National Advertisers, Magazine Publishers Association, National Business Publications, Newspaper Advertising Executives Association, Radio Code Review Board (National Association of Broadcasters), Station Representatives Association, TV Code Review Board (NAB)

Source: Courtesy of the American Association of Advertising Agencies.

The Advertising Press

Public opinion about questionable advertising practices is influenced by the press. In addition to stories that often appear in national and local news media, the advertising industry has a vigorous trade press of its own, a press that is not afraid to spotlight excesses in the business. *Advertising Age*, like its predecessor *Printers' Ink*, has waged a consistent battle for more truthful and tasteful advertising. By publicizing excesses, the press exerts indirect pressure for advertisers to comply with governmental and self-regulatory rules and guidelines.

Future Trends

Advertising Under Siege: Major Issues Facing Advertising

Daniel Jaffe, the Association of National Advertisers' vice president of government relations, has identified three major regulatory threats to the advertising industry:

1. The threat that advertising will be further seen as a major new source of revenue for cash-starved governments. In 1990 and 1991, 24 ad-tax-proposals were introduced in 18 states, and a federal tax on all commercial advertising was proposed by a U.S. House task force looking for sources of public money to fund federal election campaigns.

2. The continued threat of warnings and restrictions. Once reserved for tobacco, warnings and restrictions now are proposed for alcoholic beverages, food, children's advertising, telemarketing, outdoor advertising, airlines, rental cars, and on and on and on.

3. The growing threat of environmental claim legislation and regulations. Already, six states—California, New York, Rhode Island, Indiana, New Hampshire, and Maine—have enacted environmental advertising and labeling laws, and more states are considering similar legislation. However, there are no national guidelines to counter the hodgepodge of arbitrary and conflicting laws at the state level.

These threats, according to Jaffe, will require more work, more stamina, and more resources deployed across a wider arena.

Source: Daniel L. Jaffe. "Advertising Under Siege: Significant Trends and Major Issues Facing the Industry Today." *The Advertiser* (Fall 1991): 79–81.

Summary

Advertising is one of the consumer's most important sources of market information. Yet some of this advertising-supplied information may be unfair and deceptive. To protect both consumers and competitors, control over advertising is exercised by the combined efforts of government and self-regulatory authorities.

By far the most significant and predominant force in government regulation is the Federal Trade Commission. Most state and municipal authorities are patterned after the FTC.

The FTC's main activities focus on advertising deception. The commission can stop a campaign if ads communicate—by statement, implication, or omission—claims that are at variance with the facts. The FTC is not required to prove deception, just that false information with the capacity or likelihood to deceive was communicated. Deceptive advertising is stopped by consent orders or cease and desist orders, both of which can require the dissemination of corrected market information through affirmative disclosure and corrective advertising.

Laws and administrative decisions are subject to court interpretation. As a consequence, control may be influenced by changes in law and by their administration and interpretation. A great many regulatory changes have occurred over the past three decades. The 1970s was the decade of active regulatory involvement, while the 1980s have been the decade of deregulation. So far, the 1990s have shown an interest in reviving many consumer protection programs.

Industry controls over advertising are exercised by advertisers, agencies, trade associations, and media, working independently or as part of some industry group.

Self-regulation activities have at their core the desire to avoid the involvement of governmental controls and to enhance advertising effectiveness by policing image-damaging advertisers. The upper limit of self-regulation remains the strength and power of the government, for the mere existence or threat of government intervention itself is a market force.

The most celebrated self-regulatory mechanism is the National Advertising Division/National Advertising Review Board, which represents all segments of the advertising business. One of the oldest forms of self-regulation is media clearance, which is exercised individually by media vehicles and collectively by media associations. Advertising media have the right and power to reject any ads (except broadcast spots placed by political candidates). Some media impose very stringent standards on types of ads they will accept for electronic transmission or publication.

Questions for Discussion

1. What is deception in advertising? How do most state laws on deception differ from federal law?
2. How are each of the following organizations currently involved in the "regulation" of deceptive advertising content? How are they involved with issues of offensive or obscene advertising?

> Federal Trade Commission (FTC)
> Food & Drug Administration (FDA)
> Federal Communications Commission (FCC)
> National Advertising Division (NAD)
> National Advertising Review Board (NARB)
> National Association of Broadcasters (NAB)

3. What does it mean to say that the FTC cannot be punitive in its remedies?
4. What is corrective advertising? Why do consumerists consider it such an important innovation?
5. What are the differences between an FTC cease and desist order and a consent decree in content, legal procedures, and legal force years later?
6. What is The Advertising Substantiation program? Why would such a program be desirable for advertisers? For government regulators?
7. "Self-regulation is all we really need to best influence advertising content for the consumer's benefit." Counter or defend this statement.
8. Your advertising campaign is ready for launch. After the release of the first ads, however, the NAD has contacted you with a complaint that your ads are deceptive. You reply that the claims in question are adequately substantiated, but the NAD does not accept your arguments. Outline the issues and possible strategies of what you should do next.
9. Explain the basic concepts behind the FTC's affirmative disclosure, corrective advertising, and advertising substantiation programs.
10. Explain how an individual advertiser can regulate competitor advertising.

Notes

1 J. Robert Moskin, *The Case for Advertising: Highlights of the Industry Presentation to the Federal Trade Commission* (New York: American Association of Advertising Agencies, 1973), 8.

2 Robert B. Ekelund, Jr. and David S. Saurman, *Advertising and the Market Process: A Modern Economic View* (San Francisco: Pacific Research Institute, 1988).

3 Don R. Le Duc, "Deregulation and the

Dream of Diversity," *Journal of Communication* 32 (Autumn 1982): 164–178.

4 *Elimination of Unnecessary Broadcast Regulation,* 57RR, 2d ed., 913–925, January 18, 1985.

5 Rader Hayes and Herbert J. Rotfeld, "Infomercials and Cable Network Programming," *Advances in Consumer Interest* 1 (1989): 14–22; Patrick R. Parsons and Herbert J. Rotfeld, "Infomercials and Television Station Clearance Practices," *Journal of Public Policy and Marketing* 9 (1990): 62–72.

6 Ivan L. Preston and Jef I. Richards, "The Relationship of Miscomprehension to Deceptiveness in FTC Cases," in *Advances in Consumer Research*, vol. 13, ed. Richard J. Lutz, (Provo, UT: Association for Consumer Research, 1986), 138–142; Herbert J. Rotfeld, "What Is Misleading?" in *Information Processing Research in Advertising*, ed. Richard J. Harris (Hillsdale, NJ: Erlbaum, 1983), 169–175.

7 Hayes and Rotfeld, "Infomercials and Cable Network Programming," 1989.

8 Parsons and Rotfeld, "Infomercials and Television Station Clearance Practices," 1990.

9 U.S. House of Representatives, Subcommittee on Regulation, Business Opportunities and Energy of the Committee on Small Business, *Consumer Protection and Infomercial Advertising* (Washington: U.S. Congress, 1990), 178–204.

10 Jeffrey P. Singdahlsen, "The Risk of a Chill: A Cost of Standards Governing the Regulation of False Advertising Under Section 43(2) of the Lanham Act," *Virginia Law Review* 77 (March 1991), 339–395.

11 Arthur Best, "Controlling False Advertising: A Comparative Study of Public Regulation, Self-Policing, and Private Litigation," *Georgia Law Review* 20 (Fall 1985), 1–72.

12 Sidney A. Diamond, "Copyright Notices Will Protect Your Ads against Imitation," *Advertising Age*, May 28, 1973, 38; "How Copyrighting Your Ads Can Protect against Infringement," *Advertising Age*, August 13, 1975, 29.

13 Michael Pertschuk, *Revolt against Regulation: The Rise and Pause of the Consumer Movement* (Berkeley, CA: University of California Press, 1982); "FTC Review, 1977–1984," Report to the Subcommittee on Oversight and Investigations of the Committee on Energy and Commerce, U.S. House of Representatives (Washington, DC: U.S. Government Printing Office, 1984); Louis W. Stern and Thomas L. Eovaldi, *Legal Aspects of Marketing Strategy: Antitrust and Consumer Protection Issues* (Englewood Cliffs, NJ: Prentice-Hall, Inc., 1984).

14 Herbert J. Rotfeld and Ivan L. Preston, "The Potential Impact of Research on Advertising Law," *Journal of Advertising Research* 21 (April 1981): 9–17.

15 Ivan L. Preston, "Extrinsic Evidence and Federal Trade Commission Deceptiveness Cases," *Columbia Business Law Review* 3 (1987): 633–694; Preston and Richards, "The Relationship of Miscomprehension to Deceptiveness in FTC Cases," 138–142; Rotfeld, "What Is Misleading?" 169–174.

16 Preston, "Extrinsic Evidence and Federal Trade Commission Deceptiveness Cases."

17 Ivan L. Preston, *The Great American Blow-Up: Puffery in Advertising and Selling* (Madison, WI: University of Wisconsin Press, 1976), 25–26.

18 Herbert J. Rotfeld and Leonard N. Reid, "Advertiser Supplied Message Research: Extending the Advertising Substantiation Program," *Journal of Consumer Affairs* 11 (Summer 1977): 128–134.

19 Preston, *The Great American Blow-Up*, Chapter 9.

20 Eric J. Zanot and Herbert J. Rotfeld, "A Comparison and Contrast of Clearance Procedures in Four Advertising Agencies," in *Proceedings of the American Academy of Advertising*, ed. Donald W. Jugenheimer (Lawrence, KS: American Academy of Advertising, 1983), 47–51.

21 William L. Wilkie, "Affirmative Disclosure: Perspectives on FTC Orders," *Journal of Marketing and Public Policy* 1 (1982): 95–110; "Affirmative Disclosure at the FTC: Objectives for the Remedy and Outcomes of Past Orders," *Journal of Public Policy and Marketing* 4 (1985): 91–111.

22 John S. Healy and Harold H. Kassarjian, "Advertising Substantiation and Advertiser Response: A Content Analysis of Magazine Advertisements," *Journal of Marketing* 47 (Winter 1983): 107–127.

23 Ibid., 128–129.

24 Thomas E. Barry, "A Framework for Ascertaining Deception in Children's Advertising," *Journal of Advertising* 9 (1980): 12.

25 Jef I. Richards, "FTC or NAAG: Who Will Win the Territorial Battle?," *Journal of Public Policy and Marketing* 10 (Spring 1991): 118–132.

26 J. J. Boddewyn, "Advertising Self-Regulation: Private, Government and Agent of Public Policy," *Journal of Public Policy and Marketing* 4 (1985): 131; Priscilla A. LaBarbera, "The Diffusion of Trade Association Advertising Self-Regulation," *Journal of Marketing* 47 (Winter 1983): 58–67.

27 Gary M. Armstrong and Julie L. Ozanne, "An Evaluation of NAD/NARB Purpose and Performance," *Journal of Advertising* 12 (1983): 15–26.

28 Ibid.

29 Herbert J. Rotfeld, "Media Standards for Acceptable Advertising and Potentially Desirable 'Chilling Effects' on Advertising Free Speech," *Proceedings of the 17th Annual Macromarketing Seminar*, T. A. Klein, R. W. Nasson, L. D. Dahringer, eds. Breukelen, The Netherlands: Nijenrode University, 1992: 335–352.

30 Bruce A. Linton, "Self-Regulation in Broadcasting Revisited," *Journalism Quarterly* 64 (Summer–Autumn 1987): 483–490; Lynda M. Maddox and Eric J. Zanot, "Suspension of the NAB Code and Its Effect on Regulation of Advertising," *Journalism Quarterly* 61 (Spring 1984): 125–130, 156.

31 Patrick R. Parsons, Herbert J. Rotfeld, and Todd Gray, "Magazine Publisher and Advertising Manager Standards for Acceptable Advertising," *Current Issues and Research in Advertising*, 10 (1987); 199–211.

32 Linton, "Self-Regulation in Broadcasting Revisited," 484; Maddox and Zanot, "Suspension of the NAB Code and Its Effect on Regulation of Advertising," 126; Eric J. Zanot, "Unseen But Effective Advertising Regulation: The Clearance Process," *Journal of Advertising* 4 (1985): 44–51, 59, 68.

33 Herbert J. Rotfeld, "The Power and Limitations of Media Clearance Practices and Advertising Self-Regulation," *Journal of Public Policy and Marketing* 11 (Spring 1992): 87–95.

34 Richard L. Gordon, "Networks Hit for Ad Clearance Cuts," *Advertising Age*, September 12, 1988, 6.

35 Kathleen T. Lacher and Herbert J. Rotfeld, "Reading Between the Lines: Potential Advertiser Influence on Newspaper Content Revealed in Publications' Standards For Acceptable Advertising," unpublished manuscript, 1992.

36 Herbert J. Rotfeld and Patrick R. Parsons, "Self-Regulation and Magazine Advertising," *Journal of Advertising* 18 (Winter 1989): 33–40.

37 Ibid.

38 Parsons, Rotfeld and Gray, "Magazine Publisher and Advertising Manager Standards for Acceptable Advertising," 15.

39 Lawrence B. Chonko, Shelby D. Hunt, and Roy D. Howell, "Ethics and the American Advertising Federation Principles," *International Journal of Advertising* 6 (October 1987): 3, 265–274.

40 LaBarbera, "The Diffusion of Trade Association Advertising Self-Regulation," 65–67.

Armstrong, Gary M., and Julie L. Ozanne. "An Evaluation of NAD/NARB Purpose and Performance." *Journal of Advertising* 12 (1983): 15–26.

Middleton, Kent R., and Bill F. Chamberlin. *The Law of Public Communication.* 2d ed. White Plains, NY: Longman, 1990. Chapter 7.

Preston, Ivan L. *The Great American Blow-Up: Puffery in Advertising and Selling.* Madison, WI: University of Wisconsin Press, 1976. Chapter 9.

Rotfeld, Herbert J., and Ivan L. Preston. "The Potential Impact of Research on Advertising Law." *Journal of Advertising Research* 21 (April 1981): 9–17.

Rotfeld, Herbert J. "Power and Limitations of Media Clearance Practices and Advertising Self-Regulation." *Journal of Public Policy and Marketing* 11 (Spring 1992): 87–95.

Stern, Louis W., and Thomas L. Eovaldi. *Legal Aspects of Marketing Strategy: Antitrust and Consumer Protection Issues.* Englewood Cliffs, NJ: Prentice-Hall, 1984. Chapter 7.

Zanot, Eric J. "Unseen But Effective Advertising Regulation: The Clearance Process." *Journal of Advertising* 14 (1985): 44–51, 59, 68.

Suggested *Readings*

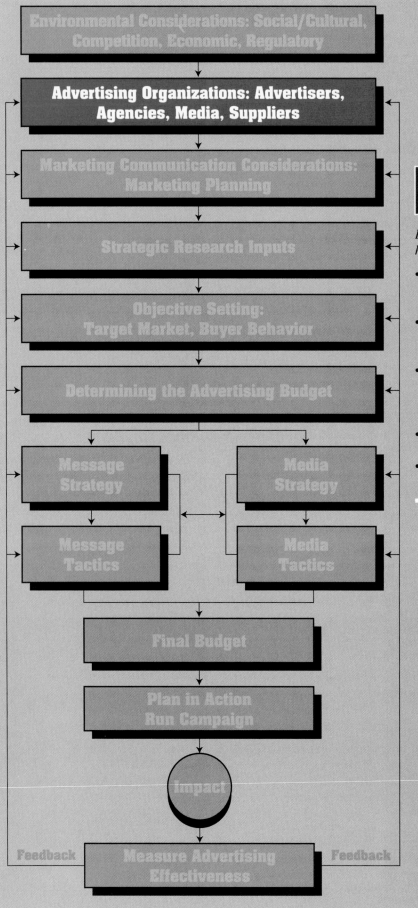

Chapter 6

Organizational Structure

CHAPTER TOPICS

ADVERTISERS
National Advertisers
Local (Retail) Advertisers
ADVERTISING AGENCIES
What Advertising Agencies Do for Their Clients
Functions of the Modern Agency
Agency Compensation
Handling Competing Accounts

MEDIA
Media Advertising Department
Media Representatives
RELATED ADVERTISING ORGANIZATIONS
Specialized Services
Production Services
Art Studios
Research Companies

In Chapter 1, we introduced you to the five interacting organizations that form the structure of the advertising business: advertisers, agencies, media, specialized services, and suppliers. The major participants in most advertising are the *advertiser* who pays the bills and whose identity appears in the ads, the *agency* that plans, creates, and places the advertising, and the *media* that deliver the ads to targeted consumers. Sometimes the agency is not used by the advertiser to create and place advertising. Instead, the advertiser may use an internal operation known as a house agency or go outside to specialized creative and media services known as creative boutiques and media buying services. More often than not, whether advertising is handled in-house or externally, suppliers such as production houses, art studios, and research companies are brought in to facilitate the advertising process.

In this chapter, we examine the organizations of advertising in greater detail. An examination of how the five organizations operate and how they are structured will help you better understand how advertising works and may also help you to decide where you might want to work in the industry.

Advertisers

Virtually every business, whether for-profit or not-for-profit, uses some form of advertising. There are two basic categories of advertisers: national advertisers and local (retail) advertisers.

National Advertisers

National advertisers—such as Procter & Gamble, General Mills, Philip Morris, and Delta Airlines—typically sell their products or services throughout the country or, in some cases, in specific regions only. Usually they spend advertising money through independent, outside advertising agencies, although some, including a few large advertisers, operate their own house agencies.

Procter & Gamble tops the list of leading advertisers in 1991, spending almost $2.3 billion. Expenditures of the top 20 companies are given in Table 6.1. Three of them—Sears, McDonald's, and Kmart—are retailers who operate or franchise their own retail stores, where they sell only their brands or their brands as well as other brand-name goods.

The Advertising Manager

The position of the advertising manager within the corporate structure varies from company to company. For example, in a small organization that does little advertising—perhaps a company producing a highly technical piece of equipment for a specialized industry—the advertising manager (if there is one at all) may report directly to the chief executive officer of the company. As an alternative, especially in a company that focuses heavily on the sales function, the advertising manager may head a department under the chief sales executive.

More typically, however, advertising is viewed as one of several marketing functions, and the advertising manager reports to a director of marketing (as shown in Figure 6.1). Under this organizational approach, the three major functions of business—production (or manufacturing), finance, and marketing—are represented at the level just below the chief executive. Advertising in turn is placed alongside other marketing functions, such as distribution, sales, marketing research, and product planning. The advertising manager typically coordinates the company's advertising with an outside advertising agency (or with a house agency, if one is used).

The specific duties of the advertising manager vary widely according to the size of the firm, the importance of its advertising, and the nature of the product. Certain duties, however, are common to most advertising managers:

TABLE 6.1

Advertising Expenditures of the Top 20 U.S. Advertisers, 1991[a]

1. Procter & Gamble Company	$2,149.0
2. Philip Morris Companies	2,045.6
3. General Motors Corporation	1,442.1
4. Sears, Roebuck & Company	1,179.4
5. PepsiCo	903.4
6. Grand Metropolitan	744.7
7. Johnson & Johnson	733.0
8. McDonald's Corporation	694.8
9. Ford Motor Company	676.6
10. Eastman Kodak Company	661.4
11. Warner-Lambert Company	656.5
12. Toyota Motor Corporation	632.2
13. AT&T Company	617.3
14. Nestlé SA	600.5
15. Unilever NV	593.7
16. Time Warner	587.5
17. Kellogg Company	577.7
18. RJR Nabisco	571.0
19. General Mills	555.6
20. Chrysler Corporation	531.1

Source: *Advertising Age,* January 4, 1993, 16.
[a] Expenditures are in millions of dollars.

FIGURE 6.1

An Organization Chart with Advertising as a Marketing Function

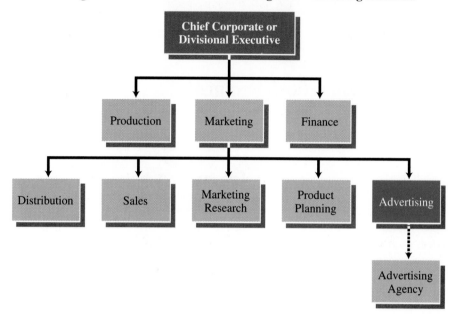

1. Planning the campaign is the manager's most important job. To do this, the manager must engage in long- and short-range planning and be knowledgeable about marketing as well as about advertising.
2. The manager supervises the execution of this plan by subordinates and the agency.
3. The manager helps select and evaluate the work of the agency. In the selection, the manager will probably have to work with the management of the company, certainly with the top marketing executives.
4. The manager informs top executives of advertising matters and advises them on related problems, which requires knowledge of all phases of marketing and communication.
5. The manager coordinates advertising and other marketing functions. The ad manager must work closely with the staff to make sure that the company's advertising stresses the most salable features of its products and that the ads appear in the media that will be most helpful to the sales personnel. The manager may help prepare portfolios for the company's salespeople and sales promotion material (point-of-purchase displays, newspaper mats, and the like) for dealers.
6. The manager must work with the production department to determine the best colors, type of packaging, and so on.
7. With the public relations department, the manager plans and executes the communication program. In institutional advertising, the ad manager will certainly need the help of the public relations people. In one large soap company, the public relations director reviews all ads (product as well as institutional), primarily to make sure that they contribute to the desired corporate image.
8. The manager coordinates the work of other departments with that of the advertising department. In a proposed contest, the ad manager checks with the legal department for possible violations of the Federal Trade Commission (FTC) regulations or of the lottery laws. The manager may also work with the accounting department to monitor media and advertising costs or to see that bills are paid.

Evaluating Agency Performance

Stephen W. Rutledge, vice president of advertising for Kraft General Foods, offers the following suggestions for conducting an evaluation of agency performance:

1. *Focus on what's important* The key question is whether advertising is contributing to business growth. Evaluate four areas: (1) overall assessment of agency's annual performance, (2) performance by key functional areas, (3) how the creative process is working, and (4) creative development priorities for the year ahead.

2. *Be objective* Evaluate how advertising is working based on clearly understood and objective, evaluative criteria, not on personality characteristics and personal preferences.

3. *Look forward as well as backward* Build on annual experience to plan for coming years, and by all means, involve the agency as a planning partner, not as a supplier.

4. *Do it in writing* A written report makes you think deeply about the agency's performance and communicate exactly what you mean. The description of the performance evaluation is the record.

Is advertising helping the business grow?

Source: Stephen W. Rutledge, "The Value of Evaluating Agency Performance," *The Advertiser*, Fall 1991, 53–56.

9. The manager works on the budget as a joint effort with the agency and other top executives of the company.
10. The manager conducts the evaluation of agency performance (see the Ad Insight entitled "Evaluating Agency Performance").

Brand and Category Management

A company that markets several brands may want to encourage the competition of these brands within the company itself. Management may feel that it can gain a larger share of the total market for a product if it maintains two or three brands instead of one. Procter & Gamble, for example, markets a number of different brands of heavy-duty laundry detergent—Bold, Cheer, Dash, Era, Oxydol, Solo, and Tide. A popular way to accomplish these objectives is to appoint a **brand manager.**

Under a brand-management arrangement, the brands usually have different advertising agencies and separate advertising budgets. Brand managers compete just as

5. *Focus the evaluation at the senior level* Agency performance deserves top management attention, and the person directly responsible for advertising planning should be responsible or at least involved.

6. *Take your own medicine* Be responsive to constructive criticism. Partnership is a two-way street and the agency's perspective and candid feedback is vital to communication.

7. *Do the evaluation early in the year* Have the evaluation done in the first or second month of the fiscal year. This allows timely feedback and sufficient time for planning.

8. *Hold interim progress checks* Monitor agency progress against objectives on a periodic basis.

The benefits of conducting an agency evaluation are:

- it provides a benchmark for measuring future progress.
- it clearly establishes expectations and priorities.
- it provides a means of tracking progress as the year unfolds.
- it helps foster and perpetuate honest and open communication.
- it lets the agency know that you think advertising is vital.

There are also things that "should not be done" when conducting an agency performance evaluation:

1. Don't let the agency know ahead of time what you're going to evaluate them on.
2. Exclude senior management.
3. Keep it subjective and don't bother with evidence to support your conclusions.
4. Don't ask for agency feedback—or listen closely to it if you get it.
5. Evaluate every dimension of the agency's operation equally.
6. Don't say what you mean. Pull your punches so the agency thinks everything is OK when it isn't.
7. Make the formal evaluation the only opportunity for dialogue about performance and relationship.
8. Tell the agency one thing and your internal management another.
9. Conduct the evaluation when you can get around to it.
10. Drag out the process so it takes a lot of time and effort for both your people and the agency.

These can "kill" a good agency evaluation, according to Rutledge.

vigorously with other brand managers in the company as they do with outside companies. The brand manager is, in effect, the marketing manager for a brand and makes most of the advertising decisions for that brand. The company's general advertising manager can then operate with a relatively small department, because it is primarily concerned with policy decisions.

Although a popular form of organization for many years, the brand management system has recently undergone changes. The major change has been to add a layer of management above brand managers in order to have more coordination of groups of product categories. As an example, the organization of Procter & Gamble's packaged soap and detergent division is initially divided into three category management groups—dishwashing, laundry, and specialty products. Each brand within a category has an advertising manager as well as a brand manager. Generally called a **category management system,** this system of organization is illustrated in Figure 6.2. The advantages are that (1) brand managers can focus more on strategy and are less involved with advertising detail; (2) advertising, because of its complexity, is handled by an expert; and (3) the company can present its products in categories to the retail trade rather than have each brand compete individually.

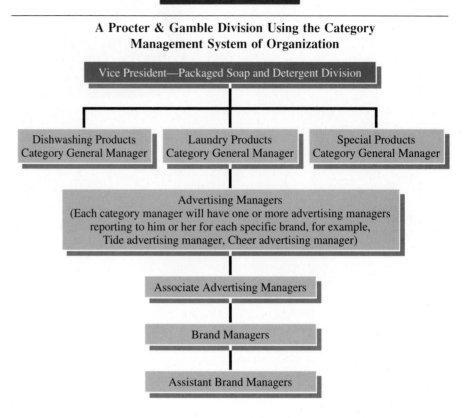

FIGURE 6.2

A Procter & Gamble Division Using the Category Management System of Organization

Vice President—Packaged Soap and Detergent Division

Dishwashing Products Category General Manager

Laundry Products Category General Manager

Special Products Category General Manager

Advertising Managers
(Each category manager will have one or more advertising managers reporting to him or her for each specific brand, for example, Tide advertising manager, Cheer advertising manager)

Associate Advertising Managers

Brand Managers

Assistant Brand Managers

The Advertiser and the Agency

One of the advertiser's most important jobs is choosing an advertising agency and then doing everything possible to maintain good relations with it. Conflicts between clients and agencies have always been a problem in the advertising business, as noted in the Ad Insight entitled "Clients Jump Ship Quickly." Selecting an agency may involve many criteria, and some companies have elaborate procedures for making such a decision. Important things to consider include the following:

1. *Compatibility*   Does the agency have a philosophy of doing business and is it compatible with your company and/or brand? This may involve the matter of product conflict.
2. *Personnel*   Who works for the agency and what is their reputation in the business? More specifically, who will be working on this particular account? What other assignments will they have? Are enough people being assigned to the account to service it properly? What is the agency's record on employee turnover?
3. *Stability*   What is the agency's record in terms of stability—specifically, its financial record, length of service for existing clients, amount of business held from year to year?
4. *Performance*   How has the agency performed for past and present clients? What are its strengths and weaknesses in terms of overall campaign planning, creative strategy, media planning and execution, research formulation, and coordinating all the elements of a marketing/communication program?
5. *Compensation*   Will the agency's compensation for working on the account be fair to it as well as to your company? How will future assignments to the agency be handled?

Clients Jump Ship Quickly: Key Is Growing Existing Accounts

Given half a chance, ad executives will wax eloquently about their loyal clients. J. Walter Thompson brags about the 90 years it has served Lever Bros, and the 70 years it has spent with Kraft, while Leo Burnett boasts of its 42-year honeymoon with Kellogg.

But as for the average client? "Loyal" is perhaps the last word that should come to mind, surprising new research suggests.

In the past five years at the 50 biggest ad agencies, a stunning 67 percent of clients have parted ways, concludes a study by Sanders Consulting Group of Richmond, Virginia.

"There's very little loyalty to agencies any more," observes R. Quigg Lawrence, the senior consultant who conducted the study. "Long-term relationships in many cases seem to have gone by the boards."

The study has already prompted criticism from ad executives. Critics point out that the research wrongly gives equal weight to all clients, from the puniest to the largest, and fails to consider new business wins. Others insist the results are exaggerated, as many of the clients deemed "lost" were in fact one-time projects or tiny start-up ventures that failed.

Still, even most ad agency executives interviewed say that, whatever its shortcomings, the study points up an urgent problem facing the ad business today. The protracted recession has made clients quick to jump ship and to blame their ad agencies for their own problems. Ad agencies have made the situation worse by trying to raid rivals' most coveted clients in a desperate bid for new business.

"The environment for clients and ad agencies has become unstable" over the past five years, says Paul Kurnit, president of Griffin Bacal. He pins only part of the blame on the economy. Other culprits, in his view: Clients' increasing reliance on promotions rather than advertising, and ad agency mergers, which made clients feel "that agencies were less dedicated and loyal to their business."

Not surprisingly, the agency that fared best of all in the study was Leo Burnett, which had a loss rate of just 24 percent, or six out of 25 clients listed in 1987. Burnett is legendary in the ad business for catering to clients, and for growing with new assignments from existing clients rather than by accumulating new clients.

Chasing after new business "isn't to get in the way of growing our existing clients' businesses—that's our No. 1 priority," declares William Lynch, the world-wide agency's president. He says Burnett's turnover rate is even lower than the study suggests; now-defunct Beatrice counted as one of the agency's losses, even though Burnett still handles former Beatrice brands Tropicana and Samsonite.

Burnett's old-fashioned approach is much-admired in the ad business, and the results of the study may prompt more agencies than ever to imitate it. "The priority always has to be growing existing business" and keeping current clients happy, says Ed Wax, Saatchi's chairman and chief executive officer. "That's your heart and soul."

Source: Joanne Lipman, "Study Shows Clients Jump Ship Quickly," *The Wall Street Journal*, May 21, 1992, B4.

Once the agency is chosen, almost all practitioners agree that the nature of the advertiser-agency relation is extremely important to the success of any advertising campaign. Some of the essential factors that serve as a basis for a strong relationship are these:

- The advertiser and the agency should operate as peers.
- The advertiser's organization and the agency team should complement each other in the performance of the advertising task.
- Both organizations must have mutual regard for their respective expertise.
- The advertiser and the agency should have mutual trust and should understand the confidentiality of the relationship.

- Both organizations should be clear as to the goals that are to be accomplished through advertising.
- The advertiser and the agency need to understand their respective views on issues of ethics and integrity, and these issues must be compatible.
- Although the relationship may endure for many years, both sides should understand the conditions that warrant a separation.

The Ad Insight entitled "Getting the Best From an Advertising Agency" offers suggestions for building a strong and productive agency-client relationship.

Use of a House Agency

A house agency, also called an "in-house" agency, exists when a company does its own advertising—in whole or in part—through a separate organization established by the advertiser. The advertising function is most frequently taken in-house for industrial products, services, and retailers. Consumer-goal firms, however, tend to rely more on full-service agencies, especially for creative concepts and production of advertising materials.[1]

Whether a company sets up a house agency, of course, depends on a host of marketing and advertising factors. Some of the key arguments for and against this approach are the following:

For

Cost Savings   House agencies typically can get media commissions and therefore may be able to perform the advertising function at less cost than if the advertiser used an outside, full-service agency.

Confidentiality   Companies that prefer to keep certain marketing and advertising information confidential may feel more comfortable working with an in-house group rather than an independent agency. Also, the house agency would then have more access to complete data for campaign planning.

Communication   Lines of communication between an advertiser and its agency can become complicated and problems can occur. The in-house group may have more direct contact with key company executives.

Coordination and Control   Some top executives feel the in-house approach functions better in terms of coordinating the advertising effort with the marketing plan and controlling advertising expenditures.

Company and Product Familiarity   As employees of the advertiser, in-house personnel have more knowledge of the company's products and its philosophy of doing business.

Against

Objectivity   Outside, independent agencies can bring objectivity to their view of advertising problems; they often represent many different kinds of clients, with varied marketing situations. In-house people may become narrow in their thinking (which could inhibit creativity) as a result of being too close to the problem.

Quality/Expertise   Although the cost to have an in-house group may be less than for an outside agency (it also could cost more), the matter of "quality" of advertising effort also has to be considered. The question hinges on who does the better job.

Specialized Personnel   In-house agencies may not have as extensive a group of highly skilled specialists as an independent agency. The company may have to hire

Getting the Best from an Advertising Agency

Getting the best from an advertising agency is the product of effective management. James D. Speros, brand management director for AT&T, offers the following step-by-step system for building a strong and productive agency-client relationship:

1. Treat your agency as a partner, not as a vendor.
2. Make certain your agency is adequately compensated for their talent and contributions; don't squeeze your agency's profit margin to the point that profitability is nearly impossible.
3. Establish expectations at the beginning of the relationship.
4. Take time to meet all of the agency people working on your business—not just account people, but traffic, production, media, creative, and research specialists.
5. Educate your agency on your business, opportunities and competitors, and its problems.
6. Let creatives experience your products first-hand, or see it being used. Experience will make the assignment tangible for them and will involve them on a personal level.
7. Establish clearly defined objectives and measurement standards prior to initiating any work.
8. Demand excellence and set high standards. Never settle for mediocrity.
9. Gain agreement on strategy prior to creative work, and put it in writing.
10. Develop a sound understanding of the lead time necessary to create and place advertising for various media.
11. Make yourself accessible.
12. Give clear and constructive feedback when reviewing agency work.
13. Provide the agency with a forum for doing its work—be completely satisfied with the work, presell it, and make sure top agency and client people are present at presentations.
14. Don't be something you are not—a media buyer or a creative director.
15. Invest in professional development—encourage formal training and development seminars.

Source: James D. Speros, "How to Get the Best from Your Advertising Agency," *The Advertiser,* Summer 1992, 34–42.

outside talent to provide many of the special services needed for the creation and production of advertising.

Working Relationship Company management may find it easier to deal with an outside company; an in-house agency is another unit that must be managed. Also, an outside agency can be discharged if the client isn't satisfied, but it can be difficult to discharge workers in a house agency when their work is found to be unsatisfactory.

Many companies that have house agencies often use them for limited and specialized purposes. For example, a company selling several brands may find it useful to have its own group handle a brand that is placed in test markets. Until management knows how a brand will be perceived by consumers, the company may not be able to assign intelligently the brand to one of its several outside agencies. Also, if an agency is compensated on a commission system, a test market—with a small dollar media outlay—may not be sufficiently profitable to handle.

Regardless of the arguments for and against house agencies, an overwhelming percentage of advertisers use independent advertising agencies and are likely to continue this pattern for some time in the future.

Local (Retail) Advertisers

Retail advertisers operate in particular markets and include such businesses as department stores, supermarkets, banks, and restaurants. Some advertisers operate in local markets only; others operate in both national and local markets. For example, Ripley's Baseball Card Shop uses local advertising to build traffic for its two Athens, Georgia, locations; Kmart uses both local and national advertising to build traffic for its national chain of stores, including the two in Athens. Both are retail advertisers because they use advertising in an effort to persuade people to buy merchandise at their particular retail outlets.

Nonstore retailers account for about 10 percent of all retail sales. They include businesses engaged in direct selling (house-to-house retailers, such as the local home-delivered newspaper), direct-response retailers (mail and telephone merchandisers, such as Land's End and L.L. Bean), and automatic merchandising (vending machines). Any of these businesses can, of course, advertise to prospects in a particular locale, although those selling products and services through telephone and mail order are the most likely users of advertising.

A look through a local newspaper will reveal the wide variety of retail stores that utilize advertising in their promotional mix. The most typical local advertisers are the following:

Appliance stores	Food stores	Shoe stores
Banks	Hardware stores	Stock brokers
Department stores	Jewelry stores	Variety stores
Drugstores	Clothing stores	Eating and drinking places
Furniture stores	Specialty shops	

Local advertisers, unlike national advertisers, do not regularly use advertising agencies. Instead, they frequently prepare their own advertising or, in the case of small retail stores, depend heavily on the media for help. This reluctance to use agencies stems from four characteristics of local advertising:

1. A heavy percentage of local advertising goes into newspapers at local rates. Because these are ordinarily lower than national rates and not commissionable, any agency that handled the account would charge a fee for its services. Many agencies have found it difficult to get stores to pay such a fee.
2. The local advertiser ordinarily operates on a day-to-day basis. Workers in an advertising department of this kind probably work today on the ad that will appear in the newspaper the day after tomorrow, or on the television commercial that may be on tonight's late news. A sudden change in merchandising policy or in the weather—or some other late development—may necessitate revisions at the last minute. A department in the store, close to buyers and merchandise managers, is in a better position to adapt quickly to such changes than is an outside organization.
3. Retail stores, unlike manufacturers, usually handle a wide variety of products. A department store may have thousands—or tens of thousands—of different items sold by the one advertiser. Although only a fraction of the store's offerings would be advertised on any one day, 10 or 20 items may appear in a single ad. How can an agency account executive (or copywriter) get to know these items well? The account executive who handles a product for a manufacturer comes to know the product and the market intimately.
4. Retailers depend heavily on manufacturers and the media for help with their advertising. A high percentage of their advertising consists of finished artwork supplied by the manufacturers of products they sell. They often have to use this art as furnished if they are to qualify for cooperative deals in which the manufacturer pays a share (usually at least 50 percent) of the cost of the advertising.

Although some local advertisers do of course use advertising agencies, most experts in the field do not foresee a major movement toward use of agencies in the near future.

The Retail Advertising Organization

Large and small stores have different types of advertising organization. In a large department store or specialty store, the advertising department is really an agency within the store and carries out a full array of advertising services.

The advertising department typically is grouped under a vice president in charge of sales promotion (see Figure 6.3). The sales promotion activity includes special events, publicity, and display, in addition to advertising. Because of the close relation of these functions, overall coordination is needed.

The advertising department is responsible for both the planning of the advertising and its execution. The planning is done by the advertising manager in concert with the store's merchandising executives. Once the plan is in place, specialists within the department execute the plan by creating the layout and artwork of an advertisement, writing the copy, and supervising production of the ad.

The advertising department mainly does print advertisements—those appearing in the local newspaper and perhaps direct-mail pieces. Many advertising departments of large stores also can handle radio and television commercials, but a number of retail advertisers call on an agency for help in broadcast campaigns.

The advertising department in a small store usually consists of only a few people. In many small establishments the store manager also serves as the advertising manager. Whether the store has a small advertising department or none at all, the manager is likely to call on certain outside sources for fairly regular help:

1. *Media* Newspapers and radio and television stations will help the manager plan the campaign, lay out the ad, and write copy. All this is normally done without charge.
2. *Manufacturers* Manufacturers of brands sold by a particular retailer will frequently supply artwork, point-of-purchase display material, films or tapes for the broadcast media, display materials, and even planning guides.
3. *Syndicated art services* Certain companies produce artwork that they sell to retailers and to newspapers. A retailer who does not want to prepare copy and layout can order advertisements from the company's proof book, which shows a wide variety of all shapes and sizes and for all types of merchandise. Most

FIGURE 6.3

The Sales Promotion Division of a Typical Department Store

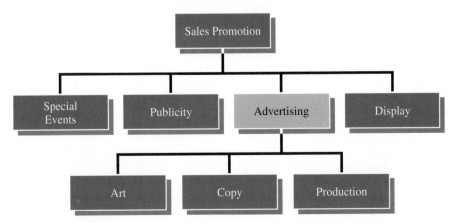

newspapers subscribe to one or more of these services, and the retailer may use the service offered by the paper.

4. *Trade associations*   Most retailers belong to at least one trade association. Many of these supply copy ideas and layouts to their members and make suggestions about how to formulate advertising plans.

A further discussion of retail advertising is presented in Chapter 20.

Advertising Agencies

When we speak of an advertising agency, we typically mean an organization that performs a wide variety of advertising functions for particular advertisers and their brands and that operates independently from the advertiser. A more accurate name for this would be a full-service advertising agency. Other types of advertising services limit their activity to one or a very few of the major functions. As mentioned earlier, for example, creative boutiques are organizations that specialize in the creative function, whereas media buying services focus on one or more aspects of the media function. The key distinction between the agency and these other two services is that the agency does not concentrate on any one advertising function, although it may agree to perform one special service, such as creative, media, or research.

TABLE 6.2

Top U.S. Cities Based on Local Billings of 500 Advertising Agencies, 1992

Rank	City	Local-Office Billings[a]	No. of Local Offices
1	New York	$25,480	147
2	Chicago	7,143	60
3	Los Angeles	4,740	52
4	Detroit	4,101	30
5	San Francisco	2,325	31
6	Dallas	1,432	18
7	Boston	1,369	20
8	Minneapolis	1,255	17
9	Atlanta	1,009	24
10	Philadelphia	1,007	21
11	St. Louis	743	11
12	Cleveland	674	11
13	Stamford, CT	589	16
14	Houston	459	12
15	Kansas City, MO	416	11
16	Washington, DC	376	9
17	Baltimore	362	7
18	Milwaukee	326	10
19	Pittsburgh	298	10
20	Seattle	295	7

Source: *Advertising Age,* April 14, 1993, 8.
[a] Dollars are in millions.

Most people think that virtually all advertising agencies are located on Madison Avenue in New York City or Michigan Avenue in Chicago. In fact, agencies are scattered throughout the United States, and most cities of any business importance can claim at least one. However, the agency business is concentrated in a few large markets and in a relatively few states. Table 6.2 lists the top 25 cities by billings, which include media expenditures for a client as well as charges for materials and services (for example, artwork and outside research).

Specific advertising agencies in the United States are listed in Tables 6.3 and 6.4, which present information on the top 20 as well as for the 20 ranked from 301 to 320. The top 20 primarily are headquartered in New York, whereas the smaller group is more scattered across the country. Income and billings of the two groups of agencies vary greatly, as do the number of people they employ.

According to the American Association of Advertising Agencies (AAAA), an agency's general purpose is to interpret to the advertiser's desired audience the advantages of a product or service. This, according to the AAAA, includes the following services:

1. A study of the client's product or service, to determine the advantages and disadvantages inherent in the product itself and its relation to the competition.
2. An analysis of present and potential markets for which the product or service is adapted.

What Advertising
Agencies Do
for Their Clients

TABLE 6.3

Gross Income and Billings of the Top 20 U.S. Advertising Agencies for 1992

Rank	Agency	Headquarters	Worldwide Gross Income	U.S. Gross Income	Worldwide Billings	U.S. Billings
1	Young & Rubicam	New York	$994.0	$431.3	$7,356.8	$3,466.2
2	McCann-Erickson Worldwide	New York	935.8	250.2	6,241.1	1,668.7
3	BBDO Worldwide	New York	835.8	334.1	6,030.4	2,564.3
4	J. Walter Thompson Co.	New York	815.4	309.4	5,690.5	2,163.4
5	Ogilvy & Mather Worldwide	New York	789.1	296.4	5,494.1	2,016.6
6	Saatchi & Saatchi Advertising	New York	783.6	366.2	5,335.5	2,503.1
7	DDB Needham Worldwide	New York	777.1	361.5	5,838.9	2,946.5
8	Lintas: Worldwide	New York	763.0	275.9	5,100.2	1,839.3
9	Foote, Cone & Belding Communications	Chicago	682.7	287.2	5,197.8	2,646.2
10	Grey Advertising	New York	673.8	285.5	4,504.5	1,904.0
11	Backer Spielvogel Bates Worldwide	New York	656.0	193.2	4,432.2	1,331.8
12	Leo Burnett Co.	Chicago	643.8	313.2	4,304.3	2,104.1
13	D'Arcy Masius Benton & Bowles	New York	558.4	274.6	4,700.7	2,597.7
14	Lowe Group	New York	248.3	72.3	1,720.2	546.9
15	Bozell	New York	231.0	174.0	1,805.0	1,425.0
16	N W Ayer	New York	175.0	94.0	1,581.5	888.1
17	TBWA Advertising	New York	158.7	48.8	1,122.2	325.6
18	CME KHBB	Minneapolis	157.1	136.0	1,141.3	1,008.5
19	Ketchum Communications	Pittsburgh	132.8	116.9	1,002.0	896.2
20	Chiat/Day	Venice, CA	120.8	105.4	906.4	811.6

Source: *Advertising Age*, April 14, 1993, 42.
Note: Dollars are in millions.

TABLE 6.4

Gross Income and Billings of U.S. Advertising Agencies Ranked 301 through 320 for 1992

Rank	Agency	Headquarters	Gross Income	Billings
301	Goldberg, Marchesano, Kohlman	Washington	$4,010.5	$26,750.0
302	Paolin & Sweeney	Cherry Hill, NJ	4,000.0	17,000.0
303	Jayme Organization	Cleveland	3,951.6	31,082.0
304	Lipman, Richmond & Greene	New York	3,925.8	24,044.9
305	Berline Group	Bingham Farms, MI*	3,900.0	32,500.0
306	GS&B: Lintas	Coral Gables, FL	3,895.0	25,980.0
307	Bonneville Communications	Salt Lake City	3,870.0	40,397.0
308	Arian, Lowe, Travis & Gusick	Chicago	3,822.2	32,392.9
309	Karakas, Vansickle, Ouellette	Portland, OR	3,800.0	25,800.0
310	Italia/Gal Advertising	Los Angeles	3,800.0	36,000.0
311	St. George Group	Pittsburgh	3,775.4	32,485.1
312	Stephan & Brady	Madison, WI	3,753.5	30,337.6
313	Lockhart & Pettus	New York	3,734.0	24,893.0
314	Reeves Agency	Baltimore	3,706.3	22,209.3
315	Quest Business Agency	Houston	3,657.3	23,701.0
316	Hoffman/Lewis	Oakland, CA	3,611.0	25,639.0
317	Leslie Advertising	Greenville, SC	3,602.5	25,208.1
318	Gerber Advertising Agency	Portland, OR	3,594.1	23,960.5
319	Sawyer Riley Compton	Atlanta	3,545.3	31,587.2
320	Louis London	St. Louis	3,533.2	25,476.0

Source: *Advertising Age,* April 14, 1993, 17.

Notes: Dollars are in thousands.

* Indicates that gross income figures are AA estimates.

3. A knowledge of the factors of distribution and sales and their methods of operation.
4. A knowledge of all the available media and means that can be used profitably to carry the interpretation of the product or service to consumer, wholesaler, dealer, contractor, or others.
5. Formulation of a definite plan and presentation of this plan to the client.
6. Execution of this plan through (a) writing, designing, and illustrating the advertisements; (b) contracting for the space, time, or other means of advertising; (c) incorporation of the message in mechanical form and forwarding it to the media; (d) checking and verifying insertion, displays, and so forth; and (e) auditing and billing for the service, space, and preparation.
7. Cooperation with the client's sales force.

These are generally accepted as the basic services of agencies. However, many agencies branch out, offering their clients services in package designing, sales research, sales training, preparation of sales and service literature, direct-response marketing, design of merchandise displays, public relations, and publicity.

Functions of the Modern Agency

Mass media portrayals of advertising imply that agencies exist primarily to write clever slogans and cater to demanding clients. Actually, any agency, regardless of its size or type of organization, must include a variety of skilled specialists. Figure

6.4 is a typical agency organization chart by function. Although the number of specialized departments varies widely from agency to agency, almost any agency has the following functions: planning, account services, creative services, trafficking, marketing and management, and financial services.

Planning

A client should expect an agency to make recommendations about the objectives and strategy of an advertising campaign and how it intends to use its skills in executing its recommendations. Many agencies accomplish this through a plans board or an executive committee, others through informal meetings. An important part of campaign planning is preparation of the advertising budget.

FIGURE 6.4

A Typical Advertising Agency Organization Chart by Functions

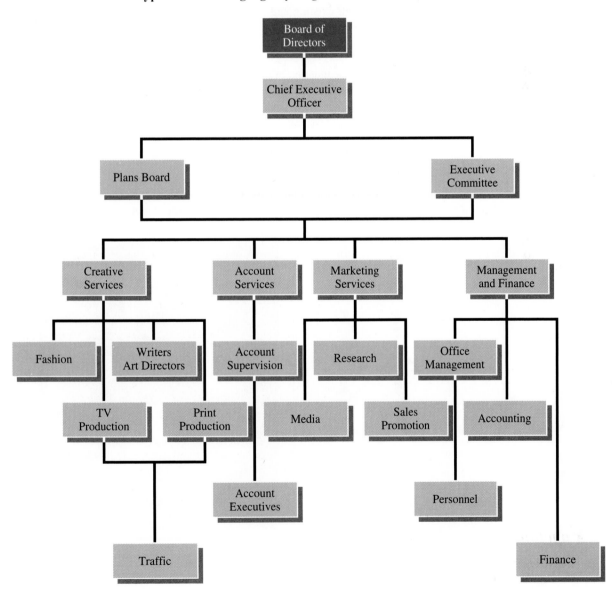

Account Services

Account services acts as the conduit between the client and agency. Its role is to ensure that agency resources meet the advertising needs of clients.

The person directly responsible for the day-to-day activities of an account is the **account executive,** also known as the **AE**. The AE is a liaison who coordinates the planning and execution of an advertising campaign and maintains contact with the client. AEs need not be specialists in all phases of advertising; however, they must be able to inspire agency personnel to produce good work, they must know as much as possible about their clients' business, they must be able to tell a good creative effort from a bad one, and they must get the work approved by the client.

The account executive usually is assisted by an assistant account executive, who is an entry-level employee learning the business. Typically, several account executives, each working on separate client assignments, report to an account supervisor. The supervisor is a senior management person who coordinates a number of agency accounts.

The person in charge of all agency accounts is usually the management supervisor. This person reports to upper management, manages and develops account services, and looks for new business opportunities. Figure 6.5 presents a series of ads for J. Walter Thompson. The ads appeared in a number of trade publications and were created to tell existing and prospective clients about the successes of the agency.

Creative Services

Another major function of the advertising agency is to provide creative services for the advertiser. These services typically include copywriting, art design, and production of the finished ads and commercials.

FIGURE 6.5

Client-Pitch Ads Produced and Placed by J. Walter Thompson, One of the World's Oldest and Most Respected Advertising Agencies

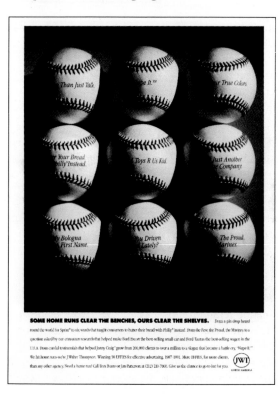

The creative people in an agency typically hold one of the following titles: creative director, creative department manager, copywriter, art director, and producer. The creative director serves as the executive-in-charge of the agency's total creative output. The creative department manager is responsible for the day-to-day management of creative services. Copywriters, the people who write the copy; art directors, the people who draw ideas and; producers, the people who translate words and drawings into finished messages, usually work together as a creative group for a particular assignment.

Traffic

The traffic department is responsible for tracking projects to ensure that they meet their assigned deadlines. Typically a traffic manager works with account and creative people to coordinate the planning and execution of the planned campaign.

Marketing Services

Almost all full-service agencies offer media and research services. In addition, a number of agencies provide client consultation regarding sales promotion programs and direct marketing.

Media The media department plans the placement of the ads and commercials in the various media and sees to it that the media plan is executed properly. Media planners and media buyers usually staff the agency media department. The media planner is the person who formulates a media plan, and the media buyer is the person who executes it.

The media department is expected to devise a plan that will meet the campaign's marketing and communication objective. This means media experts must know all about various media and their coverage as well as the audiences the advertiser is trying to reach. After the agency makes its recommendations, it prepares a schedule of advertising, showing the publications and dates of print ads and the times and stations of television and radio appearances. It then makes contracts and, finally, pays the bills from the media.

Research Every agency does some basic research to satisfy both agency planners and clients' constant need for facts. In some agencies, the function is carried out by a fully staffed research department; in others, the function is handled within other departments. If an agency has a research department, the person responsible is often called the research director.

In recent years, some agencies have adopted the British concept of account planning.[2] As a management system, account planning attempts to channel a consumer-based view to the agency's creative staff throughout the entire campaign planning process. The person responsible for presenting the consumer view is the account planner. Instead of simply reporting research results, this person bridges the traditionally separate relationship between research, account, and creative personnel by working as a part of an account team. Those agencies that have adopted this system believe better creative work is produced because the account planner knows the targeted consumer better than either client or other agency personnel. The Ad Insight entitled "Account Planning: The 13 Myths" attempts to debunk some of the myths associated with account planning.

Sales Promotion The agency often works with advertisers and dealers in planning and coordinating retail promotions, point-of-purchase materials, and any other promotional activities that may make advertising more productive. In some cases, agencies actually create sales promotion materials and work with sales and marketing managers to get the materials into the hands of salespeople and dealers; in other cases, agencies help coordinate the work of outside sales promotion specialists.

Account Planning: The 13 Myths

The proliferation of account planning in American advertising agencies has created significant interest on the part of those who feel it would enhance their agencies' competitive positions and service to clients. It has also created notable antagonism on the part of those who are threatened by it or consider it to be simply a duplication of what is already in place. Whatever your view, let's debunk some of the myths associated with account planning.

Myth No. 1: Account planning is the solution to the advertising industry's malaise. Account planning can certainly strengthen an agency's creative product but no one agency discipline can single-handedly correct the larger problems of an agency or the advertising industry as a whole.

Myth No. 2: Account planning leads to breakthrough creative. Breakthrough creative rests largely with the talents of the breakthrough creative staff. Account planning can provide the background and consumer profile needed to develop creative that works hard, and can help sell it to clients.

Myth No. 3: Account planning is the key to winning the new business pitch. This is a dangerous myth. Pitching is a team sport, and the winning strategy is likely to come from any agency discipline. An account planner *can* be a quick study on the brand and the consumer's relationship to it, and an effective presenter of the relevance of the strategic solution to the consumer.

Myth No. 4: There is a process for account planning. There are as many ways to do account planning as there are account planners. Its nature is to be fluid and responsive, rather than a processed checklist. Intuitive skills, a passion for advertising and a deep, personal involvement in the brand are the real essence of planning.

Myth No. 5: Account planning is a continuous process. Having someone devote his or her career to better understanding how people behave relative to two or three brands doesn't come cheap. Unless the agency can get the planner's time built into the fee, few clients will support this myth and even fewer account people will fight for it.

Myth No. 6: Account planning is a new name for research, qualitative or otherwise. This ever-enduring myth requires severe debunking. Research is one of the many tools used by account planners and the only tool used by researchers. Account planners have to assume responsibility for creative in a way which researchers

Source: George H. Creel II, "Account Planning: The 13 Myths," *Advertising Age,* September 16, 1991.

Management and Financial Services

An agency is no different from most other businesses that require management and financial services. An office management staff will see that the various clerical functions needed by the agency are delivered in an efficient way. The personnel department deals with hiring and firing, college recruitment, employee morale, benefit programs, and the like.

The accounting department keeps track of expenses and revenues. It is responsible for paying the agency's bills. It pays taxes and collects money owed the agency. The department handles invoices, such as purchase orders and bills, from freelance artists and other suppliers. It controls the payroll and the agency's internal operating budget.

Finance personnel are concerned with the manner in which the agency conducts its business from a fiscal standpoint. It may develop and recommend to top management the agency's internal budget, deal with problems of cash flow, develop investment policies for the agency, and analyze profit and loss statements.

Agency *Compensation*

In this section, we will first discuss types of compensation and then problems in compensation.

never do. Planners must have a strong and enduring bias toward the consumer; researchers must avoid bias at all costs. And finally, account planners don't have to be good researchers and researchers aren't necessarily good account planners.

Myth No. 7: Account planning and research departments can coexist. This may or may not be a myth dependent upon the agency model. What must be in place is a clear definition of each department's role. It also helps to know who is in charge of whom.

Myth No. 8: Clients like account planning. Clients *love* account planning (if it's free!).

Myth No. 9: Account planning is the role of the account planner. Some of the better account planners I've worked with are creative or account people who would never consider themselves account planners but use all of its principles in their day-to-day jobs of making advertising. Good solutions can come from anywhere.

Myth No. 10: Account planning is glamorous. Yep. That's why I buried this myth so deep into the article. It's fun, too, if you can fight like hell for your beliefs.

Myth No. 11: Account planners sit in the room while the ads are made. The account planner needs to articulate

the strategy before the ad is made and probably will not be around for the noodling part. The concept of a true *menage a trois* with the creative team is a goal but not a given.

Myth No. 12: Good account planners are hard to find. Account planners come from all disciplines and backgrounds. A comfort with the consumer, an ability and enthusiasm for articulating what has been learned and the ability to think strategically are the most important attributes. Look around your own agency and you will probably find quite a few people who fit the bill . . . perhaps some creatives, possibly some account people and maybe, just maybe, even a researcher or two!

Myth No. 13: The best account planners are English. This final myth is dedicated to the American agencies that have made ceremonial pilgrimages to mother England to learn the discipline of account planning and to those American agencies who have paid headhunters obscene amounts of money to import and "green card" English planners. Suffice it to say that at the end of the day no particular culture, race, religion, sex or national origin is decidely better at account planning than another. It's very much a function of the individual.

How Agencies Are Compensated

Agencies are normally compensated in three ways: (1) commissions, (2) percentage charges on materials and services purchased for clients, and (3) fees. These three methods are not mutually exclusive. For example, an agency may receive from a particular client both media commissions and percentage charges on materials and services.

Commissions from Media   The commission system is a holdover from the early days of advertising, when agents were primarily space brokers. This is the way it works:

> Suppose you operate an agency and prepare a full-page magazine advertisement for your client. The magazine has a published rate of $10,000 for this page. But because your agency is "recognized" by the magazine, you are entitled to a commission of 15 percent (most media offer agencies 15 percent, but there are exceptions). You therefore collect $10,000 from the client and pass on $8,500 to the magazine, keeping $1,500 to cover your expenses and (hopefully) make a profit.

Agency Charges   There are other out-of-pocket costs to the agency besides the cost of space or time. For print media, an agency may buy artwork, typographic composition, and printing plates from outside suppliers. With broadcast media, it is likely to have expenditures for talent, production, free-lance writers, and filming or taping. Often research is commissioned and managed for clients. To recoup these charges and to compensate itself for its involvement, the agency usually adds a percentage to the bills. The rate is usually either 15 percent, or 17.65 percent of the net cost, which would equal 15 percent of gross.

Fees Agency income is also derived from the fees it charges advertisers. One kind of fee is that charged for a specific noncommissionable service. If, for example, the agency prepares a market survey or a mailing piece, there is no agency commission involved. The agency may then charge the client a flat fee based on agency costs. But it may also decide to absorb the cost if the account is a particularly profitable one in other respects.

A fee charged to a client for a noncommissionable service is a form of agency compensation that has been used for many years. But when we talk about the fee system of compensation, we usually have something else in mind: a general fee for all services rendered, much like an accountant's bill to a client for professional advice and counsel, including perhaps the preparation of tax returns.

Although many types of fee arrangements are used, we can group them into two broad categories: (1) the fixed fee and (2) the cost-plus method. The fixed fee arrangement is one in which the advertiser and the agency agree on the amount of money that will be paid the agency for doing a prescribed amount of work. Usually a yearly fee is decided upon, and the agency is paid in equal monthly installments regardless of how much work is done in any given month.

The second category is the cost-plus method. Here, the agency keeps careful records of the costs incurred for serving a particular client—including hourly costs of its personnel who work on the account—and periodically bills the client for these costs, plus some agreed-upon profit margin (for example, a percent of total cost). Under this arrangement, many advertisers audit the books of their agency to verify costs.

A third category could be some variant of the two methods. Under all of these methods, if media commissions are received by the agency because of buying time and space, the commissions earned are credited against the fee (for example, if an advertiser and agency have agreed to a fixed fee of $100,000, and the agency's commissions from media were $60,000, the advertiser would pay the agency only $40,000).

Problems in Agency Compensation

There has been considerable concern about the ethics and economics of the system by which agencies are compensated. Many studies have been conducted to determine industry practices and attitudes toward the various methods of compensation.

One of the main reasons that the commission system has endured is its simplicity. It is easy to compute agency commissions. Thus, there is less reason for haggling, so the emphasis in competition is on nonprice factors rather than on the price of services rendered. The system is more flexible than it might seem at first glance, because the agency may include many services without extra charge if the account is particularly profitable; conversely, it may provide only basic copywriting, layout, and media selection for a less profitable account.

In recent years, many advertisers and even some agency leaders have criticized the commission system, saying that it may tempt an agency to recommend an advertising program using expensive media or, conversely, a program in which few services are provided. It is often true that the time spent on an account is not necessarily in proportion to the dollar expenditures of that account. For example, a $50,000 page in a magazine may not require any more agency time and effort than a $500 one in a trade paper.

Much of the concern today with agency compensation focuses on the strict adherence to the straight 15 percent commission system. Whereas only a few years ago three-fourths of all advertiser–agency arrangements used this system, presently an estimated one-third do so.

An agency does not ordinarily handle competitive accounts because of the confidential nature of the business. Thus, an agency that has an automobile account does not usually handle another automobile account. But what about truck and automobile accounts? The decision will probably depend on whether the original client thinks the new account would be competitive. This does not mean that a national agency would avoid a local meat packaging account, which it could handle out of its San Francisco office, because it had another meat packaging account with distribution only in the East. But it does mean an agency is limited in the number of national accounts it can solicit.

*H*andling Competing *Accounts*

Several years ago, the American Association of Advertising Agencies suggested that the "ideal agency–client policy on account conflicts is one which is based on individual product category rather than the total line of products of any given client." Under such a policy, an agency would not handle brands that are directly competitive. But it could handle an automobile account for one client and a refrigerator account for another client, even though the automobile client happened to make a competing brand of refrigerators.

Beyond these general guidelines, however, there are a number of specific situations under which client–agency conflicts are difficult to predict. For example, a few years ago Hallmark Cards ended its two-year relationship with Young & Rubicam because it perceived a conflict with the agency's recently acquired AT&T Communications international long-distance account. A Hallmark executive stated that the two accounts have "such similar values and high quality standards" and use the "same type of advertising" as to constitute a conflict. He described the type of advertising as "highly motivational through sentimental and heartfelt emotions."

A study of client–agency conflicts found that the majority of top managers in client and agency organizations feel conflicts will become more frequent.[3] An underlying reason for this expectation is the proliferation of products and growth of competing entries in many product categories.

Another factor in the issue of product conflict is the accelerating trend among companies to merge or to acquire other companies. For example, Procter & Gamble bought Richardson-Vicks and R. J. Reynolds acquired Nabisco. On the agency side, several large groups of agencies, usually called mega groups, have recently been formed, including Saatchi & Saatchi PLC, Omnicom Group, and the WPP Group PLC. The outcome is that a number of once independent agencies are now owned and operated by a controlling company.

The story of several agencies mergers is told in the "Family Trees" in Figure 6.6. BBDO Worldwide began in 1891 as the George Batten Company. Once the largest agency in the world, in 1987 J. Walter Thompson became a part of the WPP Group.

The merger trend already has had a significant impact on how an advertiser assigns different brands to an agency in order to avoid conflicts, and the matter is yet to be totally resolved. The trend, and the problems associated with it, will continue having an impact in future years. A look at the world's largest advertising agency organizations is presented in Table 6.5.

Media

The third major participant in advertising is the medium that carries the advertisement or commercial. In a typical advertising budget, at least 80 percent of the total dollars are allocated to time and space in the various advertising media.

FIGURE 6.6

Evolution of Some Large Agency Organizations: Family Trees

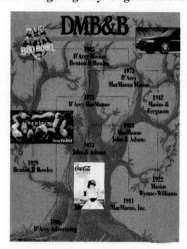
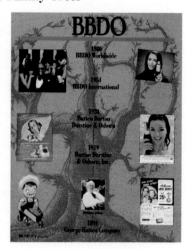

TABLE 6.5

World's Top 25 Advertising Organizations

Rank 1992	Advertising Organizations	Headquarters	U.S.-Based Agency Brands Included	Worldwide Gross Income 1992
1	WPP Group	London	**Ogilvy & Mather Worldwide;** Cole & Weber; Ogilvy & Mather Direct; Ogilvy & Mather Yellow Pages; A. Eicoff & Co.; **J. Walter Thompson Co.;** Brouillard Communications; J. Walter Thompson Direct; Thompson Healthcare; Thompson Recruitment Advertising; **Scall, McCabe, Sloves;** Fallon McElligott; Morton Goldberg Associates; Martin Agency; Steinrich Group	$2,813.5
2	Interpublic Group of Companies	New York	**McCann-Erickson Worldwide;** McCann Direct, McCann Healthcare; **Lintas:Worldwide;** Lintas: Marketing Communications; Dailey & Associates; Fahlgren Martin; GS&B; Lintas:MGI; Long, Haymes & Carr; **Lowe Group;** Lowe & Partners; Lowe Direct; Laurence, Charles, Free & Lawson	1,989.2
3	Omnicom Group	New York	**BBDO Worldwide;** Baxter, Gurian & Mazzei; Frank J. Corbett Inc.; Doremus & Co.; Lavey/Wolff/Swift; Tracy-Locke; **DDB Needham Worldwide;** Bernard Hodes Group; Kallir, Philips, Ross; **(shared shops):** Rainoldi Kerzner Hadcliffe, Rapp Collins Marcoa; Alcone Sims O'Brien; Harrison, Star, Wiener & Beitler; **(other independent units):** TBWA Advertising; Goodby, Berlin & Silverstein; Altschiller Reitzfeld	1,806.7
4	Saatchi & Saatchi Co.	London	**Saatchi & Saatchi Advertising Worldwide;** Conill Advertising; Cliff Freeman & Partners; Klemtner Advertising; Rumrill-Hoyt; Team One; **Backer Spielvogel Bates Worldwide;** AC&R Advertising; Kobs & Draft; **CME KHBB**	1,696.5
5	Dentsu	Tokyo	Dentsu Corp. of America	1,387.6
6	Young & Rubicam	New York	Young & Rubicam; Chapman Direct, Creswell, Munsell, Fultz & Zirbell; Muldoon Agency; Sudler & Hennessey; Wunderman Cato Johnson Worldwide	1,072.3

Figure 6.6 (*continued*)

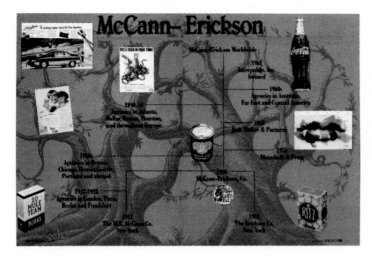

Rank 1992	Advertising Organizations	Headquarters	U.S.-Based Agency Brands Included	Worldwide Gross Income 1992
7	Euro RSCG	Neuilly, France	Robert A. Becker, Inc.; Cohn & Wells; Comart-KLP; Lally, McFarland & Pantello; Messner Vetere Berger McNamee Schmetterer/Euro RSCG; Tatham Euro RSCG	$951.2
8	Grey Advertising	New York	Grey Advertising; Beaumont Bennett Group; Font & Vaamonde; Gross Townsend Frank Hoffman; Grey Direct International	735.4
9	Foote, Cone & Belding Communications	Chicago	Foote, Cone & Belding Communications; FCB Direct/U.S.; IMPACT; Krupp Taylor U.S.A.; Vicom/FCB; Wahlstrom & Co.	682.7
10	Hakuhodo	Tokyo	Hakuhodo America Advertising	661.1
11	Leo Burnett Company	Chicago	Leo Burnett Co.	643.8
12	Publicis-FCB Communications	Paris	Publicis, Inc.	590.1
13	D'Arcy Masius Benton & Bowles	New York	D'Arcy Masius Benton & Bowles; Medicus Intercon International, Clarion Marketing Communications	558.4
14	BDDP Worldwide	Paris	McCracken Brooks Communications; Wells Rich Greene BDDP	293.0
15	Bozell, Jacobs, Kenyon & Eckhardt	New York	Bozell; Poppe Tyson; Temerlin McClain	231.0
16	Tokyu Agency	Tokyo	NA	179.4
17	Daiko Advertising	Osaka, Japan	NA	175.9
18	N W Ayer	New York	N W Ayer; Ayer Direct	175.0
19	Asatsu	Tokyo	Asatsu America	165.9
20	Dai-Ichi Kikaku	Tokyo	Kresser Craig/D.I.K.	151.4
21	Ketchum Communications	Pittsburgh	Ketchum Advertising; Botto, Roessner, Horne & Messinger; Di Franza Williamson	132.8
22	Dentsu, Y&R Partnerships	New York/Tokyo	Lord, Dentsu & Partners	132.3
23	Chiat/Day	Venice, CA	Chiat/Day; Chiat/Day Direct	124.9
24	Ross Roy Group	Bloomfield Hills, MI	Ross Roy Inc.; Calet, Hirsch & Ferrell; Griswold	111.5
25	I&S Corp.	Tokyo	NA	107.4

Source: *Advertising Age*, April 14, 1993, 12.

Media organizations vary in size from billion-dollar corporations that own and operate several different types of media to the small businesses that publish weekly newspapers in rural towns across America. Table 6.6 lists the top 20 media companies in the United States. Some of these companies concentrate on one type of media whereas others are less focused. For example, General Electric's sole media operation is the NBC television network. Time Warner received its media revenues from magazine and cable television operations in about a 40–60 split. The Hearst Corporation received revenues from all categories shown, although almost half came from magazines.

Media Advertising Department

The advertising department of any medium is primarily a sales department, and the people who work for it or for the medium's national representative are primarily salespeople. In fact, the head of the advertising department is often called the advertising sales manager or, in the case of broadcast media, simply sales manager.

The sales function, however, is not the only task of a medium's advertising department. Most media sponsor research that they view as a form of promotion to help sell space or time. A medium's advertising department may also offer its customers a variety of services, such as copywriting, artwork, and production of a finished commercial. In addition, a medium may choose to advertise itself to prospective advertisers, their agencies, and even ultimate users of the medium (such as newspaper or magazine subscribers and listeners of a radio station). Many media have their own departments, typically called promotion departments, to accomplish this task, but others use an advertising agency.

Newspapers

Newspaper advertising departments vary in size from the one-person department in the small-town weekly to metropolitan departments that have more than 500 employees. The advertising department of a newspaper typically includes retail, classified, and general advertising units. The functions of a typical newspaper advertising department are shown in Figure 6.7.

Retail Advertising This department, also known as local display, sells advertising to retail stores, local banks and service organizations, and the like. Retail salespeople, who are marketing as well as advertising specialists, help customers plan their advertising and often write the copy, lay out the ad, and oversee the final production. They help local advertisers coordinate their promotional effort in line with research information that is available from the newspaper and other sources.

The retail department may have an individual who is responsible for coordinating cooperative advertising funds. Such an individual keeps retail advertisers apprised of funds that are available from national advertisers.

Classified Advertising The classified advertising department sells, prepares, and services both individuals and business firms that use the **classified** section of the newspaper. Most classified ads by individuals to advertise, say, a garage sale or sell a motorcycle are straight lines of copy. But businesses often use classified ads that contain illustrations as well (for example, a local automobile dealer shows pictures of the cars as well as describes them and lists prices). The department usually has a staff of people who sell advertising space by telephone as well as salespeople who go out and deal directly with their customers (street sales).

General Advertising Usually, this is the smallest unit in the advertising department and deals solely with national advertising. National ads typically are sold by representatives who maintain offices in major advertising cities. The general advertising staff ensures that the national advertiser's requests (for example, the specific placement of

TABLE 6.6

Percent of Revenues by Media Type, 1990

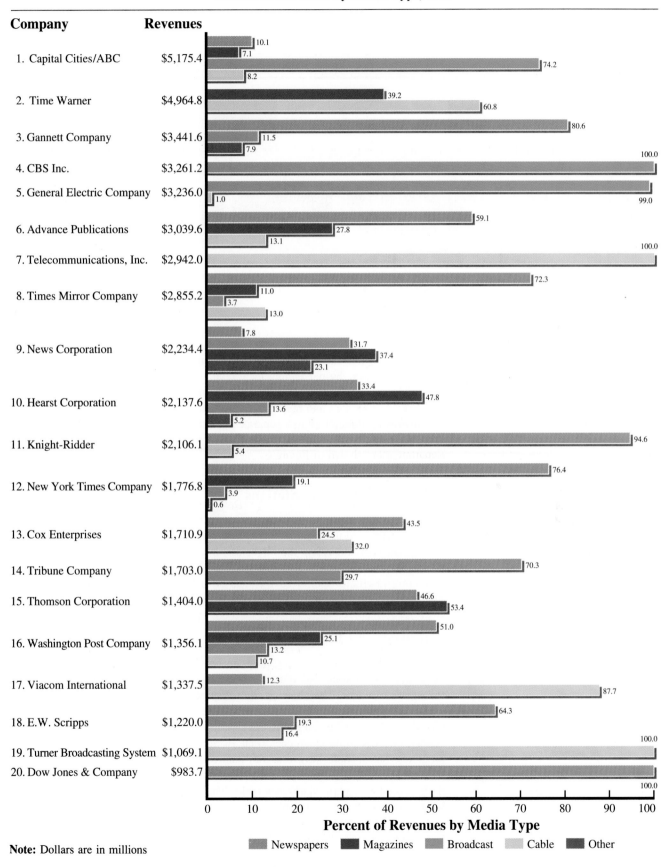

Company	Revenues	
1. Capital Cities/ABC	$5,175.4	
2. Time Warner	$4,964.8	
3. Gannett Company	$3,441.6	
4. CBS Inc.	$3,261.2	
5. General Electric Company	$3,236.0	
6. Advance Publications	$3,039.6	
7. Telecommunications, Inc.	$2,942.0	
8. Times Mirror Company	$2,855.2	
9. News Corporation	$2,234.4	
10. Hearst Corporation	$2,137.6	
11. Knight-Ridder	$2,106.1	
12. New York Times Company	$1,776.8	
13. Cox Enterprises	$1,710.9	
14. Tribune Company	$1,703.0	
15. Thomson Corporation	$1,404.0	
16. Washington Post Company	$1,356.1	
17. Viacom International	$1,337.5	
18. E.W. Scripps	$1,220.0	
19. Turner Broadcasting System	$1,069.1	
20. Dow Jones & Company	$983.7	

Percent of Revenues by Media Type

Newspapers ■ Magazines ■ Broadcast □ Cable ■ Other

Note: Dollars are in millions

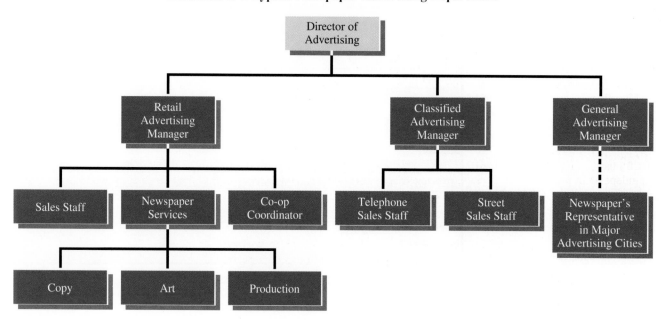

FIGURE 6.7

Functions of a Typical Newspaper Advertising Department

an ad) are carried out. In some instances, this department helps "merchandise" general advertising by persuading local retailers to tie in with national campaigns.

In addition to the retail, classified, and general advertising units, a newspaper may have a promotion and research department as well. Whether it is placed under the advertising director or in a separate department, the department researches the paper's effectiveness as an advertising medium and communicates to prospective users.

Television and Radio Stations

Local television and radio stations operate much like local newspapers. Like the newspaper, the station ordinarily has managers for both retail and national advertising (see Figure 6.8) and offers the buyer of time some help in writing commercials, merchandising, and research. Some stations offer a substantial amount of help in promoting programs sponsored by local advertisers and by network advertisers. There is no counterpart to the classified advertising department in the local station.

Television and Radio Networks

The **network** focuses its selling program on the national advertisers (particularly those that have national distribution). The salespeople (or account executives) work for a sales manager. They have at their disposal a myriad of services to persuade the prospective time buyer. Whatever the advertisers' problems, the sales staff can provide a solution to fit their needs—everything from a completely packaged program series to desired time clearances (that is, agreement by local stations to use the program). Salespeople have research data to help the buyer and, incidentally, to indicate what a good buy their network is. A network may offer free merchandising if the account is particularly desirable. The network also employs promotional writers to prepare material publicizing the network.

A unique aspect of broadcast networks is the fact that the price of commercials and other aspects of buying is not as fixed as in many of the other media. Thus, network salespeople engage in an elaborate negotiating process in selling their commercial time to broadcast buyers. The cost of a single commercial on a particular network program may depend on how many commercials totally are bought, when the agreement to buy is made (for example, early in the buying season, known as "up front" buying), the number of people to be delivered by a particular broadcast, and a host of other factors.

It should be pointed out that by television networks we also mean cable networks as well as the more traditional types (that is, ABC, CBS, and NBC). With the growth of cable television systems in cities across the country have come cable networks that provide the local systems with a host of broadcasting programming. Current cable networks include ESPN, Cable News Network (CNN), Lifetime, Nickelodeon, USA Network, and the Weather Channel.

Independent Program Producers

The independent producers who create, produce, and distribute television programs are an important part of the industry. Television production houses usually specialize either in developing programs for the networks or in producing shows for sale to individual stations. Some, of course, do both. M*A*S*H, for example, produced by Twentieth Century-Fox, was a longtime weekly series on the CBS television network and now is offered in syndication. A **syndicated program** is one that the producer sells to individual television stations throughout the United States to be shown at a time the station chooses.

An independent producer may also specialize in certain types of programming. Several produce nothing but game and quiz shows, which typically are sold via syndication to individual stations in as many markets as possible.

Magazines

Like newspapers and the broadcast media, magazines (whether consumer or business) provide three major types of services to the national advertiser: personal help with

FIGURE 6.8

Typical Television Station Organization

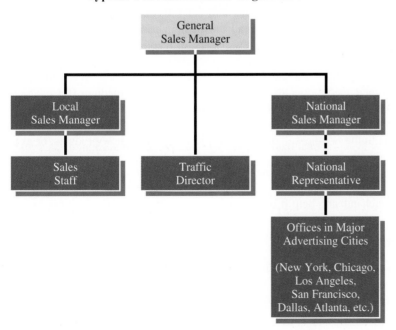

advertising problems, research, and merchandising. Like the networks, they typically deal directly with advertisers and agencies rather than through representatives. Most magazine business offices are located in New York or Chicago, and those that are not have sales offices there. From these central offices the salespeople call on their prospects.

The sales personnel are aided by a wealth of promotion material, prepared mostly by people who work for the magazine. Copywriters may create direct-mail pieces, which are sent out regularly to space buyers in agencies. Other promotional people put together selling aids to be used in presentations.

The magazine's research department works closely with sales and promotion personnel. But many of the larger research studies are made by outside organizations, because they are more objective and their findings are not suspect. Simmons Market Research Bureau (SMRB), for example, regularly conducts studies of media audiences.

Merchandising services include visits to stores around the country to tell retailers about brand promotions that will appear in the magazine. The purpose is to persuade local dealers to "tie in" with the national magazine advertising. In some instances, a magazine may merchandise an advertiser's campaign by sending direct mailings to retailers.

Outdoor Advertising

The important people in the outdoor advertising industry (which includes posters and painted billboards) are the local plant operators. They lease promising sites for their units and place boards on these sites. Then, either through their own salespeople or the industrywide sales organization, they sell the space to agencies or directly to advertisers.

Media Representatives

Media representatives sell most of the newspaper space and the spot television and radio time that is bought by national (general) advertisers. These representatives handle only one paper or station in a market and have exclusive rights to sell their paper or station at the national level. They provide the only regular contact that most advertisers and media buyers in agencies have with the local medium. Some of the media do not use a media representative but rather handle their own national sales. For example, a large metropolitan newspaper, such as *The New York Times,* may staff its own sales offices in major advertising cities. Or a television station that is part of a chain may rely on a staff that sells time for all of the chain's stations.

The economic justification for a local medium using a media rep is that a salesperson representing a number of newspapers, or television or radio stations, can do a better job at less cost than the medium could by itself.

Media reps have a threefold job: to sell the medium itself, to sell the markets in which their media operate, and to sell their particular medium (for example, *The Atlanta Constitution* or television station WWBT in Richmond) in that market against the competition. The media rep may sell the city as "the fastest-growing market in the Southeast," or as an ideal test market for new products, or as a high-income area.

In trying to outsell the competition, media reps may sell their medium as more efficient than the competition, or they may sell the high quality of its audience, or the merchandising help it offers, or the sheer number of people it reaches.

Compensation

Media representatives typically work on a commission basis, whereby their income is keyed to the amount of sales they generate for the medium. Newspaper reps generally receive from 10 to 15 percent whereas broadcast reps operate on a 7 to

15 percent commission. If a newspaper has a page price of $2,000 for a national advertiser and works with a rep on a 15 percent commission basis, the rep will receive $300. Too, if the advertiser uses an agency (or has a house agency), the agency will also receive a 15 percent commission, or $300. Thus, for a $2,000 page, the newspaper actually receives $1,400. A medium must take this into account when setting prices for advertising space and time.

Related Advertising Organizations

In addition to the three major segments of the advertising industry—the agencies, the advertisers, and the media—many other organizations are closely related to the industry. As we have previously mentioned, they provide useful services to the three major segments and facilitate the advertising process.

Creative boutiques and **media buying services** have been around for several decades. Such companies are specialists in the creative and media functions, respectively, and it can be argued that they are in fact advertising agencies with a limited focus. They are like a department in a full-service advertising agency that is pulled out and organized as a separate company. (In fact, many such companies are headed and staffed by people with experience in a full-service agency.)

The interrelationship of several advertising organizations is shown in Figure 6.9. Agency people in the various functional areas work with a variety of specialists to provide the services necessary for the execution of an advertising campaign. As an alternate to using a full-service agency, the advertiser might separately employ companies to perform the various agency functions—for example, a creative boutique, a media buying service, a production house, or a researcher supplier, to name a few.

Specialized Services

Producing finished ads and commercials requires a host of skilled specialists. Often, they work directly for an agency or advertising department or medium, but many organizations exist that provide only a particular specialized service.

In the print field, typographers specialize in setting the type—both headline type and body copy—that will be pasted into a final layout by others. Photoengravers take artwork and, through detailed photographic and chemical processes, convert it into metal so that it can be printed back onto paper. The printing service produces the final advertisement in newspapers, magazines, and direct-mail pieces. We will discuss the specifics of these tasks in Chapter 15.

In the field of television commercials, even more specialized organizations exist. Some companies specialize in taping or filming commercials of a certain type. For example, one New York firm produces mostly food commercials that are shot indoors in a studio. Another company does on-location production exclusively. Still other companies specialize in writing and producing commercial music, provide the talent used in commercials, and supply special effects.

Although many of the specialists mentioned here deal only with advertising, quite a few of them do nonadvertising work as well.

Production Services

The art studio produces finished artwork for advertisements. These specialists typically work closely with the ad agency's art director in developing the art needed for a particular campaign. Some artists are expert in watercolor drawings, others in ink drawings, others in oil paintings, and still others in photography.

Art Studios

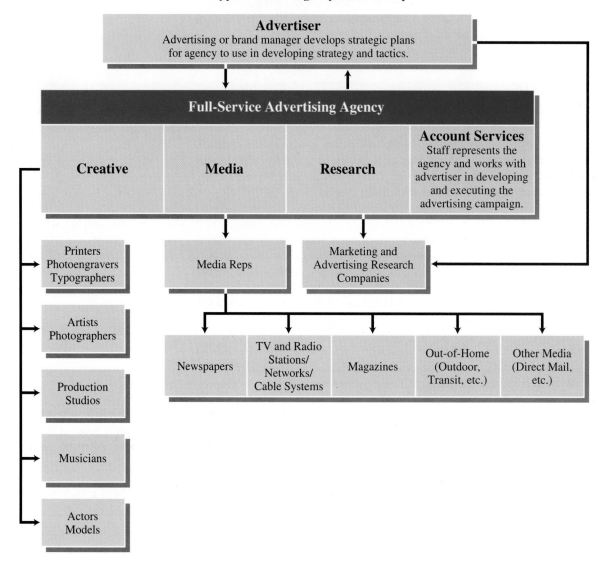

FIGURE 6.9

A Typical Client-Agency Relationship

Research Companies

Some observers of the advertising scene note application of the truism, "When in doubt about what to do, call in research." And, indeed, research is a vital component of the advertising decision process. Most agencies, advertisers, and media include the research function as part of their advertising department or have it readily available to the department.

But there are also literally thousands of independent research companies that can be hired to assist in the process. The kinds of research these companies do—as well as the range of their services—are quite extensive. For example, some firms concentrate on marketing research, such as measuring brand shares and distribution patterns. Others study consumer motivations and attitudes, which may form the basis for an advertising appeal. Still other companies specialize in pretesting ads and commercials before they are run in media. Trade ads for two research suppliers are presented in Figure 6.10. More on research companies will be said in later chapters.

Martin Mayer Returns: Suggestions for the Future of the Agency Business

Thirty-three years after *Madison Avenue, U.S.A.* became a best seller, Martin Mayer wrote another book about the advertising business, *Whatever Happened to Madison Avenue? Advertising in the '90s.* While Mr. Mayer remains steadfast in his belief that advertising builds brands by adding perceived value and promotes consumer choice, his new book left him feeling pessimistic about the future of advertising.

Fragmenting national media, the rise of data-base marketing, and the failure of agencies to nurture unique consumer research talents have put agencies in a bind, Mr. Mayer believes. Following are some of Mr. Mayer's observations about today's advertising business:

1. In the past advertising leaders had access to each other. They talked directly to each other—they picked up the phone and called. Today, they can't get each other on the phone.
2. There is a negative trendline and advertising needs to reestablish its role in marketing. Agencies need to stop thinking about "just advertising something"; they need to make an investment in selling the imaginative qualities of the advertising business.
3. Agencies are not getting the information they need from clients. Agency people must become more involved in the design and commission of research studies.
4. There is decreasing willingness on the part of clients to let agency people take the leading role in the production of advertising, particularly television advertising. Agencies need to reassert themselves—they need to take a leadership role.
5. Agencies have got to spend the money to get syndicated research data, and then they have to massage the data to find out what they need to know. They can't simply say that it's the client's domain and expect to have some control.
6. Today, clients are less willing to accept the agency's judgment about spending their money.

7. Agencies have lost leverage with clients because they have given up their research role. They need to reinvest in themselves, which they are not doing.
8. Agencies have to get creatives out into the streets—pumping gas, selling cosmetics. They need to talk with people in a real-world setting, not just listen to focus groups.
9. Agencies need to be loyal to clients, not to their mass media roots. Today, agencies are in danger of losing their special status with clients. With the mergers and buyouts, advertising is a much more cold-nosed business than it once was.
10. Agencies used to have to make a larger commitment to a creative idea. Today, the risks they take are much smaller.
11. There is not enough partnership between clients and agencies. Clients are doing most of the marketing and research today. Agencies need to stand between the client and the consumer as the cynical intermediary.
12. The agency business needs to make an investment in building brands through advertising rather than extending them.
13. Today, the agency business is much less geographically concentrated. New York and Chicago are no longer everything to the advertising business. Agencies in places like Richmond and Minneapolis seem to be more in touch with clients than those in New York and Chicago.
14. Agencies need to stop operating on the client's plan. They need to go to meetings with their own ideas and facts, and they must persuasively say "You don't know" to the client.
15. Agencies should not be publicly held; they should be owned by people who have a stake in their well-being rather than by people looking for a return on their investments.

Source: Adapted from "Martin Mayer Returns," *Advertising Age* (March 25, 1991): 1, 16–17.

Summary

FIGURE 6.10

Trade Advertisements Describing Some of the Research Services Offered by McCollum Spielman Worldwide and AHF Marketing Research

The three organizations that perform the major advertising functions are the advertiser, the advertising agency, and the media in which advertising is placed. In addition to these, there are a number of related organizations that supply services to support the process.

Advertisers are of two main types: national (general) and local (retail). The advertising manager of a business is usually the top person in advertising policy and execution, working with other top company executives and often with an advertising agency as well. The brand-manager system has become popular in many national advertising companies. Under this arrangement, the brand manager becomes in effect the marketing manager for one of the company's several brands. Because of the changing nature of marketing, brand management systems have been modified to include category managers as well as brand managers.

When advertisers use an outside advertising agency, they must be careful in choosing the agency and maintaining good relations. In those instances when a company elects to do the complete advertising task itself, a house agency is established. Each advertiser has to decide on the approach that best fits its particular needs. Retailers generally do not use agencies and perform most of the agency's normal functions within the store, although most rely on help from manufacturers, art services, trade associations, and the local media.

Advertising agencies, in particular full-service agencies, perform a wide variety of advertising functions for their client advertisers, including planning, creative services, account liaison, research, and media strategy and execution. An agency is compensated for its work through the receipt of media commissions, charges on materials and services purchased on behalf of its clients, and/or fees paid by a client for specific work performed. Although the straight commission system has been the mainstay of agency compensation for many years, its use has diminished recently and new compensation methods will likely be used in the future. As more and more companies and agencies broaden their business base through acquisitions and mergers, the matter of product conflict will continue to be a problem in future advertiser–agency relations.

Media advertising departments are strongly sales oriented, although they also do other things—such as creative services and research—for users of their medium. The local media (for example, newspapers, television, and radio stations) provide their own staffs for selling and servicing local accounts, but their national representatives sell the national advertisers and their agencies. These media reps have exclusive rights to the local medium and will handle only one newspaper or station in a given market. They are compensated by a commission received from the medium for space and time bought by national advertisers and agencies.

Several other types of organizations are closely related to the advertising industry. Creative boutiques and media buying services offer specialists to advertisers who do not need a full-service agency. Production companies assist in putting an advertising idea into the necessary mechanical form. Art studios, and similar suppliers, specialize in executing the creative strategy through providing final artwork and finished commercials. Research companies do the studies that help formulate marketing and advertising strategy, as well as measure the results of advertising efforts.

Questions for Discussion

1. To what extent should an advertising department concern itself with checking the work of its advertising agency?
2. Would you advise a company marketing five different products, with an advertising department organized according to each product, to install a brand-manager system? Why? Why not?
3. If you were an advertiser negotiating with an agency, which compensation method would you prefer? Why? Why not?

4. Why has the agency business become so centralized in our larger cities?
5. Does it seem logical to you that an agency should have to turn down an account if it already has a competitive account? Is this situation any different from that of the newspaper or television station that sells space or time to competing advertisers?
6. Try to schedule a visit to an advertising agency in your community or one in a nearby city. While visiting the agency try to visit each department. Also, try to learn the following:
   a. How the agency is organized; what particular functions are performed
   b. How the agency is compensated by its clients and the agency's viewpoint on the various compensation systems
   c. If the agency has had problems with account conflicts and, if so, how they were handled
7. Go to your library and find the most current *Advertising Age* issue that lists the "100 Leading National Advertisers" (typically printed in September). Look up the listing of one company that sells a number of different brands (for example, Procter & Gamble, General Foods, General Mills). Study the list of brands advertised, as well as the advertising agencies that handle these brands, and then write a policy statement the company could use regarding account conflicts.
8. If you were the national representative for your hometown newspaper, what information would you want from the newspaper to help you sell space to national advertisers? Where would it get such information?
9. Visit a local medium, such as a television or radio station or your community newspaper, and find out how its advertising department is organized. How many employees handle the advertising function and what are their tasks on a typical day?

Notes

1. M. Louise Ripley, "What Kind of Companies Take Their Advertising In-House?" *Journal of Advertising Research* 31 (October/November, 1991): 73–80.
2. Thomas E. Barry, Ron L. Peterson, and W. Bradford Todd. "The Role of Account Planning in the Future of Advertising Agency Research," *Journal of Advertising Research* 27 (February/March 1987): 15–21.
3. Herbert Zeltner, "Client–Agency Conflicts," *Advertising Age,* March 5, 1984, M64–M68.

Suggested Readings

Aaker, David A., Rajeev Batra, and John G. Myers. *Advertising Management.* 4th ed. Englewood Cliffs, NJ: Prentice-Hall, Inc., 1992.

Barry, Thomas E., Ron L. Peterson, and W. Bradford Todd. "The Role of Account Planning in the Future of Advertising Agency Research." *Journal of Advertising Research* 27 (February/March 1987): 15–21.

Bloede, Victor G. *The Full-Service Advertising Agency.* New York: American Association of Advertising Agencies, 1983.

Buell, Victor P. *Organizing for Marketing/Advertising Success.* New York: Association of National Advertisers, 1982.

Engel, James F., Martin R. Warshaw, and Thomas C. Kinnear. *Promotional Strategy.* 7th ed. Homewood, IL: Irwin, 1991.

Gamble, Frederic R. *What Advertising Agencies Are—What They Do and How They Do It.* New York: American Association of Advertising Agencies, 1976.

Jugenheimer, Donald W., Arnold M. Barban, and Peter Turk. *Advertising Media: Strategy and Tactics.* Dubuque, IA: Brown & Benchmark, 1992.

Boone, Louis E. and David L. Kurtz. *Contemporary Marketing.* 7th ed. Hinsdale, IL: Dryden Press, 1989.

Mayer, Martin. *Whatever Happened to Madison Avenue?* Boston: Little, Brown and Company, 1991.

Weilbacher, William. *Choosing an Advertising Agency.* Chicago: Crain Books, 1983.

P A R T 2

Advertising Campaign Planning: Strategy

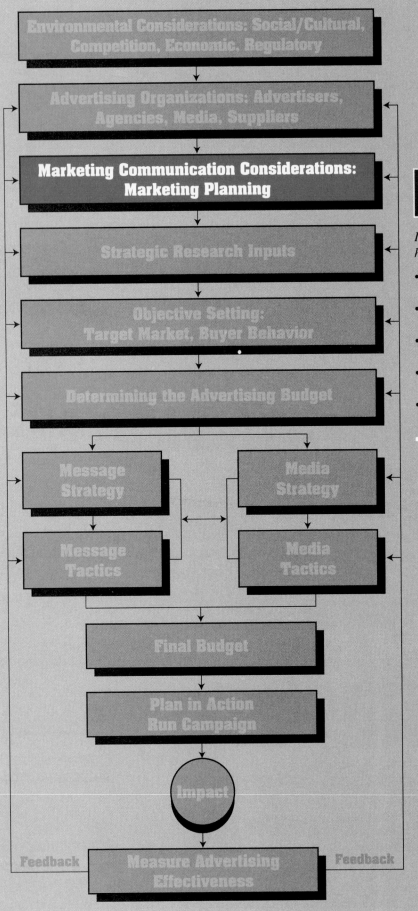

LEARNING OBJECTIVES

In your study of this chapter, you will have an opportunity to:

- Understand the concept of an advertising campaign.
- Determine the elements of a successful advertising campaign.
- Understand how advertising works in the marketing mix.
- Understand integrated marketing communications.
- Learn the planning sequence for a campaign.

Chapter 7

Overview of Campaign Planning

CHAPTER TOPICS

WHAT IS AN ADVERTISING CAMPAIGN?
THE MARKETING MIX: BASIS FOR CAMPAIGN
   PLANS
     Product
     Price
     Channels of Distribution (Place)
     Promotion
INTEGRATED MARKETING COMMUNICATIONS

THE PLANNING OF ADVERTISING
   Strategic Research Inputs
   The Setting of Objectives
   The Advertising Budget
   Message and Media Strategy
   The Plan in Action
   Measuring the Effectiveness of Advertising
   Adjustments to the Campaign

Part 1 dealt primarily with the environment in which advertising must function and with the key organizations responsible for the creation and dissemination of advertising. Chapters 2 through 5 offered a macro viewpoint that related the process of advertising to marketing communications, to social and economic conditions, and to the regulatory environment. Chapter 6 described the institutions responsible for the actual development of advertising.

Part 2 builds on that background information and provides a microperspective of advertising. It examines the concepts that are applied to planning and executing an effective advertising campaign as they relate to national advertisers, retail advertisers, government, and nonprofit organizations.

Chapter 7 provides an overview of the total campaign planning process. Chapters 8 through 12 describe key decision areas that precede the campaign and research that evaluates the success of the campaign.

What Is an Advertising Campaign?

An **advertising campaign** is defined as a series of advertisements with an identical or similar message, placed in one or more of the advertising media over a particular period of time. A campaign is designed to achieve a "look" or "feel" that communicates an image or idea in a consistent fashion. The Range Rover campaign in Figure 7.1 shows advertisements using similar layout, headline, and copy approaches to communicate a rugged, outdoor image.

FIGURE 7.1

Advertisements from the Range Rover Campaign

All advertisements have the same overall approach.

Lots of people use their Range Rovers just to run down to the corner.

Sometimes you have to get out and push a Range Rover.

A campaign involves more than the creation of a series of related advertisements disseminated via advertising media. A broader and more useful definition is this:

> An advertising campaign consists of an analysis of marketing and communication situations in order to establish objectives and make strategic decisions to be carried out in a series of advertising messages to be placed in advertising media.

Figure 7.2 provides a more complete look at the foundation of campaign planning. The campaign planning process is like an iceberg (the iceberg analogy was also depicted in Chapter 1). Only the advertising messages are seen by consumers. Yet, the finished messages are built on a solid base of objectives and strategies developed by marketing and advertising decision makers.

This chapter explores the key factors involved in formulating an advertising campaign. They can be divided into three major categories: marketing mix considerations, integrating marketing communications, and the planning of the advertising.

The Marketing Mix: Basis for Campaign Plans

One of the first and most critical steps advertising planners must take is to analyze the marketing framework within which advertising decisions are made. The successful

FIGURE 7.2

The Advertising Strategy and Planning Process

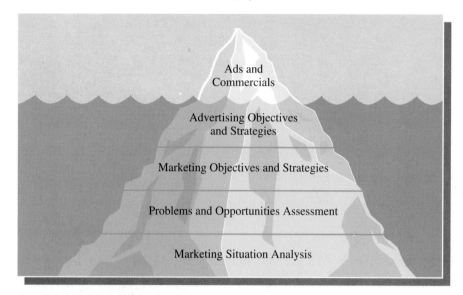

advertising campaign evolves from a clear understanding of the firm's marketing mix.

The combination of ingredients that a company chooses in its effort to satisfy the needs or wants of a particular group of customers is the marketing mix. Any number of ingredients may be considered in developing the mix. The number of factors involved depends on the situation as well as on how the particular factors are defined. Here, we consider four major ingredients: (1) the product to be marketed, (2) the price of the product, (3) the channels of distribution through which the product is sold (referred to as place), and (4) the promotion used for advertising and selling the product. They comprise the 4Ps of the marketing mix.

Product

As an ingredient of the marketing mix, the term *product* is used in a broad sense to mean several types of marketing decisions. The development and planning of the product itself is a vital factor and is obviously a key marketing consideration. A recent study of the fifty largest U.S. firms indicates that most companies will rely more on quality and customer satisfaction than price reduction in order to compete.[1] For example, Fischer Price started as a small, regional toy company with a commitment to quality toys that could be trusted with a baby. Consistent product development has led the company into the *Fortune* 500 of the largest companies in the United States.

The term *product* is also used in marketing situations that involve, not physical goods, but service and idea concepts. Figure 7.3 shows an ad for a service. In developing product strategy, such organizations apply many of the same concepts that are applied to a physical brand.

Packaging is another aspect of product policy that bears directly on the marketing mix. In many industries, the package is a powerful selling force, because it constantly competes with other packages for the customer's attention in self-service and self-selection situations. For a few products (for example, certain types of cosmetics), the package costs more and is frequently more important than the product itself in inducing potential customers to buy. Often the physical appearance of the package directly affects major marketing and advertising decisions. When L'eggs pantyhose

FIGURE 7.3

An Advertisement Promoting a Service

was first introduced, the plastic egg-shaped package was a focal point of the advertising. The company has recently changed to a biodegradable cardboard package because of concern for plastics and the environment.

Brand name is another important concept related to product. The intent of the brand name is to be easily remembered in a marketplace that has over 35,000 such names. Brands such as Budweiser, Converse, Coke, Crest, and Reebok were, in part, established from advertising that helped to create and reinforce them. Marketers put a great deal of effort into finding distinctive names that will stand out from the crowd.

In some instances, a manufacturing company chooses not to market a product under its own brand name, but instead sells the product to retailers who assign their own brand name. For example, Kroger contracts with many manufacturers to produce products that it sells under the Kroger brand.

Price

The setting of price and its importance in the marketing mix are indeed complex. They depend partly on the appraisal of consumer behavior toward possible prices and overall marketing strategy. When introduced, the overall prices for the Saturn

·cars were lower than expected. Industry experts believed that General Motors'
pricing strategy was set to reflect a high-volume strategy rather than a high-revenue-
per-car strategy. The decision reflected a desire to gain market share rather than
higher revenues on a per-car basis.[2]

From an advertising standpoint, the price charged for a brand affects several
decisions. For example, price often relates to the size of the advertising budget. If
a product's price allows a large margin of gross profit, increased advertising dollars
may be feasible. The media that are chosen also may relate to pricing policy. A
brand priced at the high end of a price range may require media selections that
convey this image. For example, consider the pricing of watches. The high-priced
brands such as Rolex are more consistently advertised in publications that appeal
to upper income segments of the population. And, of course, the type of message
used in the advertising will be affected by pricing strategy.

Channels of Distribution (Place)

The marketer has a choice of several methods of distribution. Selling can be direct
to consumers. Advances in direct marketing, such as catalog sales and 800 numbers,
have accelerated the growth of shopping without going to a retail store. Land's End,
L.L. Bean, Eddie Bauer, and J. Crew are all examples of successful marketers that
compete in the market for casual clothes.

More traditional forms of distribution consist of manufacturers, wholesalers, and
retailers. Or it may involve only manufacturers and retailers. Regardless of the
channel of distribution used, the marketer must blend this ingredient of the mix
with the other elements. Thus, a brand marketed by a company that seeks to establish
high prestige through its product, pricing, and advertising policies must follow suit
by selecting retail outlets that match the total strategy. Certain types of discount
stores, which focus heavily on low price and minimum service, would not be a
good channel outlet.

Channel decisions and advertising planning are further entwined by the degree and
type of advertising support that dealers give brands. Some retailers may extensively
advertise a national brand available in their store. This often happens when a retailer
carries a brand on an exclusive basis. A marina or boat store, for example, may be
the only retailer in the area that handles Sea Ray boats and may be willing to
advertise this fact extensively.

Many marketers provide their dealers with advertising materials and subsidies to
encourage support at the retail level. Additionally, marketers may devote part of
the budget for advertising to channel members or prospective dealers; this is called
trade advertising. Trade advertising may accomplish any number of marketing
objectives, such as getting a brand into a retail outlet, enlisting retailer aid in
promoting the brand, and paving the way for calls by the company's sales staff.
Chapter 20 discusses both retail and trade advertising.

Promotion

Promotion in the marketing mix traditionally consists of four areas: personal selling,
sales promotion, advertising, and public relations. Discussion in this section briefly
touches on personal selling, sales promotion, public relations, and advertising. Sales
promotion and public relations are covered more completely in Chapter 19.

The role personal selling plays in the marketing mix depends on a number of
factors. The complexity of the product is one factor to consider. For many business-
to-business goods, the prospective buyer needs technical explanations of how they
work, and personal selling often is the dominant promotional tool. Among goods
sold at the retail level, those with hidden qualities and complicated features benefit
from personal sales effort. Many buyers of stereo equipment, for example, will seek
a store that is noted for the quality of its sales staff. As in the case of other mix
ingredients, the type and extent of personal selling affects advertising decisions.
Because advertising and personal selling are both forms of promotion, the need for

their coordination is critical. In many cases, salespeople use advertising material when they call on a customer.

Sales promotion is the most rapidly increasing form of promotion. Expenditures for sales promotions surpass the expenditures for advertising media.[3] Sales promotion can take the form of either consumer promotions or trade promotions. Consumer promotions are aimed at customers who use the product. Coupons, rebates and sweepstakes are typical consumer promotions. Trade promotions are directed to channel members, such as retailers and distributors, in order to get them to carry and sell the product. Common forms of trade promotions, those activities directed to wholesalers, distributors, and retailers, are case discounts and trade shows.

Sales promotion activities are generally undertaken to add to the basic value of the product for a limited time period, and thus, stimulate consumer purchasing and sales force and dealer effectiveness. Consumers, salespeople, and dealers are motivated in the short run. Therefore, sales promotion efforts can be an effective strategy for quick, positive results.

The transient nature of sales promotion makes it inappropriate for building brand loyalty and long-run sales. Sales promotion is associated with non-consumer-franchise activities that employ nonunique incentives (a price cut is seldom unique) to speed up the buying decision or to obtain distribution and trade support.

Public relations refers to the firm's communication and relationships with various publics, including customers, stockholders, employees, suppliers, government, and the society in which it operates.[4] Public relations seeks to help build prestige and favorable image for all aspects of the corporation. While the goals of public relations are broader than advertising, both are working to enhance image and sales and therefore need to work together. The next section will demonstrate how advertising and other communication elements are coordinated.

Integrated Marketing Communications

We have noted a number of marketing communications tools that can be used to reach customers and channel members. **Integrated marketing communications** is concerned with the strategic coordination of all marketing communications tools used by the firm. Many feel that such coordination will be the key to effective planning in the 1990s.

> Integrated marketing communications—the coordination of media advertising, direct marketing, promotion, or public relations for a brand—has become the hot marketing issue of the 1990s.[5]

The purpose of integrated marketing communications is to provide an orchestrated message to all customers, dealers, and other publics. Such coordination has been termed "one voice marketing" because all efforts are coordinated to present a clear and consistent message. Figure 7.4 shows many of the activities that enable marketing communicators to speak in one voice.

While the idea of providing clear and consistent messages across marketing communications channels is not altogether new, changes in technology and market strategy have provided new opportunities and challenges. The following are some of the major changes that have increased the opportunity and need for coordination:

• The rise in direct marketing whereby marketers have direct communication with customers, for example, through catalogs and direct mail. Many marketers have created their own data bases or lists of specific customers that are contacted directly.

FIGURE 7.4

Integrated Marketing Communications

All forms of communications are integrated to present clear and consistent
marketing efforts that speak in one voice.

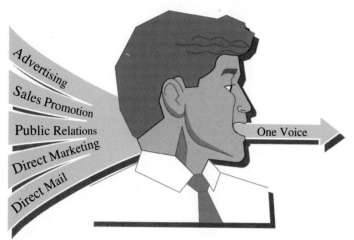

- The sophistication of direct-mail targeting. Computerization of lists and printing allows marketers to reach consumers on a routine basis.
- The proliferation of select broadcast media, such as specific cable channels, that allow for greater definition of target markets.
- Increased telecommunication activity—such as the use of 800 numbers—to facilitate direct selling and ordering.
- Greater use of sales promotion requiring greater coordination with advertising.

The two following examples, each using different forms of integrated marketing, illustrate the above changes and opportunities.

Advertising Works With Direct Mail, Data Based Marketing

Audi of America shifted the majority of its magazine budget to Time Inc. Audi used Time Inc.'s major magazines, *Time, Sports Illustrated, Fortune,* and *Money* to advertise its automobiles. Additionally, Audi tapped the publishers data base and used selective-binding and ink-jet printing to create a highly targeted direct-mail effort. Merging information from Time Inc.'s subscriber data base allowed for a profiling of likely Audi buyers who could be targeted for a special incentive to test drive an Audi.[6]

Advertising Works With Select Cable, 800 Numbers

Ryder Trucks used integrated marketing communications to help sell used rental trucks. Ryder's advertising agency, Ogilvy & Mather, combined a mixture of direct response and direct mail, creating television ads that included an 800 number. Viewers were urged to call for a free booklet on how to buy a used truck.[7]

Kellogg's Coordinated Effort, Integrated Marketing Communications at Work

During the introduction of Kellogg's Frosted Bran and Low Fat Granola, the company integrated three forms of promotion: print advertising, free samples, and cents-off coupons. The three forms of promotion were coordinated to arrive at the same time. Consumers in the Atlanta area received all three items in the Sunday newspaper.

The advertisement took one full page in the newspaper and the coupon was distributed in a separate coupon section called a free-standing insert. The free sample was attached to the paper.

Using this coordinated strategy, Kellogg's was able to have the reader–(1) become aware of the product, (2) try the product, and (3) have an incentive for further use— all at the same time!

The above Ad Insight entitled "Kellogg's Coordinated Effort, Integrated Marketing Communications at Work" illustrates how advertising, free samples, and cents-off coupons were all coordinated to arrive on the same day. Such coordination requires a great deal of planning. As noted by James C. Reilly, General Manager, Marketing Services and Communications, IBM, United States, "Integrated marketing communication, by definition, requires planning across a number of communications, from advertising to public relations to trade shows, and so on."[8]

The Planning of Advertising

Marketing mix planning and integrated marketing communication planning enhance our ability to focus on advertising campaign planning. The planning of a successful advertising campaign requires a number of elements organized in a logical procedure. This section provides an overview of the factors that contribute to the process. Figure 7.5 shows the elements involved in campaign planning and the order in which they usually appear. Chapters 3 through 5 showed that advertising operates in a larger economic and regulatory environment. Chapter 2 and the preceding section of this chapter point out that advertising operates in a larger marketing and communications context.

The planning elements are shown in Figure 7.5. They include marketing communication considerations, such as the marketing mix and integrated marketing communication, strategic research, objective setting, budgeting, strategic message and media decisions, tactical message and media decisions, final budget, running the campaign, and measuring the campaign's effectiveness. Each element is briefly discussed in the following pages of this chapter.

Later chapters in Part 2 and Part 3 will be devoted to further discussion of each of the highlighted elements shown in Figure 7.5. And following Chapter 12, an Appendix containing an advertising campaign will illustrate how advertisers and their agencies actually create campaigns.

FIGURE 7.5

Campaign Planning Framework

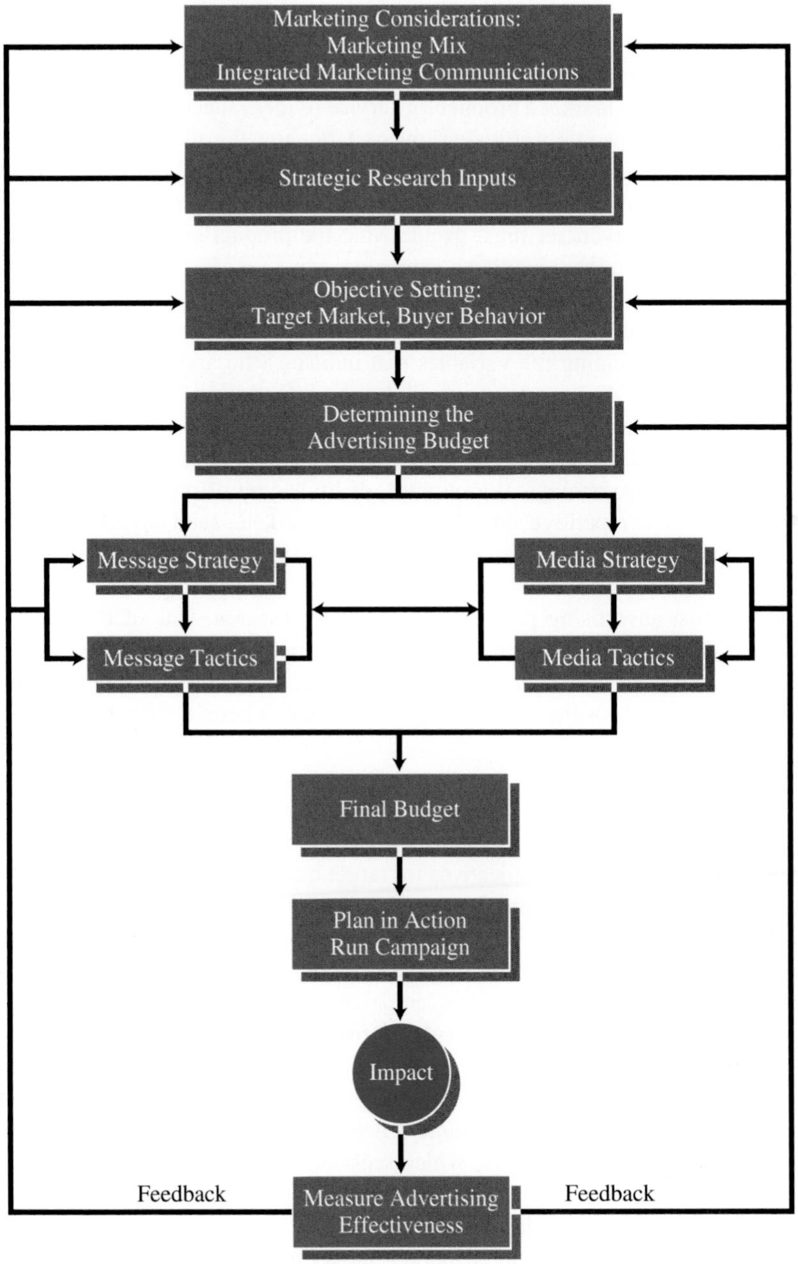

```
        ┌──────────────────────────────────────┐
        │ Marketing Considerations:            │
        │ Marketing Mix                        │
        │ Integrated Marketing Communications  │
        └──────────────────────────────────────┘
                        │
        ┌──────────────────────────────────────┐
        │ Strategic Research Inputs            │
        └──────────────────────────────────────┘
                        │
        ┌──────────────────────────────────────┐
        │ Objective Setting:                   │
        │ Target Market, Buyer Behavior        │
        └──────────────────────────────────────┘
                        │
        ┌──────────────────────────────────────┐
        │ Determining the                      │
        │ Advertising Budget                   │
        └──────────────────────────────────────┘
            ┌───────────────────┴───────────────────┐
     ┌──────────────┐                        ┌──────────────┐
     │ Message Strategy │                    │ Media Strategy │
     └──────────────┘                        └──────────────┘
     ┌──────────────┐                        ┌──────────────┐
     │ Message Tactics │                     │ Media Tactics │
     └──────────────┘                        └──────────────┘
            └───────────────────┬───────────────────┘
                    ┌──────────────┐
                    │ Final Budget │
                    └──────────────┘
                    ┌──────────────┐
                    │ Plan in Action │
                    │ Run Campaign │
                    └──────────────┘
                        ( Impact )
     Feedback   ┌──────────────────────┐   Feedback
                │ Measure Advertising  │
                │ Effectiveness        │
                └──────────────────────┘
```

Advertising planners should begin with strategic research. Research, when done properly, minimizes guesswork and allows decision makers to develop a plan as scientifically as possible. But research should not be a substitute for careful analysis or "creative" solutions to problems. Of the various kinds of research, each has its own potential uses. Four major areas of advertising research—consumer research, product research, market analysis, and the competitive situation—are introduced here. Chapter 8 will provide an in-depth discussion of each.

Strategic Research
Inputs

The value of consumer research should be especially clear. The marketing concept stresses the sovereignty of the consumer. Systematic applications of the behavioral sciences have led to better ways of understanding the consumer. Consumer research can give guidance in a number of planning areas, such as setting objectives, defining target markets, and developing message (creative) and media strategies.

Product research is a special kind of consumer research that concentrates on consumers' opinions and preconceptions about the product, service, or idea that is being advertised. To market a product (or service or idea) successfully, the advertiser must learn not only people's attitudes toward it, but how the attitudes are symbolized in a brand or corporate image. (The use of imagery and symbols in advertising is most important in the development of message strategy and is further discussed in Chapter 11.) The advertiser must decide what the product's strong points are and capitalize on them in the advertising campaign. Most successful campaigns emphasize product strengths and minimize product weaknesses.

Market analysis is a type of research that helps locate markets for a particular brand. It involves finding the variables that indicate who and where the product's best prospects are. Market analysis provides the information from which a planner can decide on a target market. Target markets can be defined in any number of ways—for example, by the demographic characteristics of consumers, by geographic location, by sociopsychological groupings, or by degree of product usage.

Analyzing the competitive situation allows the marketer (and advertising planner, which are used interchangeably) to examine the strategies of competitors. Such an examination allows the marketer to make adjustments according to the competitive situation. Most advertising planners do use some research. One of the first things a planner often wants to know before developing the campaign is how well various brands are doing in terms of market share. Information would be valuable in understanding the sales position of leading brands and where a new brand may be positioned in the market.

The Setting of Objectives

After developing a number of strategic research inputs, decision makers are ready to develop specific advertising objectives for target markets. Clearly, every advertising campaign should contain a precise set of objectives. Advertising objectives serve to give everyone working on the campaign a clear sense of direction and an understanding of what should be accomplished. Advertising objectives also serve to help coordinate everyone working on the campaign.

Understanding buyer behavior results in realistic objectives. The most common advertising objectives fall into three categories: (1) learning objectives, which serve to make consumers aware of or knowledgeable about the product; (2) feeling objectives, which attempt to have consumers develop a favorable attitude toward the product; and (3) doing objectives, which seek to have consumers take some action toward the product. A detailed explanation of the kinds of objectives that advertisers commonly develop is provided in Chapter 9.

Determining the specific target market allows marketers to write more precise objectives. Target markets can be segmented along a number of lines—demographics, psychographics, and product usage, for example. The development of a target market is critical to advertising planning.

The Advertising Budget

Determining the amount of money to be spent on the advertising campaign is a key decision in the campaign planning process. A primary time for budget decisions occurs after the planner develops specific objectives. This sequence allows the advertiser to assess the cost of meeting the stated objectives. However, budgeting decisions are often made at other points in the planning process. For example, many advertisers develop a budget based on last year's sales or what they anticipate will happen to sales next year. At times advertisers will spend an amount of money thought necessary to match the competition. Other advertisers use sophisticated budgeting techniques based on market tests.

Decisions about advertising budgets often involve top-level management. In fact, advertising campaign planners are not always responsible for determining the amount of money to be spent. Rather, the expenditure is established by the top marketing executive or even the top official in the company. Regardless of who makes the decision, campaign planners need to provide as much input as possible. The campaign planner's research, target market, and objective-setting decisions provide the framework for sound budget decisions.

As Figure 7.5 indicates, a final budget is constructed after all of the media and creative decisions have been made. The budget is both a procedure for arriving at an allocation—the total number of dollars devoted to advertising—and a detailed account of how the allocation will be spent. Chapter 10 details the methods used to determine advertising budgets and the factors that affect the allocation.

Message and Media Strategy

Developing a campaign theme for the message and selecting media for disseminating the message are the heart of campaign planning. All of the carefully researched inputs, defined markets, objectives, and budgets set the stage for the creation and dissemination of the advertising message. Message development and media planning usually take place concurrently.

Message planners and media planners work in concert to create a solid campaign. Distinct message ideas and images that are effectively conveyed through media are invaluable to a company. For example, 9-Lives cat food has used Morris the Cat to convey the message, "even finicky cats can't resist 9-Lives." Television is used as the primary medium because it allows for a close view of Morris and the product.

Once key strategic decisions are made, someone must decide how to execute them. The planning model shows that both message and media tactics are directly derived from message and media strategies. Part 3 of the text closely examines the development and execution of message and media tactics and the host of production decisions that must be made.

The Plan in Action

After the essential background information has been gathered through research, the advertising objectives have been set, and the strategy and tactics have been developed, the plan is put into action. Advertising may be scheduled for the entire target market (for example, the whole country for a national advertiser or a metropolitan area for a retailer's campaign) or it may be tested in only a few selected markets. Putting the plan into action can produce a market impact that is positive, negative, or neutral, depending on the plan's objectives and how well they are executed.

Measuring the Effectiveness of Advertising

Measuring advertising effectiveness is the primary way to understand the success of the advertising plan. This involves how well the advertising campaign met the desired message and media objectives. For example, if an advertising goal is to increase product awareness among a target market from 25 percent to 50 percent, this can be measured. Chapter 8 provides a detailed look at the techniques used to measure advertising effectiveness.

Adjustments to the Campaign

Once a campaign has been planned and executed and the market impact has been measured, planners must conduct an analysis to determine: What actions were successful? Why? If we had done certain things differently, would results have been drastically changed? If so, why?

The purpose of measuring the effectiveness of advertising, and making evaluations, is to provide the planner with feedback on the total process. This feedback then logically serves as a research input for the next stage of the campaign. Thus, each successive campaign plan should benefit from its predecessor.

Summary

A logical and systematic approach is needed in the planning of an advertising campaign. One of the first things the planner does is to assess the social, cultural, and regulatory environments. This is followed by a careful examination of the company's marketing mix (product planning, pricing, channels of distribution, and promotion) and how all of the marketing communication tools will be integrated.

Strategic research is used to define target markets and set advertising objectives. Budgeting considerations must be closely tied to the objective setting process. Planners then develop media and message strategies—"the heart of a campaign."

Following implementation of the plan, the market impact of an advertising campaign should be assessed through techniques that measure advertising effectiveness. The planner can incorporate this feedback in subsequent campaigns.

Questions for Discussion

1. What is the relation of advertising to the other ingredients of the marketing mix?
2. Why has integrated marketing communications become an important issue in the 1990s?
3. Why are advertising objectives important?
4. What sequence of events does an advertising planner go through?

Notes

1 Howard Schlossberg, "U.S. Firms: Quality Is the Way to Satisfy," *Marketing News,* February 4, 1991, 1.
2 George Leaming, "Saturn Strategy: On Solid Ground or Up in the Stars?," *Marketing News,* November 6, 1990, 8.
3 Scott Hume, "Trade Promotions Devour Half of All Marketing $," *Advertising Age,* April 13, 1992, 3.
4 Louis E. Boone, and David L. Kurtz, *Contemporary Marketing,* 7th ed. (Ft. Worth, TX: Dryden Press, 1992), 533.
5 Scott Hume, "New Ideas, Old Barriers," *Advertising Age,* July 22, 1991.
6 Scott Donaton, "Audi Turns to Time Inc. for $5M Targeted Effort," *Advertising Age,* June 1, 1992, 50.
7 "The New Advertising," *Agency,* Fall, 1990, 28–33.
8 James C. Reilly, "The Role of Integrated Marketing Communications In Brand Management," *A.N.A./The Advertiser,* Fall, 1991, 32–38.

Boone, Louis E., and David L. Kurtz. *Contemporary Marketing,* 7th ed. Ft. Worth, TX: Dryden Press, 1992. Chapters 16–18.

Kotler, Philip. *Marketing Management.* 7th ed. Englewood Cliffs, NJ: Prentice-Hall, 1991. Chapters 21–23.

Kurtz, David L., and Louis E. Boone. *Marketing,* 3d ed. Hinsdale, IL: Dryden Press, 1987. Chapters 2, 9–20.

Schultz, Don E., *Strategic Advertising Campaigns,* 3d ed. Lincolnwood, IL: NTC Business Books, 1990.

Suggested Readings

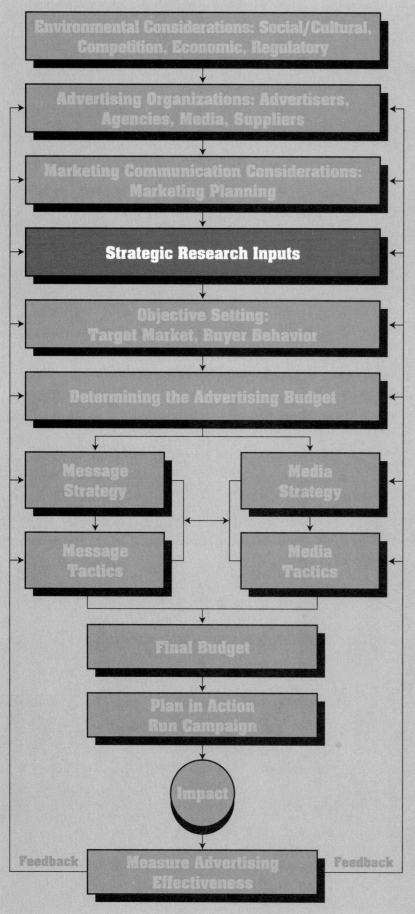

LEARNING OBJECTIVES

In your study of this chapter, you will have an opportunity to:

- Learn the steps in the research process.
- Examine the key research inputs for campaign planning.
- Understand how advertising effectiveness tests relate to campaign planning.
- Appreciate the difference between communication-effect and action-effect tests.
- Learn about the different methods available for advertising effectiveness testing.

Chapter 8

The Research Process

CHAPTER TOPICS

THE RESEARCH PROCESS
  Information Needs
  Secondary Sources
  Primary Sources
  Data as Input
STRATEGIC RESEARCH
  Consumer Research
  Product Research

Market Analysis
Competitive Situation
MEASURING ADVERTISING EFFECTIVENESS
  Some Barriers to Testing
  Classification Schemes for Measuring Effectiveness

Any advertising decision maker is confronted with numerous questions, decisions, and choices concerning the planning and implementation of a campaign. The following are some of the major questions that need to be answered: To what group or target market should we direct the campaign? What should be our objectives? How much should we spend? What should we say? Which media should we use? How much media should we use? Did my advertising work?

Research is an essential ingredient that answers questions and assists in the decision-making process. A great deal of time, effort, and money is spent on research-assisted advertising decisions. In fact, the 50 largest advertising and marketing research companies had annual worldwide revenues of approximately 3.5 billion dollars in 1992.[1]

In Chapter 7, the campaign planning model, Figure 7.5 on page 207, indicates that research is used initially for strategic decisions and finally to measure the impact of advertising effectiveness. Information learned from effectiveness research is then used as feedback into the planning process. This chapter provides an overview of the research process and then addresses the key areas of strategic research and measuring advertising effectiveness.

The Research Process

The research process consists of several separate steps. The researcher (1) establishes the need for information and develops research objectives, (2) determines sources of data, (3) develops data collection forms and designs the sample, (4) collects and processes the data, (5) analyzes the data, and (6) presents research results.[2] Figure 8.1 shows how these steps relate to the research process.

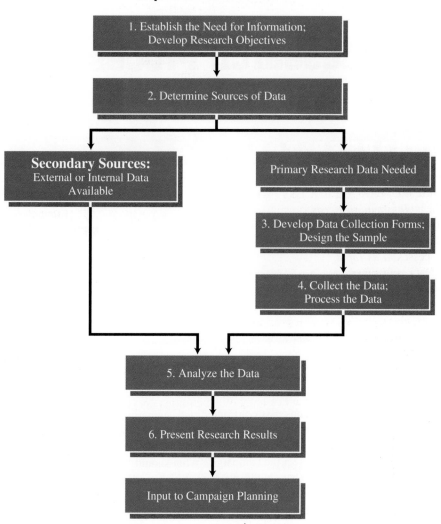

FIGURE 8.1

Steps in the Research Process

1. Establish the Need for Information; Develop Research Objectives

2. Determine Sources of Data

Secondary Sources: External or Internal Data Available

Primary Research Data Needed

3. Develop Data Collection Forms; Design the Sample

4. Collect the Data; Process the Data

5. Analyze the Data

6. Present Research Results

Input to Campaign Planning

Source: Adapted from Gilbert A. Churchill, Jr., *Marketing Research*, 5th ed. (Hinsdale, IL: Dryden Press, 1991), 69.

Information Needs

Establishing the need for information is a critical initial step that is more difficult than it may seem. The researcher must know *why* the information is needed and *how* the research will assist the various areas of advertising campaign planning and execution. Research can be used throughout the development, execution, and evaluation of the campaign. It is important to understand to which specific area of the campaign the information will be applied.

When the need for information is established, the next step is to specify research objectives. Research objectives are written to specifically determine the information needs for the project. Objectives serve as a guide to the questions that will be answered.

Following the establishment of research objectives, the planner determines how to obtain the necessary information. This often involves a decision regarding whether the information can be obtained from an existing source or whether the information needs to be specifically researched for the company.

As noted in Figure 8.1, secondary research, which uses data already available from inside or outside sources, follows the path at the left. The researcher first determines whether the data needed are already available from **secondary** research consisting of internal or external sources. Previous company research studies and company records serve as internal sources. There are 6,000 corporate libraries in the United States, many of which specialize in secondary research. The use of secondary research extends far beyond the United States. A recent study indicates that Japanese planners use secondary research extensively.[3]

External sources include commercially produced research reports, trade reports, and government data. A number of external data sources used in campaign planning will be discussed later in the chapter in the Ad Insight entitled "Sources for Strategic Research."

Secondary Sources

Primary research, which involves the gathering of original data, follows the path at the right of Figure 8.1. There are many different methods of primary research. The most common methods include mail and telephone surveys, personal interviews, field tests, and field observations. Most of these techniques are discussed throughout the chapter. The use of these methods involves steps 3 through 4 of the research process.

Data collection forms or observation formats must be developed for use in obtaining the information needed. The forms constitute the way researchers ask the questions or observe consumers. Much of the time we think of the forms as questionnaires, although they may be as simple as a tally sheet or written notes taken from trained observers.

Sample design concerns the selection of people to be studied. The researcher must establish the population of individuals from which to draw a **sample** and also the size of the sample.

Data collection is the actual obtaining of the information. Researchers are careful to select and train skilled interviewers or observers to collect the data. Data processing is used to edit and code the data in order to analyze the information. Editing involves looking at the data to make sure it is consistent. It can then be coded—that is, placed into appropriate categories.

Primary Sources

As Figure 8.1 indicates, whether the data are obtained from primary or secondary sources, they must be analyzed. Data analysis is conducted to determine that the information obtained in the study actually meets the research objectives. At this point, the researcher is obtaining answers to the original questions asked.

The information obtained, when organized in a clear and concise way, becomes the presentation of the results. Results are presented in a written or an oral report, and often both.

Although the researcher may make specific recommendations, management is ultimately responsible for making final decisions. It is important to understand that people, not research data, actually make the decisions. When used properly, information obtained from the research process should ultimately provide a valuable input to campaign planning.

Data as Input

Strategic Research

Strategic research generates information that is the foundation of an advertising campaign. The results of the research allow advertising managers to make decisions that are transformed into objective setting, budgeting decisions, message strategy and tactics, and media strategy and tactics.

These inputs provide a planner with (1) an understanding of the targeted consumer to be reached by the campaign, (2) the product and brand attributes as perceived by consumers, (3) a knowledge of which markets provide which opportunities, and (4) the ways competing brands are operating in the marketplace. Collectively, this kind of research is a base on which to build campaign objectives and strategies.

Strategic research should precede both objective setting and budgeting. It allows for the development of marketing and advertising strategy. While strategic research is used primarily in the planning stages, it can also be used throughout the campaign to monitor overall trends. Four common types described briefly in Chapter 7 will now be discussed in more detail: consumer research, product research, market analysis, and the competitive situation.

Consumer Research

Understanding the consumer in terms of the influences on purchase decisions is one of the first, and most basic, steps in planning an advertising strategy. It affects various elements of an advertising campaign, including the setting of objectives, defining target markets, developing the creative strategy, and planning media selections. The more we know about consumers—what motivates them to buy a product, their perceptions about advertising, and the people who influence their brand choice—the better able we are to choose meaningful targets for our campaign, write effective advertisements and commercials, and select media.

Research and other aspects of consumer behavior are often taught at the college level as a separate course. **Consumer behavior** focuses on why and how people purchase and use products and services. The underpinnings of consumer behavior are the fields of human behavior, namely, psychology, sociology, and anthropology.

In psychology, we focus attention on individual factors. Our concern is with motives (what causes a person to want certain products?): personality, learning, attitudes and beliefs, and perception. For example, researchers discovered that many chocolate lovers kept secret stashes of the product hidden throughout the house. The finding resulted in the advertising campaign theme, "True Confessions of Chocoholics."[4]

FIGURE 8.2

Advertisement Conveying the Social Appeal of Fun in a Group Activity

Sociology is concerned with groups and, specifically, how people interact in certain situations. Social factors are the basis for understanding consumer behavior through reference groups, the family, and the role of peer and group influence. Figure 8.2 shows a product that is oriented to the social appeal of fun in a group activity.

Anthropology (especially cultural anthropology) focuses on a unit of even broader consequence than the group—the sociocultural environment of a total society. Consumers are often observed in their natural habitat (for example, at home or during leisure activities) to understand the cultural significance of using the product. Grey Advertising employed such a technique in investigating how women used Crisco. Researchers at Grey discovered that baking a pie was the act of creation and celebration rather than just making dessert. This resulted in the campaign theme, "Recipe for Success."[5]

A simple overview of the consumer decision process presented in Figure 8.3 shows many individual, social, and cultural factors that influence a consumer's purchasing behavior and the process by which decisions are made. For example, an advertisement or other stimulus input may get you to consider purchasing the advertised brand. Before making a final decision, however, you may weigh several individual, social, and cultural factors: Do I need the product? How does the product fit or enhance my image or personality—is it me? How will my family or friends react? After purchasing the product, you may actively assess how well the product met your expectations. The postpurchase assessment becomes feedback for later decisions.

Product research focuses on how the consumer perceives the total product, including the physical, service, and symbolic attributes. In developing the advertising campaign, planners must keep in mind what consumers know about the product and what consumers like and expect from a product.

Product Research

FIGURE 8.3

An Overview of the Consumer Decision Process

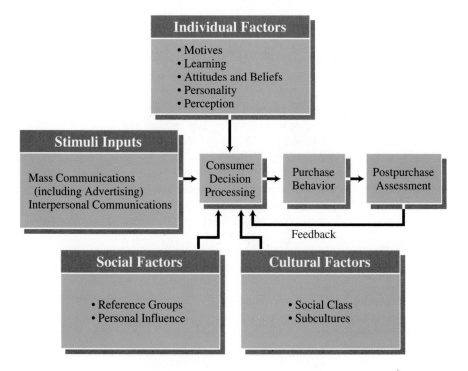

Understanding consumer desires and expectations are often integral parts of product design. For example, Mazda created Miata with the expectation of creating a two-seat roadster reminiscent of the Lotus and Triumph that many affluent baby boomers grew up admiring. Mazda engineers researched and matched the sound of the Miata to actual consumer perceptions of what a roadster was supposed to have sounded like. This type of product research is one reason the Miata was such a success upon its introduction.[6]

Product **positioning** involves developing a strategy aimed at a particular market segment and designing it to achieve a desired position in the customer's mind.[7] Positioning research seeks to understand what consumers think of existing products, proposed new products, and competing products.

Advertising strategists can use research findings to position products with advertising.[8]

For example, positioning research for 7-Up indicated that consumers categorized products in the soft drink category as colas or noncolas. This finding led to advertising 7-Up as the uncola.[9]

*M*arket Analysis

A third strategic research area, market analysis, helps identify market opportunity by spotting trends. The knowledge gained from this research input bears directly on defining target markets, developing products, and creating effective campaigns. Market analysis provides information that reveals a "picture" of the marketplace. The planner uses this information to decide which markets provide the greatest opportunity for development.

An initial approach to market analysis is to examine demographic characteristics of consumers. One excellent source is the national census of the population conducted every ten years by the U.S. Bureau of the Census. Some figures are updated annually. The census provides extensive information: the age distribution of the population, how much people earn, their level of education and occupational levels, and the like. For example, the 1990 census revealed that 10 percent of the U.S. population (approximately 24 million individuals) are Hispanic. The Census Bureau predicts that the Hispanic market will grow to 13 percent and that most Hispanics live in Los Angeles, New York, Miami, Chicago, and Texas.[10] This market analysis shows a growing market concentrated mostly in metropolitan areas, thus providing a great deal of opportunity for developing products and services.

For many U.S. firms, market analysis takes on global dimensions. Table 8.1 shows market opportunity for soft drinks, fast food, athletic footwear, and blue jeans among young adults between 14–34 years of age. The study was conducted for MTV: Music Television by Yankelovich Clancy Shulman researchers. Young adults of these ages around the world are most apt to watch MTV.[11]

There are several sources of information available on product use. An overview of many of these services is provided in the Ad Insight "Sources for Strategic Research." Two of the leading services providing product and market information are Standard Rate and Data Service (SRDS) and the Survey of Buying Power Index provided by Sales and Marketing Management. These services provide national, regional, and local data in such areas as household income, consumer spendable income, retail sales, and consumer demographics. Two firms, Simmons Market Research Bureau (SMRB) and Mediamark Research Inc. (MRI), specialize in providing information on product usage, media usage, and demographic characteristics.

*C*ompetitive Situation

A fourth research input to the campaign process involves monitoring the efforts of the competition. Information regarding competitive efforts is becoming increasingly important. Leo Bogart, a well-known advertising researcher, comments, "In a complex market—and all markets are complex these days—the way in which consumers respond often reflects not what the advertiser does but what the competitors do."[12]

TABLE 8.1

MTV: Music Television
Global Market Analysis: What Young Adults Buy

Participants were asked: "Which of the following have you purchased in the past three months?" *

Product	% in U.S.	% in Australia	% in Brazil	% in Germany	% in Japan	% in U.K.
Soft drinks	96	90	93	83	91	94
Fast food	94	94	91	70	86	85
Athletic footwear	59	40	54	33	30	49
Blue jeans	56	39	62	45	42	44

[1]Source: Yankelovich Clancy Shulman, *Advertising Age*, (November 18, 1991): 64.
*Young adults 14–34.

Many research organizations regularly collect information regarding major competitors. The cost of such research is considerably cheaper than research done by an individual company. The syndicated research is able to gain some economies of scale by repeatedly doing a certain kind of research; also, by selling the results to a number of clients, the researcher reduces the unit cost of the research. The Ad Insight entitled "Sources for Strategic Research" shows a number of these services.

When analyzing the competitive situation in terms of market shares and other related factors, many advertisers use the Nielsen Retail Index System. The service provides an audit of retail stores and a great deal of data concerning retail activity. Some of this information includes sales to consumers, retail inventories, number of day's supply, prices, and dealer support in such areas as displays, local advertising, and coupon redemption.

Advertisers also monitor the competitive situation by systematically following how much their competition spends in various advertising media. A number of research companies provide such syndicated research, including Leading National Advertisers (LNA), Broadcast Advertisers Report (BAR), Media Records, and Radio Expenditure Report (RER). LNA/Arbitron Multi-Media Report Service offers one of the most complete services in that it reports expenditures for major advertising media.

Many advertisers monitor and examine the message strategy of the competition. The purpose of such monitoring is to understand the competitors approach or positioning statement. For example, Avis has traditionally positioned itself as the number two car rental agency and stated that because they are number two, "At Avis, we try harder." In response, Hertz, the leader, has positioned itself as, "Hertz, the best never rests."

Measuring Advertising Effectiveness

Advertising agencies, advertisers, and media spend millions of dollars annually in an attempt to gauge the effectiveness of advertising. Specifically, they try to discover whether a particular advertisement or campaign will accomplish, or has

Sources for Strategic Research

A number of research companies provide valuable information for campaign planning. Below is a list of major sources and some of the information they provide. The sources have been placed in categories by which they are commonly used for strategic research and planning; however, in several cases they provide information that can be used for many purposes.

GENERAL MARKET PLANNING

Survey of Buying Power Data Service Regional data for household income and buying power, demographics, general retail sales, retail sales by store type and merchandise type. Provides market rankings in a number of categories and is available in a printed and a CD-ROM format.

Standard Rate and Data Service (SRDS) National, regional, and local data on number of households, consumer spendable income, retail sales, automobile registrations, and farm population. Provides market rankings in a number of categories.

UNDERSTANDING PRODUCT AND MEDIA USAGE

Simmons Market Research Bureau (SMRB) Demographic and psychographic information on heavy, medium, and light users of more than 5,100 brands in more than 800 product categories is combined with media use.

Mediamark Research Inc. (MRI) Drawing from a list of 70 million households, MRI's sample consists of demographic information on 20,000 heavy, medium, and light users of approximately 5,700 brands in 450 categories.

COMPETITIVE INFORMATION

Nielsen Retail Index System Consumer sales relative to competition, average retail prices of your product and competition, merchandise purchased by retailers for brand, product class, and store type.

Leading National Advertisers (LNA) Provides data on advertising expenditures by brand in specific magazines, outdoor advertising, and newspapers.

Broadcast Advertiser Reports (BAR) Data on competitive expenditures in network and spot television, syndicated television, cable television, and network radio.

LNA/ARBITRON Multi-Media Report Service General advertiser expenditures for nine different media.

Media Records Data on advertiser expenditures in newspapers.

Radio Expenditure Reports (RER) Data on advertiser expenditures in spot radio

accomplished, its objectives. Advertising research can be thought of as a way to help ensure that the money invested in advertising is well spent. Advertising effectiveness measures are key inputs to all elements of the planning process, as noted previously in Figure 7.5.

Several reasons account for the large sums allocated to advertising research. The growth in the scale of advertising expenditures has prompted marketers to be more knowledgeable concerning the impact of their campaigns. Some advertisements and campaigns are more effective than others, and managers are always trying to determine what is and what is not working. The development of more accurate measurement techniques has allowed managers to select from a wide array of testing services.

Some barriers to testing exist. Isolating the effects of advertising from the many other variables that produce a sale is difficult. Often the goal of the researcher is to point and say, "This ad produced that sale." The numerous factors that influence a sale make this a very difficult task. Instead of concentrating on sales, other communication factors are measured—such as readership, recall, consumer opinion, attention, and comprehension. The assumption is that such factors are related to sales.

Good research can be both expensive and time consuming. The advertising business is fast paced and it is often difficult to spend large sums of money for effectiveness results that may come six months or even a year into the future.

At times, creative people (although by no means all of them) object to the many measurement techniques and feel that researchers try to interfere with the creative process. They fear that certain writers may take research findings too literally and try to repeat only the "best-read" or "highest-rated" ads and, in the process, lose the unique or creative appeal necessary for effective advertising. Some creative people argue that consumers are so complex and unpredictable that no method can accurately assess the impact of advertising. By and large these fears are not well founded. Few researchers claim to be as infallible and are usually not as interfering as some creative individuals would believe. The key is to meld the sometimes complex input of advertising research into the copy and art of the creative process.

Finally, advertising people are at times understandably confused by the disagreements among researchers over the validity of the different methods of measuring audience response. There is no one correct method; instead, a number of methods measure different aspects of advertising effectiveness, often in combination.

Some Barriers to Testing

While we would like to know how much each element contributed to the advertising campaign, this is not always possible. The time consumed, the expense, and some of the uncertainty involved in testing means that the marketer must concentrate on the important problems that can be measured with some exactness. Most of the effectiveness measurements have to do with the message, the media, or the level of expenditure.

One way to approach the problem is to look briefly at two of the various schemes used to classify measurement methods. This will give some insight into several of the key variables that are likely to be influential in testing.

Classification Schemes for Measuring Effectiveness

Pretesting and Posttesting

A most useful approach in measuring advertising's effectiveness is to categorize tests according to whether they are conducted before the advertising is exposed to a final audience (pretesting) or after exposure (posttesting). Many advertisers examine customer reactions to proposed campaigns and use the results to help copywriters finalize the advertising appeal or campaign. Once the advertising actually is run in the media, a follow-up with posttests is conducted to determine message effectiveness.

Communication and Action Effects

A second method of classifying tests is to divide them into communication-effect and action-effect tests. Communication-effect research is based on the premise that many advertising objectives are communication oriented. Many of the traditional testing services are in the communications effectiveness area. The Ad Insight "Communication Effectiveness Measures" indicates just a few of the companies and the communication measurement provided. Action-effect research determines the impact advertising has on inquiries, sales, or some other action-based objective. No one approach is correct.

Communication Effectiveness Measures

A number of companies provide services to evaluate the communication effectiveness of advertising. This list examines some of the major services. The following sources have been placed in broadcast and print categories.

BROADCAST

ASI Market Research Provides television commercial testing for finished or rough commercials. Between 100 and 200 respondents are asked to view a commercial placed on an unused local cable channel. The test commercials are placed within the program in a typical format. Respondents are contacted the day after the program is aired to test for recall.

Gallup & Robinson Inc. Provides on-air pretesting of new commercials and posttesting of existing commercials set within prime time programming. The service can measure the commercial's ability to make an impression, the feelings that the commercial evokes, the commercial's ability to persuade, and its overall effectiveness.

Starch INRA Hooper Helps uncover the meanings that people find in commercials. The emphasis is placed on the commercial itself rather than on a comparison among other commercials or advertisements.

PRINT

ASI Market Research Print Plus Places test advertisements in selected magazines and asks respondents to read the magazine one evening and participate in a telephone survey the next evening. Measures day-after recall, persuasion, and product interest.

Gallup & Robinson Inc. Uses a sample of 150 adults for its Magazine Impact Research Service (MIRS) and its Rapid Ad Measurement (RAM). MIRS posttests ads by assessing the performance of individual ads, overall print campaign effectiveness, and assesses general patterns in creative strategies. RAM pretests magazine ads for proved name recognition, idea communication, and buying attitude.

Starch INRA Hooper Includes the Starch Readership Report, which studies 75,000 ads in 1,000 individual magazines. Face-to-face interviews zero in on recognition of the test ads. The Starch Impression Study asks respondents to tell what the ads mean to them. The Starch Ballot Readership Study measures the readership of advertisements in business magazines.

Harvey Research Organizations Inc. The Harvey Communications Measurement Service evaluates readership and impact of advertisements in business publications through face-to-face interviews. The Harvey Ad-Q examines advertising effectiveness among readers with buying influence.

Readex Readership Research Examines readership in advertisements and editorial items in business, professional, and farm publications. The Reader Interest Plus Report measures interest in ads and editorials that are at least one-half page. The Readex Red Report highlights certain articles and advertisements with red stickers placed in duplicate copies of the magazine. Readers are asked to comment on those articles and ads. The Message Impact Report looks at the performance of the advertisement.

Source: From A.D. Fletcher and T.A. Bowers, *Fundamentals of Advertising* (Belmont, CA: Wadsworth, 1991), 222–268.

Many advertisers use a communication-effect measure because of the difficulty in measuring action effects attributed to advertising. Yet others feel that the action or sales effectiveness of a campaign can be measured. The most important issue is to measure the success of the ad based on the prestated objective of the ad. Therefore, if an ad had a stated objective of awareness, then awareness should be used to measure whether the ad was successful. Obviously, measurement becomes more difficult in situations in which advertising objectives are stated as sales or some other action.

The pretesting/posttesting and the communication-effect/sales-effect classifications are combined in Figure 8.4. The resulting matrix groups advertising effectiveness measures by classification. Given the wide array of tests, we have selected only some of the more commonly used ones for discussion. Some of the tests can be placed in more than one location in the matrix. The decision about where to place a particular test is based on the typical use of that measure.

Communication Effects—Pretesting

Much advertising is assigned the task of accomplishing specific communication objectives. Accordingly, a number of pretests and posttests are available. Communication pretesting techniques have been the most widely used by advertisers. A number of methods, as we will discuss below, have been developed to test the effectiveness of the ad or campaign before it is run.

Dummy Advertising Vehicles This technique involves placing an ad in a dummy vehicle. Each issue of the dummy vehicle contains a full complement of editorial material and advertisements. Subjects are asked to read the magazine as they would an actual publication. They are then questioned on both the editorial content and the advertisements. Advertisements are evaluated on recall, the extent to which the copy was read, or the favorable opinions generated. This method can also be used for broadcast commercials when inserted in an actual television program (usually a pilot program that was not used by the network).

Dummy vehicles are widely used and, in the case of magazines, present a realistic testing situation (because readership is in the home). However, some concern exists that such tests measure product interest rather than interest in the creative approach.

Focus Groups Small group discussions are termed focus groups. Usually a focus group has between 8 and 12 subjects who have been specifically recruited to attend a meeting at a research facility. Subjects are often asked to discuss how they feel about a specific ad or campaign. Usually the ads are in rough or unfinished form, which saves final production costs.

Figure 8.5 shows ads tested in a research project sponsored by the American Cancer Society. The example on the left shows an advertisement with a currently

FIGURE 8.4

Classification of Advertising Effectiveness Measures

	Communication Effects	**Action Effects**
Pretesting	Dummy Advertising Vehicles/ Focus Groups Theater-type Tests On-the-Air Physiological Measures Projective Techniques	Inquiry/Direct Response Market Tests Single Source Services
Posttesting	Readership Tests Recall Tests Awareness and Attitude Tests	Inquiry/Direct Response Market Tests/Monitoring Single Source Services

FIGURE 8.5

**Two Advertisements Tested in Focus Groups to Determine the Impact
of Existing and Test Tobacco Warnings**

mandated Surgeon General's Warning (lower right). The advertisement on the right contains a test warning. Focus groups with teenagers were conducted to determine how young people make decisions about smoking and to see if newly created cigarette warnings would be more effective than the existing Surgeon General's warnings. Results revealed that teenagers did not relate to the Surgeon General's warning and that simple, more direct warnings worked best.

Focus groups are an excellent way to gain in-depth information; however, some problems are associated with these techniques because of the artificial nature of the sessions. Also, subjects may go along with the group and not reveal what they really think.

Theater-Type Tests   A number of research firms, such as ASI Market Research Inc., test commercials in a theater environment. Some use electronic recording equipment whereby each audience member has a control device to signify whether he or she likes or dislikes the commercial. Another technique asks direct and indirect questions about the commercial content. More recently the trend has been to test commercials on-site. To do this, research companies situate specially equipped trailers near shopping malls, or they set up equipment within shopping malls. Subjects are recruited to watch and rate commercials.

The strength of the technique centers around the subject's ability to view and respond in a controlled situation. Researchers, then, are assured that subjects are exposed to the commercial. On the other hand, the artificial nature of the situation may force consumers into paying more attention, than normal, to a commercial.

On-the-Air Techniques   ASI's Day After Recall (DAR) and Recall Plus measure responses to ads that are placed within broadcast programs. DAR tests about 200 subjects who are contacted by phone and who claim they watched a particular program the previous evening. The measures are either aided recall or unaided recall. Subjects are asked whether they remember seeing a commercial for a product in the product class of interest; for example, "Did you see an ad for hand soap?" This is termed unaided recall, because the particular brand is not mentioned. If they do not remember, subjects are asked whether they remember seeing a commercial for the specific brand. This is termed aided recall, because the specific brand is mentioned. Those who recall the ad are asked if they remember specific copy points. Recall Plus is a similar technique except that cable respondents in test cities are recruited and asked to preview an upcoming program in their homes. The use of cable allows ASI to use special programming. ASI then makes an appointment for a second interview for the day following the program. The prior recruiting and cable programming techniques offer the researcher more control.

On-the-air tests are widely used. A strength of these tests is that subjects have viewed the ad in their own home and that the testing situation is not artificial. However, critics claim that recall does not really mean consumers understand or like the message.

Physiological Methods   A number of techniques measure how subjects react to messages. These methods are gaining a great deal of interest among researchers. The following notes a few of the measures.

Applied Science Laboratories (ASL) utilizes eye tracking techniques to determine how the eye moves across the page. Subjects wearing a lightweight headset are monitored by a computer/VCR system that records the pattern of movement, pupil dilations, and length of viewing. Results determine the illustrations and copy points that are seen. Figure 8.6, top photo, shows a subject with an ASL headset and how the technique operates. The bottom photo gives an example of what the reader sees when using the apparatus.

Galvanic skin response (GSR) measures skin reactions by attaching electrodes to the subject (usually on the hand and forearm). The instrument measures changes in electrical resistance brought on by skin moisture as subjects read or view the advertising. Skin moisture is thought to be related to arousal or interest.

The tachistoscope, a mechanical device, is used to measure perception and allows the researcher to understand at what point the ad is perceived. The technique relies on a shutter that is placed on a slide projector. The shutter varies the amount of time that a picture is shown on the screen. The purpose is to determine how long it takes respondents to get the intended idea of the illustration or copy, an important factor in print and outdoor advertising. This technique is different from the GSR technique because it measures perception (when respondents note the information) rather than physiology.

Physiological measures have an advantage in that respondents have a limited chance to hide their true response. Recent advances such as the eye scanner have excellent potential in the understanding of reading and viewing behavior. However, there are some problems. The techniques are extremely artificial because subjects are asked to view or read while hooked to machines in a laboratory setting. Additionally, in the GSR, no one is really sure what is meant by interest or arousal and whether subjects are responding positively or negatively to the message.

Projective Techniques   These techniques avoid the pitfalls of direct questioning ("Do you like the ad?") and permit subjects to indirectly project their feelings. A trained interviewer probes individuals or small groups about their feelings and motivations concerning both products and messages. Researchers attempt to discover underlying feelings by asking questions that encourage subjects to project themselves into the situation. Typical questions are: What thoughts come to your mind?, and What does this ad tell you about yourself?

In many cases respondents are asked to complete sentences or to draw pictures. For example, researchers at McCann-Erickson used the projective technique to investigate the images of certain brands of cake mix. Subjects were asked to sketch

FIGURE 8.6

Tracking Device Used to Determine Eye Patterns during Reading

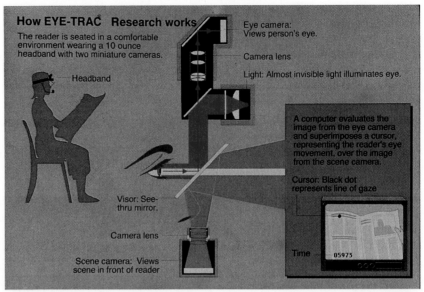

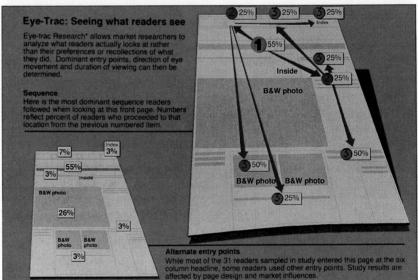

Source: Courtesy of Applied Science Labs, a division of Applied Science Group, Inc.

the typical brand users for two leading brands. Subjects portrayed Pillsbury customers as apron clad and grandmotherly and Duncan Hines users as more contemporary. This type of information can be helpful in understanding the brand image and creating advertising campaigns. Figure 8.7 reflects these portrayals.

Projective techniques can provide excellent insight and depth. However, the results depend heavily on the skill of the moderator. The information gathered is highly subjective and open to interpretation.

Communication Effects—Posttesting

Major forms of communication-effect posttesting are readership tests, recall tests, and awareness and attitude tests.

FIGURE 8.7

**The Results of a Projective Technique Used to Examine Consumers'
Underlying Feelings about Brands of Cake Mix**

Who Baked the Cake

*When asked to sketch figures of typical cake-mix users, subjects portrayed Pillsbury
customers as grandmotherly types and Duncan Hines buyers as svelte and contemporary*

McCANN–ERICKSON

Source: From *Newsweek* (February 27, 1989): 46.

Readership Tests   These widely used techniques measure recognition of magazine
ads. Starch INRA Hooper is the largest of the services and covers almost all of the
major magazines. A minimum of 100 readers of each sex are interviewed in their
homes or offices to determine the extent of readership for selected ads. Subjects
are asked if they have read the specific study issue of a particular publication. If
the answer is yes, the subjects are asked questions about the ads. The test is sometimes
referred to as "recognition" because subjects are shown the actual ad as it appeared
in the studied publication. Figure 8.8 shows a copy of an ad that has been scored.
Three scores are obtained:

- *Noted*   The percentage of issue readers who remembered having previously
  seen the ad in the issue being studied
- *Associated*   The percentage who remembered seeing some part of the ad that
  clearly indicated the brand name or advertiser
- *Read Most*   The percentage who read half or more of the material in the ad

The expense of the testing is partially borne by the magazines that use the data
as a sales tool to attract advertisers. Thus, the cost to the agency and client is fairly
low. The test is based on the premise that an ad must be seen or read before it can
have an impact on its audience. Results are often used to compare different ads in
the same product category in order to determine the effectiveness of different creative
approaches. To a degree, the technique measures the attention-getting value of the ad.

Starch has been subject to criticism because respondents are often thought to
confuse ads being measured in a specific issue with similar ads they may have seen

FIGURE 8.8

An Advertisement That Was Scored as Part of a Starch Readership Survey

before. However, while Starch has always recognized that some respondents may not be sure whether they saw a specific ad in the study issue or some other issue or publication, it employs two safeguards to minimize this problem. First, there is a screening procedure to qualify individuals as readers of the specific issue under study. Secondly, in the through-the-book interviewing procedure, respondents are questioned about whether a specific ad was seen or read in that particular issue. It is important to note that Starch interviews issue readers about that particular issue and does not purport to measure exposure to an ad without these restrictions.

Recall Tests   The recall test is closely related to the recognition test because both rely on memory. However, the recall test does not aid the reader as much. Hence, it is sometimes termed unaided recall. Gallup and Robinson offer an "Impact" service designed to show which ads are best at gaining and holding attention. Before subjects are interviewed, they must prove they have read the magazine by giving the details of at least one article or feature. Subjects are then handed cards showing the names of products advertised and asked to make a list of the ads they have seen. For each ad on a subject's list, he or she is asked a series of questions about content and persuasive power. Ads are scored on proved name recognition, idea communication, and favorable attitude.

By providing information on penetration of copy, recall tests give guidance on whether the subjects understood the idea of the ad. Information is supplied on "correct" and "incorrect" impressions of the ad. A problem is that the tests rely heavily on memory, and this may understate the effectiveness of some ads, particularly those who rely on low-level learning and imagery.

Awareness and Attitude Tests   In many cases advertisers conduct their own research to determine the effectiveness of a campaign. Prior to a new campaign the advertiser obtains a benchmark measure of awareness and attitudes toward the product. After the advertising campaign, a second measure is taken to determine if and how much awareness and attitudes have changed as a result of the advertising. The key to developing meaningful communication posttests is to make sure that the research measures the stated communication objective.

For example, the U.S. Postal Service (USPS) developed the "We Deliver" campaign with specific objectives: (1) to promote awareness and (2) to develop a positive image about the postal service and Express Mail (the overnight service). The benchmark research revealed that potential users had some negative perceptions concerning the USPS. The USPS was perceived as bureaucratic and institutional. After the new "We Deliver" campaign, a posttest measure was developed to see if the campaign had met the stated objectives. Posttest research indicated that awareness of the Express Mail service jumped from 76 percent to 86 percent. Additionally, following the campaign 67 percent of the potential users felt the USPS provided good service.

Action Effects—Pretesting

Ultimately, marketers view sales or similar forms of action, such as inquiry or trial, as the key to a campaign's success. We have noted the difficulty in understanding the contribution of advertising to actions in the market. However, a number of techniques can begin to assess this relationship. Pretesting techniques provide an understanding of the advertising on a reduced-scale basis by examining a testmarket environment to determine which advertising approach is potentially most profitable.

Inquiry/Direct Response Inquiry tests are used to check the potential sales effect of advertisements. Indeed many marketers will calculate the percentage of inquiries that are converted to sales.

Checking potential sales through inquiries can be very straightforward. Advertisers run ads and offer a certain inducement to reply, such as a gift or sample of the product. The usual approach is to divide the cost of the advertisement by the number of inquiries to find the cost of each inquiry. One variation is the split-run test, in which advertisers run two or more versions of an ad to determine the approach that garnered the most inquiries.

The rise in 800 (toll-free) numbers coupled with direct marketing that results in consumer purchases over the phone has led to a good deal of inquiry testing. A marketer can vary the appeal and determine which generates the most calls.

Inquiries certainly provide an understanding of subjects seeing or hearing the message. In many cases the advertiser can determine which approach worked the best. However, some inquiries may not represent sincere interest in the product. The use of inquiries and leads are not appropriate for all marketing situations. Also, unless a single element is being tested, such as one headline versus another, the results do not really determine an understanding of how the ad worked or which element worked. Finally, inquiry tests can be time consuming, taking several months for the final results.

Market Tests The purpose of market tests is to establish the potential impact of a national marketing program before a company invests large sums of money. Market tests take many different forms and examine a number of marketing variables, including new product testing, pricing, sales promotion strategies, and advertising. Advertising tests typically determine either (1) the best advertising approach or (2) the amount of advertising that is most productive in terms of sales, trials, or inquiries.

Market tests can take many forms. In a standard market test, an advertiser examines the impact of a promotional program on a limited basis to gauge what the reaction may be on a national level.

Single Source Services These services obtain a range of marketing information from the same company. Advances in television testing and supermarket scanning

Anthropologists in Advertising

Many companies attempt to sell values rather than product benefits. As a result, advertisers are beginning to research the cultural meanings of brands. This type of research uses anthropologists, who choose to observe consumers rather than ask questions of them. The cultural perspective reveals that people cannot always state "why" they use products and that we can understand consumers by watching them in a natural environment.

Following are some current examples of cultural studies:

Anthropologists were used to discover the "essence of Jeepness" or why upscale consumers were so loyal to Jeep.

Anthropologists found that rural letter carriers are seen as contacts with society and an antidote for loneliness. This led to the U.S. Postal Service to extend their theme to "We deliver for you."

Anthropologists watch mothers in a grocery store to determine the influence of children on purchasing.

Source: Gary Levin, "Anthropologists in adland." *Advertising Age,* February 24, 1992, 3.

equipment have fostered a number of single-source market test services that can be used on a test market basis. The information includes **people-metered** television viewing, which electronically measures television viewing and scanning equipment, which measures actual purchases. These developments have led to the electronic test markets that utilize a panel of households in a test area. People in these panels are given identification cards to show when checking out at the grocery store. All purchases are automatically recorded via the electronic scanners. Panel members are also monitored in terms of television viewing. Marketers correlate (associate) exposure to test commercials with purchases. The combination of measures can examine the impact of the amount of advertising, different forms of promotion, and new products.[13] A number of larger research companies, Nielsen, Arbitron, Information Resources Inc., and SAMI/Burke are all developing or offering such services.

Single source services are rapidly changing due to technology and market acceptance. Because these services are time consuming and expensive, they are not accessible to all advertisers. It should be cautioned that although the services can provide up-to-date information regarding viewing and purchasing, we cannot always assume that viewing leads to purchasing. Therefore, even with sophisticated market measures, we must rely on logical thinking to determine how we think advertising works. Chapter 9 provides a discussion of how advertising works.

Action Effects—Posttesting

Because advertising is an ongoing investment for most marketers, a need often exists to continually monitor the sales effectiveness of advertising.

Market Tests/Monitoring A great deal of market monitoring is used to continually update sales information through the use of scanning data. For example, Information Resources Inc. (IRI) has a national sample of homes on a panel that collects purchasing information via supermarket scanners. Panel members show their card when purchasing products. The national sample includes homes in many different markets around the country. This allows marketers to correlate promotional strategies with

Electronics

Overall, research spending will increase. This is due to the fact that marketers will have a pressing need to justify expenditures. Over the last few years, there has been an increase in measuring action effects, such as sales, in relation to advertising. This trend will increase:

There will be an increase in the use of electronic measurement techniques, such as people meters. People meters allow

for electronic measurements of all individuals in the room watching a program. Such techniques will be combined with viewing information on household shopping data obtained from supermarket scanners.

Large companies, such as Nielsen and Information Resources Inc. (IRI), will be introducing in-home scanning devices. Such devices, termed "wands," will allow for shoppers to easily record purchases in the home.

---

sales. Because the sample is large and over different markets, at times it is possible to vary the advertising approaches in separate areas to determine effectiveness.

Measures of Past Sales   A number of research services collect data useful in relating sales to advertising. The Nielsen Retail Index monitors retail sales, inventory, share of market, prices, displays and promotional effort. Another Nielsen system, ScanTrack, combines supermarket scanning data with regular visits to stores in order to monitor displays and other promotions. This is a rapidly changing area with new services continually entering the market.

Other research companies measure sales through consumer panels rather than retail store sales. NPD Group has a panel of 15,000 households that uses a preprinted diary to record purchases in 50 product categories.[14] Specialized panels are also used; for example, the Farm Research Institute maintains a panel who report purchases of agricultural products.

Retail audits and panel data are important sources of research sales. These systems do not provide a controlled test environment, but rather a way to monitor market action and promotional effort. In many cases, careful analysis can relate sales to promotional effort. However, many nonadvertising variables also influence sales and make it difficult to fully understand the impact of advertising.

Summary

Strategic research deals with the research elements that form the foundation of an advertising campaign. The research process involves a series of steps: (1) establishing the need for information and specifying objectives, (2) determining data sources, (3) developing data collection forms and designing the sample, (4) collecting and processing data, (5) analyzing the data, and (6) presenting research results. All of the steps are used in primary research; however, many syndicated sources of information may be utilized by advertising planners.

Research inputs provide the advertising decision maker with the base on which to build plans. There are different types of research, each providing somewhat different kinds of information. Consumer research, for example, can provide the planner with insights into how consumers behave in the marketplace and some of the reasons for such behavior. Product research also involves consumer responses, but looks more specifically to the relationships between such responses and elements of the product. Market analysis is a research input that assists a planner in identifying market opportunities, usually on the basis of demographic, geographic, or product usage dimensions. Analysis of the competitive situation through the monitoring of brand sales and advertising strategies is yet another area of strategic research that can assist the planning function.

A variety of measurement techniques provide feedback from advertising. They provide insights as to whether ads, media, or level of expenditure are communicating effectively and producing action such as sales, trials, or inquiries. Testing need not inhibit the best creative efforts of advertising people; instead, it should make their efforts more productive.

Advertising testing methods may be classified in a number of different ways. In measuring communication or action effects, we can choose either pretesting or posttesting methods. The most commonly used methods of pretesting communication effects are dummy vehicles, focus groups, theater-type tests, on-the-air tests, physiological methods, and projective techniques. Posttesting such effects can be accomplished by recognition tests, recall tests, and awareness and attitude tests.

The most typical pretests of action effects are inquiry tests and the use of inquiry and market tests. Posttesting action effectiveness involves both marketing/testing/monitoring and measuring of past sales.

Questions for Discussion

1. Discuss the value of strategic research in developing an advertising campaign.
2. How can a planner be assured that the research will be put to good use in campaign planning?
3. What is the difference between secondary (external or syndicated research) and primary research?
4. What is the broad definition of product?
5. Why is research on competitors important when planning an advertising campaign?
6. What is the difference between a pretest and a posttest?
7. What is the difference between communication-effect and action-effect tests?
8. What is a theater-type test?
9. What do physiological tests measure?
10. Why is a Starch test considered an aided recall test? Clip from a current magazine two advertisements that you feel would have a high "noted" score. Why do you think so?
11. Which posttest measures are undergoing the most rapid development and change? Why?
12. Is there a conflict between research and creative testing?

Notes

1. Jack J. Honomichl, "The Honomichl 50," *Marketing News*, June 7, 1993, 2.
2. Gilbert A. Churchill Jr., *Marketing Research Methodological Foundations*, 5th ed. (Hinsdale, IL: Dryden Press, 1991), 5.
3. Tim Powell, "Despite Myths, Secondary Research Is a Valuable Tool," *Marketing News*, September 22, 1991, 28.
4. Annetta Miller, Bruce Shenitz, and Lourdes Rosado, "You Are What You Buy," *Newsweek*, June 4, 1990, 60.
5. Ibid., 59–60.
6. Howard Schlossberg, "Pepperidge Farm Wins Grand Edison Award, AMA also cites 10 best new products for 89." *Marketing News*, March 14, 1990, 12.
7. Louis E. Boone and David L. Kurtz, *Contemporary Marketing*, 7th ed. (Ft. Worth, TX: Dryden Press, 1992), 560.
8. Alan D. Fletcher and Thomas A. Bowers, *Fundamentals of Advertising Research*, 4th ed. (Belmont, CA: Wadsworth, Inc., 1991), 27.

[9] Fletcher and Bowers, *Fundamentals of Advertising Research*, 27.

[10] Joaquin F. Blaya, "The Hispanic Market—Why You Need to Understand It," *A.N.A/The Advertiser*, Fall, 1991, 45.

[11] Nancy Giges, "Global Spending Patterns Emerge," *Advertising Age*, November 18, 1991, 64.

[12] Leo Bogart, "Advertising: Art, Science or Business?" James Webb Young Address Series. Department of Advertising, University of Illinois, 1988.

[13] Gilbert A Churchill, *Marketing Research Methodological Foundations*, 5th ed. (Hinsdale, IL: Dryden Press, 1991), 207.

[14] Ibid., 269.

Suggested Readings

Boone, Louis E., and David L. Kurtz, *Contemporary Marketing*, 7th ed. Hinsdale, IL: Dryden Press, 1992, Chapters 16, 17.

Churchill, Gilbert A. *Marketing Research Methodological Foundations*, 5th ed. Hinsdale, IL: Dryden Press, 1991.

Engel, James F., Roger D. Blackwell, and Paul W. Miniard. *Consumer Behavior,* 6th ed. Hinsdale, IL: Dryden Press, 1990.

Fletcher, Alan D., and Thomas A. Bowers. *Fundamentals of Advertising Research,* 4th ed. Belmont, CA: Wadsworth, 1991. Chapters 1, 2, 12–17.

Haller, Terry. *Danger: Marketing Researcher at Work*. Westport, CT: Quorum Books, 1983. Chapters 4–6.

Kotler, Philip. *Marketing Management*, 7th ed., Englewood Cliffs, NJ: Prentice-Hall, 1991. Chapters 4, 5, 6, 8, 9.

Ward, Jean, and Kathleen A. Hansen. *Search Strategies in Mass Communication*. West Plains, NY: Longman, 1987. Chapters 6, 8.

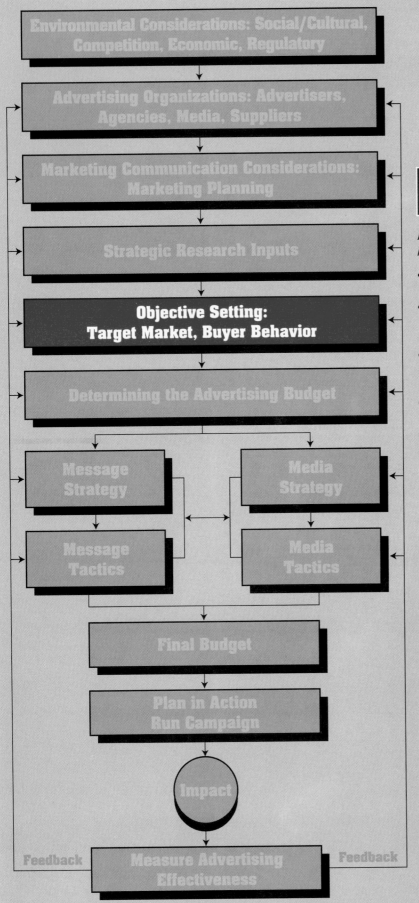

LEARNING OBJECTIVES

In your study of this chapter, you will have an opportunity to:

- Understand why advertising objectives are important.
- Learn how advertising objectives function and what constitutes a good advertising objective.
- Understand how advertising objectives are related to target markets and the criteria for determining target markets.
- Learn about different ways advertising can work to facilitate marketing goals.
- Learn how objectives are related to the buyer behavior process.

Chapter 9

Advertising Objectives

CHAPTER TOPICS

ADVERTISING OBJECTIVES
The Function of Advertising Objectives
Understanding Advertising: Key Inputs to Objective
Setting
TARGET MARKETS
The Advantages of Targeting
Basis for the Targeting Decision
Types of Targeting Strategies
Defining Target Markets

UNDERSTANDING HOW ADVERTISING WORKS
How Advertising Can Work to Facilitate
Marketing Goals
Specific Advertising Objectives
Different Buying Processes

Ruben Solanot, General Manager, INTI S.A., a Coca-Cola–owned bottler in Cordoba, Argentina, was recently participating in an executive development seminar for marketers at The University of Georgia. Mr. Solanot had risen to the top of his organization as a production expert and was seeking to broaden his knowledge of marketing and advertising. During one of the sessions, Mr. Solanot expressed two major advertising concerns. He asked, "How does my advertising work?" "How do we set advertising objectives that are appropriate for our target markets?" Mr. Solanot's questions are insightful because they are of critical concern to all advertisers. A key to successful advertising is good objective setting. The key to good objective setting is understanding how advertising works in each specific business situation.

Objectives serve as the critical starting point and establish a tone and structure for the total campaign. Objectives answer the question, Where do we want to go? They serve as the base for the campaign's strategy and tactics, as well as the basis for measuring the effectiveness of advertising. Once objectives are clearly in place, the planner can proceed to strategic decisions. Strategic development answers the question, How do we get where we want to go?

This chapter illustrates the importance of advertising objectives and how they are utilized. Two key inputs, target markets and buyer behavior, are discussed to provide an understanding of how advertising works and how objectives are developed.

Advertising Objectives

Recall that Chapter 2—which dealt with the marketing communication environment in which advertising functions—included a brief discussion of objectives and goals.

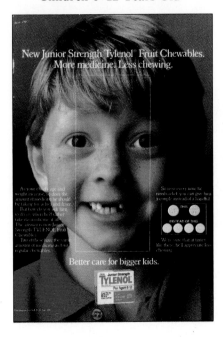

Advertisement with the Objective of Introducing a New Product to a Specific Market: Parents of Children 6–12 Years Old

A distinction was made between marketing and advertising objectives. Marketing objectives, generally considered to be broader and long range, relate to what is sought from the entire marketing program through the workings of the 4Ps of the marketing mix. A typical marketing objective is the market share sought for a particular brand ("to increase market share from 8 percent to 10 percent in three years").

Advertising strategy, as a part of the total marketing program, has a somewhat narrower focus, and objectives are set with this in mind. Typically, advertising objectives are somewhat shorter range and deal with what can be accomplished through communication. At times, we can use market actions, such as trial, inquiry, or even sales, as appropriate advertising objectives. In these instances we can assign advertising the sole or major responsibility for producing sales or action, as in the case of direct-response advertising. Yet, mostly, advertising works in concert with other marketing variables in yielding sales, and this should be taken into account when setting advertising objectives.

An example involving a Tylenol product will illustrate the difference between marketing and advertising objectives (see Figure 9.1). With the introduction of Junior Strength Tylenol for ages 6–12, parents could continue to offer nonaspirin medicine to their children, who they perceived were too old to take the children's products and too young to take the adult product. The marketing objective is to provide a product and create sales in a specific market niche. The advertising objective is to communicate a new product made specially for older kids.

Marketing objectives are often stated as sales goals or market share goals. They are expressed as a percentage ("to increase market share by 2 percent") or as a specific number ("to sell 50,000 units in the next year"). Advertising objectives are usually expressed in a similar fashion using communication variables ("to increase product awareness by 25 percent").

Also to be considered in establishing advertising goals is the difference between general and specific objectives. General objectives are those set for the whole campaign. They deal with the interrelation of all of the campaign factors and tie directly into the overall marketing program. The general objectives transfer marketing objectives into advertising objectives. For example, in order to achieve a 5 percent increase in sales we may need a 25 percent increase in awareness among the target market.

Specific advertising objectives are those that deal with the two strategic decisions that are considered the heart of a campaign: the message formulation and the media plan. Here planners outline what they want to achieve from specific advertisements and commercials as well as from the media used to carry the advertising.

The Function of Advertising Objectives

Advertising objectives serve three key areas: (1) communication and coordination, (2) decision making, and (3) evaluation of the campaign.[1]

By serving as communication and coordination devices, the objectives allow a large number of individuals working on the same project to stay on target toward a common goal. In many instances the advertising agency account team, creative team, media buyers, research specialists, and the marketing team from the advertiser are all working on the project at the same time. The objectives serve as a source of continuity and a way to communicate the status of every element of the project.

Objectives serve as criteria for decision making. The planning and execution of a typical campaign involves a large number of decision areas. Setting advertising objectives draws attention to the many specific elements in a campaign and allows planners to evaluate alternatives and make decisions. When more than one approach or creative concept is presented, a look at the objectives should guide the planner toward the one best suited to the campaign.

Objectives also provide a base for measuring and evaluating the results. The setting of advertising objectives assists in making explicit just what is to be accom-

The Basics of Writing an Advertising Objective

Successful advertising objectives share some basic characteristics. To be sure, not all successful objectives have every one of the following characteristics; however, they can contribute to success.

Hierarchical The advertising objective is guided by a larger marketing objective. Therefore, the advertising objective "serves" a marketing objective.

Precise The advertising objective is written in a precise way to reflect both an action and a time period. For example, "we wish to increase awareness among our target market by 20 percent in the coming year."

Measurable The objective should have an element that can be measured in order to establish if the goal is achieved. If we wish to increase awareness by 20 percent, we must know the current awareness level and how we intend to measure awareness.

Realistic Good research and market experience help create realistic objectives. The planner must have a sense of what can realistically be accomplished. If we set goals too high, we can become frustrated when they are not

achieved. If goals were set too low, we might have been able to accomplish more. No "right" answer is available for creating realistic objectives; however, there is usually information about what happened in the past and research to guide what may happen in the future. No substitute exists for experience in the market.

Flexible Dealing with the future may involve a lot of uncertainties. The planner needs to remain flexible and not have all objectives "set in stone." At times, it is acceptable to change and adjust the objective.

Long Term We often set advertising objectives within a limited time frame, but our advertising communication does not stop working when the campaign period ends. People remember our messages for long periods of time. Therefore, planners often think about how the campaign can continue in the following years. They consider it important to have a campaign they can build on. For example, Michelob beer extended the campaign "Weekends are made for Michelob" to "Put a little weekend in your week," and then to "The night belongs to Michelob."

---

plished through a particular campaign. Objectives allow the planner to assess the relative successes and failures of certain strategies.

Writing good objectives requires both discipline and knowledge. The basics of writing an advertising objective are provided in the accompanying Ad Insight entitled "The Basics of Writing an Advertising Objective." The elements demonstrate how to approach writing good objectives.

Through the careful setting of objectives and the systematic measuring of results, a great deal can be learned about how advertising works. Setting advertising objectives forces the decision maker to seek an understanding of the entire campaign planning process. The decision maker needs to understand not only the factors that are part of the campaign but also how the factors relate to one another. In other words, the objective setting process calls attention to the critical question, How does advertising work in my situation? As will be seen later in the chapter, there is an emphasis on the particular situation because advertising cannot be expected to work the same way in every case.

Understanding Advertising: Key Inputs to Objective Setting

Marketers are always learning how their advertising operates in a particular situation. A major part of objective setting depends on how we regard advertising as a component of the buying process. In other words, advertising works differently depending on the specific target market and buying situation. Retailers often feel that advertising should have an immediate response by bringing customers into the store. Therefore, a local pizza parlor will place an advertisement containing a coupon in the paper and evaluate the effectiveness of the promotion by the number of coupons redeemed. An automobile manufacturer probably envisions car buying to be a longer purchasing process than for many other products. We certainly buy fewer cars than pizzas! In view of the longer, complex purchasing decision, the automobile manufacturer often turns to image-based advertising in the hope of developing a strong attitude in order to help persuade the consumer. The results of automobile advertising usually cannot be evaluated in a short-term period.

In order to construct advertising objectives that apply to a specific situation, two major areas must be addressed. Figure 9.2 notes these major areas.

Defining target markets is concerned with locating and determining the group to which we are marketing our product, service, or idea. The major factors for defining target markets are demographics, geography, psychographics/lifestyle, and the benefits derived from these factors.

Understanding behavior is a two-part process. Initially it is concerned with identifying the desired behavior within that target market that advertising is attempting to precipitate, reinforce, change, or influence.[2] For example, do we want people to try the product, remain loyal to the product, or increase use of the product? Secondly, is it concerned with identifying the process that will lead to the desired behavior and the role that advertising plays in the process. For example, is it necessary to create awareness, communicate information about the brand, or create an image or attitude?

The final two sections of the chapter are devoted to providing answers to the inputs shown in Figure 9.2. First is a discussion about target marketing and segmentation methods used to define target markets; then we will discuss how buyer behavior is related to objective setting.

Target Markets

Common sense tells us that we cannot please everybody. Most companies attempt to match their resources with particular market segments. Once the groups have

---

FIGURE 9.2

Key Inputs to Objective Setting

Defining Target Markets—Who is the target?

- Demographic Segmentation
- Geographic Segmentation
- Psychographic/Lifestyle Segmentation
- Benefit Segmentation

Understanding Buyer Behavior—How does advertising influence behavior?

- What is the desired behavior in the target market that advertising is attempting to precipitate, reinforce, or change? (Trial, Loyalty, Increase Use, New Use)
- How can advertising influence the desired behavior?
  Cognition—Learning
  Affective—Attitude/Feeling
  Conative—Doing/Actions

Target Marketing and Objective Setting: Partnership for a Drug-Free America

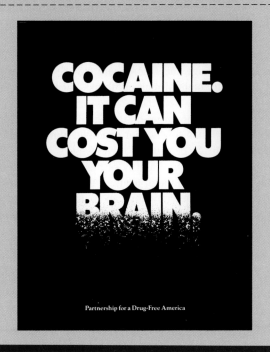

Dailey & Associates, Los Angeles, created "Cocaine. It can cost you your brain," as part of the Partnership for a Drug-Free America program. Before creating the ad, the agency developed the following general target market profile and communication objectives.

Target Market Middle-income and upper-income groups who live by using brain power. Professional and white-collar groups.

Objective Educate and remind the target group that cocaine can cost them everything.

been identified, the company can develop a plan to reach them. This section explores how a planner goes about deciding which target markets or segments should receive the advertising campaign. The Ad Insight on an anti-cocaine ad demonstrates how a target market profile and the advertising objective are combined.

The campaign planner, after finding out through market research as much as possible about the characteristics of the marketplace, makes specific decisions about which target market or markets to focus on. These target market decisions, in turn, affect the campaign message and media strategies.

The segmenting of target markets provides several advantages for the marketer. First, sellers are in a better position to spot and compare market opportunities. They can examine the needs of each segment in the light of the current competitive offerings and determine the extent of current satisfaction. For example, Goodyear developed the Goodyear's Certified Auto Service campaign to communicate that the company had updated its retail car service outlets. Low customer satisfaction levels presented an ideal opportunity to define the target market:

The Advantages of Targeting

> Research showed that while 60 percent of car owners were satisfied with whoever was servicing their cars, 40 percent were dissatisfied. Right away, the latter (dissatisfied customers) was chosen as the target (market).[3]

Second, sellers can make finer adjustments of their product and marketing appeals. Instead of one marketing program aimed to draw in all potential buyers, sellers can create separate marketing programs aimed to meet the needs of different buyers.

Third, sellers can develop marketing programs and budgets based on a clearer idea of the response characteristics of specific market segments. They can allocate funds to the different segments in line with their likely levels of purchase response.

The Kotex advertisements in Figure 9.3 indicate the use of different Kotex products for various market segments. Note how the products and advertising appeals change to meet the various target markets.

Basis for the Targeting Decision

The target decision is based on a number of features of the market segments involved. Some of the most important are the following:[4]

- *Measurability* is the degree to which the target market can be measured. Certain criteria or factors, such as age and income, are easy to measure. Other criteria or factors, such as how a potential market "thinks" or its attitudes, are much more difficult to measure.
- *Accessibility* is the degree to which the target market can be reached. Some target markets are easier to reach than others. For example, many busy executives are more difficult to reach because of travel.
- *Substantiality* is the size and potential profitability of the segment. In some instances the market may not be large enough to merit a specialized program.
- *Actionability* is the degree to which the company can design effective programs for different target markets. At times, the staff and resources of the company allow it to serve only a portion of the available segments.

Types of Targeting Strategies

The basic types of market coverage strategies are concentration, differentiation, and undifferentiation. In concentration, the advertiser focuses on one particular market

FIGURE 9.3

Advertisements for Kotex Show How Products and Appeals Are Geared to Specific Target Markets

segment and develops a marketing and advertising program directed to it. Rather than seek a small share of a large market, advertisers attempt to capture a sizable share of a particular segment. For example, Jaguar has concentrated on the luxury touring-car market.

The second targeting approach, differentiation, identifies two or more subgroups, and marketing programs are developed for each. Nike offers a highly differentiated line of athletic shoes including several separate product offerings for jogging, tennis, walking and cross training. Kotex (Figure 9.3) has identified a number of different marketing programs for subgroups in the feminine protection market.

A third approach, undifferentiation, ignores market segment differences and develops a single marketing program for all groups. Using this method, the firm emphasizes mass distribution and mass advertising to accomplish its goals. Although an undifferentiated approach can achieve certain cost efficiencies, many analysts believe that such a strategy is untenable for most marketers.

As Figure 9.2 indicates, target markets are often defined on the basis of demographic, geographic, psychographic/lifestyle, and benefit factors. Generally, advertisers use more than one characteristic in defining a target market. Segmentation strategies usually include more than one demographic variable in conjunction with geographic, psychographic/lifestyle, and benefit approaches. The following will discuss these approaches.

Defining Target Markets

Demographic Factors

The most frequently used method of dividing markets is by demographic factors. Consequently, many of the available data on both markets and media audiences are broken down by demographic classifications.

Age The primary method of analyzing markets by age is to divide the population into age groups and analyze the wants and needs of each group. Advertisers are extremely interested in population changes. For example, Table 9.1 indicates that

Projected U.S. Population by Age Group (Millions)				
	1995	**2000**	**2005**	**2010**
Total Population:	260	268	276	283
Age Group:				
Under 5	18	17	17	17
5–17	48	49	47	46
18–24	24	25	27	27
25–34	41	37	36	38
35–44	42	44	41	37
45–54	31	37	42	43
55–64	21	24	30	35
65–74	19	18	19	21
75 and over	16	17	19	19

Source: U.S. Department of Commerce, Bureau of the Census, *Statistical Abstract of the United States*, 1991, 16.

two categories—45–54 and 55–64—are projected to increase the fastest by the year 2000. This section of the population is sometimes referred to as "baby boomers," who were born from 1946–1964. As they entered their peak spending years in the 1980s, baby boomers were key target markets for VCRs, minivans, and microwave ovens. Now, this same group has shifted their focus from spending to saving—saving for their children's education and for retirement.[5] Other projections indicate that for the years 2005 and 2010 a larger portion of the population than ever before will be older. This rise can be categorized as the "graying of America." No doubt changing age levels will mean an increase in products and advertising aimed at older Americans.

Gender The marketplace and workplace are reflecting a major shift in the role of women. The full-time homemaker represents less than 30 percent of all women in the United States. An increasing number of women are in two-paycheck homes in which couples share the decision making on how they are going to spend those paychecks. There is a major push by automobile manufacturers to design cars for women. This is in sharp contrast to an industry that had previously been oriented toward men.

Income Purchasing power is a major outgrowth of income. In some product categories, like cars, furnishings, and appliances, expenditures rise with income. Luxury automobiles, specialty clothing, exotic travel, and expensive homes are all associated with high income. For example, Figure 9.4 shows an advertisement for Hermès Paris retail stores that features $110 ties. In certain situations, if we know a person's income we can predict spending patterns. Or we can estimate how much of our product we should sell if we know how many households in the market are

FIGURE 9.4

Advertisement Appealing to High-Income Shoppers

This ad appeared in *Forbes*, April 6, 1992, 19.

in each income group. Fortunately, we have a great deal of data on the relationship of income to purchasing power. Usually, income data are combined with other demographics to give a more complete picture.

Education In general, the higher a person's education, the more likely he or she is to have a high income. Consequently, for many types of products, the markets can be divided by either income or education. Many studies indicate that the highly educated spend more on the average than do the poorly educated for housing (rent, mortgage, taxes), communication (for example, telephone and magazines), recreational products, and consumer electronics.

For many years, a trend has existed toward relatively higher levels of educational achievement. Table 9.2 shows the percentage of the population, 25 years and older, who have completed a certain level of education. In 1970, only 10.7 percent had four or more years of college. This figure grew to 21.1 percent in 1990.

Occupation Like education, occupation is related to income in that certain occupations are traditionally better paid than others. The differential between white-collar and blue-collar incomes has been steadily decreasing, yet spending patterns among different occupational groups earning roughly the same income can be quite different. For example, the white-collar, clerical, or salesperson spends substantially more for clothing and home furnishings than the craftworker or supervisor.

Family Life Cycle The consumption of products and services will vary by family life cycle and number of people in the home. Family life cycle combines the characteristics of age, marital status, number of children, and ages of children. Each stage has different buying needs. Young marrieds with children are focusing on family-oriented appliances and baby products whereas young marrieds without children are apt to have more money to spend on new fashions and recreation. Additionally, the number of individuals within the home is expected to decline. Fewer children per household will mean less food consumed at home. The smaller household, along with the family in which both adults work, will be eating many more meals away from the home.

TABLE 9.2

Years of School Completed for Persons 25 Years Old and Over

| | Percent Completing | | |
Years Completed	1970	1980	1990
Elementary			
0–4 years	5.5%	3.6%	2.5%
5–7	10.0	6.7	4.1
8	12.8	8.0	5.0
High School			
1–3 years	19.4	15.3	11.5
4	13.6	31.1	38.5
College			
1–3 years	10.6	15.7	12.3
4 or more	10.7	16.2	21.1

Source: U.S. Department of Commerce, Bureau of the Census, *Statistical Abstract of the United States*, 1991.

FIGURE 9.5

**The Singles Boom—Americans
Living Alone, by Age**

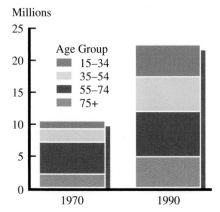

Laura Zinn, "Home Alone—with $660 Billion" *Business Week,* July 29, 1991, 77.

There has been a growth in the number of single Americans. Figure 9.5 shows that the growth of singles has doubled in the last 20 years. J. Walter Thompson, one of the world's largest advertising agencies, has conducted extensive research on the singles market and estimates the earning power to be $660 billion.[6] As shown in Figure 9.6, specific products and appeals are developed for the singles market. Saturn automotive recently ran billboards in California showing a snazzy two-door Saturn with a caption that read, "Single, Bright, and Available." Saturn's director of consumer marketing, Thomas W. Shaver, stated: "If we catch people early—when they're single—maybe we can have a long-term relationship."[7]

Religion and Race   Determining whether purchasing differences are due to religion or race or other demographic variations such as income is often difficult. Advertisers are always at risk and need to be very careful about stereotyping various ethnic groups. Nevertheless, specific groupings do represent substantial target market opportunities. African-Americans represent the largest racial/ethnic grouping; the second largest ethnic group is Hispanic, and Asian Americans represent the fastest growing ethnic grouping.

As noted, marketers need to be very careful not to stereotype each of the ethnic groups into one homogeneous market. For example, the Hispanic population comes from a very diverse variety of regions and national backgrounds—South and Central America, Puerto Rico, Cuba, Mexico, and other regions. The rapid growth of the Hispanic population, 24.1 million or 10 percent of the U.S. population (an increase of 8 times the rate of the rest of our population) has fostered a number of Hispanic radio stations, magazines, and newspapers. Coca-Cola special sweepstakes "El Super Concurso de El Magnate" (Millionaire Sweepstakes) for Coca-Cola Classic generated 500,000 responses from Hispanic viewers.[8]

Recent research on viewing habits indicates that African Americans in the United States view more TV than other households, 69.8 hours a week compared to non-African American households 47.1 hours. Two of the highest-rated prime time series among these viewers are "A Different World" and "Fresh Prince of Bel Air," which feature African Americans. Other hit prime-time shows, such as "Roseanne," and "Murphy Brown," rate much lower with these audiences. These viewers want to see a world that acknowledges African Americans, even if they are not the stars. Ken Smikle, president of the African-American Marketing & Media Association, an organization of African-American–owned advertising agencies and communication

FIGURE 9.6

Saturn Appeals to the Singles Boom

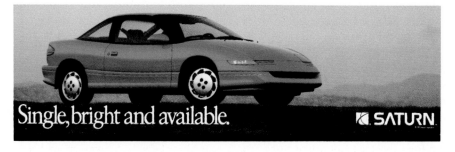

companies noted, "The more advertisers are interested in reaching this audience, the more networks and independent stations will be interested in delivering this audience."[9]

Geographic Factors

Geographic segmentation is the dividing of the overall market into groups on the basis of population location. Marketers rely on geography for a variety of decisions related to segmentation. In the United States, general regional sales data are available for most major products. Sales breakdowns by region allow the marketer to decide which markets present the best opportunity. Many companies take a global perspective. Table 8.1 in the previous chapter shows that over 90 percent of young adults in the United States, Australia, Brazil, Japan and the United Kingdom purchase soft drinks regularly. This allows soft drink manufacturers to target such countries as areas for growth.

Geography can be used to isolate both differences and similarities in the market, based on location. For example, in the United States a number of regional differences exist based on market use and consumer tastes. Mexican food is sold more heavily in the South and Southwest. Biscuits are sold more in the South. Cola drinks are commonly used as a breakfast beverage in the South. Midwest consumers use more dairy products per capita. The Northeast prefers a white-colored cheddar cheese, whereas the rest of the country favors a yellow cheddar cheese. A number of similarities in terms of group concentration can also be found. For example, the Hispanic market tends to concentrate in Los Angeles, New York, Miami, Chicago, and Texas. As a result, marketing campaigns directed at this group are invariably conducted in these markets.[10]

Psychographics and Lifestyle

Consumers who are in the same demographic category often have different attitudes and lifestyles. Understanding the way consumers think and live can be important in developing marketing strategies and advertising appeals. The technique used to define consumers according to personality is called psychographics. Personality characteristics are often related to product buying and media use. For example, Simmons Marketing Research Bureau (SMRB) classifies individuals by self-concept, or how they evaluate their own personality. Personality traits—such as affectionate, creative, funny, and trustworthy—are related to products purchased and media used.

Advertising executives have noted that consumer attitudes have changed dramatically from the 1980s to the 1990s. To create ads in the 1990s, advertisers need to continually understand how consumers think and feel. Figure 9.7 shows a print advertisement for Michelob, which stresses a very definite psychographic appeal to women. The advertisement was created to stress that self-help is not as important today as it used to be in the 1980s. The goal is to poke fun at all that self-help stuff and to say, "Don't get so hung up about it. Enjoy yourself," says Bob Goughenur, Michelob's Brand Director.[11]

Media and advertising research is continually looking for personality profiles that will enhance the understanding of target markets. For example, in a recent marketing/ advertising survey for Popular Mechanics magazine, it was found that many consumers rely on a psychographic group of "must know" men for information and advice about products and brands. "Must know" men are do-it-yourselfers who get intrinsic satisfaction from the doing of an activity, such as home improvements, electronics, and computers. This psychographic characteristic goes across many different incomes and occupations. The group can influence the purchasing habits of up to 85 million consumers.[12]

The way consumers see themselves in relation to their job, leisure activities, and buying habits results in lifestyle segmentation. Many advertisers use **values and**

FIGURE 9.7

Psychographic Appeal by Michelob Pokes Fun at Trendy Self-Help Messages

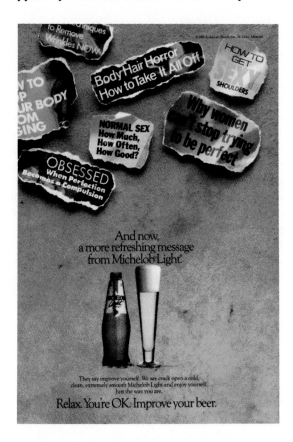

lifestyles (VALS) marketing data by SRI International. Figure 9.8 shows the VALS 2 typology, a psychographic system for segmenting American consumers and predicting consumer behavior. VALS 2 is built on the concept of self-orientation. It states that consumers pursue and acquire products that provide satisfaction and give shape, substance, and character to their identities. They are motivated by one of three self-orientations: principle, status, or action.

Benefit

A fourth approach to segmentation focuses on the attributes that people seek in a product and the benefits that they perceive an existing product to possess.[13] Joseph T. Plummer, executive vice president of D'Arcy Masius Benton & Bowles (DMB&B), one of the world's largest advertising agencies, notes that benefit segmentation is the key to successful advertising:

> Understanding the desired consumer benefit, delivering it with your brand, and communicating that benefit to the consumer through your advertising is what marketing is all about.[14]

Benefit segmentation uses both product usage rates and product benefits derived from the product or service.

Usage Rates Segments are often broken down into heavy, moderate, or light users. For example, Suave shampoo customers tend to be heavy shampoo users. Grocery store audits indicated that Suave customers accounted for 21 percent of the buyers purchasing shampoo. However, the same 21 percent of the buyers accounted for 38 percent of the total ounces of shampoo purchase. The following demographics comprise the typical Suave purchaser: a female head of household who is 18–45, large family with young children, middle income and blue-collar occupation.[15]

Product Benefits   Segments are also identified by the product benefits that are expected from the brand. The same product category or service can offer different benefits to consumers. Timex markets watches based on durability and price, Rolex markets watches as jewelry with prestige and accuracy, and Seiko markets watches as general product quality.

Benefits are not always new to the product, yet can be made new to the consumer. Cheerios, a longstanding cereal brand, has increased market share in the 1990s by emphasizing the benefit of oat bran.[16]

Benefit segmentation can endure over a number of years. A classic example of this results from a study originally conducted in 1964 and updated in 1990. It is

FIGURE 9.8

Lifestyle Segmentation: The VALS 2 Network

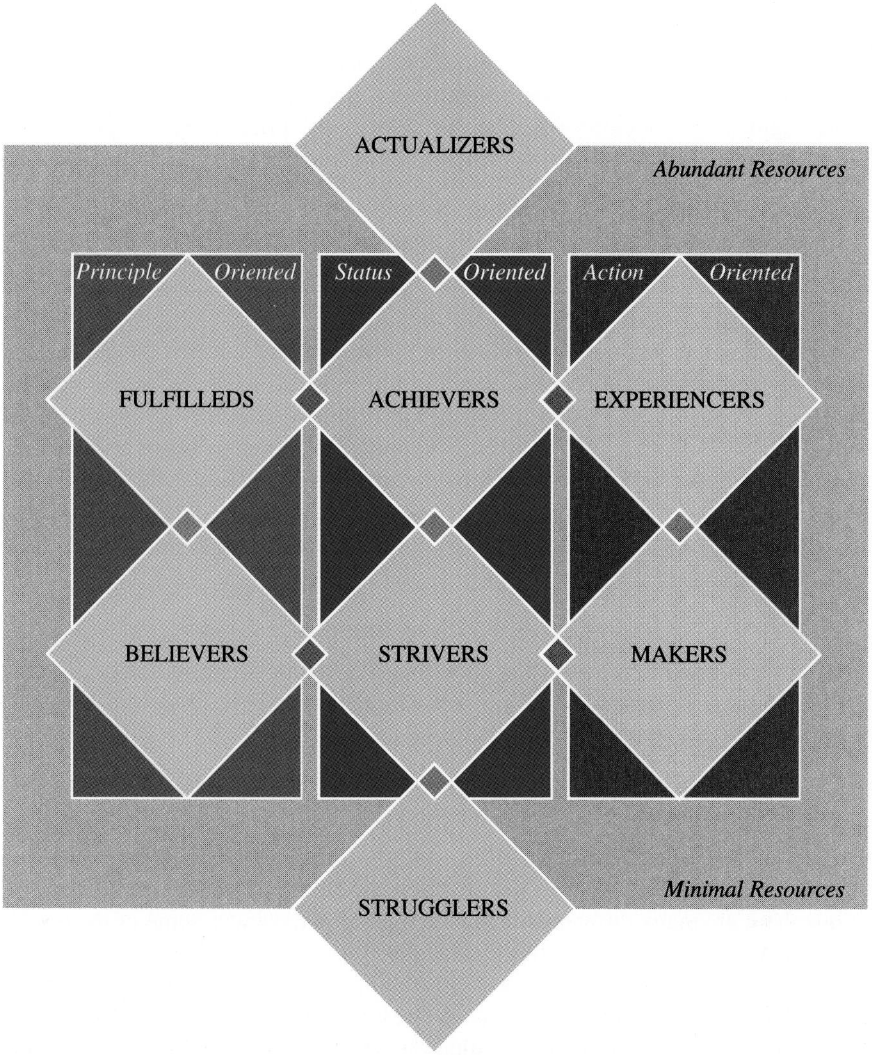

Source: Courtesy of the VALS™ Program at SRI International, Menlo Park, CA, 94025.
BLACK

	TABLE 9.3			
Benefit Segmentation in the Toothpaste Market				
Benefit Segments	**Demographics**	**Behavior**	**Psychographics**	**Favored Brands**
Economy (low price)	Men	Heavy users	High autonomy, value oriented	Brands on sale
Healthy teeth (decay prevention)	Large families	Heavy users	Hypochondriac, conservative	Crest
Cosmetic (bright teeth)	Teens, young adults	Smokers	High sociability, active	Aqua-Fresh, Ultra Brite
Taste (good tasting)	Children	Spearmint lovers	High self-involvement, hedonistic	Colgate, Aim

Source: Russell I. Haley, "Benefit Segmentation: A Decision Oriented Research Tool," *Journal of Marketing,* July 1963, 30–35. See also Joseph T. Plummer, "Outliving Myths," *Journal of Advertising Research,* February/March 1990, 27.

illustrated here as Table 9.3. The table shows toothpaste consumers differing over the anticipated benefit. Crest users want healthy teeth (decay prevention), whereas other segments are looking for bright teeth, taste, or price. Crest's segmentation approach with respect to medicinal benefits has remained constant for three decades!

Understanding How Advertising Works

After defining the target markets, planners investigate how advertising can be used to influence the buying decision process. Leading professionals and academics feel that consumers go through different stages prior to and after the use (purchase) of a product, service, or idea. The process is commonly referred to as **buyer behavior,** or consumer behavior. Understanding buyer behavior is a difficult task that includes lengthy discussions in motivation and persuasion. The purpose of this section is not to explain all of the elements in the buying process but rather to highlight the role advertising can play in the process.

How Advertising Can Work to Facilitate Marketing Goals

Both academics and professionals agree that advertising works in many different ways. Rossiter, Percy and Donovan, a research team comprised of well-respected advertising professionals and university researchers, noted:

> There is much debate and conflicting evidence about "how ads work." What is clear is that there is no *one* way in which ads work. Rather, it depends on the advertising situation.[17]

It is very evident that the specific situation dictates the way advertising works. While there are many different situations, Figure 9.9 illustrates some of the typical ways advertising can work. On the left side we see exposure to advertising indicating that the target market is exposed to the ad campaign. The middle category shows some of the typical mental actions that can result from advertising exposure. These mental actions are usually communication oriented because they include such factors as product awareness, knowledge, attitude, and image. As will be shown in the next section, the communication factors are often used as advertising objectives.

The column on the right indicates some of the typical market actions that can be partially attributed to effective advertising. These include: inquiry about the product, product trial, product purchase, and loyalty, which refers to repurchasing the product. The following is a brief description of the routes shown in Figure 9.9:

1. Advertising can develop brand awareness, which can directly lead to having the consumer inquire about the product, try the product, purchase the product, or remain loyal to the product.
2. Advertising can play a role in both consumer awareness and knowledge about brand attributes or benefits. The consumer is learning more. Such learning plays a role in product inquiry, trial, purchase, or loyalty. The Traveler's Insurance advertisement in Figure 9.10 builds awareness about company assets to create a knowledge base that serves as protection for their customers.
3. Advertising can help develop or enhance a favorable attitude about the brand. Consumers *like* the product or have an intention to buy the product. The development of such an attitude is likely to play a role in the initial trial, purchase, or repurchase of the brand. Attitude studies indicated that while Jim Beam had a smaller market share than Old Crow, younger consumers moving into the bourbon market *liked* Jim Beam better. As the younger market matured, this liking translated into sales, moving Jim Beam far ahead of Old Crow.[18]

FIGURE 9.9

Examples of How Advertising Can Work

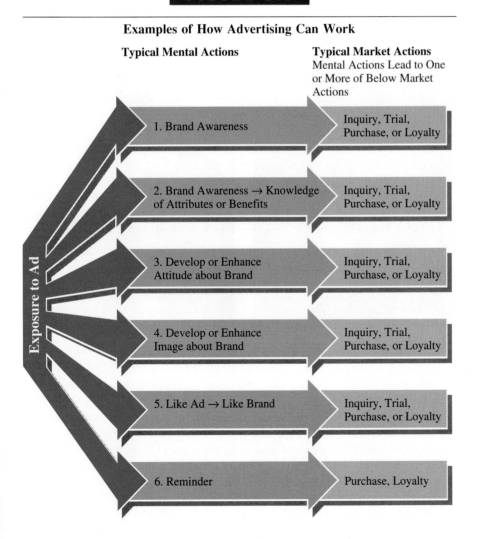

FIGURE 9.10

Examples of Advertising Objectives

Awareness

Interest

Knowledge

Feeling

4. Advertising can help develop and enhance an image or feeling about the brand. The image creates a portrait or feeling about the brand or an association with an experience (note the up-scale feeling for Chanel shown in Figure 9.10). Also, many advertisers feel that a distinct image is a critical asset that leads directly to trial, purchase, and loyalty. Tony the Tiger and Charlie Tuna are well-defined images that portray the product. The Ad Insight entitled "Objective Setting and Target Marketing at Work" shows how Maybelline developed a new image.

Objective Setting and Target Marketing at Work:
Maybelline Updates Its Image

Maybelline developed the campaign theme, "Maybe she's born with it. Maybe it's Maybelline," to solidify its image with a more mainstream target market.

The new, upscale image is a conscious effort to try to get department store customers who are trading down. Maybelline President Bob Hiatt noted that Maybelline's previous image was positive but not well defined. "It (Maybelline) didn't have the clear positive attributes of Cover Girl or Revlon. Maybelline was regarded as a brand whose products perform but were not top of the line."

Maybelline's advertising objective is to give itself a sharper focus and to glamorize its image among cosmetics users. In short, to move from a brand considered functional to a brand considered upscale. Model Christy Turlington is featured to make the product more current.

Sources: Pat Sloan, "Maybelline makeover," *Advertising Age* (September 9, 1991): 4; Martha T. Moore. "Maybelline Flirts with Sexier Image," *USA Today* (September 6, 1991): B–1.

5. At times, a favorable attitude toward the advertisement plays a role in the development of positive feelings about the brand. Studies have found a strong correlation between brand attitude and attitude toward the ad.[19] In other words, liking the ads leads to liking the brand. This, in turn, can lead to any of the typical outcomes: inquiry, trial, purchase, or repurchase.

6. Advertising can also serve as a reminder to prompt reuse, especially for those products that are continually or routinely purchased. Advertising serves as a reminder to buy the specific brand, which can lead to loyalty. Many well-established brands, such as Budweiser and Coke, use reminder advertising as part of their overall strategy.

In addition to general objectives, advertisers are always trying to determine the most appropriate specific objective for a campaign. Usually advertising objectives are characterized as communication oriented, preceding some form of action such as purchase or sales. In some instances advertising objectives can be action oriented. Three distinct kinds of advertising objectives are described in Figure 9.11.

Learning (cognitive) objectives are oriented toward awareness, knowledge, and comprehension. The purpose of such objectives is to communicate or let the consumer know about the product in general or some aspect of the product. Learning objectives may vary in levels from awareness that the product exists to detailed

Specific Advertising
Objectives

FIGURE 9.11

A Classification of Advertising Objectives

Learning (Cognitive)	Feeling (Affective)	Doing (Conative)
Attention	Favorable Attitude	Inquire Trial
Awareness	Liking	Purchase
Knowledge	Preference Conviction Desire	Loyalty (Repurchase)
Comprehension	Image	Allow Salesperson in Home
Understanding		

comprehension and understanding. Regardless of the specific level, many experts feel that some form of awareness is a necessary precondition prior to such things as brand attitude.[20]

Feeling (affective) objectives are attitude oriented and are concerned with having consumers like the product or form a favorable impression. Although all advertising is ultimately aimed at persuasion, feeling objectives are specifically developed to have the consumer like or desire the product. Much of what is termed *image advertising* is created to develop an atmosphere for the product that will lead to favorable attitudes.

Doing (conative) objectives seek an action. These objectives ask the consumer to do something. Earlier discussions (Chapter 2) illustrated the difficulty in understanding how advertising directly influences sales because of the many factors that are involved in the purchase process and the limited scope of advertising. However, in some cases advertising objectives are oriented toward action. A number of separate behaviors are associated with action objectives, such as purchasing, repurchasing (loyalty), trial, and allowing the salesperson in the door. The rise in toll-free 800 numbers has prompted advertisers to request that customers "call in" for more information. Examples of four advertising objectives are illustrated in Figure 9.10: awareness, interest, knowledge, and feeling.

Different Buying Processes

Recall that in Figure 9.2 there are two key questions or inputs used to define advertising's role in buyer behavior.

What is the desired buyer behavior in the target market that advertising is attempting to precipitate, reinforce, change, or influence?

How can advertising influence the desired behavior?

Four widely accepted processes or models of buyer behavior are shown in Figure 9.12. Each model uses the basic concepts of learning (cognitive), feeling (affective), and doing (conative) described in Figure 9.11. However, each model shown in Figure 9.12 uses a different order to explain how the purchase process can shift according to a particular situation and the role advertising can play. The planner can select the model that is most appropriate for the situation.

FIGURE 9.12

Four Models of Advertising and the Buying Process

Learn Feel Do "High Involvement" Information	Feel Learn Do "High Involvement" Affective	Learn Do Feel "Low Involvement"	Do Feel Learn "Dissonance Attribution"
Buyer Behavior			
Consumer goes through learning and attitude before purchase.	Consumer goes through emotion first and then learning before purchase.	Consumer goes through low-level learning before purchase. Attitude development is after purchase.	Consumer purchases product, then forms attitudes to learn the decision was correct.
Conditions			
Products with a high degree of differentiation: Consumer is active or involved in the buying process.	Products can have high psychological or tangible differentiation: Consumer is active or involved in the buying process.	Products with a low degree of differentiation: Consumer is not active or involved in the buying process.	Products appear the same, yet have hidden or unknown qualities: Consumer realizes it is an important buying process.
Examples of Objectives			
Awareness Comprehension Attitude Development Image	Attitude Development Image Awareness Comprehension	Exposure Awareness Image	Reinforcement Supportive Information

Learn-Feel-Do Model

This is sometimes referred to as the "high involvement" or a learning hierarchy model. Richard Vaughn, senior vice president of Foote, Cone & Belding advertising, calls this as an "information" model because the first thing we do is learn about the product and brand.[21] The buying process occurs in a logical order: the consumer initially learns about the product and then develops a favorable feeling or attitude. An action (doing), such as purchase or trial, is the result of learning and attitude change. In this situation the consumer is more involved or active in the buying process and products can be differentiated over some tangible or psychological issues. The search for product information is active. Advertising objectives are designed to create both learning and positive attitudes.

One of the most widely accepted and enduring approaches within the learn-feel-do model is **DAGMAR,** developed by Russell Colley.[22] DAGMAR stands for Defining Advertising Goals for Measured Advertising Results. DAGMAR views advertising as a means of communication and suggests that objectives be set within the context of a hierarchy of effects. Colley assumes that advertising is a communication force and its purpose is to create a state of mind conducive to purchase. Advertising is one of several communication forces that, "acting singly or in combination, move the consumer through successive levels of what we have termed the communications spectrum."[23]

The levels that Colley hypothesized are shown in Figure 9.13 and serve as the basis for the approach. Awareness, the minimal level for advertising goals, means that consumers recognize the existence of a brand, service, or idea. One level above awareness is comprehension, the state in which the consumer has a deeper understanding of the product in terms of benefits and attributes.

The DAGMAR Approach to Advertising Objectives

Marketing Forces
(Moving People toward Buying Action)

- Advertising
- Promotion
- Personal Selling
- Publicity
- User Recommendation
- Product Design
- Availability
- Display
- Price
- Packaging
- Exhibits

Action

Conviction

Comprehension

Awareness

Unawareness

Countervailing Forces

- Competition
- Memory Lapse
- Sales Resistance
- Market Attrition

Note: *DAGMAR was developed at a much earlier date than the formal learning hierarchies. It is often considered the earliest use of a hierarchy or sequence.*

Source: Russell H. Colley, *Defining Advertising Goals for Measured Advertising Results* (New York: Association of National Advertisers, Inc., 1961), 55.

At the conviction level, consumers have some mental commitment to the brand. They may be convinced to buy the brand in the future, or they may state a preference for a particular brand. Once the consumer has made an overt move toward the purchase of the brand, the final level, action, is reached. Action may take many forms such as inquiry, trial, or meeting with a salesperson. The idea is that advertising will have induced action just short of an actual sale, as the final sale results from many other nonadvertising variables.

Feel-Learn-Do Model

This model is a variation of the previous high-involvement model. In this situation the consumer is still active and highly involved in the buying process. However, the model is affective because feeling and emotion precede learning.[24] Such items as jewelry, fashion clothing, and cosmetics are examples of situations where emotion plays a larger role in the start of the process. It is likely that products in this situation have a high degree of tangible or psychological differentiation. Advertising objectives are more likely to be oriented to attitude development and image. However, awareness and comprehension objectives can be successfully used to illustrate key product benefits that focus on emotion or feeling. For example, the Ad Insight for Maybelline shows a situation where emotion and feeling may precede learning.

Learn-Do-Feel Model

The model is often called "low involvement." It assumes that in many instances consumers are not heavily involved and are less active in the buying process; therefore, the search for product information is not active. Herbert Krugman initially developed the model in order to help explain how individuals view television advertising.[25] Krugman felt that in many instances advertisements are seen by individuals but that the information is not actively processed in terms of viewing or close attention. Individuals may be watching the commercial but not really paying attention. Therefore, the level of learning is low. Michael Ray extended the model beyond just television advertising.[26] Ray included involvement or activity with the product as well as the commercial. He reasoned that in certain situations a great deal of mental effort is not focused on the product or the advertising for the product.

Generally, the model is characterized by products or services that are well established in the market, yet do not have a great deal of product differentiation between the competitors. Products such as dish soap, chewing gum, and floor wax are often purchased on a regular basis and may not be given a great deal of consideration prior to purchase. Advertising objectives are designed to create limited awareness and help remind the consumer of the brand at the time of purchase. At times, such objectives may be image based when image is taken to mean an easy way to think about or stereotype the product. Advertising objectives are not focused on changing or developing attitudes. Attitudes are formed as a result of using the product or service.

The low-involvement situation offers an alternative perspective when setting advertising objectives. The focus is on lower level learning, such as awareness, positive images, and exposure to advertising.

Do-Feel-Learn Model

This is termed a "dissonance-attribution" model because it deals with removing potentially uneasy feelings (dissonance) after the purchase process for an important product or service. The model explains postpurchase behavior—the search for product information after the purchase—as a way to determine the causes of the decision (attribution). Hence, product information such as advertising is used to confirm, rationalize, or justify a decision.

Individuals are often placed in a situation in which they are forced to make a choice between two products that appear close in quality but are complex and have many unknown benefits. In other words, the decision appears to be a "close call" for an important product or service choice.

> When the choice (product or service decision) is important enough, the very act of making that choice leads a person to try to bolster or rationalize the decision that he or she has made by *developing an improved attitude on the chosen alternative* [emphasis added].[27]

Information is used to assist attitude development after the choice. In effect, the outcome of the process is that individuals learn that they have made the right decision. Individuals will seek out information that is consistent with their decision and avoid information that goes against the decision. For example, the person who recently purchased a new car is most likely to read advertisements or pay attention to commercials for the new car in order to feel good about the purchase. Advertising objectives are focused on reassuring and reinforcing the individual that he or she made the right choice.

Summary

Advertising objectives serve as the base for much of a campaign's strategy and tactics as well as the basis for measuring the effectiveness of advertising. Objectives also play a key role as communication devices for everyone involved in campaign planning. Objective setting requires two important inputs: (1) understanding of the target market and (2) understanding the role advertising plays in the buyer's decision-making process.

Defining target markets permits the planner to spot and compare opportunities, to make adjustments in marketing and advertising appeals, and to allocate funds more efficiently. The four principal types of segmentation are demographic, geographic, psychographic, and benefit.

Most professionals and academics agree that advertising can work in a number of different ways. Advertisers utilize three kinds of objectives—learning, feeling, and doing. Learning objectives are termed "cognitive" because they are based in awareness, knowledge, and comprehension. Feeling or "affective" objectives are geared toward developing attitudes, such as liking, desire, or conviction. Doing objectives are termed "conative" and are based on action such as trial or purchase.

We know that the buying process is apt to be different in various buying situations. Because the buying process differs, the marketer must understand how advertising can be utilized in a given situation. Four different buyer behavior models are used to explain the role of advertising. The learn-feel-do, high-involvement "information" model emphasizes both learning and attitude-change advertising objectives. The feel-learn-do, high-involvement "affective" model emphasizes emotion prior to learning and purchase. The learn-do-feel, low-involvement model emphasizes low-level learning objectives. The do-feel-learn, dissonance-attribution model emphasizes advertising objectives that reinforce prior behavior.

1. Explain how objective setting contributes to the overall campaign plan.
2. What are the key elements in writing an advertising objective? Write a hypothetical advertising objective.
3. What is a target market? Why is it important for advertisers to define target markets?
4. Why is lifestyle an important target market technique?
5. What is DAGMAR?

Questions for Discussion

6. Clip ads that you feel have a learning objective, a feeling objective, and a doing objective.
7. Give an example of a buying process that illustrates learn-feel-do.

Notes

1. David A. Aaker, Rajeev Batra, and John G. Myers, *Advertising Management*, 4th ed. (Englewood Cliffs, NJ: Prentice-Hall, 1991), 79–80.
2. Ibid., 82–83.
3. Martin Siegel, "Goodyear Ad Campaign Makes Car Service Something to Smile About," *Marketing News*, April 25, 1988, 6.
4. Philip Kotler, *Marketing Management*, 7th ed. (Englewood Cliffs, NJ: Prentice-Hall, 1991), 278.
5. "Demographics," *USA Today*, February 12, 1992, 5B.
6. Laura Zinn, "Home Alone–With $660 Billion," *Business Week*, July 29, 1991, 76–77.
7. Ibid., 77.
8. Carrie Goerne, "Targeting Hispanics: NutraSweet Educates while Coke Titillates," *Marketing News*, November 11, 1991, 1.
9. "Blacks Reveal TV Loyalty," *Advertising Age*, November 18, 1991, 236.
10. "Joaquin F. Blaya, "The Hispanic Market—Why You Need to Understand It," *A.N.A./The Advertiser*, Fall 1991, 45.
11. Stuart Elliot, "Marketers Cast About for Themes." *USA Today*, March 18, 1991, 1B.
12. Carrie Goerne, "Survey: If You Must Know, Just Ask One of These Men," *Marketing News*, March 30, 1992, 13.
13. Louis E. Boone and David L. Kurtz, *Contemporary Marketing*, 7th ed. (Ft. Worth, TX: Dryden, 1992), 277.
14. Joseph T. Plummer, "Outliving The Myths," *Journal of Advertising Research*, February/March, 1990, 27.
15. John A Quelch and Paul Farris, *Cases In Advertising and Promotion Management*, 3d ed. (Homewood, IL: Irwin, 1991), 558–564.

16. Plummer, "Outliving the Myths," 27.
17. John R. Rossiter, Larry Percy, and Robert J. Donovan, "A Better Advertising Planning Grid," *Journal of Advertising Research*, October/November, 1991, 11.
18. James F. Engel, Roger D. Blackwell, and Paul W. Miniard, *Consumer Behavior*, 6th ed. (Hinsdale, IL: Dryden Press, 1990), 305.
19. Aaker, Batra, and Myers, *Advertising Management*, 232.
20. Rossiter, Percy, and Donovan, "A Better Advertising Planning Grid," 12.
21. Richard Vaughn, "How Advertising Works: A Planning Model Revisited," *Journal of Advertising Research*, January/February, 1986, 57–66.
22. Russell H. Colley, *Defining Advertising Goals for Measured Advertising Results* (New York: Association of National Advertisers, Inc., 1961).
23. Ibid., 53.
24. Vaughn, "How Advertising Works: A Planning Model Revisited," 57.
25. Herbert E. Krugman, "Memory Without Recall, Exposure Without Perception," *Journal of Advertising Research* 17 (August 1977): 7–12; and "The Impact of Television Advertising: Learning Without Involvement," *Public Opinion Quarterly* 29 (Fall 1965): 349–356.
26. Michael L. Ray, *Advertising and Communication Management* (Englewood Cliffs, NJ: Prentice-Hall, 1982), 184–187.
27. Ibid., 185.

Aaker, David A., Rajeev Batra, and John G. Myers. *Advertising Management,* 4th ed. Englewood Cliffs, NJ: Prentice-Hall, 1992. Chapters 3, 4.

Boone, Louis E., and David L. Kurtz. *Contemporary Marketing,* 7th ed. Ft. Worth, TX: Dryden Press, 1992. Chapter 4.

Colley, Russell H. *Defining Advertising Goals for Measured Advertising Results.* New York: Association of National Advertisers, 1961.

Engel, James, F., Roger D. Blackwell and Paul W. Miniard. *Consumer Behavior,* 6th ed. Ft. Worth, TX: Dryden Press, 1990. Chapters, 2, 3, 9, 15, 16.

Kotler, Philip. *Marketing Management,* 7th ed. Englewood Cliffs, NJ: Prentice-Hall, 1991. Chapters 6, 10, 21.

Plummer, Joseph T. "Outliving The Myths." *Journal of Advertising Research* (February/March 1990): 26–28.

Ray, Michael L., *Advertising and Communication Management.* Englewood Cliffs, NJ: Prentice-Hall, 1982.

Vaughn, Richard. "How Advertising Works: A Planning Model Revisited." *Journal of Advertising Research* (January/February 1986): 57–66.

Suggested Readings

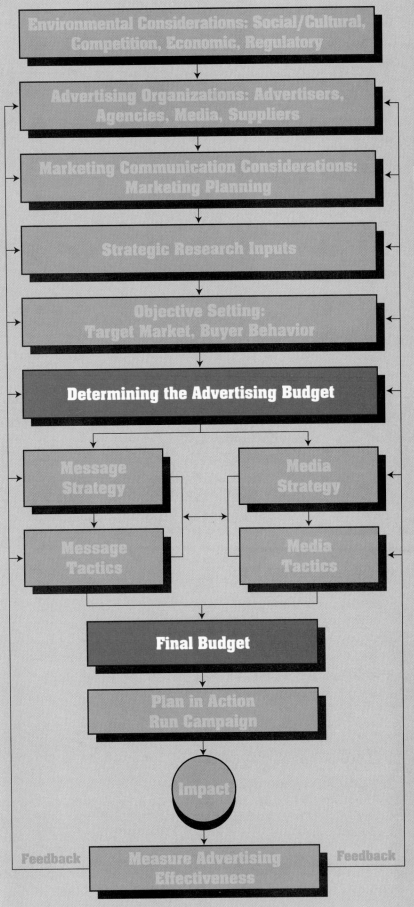

Environmental Considerations: Social/Cultural, Competition, Economic, Regulatory

Advertising Organizations: Advertisers, Agencies, Media, Suppliers

Marketing Communication Considerations: Marketing Planning

Strategic Research Inputs

Objective Setting: Target Market, Buyer Behavior

Determining the Advertising Budget

Message Strategy

Media Strategy

Message Tactics

Media Tactics

Final Budget

Plan in Action Run Campaign

Impact

Feedback   Feedback

Measure Advertising Effectiveness

Chapter 10

The Budgeting Process

CHAPTER TOPICS

DETERMINING THE ADVERTISING BUDGET
THE BUDGETING PROCESS
ADVERTISING AS AN EXPENSE AND AS AN
   INVESTMENT

BUDGETING METHODS
   Objective and Task
   Percent of Sales
   Unit of Sale
   Competitive Spending
   Quantitative/Experimental
   Affordable and Arbitrary Methods
BUDGETING INFLUENCES

Determining the Advertising Budget

Remember from the previous chapter Mr. Ruben Solanot, General Manager, INTI S.A., a Coca-Cola–owned bottler in Cordoba, Argentina? It was noted that Mr. Solanot had risen to the top of his organization as a production expert and was seeking to broaden his knowledge of marketing and advertising. Mr. Solanot's first questions involved how advertising works and how he should set objectives. Next, Mr. Solanot noted a real very real issue that is of concern to anyone in charge of marketing spending:

> I never really know how much to spend on advertising. My brand managers ask for a certain amount of money and I never know if I am spending too much or too little.

Determining the amount of money to spend on advertising is a critical decision that has an impact on the total campaign. One of the most difficult aspects is to know how much money needs to be spent in order for the campaign to be effective.

The campaign planning framework in Figure 7.2 (page 207) indicates that budgeting considerations logically follow objective setting. Advertisers in the United States and abroad are keenly aware of the budget and how it relates to objective setting. This chapter will review the budgeting process and the methods used in determining the budget.

The Budgeting Process

A distinction can be made between the advertising **appropriation**, which is the total amount of money to be spent, and the **budget**, which includes the specific items to be funded, the schedule of spending, and the total amount of money. Although both practitioners and academics often use these terms interchangeably, a budget includes strategies for spending the money as well as the total appropriation.

Budgeting is an ongoing process that usually begins with appropriate objectives and is finalized when the last details of media and creative strategy and tactics are completed. This is illustrated in the campaign planning framework in Figure 7.2 (Chapter 7).

In most situations, the advertising planner does not, in the final analysis, decide how much money will be appropriated. The planner submits a detailed budget proposal, which includes the rationale for including the items. The final budget decision is usually made by the marketing manager or the vice president of marketing, who also evaluates the requests of other departments. In effect, the dollars spent on advertising are competitive with the money spent in many other areas of the firm. Like other departments, advertising must justify the proposed expenditures.

In recent years there has been a push to spend a greater portion of marketing dollars on other forms of promotion other than media advertising. In 1981, approximately 43 percent of the marketing budgets was spent on advertising and 57 percent on sales promotion. Companies are now spending approximately 30 percent of their budgets on advertising and 70 percent on sales promotion.[1] The shift signifies that advertising has to be coordinated with other forms of promotion and that other forms of promotion, such as contests and premiums, often rely on some form of advertising to carry forth the message.

The actual advertising budget has been expanded to include other forms of promotion and corporate communications. What used to be referred to as the advertising budget is now often referred to as the advertising and sales promotion budget. In most consumer advertising, the largest item in the budget is the amount spent on media time and space. Figure 10.1 shows many major items typically found in the advertising and sales promotion portions of the budget. Chapter 19 specifically covers the specific elements of sales promotion.

The trade-off between advertising spending and spending on other items is not limited to large firms. Anyone who decides to spend money on advertisng does so in the belief that the advertising expenditure will better serve the firm than spending in another area.

Ultimately, the specific marketing situation will influence whether expenditures are to be considered in the advertising budget. Business-to-business marketers (those whose products and services will be used by other businesses) certainly consider catalogs for customers and salespeople to be a critical component of the budget. Retailers regularly use coupons and include them in the advertising budget.

Advertising as an Expense and as an Investment

An important question related to advertising appropriations is their impact on the bottom line, or profits. Advertising appropriations have variously been described as both an expense and an investment. The combined amount of national and local money spent on all advertising in the United States through 1997 is expected to grow at a rate of at least 4.5 percent per year. The projected totals are shown in Table 10.1. Many advertisers have found that a decrease in the advertising allocation, even during a recession, can have a negative impact on sales and profits. During a recession or period when sales are slumping, the initial reaction of some marketers

FIGURE 10.1

Items Typically Found in the Advertising and Sales Promotion Budgets

Advertising	Sales Promotions and Other Corporate Communications
Space and time costs in media	Premium handling charges
Media costs for consumer contests, premium and sampling promotions	House-to-house sample distribution
Direct mail	Packaging charges for premium promotions
Subscriptions to periodicals	Showrooms
Catalogs for customers	Testing new labels and packages
Advertising aids for salespeople	Package design and artwork
Cooperative advertising costs	Corporate/product/publicity
Ad department travel and entertainment expenses	Factory signs
Ad department salaries	Signs on company-owned vehicles
Ad testing	Samples for intermediaries
Advertising consultants	Sales promotions/Public relations consultants
Industry directory listings	Coupon redemption costs
	Corporate publicity
	Exhibit personnel
	Gifts of company products
	Sponsoring recreational activities
	House organs for employees
	Entertaining customers and prospects
	Plant tours
	Annual reports

is to decrease advertising in order to hold down costs. However, cutting advertising expenditures to save money in the short run can be risky. Studies show that companies who advertise during a recession have better short- and long-run sales than companies that do not.[2]

TABLE 10.1

Advertising Expenditures in the United States, 1992–1997

Year	Total (In Billions)
1992	$132.10
1993	138.04
1994	144.25
1995	150.74
1996	157.52
1997	164.60

Source: Initial figures from *Marketing News* (January 4, 1993): 5. Projections are based on 4.5 percent annual increases.

FIGURE 10.2

Advertising As an Investment in Building a Brand

"The remarkable thing is, when you think about McDonald's you've got to think about people. A friendly crew person welcoming you. Kids, moms and dads having a good time at McDonald's, even a funny clown named Ronald." Those pictures in your mind are advertising at work.

"Without advertising, everybody would think Ronald was just the name of a former president."

Our advertising is people to people—an invitation from our people to our customers to come in and visit. Personal, friendly, and above all, real.

I'm told there are business people out there who don't believe in the power of advertising. For them, two facts: First, McDonald's is one of the most advertised brands on this planet. Second, McDonald's is the only company listed in the current Standard and Poor's 500 to report combined increases in revenues, income, and earnings per share for more than 100 consecutive quarters since 1965. Frankly, Ronald and I like to think there's a connection here."

Mike Quinlan, Chairman, CEO McDonald's (left)

AAAA
American Association of Advertising Agencies

Even though the results of advertising are not always traceable, marketers understand that advertising expenditures are necessary. In the most basic way, advertising is treated as an **expense**. More specifically, advertising is often viewed as a variable expense as opposed to a fixed expense—something to increase or decrease depending on the current status of the market situation.[3] Like many other expenses advertising is viewed as a short-term cost of doing business and taken out of the firm's annual operating budget. At the end of the year the costs of advertising are included with other marketing and production costs. Therefore, for accounting purposes, advertising is considered an expense.

In a larger sense, advertising appropriations can be thought of as an **investment** that goes beyond a short-term cost of doing business. Moneys allocated to advertising are expected to generate future benefits. In most cases the benefits are seen as advertising objectives, such as: product awareness, favorable attitudes, and sales. A major study by Information Resources Inc. indicates that advertising can at times produce long-term sales even two years after a campaign ends.[4] Although it is very difficult to precisely know advertising's long-term impact, it is clear that allocations can work toward future goals that extend well beyond a one-year period.

A strong brand can become the companies most valued asset. It is the brand recognition and image, enhanced and maintained by advertising, that can continually generate sales. To their corporate owners, brands are more valued than such tangible assets as factories.[5] In short, brand name is an extremely valuable financial asset. The American Association of Advertising Agencies (AAAA) has developed a campaign that focuses on advertising's ability to develop long-range profitability. Figure 10.2 shows an advertisement featuring the CEO of McDonald's. He points out the value of advertising as an investment in terms of building brands and producing long-run sales. A similar ad with the chairman of Apple Computer is found in Chapter 4, Figure 4.8.

A study by the Strategic Planning Institute and the Ogilvy Center for Research and Development looked at 700 consumer businesses and the role of advertising in relation to sales. This is called the advertising-to-sales ratio (A/S), or percent of money spent on advertising relative to sales.[6] Two key conclusions were drawn from the study:

- Businesses with higher advertising-to-sales ratios earn a higher return on investment.
- Businesses with higher advertising-to-sales ratios generally have higher market shares.

Table 10.2 shows the sales per dollar of advertising for selected national products and services. Note how the relationship between sales and one dollar of advertising differs for these well-known companies. In general, the categories with higher priced items that are not purchased frequently, such as appliances and autos, have higher revenues per dollar spent on advertising. More frequently purchased, lower cost items—such as soft drinks, soaps, and fast foods—require more advertising per dollar of sales.

Budgeting Methods

A number of methods are used to determine the amount of money allocated to advertising. Table 10.3 offers a global perspective by illustrating the percent of time different budgeting methods are used by consumer marketers in both the United States and England. It can be seen that in both the United States and England most businesses use a combination of methods.

TABLE 10.2

Sales Per $1 of Advertising for Selected National Advertisers

Product Category	Advertiser	Sales for $1 Advertising
Airlines	Delta Airlines	$ 65.87
Appliances	General Electric	265.65
Automotive	General Motors	85.33
Food	General Mills	13.99
Restaurants	McDonald's Corp.	9.63
Retail	Sears, Roebuck	48.53
Soaps	Procter & Gamble	13.66
Soft Drinks	Coca-Cola	31.49
Wine, Beer, and Liquor	Seagram	22.71

Source: Based on *Advertising Age* (September 23, 1992).

Objective-and-task, competitive spending, and quantitative/experimentation techniques are more information oriented because they require the marketer to gather information or place a value on certain objectives in order to set the budget. Percentage of past or anticipated sales, unit of sale, and arbitrary/affordable techniques are considered to be more rule of thumb or judgment oriented because they use the judgement of executives based on traditional norms and patterns. In general, the information-oriented techniques are noted to be more sophisticated because they require more comprehensive planning.[7] Recent years have seen a movement toward the use of

TABLE 10.3

Budgeting Methods Used by Consumer Marketers in the United States and England

	Percent Using Each Method	
	United States	**England**
Objective and Task	63%	56%
Percent of International Sales	53	30
Percent of Past Years' Sales	20	30
Unit of Sale	21	—
Competitive Spending	24	11
Quantitative/Experimentation	51	24
Affordable/Arbitrary	24	50

Sources: Vincent J. Blasko and Charles H. Patti, "The Advertising Budgeting Practices of Industrial Marketers," *Journal of Marketing* 21 (Fall 1984): 107. James E. Lynch and Graham J. Hooley, "Increasing Sophistication in Advertising Budget Setting," *Journal of Advertising Research*, February/March 1990, 72.

budgeting techniques that emphasize greater sophistication. Both task objective and quantitative/experimental approaches have been increasing in the United States.

Objective and Task

Objective-and-task budgeting is the most widely practiced method. The marketer starts with a thorough understanding of how advertising is utilized as an influence in the buying process. After establishing key objectives, the marketer determines the tasks necessary to achieve the objectives and the costs associated with each task. The sum of all of the costs establishes the total appropriation and also how the money will be allocated. The following table gives very brief examples of how the method works.

Marketing Objective	Advertising Objective	Advertising Task	Budget
Retailer: Introduce a new kind of pizza—sell 200 pizzas over the weekend	Make current customers aware— get them to try the pizza	Use newspaper ad with coupon	$250.00 for 1/2-page ad with coupon
Manufacturer: Introduce a new frozen pizza	Make 50% of target market aware—create favorable image	Use national magazines to create awareness and image	$1,000,000 for magazine space

The objective-and-task approach emphasizes building the budget from the ground up and logically places advertising as an element that works toward meeting a marketing objective. By defining the role of each objective and task and the respective cost, the method allows for a justification of the advertising budget. Advertising appropriations are seen as an investment that will generate a future benefit.

Percent of Sales

The **percent-of-sales** method utilizes a fixed percentage of either past sales or anticipated sales. The method has been heavily used by marketers because it is easy and does not require a great deal of knowledge to implement. Additionally, the method provides managers with a feeling that they can spend what is afforded based on past or potential sales. At times the method can limit excess spending and create market stability if competitors spend approximately the same percent. The percent-of-sales approach is often seen as a starting point for comparison and used in conjunction with other methods. Advertising as a percent of sales for some major food marketers is shown in Table 10.4.

The disadvantages of using only this approach outweigh the advantages. Using a percent of past sales is illogical because it assumes that advertising is a result rather than a cause of sales. It is also inflexible because it does not allow for the possibility that sales may decline because of too little advertising or that sales do not take advantage of a rising potential. There is much variation in the productivity of advertising at different levels of operation, so it is entirely possible that the return on extra advertising expenditures may diminish rather than increase after a certain level of sales has been reached. A company using this approach may therefore underspend when potential is great and overspend when potential is low.

TABLE 10.4

Total U.S. Advertising Appropriations and Advertising as a Percent of U.S. Sales for Selected Marketers

Company	(Dollars in Millions) Ad Spending	Sales	Percent of Sales
RJR	$636.1	$12,125	5.2%
Kroger	131.1	20,261	.6
Coca-Cola	377.2	3,931	9.5
Kellogg	577.7	3,043	18.9
H.J. Heinz Co.	307.9	3,863	7.9

Source: *Advertising Age* (January 6, 1992): S–2.

Using a percent of future sales recognizes that advertising precedes sales. The approach depends heavily on the sales forecast. A major shortcoming is that the approach does not really attempt to understand or justify advertising contribution. By focusing on short-term sales, it does not allow for long-range planning.

Unit of Sale

Unit of sale is, in many respects, a variation of the percentage of sales approach. Instead of dollar sales, the base is the physical volume of either past or future sales. A fixed amount is multiplied by the number of units of the product sold or to be sold. Marketers of durable goods with a high unit value, such as automobiles, often determine the cost of advertising on a per-unit basis.

A variation of this method is to know the cost of advertising per user or prospective user. For example, studies for Gerber's baby foods have estimated that it loses 10,000 customers per day because they outgrow the market. At the same time Gerber's has 10,000 new customers enter the market every day, or about 350,000 new customers per year. Advertising costs are $35 million per year, or about $10 per baby.[8]

Competitive Spending

At times, marketers base their budgets primarily on the expenditures of their competitors. The **competitive spending** method is often viewed as one consideration in the budgeting decision because it allows for an understanding of spending relative to other entrants. For example, the data given in Table 10.4 could be used by a food marketer to understand what competitors with similar brands are spending.

Using only this method would have inherent disadvantages. First, it assumes that the company's objectives are the same as those of competitors, and this may be a very incorrrect assumption. Second, it does not allow the company to determine its own optimal level of expenditure; it assumes its competitors are advertising efficiently and that by following suit the company will achieve efficiency. Last, information on competitive spending is usually available only after it has been spent. Thus, the company is committed to following the past results of another company.

Quantitative/ Experimental

The term quantitative methods encompasses a number of statistical models and field experiment techniques. The main purpose of any of these methods is to understand when advertising dollars are operating at peak efficiency. The marketer appropriates funds as long as the money invested returns more or at least an equal amount of

FIGURE 10.3

Determining the Advertising–Sales Relationship

The green area indicates spending levels where advertising expenditures are contributing to sales. The blue area indicates where advertising will no longer be valuable in increasing sales. X is the saturation point beyond which advertising appropriations should not be increased.

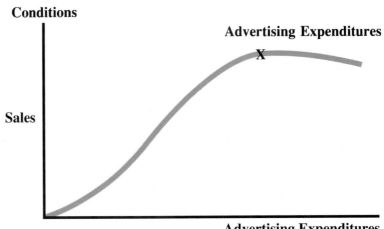

sales. The marketer seeks to determine the point at which advertising appropriations no longer contribute to sales.

An example of the advertising–sales relationship is shown in Figure 10.3. The curved line indicates a typical sales curve where initial sales are slow, then begin to build rapidly and finally level off. The bottom (horizontal) line indicates the amount of money spent on advertising. Notice how advertising dollars appear to be contributing to sales (vertical line) up to point X.

Beyond point X, the marketer is not gaining any additional sales for the money spent on advertising. Therefore, it would not pay to spend money beyond that point.

Field or market experiments use different amounts of advertising spending to determine the most efficient level. An advertiser would vary the level of advertising spending in different markets (test areas) to determine the impact. For example, City A would receive one level of expenditures while City B would receive another level of expenditures. Results such as awareness, attitude change, or sales would be compared to determine the best level of advertising. Market experiments require a high level of research sophistication in order to make sure the results are valid. The major drawbacks are time and costs involved. A market experiment usually takes at least six months and can in many cases take a year. The costs associated with the method usually limit its use to national advertisers with large budgets.

Historical data are sometimes used to develop a statistical model of the advertising–sales relationship. Prior sales records and advertising appropriations are analyzed to understand the impact of advertising on sales. This method requires a good deal of past sales, advertising, and marketing data in order to develop an accurate picture. For this reason its use has been very limited.

Affordable and Arbitrary Methods

The affordable method allows an appropriation for advertising only after all other expenses and investments. The technique relies on the money that is left over and can therefore be afforded by the company. The method ignores the role of advertising as an investment in future objectives. Certainly, it leads to an uncertain budget and the lack of long-range planning.

The arbitrary method does not rely on any planned system to allocate appropriations. It is sometimes used by inexperienced marketers who have not investigated the value of advertising.

Budgeting Influences

In deciding the various approaches to use, and in setting upper and lower limits on spending, the marketer will be influenced by several key considerations. The considerations vary according to whether the situation is consumer, retail, or business-to-business based. Some examples of advertising as percent of sales for consumer, retail, and business-to-business marketers are shown in Table 10.5. In general, consumer advertising has the highest percentage of advertising to sales, while business-to-business marketers have the lowest percentage.

A number of factors need to be considered when determining the amount to be spent on advertising. Separate checklists for consumer, retail, and business-to-business marketers are provided in Figures 10.4, 10.5, and 10.6. As the consumer and business-to-business checklists indicate, uniqueness is important in determining when to advertise. Figure 10.7 is an example of such advertising—Grey Poupon Dijon emphasizes the unique taste of its mustard with white wine.

Summary

One of the most critical campaign decisions is the amount of money spent on advertising. Advertising expenditures are considered an expense because they are taken out of the annual operating budget. However, advertising is also considered

TABLE 10.5

Advertising as a Percent of Sales for Selected Consumer, Retail, and Business-to-Business Marketers

	Ad Dollars as a Percent of Sales
Consumer Marketers	
Beverages	8.2%
Canned and Frozen Fruit and Vegetables	7.6
Malt Beverages	5.6
Retail	
Home Furniture and Equipment	3.0%
Department Stores	2.5
Auto- and Home-Supply Stores	1.4
Business-to-Business Marketers	
Agricultural Chemicals	1.5%
Pumping Equipment	1.4
Surgical and Medical Supplies	1.3

Source: *Advertising Age* (July 26, 1993): 27.

Future Trends

Advertising-Promotion Gap to Narrow by 1996

The decade from 1980 to 1990 has seen a shift from advertising to promotion, whereby 30 percent of the spending went to advertising and 70 percent to other forms of promotion. During the decade marketers increasingly placed more emphasis on sales promotion including coupons, contests, and retailer incentives.

Industry forecasters, Veronis, Suhler & Associates, now feel this trend will reverse, and the spending between promotion and advertising will narrow by 1996. Again, there will be greater emphasis on advertising due to the fact that media advertising expenditures are expected to grow more rapidly.

Source: Joe Mandese and Scott Donaton, "Media, Promotion Gap to Narrow," *Advertising Age,* January 29, 1992, 16.

FIGURE 10.4

Checklist of Budgeting Considerations for Consumer Products and Services

Newness of Product   It takes substantially more money to launch a new product than to keep an established product going.

Product Uniqueness   A higher percentage of advertising is invested in products that have unique factors that can be differentiated.

Hidden Qualities   If the basis for differentiating a product is hidden and cannot be readily judged at the time of purchase, then more money is usually spent on advertising.

Absence of Strong Price Competition   If products are sold primarily on price, marketers are reluctant to spend money creating brand preference.

Opportunity for Strong Emotional Appeal   Products that can be sold through strong emotional appeals have a great opportunity to benefit from advertising (that is, perfumes, cosmetics, and baby products).

Favorable Primary Demand   If a product class in general is in high demand, it is easier to stimulate brand preference through advertising.

Retailer Not Involved in Advertising   Some marketers prefer to build demand through a heavy amount of advertising to the customer, and the retailer does little to promote the product. Usually this is characterized by low retail margins and no one retail store is of critical importance to the marketer.

Retailer Involved in Advertising   The retailer is more active and takes on a great deal of the sale and promotion effort. Usually, this is characterized by high retail margins.

Scope of Market   Companies who cover a national or regional market rather than a local one will obviously have to spend more money.

Competition   Highly competitive situations, where other marketers are spending a great deal on well-directed advertising, generally require us to spend more money.

FIGURE 10.5

Checklist of Budgeting Considerations for Retailers

Age   In general, a new store must invest more in advertising than does an older, more established one. The new store must win the confidence of consumers and make the store and the merchandise known in the community by advertising.

Location   A store located in a major shopping area usually does not require as much advertising to generate traffic. A store located in a less convenient location will need more advertising to attract customers.

Merchandising Policies   Promotional (bargain appeal) stores depend heavily on low price. Consequently, they require a higher advertising investment than do stores enjoying a steady business in regular-price merchandise. Also, a store that emphasizes fashion merchandise, which must be sold quickly, will need larger advertising budgets.

Competition   If the competition is keen, a store manager must continually advertise to maintain existing customers and attract new ones. Additionally, the manager must monitor the success and failure of competitive advertising.

Type of Media Available   Communities vary greatly in the number and quality of media and in the advertising rates charged. Retailers in a town with limited local newspapers and broadcast media will spend less on advertising.

Scope of Trading Area   Normally, the larger a store's trading area, the more money it will spend on advertising. The dominant department and specialty stores in an area attract customers from the city's entire trading area and spend more on advertising.

Type of Merchandise Handled   Variety stores depend on impulse buying of high turnover items for the bulk of their business. Stores with goods that are more shopping oriented such as furniture, jewelry, and appliances do considerably more advertising on a per-unit basis. Prospective customers commonly consult the local media advertising to check the availability, quality, and even the price of such shopping goods.

Support from the Manufacturer   Many retailers gear their advertising to the advertising efforts of the companies whose brands they carry. If a retailer is an exclusive dealer for a brand that is heavily advertised, then there is less need for retailer sponsored advertising. Many retailers take advantage of cooperative advertising programs offered by the manufacturer. The manufacturer provides ads that can be run in local media with the retailer's name. Many manufacturers also provide point-of-purchase materials that can reduce the retailer's display cost.

an investment because it contributes to the long-range profit of the company. In recent years the advertising budget has been expanded to the advertising and sales promotion budget. The largest item in the advertising budget is the amount spent on space and time in the various advertising media.

Advertisers use a variety of approaches in determining their budgets. Among the most common are objective and task, percent of sales, unit of sale, competitive spending, and quantitative/experimental. Most advertisers use a combination of approaches. The most logical approaches are those based on an investigation of the sales potential and the assumption that advertising precedes rather than follows sales.

Some firms consistently spend a higher percentage of sales for advertising than do others. Among the more important factors determining the amount to be spent are newness of the product advertised, the opportunity to differentiate the product, the presence of hidden qualities, amount of price competition, importance of the retailer, scope of the market, and what competitors are doing.

FIGURE 10.6

Checklist of Budgeting Considerations for Business-to-Business Products and Services

Product Quality Products with a noted high standard of quality usually allocate a higher percentage of sales to advertising. This allows the advertiser to promote the quality.

Product Uniqueness If a product has a unique design or special application that sets it apart from the competition, a higher percent of advertising is used to communicate the special factors.

Frequency of Purchase Products that are purchased more frequently generally have more advertising. Products purchased less frequently rely more heavily on personal sales.

Newness of Product Similar to consumer goods, new business-to-business goods require a higher percentage of advertising to sales in order to introduce and establish the product in the market.

Market Share As market share increases, the amount of advertising on a percentage of sale basis usually declines.

Growth in Customer Base As the customer base grows, the total advertising outlay will grow in order to continue reaching a larger number of customers.

Amount of Purchase Less advertising and more personal sales are used for products that are more expensive on a per-unit basis.

Price As price goes up relative to the competition, a higher percent of advertising is used to support product quality and uniqueness claims.

Source: Michael L. Ray, *Advertising and Communication Management* (Englewood Cliffs, NJ: Prentice-Hall, 1982), 161–162.

FIGURE 10.7

Products with Unique Appeal Present a Good Opportunity to Advertise

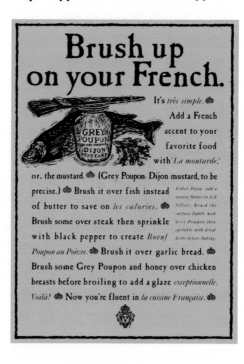

1. Of the various approaches to budgeting, which one would you recommend for use by a manufacturer of VCRs? By your local department store? Why?
2. What are the principal reasons for the substantial variations in percentage of sales devoted to advertising from one product class to another? From one type of retail store to another?
3. Why is the presence of hidden qualities a help in advertising a product?
4. Why is advertising considered an "investment"?
5. Why is the objective–task approach favored by advertisers?
6. What are the advantages and disadvantages of the percent of past sales approach?
7. What are some of the key factors influencing advertising spending for consumer goods? Retail goods? Business-to-business products?

[1] Mark Landler, "What Happened to Advertising?" *Business Week*, September 23, 1991, 71.

[2] "Recession and the Budget Axe," *American Advertising*, Fall, 1991, 10.

[3] Ibid., 11.

[4] Gary Levin, "Tracing Ad's Impact, Study Shows Long-term Effects of Campaigns," *Advertising Age*, November 4, 1991, 49.

[5] Bernard Ryan Jr., "It Works! How Investment Spending in Advertising Pays Off," American Association of Advertising Agencies, Inc., New York, NY, 1991, 7.

[6] "Does Advertising Pay? The Impact of Advertising Expenditures on Profits for Consumer Business," *Ogilvy and Mather Viewpoints*, January–February, 1988, 7.

[7] James E. Lynch and Graham J. Hooley, "Increasing Sophistication In Advertising Budget Setting," *Journal of Advertising Research*, February/March, 1990, 67.

[8] "Gerber Targets New Moms with Direct-Mail Packages," *Marketing News*, May 23, 1988, 13.

Aaker, David A., Rajeev Batra, and John G. Myers. *Advertising Management*. 4th ed. Englewood Cliffs, NJ: Prentice-Hall, 1992. Chapter 16, 17.

Blasko, Vincent J., and Charles H. Patti. "The Advertising Budgeting Practices of Industrial Marketers." *Journal of Marketing* 21 (Fall 1984): 104–110.

"Does Advertising Pay? The Impact of Advertising Expenditures on Profits for Consumer Business." *Ogilvy and Mather Viewpoints*, January–February 1988.

Kotler, Philip. *Marketing Management*. 8th ed. Englewood Cliffs, NJ: Prentice-Hall, 1991. Chapter 21.

Lynch, James E., and Graham J. Hooley. "Increasing Sophistication in Advertising Budgeting Setting." *Journal of Advertising Research* (February/March 1990): 67–75.

Ryan, Bernard, Jr., "It Works! How Investment Spending in Advertising Pays Off," American Association of Advertising Agencies, Inc., New York, 1991.

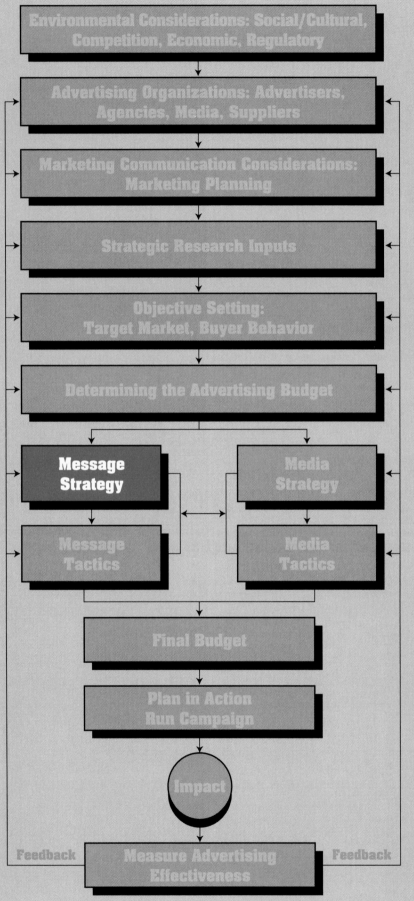

Chapter 11

Message Strategy

CHAPTER TOPICS

MESSAGE STRATEGY DEFINED
    Message Strategy as Differentiated from Tactics
    Determining the Message Idea
    The Copy Platform: The Creative Blueprint
    Message Tactics: Elements of Ad Execution

TYPES OF MESSAGE STRATEGIES

CLASSIC CREATIVE APPROACHES
    Burnett's Inherent Drama
    Reeves's Unique Selling Proposition
    Ogilvy's Brand Image
    Bernbach's Execution Emphasis
    Trout and Reis's Positioning
    FCB's Message Matrix
    Creative Style of the 1980s

CREATIVE OBJECTIVES
    Long-Range versus Short-Range Objectives
    Hierarchy of Creative Objectives
    General versus Specific Objectives

JUDGING MESSAGE IDEAS AND EXECUTIONS

CREATIVITY AND MESSAGE STRATEGY

IDENTIFYING SYMBOLS
    Trademarks, Brand Names, and Trade Names
    Licensed Names
    Trade Characters
    Slogans

OBTAINING AND RETAINING PROTECTION FOR IDENTIFYING SYMBOLS

GUIDELINES FOR USING IDENTIFYING SYMBOLS

Advertising creativity, the force that drives message strategy development and execution, is the one aspect of advertising that has defied mathematical treatment. Gordon E. White, a former creative director, calls creativity the *X* factor in the advertising planning equation because, unlike media planning and budgeting decisions, the potential efficacy of various creative approaches cannot be plugged in as the "message" variable of some advertising formula.[1] As experience has taught advertising practitioners, different creative approaches will produce different results even when backed by the same number of advertising dollars in the same media. Yet, though message strategy is indisputably the least scientific aspect of advertising, it is the most important. As so poetically described by creative genius Leo Burnett in his famous speech, "Finally Somebody Has to Get Out an Ad," the life, core, and heart of the advertising business is making ads.[2]

This chapter will provide guidance for working out the message strategy for an advertising campaign. It will show how message strategy is built and the role that such important inputs as creativity, marketing decisions, and message characteristics play in working out that strategy. Message strategy is an extension of the marketing plan and must be coordinated with media and budgeting strategies to provide a blueprint for executing the specifics of an advertising campaign.

Message Strategy Defined

In theory, creating effective advertising would seem a simple business—getting the right message to the right audience at the right time. In practice, however, the business of advertising is not so simple; other advertisers are trying to reach the same audience.[3] To overcome competing voices as well as the audience's general defensive tendencies, the key to effective advertising—getting people's attention and then motivating them to process the sales message—is the development and execution of the right message strategy. According to John O'Toole, former chairman of one of the world's largest agencies, an advertising campaign cannot succeed with the wrong message strategy.[4] Examples of how two classic message strategies were conceived are presented in the Ad Insight entitled "Two Moments of Creation."

Message Strategy as Differentiated from Tactics

Message planning involves two interrelated decisions: the determination of message strategy and of message tactics. Message planning has been defined in a variety of ways by advertisers. Some call it copy strategy; others call it creative strategy. However, regardless of what it is called, all agree that message strategy involves the determination of "what the advertising is to say" and that message tactics involve the matter of "how the strategy is executed." As a basic component of campaign planning, message strategy provides a logical progression from marketing to communication objectives to message content to tactics for conveying the advertising message in the form of finished advertisements.

The "what to say" decision involves the formulation of a main message idea that will communicate the benefit or problem-solving capabilities of the advertising object—the product, service, or idea—to the identified target audience. It spells out what advertising is expected to communicate, but it does not specify how the message will be delivered. To one agency creative head it is "a kind of route map laying down how we will get from Point A to Point B—Point A being what our prospects think today, Point B being what we want them to think one, two, three years from now."[5] Put another way, it is the "Big Idea," described in the accompanying Ad Insight, that captures the want-satisfying qualities or benefits of an advertised object, which is translated into attention-getting and memorable ads.

Consider, for example, the message strategy of the recruiting campaign of the U.S. Army.[6] First introduced in 1981, "Be All You Can Be" was chosen as the main theme to communicate the benefits of personal growth and development that could be derived through Army enlistment. Since then, only minor changes in some lyrics and subthemes have been necessary, mainly to reflect subtle changes in message targeting. For the first two years of the campaign, the subtheme "Because We Need You in the Army" was paired with the main theme to reflect a "your country needs you" attitude. Two years later, the subtheme was changed to "You Can Do It in the Army," a claim more in line with the "individual development" emphasis of the campaign's main strategy. In 1985, "Find Your Future in the Army" became the subtheme, a theme that reflected individual challenge and career training. That subtheme was extended several years later with "Get an Edge on Life."

Today, the Army's campaign strategy is still alive and well, using the original theme "Army. Be All You Can Be" (see Figure 11.1). The campaign is testimony to the fact that, once the right message idea is determined, it can be retained and built on for years.

Determining the Message Idea

The most effective message idea is the product of an accumulation of facts—about products, markets, consumers, and competitors. The common denominator of all advertising creative efforts is background information. Writers, artists, and others involved in the creation of advertising need to understand such things as how the

Two Moments of Creation: Visits with the Creators of Two Classic Campaigns

(1) There was no hair-coloring business in 1955. If you used haircoloring, it was blotchy looking and uneven; for a woman to *admit* to coloring her hair was a frightful shame. But I knew that women would consider using this new product if it looked natural. I had some cosmetic experience, so the account had been given to me. We had to wait nine months [for the agency to complete its research], and I thought about it a lot during that time. Things stay in your subconscious mind, and I believe that everything you have back there is usable, if you just have sense enough to use it. In 1933, just before I was married, my husband had taken me to meet the woman who would become my mother-in-law. When we got in the car after dinner, I asked him, "How'd I do? Did your mother like me?" and he told me his mother had said, "She paints her hair, doesn't she?" He asked me, "Well, do you?" It became a joke between my husband and me; anytime we saw someone who was stunning or attractive we'd say, "Does she, or doesn't she?" Twenty years later, I was walking down Park Avenue talking out loud to myself, because I have to hear what I write. The phrase came into my mind again. Suddenly, I realized, "That's it. That's the campaign." I knew that anyone who came in competitively couldn't find anything better. I knew that immediately. When you're young, you're very sure about everything.

(2) In trying to figure out how to appeal to the less-than-45-year-old audience (those we had in spades), the

copywriter [Robin McLaughlin], decided to use the word "lovers" in the context of a series of ads, each of which would focus on a particular attraction in the state: beaches, mountains, gardens, etc. The first ad read, "Virginia is for history lovers." When she showed the ad to [art director] George Woltz and me, we said, "This isn't going to work." It wasn't practical, we said, to devote a whole ad to each aspect. We had to have all the attractions in the same ad to highlight all the things people could do and see. So, we decided to just drop the modifiers and make it, "Virginia is for lovers." It was like the hula-hoop. "Lovers" was a "naughty" word back in 1969. But the campaign hit at a time when love was topical, and very much on people's minds. The Vietnam War slogan, "Make love, not war," had been popularized by peace demonstrators, and there was interest in trying to be in sync with your fellow human beings. We thought we had a nice line that fit the strategic objective, but we didn't realize the line had magic like no other. It caught the imagination. It suggested all kinds of things without being specific. When we presented it, everyone was shocked. Their jaws really dropped. But the chairman of the state's board saw that this would be the kind of thing that would set the state apart. It was an on-the-edge idea that has since entered into the culture of Virginia. I knew we had a winner at a convention in San Diego, when people started gobbling up buttons and sweatshirts.

Source: *Agency,* May/June 1991, 32–35.

The "Big Idea"

*A spot of color
and a bit of humor
work in this print ad, one of
a series for Pepto-Bismol.*

*Product demonstration
without words broke
the detergent
mold ad for Cheer.*

Sources: Used with permission of Whitey Herzog and The Procter & Gamble Company. Used with permission of The Procter & Gamble Company and actor, JoBe Cerny.

"Trends in advertising come and go, but one rule remains intact and unchallenged: The Big Idea makes a big difference," according to Fred Danzig, editor of *Advertising Age*. "Advertisers pay their agencies big money and hope that at some point, a Big Idea—that awesome bolt of creative lightning that can cut through the clutter and power sales to higher levels—will strike."

Simply put, the "Big Idea" is what advertising is all about. It makes brands and product categories flourish; it creates new jobs, overtime, and capital investments; and it attracts new clients to agencies that have the capacity to produce "Big Ideas."

The modern history of the advertising business is dotted with "Big Idea" campaign successes:

Clairol's "Does she . . . or doesn't she?"
Armour's "Aren't you glad you use Dial?"
Avis's "We try harder."
Continental Baking's "Wonder Bread helps build strong bodies 12 ways."
Colgate-Palmolive's "Colgate cleans your breath while it cleans your teeth."
McDonald's "You deserve a break today."
Marlboro's "Marlboro Country."
Coca-Cola's "It's the real thing."
International Ladies Garment Workers' "Look for the Union Label."
GM's "Baseball, Hot Dogs, Apple Pie, and Chevrolet."
Miller Lite's "Tastes Great, Less Filling."
United's "Fly the Friendly Skies."

Source: Fred Danzig, "The Big Idea," *Advertising Age* (November 9, 1988):16, 140, and 188.

consumer sees the product in relation to competitive offerings; what specific attributes, usage situations, or user characteristics are important to the consumer when considering purchase; what competitors are saying about their products in their advertising campaigns; and whether particular product attributes or usage situations have been overlooked by competitive advertising messages.

The necessary information comes from two sources: (1) intuition and acquaintance with the product or service and (2) scientifically collected research data, which is often detailed in the situation analysis and strategies of the marketing plan. Intuition

FIGURE 11.1

Advertisements from the U.S. Army's "Be All You Can Be" Campaign

*The ads demonstrate the successful development
and maintenance of message strategy.*

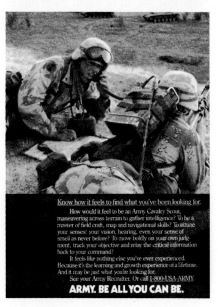

and acquaintance are the accumulation of facts through firsthand experiences with the product and its users or reliance on professional judgment and familiarity. Research data is the accumulation of facts through secondary analyses of published data or through commissioned consumer surveys, in-depth interviews, observations, or **focus groups.** Neither information source can determine the best answer to the message idea question; however, both can provide valuable insight that may lead to the "Big Idea"—that one idea, like "Be All You Can Be," that will guide a campaign for years.

What the advertising planner is searching for is what Kenneth Longman calls the differential-copy advantage—the characteristic or set of characteristics, either real or perceived, that will allow advertising to differentiate the product or service from the competition.[7] A real advantage exists when something is actually different about the product or service, such as superior performance, a special ingredient, or a cost-saving feature. A perceived advantage, on the other hand, exists when the consumer sees a difference, although in actuality the difference is slight or even nonexistent. Both types of advantages are natural outgrowths of the fact that all products and services consist of objective and subjective features. For example, when women buy perfume, they do not buy just a fragrance; they buy psychological and interpersonal benefits. Beer drinkers do not buy simply liquid refreshment; they buy a reward for a hard day's work; they buy a lifestyle. Once found, that differentiation will become the basis for the campaign's message idea.

A differential-copy advantage is based on three differences that exist in all products and services:

1. *Physical differences*   The actual composition of the product or service, such as ingredients, styles, or features.
2. *Functional differences*   The operational consequences of product/service consumption, such as ease of operation or performance.
3. *Characterizational differences*   The psychological consequences of product/ service consumption, such as how it makes consumers feel or see themselves in relation to the product/service or in relation to others.

How a differential-copy advantage is determined is shown in Figure 11.2. Three things that should be noted about this example are true of all approaches to message idea development:

1. All products and services have many physical, functional, and characterizational differences that can be generated; however, not all are unique or relevant to the target audience. For example, although Colombian

---

FIGURE 11.2

Determining a Differential-Copy Advantage: An Analysis of Colombian-Grown Coffee Beans

Product: Colombian-grown coffee beans

Physical Features:
100% Colombian coffee
Full-bodied flavor
Rich aroma

Functional Features:
Fewer poor pots of coffee
Please spouse or guests
Please self
Relaxing and soothing

Characterizational Features:
Coffee-growing tradition
From mountains of Colombia
Early morning enrichment

Source: Kenneth A. Longman, *Advertising* (Orlando, FL: Harcourt Brace Jovanovich, 1971), 172.

coffee is rich in aroma, the attribute may not be very important to the coffee buyer. Or another major brand of coffee may have based its advertising campaign on rich aroma for years. As a result, no opportunity exists for message differentiation, unless a "me-too" message strategy is desired.

2. Physical, functional, and characterizational differences are interrelated; the decision to focus on one or any combination must be determined by relevancy and opportunity. For example, drinking pleasure is derived from the knowledge that Colombian coffee, with its full-bodied flavor, is grown and harvested under special and unique mountain conditions.

3. The targeted consumer is the final judge of which physical, functional, or characterizational differences are important; therefore, any differential-copy advantage must be selected based on how the consumer sees the product, not how advertising professionals or clients see the product.

In practice, the differential-copy advantage that is selected is expressed as part of a copy platform. Although creative managers do not necessarily agree on the form of the copy platform, most would agree on at least the following:

The Copy Platform: The Creative Blueprint

1. The copy platform should be consistent with the marketing plan's strategies and objectives.
2. The copy platform should state clearly and specifically the message or creative objectives (advertising communication objectives).
3. The creative objectives should include a statement of which market segments are to be targeted and which product/service/idea attributes are to be communicated.
4. The copy platform should be coordinated with media and budgeting strategies.
5. The copy platform should provide guidelines for creating the ad executions.

An example of one agency's creative work plan is shown in Figure 11.3. McCann-Erickson, another major advertising agency, refers to its plan format as a creative contract. Regardless of what it is called, a good copy platform should address five specific points, each of which must be consistent with the previously formulated marketing plan:[8]

1. *Creative objectives* What the message strategy should accomplish. How does the advertiser want targeted consumers to think, feel, or act as the result of exposure to the message?
2. *Target audience* The individual that the advertising should directly address. Based on market statistics, who is the typical targeted consumer?
3. *Key benefit* Why the consumer should buy or lease the product/service or adopt the advocated idea; that is, the selected differential-copy advantage. What want-satisfying feature differentiates the product from the competition?
4. *Tone* The manner or direction the message idea should convey. Should the message be strong and forceful or understated and implicit? Should it be humorous or serious?
5. *Message idea statement* A terse and precise statement of what the advertising should say and how it should be said. In essence, the message idea statement brings together the other four points of the platform.

The objectives specify exactly how the key benefit—the selected differential-copy advantage—is related to the desired responses from the target audience. The tone gives direction to the differential-copy advantage, and the message idea statement provides a summary position.

As noted by Michael Ray, a tone statement should deal with three broad questions:[9] (1) whether and to what extent advertising should be emotional as opposed to

FIGURE 11.3

Example of a Creative Work Plan

CLIENT: ___STAR APPLIANCE COMPANY___

PRODUCT/SERVICE: ___Star Line of Cordless,___

___Rechargeable Appliances___

PLANNING PERIOD: ___Fall 1989___   DATE: ___April 18, 1989___

I. KEY FACT *(The one most important fact upon which the creative strategy will be based.)*

Research indicates a strong consumer interest in cordless, rechargeable appliances; Star line will include: hand mixer, knife, and can opener.

II. CONSUMER PROBLEM THE PRODUCT SOLVES *(Problem consumer is having in buying or using the product or service. It's a problem the client's product solves and advertising can address.)*

Consumers believe that cordless products do not provide the power that is required to complete their intended tasks.

III. COMMUNICATION OBJECTIVE *(What the advertising needs to do to solve the consumer problem and the response desired from the consumer.)*

—Introduce Star's New Freedom line of cordless appliances
—Convince consumers that Star's products offer superior benefits

IV. CREATIVE STRATEGY DEVELOPMENT

A. Target Group Definition *(The characterization of the target consumer.)*

1. Demographics: —women ages 25—54
—college educated
—HH income $20M+

2. Psychographics: —convenience oriented
—organized
—likely to try new products

B. Principal Competition *(The market segment which the product will be positioned against.)*

—Black & Decker (knife and mixer)
—Norelco (can opener)
—Hamilton Beach (knife)

C. Consumer Benefit *(What the product promises to do for the consumer that **solves** the consumer's problem.)*

An entire line of new cordless appliances that <u>always</u> provides the <u>power you need and the freedom you want</u>

D. Reason Why *(The key ideal(s) or fact(s) that justify the consumer benefit allowing the advertising to make the product's claim.)*

—Products are powerful
—Exclusive interconnect system
—Products are stored in recharging stands
—Freedom from cord restriction

E. Tone of Advertising *(The feeling the advertising should convey.)*

Introductory—implied superiority

V. Requirements *(All elements that are required to appear in the advertising.)*

—Strong Star brand identification
—Legal requirements: A. ® Star TM Interconnect System disclaimer
                      B. © 1985 Star Appliance Company
                      C. Star Logo

rational, (2) whether and how competition should be considered in advertising, and (3) how strong the advertising message should be. The question of emotional tone involves deciding where to situate the advertising on the factual–feeling continuum. In today's terminology, the continuum is anchored by two forms of advertising:

- *Informational advertising,* which provides consumers with factual, relevant information in a clear and logical manner so that they have greater confidence in their ability to make reasoned purchase decisions.
- *Transformational advertising,* which associates the experience of consuming the product or service with psychological characteristics so that emotions and feelings are experienced.[10]

Whether factual- or feeling-based, tone can be positively or negatively directed. One of the most recognized forms of feeling-based tone is the use of threat appeals in advertising (see Figure 11.4).

Competitive tone deals with the decision of how to treat the competitive environment encountered by the advertising campaign. One option, of course, is to employ a positive, noncompetitive tone in advertising. The use of this option ignores the potential countervailing effects of competitive claims. If the decision is made to address the competitive environment, the advertising strategist has two viable options:[11]

1. Position the product or service in relation to competitive offerings by implicitly or explicitly mentioning competitors.
2. Use a refutational approach to attack consumer-held beliefs that are counter to the established message strategy or competitive counterclaims.

The question of message strength involves deciding how strongly the message should be communicated. Advertisements can be designed with great intensity, moderate intensity, or little intensity. In advertising terms, they can be hard sell, soft sell, or somewhere in between the two extremes. The optimal degree of message strength stimulates interest, but not incredulity.[12]

The message idea, often expressed as a theme, serves as a written guide for the creation of ads and as a gauge for measuring whether the creative output of the campaign is on strategy. As a rule, numerous theme alternatives should be generated and tested among representatives of the target audience in focus group sessions or

FIGURE 11.4

Two Ads from Allstate Insurance Effectively Using Threat Appeal

in-depth interviews to determine the best campaign theme. As with the search for the differential-copy advantage, the generation and selection of a theme must be based on the consumers' perspective—what the theme communicates to them. Later in the chapter we will return to the role of message strategy in evaluating effective advertising.

Message Tactics: Elements of Ad Execution

Once the message idea has been selected, tactical decisions must be made about the verbal and visual character of ad executions. As noted in Chapter 2, an advertisement is composed of verbal and visual signs—words, pictures, and sounds—that are arranged by copywriters, composers, directors, and artists. As shown in Figure 11.5, tactics form the creative mix, which flows from the campaign's objectives. Guidelines for the proper mixing of verbal and nonverbal signs in the creation of effective print and electronic advertising are dealt with in Chapters 13, 14, and 15.

Which is more important—message strategy or tactics? Some experts have argued that strategy is more important on the grounds that strategy directs executions. It is possible to get by with mediocre executions if the strategy is on target, but not possible to get by with brilliant executions if the strategy is wrong. On the other hand, brilliant executions could turn a mediocre strategy into a winner; or a brilliant strategy could be diminished by weak executions. All things considered, the answer to the question is simple: they both are important. Like all aspects of advertising planning, both strategy and tactics must work together. They must build on the marketing and advertising strategies and complement each other.

Types of Message Strategies

A number of classification schemes have been developed as a means of identifying various types of message strategies. One of the most useful, developed by Charles Frazer, is shown in Figure 11.6. As in other classification schemes, Frazer's seven alternatives are neither exhaustive nor mutually exclusive. However, the scheme does provide a useful way of looking at and evaluating the general nature and character of message approaches.

Classic Creative Approaches

Over the past century, advertising has been influenced by the thinking of many creative giants. Figure 11.7 lists some of the most influential and their contributions to creative thinking. Six of the most distinct and enduring approaches to message strategy are: Leo Burnett's inherent drama, Rosser Reeves's unique selling proposition, David Ogilvy's brand image, William Bernbach's execution emphasis, Jack Trout and Al Reis's positioning, and Richard Vaughn's message matrix (see the Ad Insight entitled "Heroes," for thoughts on the contributions of Burnett, Hopkins, Ogilvy, Reeves, and Bernbach).[13] Five of these six approaches are dealt with in Frazer's classification scheme. The exception is Bernbach's execution emphasis. All of the others focus on the "what is said" component of message strategy.

Burnett's Inherent Drama

Leo Burnett, founder of the Leo Burnett agency and father of the Chicago School of Advertising, believed that the secret to effective advertising was finding the inherent drama in a product. To him, this meant the identification of the "reason" why a manufacturer made a product and why the consumer purchased it. Once it

FIGURE 11.5

Evolution of the Creative Mix

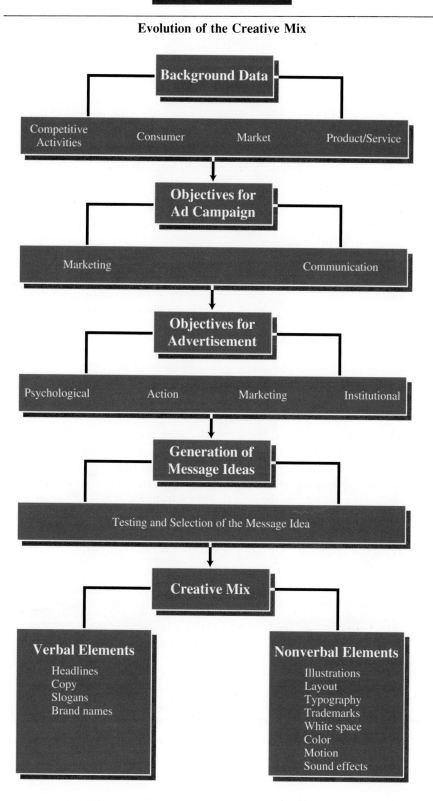

was found, the job of advertising was to take the Inherent Drama—the product–consumer interaction—and produce arresting, warm, and believable ads without relying on gimmicks, tricks, or borrowed interest.

FIGURE 11.6

Summary of Creative Strategy Alternatives

Alternative	Most Suitable Conditions	Competitive Implications
Generic Straight product or benefit claim with no assertion of superiority	Monopoly or extreme dominance of product category	Serves to make advertiser's brand synonymous with product category; may be combated through higher order strategies
Preemptive Generic claim with assertion of superiority	Most useful in growing or awakening market where competitive advertising is generic or nonexistent	May be successful in convincing consumer of superiority of advertiser's product; limits response options for competitors
Unique Selling Proposition Superiority claims based on unique physical feature or benefit	Most useful when point of difference cannot be readily matched by competitors	Advertiser obtains strong persuasive advantage; may force competitors to imitate or choose more aggressive strategy (that is, "positioning")
Brand Image Claims based on psychological differentiation, usually symbolic association	Best suited to homogeneous goods where physical differences are difficult to develop or may be quickly matched; requires sufficient understanding of consumers to develop meaningful symbols/associations	Most often involves prestige claims, which rarely challenge competitors directly
Positioning Attempts to build or occupy mental niche in relation to identified competitor	Best strategy for attacking a market leader; requires relatively long-term commitment to aggressive advertising efforts and understanding consumers	Direct comparison severely limits options for named competitor; counterattacks seem to offer little chance of success
Resonance Attempts to evoke stored experiences of prospects to endow product with relevant meaning or significance	Best suited to socially visible goods; requires considerable consumer understanding to design message patterns	Few direct limitations on competitor's options; most likely competitive response is imitation
Affective Attempts to provoke involvement or emotion through ambiguity, humor or the like, without strong selling emphasis	Best suited to discretionary items; effective use depends upon conventional approach by competitors to maximize difference; greatest commitment is to aesthetics or intuition rather than research	Competitors may imitate to undermine strategy of difference or pursue other alternatives

Source: Charles F. Frazer, "Creative Strategy: A Management Perspective," *Journal of Advertising* 12 (1983): 40. Reprinted with permission.

One of the best examples of the inherent-drama approach is Burnett's work for Green Giant peas. To communicate the special care taken in the company's harvesting and packaging process and the consumer's desire for freshness, Green Giant peas were advertised as "harvested in the moonlight." A more contemporary example is Starkist's "Charlie, the tuna," who is not good enough for Starkist, but who neverthe-

FIGURE 11.7

Approaches of some of the Greats of Advertising Creativity

Creative Greats	Approach
John E. Powers, 1880s	• First person hired full-time to write copy. Believed in truth-telling and writing about products as news.
Earnest Elmo Calkins, 1890s	• Introduced the concept of image advertising; emphasized the power of graphics.
John E. Kennedy, 1904	• Wedded the idea of salesmanship in print to news, creating the philosophy that advertising had to convey reasons-to-buy.
Claude Hopkins, 1904	• Believed in systematic research to determine basic copy principles; advocated advertising to the individual, not to the masses. Introduced the preemptive claim and believed in hard-sell copy.
Theodore McManus, 1910–15	• Leading advocate of impressionistic or atmosphere advertising. Believed in softsell, visual approach without Calkin's corny jingles and trade characters.
Helen Lansdowne, 1911	• First woman to be successful in writing copy.
Helen Resor, 1916	• Copywriter who blended visual appeal with reason-why copy; believed in status appeals.
James Webb Young, 1920s	• Copywriter who developed technique for generating ideas; believed in intuition instead of social science.
John Caples, 1930s	• Believed in hard-hitting, hard-selling advertising; introduced findings on the pulling power of headlines.
Raymond Rubicam, 1930s	• Stressed ethics and creativity; advocated humor and originality to make ads interesting and convincing.
J. Sterling Getchell, 1930s	• Focused on the use of photos and stark realism; introduced comparative ads.
Clyde Bedell, 1930s	• Identified "selling points," calling attention to the relationship between product attributes and consumer benefits.
Alex Osborne, 1940s	• Introduced creative brainstorming as a method for producing ideas.
Howard Gossage, 1960s	• Advocated unorthodox and unconventional advertising; used sophisticated humor in contrast to the serious, bombastic approach.
Mary Wells, 1960s	• Produced very creative campaigns; started Wells Rich & Green, a very influential and creative agency.
Philip Dusenberry, 1970s–80s	• Believed that advertising has to be heavy in emotion and warmth, and be entertaining.
Lee Clow, 1980s	• Designed ads with impact and honesty, but with respect for consumer intelligence.
Hal Riney, 1980s	• Designed ads that contained realism and appealed to genuine human emotions.

Source: David A. Aaker, Rajeev Batra, and John G. Myers, *Advertising Management*, 4th ed. (Englewood Cliffs, NJ: Prentice-Hall, 1992): 396–401; Sandra E. Moriarty, *Creative Advertising; Theory and Practice*, 2nd ed. (Englewood Cliffs, NJ: Prentice-Hall, 1991): 11–16.

less keeps trying to get caught. Charlie knows, as the advertising campaign has driven home for decades, that Starkist uses only the "best" tuna in its product.

Heroes: Advertising's Creative Greats

Never confuse a mentor or a role model with a hero. Mentors or role models are people who lead by example. You find them most often as supervisors and their presence drives you to match their level of performance.

Heroes, on the other hand, are people who may be admired from afar. They set examples not just for an office or a company, but for a wider universe of performers. And, perhaps most importantly, they never go away. They not only were good, they remain just as good in memory as well as in example. They never leave for another position or take a job in a different industry. You can stop being a mentor; you never cease being a hero.

Who made the biggest difference in your business life? We ask some past A.A.A.A. chairmen about their idols. (Years indicate when they were A.A.A.A. chairmen.)

CUMMINGS ON BURNETT

(Barten A. Cummings, 1969, Chairman, Compton Advertising, Inc.)

Other than my father, who ran a very successful, small advertising agency in my hometown of Rockford, Illinois, I most admire Leo Burnett, who surely is one of the greatest advertising men of all time.

Under his leadership, the Burnett agency flourished and grew to become the largest in the world—and today, the principles that Leo established during his tenure continue to assure the success of the Burnett Company.

The amazing thing about Leo's great creativity is to note that so many of his basic campaign ideas continue even to this day, many years after his passing, such as Marlboro Country, the Jolly Green Giant, the Good Hands of Allstate, Tony the Tiger, the Pillsbury Dough Boy, Charlie the Tuna, and many others.

No other renowned creative person has ever had so many basic creative campaign ideas continue decade after decade—not Ogilvy, not Bernbach, not Brower—not one other person can come close to equaling Leo Burnett's continuing successful campaigns.

That is why I believe Leo Burnett is the greatest of them all! God bless him for the many contributions he made to our profession.

O'TOOLE ON HOPKINS

(John O'Toole, 1984, Chairman, Foote Cone & Belding Communications, Inc.)

A "Hero"? How about this: a copywriter once described as "a shy mouse of a man" who spoke with a lisp and, despite his generous income, refused to pay more than $6.50 for a pair of shoes.

That was Claude Hopkins, whose insights into the nature and practice of advertising in the first decades of this century were key to unleashing its real power. Hopkins was among the first to equate the role of an ad with that of a personal salesman, the first to use a test market, the innovator of the "preemptive claim" and "reason why" copy, the first to use a demonstration in advertising, the first to use copy testing.

Hopkins' book, *Scientific Advertising*, is to this day the most valuable work on the subject extant and the first I recommend to aspiring copywriters. That doesn't mean that I agree with every premise or that some of it hasn't been overtaken by time and technology. He published it, after all, in 1923. But if you examine current writings about the craft in trade and popular-culture journals, you can usually find contemporary insights into the reality of advertising, those epiphanies encountered by today's observers, somewhere in your dusty copy of *Scientific Advertising*.

My "hero" was a compulsive worker, poorly educated and defensive about it and, it would appear, somewhat humorless. An odd choice. Unless you are one of those whose understanding of his craft was illuminated by Hopkins' admonition to make every ad so personal that it will have "the impact of a bellboy paging a man in a crowded room."

NEY ON BERNBACH, OGILVY

(Edward S. Ney, 1977, President, Young & Rubicam)

I chose these two men for really quite similar reasons—(a) both started agencies in post World War II years and (b) the agencies were built on great creative work. Bill Bernbach insisted that the central creative persuasion come from the product, which was always presented with flair and wit. David Ogilvy, because of his Gallup background, was a believer in research, and insisted on creative persuasion being capable of sustaining great *campaigns*.

Very importantly, they both built organizations of quality and integrity. They contributed greatly to the business by the fact that they had such excellent training programs in their companies, and they themselves became the sym-

Bill Bernbach

bol of creative leadership. Their people and their disciples are all over the agency business, with brilliant records. As businessmen, they both understood the necessity to build international organizations in a world that was moving towards open world trade. As usual, they were right.

Above all, they were great leaders. They spoke for the industry, and they loved the business. Beyond being brilliant in their craft, they were revered by the people in their companies, deeply admired by everybody in the business, and made lots of clients very, very happy. In addition, they used their great skills on some of the world's great challenges, for example, Bernbach for Israel, Ogilvy for the World Wildlife Fund, et al.

Bill Bernbach and David Ogilvy represent the advertising agency business at its best. Fortunately, David is still with us, as we all so well know, and continues to make his pungent and brilliant comment available to one and all. Bill's legend continues to grow as the Leukemia Society gives its Bernbach Award to top people in the business.

I doubt that we will *ever* see two people who contributed more to business and the world community.

REINHARD ON BERNBACH

(Keith L. Reinhard, 1990, Chairman & CEO, DDB Needham Worldwide, Inc.)

You didn't have to be Jewish to love Levy's Rye Bread. Nor did you have to be a New Yorker to love Ohrbach's. The work of Doyle Dane Bernbach ignited the imaginations of a generation of creative people, no matter where they lived or worked.

Bill Bernbach was my hero, as he was the hero of every creative person I knew.

Bernbach was the Picasso of our business. He changed forever the direction of all advertising by destroying old conventions and hoary restrictions; by rethinking how advertising works. The campaigns inspired by his vision remain unchallenged as classic examples of our industry at its best.

Helmut Krone once told me that creative people would willingly work around the clock in pursuit of an idea

which might gain a smile of approval from Bill. I never had that chance, so I will spend my energies doing what I can to interpret Bernbach's insights for a dramatically changed world and attempt to prove the truth of his prediction that "the future, as always, belongs to the brave."

KUMMEL ON REEVES

(Gene Kummel, 1980, Chairman, McCann-Erickson)

Like Branch Rickey's description of the ideal baseball player who could run, throw, hit, and hit with power, Rosser Reeves "could do it all!"

He ran a great business as CEO of Ted Bates. He created and employed a philosophy . . . "the Ultimate Selling Proposition" (USP) . . . that not only was so forceful with his clients but was adopted by other clients as well. He was a truly great New Business rainmaker . . . ask any of us who competed against him.

And above all else, he was a great copywriter who himself wrote or inspired great campaigns that lasted for many years in their effectiveness: Colgate toothpaste: "Cleans your breath while it cleans your teeth!", M&M candies: "Melts in your mouth . . . not in your hands!"; Wonder Bread "Helps build bodies 12 ways."

Forgetting all of the above, Rosser Reeves would have been a hero of mine for one story alone about him, although it may have been apocryphal. I heard that the CEO of Continental Baking called Rosser to his office one day and declared: "Rosser, we are now in our 15th year with "Helps build bodies 12 ways" for Wonder Bread. Why do we keep paying you 15 percent each year for the same campaign?"

Replied Rosser: "To keep you from changing it."

At the close of his life, I heard that Rosser planned to move from his retirement home in the island of Jamaica to Chapel Hill, North Carolina, so I called my friend, Professor Jay Klompmaker of the North Carolina Business School, to suggest Rosser Reeves as a frequent guest lecturer on advertising. Jay was instantly enthusiastic, but before the series could be instigated, Rosser died.

It was a pity. Those young people at the Carolina business school would have found a hero who "could do it all!"

WEITHAS ON BURNETT

(William Weithas, 1988, Chairman, Lintas: Worldwide)

"I am often asked how I got into this business. I didn't. The business got into me." Leo Burnett.

I have always had heros, men I looked up to and admired.

Early on there were the baseball greats, Williams and DiMaggio. During the War, the famous generals became my idols: MacArthur, Patton, Eisenhower.

Brilliant statesmen and political leaders that I read about—Roosevelt, Churchill—filled me with awe and became models of dedication.

Continued

But that was before I entered the real work-a-day world of advertising and discovered a whole new breed of outstanding men—Bernbach, Ogilvy, Brower, and the greatest of all, Leo Burnett.

I met Leo only once. As an assistant account executive for BBDO on the Campbell's business, I was carrying the black bag out to a client meeting and ran into him in the lobby. He asked who I was and about my work and introduced himself, spattering ashes over his vest.

It was a great moment.

Leo's legacy consists of the principles he lived by and the standards he set for our business.

"A good art director," he said, "is either a plagiarist or a revolutionist."

He warned against talking down to your audience: "Too many ads that try not to go over the reader's head end up beneath his notice."

"The greatest thing to be achieved in advertising," he said, "is believability and nothing is more believable than the product itself." He encouraged his creative people to find the inherent drama in the product. To this day, Leo's philosophy lives on in the agency he founded.

He urged that advertising be simple, inviting, likeable. That advertising people should be loyal to their clients' products; curious about everything; never sacrifice their integrity; and "work like hell and love, honor, and obey your hunches."

"Remember what our business is all about," said Leo, "making better ads and attending to clients."

I can live with these words and "the strong, insistent voice of integrity" Leo believed you should never be tempted or threatened to ignore.

McCAFFREY ON OGILVY

(James J. McCaffrey, 1972, Chairman, McCaffrey & McCall, Inc.)

When David Ogilvy arrived on the scene in the late 1940s, he had going for him a keen mind, a burning desire to succeed, a plan on how to go about it, an enormous capacity for hard labor, something more than a soupçon of self-confidence, a finely tuned sense of the dramatic, and the guts of a cat burglar.

The business world remembers him primarily as a brilliant writer. The early Hathaway, Schweppes, and Rolls-Royce campaigns alone are enough to assure him advertising immortality. He was the ultimate perfectionist. The invariable result was highly literate, compelling work couched in impeccably clean, spare language.

But David was far more than a superb craftsman. He was an innovator and an industry leader.

He stood virtually alone in favor of fee compensation and against the agency commission system when this made him as popular as smallpox among his peers.

And it was he who engineered the appointment of John Crichton as A.A.A.A. president, an event that ushered in a new era of progress, stability, and pride in the business.

David Ogilvy was a great teacher and a canny manager. In less than two decades, he led his agency from scratch to a place in the top five in billings and profits. And he left it well manned to carry on, because he had selected and taught his successors well.

Not bad for a young Scot on foreign soil.

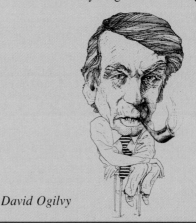

David Ogilvy

Reeves's Unique Selling Proposition

Neil Borden emphasized the importance of looking for the differentiating qualities of product to determine how advertiseable it is. The more product differentiation possible, the more advertiseable the product will be. Rosser Reeves, then of the Ted Bates agency, put Borden's notion in action as the "unique selling proposition." To his way of thinking, a successful advertising campaign had to be built on the product's Unique Selling Proposition (USP), which he described as having three parts:

1. Each advertisement must make a proposition to the consumer. Not just words, not just product puffery, not just show-window advertising. Each advertisement must say to each reader, "Buy this product and you will get this benefit."
2. The proposition must be one that the competition either cannot, or does not, offer. It must be unique either in the brand or the claim.

3. The proposition must be strong enough to move the mass millions, that is, pull new customers to your product.

Once it was identified, Rosser believed that the USP should be hammered away at repeatedly in advertisements and retained indefinitely in a campaign. One of Reeves's most famous USP's was M&M candies' claim, "melts in your mouth, not in your hands."

Product personality is the total impression people have of a product, and it is commonly called an image. It is what comes to mind upon hearing the names IBM, Sears, Delta Airlines, Transamerica Corporation, or UPS (see Figure 11.8). David Ogilvy, one of the most respected creative people in the history of advertising and co-founder of the agency, Ogilvy & Mather, believed that a brand image could be developed or cultivated through advertising for every product. He based his approach on the belief that images are not inherent in products, but are instead qualities that the consumer associates with them. To Ogilvy, people buy physical and psychological benefits, not products, and advertising should therefore be built on the long-term investment in the development and retention of a brand image, even if the approach meant short-run sacrifices.

> Every advertisement should be thought of as a contribution to the complex symbol, which is brand image. The manufacturer who dedicates his advertising to building the most sharply defined personality for his brand will get the largest share of the market at the highest profit. By the same token, the manufacturers who will find themselves up the creek are those shortsighted opportunists who siphon off their advertising funds for promotions.[14]

Over the years, brands such as Betty Crocker foods, Marlboro cigarettes, and Budweiser beer have conjured up strong images in the public mind as their advertising has built on unique and well-defined brand images. Marlboro was, at one time, a filter-tipped cigarette with definite feminine appeal. Then a new campaign set out to build an image of Marlboro as the cigarette for outdoor men "who came up the hard way." Illustrations and other visuals showed only rugged-looking men

O_gilvy's Brand Image_

FIGURE 11.8

Image-Building Ads for Range Rover, Absolut, and American Express

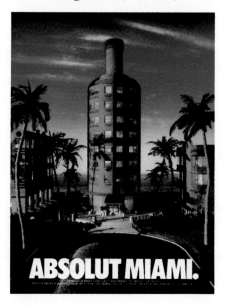

(cowboys, tattooed laborers), and in print or on television, each told something of his outdoor life and explained why he chose Marlboro. Although the Marlboro man appears only in print in America today, he continues to ride the range in some foreign countries where television commercials for cigarettes are not banned.

Bernbach's Execution Emphasis

In the early 1950s, William Bernbach began creating advertising based on an approach quite different from the approaches of Burnett, Reeves, and Ogilvy. Bernbach, one of the founders of the then Doyle Dane Bernbach agency, believed that execution—the "how you say it" component of message strategy—could become content in and of itself. To him, execution style was the dominant feature of advertising, and he believed that the secret to effective advertising was taking a problem and turning it into an advantage with dramatic visuals and honesty. Sound execution had to be based on four points:

1. The audience must be respected; ads should not talk down to the people they are trying to reach.
2. The approach must be clean and direct.
3. Advertisements must stand out from others; they must have their own character and style.
4. Humor should not be ignored; it can be effective in gaining attention and providing a listening, viewing, or reading award.[15]

One of the best-known examples of Bernbach's Execution approach is his early work for Volkswagen. When first introduced in the United States, the VW had four negative features: it was small, ugly, rear-engine powered, and foreign produced. Bernbach took these negatives and created humorous and distinctive advertisements that are regarded as some of advertising's all-time best creative output.

Trout and Reis's Positioning

In 1972, Jack Trout and Al Reis, founders of the Trout & Reis agency, introduced the **Positioning** approach to message strategy. They believed that advertising should be created to gain a perceptual foothold in the consumer's mind by establishing something memorable and distinctive about the product relative to competition. To support their approach, they offered Crest's ADA Seal of Approval, Avis' "We're No. 2, but Trying Harder" theme, and Michelob's "first American-made premium beer" claim as evidence of effective perceptual positioning through advertising. Like the approaches of Burnett, Reeves, and Ogilvy, the positioning approach is based on "what should be said," and once identified and communicated should be recalled every time the consumer needs the kind of benefit or problem solution the product offers.

The problem is to decide which positioning strategy is most likely to be successful. Among the possible approaches to the positioning strategy:

1. Product characteristics or customer benefits (Miller beer's cold-filtering process)
2. Price–quality relationship (Sears as a family-oriented, middle-class store offering top value)
3. Use or application (IBM PCs for desk-top publishing and graphics)
4. Product user (positioning Busch as the heavy-drinking, working man's beer)
5. Product category (positioning domestic wines as an alternative to foreign wines)
6. Cultural symbols (American cowboy as the symbol of Marlboro cigarettes)
7. Competitor (Avis positioning itself as the number-two rental car company)

The positioning approach is sometimes confused with the brand-image approach, but it is actually a broader concept. Positioning involves identifying competition, relevant attributes, competitor position, and market segments. In effect, it is the logical outgrowth of image analysis in that it involves applying what is known about the brand's image, the competition, the target audience, and how members of the audience are motivated to respond. As a consequence, it is helpful to analyze brand image before it is converted to a positioning strategy, which states how the product position is to be communicated.

In 1979, Richard Vaughn outlined Foote, Cone & Belding's approach to the planning, creation, and execution of advertisements.[16] The approach, called the FCB Strategy Planning Model, has been refined over the years and is now utilized by many agencies and advertisers, although it is often called something else. The model consists of a "message matrix" anchored on two continuums: thinking/feeling and high/low importance (involvement). We refer to the model as the message-matrix approach because it forces the planner to match product characteristics with consumer styles when searching for the "Big Idea"—the differential-copy advantage.

The matrix, with its four planning quadrants, is depicted in Figure 11.9. Each quadrant relates the type of product to consumer involvement; suggests how advertising should be processed; and offers creative, media, and testing implications. According to Vaughn, the purpose of the approach is to identify the information, emotion, or action leverage for a particular product; build the appropriate model for the advertising situation; and then execute it.

F*CB'S Message Matrix*

FIGURE 11.9

FCB's Message Matrix: A Modern Creative Approach

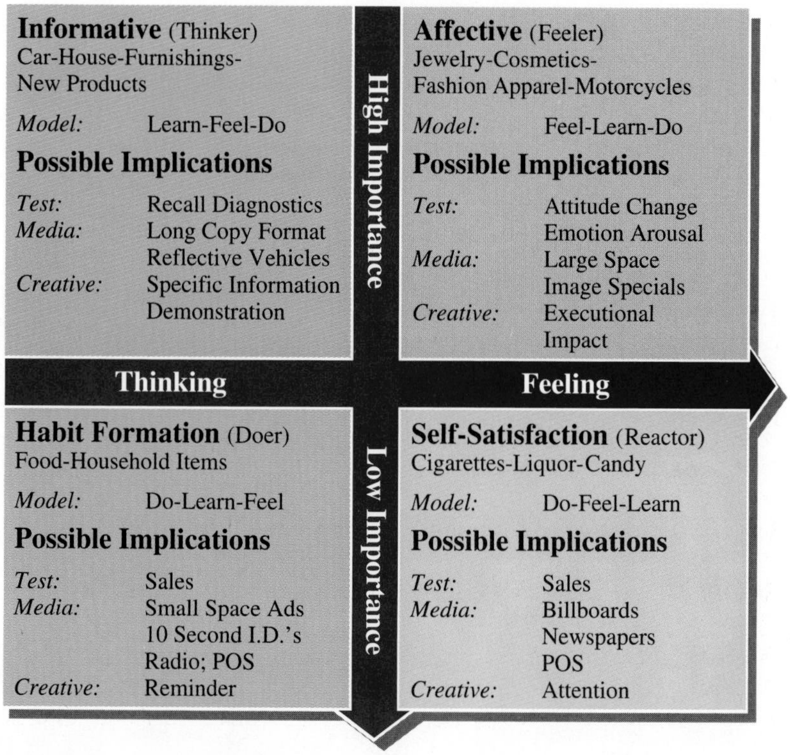

Informative (Thinker) Car-House-Furnishings-New Products	**Affective** (Feeler) Jewelry-Cosmetics-Fashion Apparel-Motorcycles
Model: Learn-Feel-Do	*Model:* Feel-Learn-Do
Possible Implications	**Possible Implications**
Test: Recall Diagnostics *Media:* Long Copy Format Reflective Vehicles *Creative:* Specific Information Demonstration	*Test:* Attitude Change Emotion Arousal *Media:* Large Space Image Specials *Creative:* Executional Impact

High Importance — **Thinking** / **Feeling** — **Low Importance**

Habit Formation (Doer) Food-Household Items	**Self-Satisfaction** (Reactor) Cigarettes-Liquor-Candy
Model: Do-Learn-Feel	*Model:* Do-Feel-Learn
Possible Implications	**Possible Implications**
Test: Sales *Media:* Small Space Ads 10 Second I.D.'s Radio; POS *Creative:* Reminder	*Test:* Sales *Media:* Billboards Newspapers POS *Creative:* Attention

Source: *How Advertising Works: An FCB Strategy Planning Model,* Foote, Cone & Belding Communications, Inc., 1979.

Creative Style of the 1980s

FCB's "message matrix" represents a strategic approach to the development of creative strategy. Although introduced in the late 1970s, it no doubt has played a significant role in the planning of advertising throughout the 1980s and the early 1990s. However, the most visible creative style in modern advertising is represented in the work of Philip Dusenberry, Lee Clow, and Hal Riney, the last three individuals listed in Figure 11.7. The style does not yet have an agreed-upon industry name, so we will refer to it as the "executional-impact" approach.

Introduced in the mid-1980s, ads associated with the executional-impact approach placed greater emphasis on "how an ad communicates than on what the ad communicates." Strategic thinking was not necessarily abandoned; however, human emotions, honest dialogue, realism, executional impact, and entertainment value were thought to be as important or more important than creative strategy when creating effective advertising. A TV commercial which typifies the executional-impact approach of the 1980s is presented in Figure 11.10. Other well-known ads associated with the approach include Nike's "Bo Knows" campaign, Gallo Wines' Frank Bartles and Ed Jaymes campaign, and Pepsi's celebrity campaign featuring stars such as Michael Jackson. Some provocative thoughts on the value of entertainment in modern ad creation are presented in the Ad Insight entitled, "That's Entertainment: Creative Coverage for Second-Tier Brands."

Creative Objectives

Without knowing the objectives of an advertisement, it is impossible for copywriters and artists to produce a successful advertisement or to judge how good it is on the criterion of communication effectiveness. As earlier chapters have indicated, objectives provide planning guidance and a means of evaluation. When restated in the copy platform, advertising objectives serve a guidance purpose: They allow creative people to see the response an advertisement is supposed to evoke and to design content and format to best bring about the desired response.

FIGURE 11.10

A Nike Commercial That Makes Viewers "Feel" the Energy

In this section, we will visit advertising objectives once again to show how communication response is related to message strategy. Creative objectives are discussed on three dimensions: long-range versus short-range, hierarchical character, and general versus specific communication response.

When planners emphasize communication, their focus is primarily on short-range objectives. But when sales are emphasized, planners are adopting a long-term outlook, because they realize that it takes time for advertising to affect sales even though it can produce communication effects in the short term.

Agency executive William Wells urges advertising practitioners to be more sensitive to the differences between communication and marketing objectives.[17] He believes overemphasis on marketing objectives causes creative people to sacrifice "creative sensitivity" in their haste to cram as many claims as possible into an advertisement, without proper regard for the ad's communicative role in the larger marketing plan. To Wells, the trick is to decide in the short term how advertising can contribute to long-term marketing success.

Long-Range versus Short-Range Objectives

Michael Ray maintains that advertising creatives use a hierarchy of objectives, however inadvertent that use may be.[18] He analyzed the philosophies and style of Rosser Reeves, Leo Burnett, David Ogilvy, and William Bernbach. Ray discovered that Reeves worked predominantly in the low-involvement hierarchy of objectives with products in the mature stage of the life cycle. Ogilvy dealt more with the learning hierarchy in his early work with products, such as Rolls-Royce and Hathaway shirts, but later in the low-involvement hierarchy as he moved more to mass-consumption products. Like Ogilvy, Burnett favored the learning hierarchy, trying to get across the naturally involving nature of products, which he called inherent drama. Bernbach, in contrast to the others, had no implicit allegiance to any hierarchy; instead, he relied on tactics and executional devices such as humor and format to communicate the virtues of products. The hierarchical nature of objectives are built into Vaughn's message-matrix approach and guide all creative thinking at Foote, Cone & Belding. Based on his analysis, Ray notes that objectives must be response-oriented and that message content and tactics must be adapted to each advertising situation using research findings as a guide.

Hierarchy of Creative Objectives

To say that we want to create awareness, increase comprehension, build conviction, or move people to action is not enough. Sound advertising objectives must specify the exact nature of the desired responses and in a manner that they can be measured. They must also, as we have previously discussed, be ordered on the basis of how we think advertising-presented information will be processed: from comprehension to action to conviction as suggested by the "learn-do-feel" model or from comprehension to conviction to action as suggested by the "learn-feel-do" model.

General versus Specific Objectives

Awareness

A fundamental objective of most advertisements is to create immediate awareness of a theme or a brand name. But planners must decide on the awareness they hope to achieve and with what target audience. They must specify what they want the audience to be aware of, and to what extent they will appeal to the audience's predisposition to attend encountered advertising.

Often consumers select stimuli in one quick glance or after hearing a few syllables. In that instant, an advertisement either creates awareness or loses the prospect. In less time than it takes to turn a page or flip a dial, an advertisement must engage

That's Entertainment: Creative Leverage for Second-Tier Brands

Like the leaders, brands that are second, third, or worse need to be consistent with advertising, but they need something more: creative leverage.

That's the memory power that propelled the California Raisins to top of mind and made them the most popular commercial in the country for three years in a row.

Two important points about creative leverage:

- It concentrates on a competitive difference, perceived or real, usually identified through consumer qualitative research. The resulting "core idea" is dramatized and camouflaged under a cloak of entertainment that's fashioned with the finest art techniques that can be deployed.
- It is not a one-night stand. Once a unique method has been found to deliver the core idea, the smart advertiser sticks with it, changing only to keep the commercials fresh and relevant.

  The brand mystique is massaged into consumer consciousness through consistent impressions delivered over a long period of time.

For example, in the late 1940s, David Ogilvy gave us The Man in the Hathaway Shirt, an ad laden with product benefits and reasons to buy. The eye patch lives on today in the pages of national magazines.

Product positioning is not disposable. Memories are too short, and advertising is too expensive, for campaigns to change with every new creative team. Brand mystique is formed over time, from a kaleidoscope of images bound together by a strong common element I call the "core idea," the dominant value point that sets the brand apart and gives it value beyond price alone.

The purpose of every ad is to sell the client's product. Some think every ad should return sales to pay for the cost of the insertion. Others see advertising as a way to build brand franchise.

The question is, what is the best way to do either one today given the circumstances we face in this over-advertised, over-produced, competitive society?

Ogilvy tells us in the first sentence of his book, *Ogilvy on Advertising*, that "I do not regard advertising as entertainment or an art form, but as a medium of information."

He's right and he's not. Information—persuasion— is the thing, of course. But TV advertising must entertain, it must have artistic value. Both are necessary in today's world to generate the attention necessary to convey information.

There are three compelling reasons why entertainment, art, and information are essential ingredients for today's advertising:

- **Entertainment** Today's consumers are jaded. At the very least, after 25 years before the tube, they've seen and judged 450,000 commercials. They are exposed to 81 spots every evening.

Source: David N. Martin, "That's Entertainment: Creative Leverage Uses Art, Information to Produce Memorable Ads and Brands," *Marketing News*, 23:3 (November 6, 1989): 24.

the prospect's interest. The power to create awareness is the power to distract, and then arrest, an audience.

How, then, can we determine whether an advertisement will create awareness or be ignored? We know from communication research that people are stopped by a message either because they see in it some promise or reward or because it is easier to notice than to ignore (the principle of least effort). Awareness created by advertising comes from a sound message idea dramatically presented and from the right media environment.

We know that awareness is a relative quality. Most advertisements achieve some level of awareness with some people. Others attract mass attention. The question is not, Will this advertisement create awareness? It is, Will the advertisement create all the awareness about the theme, brand name, or product feature that it should? The question is not presence, but power; not general awareness, but specific awareness.

Viewers have thrown up defenses, and the only way to get around them is to entertain. The only way to be remembered is for your spot to be the best entertainment they see during the three hours they spend each day before the tube.

- **Art**   The people who create advertising do so for love of the art. Copywriters and art directors are motivated by artistic expression and buoyed by peer acclaim. Their art makes the message stand apart.

  Music, photography, actors, and ideas create dramatic moments that are remembered long after hundreds of other images in adjacent minutes are forgotten. Art, skillfully applied, touches human emotions.

- **Information**   This is the paradox: Consumers want information, but they do not believe or take notice when it is spelled out for them in advertising.

  When in doubt, they will always buy the established brand.

  Our own extensive consumer interviews tell us we must demonstrate why the product or service we're selling is better than the competition. Consumers want facts, just as they need strong medicine when they get the flu, but the facts need to be sugar-coated.

So how do we blend entertainment, art, and information?

Smart advertising "camouflages" the product's dominant value point. The distinctive reason to try the brand is there hidden under a cloak of entertainment.

With commercial camouflage, instead of using words like "Quality you can depend on," such marketers as Frank Perdue say, "It takes a tough man to make a tender chicken." Quality is implicitly, rather than explicitly, stated.

Perdue has been saying quality in this way for 17 years. Like Pepperidge Farm, the brand image has been protected and cultivated through the years to the point where nine out of 10 people can now recall the Perdue name and this selling proposition without prompting.

With commercial camouflage, consumers discover the dominant value point for themselves. A good reason to trust and try the brand is there, but consumers are invited to join in the game and find it.

Many major advertisers see advertising as a commodity. They produce test commercials, or even go to full production, and conduct day-after recall tests. Then they throw media weight at the market, dominating category share of voice.

It works for the leaders. Most of the brands we deal with don't have the bucks to do it. So what do we do instead?

Second-tier brands gain ground through the use of implicit copy. They must, because usually they can't afford to have the strongest share of voice in the product category.

Awareness is also influenced by the inherent interest of products. Some products are simply more interesting than others. For example, a BMW is more appealing to most people than a Ford Escort; and if both are advertised in the same publication, chances are that the BMW ad will attract more attention than the Escort ad, all things being equal. A major function of message strategy is to make sure that the other things are not equal. It is the job of strategists, copywriters, and artists to create attention-grabbing advertising that makes a product more interesting.

Comprehension

The process of learning from an ad is complex. What elements must the creative person include to make comprehension easy and thorough? To a considerable extent, the key is knowing how much information the audience has and is likely to seek.

Research has shown that people look for market information, but they usually do not work too hard to find it. The decision facing creatives is to identify what the advertiser specifically wants the audience to comprehend and then to decide how to best present the information—in a highly structured executional format or in a loosely structured format.

A highly structured format takes the audience by the hand and leads them through the ad in an effort to reduce subjective interpretation and miscomprehension. A loosely structured format allows for some desired level of audience interpretation, so that the audience projects their experiences and knowledge when processing the ad. Examples of the two types of formats are shown in Figure 11.11. Miscomprehension is a real problem for advertisers, and ads must be created and designed to enhance comprehension in the direction and manner stated in the advertising plan.

Conviction

Most creative people would like to create in an audience a favorable disposition (emotional or rational) toward the purchase of the advertised product or brand. However, there is no unanimity on how to achieve it, other than to say that it is difficult to do through advertising alone. Advertising can create awareness and convey information; but conviction is generally built from experience, not advertising. What advertising usually does is reinforce conviction, which is acquired more readily through experience or from information obtained from more objective and personal information sources. As a consequence, the question facing advertising creatives is: Will the specific content and format elements contribute to creation or maintenance of conviction?

FIGURE 11.11

Examples of Highly Structured (EASTPAK) and Loosely Structured (Bugle Boy) Ads

The EASTPAK ad leads the reader through the ad and to the same conclusion—the backpack's quality will endure four years of college. The Bugle Boy ad begs for reader interpretation—What's going on here?

Action

In judging an advertisement for impulsion to act, the key question is, Will this advertisement move people we are trying to reach to behave in the desired manner? Advertising is only one of the host of marketing and nonmarketing factors that influence sales, and it is much more important in some marketing mixes than in others. Its impelling action must therefore be coordinated with other marketing and communication elements. There must be some reason to believe that advertising will contribute, either directly or indirectly, to consumer action; otherwise, the money spent for advertising should be allocated to another element of the promotion mix.

Consumer motivation is a complex and sometimes perverse process. Consumers sometimes behave on impulse; at other times, they behave on reason. Sometimes they know why they behaved in a certain way; at other times, they cannot articulate a reason. However, in most situations, the impulsion to act comes from one basic force: a conviction that an advertised product or brand will satisfy one or more of their basic needs or wants.

In product trial situations, content and format must be designed to get people to take some initial action; for example, to get them to pick up a brand of beer because it has that "original draft taste." In commitment situations, on the other hand, message strategy and tactics must work to reinforce or legitimize how consumers already see products and themselves.

Judging Message Ideas and Executions

Not all individuals are blessed with the ability to look at message ideas and executions and know that they are winners. Some have the ability by instinct. Others have to develop it. Fortunately, for those without instinctive ability, rules can be applied in judging advertising creativity. Message ideas can be judged on seven criteria:

1. *Strategy fit* Is the idea consistent with the already established marketing and advertising strategies? Can the idea be established with the allocated number of media dollars? Will it cause consumers to act in the desired manner? Does it fit the company's image?
2. *Target segment fit* Is the idea aimed at the appropriate segment? Is it consistent with the problems and language of the target audience? Does it speak to the buyer that the advertiser wants to reach?
3. *Total promotion mix fit* Is the idea coordinated with the message of other promotion elements? Is the idea conveying "exclusivity" while sales promotion is communicating "cheap"?
4. *Leverage* Will the idea stand out under competitive media conditions? Does it have the power to grab the attention of the target segment?
5. *Specificity* Is the idea to the point? Or is it too generic?
6. *Resistance to counterattack* Is the idea vulnerable to competitive claims?
7. *Durability* Does the idea have legs? How long will it last before it wears out?[19]

Ad executions can be evaluated on four dimensions:

1. *Strategy adherence* Make sure the ads adhere to the stated message idea.
2. *Single-mindedness* Make sure the ads convey the main benefit, attribute, function, or character of the product in a succinct and simplistic manner.
3. *Message dominance* Make sure the ad tactics do not overpower the product message.
4. *Image consistency* Make sure the ads do not change the product's image, unless image change is the strategic objective.[20]

Creativity: Do You Have It?

Can a person's creativity be measured? Morris Stein, of New York University, one of the world's leading authorities on creativity, thinks that advertising professionals can use the following items to identify the creative thinker.

- More- and less-creative people do not differ significantly from each other in tests of verbal intelligence.
- More-creative people are not as anxious as the less-creative.

- More-creative people are more autonomous, more dynamic, and more integrative than their less-creative colleagues.
- More-creative people see their attitudes as being more different from others.
- Less-creative people are more authoritarian than the more-creative.
- More-creative people place a higher value on practical matters and utility, more emphasis on harmony and form, and less on mystical values.
- More-creative people are more oriented to achievement and acceptance of their inner impulses; less-creative people are more oriented to avoiding situations in which they might be blamed for their activities.
- More-creative people are more apt to show their psychological well-being than less-creative people.
- Less-creative people tend to take risks, where risks may be less warranted, more than is true of the more-creative.
- When solving problems, the more-creative tend to work slowly and cautiously while analyzing data. However, once a more-creative person obtains needed data and approaches the point of synthesis, he works quickly. Less-creatives spend less time analyzing problems, but more time attempting to synthesize material.

Source: Emanuel H. Demby, "Creativity: Do You Have It?" *Marketing News* (November 8, 1985): 44, 47. Adapted with permission from *Marketing News,* published by the American Marketing Association.

Strict adherence to these rules is not a guarantee of creative success. The perfect message idea or the unique ad execution comes with ability and experience. A checklist for identifying the creative thinker is provided in the Ad Insight entitled "Creativity: Do You Have It?"

Creativity and Message Strategy

No other aspect of advertising is quite so surrounded by myths as the subject of creativity. Some contend that highly creative advertisements result from pure inspiration. Others contend that creativity requires a certain standardized way of thinking. And still others contend that the secret ingredient is hard work, an open

Kenneth Roman on How to Manage Ideas

The man in the Hathaway shirt

AMERICAN MEN are beginning to realize that it is ridiculous to buy good suits and then spoil the effect by wearing an ordinary, mass-produced shirt. Hence the growing popularity of HATHAWAY shirts, which are in a class by themselves.

HATHAWAY shirts wear infinitely longer—a matter of years. They make you look younger and more distinguished, because of the subtle way HATHAWAY cut collars. The whole shirt is tailored more generously, and is therefore more comfortable. The tails are longer, and stay in your trousers. The buttons are mother-of-pearl. Even the stitching has an ante-bellum elegance about it.

Above all, HATHAWAY make their shirts of remarkable fabrics, collected from the four corners of the earth—Viyella and Aertex from England, woolen taffeta from Scotland, Sea Island cotton from the West Indies, hand-woven madras from India, broadcloth from Manchester, linen batiste from Paris, hand-blocked silks from England, exclusive cottons from the best weavers in America. You will get a

great deal of quiet satisfaction out of wearing shirts which are in such impeccable taste.

HATHAWAY shirts are made by a small company of dedicated craftsmen in the little town of Waterville, Maine. They have been at it, man and boy, for one hundred and fifteen years.

At better stores everywhere, or write C. F. HATHAWAY, Waterville, Maine, for the name of your nearest store. In New York, telephone MU 9-4157. Prices from $5.95 to $25.00.

"Managing creativity starts with the principle of tolerance of error," according to Kenneth Roman, Chairman of Ogilvy & Mather Worldwide. In his view, "risk is the heart of creativity," and outstanding advertising is the product of *the right to be wrong.* "Outstanding creative work is original in concept and execution. Original means untried, and therefore entails risk."

At Ogilvy & Mather, Roman's philosophy of creative risk is put into action by practicing nine management principles:

1. **Protect new ideas**   Ideas, like babies, are born small, immature, and shapeless. The entrepreneurial company protects ideas until they mature, for almost no idea has zero value or is born fully formed.
2. **Be prepared to be shocked**   A measure of originality is the "surprise effect." Ideas represent change and often challenge an organization's status quo. The more original the idea, the more obvious it seems after the fact.
3. **Look for magicians as well as plumbers** Organizations need those who create and those who keep the machinery running. Judge people on the results they produce and their accomplishments.
4. **Create an environment for ideas**   Try to *listen* and to separate the evaluation of ideas from their generation.
5. **Don't confuse research with innovation**   Too often research is misused. Research can help think through ideas, but it seldom creates them.
6. **Stay tuned**   Stay tuned to the world as it is—not as you would like it to be. Ideas happen quite often by chance and are seized by the prepared mind.
7. **Turn data into meaning and meaning into strategies**   We are swamped by statistics. Look beyond the numbers to find what they mean to the consumer and his or her everyday experiences.
8. **Try to reinvent the wheel**   Find a way to rethink good ideas. The wheel that works best in the advertising business is the one you think you invented yourself.
9. **Smile a little**   Creative types have well-developed senses of humor. Laugh along with them.

Source: Kenneth Roman, "How to Manage Ideas," *Viewpoint* (the Ogilvy & Mather journal of opinion and commentary), January/February 1988, 3–5. Reprinted with permission.

Ogilvy & Mather's management philosophy has produced ideas—like the Man in the Hathaway Shirt—that could easily have been killed.

mind, and ungovernable curiosity. Kenneth Roman, whose somewhat different approach to creativity is presented in the Ad Insight "Kenneth Roman on How to Manage Ideas" believes that outstanding advertising is the product of the right to be wrong.

All of these views, as well as others, certainly contain some truth. But what does the research tell us? Five basic propositions can be gleaned from the research on creativity.

An organized approach helps but does not ensure creative success. For example, many have praised the idea-generating approach of James Webb Young, a pioneer in creative thinking. Leo Burnett thought it the finest spur to creativity, and David Ogilvy identified Young as one of the five giants in the history of advertising copywriting. The organized approach is still regularly used and has influenced thousands of working ad people.[21]

The Young model has five distinct states:

1. *Immersion* The collection and analysis of information pertinent to the communication problem
2. *Digestion* The "turning over in the mind" of bits of information
3. *Incubation* The placing of the problem on "conscious hold" to let the subconscious work
4. *Illumination* The point when the light goes on, with creative ideas surfacing as the result of the first three stages
5. *Verification* "The cold grey dawn of the morning after," when doubt creeps in

FIGURE 11.12

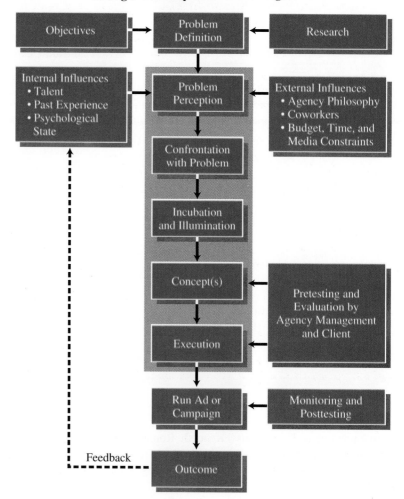

Young's Technique for Producing Ideas

As shown in Figure 11.12, Young's approach is an integral part of the way creativity is conceptualized by advertising scholars and is grounded in the notion that research is an important antecedent to creativity.

The brainstorming technique was developed by another famous advertising agency executive, Alex Osborne. The key to his approach is the generation of ideas by a group and deferred judgment of the generated ideas—the separation of idea generation and idea evaluation. Some studies have validated the brainstorming approach; others have raised doubts.

Some types of individuals are more likely to be creative than others. Successful creative types are significantly more open to experience, more flexible, more unconventional, more playful, more aggressive, more independent, more inner-directed, and rank higher on self-image, sense of humor, risk taking, and curiosity than less creative individuals. No direct relationship, however, has been found between intelligence and ideation, or creativity.

Creative people produce better ideas when they are in a structured group than when they participate voluntarily in unstructured groups. Groups of up to 12 members help to stimulate creativity. Individuals in group situations seem to be more fluent, more flexible, and more original than when they are in individual situations. To a certain extent, this explains why most large agencies use creative planning or creative review boards to judge both components of message strategy: "what is said" and "how it is said."

Training tends to increase the production and quality of ideas. In spite of the widely held belief that creativity cannot be taught, some evidence suggests that training definitely helps. Studies indicate that people in training programs signficantly differ from comparable individuals in their ability to produce and evaluate ideas.

The desire to create is more important than the environment. Some work best under pressure; some create their own pressure. But all good creative people have an inner compulsion to create. As William Marsteller put it in his observations about the great creative people in advertising:

> They did not need a certain kind of office, certain time of day, phase of moon, soft music, sharp pencils, three martinis or light covering of dandruff in order to be inventive. Their fame is rooted in their ability to be fresh and interesting and relevant and original over a long period of time for a wide variety of purposes.[22]

Identifying Symbols

Trademarks, brand names, trade names, and slogans are symbols that, over time, come to stand for a product, organization, or concept. Once created and accepted, they often become the one consistent and unifying feature of all forms of marketing communication, including advertising. Because of their enduring nature, here we will examine the communicative functions of the four identifying symbols and the principles involved in integrating them into message strategy.

As defined by the **Lanham Trade-Mark Act** (1946), which regulates registration of identifying marks, a trademark is "any word, name, symbol, device or combination thereof adopted and used by a manufacturer or merchant to identify the origin of a product and distinguish it from products manufactured or sold by others." The mark need not be physically affixed to the product. The Lanham act also covers service marks (used to distinguish services rather than products), certification marks (used by persons other than the owner to certify geographical origin, grade, or quality), and collective marks (used to indicate membership in some organization) as well as product marks.

Trademarks, Brand Names, and Trade Names

A trademark is a broader term than brand name, store name, or trade name because it is protected by law and subsumes these other related terms under its legal umbrella. Its basic intent is to protect owners from the unlawful use of their property by others and to protect the public from being deceived.

A registered trademark is the name by which the manufacturer has branded a product to distinguish it from competitors' products. In marketing terms, it is called a brand name. The brand name is often paired with a graphic or pictorial design, which is called a **logotype,** or logo.

The term *trademark* should not be confused with the term *trade name*. A trade name is the name under which a company does business. For example, Nestlé is the trade name of an international company that markets tea under the brand name of "Nestea." Winn-Dixie is the trade name (store name) of a retailer that markets food products under its store brand, Thrifty Maid.

Trademarks, brand names, and trade names may come from many sources. Generally speaking, they are likely to come from one or some combination of the following, although, as will be pointed out later, some of the sources should be avoided.

Identifying symbols perform four important communication functions:

1. Buyers of most mass-produced merchandise have little or no direct contact with manufacturers or sellers of products and look for some sign indicating reliability and quality. Trademarks, brand names, and trade names signify these two features.
2. Many products have qualities that are hidden by packaging or are too complex to judge by appearance. Trademarks, brand names, and trade names identify products that may be trusted.
3. Many products are sold by self-service retailers. Trademarks, brand names, and trade names often presell products before purchasers go into the store.
4. Mass communication makes it possible for manufacturers and sellers to capitalize on identifying marks. Trademarks, brand names, and trade names are used inexpensively in advertising and other forms of promotion to build and maintain name recognition and to unify marketing communication messages.

Licensed Names

A special kind of identifying symbol is the licensed name. In recent years, there has been an increase in the use of "rented" names in advertising and other forms of promotion—NFL football teams, Disney characters, and movie characters (Batman, Roger Rabbit), to name a few. Advertisers who use licensed names capitalize, of course, on the wide acceptance and popularity of that name, but they must pay a fee for using the name and must conform to certain licensing standards.

Source	Examples
Dictionary Word	United Airlines, Dial soap, Crest toothpaste, Sure antiperspirant.
Coined Word	Exxon gasoline, Amtrak rail service, Gleem toothpaste, Ultima II cosmetics, Xerox information services.
Personal Name	Ford automobiles, Calvin Klein clothing, Campbell's soup, Heinz foods.
Geographical Name	USAir, Pittsburgh paint, Atlanta dairies, California Cooler.
Foreign Word	Ciara perfume, Monte Carlo automobile, Popov vodka.
Initial and Numbers	IBM computers, 3M tape, A-1 steak sauce.

Another visual identifying symbol often associated with advertising is the trade character. The trade character can be registered as a trademark and is often an animal, cartoon character, distinctive personality, or inanimate object. Once adopted, a trade character can build product, company, or brand recognition, sometimes even after the particular trade character has been abandoned. (Remember the Campbell's twins or Speedy Alka-Seltzer?) Examples of popular and enduring trade characters are the Prudential Rock, Kellogg's Tony the Tiger, McDonald's Ronald McDonald, Budweiser's Clydesdales, and Juan Valdez (see Figure 11.13).

Slogans are repeated creations of advertising people that are utilized to establish or perpetuate some basic idea or theme over a long period of time. Like trademarks, they serve to identify advertisements with products, manufacturers, or sellers. To be effective, slogans must be consistent with the purpose of campaigns and must be changed or modified when campaigns drastically change their message strategies. Some widely used slogans are listed in Figure 11.14.

In structure, slogans are similar to headlines, which will be dealt with in Chapter 13. Many slogans, in fact, evolve from headlines that prove successful; but the slogan's purposes are generally different from those of the headline. The two most common purposes of slogans are: (1) to provide continuity for a campaign, perhaps for a year, perhaps for many years, and (2) to crystallize in a few memorable words the message idea [theme] that the advertiser wants to associate with the product.

The two main types of slogans are those that emphasize a product (institutional) reward and those that emphasize action to be taken.

Trade Characters

FIGURE 11.13

Two Ads Featuring Well-Known Trade Characters: Tony the Tiger and Juan Valdez

Slogans

FIGURE 11.14

Some Widely Used Slogans

Suggestion: Cover the right-hand column and see how many slogans you can name without peeking.

Brand or Company	Slogan
Hallmark	When you care enough to send the very best.
Delta Air Lines	We love to fly and it shows.
Maxwell House Coffee	Good to the last drop.
American Express card	Don't leave home without it.
Toyota	I love what you do for me.
Advil	Advanced medicine for pain.
American Airlines	Something special in the air.
Volvo	A car you can believe in.
DuPont	Better things for better living.
Saturn	A different kind of company. A different kind of car.
BMW	The ultimate driving machine.
Allstate Insurance	You're in good hands.
Embassy Suites	Twice the hotel.
Northwestern Mutual	The quiet company.
Sure deodorant	Anything less would be uncivilized.
ESPN	The total sports network.
Diet Coke	Just for the taste of it.
MasterCard	Master the moment.
RCA	Changing Entertainment Again.
Miller Lite	It's it and that's that.

Reward Emphasis

"You're in good hands" (Allstate)
"Just for the taste" (Diet Coke)

Action Emphasis

"Don't leave home without it" (American Express card)
"The right choice" (AT&T)

Advertising research indicates that slogans are more effective when aimed at product users and adolescents and work best with products of the impulse type—like beer, soap, and potato chips—that are low in price and are purchased without much thoughtful deliberation.

From the various studies of slogans, certain general rules for slogan writing seem to emerge:

1. Make the slogan easy to remember and unlikely to confuse.
2. Make it help differentiate the product from the competition.
3. Make it provoke curiosity, if possible.
4. Make it emphasize a reward or an action.
5. Use rhyme, rhythm, or alliteration.

Obtaining and Retaining Protection for Identifying Symbols

The big problem with using any identifying mark is how to avoid conflict with earlier users. No complete directory exists of brand names, slogans, trademarks, and other identifying symbols, but trademark lawyers have access to a number of sources of information, including Patent Office records and trade directory listings. Reports and opinions can be obtained indicating whether a proposed trademark will be considered confusingly similar to one already in use.

Any identification symbol should be registered. If the mark meets the legal requirements for registration, it will probably also "stand up" in court if necessary. If a trademark is registered, it is considered that everyone has access to information regarding the trademark, whether or not the records are actually checked. Note the registration marks in the ad in Figure 11.15.

An ever-present danger is that a brand name may become so successful that it comes to represent a whole class of products and appears in the dictionary as a generic name. Aspirin, zipper, linoleum, and escalator are examples of brand names that became generic. The American Thermos Company said in its catalog in 1910 that "thermos is a household word." More than 50 years later, the company found that it had indeed made the brand a household name, when the courts offered no protection from competitors. By contrast, General Motors has successfully defended its right to exclusive use of "Frigidaire" and Minnesota Mining and Manufacturing (3M) its rights to "Scotch Tape."

To avoid the loss of trademarks and related identifying symbols, trademark expert Sidney Diamond advises that a trademark always must be identified on packaging, in advertising, and wherever else it may appear and that infringers be sued. He writes that a trademark can be protected in five ways:

1. Use the generic name of a product in association with the trademark (for example, Q-tips cotton swabs).
2. Provide notice that the brand name, character, or slogan is a trademark by using an ® symbol or a line specifying ownership.
3. Use a special typographical design—a particular typeface, italics, or color combination.

FIGURE 11.15

Advertisements with Several Registered Trademarks

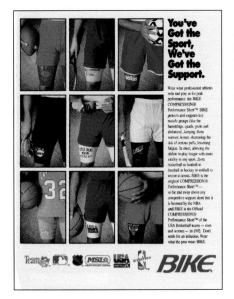

4. Present the trademark in the correct grammatical form; a trademark should not be used as a noun, in the plural, as a verb, or in the possessive.
5. Monitor competitive marketing activities for possible infringements.[23]

Guidelines for Using Identifying Symbols

Although trademarks, brand names, trade names, slogans, and other identifying symbols differ in format, certain principles apply in the creation and utilization of all of them. Some of these stem from legal requirements and some from the principles of effective communication.

1. Avoid using confusing visual and verbal elements.
2. Avoid names that describe the product.
3. Avoid family names.
4. Avoid geographical names.
5. Make symbols easy to identify.
6. Avoid unpleasant connotations.
7. Make symbols applicable to all media.
8. Make symbols international.

Summary

Advertising message planning consists of two related decisions: "what to say" in advertising and "how to say it." The first decision is called message strategy and involves the formulation of a main message idea that will communicate the benefits or the problem-solving capabilities of a product or service. The second decision is called message tactics and involves how the visual and verbal elements—the tactical tools of advertising—are utilized to most effectively communicate the message idea.

A number of schemes exist for classifying message strategy. The six best-known strategic approaches are Burnett's inherent drama, Reeves's unique selling proposition, Ogilvy's brand image, Bernbach's executional emphasis, Trout and Reis's positioning, and FCB's message matrix.

The message idea is the product of the accumulation and analysis of facts—about products, markets, consumers, and competitors. In these facts, the advertising planner hopes to find the "Big Idea," or differential-copy advantage, that will become the basis for the campaign's copy platform. The copy platform is a managerial device that serves to guide and evaluate creative efforts. It consists of five basic components: (1) statement of creative objectives, (2) definition of target audience, (3) key benefit to be communicated, (4) tone of message delivery, and (5) statement of the main message idea.

Message strategy is determined to a great extent by the already formulated marketing and advertising strategies, especially by established communication objectives. Every ad is supposed to influence how the consumer behaves, and it is expected to accomplish certain steps outlined in a specific and hierarchical fashion—awareness, comprehension, conviction, and action. Creative objectives, because they are communication objectives, tend to be short-range in nature.

The force that drives message strategy is creativity. Increased research on creativity in recent years has provided more understanding about how creativity works and how it may be encouraged. However, creativity still remains the most unscientific aspect of advertising, even though its creations are the most important products of advertising people.

Trademarks, brand names, trade names, slogans, and trade characters are identification symbols that advertisers incorporate in their advertisements and other forms of promotion. These identifying symbols are important communication assets that can be legally protected as specified by the Lanham act of 1946 and various state trademark laws.

Questions for Discussion

1. Why is it useful to define objectives for advertisements? What is the role of the copy platform?
2. Clip ten advertisements from your favorite publications and identify the main message strategy in each. Based on your knowledge of the classic approaches to message strategy, how would you classify the ten ads? What are the tactical elements of each ad?
3. What is the role of creativity in advertising message planning?
4. Describe in your own words the image of a brand that you see regularly.
5. Identify five greats of advertising creativity. What are their major contributions to creative thinking in advertising?
6. How would you define a trademark? Distinguish it from a brand name and a trade name.
7. How do slogans relate to message strategy?

Notes

1. Gordon E. White, "Creativity: The *X* Factor in Advertising Theory," *Journal of Advertising* 1 (1972): 28–32.
2. Leo Burnett, "Finally Someone Has to Get Out an Ad," in *The Role of Advertising*. Charles H. Sandage and Vernon Fryburger, eds (Homewood, IL: Irwin, 1960), 352.
3. Don Schultz, *Essentials of Advertising Strategy* (Chicago: Crain Books, 1981), 8.
4. John O'Toole, *The Trouble with Advertising* (New York: Chelsea House, 1981), 121.
5. Norman Berry, in Annual Report, Ogilvy & Mather, 1983.
6. William H. Harkey, Leonard N. Reid, and Karen Whitehill King, "Army Advertising's Perceived Influence," *Journalism Quarterly* 65 (Fall 1988): 719–725, 732.

7 Kenneth Longman, *Advertising* (New York: Harcourt Brace Jovanovich, 1971), 167–177.

8 W. Keith Hafer and Gordon E. White, *Advertising Writing: Putting Creative Strategy to Work,* 3d ed. (St. Paul, MN: West, 1989), 3–4; Kenneth Roman and Jane Maas, *How to Advertise* (New York: St. Martin's Press, 1976), 3.

9 Michael Ray, *Advertising and Communication Management* (Englewood Cliffs, NJ: Prentice-Hall, 1982), 250–272.

10 John R. Rossiter and Larry Percy, *Advertising and Promotion Management* (New York: McGraw-Hill, 1987), 165–191.

11 Ray, *Advertising and Communication Management,* 256–265.

12 Ibid., 270.

13 David A. Aaker, Rajeev Batra, and John G. Myers, *Advertising Management,* 4th ed. (Englewood Cliffs, NJ: Prentice-Hall, 1992), 384–401; Sandra E. Moriarty, *Creative Advertising,* 2d ed. (Englewood Cliffs, NJ: Prentice-Hall, 1991), 11–16; Ray, *Advertising and Communication Management,* 284–290; and Richard Vaughn, "How Advertising Works: A Planning Model," *Journal of Advertising Research* 20 (October 1980): 27–33.

14 David Ogilvy, *Confessions of an Advertising Man.* (New York: Atheneum)

15 Ray, *Advertising and Communication Management,* 288–289.

16 Vaughn, "How Advertising Works: A Planning Model," 27–33.

17 William Wells, "Creative Sensitivity Called Missing in Ad Education," *Advertising Age,* November 13, 1980, 164.

18 Ray, *Advertising and Communication Management,* 284–290.

19 Ibid., 212–215.

20 John Kiel, "Can You Become a Creative Judge?" *Journal of Advertising* 4 (1975): 29–31.

21 Timothy A. Bengston, "Creativity's Paradoxical Character: A Postscript to James Webb Young's Technique for Producing Ideas," *Journal of Advertising* 11 (1982): 3.

22 William A. Marsteller, *Creative Management* (Chicago: Crain Books, 1981), 37.

23 Sidney A. Diamond, "Protect Your Trademark by Proper Usage," *Journal of Marketing* 26 (July 1963): 17–22.

Suggested Readings

Hafer, W. Keith, and Gordon E. White. *Advertising Writing: Putting Creative Strategy to Work,* 3d ed. St. Paul, MN: West, 1989. Chapter 1.

Marra, James L. *Advertising Creativity: Techniques for Generating Ideas.* Englewood Cliffs, NJ: Prentice-Hall, 1990.

Moriarty, Sandra E. *Creative Advertising: Theory and Practice,* 2d ed. Englewood Cliffs, NJ: Prentice-Hall, 1991.

Ray, Michael. *Advertising and Communication Management.* Englewood Cliffs, NJ: Pentice-Hall, 1982. Chapters 7–9.

Roman, Kenneth, and Jane Maas. *The New How to Advertise.* New York: St. Martin's Press, 1992.

Schultz, Don E., and Stanley I. Tannenbaum. *Essentials of Advertising Strategy,* 2d ed. Chicago: NTC Business Books, 1988.

Zeigler, Sherilyn K., and J. Douglas Johnson. *Creative Strategy and Tactics in Advertising: A Managerial Approach to Copywriting and Production.* Columbus, OH: Grid, 1981. Chapter 5.

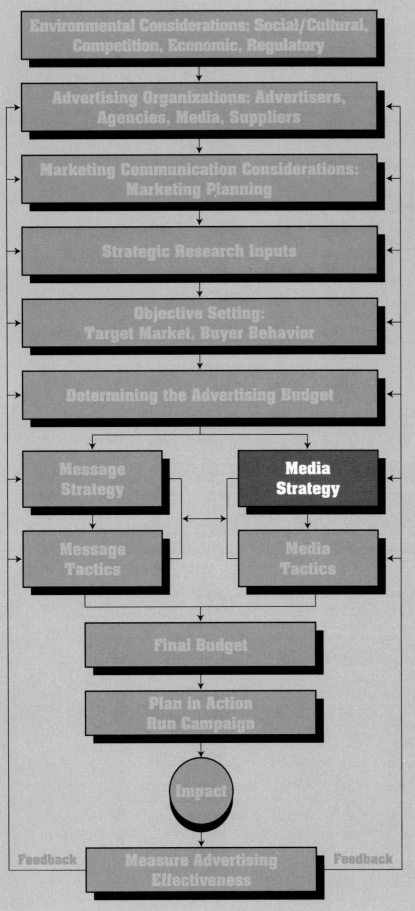

Environmental Considerations: Social/Cultural, Competition, Economic, Regulatory

Advertising Organizations: Advertisers, Agencies, Media, Suppliers

Marketing Communication Considerations: Marketing Planning

Strategic Research Inputs

Objective Setting: Target Market, Buyer Behavior

Determining the Advertising Budget

Message Strategy

Media Strategy

Message Tactics

Media Tactics

Final Budget

Plan in Action Run Campaign

Impact

Feedback

Measure Advertising Effectiveness

Feedback

LEARNING OBJECTIVES

In your study of this chapter, you will have an opportunity to:

- Assess current media trends as a backdrop to media strategy.
- Understand the relationship between media planning and marketing strategy.
- Examine the five dimensions of a media plan.
- Learn about the use of media models in media selection.
- See how an advertising agency develops a media plan for an actual advertiser.

Chapter 12

Media

CHAPTER TOPICS

MEDIA TRENDS
    Changes in Market Structure
    Increase in Complexity of Media
    Increase in Total Advertising Volume
    Changes in Buying and Selling Methods
    Availability of Product and Media Usage Data
    Growth of New Media Technology
MEDIA PLANNING AS PART OF MARKETING
    STRATEGY

DEVELOPING THE MEDIA PLAN
    Setting Media Objectives
    Defining the Target Market
    Selecting Media and Allocating the Budget
    Choosing Media Vehicles and Units
    Scheduling
USE OF MEDIA MODELS

It's 9 P.M. on a Thursday evening; you turn on your television set to one of your favorite programs. After a two-minute preview of this week's program content, there is a break for commercials. The first commercial, for a new brand of cookies, intrigues you because of its unique use of graphics and sound; you watch intently. Given this scenario, one would likely conclude that the commercial was "successful," that is, it accomplished its purpose. Yet, the big question is: What made this advertising communication successful—the product itself, the creativity of the message content, its placement in this particular program, a combination of several things, or something else?

Regardless of how one answers the above question, it is clear that before an advertisement can be effective, it needs an audience. It cannot communicate unless someone has a chance to read it, hear it, or view it. Product, service, or idea messages may, of course, reach audiences face-to-face as well as through the mass media. However, advertising is usually aimed at large audiences and consequently must depend primarily on the mass media. Most advertising planners devote a good deal of their time and effort to the complex business of formulating the best possible media mix.

Fortunately, more factual information is available on media than on most other phases of advertising, Data on **circulation, audiences, rates,** and **cost per thousand** are readily available. Frequently, media salespersons supply special data on brand usage, motivations of audiences to buy, or personal buying habits. But in spite of all the data available, media decisions are still highly subjective because of (1) the almost infinite number of different mixes available for any given campaign and (2) the fact that the ingredients of the mix are not as open to comparison as they seem at first.

Consider, for example, the number of alternative ingredients. Currently in the United States there are approximately 1,600 daily newspapers, 7,500 weekly newspapers, 1,300 commercial television stations, 12,000 AM and FM radio stations,

2,400 consumer or farm magazines, 5,400 business publications, 250,000 billboards, and 75,000 public transit vehicles. Each of these can be used in an almost infinite number of ways.

Then, too, the alternatives are not easily comparable. It can be shown that one magazine has a cost per thousand of $3.99 and another of $16.56 per thousand. Does this mean planners should buy the former? Not necessarily, because the readers of the second magazine may be wealthier, more interested in the publication, or in an area of better distribution for the product. Consequently, a large subjective element is always involved in evaluating the data.

This chapter, therefore, examines the important *strategic* decisions of planning the media strategy. All of the factors in campaign planning that are discussed in this part of the book—research, objectives, targeting, budgeting, message strategy— have a bearing on media planning. In Chapters 16, 17, and 18 we will see how the specific types of media fit into the strategy.

Media Trends

The media planner must keep abreast of trends in advertising to factor them into the media strategy for a particular campaign. Some of these current trends are discussed in this section, whereas future trends are presented at the end of the chapter.

Changes in Market Structure

The American market has undergone basic changes in the past 10 to 20 years. Among the most important changes in demographic characteristics, lifestyle trends, and subcultural influences have been shifts in[1]

- *Proportion of working women* The percentage of women in the labor force as a percentage of all women has changed from about one-half in the late 1970s to almost two-thirds currently. A higher degree—over 70 percent—of women in their twenties and thirties are employed outside the home. This evolution has had important implications for advertising decisions, including media choice.
- *Changing family composition* The "traditional" family of the 1950s—composed of a working father, a nonworking mother, and at least one school-age child— today clearly is the exception rather than the rule. With half of all marriages ending in divorce, there is a high percentage of households with one parent, as well as a noticeable number of single-household units. Further, the proportion of teenagers in the population has steadily been decreasing and will likely continue to do so until almost the end of this century.
- *Changing age composition* With the youth market decreasing in size relative to past periods, there is increased attention being devoted to the "baby boom" genera- tion, as well as older (65+) Americans. For example, today one American in eight falls in the 65+ category; by the year 2030, more than one in five will.[2] This trend is reflected in how certain media develop their editorial and entertain- ment content. For example, one of the largest circulating consumer magazines for this age group is *Modern Maturity*, published by the American Association of Retired People (AARP).
- *Male–Female role changes* In addition to some of the demographic changes noted above, there also are lifestyle trends that have implications for advertising. Among these are the changing relationships between men and women in terms of such things as child care, shopping, and household responsibilities. Examine some magazines that have high male readership—for example, *Sports Illustrated* and *Field & Stream*. You are likely to find products advertised to men that only a few years ago would have been targeted toward women only.

- *Focus on health*   Another lifestyle trend is the focus on health, nutrition, and physical fitness. Witness the boom in so-called "healthy foods." Several years ago ConAgra developed "Healthy Choice" frozen dinners after its chairman had a heart attack and needed to be on a special diet. The Healthy Choice line now extends into a whole range of products, aimed at reduced calories, cholesterol, salt, sugar, and the like. Many other companies followed with products of their own. From a media perspective, visit a local store where magazines are sold and notice the many publications that zero in on this market. Note the advertisement for Eggo Waffles in Figure 12.1 that appeared in *Cooking Light* magazine.

- *Changes in subcultural markets*   There are a number of subcultures within the United States, each with values that often distinguish them from others in the total society. For example, we can identify subcultures according to region of the country, national origin, religion, or ethnic identification. In particular, African Americans and Hispanics often are singled out for special treatment by advertisers. One reason for doing this is the sheer size of these special markets—African Americans represent 12 percent of the total population and Hispanics about 10 percent. Each subculture can be reached by general advertising media, yet each also can be reached through specialized media, such as *Ebony* and *Hispanic Business* magazines. A number of newspapers in the United States are printed in Spanish, and almost 200, mostly weekly, are aimed at African Americans. Although there is disagreement as to the degree and speed of assimilation of these subcultures into society as a whole, there is a continuous need to monitor changes within such groups.

Changes in market structure are important for media planners to understand and project into the future because they have direct impact on the way people use the mass media.

An Advertisement for Eggo Waffles, Focusing on the Health Attributes of the Product, Appeared in *Cooking Light* Magazine

Increase in Complexity of Media

The major changes in almost all types of media have served to make them more complex. For example, when network radio declined in importance because of the growth of television, the medium shifted to a local station structure, with thousands of local radio stations in individual markets. The net result has been a much more specialized medium, with particular stations aiming at certain segments of a market through their programming format. Thus we find local stations concentrating on, for example, progressive rock, country and western, all-talk, or middle-of-the-road formats.

In the magazine field, more and more specialized magazines are available. Magazines are published for virtually every conceivable type of interest group. This special-interest characteristic is a departure from the past, when the major thrust of many magazines was general editorial.

Television has undergone significant changes. The growing use of cable television, in particular, has narrowed the size of audiences for particular programming. In so doing, it has complicated the way the medium is bought for commercials. The growth of home videocassette recorders (VCRs) likewise has added complexity in measuring television audiences and assessing the implications for advertising. Not only does the VCR cause "time shifts" in viewing, but the remote control device permits speeding through commercials ("zipping").

The changing rates charged for the various media add to the complexity. Some changes are a direct result of increases in operating costs, such as for labor and paper. Other changes result from shifts in the demand for a particular medium or the increases or decreases in audience size. As the result of a general recession in the total economy in the early 1990s, many magazines discarded their standard rate cards and negotiated each purchase with an advertiser. The pattern of negotiated rates—common for many years in the broadcast media—has become fairly typical for magazines even after an economic upturn.

The media planner must constantly be aware of cost trends. For example, network television unit costs recently were about 5 percent above the previous year, whereas the comparable figure for cable television was 9 percent. This knowledge affects how a media buyer deals with the various media types in negotiating the purchase of time and space.

Increase in Total Advertising Volume

Total advertising volume in the United States has more than doubled in the past 10 years. Media buyers have had increasingly larger dollar budgets to allocate among the media, although these expenditures must be viewed in the context of the prices charged for media units. Price increases result both for the effect of inflation in the economy and from increasing audience sizes due to population growth. The astute media planner must continually strive for efficiency in media selection.

Advertising volume for 1991 and 1992 among the various media types is shown in Table 12.1 The $131.29 billion spent in 1992 represents a 3.9 percent *increase* over $126.4 billion in 1991. Figure 12.2 shows the allocation of advertising monies according to media type. Thus, newspapers are shown to be the medium with the largest percent of funds (23.4 percent), followed by television (22.4 percent), and direct mail (19.3 percent).

Usually, year-to-year changes for overall expenditures are *positive,* but during recessions decreases are likely. Some of the individual media had greater or lesser percentage increases than the overall 3.9 percent. For example, non-network cable television grew by 13.1 percent, whereas network radio advertisers spent almost 14 percent *less* in 1992 as in 1991.

In recent years, advertising growth overseas has been relatively greater than in the United States. Figure 12.3 shows these differences. Thus, only in 1984 was the growth rate higher in the United States than overseas.

Changes in Buying and Selling Methods

Media are bought and sold in more complex ways than they were a few years ago. For example, commercial time on television can be bought by the minute, or more typically by the half minute, although use of the 15-second commercial has recently increased in popularity. Advertisers are also experimenting with other time units, ranging from 10-second "news break" type commercials to "infomercials" of 5 and 10 minutes in length on cable television channels. Some infomercials are a full 30 minutes to one hour, whereby the commercial and the program are indistinguishable. (This type of program–commercial has caused considerable criticism by consumer advocates as an unfair practice!) Time can be bought for one show one time or for a combination of commercials in any number of shows on any network.

The situation has changed in the magazine field, also. At present, an advertiser is not restricted to using magazines for national coverage. Many publications can be bought in any of a large number of geographical areas. A purchase can even be limited to one or a few metropolitan markets. *Time* magazine, for example, can be purchased on a state or metropolitan basis (for example, Houston). Aside from these regional editions, several publications also offer demographic editions. In this case, media buyers purchase only the part of the magazine's circulation that goes to subscribers with certain demographic characteristics. An advertisement in *Time*, for example, may be purchased and delivered only to college student subscribers.

Newspapers have recently streamlined the way they sell advertising space to national advertisers. They have narrowed the circulation base available for many advertisers by offering zoned editions, so that an advertiser can buy space in a limited geographical part of the paper's circulation area. They have further altered the circulation base by starting or buying suburban newspapers. Another significant change was the adoption of a program of **Standard Advertising Units (SAUs)** for national advertisers. Before the use of SAUs, the sizing of an advertisement differed from one newspaper to another, and this complicated the buying process. Currently, national advertisers can choose from about 50 standard sizes.

TABLE 12.1

Advertising Volume in the United States, 1991 and 1992

	1991		1992		
Medium	Millions of Dollars	Percent of Total	Millions of Dollars	Percent of Total	Percent Change
Newspapers					
National	$ 3,685	2.9%	$ 3,602	2.7%	−2.3%
Local	26,724	21.2	27,135	20.7	1.5
Total	30,409	24.1	30,737	23.4	1.1
Magazines					
Weeklies	2,670	2.1	2,739	2.1	2.6
Women's	1,671	1.3	1,853	1.4	10.9
Monthlies	2,183	1.8	2,408	1.8	10.3
Total	6,524	5.2	7,000	5.3	7.3
Farm Publications	215	0.2	231	0.2	7.4
Television					
Network	8,933	7.1	9,549	7.3	6.9
Cable (national)	1,521	1.2	1,685	1.3	10.8
Syndication	1,853	1.5	2,070	1.6	11.7
Spot (national)	7,110	5.6	7,551	5.8	6.2
Spot (local)	7,565	6.0	8,079	6.1	6.8
Cable (non-network)	420	0.3	475	0.3	13.1
Total	27,402	21.7	29,409	22.4	7.3
Radio					
Network	490	0.4	424	0.3	−13.5
Spot (national)	1,575	1.2	1,505	1.2	−4.4
Spot (local)	6,411	5.1	6,725	5.1	4.9
Total	8,476	6.7	8,654	6.6	2.1
Yellow Pages					
National	1,162	0.9	1,188	0.9	2.2
Local	8,020	6.3	8,132	6.2	1.4
Total	9,182	7.2	9,320	7.1	1.5
Direct Mail	24,460	19.3	25,391	19.3	3.8
Business Papers	2,882	2.3	3,090	2.4	7.2
Outdoor					
National	637	0.5	610	0.5	−4.2
Local	440	0.3	421	0.3	−4.3
Total	1,077	0.8	1,031	0.8	−4.3
Miscellaneous					
National	11,588	9.2	12,124	9.2	4.6
Local	4,185	3.3	4,303	3.3	2.8
Total	15,773	12.5	16,427	12.5	4.1
National Total	72,635	57.5	76,020	57.9	4.7
Local Total	53,765	42.5	55,270	42.1	2.8
Grand Total	$126,400	100.0%	$131,290	100.0%	3.9%

Source: *Advertising Age,* (May 3, 1993): 4.

FIGURE 12.2

Allocation of Advertising Monies by Media Type, 1992

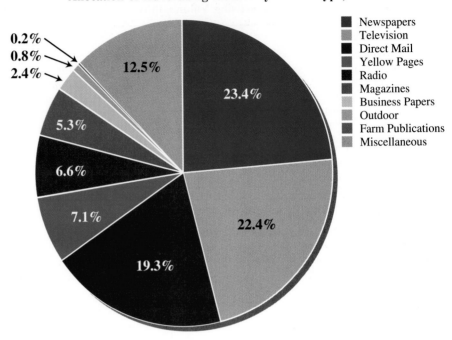

Legend:
- Newspapers
- Television
- Direct Mail
- Yellow Pages
- Radio
- Magazines
- Business Papers
- Outdoor
- Farm Publications
- Miscellaneous

0.2%
0.8%
2.4%
12.5%
23.4%
5.3%
6.6%
7.1%
22.4%
19.3%

Source: Compiled from *Advertising Age* (May 3, 1993): 4.

FIGURE 12.3

Comparison of Advertising Growth, United States versus Overseas, 1984–1991

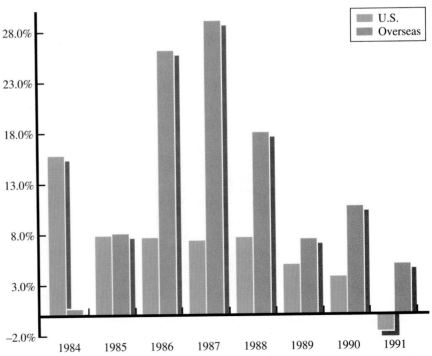

U.S.
Overseas

Source: Compiled, in part, from *ADWEEK* (June 10, 1991): 27; 1991 figures are authors' estimates.

An especially significant trend in the buying and selling of media has been the development of the independent media buying service. The **buying service** is primarily used by small advertising agencies that are unable or unwilling to establish their own full-service media departments and by advertisers who feel that the independent service can secure a better media buy than the full-service agency. A few large agencies have recently experimented with using buying services to handle their media placements during peak periods. This allows the large agency to keep its personnel at a minimum throughout most of the year and use a buying service only when needed. The media buying service works closely with local television and radio stations, its prime area of media placement.

Syndicated market research services, such as Simmons Market Research Bureau (SMRB) and Mediamark Research Inc. (MRI), provide information about the media patterns of consumers of certain products or brands. These services also provide data on the demographic, geographic, and psychographic characteristics of the users of different media types and vehicles. Such information allows the media planner to better relate target markets to media selection. It also helps in deciding on the right mix of media types.

The opportunity to use product and media usage data has been facilitated by a growing use of computers, especially personal computers (PCs). This trend toward computerization has been adopted by both agencies and advertisers' media departments. Although much computer use has been devoted to data collection and handling, more and more attention is being given to *analytical* treatment.

An increasing amount of information is available to help planners analyze the media patterns of competitive brands. If, for example, you were developing a media plan for a new diet soft drink, it would be helpful to see how Diet Coke, Diet Pepsi, and other competitors used media in past periods. Note in Figure 12.4 how the LNA/Arbitron service can provide competitive media data through the use of an office PC.

Availability of Product and Media Usage Data

FIGURE 12.4

LNA/ARBITRON Multi-Media Database Permits Media Planners to Analyze the Spending Patterns of Competing Brands via an Office PC

Growth of New Media
Technology

Perhaps the most significant current trend, as it pertains to the planning of media strategy, is the growth of new media technology. Our discussion is limited to those media types in which we believe there to be clear implications for *advertising* decisions. There are, of course, many new technologies in themselves, but most are not likely to impinge on media strategy.

Cable Television and Other Delivery Systems

Cable television was first established in the late 1940s as a means of improving over-the-air broadcast signals in remote areas with poor reception. A master antenna is erected to pick up television signals from nearby broadcast stations; these signals are disseminated to subscriber homes by coaxial cable. Since 1975, when the Satcom satellite was launched, cable systems also receive signals from very distant locations. It is through satellite transmission that a subscriber in a local area can have access to the programming offered by cable networks, such as ESPN, The Weather Channel, and USA Network. The local cable system receives satellite transmissions through its "dish" antenna and sends such programming on to its subscribers via coaxial cable. Thus, a local cable system gathers signals from several sources and disseminates them to home subscribers by wire.

Currently, around 62 percent of all U.S. homes subscribe to a cable system, paying an average of $15 to $25 per month for the service. The basic monthly fee allows a home to receive a certain number of channels. Other program offerings, such as HBO, Showtime, and The Disney Channel, are available for an additional fee (this is known as pay cable). It is estimated that by the year 2000, when virtually every home will have access to cable, about 75 percent of all households will subscribe to at least the basic service.

Cable television has greatly expanded an advertiser's media options for delivering commercials. In addition to the traditional networks—ABC, CBS, NBC, and their local affiliated stations—the advertiser also can consider the following:

1. *Superstations*   Currently, four television stations (WTBS, Atlanta; WGN, Chicago; WWOR, New York; and WPIX, New York) send their signals via satellite to subscribing cable systems around the country.
2. *Basic cable networks*   Cable networks produce programming and use satellite transmission to subscribing cable operators; included are ESPN, CBN, Cable News Network, and Arts & Entertainment.
3. *Local cable system programs*   Some cable systems produce their own programs and sell time for commercials; for example, the operator may broadcast high-school football games or local news programs. Most systems sell commercial time to local advertisers.

Satellite transmission has especially escalated in the international field, mainly in western Europe (see Chapter 21 for a full discussion of international advertising).

Subscription television (STV) differs from cable in that programming is transmitted as an over-the-air signal. The signal is "scrambled" so that only subscribing homes (with a special decoding device attached to the television set) can receive it. STV basically is used in areas that have not yet been wired for cable. As such, it is not likely to be a viable medium when cable is universal.

The **direct broadcast satellite system (DBS)** involves relaying a signal via satellite directly to the home of a subscriber who has a small receiver dish. Subscribers pay a monthly programming fee to a DBS company, much as they would to a cable system, but also must either buy or rent the receiving equipment. Predictions vary as to the future success of DBS, but there has been added interest recently in the technology due to the lowering of costs of the receiver dish. For example, "SkyPix" is a service that was initiated in 1992. Subscribers purchase a small 3-foot dish antenna for around $850, including installation charges. The SkyPix system can offer up to 250 channels, although only 80 were originally offered. In addition to regular programming, SkyPix offers a subscriber the opportunity to receive live events (for example, sports and concerts) and special-interest programs, such as educational and kids' shows.

A service similar to SkyPix is "TV Answer." TV Answer, however, does not generate programming, but rather delivers to homes a variety of services, including home banking, shopping, interactive advertising, and pay-for-view television. The system is totally interactive, permitting two-way communication between subscribers and the services offered. A transceiver, costing between $200–$300, is required to receive TV Answer, and the subscriber also pays a monthly service fee, similar to cable television.

A relatively new service, related to DBS, is **wireless cable television**. Under a wireless cable system, a satellite transmits programming to a ground-based transmitter, which in turn sends the signal to individual receiving homes via a microwave signal. Presently, about 55 such systems operate in 24 states and serve 400,000 people. Subscribers pay on the average around $75 to $100 to have the antenna system installed in the home and are charged $30 to $35 per month.

A **multi-point distribution system (MDS)** is distributed by microwave to STV and operates in about a 20- to 25-mile radius. It is used most frequently to deliver paid programming to hotel and apartment complexes and in the near future will not likely deliver a noticeable percent of all U.S. homes.

Videocassette Recorders and Videodisc Players

The **videocassette recorder (VCR)** has become an increasingly popular consumer product in the past ten years. It was present in only 2 percent of U.S. homes in 1980; by 1992 nearly 78 percent owned one. The penetration level likely will increase to 90 percent or more by the end of the century. Much of the popularity of VCRs can be attributed to their versatility. Programs can be recorded when they are received by a television set and played back at the consumer's convenience. Also, a vast range of programming (on videocassettes) is available for purchase or rental, from instructional programs to rock videos to blockbuster Hollywood movies.

Videodisc players (VDPs) are not as popular as VCRs, primarily because they do not record but merely play back a prerecorded program disc. However, improved technology will ultimately permit recording through the television set, and this feature should increase demand of the product. Advertisers currently are experimenting with placing commercials within prerecorded cassettes and discs. For example, Diet Pepsi did this in the videocassette of the movie *Top Gun*. Also being considered by advertisers is the use of the videocassette box as an advertising carrier. Presently, a number of videocassette production companies use commercials for other features they produce within a particular tape.

Videotex and Audiotex

Videotex is an interactive electronic system in which data and graphics are transmitted from a computer network over telephone or cable lines and displayed on a subscriber's television or computer terminal screen. The subscriber can receive a wide range of services, including news, weather, and sports information; at-home banking services; travel schedules and reservations; and educational directories such as the yellow pages and real estate listings. Because videotex is an interactive system, subscribers can ask for additional information and actually place orders for products and services, such as bank transfers. The system readily lends itself to use by an advertiser, and several major advertising agencies have established special groups to utilize the possibilities. Presently, one of the most extensive videotex projects is the joint venture between IBM and Sears, called Prodigy. Prodigy was developed in 1988 at a cost of $450 million and is aimed at personal computer users as well as business users. Prodigy operates in over 50 markets, with around a half-million subscribers, and more than 200 advertisers use the system.

Audiotex involves an advertiser leasing telephone lines from a carrier, such as AT&T or Sprint, and delivering advertising messages to people who call an 800 or 900 number. The caller can merely listen to the message or, with a touch-tone phone, can interact with the message, for example, requesting additional information or placing an order. A number of advertisers have used audiotex to deliver information about consumer promotions—such as contests and sweepstakes—but others use the method for disseminating regular advertising messages.[3]

Among the many advertising implications that relate to the growth of the new media, perhaps of greatest significance to the media strategist is the matter of *audience fragmentation*. Although individuals likely will spend more time in front of a television screen (or computer monitor) than they do now, the wide choice of viewing options will result in smaller audience sizes for a program unit. Yet, because so much of the viewing will be focused on content of a specific nature, markets may be segmented in more specialized ways than is currently possible. Thus, for example, a local stockbroker could use stock quotations on audiotex to reach a tightly segmented market.

In addition, increased viewing of the new media very likely will affect traditional media forms as well. For example, the amount of time spent listening to radio and reading magazines and newspapers may decline, and media planners will have to consider carefully these changes. Further, the manner of viewing may change traditional media patterns. Studies have shown that homes having VCRs recorded almost 2 hours per week without having watched any program during the recordings. Of the hours recorded, only 75 percent were played back. Thus, a certain number of recorded commercials were never seen. And this does not take into account those commercials that were lost to **zipping** (fastforwarding during playback). A recent study showed that among the homes that replayed taped programs, two-thirds (67 percent) claim they zip through the commercials; the number doing this represent over *one-fourth* of all homes in the United States.[4]

Media Planning as Part of Marketing Strategy

The development and utilization of the marketing concept by business has meant the furtherance and strengthening of the liaison between advertising and marketing plans. Overall advertising strategy can be developed logically only when marketing considerations are systematically taken into account. By the same token, the various components of advertising must be viewed within a marketing context. This is especially so in the case of the media strategy. As Barban, Cristol, and Kopec advise budding media planners: "*Media problems are marketing problems.* Your ability to make media decisions will continue to grow as you develop an understanding of the marketing and advertising influences on media planning."[5]

What, then, are some of the specific areas of marketing that have an important influence on media decisions?[6] First, the development and execution of the media plan must await *marketing objectives*. It is of little value to determine media strategy until the aims of the marketing program have been clearly delineated. Once marketing objectives are set, the media planner can coordinate the aims of the media effort.

A second important marketing factor is the basic *characteristics of the product* being advertised. The nature of some products makes them more suitable to one medium than to another. Also, the newness of a product may affect media decisions. For example, a totally new product concept usually requires a considerable amount of print advertising to explain how the product works and the ensuing consumer benefits.

The *pricing strategy* for the product can have a noticeable influence on the media plan. The high cost of network television, for example, might not be feasible for a product with a low unit sales price and limited sales potential. Or the price margins in the distribution channels may affect the amount of dealer effort that an advertiser can expect. If a retailer provides a large amount of newspaper advertising in support of a national brand, the national media mix should take this into account. Also, a high-priced product appealing to a prestige market should be advertised in media vehicles that support the prestige claim.

Channels of distribution are also important in media planning. It is logical to limit media buying to areas where the product is available for sale. Typically, it is impossible to totally eliminate waste circulation, but the usual goal is to keep such circulation to a minimum. Also, certain media vehicles can be bought to influence the dealers as well as the ultimate consumers of the product. Thus, a producer might run an advertisement for a particular brand in *Time* magazine, a high-prestige medium, to attract retailers as well as consumers.

Finally, *promotion plans* can also affect media plans. Marketing strategy typically involves decisions about the relative amount of effort devoted to advertising, personal selling, and sales promotion techniques (such as contests and couponing). For example, the importance placed on personal selling by the marketer may influence media decisions. When personal sales effort is relatively minor, the advertiser may want to advertise heavily in trade magazines to keep dealers and prospective dealers informed. Or a decision to use a particular sales promotion device (say, a 50-cent coupon) may mean the use of a specific advertising medium (for example, daily newspapers) to distribute the promotion piece.

Many other marketing factors can affect media decisions. But the five just discussed are significant in most brand situations, and they suffice to demonstrate the importance of systematically tying together media strategy and marketing strategy.

Developing the Media Plan

The actual media plan flows naturally from marketing strategy and can take many different forms and shapes. Media planning, like much of advertising planning in general, is not so highly standardized that every plan contains identical elements. Nevertheless, for our purposes here, we concentrate on five basic dimensions of the media plan: (1) media objectives; (2) target market definition; (3) the media types to be used, and their allocation; (4) media vehicles and units to be used, and their allocation; and (5) media scheduling.

Like any aspect of advertising, a media plan must begin by setting goals. And these goals should be stated as precisely as possible, so that once the plan is put into effect, results can be measured. Since media objectives often are stated in terms of **reach**, **frequency**, **gross rating points**, and **continuity**, let us first define these concepts.

*S*etting Media Objectives

Reach

Reach is the number of different persons or households exposed to a particular media vehicle or media schedule at least once during a specified time period (usually four weeks). Let us take as an example, a sample group of ten television homes (A through J) that may be watching Program X over a four-week period (see Special Exhibit A).

We see that seven of the ten homes watched Program X at least once during the four-week period (Homes C, F, and I did not watch). Thus, we can say that the reach was 7, or 70 percent (7 of 10 = 70 percent). Reach is thus a measure of the extent of a particular media buy. With several different media types and different media vehicles in a schedule, computing the reach figure can be somewhat complicated. But media analysts use a variety of source material, along with various estimating procedures, to compute their reach figures.

SPECIAL EXHIBIT A

Week	Home A	B	C	D	E	F	G	H	I	J	Total Exposure
1	NEWS 3	NEWS 3						NEWS 3			3
2		NEWS 3			NEWS 3	NEWS 3			NEWS 3		4
3	NEWS 3	NEWS 3					NEWS 3	NEWS 3			4
4		NEWS 3			NEWS 3			NEWS 3		NEWS 3	4
Total Exposures	2	4	0	1	2	0	1	4	0	1	15

Frequency

Frequency is "the number of times within the four-week period that a prospect or portion of the population is exposed to the message."[7] In our example, some homes were exposed four times (Homes B and H), some twice (A and E), and so forth. Typically, we are interested in the average frequency of a particular schedule, which is computed from the following formula:

$$\text{Average Frequency} = \frac{\text{Total Exposures}}{\text{Reach}} = \frac{15}{7} = 2.14$$

Of those television homes reached, the average number of exposures was slightly more than 2 (2.14). Frequency is thus a measure of the intensity of a particular media buy.

Gross Rating Points

Reach and frequency each describe a part of the media plan. Often it is useful to put these two concepts together to describe the total weight of a media effort. The concept used to express this combination is the *gross rating point* (*GRP*). In quantitative terms, gross rating points are equal to reach multiplied by average frequency. GRPs therefore describe the total weight of advertising that derives from a particular media buy. In our example, 70 percent of the homes were reached by Program X an average of 2.14 times within the four-week period. The total impact of this media effort can be expressed as:

$$\text{GRPs} = \text{Reach} \times \text{Average Frequency} = 70 \times 2.14 = 149.8 = 150$$

Another program might deliver more GRPs. This tells us that it has more total weight than Program X, but we also must know the specific reach and frequency levels that make up the other program before we can judge which better meets our objectives.

Continuity

Continuity has to do with how the advertising is scheduled over the planning period. In other words, continuity relates to the timing of the media insertions. For example, we might allocate 30 percent of our media budget to the introductory month, then cut back to 20 percent in each of the following two months, followed by no advertising for six months, with 10 percent allocated to each of the last three months of the one-year plan.

Approach to the Setting of Media Objectives

In terms of setting objectives, the media planner uses reach, frequency, GRPs, and continuity as a kind of shorthand to express the goals sought. Of course, which objectives are set depends on a host of background factors, especially the marketing and advertising goals. Let's look at four of the key factors: product life cycle, extent or breadth of the target market, repurchase cycle, and target market turnover. Ad Insight describes what an assistant media planner does in a typical day.

The product life cycle is one useful factor in arriving at media goals. For example, if you were introducing a product, the advertising goal might be to make a large percentage of the target market aware of your brand; the corresponding media goal probably would be to achieve a high level of reach, with moderate to low frequency levels, in the early stage of the advertising campaign. If, on the other hand, your new brand were positioned head-on against a market leader, you may decide to seek a small segment of the market currently not well covered. You probably would want to emphasize frequency against the small market segment. For established products at the maturity stage of the life cycle, planners may feel it necessary to use reminder advertising and maximize the exposures of messages to the target market.

The extent or breadth of the target market is another factor to consider in setting objectives. Markets that are widely dispersed geographically and demographically may require a greater investment of the budget for reach, leaving frequency as a secondary concern. A target that is more narrowly defined, however, may suggest a focus on the frequency dimension.

A product's repurchase cycle also affects reach, frequency, and continuity goals. For products that are purchased often, such as soft drinks, planners may need to advertise rather frequently in order to keep their brand in the minds of consumers. And, if there are seasonal sales patterns (for example, summer sales are higher for soft drinks), the overall continuity of the plan will be affected. On the other hand, some products have a long repurchase cycle, and advertising likely will have to be timed to the manner of purchase. Reach levels can be built up in advance of the purchase decision, at which time higher frequency may be sought.

Related to the repurchase cycle is target market turnover. Regardless of how often a consumer repurchases a product, that product may be useful only for a short period of time in the consumer's life. An example is baby food, which may be used for only a year or two. There could be a need to reach a large segment of new prospects at most times because of the turnover effect.

Defining the target, as discussed in Chapter 9, is an important part of the media plan. The media planner seeks primarily to match the defined markets with the media under consideration:

Defining the Target Market

> The principle underlying efficient use of advertising time and space is matching markets and media—that is, the media planner tries to invest advertising dollars in those media vehicles having audiences that closely parallel the description of the target market. The better the match, the less money wasted on delivering messages to consumers for whom the product was not intended in the first place.[8]

Further, the media specialist must be sure that target markets are defined in a way that permits matching them to media vehicles. In other words, the target typically must be defined in demographic, geographic, psychographic, and/or product usage

A Day in the Life of the Assistant Media Planner

Tuesday

8:42 Arrive at your desk with breakfast in hand—ready to go.

8:52 Start to return yesterday afternoon's phone messages while you're compiling today's list of projects.

9:15 Check in with you planners and then prioritize what needs to be done today.

9:40 Get the computer to run reach/frequencies for the magazine options you designed with the incremental money allotted to the battery account last week.

9:58 Run upstairs to the 10th floor conference room for a screening of the agency's latest commercials. A half hour later, you leave the presentation, your mind churning up ideas on where that advertising might be placed to work harder.

10:30 Head back to the computer room via the receptionist to pick up your messages. Nothing urgent, so on to the computer for a reach/frequency analysis. Susan, your planner on the battery account, stops by to fill you in on her conversation with the Account Executive. The client is coming to the agency Friday and wants the new plan with the incremental funds; therefore, current Page Four Color costs are needed for the top 15 magazines by Thursday. Having learned the hard way how long it takes to get hold of 15 representatives, you decide to call eight today and seven tomorrow morning.

11:00 Finish printing the reach/frequencies and head for your cubicle. Robert, your other Planner, catches up with you in the hallway to remind you that the client meeting is at 3:30 today and the soap budget is due in a few days. You make the time to quickly read your mail.

11:15 Back at your desk, you add to your priority list. The phone rings, and it's the Account Executive on your third account asking for the merchandising flowcharts that you've been working on. The client meeting was moved up a few hours and the AE wants you to present your recommendations ASAP. You agree, hang up the phone, grab the computer disk with the revised flowcharts on it and head for the computer again to print out fresh copies. (It's a good thing you finished the flowcharts last night. You had a feeling it was going to be a busy day!)

11:45 Start calling the first eight magazine reps, and at the same time begin extracting the important reach/frequency numbers to discuss with Susan.

12:15 Some people have gone to lunch, so the agency has quieted down, and the phones have stopped ringing. You leave messages with the last five reps because *they* are out to lunch!

12:30 Before you start on the budget, you grab a friend and go out to get your own quick lunch.

Source: Courtesy of Tony Nacinordi, Senior VP Associate Media Director, and Ogilvy & Mather Advertising, New York.

terms, because this is how most media audience data are presented. Note in Figure 12.5 that several consumer magazines are shown in terms of audiences among several education groups.

When more than one target market is defined, the planner must determine the relative importance of each. For example, for a snack item, our primary target might be parents aged 25 to 49 in households of $25,000 to $49,999 annual income. A secondary target could be children aged 4 to 12 in primary target households. The media planner, in order to select media types and vehicles as efficiently as possible, would want to weight these two targets. The planner might decide, for example, to put 70 percent of the emphasis on parents and 30 percent on children.

1:30 Back at your desk, you think through the correctness of some of your recommendations. You update your priority list of assignments. Just when you begin the budget recap for the soap account, the phone rings . . . and it's a rep returning your call. You quickly get the information you need and then back to the budget.

2:00 Finally, you've tackled the budget and discovered that the client is underbilled in Spot TV. Quickly call the spot buyer and discuss the problem. Resolved, you head towards Robert's office; but there's your phone again . . . hurray! It's the last of the magazine reps returning your call.

2:20 Once again, you take off to visit Robert. With budget in hand, you explain that there is a billing discrepancy due to an underbilling in Spot TV that, according to the spot buyer, will correct itself next month. Good catch.

2:50 You make your way to Susan's office to compare the alternate plan's reach/frequencies. You both agree on a prototypical plan and together you go meet with her boss to present the plan and discuss why it was chosen. The final decision is to put the prototypical plan on a flowchart.

3:20 You dash back to your desk to collect everything you need for the client meeting and call Robert's office to see if he's left yet. Relieved to find him there, you tell him you'll stop by. The two of you make your way to the conference room laughing about how crazy today is.

4:45 Your presentation goes smoothly and revisions are due in a week. Back at your desk, you're relieved to cross a few items off your list, but as usual you end up adding more than you crossed off. As you begin writing the budget cover letter, the phone rings—it's the Account Executive you spoke with this morning, and this time he's calling to thank you for all the work you put into the merchandising effort. The client loved the color flowcharts, approved the merchandising plan, and as a result, the meeting was a success.

5:00 Meet with your Network TV Buyer to preview the fall schedule and screen clips from three pilots.

5:35 Now the agency is starting to wind down, and you've finished the budget letter. Your secretary is busy typing somebody else's work, but you agree on a deadline suitable to your schedules. Back at your desk, you take another look at your priority list and decide what has to be done *tonight* based on deadlines as well as this week's scheduled lunches, presentations and meetings. You read your mail.

6:30 Quickly make a list of what needs to be done tomorrow, grab your coat and off to meet your friends for a private viewing of a new movie at Time Magazine's Executive Screening Room.

6:31 The phone rings . . .

Every media plan requires that specific media types be selected—network television, newspapers, consumer magazines, and so on—and the budget be allocated among those chosen. Deciding which media types to include in a media plan involves a host of factors, both objective and subjective.

Among the objective factors are (1) the match of media type to target market (does one particular medium deliver more of the target than another?); (2) the match of media type to stated objectives; (3) the relative efficiencies of the various media (what is the cost associated with reaching a particular kind of prospect via a particular medium?); and (4) the influence of competition (do you want to avoid media types used by competitors?).

S*electing Media and Allocating the Budget*

Subjective considerations include the following:

1. The perceived characteristics of media—Do consumers consider a particular medium more "dynamic" or "vital"? What is the perceived prestige value of the various media?
2. The message (creative) strategy to be employed—Certain creative approaches may be considered better in one media type than in another.
3. The media environment—What is the editorial or entertainment environment of the media types to be used? For example, if there is an abundance of violence on prime-time network television, is this appropriate for the brand, even if the specific program chosen is not violent?

The Ad Insight entitled "Toward Even Better Media Comparisons" has an interesting discussion of making media comparisons.

If the media plan involves more than one media type, the planner must allocate resources among the included types. In deciding on the relative weights, the planner will consider many of the same factors as for selecting types. The net result of these decisions is a media mix. For example, the media mix for a $30 million campaign to introduce a new cake mix might be:

Medium	Amount	Percent of Total
Daytime network television	$15,000,000	50%
Home service magazines	12,000,000	40
Daily newspapers in 50 major markets (couponing)	1,800,000	6
Contingency reserve	1,200,000	4
Total	$30,000,000	100%

Aside from allocating the budget to various media types, the planner also may need to consider geographic allocations. In fact, many advertising situations require that budgets be allocated both to media types and geographic regions simultaneously.

Let's illustrate this situation with an example. Assume your brand is sold in five regions of the United States and you want to allocate a $30 million budget to network and spot television (keeping in mind that spot television is bought on a market-by-market basis). Your goal is to spend in each region in proportion to the sales potential. Further, you have checked with the networks to determine their audience delivery in your regions. The following information summarizes the situation:

Region	Sales Potential	Network Delivery	Budget Goal (based on sales potential)
1	15%	10%	$ 4,500,000
2	25	20	7,500,000
3	20	35	6,000,000
4	30	20	9,000,000
5	10	15	3,000,000
Total	100%	100%	$30,000,000

This shows that a "problem" occurs because of an overdelivery of network television in Regions 3 and 5, with the greatest relative amount in Region 3.

A "solution" to the problem is as follows:

1. Because the greatest overdelivery of network television is in Region 3, this region will be your base for determining the total network budget.
2. Divide the budget goal for Region 3 ($6,000,000) by the network delivery percent in the region. Thus, $6,000,000 ÷ .35 = $17,142,857. This figure becomes your total network television budget, based on the region with the most overdelivery.
3. The spot television budget, therefore, will be $12,857,143 ($30,000,000 − $17,142,857).
4. The number of network dollars for each region can be computed by multiplying the network delivery percentage by $17,142,857. Thus, for Region 1: .10 × $17,142,857 = $1,714,286; for Region 2: .20 × $17,142,857 = $3,428,571, and so on.
5. Once you know the network allocation to each region, the spot television budget is derived by subtracting the network amount from the budget goal. Thus, for Region 1: $4,500,000 − $1,714,286 = $2,785,714, and so on. Region 3 does not receive spot television dollars because of adequate coverage through network ($6,000,000, which is the budget goal).

Applying steps 1 through 5 results in the following budget allocation:

Region	Sales Potential	Network Delivery	Budget Goal	Budget Allocation Network TV	Budget Allocation Spot TV
1	15%	10%	$ 4,500,000	$ 1,714,286	$ 2,785,714
2	25	20	7,500,000	3,428,571	4,071,429
3	20	35	6,000,000	6,000,000	—
4	30	20	9,000,000	3,428,571	5,571,429
5	10	15	3,000,000	2,571,429	428,571
Total	100%	100%	$30,000,000	$17,142,857	$12,857,143

Choosing Media Vehicles and Units

Once a decision is made on media types, specific media vehicles within each medium must be selected. And, further, the units of each vehicle must be chosen. For example, if daytime network television were chosen to receive $15 million, we would then decide which daytime programs to buy—*As the World Turns, The Bold and the Beautiful, Another World*, and so forth. Are we going to buy 30-second or 15-second units? And, if we buy more than one vehicle, what is the allocation among them?

These vehicle and unit decisions generally are made on the same objective and subjective bases as those used for selecting media types. Our goal is to find as much factual information as possible and make our decisions accordingly. Thus, data such as those given in Figure 12.5 can be used to determine how certain vehicles (in this case, consumer magazines) deliver audiences according to specific variables (education).

Scheduling

Much of what we decide about the timing of media insertions is related to marketing and advertising variables. For one thing, we will probably consider the seasonal sales pattern of the advertised brand. A tanning lotion, for example, may have a large percentage of its sales during warm months—and our media schedule probably will reflect this.

Toward Even Better Media Comparisons
by Ron Kaatz*

We lived in a much simpler communications environment in 1958 when the ARF's Audience Concepts' Committee began to study the issues involved in measuring media effectiveness.

Long before CNN, home video, place-based media, zapping and zipping were part of our vocabulary, *Gunsmoke* was the nation's #1 TV show, seen in 40 percent of our homes each week. Media planning was easy and an advertiser only had to buy six issues of *Life*, *Look*, and the *Saturday Evening Post* to reach 77 million different people.

In 1958, Ted Turner was 20 and Chris Whittle was a young lad of 10.

Three years later, the Committee released its model for evaluating media in a major document—"Toward Better Media Comparisons." It recognized just five basic media types (newspapers, magazines, radio, television, and outdoor) and considered the advertising message *only* as it was relevant to its means of transmission.

The Committee urged the industry to "wholeheartedly support any thoughtful experimental approaches to the problem of relating advertising to its sales response. Constructive work in this direction will constitute the most direct attack on the problem of media comparison and at the same time will provide valuable information about many other factors influencing sales."

Unfortunately, there have been few attempts to develop really better media comparisons in the 30 years since the

ARF published its recommendations. Rather than reward efforts to measure the *right* levels of communications' effectiveness, we require every new media system to deliver those same, precisely *wrong* measures of vehicle exposure as are etched in stone by Nielsen for television and by MRI or Simmons for magazines.

Today's drive for accountability and the focus on Integrated Marketing Communications makes it essential that we evaluate media opportunities in terms of the consumer response they generate rather than the number of warm bodies they reach. Although we know how many people tuned in to *Super Bowl XXVII* and how many said they read an issue of *Sports Illustrated* that reported on its outcome, these numbers say precisely nothing about what this did for Budweiser, Pepsi, McDonalds, or Nike.

Integrated Marketing Communciations demands that every communications' discipline work together to engage the consumer in a genuinely meaningful sales conversation. Advertising, sales promotion, events, direct marketing, public relations, signs and displays, packaging, etc., all must be based on a single focused strategy to achieve maximum productivity for a product or service.

Integrated Marketing Communications demands an Integrated Media Planning System. This recognizes that personal contact and word of mouth are still the most powerful media, and considers the impact of one message delivered to one consumer at one point in time. Integrated Media Planning looks beyond the traditional to nontradi-

Source: Courtesy of Professor Ron Kaatz.

The degree to which a product is repurchased is another scheduling influence. Products with a short repurchase cycle may require somewhat more constant levels of advertising than products that are purchased infrequently. Related to this factor is the product life cycle. Most products go through a prescribed cycle, from introduction to sales decline, and media scheduling is often adjusted to particular stages of the cycle.

Often media planners are concerned with what competitors are doing within various media. For example, if a competitor concentrates advertising during one time period, planners may want to consider this fact in their own scheduling.

tional media, and seeks added values via all media. Through a well-focused strategy, it delivers messages in a variety of media channels that all build toward the sale of product, a service, or an idea. An Integrated Media Planning System operates as a chain, where there can be no weak link. For example, it might consist of:

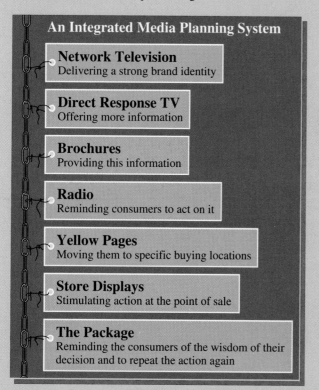

An Integrated Media Planning System

Network Television
Delivering a strong brand identity

Direct Response TV
Offering more information

Brochures
Providing this information

Radio
Reminding consumers to act on it

Yellow Pages
Moving them to specific buying locations

Store Displays
Stimulating action at the point of sale

The Package
Reminding the consumers of the wisdom of their decision and to repeat the action again

Such a system permits the logical introduction and flow of messages delivered via home video—on the computer via Prodigy—in the doctor's office—at the airport—in the classroom on Channel One and at every other decision-making point. It is based on the ability of one communication force to enhance and reinforce another.

For an Integrated Media Planning System to work, however, marketing communicators cannot base their decisions on the old, tired *input* measures of vehicle exposure. Decisions must be based on *output* in the form of information communicated and actions taken. Media that can provide such information today must be encouraged and rewarded for doing so. Every new media entrepreneur who offers these new measures of consumer response must not be penalized by being told, "Sorry. We can't use it until TV and magazines provide us with the same stuff!" This is precisely the wrong thing to do and will continue to get us precisely nowhere as we seek "Even Better Media Comparisons" in the 1990s and beyond.

*Ron Kaatz is Associate Professor in the Integrated Advertising and Marketing Communications Division of Northwestern University's Medill School of Journalism. He joined Medill following 30 years in advertising at Leo Burnett Co., the CBS Television Network, and J. Walter Thompson Co. (20 years). His teaching is joined today by writing, consulting, and speaking in areas of advertising and marketing communications.

Typically, timing schedules are either continuous, flighting, or pulsed, as shown in Figure 12.6. The continuous schedule involves spending about the same percentage of the total budget each month. A flighting approach indicates various expenditures in some months, with no media effort at other times. A pulsing approach uses advertising throughout the campaign, but with various amounts by time period.

Once the scheduling strategy is determined, the media analyst usually develops a visual flowchart so that all involved can see the plan in action. Although the media schedule does not show every detail of the entire plan, it is a bird's-eye view of some of the important elements. Figure 12.7 shows a sample media flowchart.

FIGURE 12.5

A Breakdown of Magazine Readership by Education Level

0014
M-1

EDUCATION OF RESPONDENT (ADULTS)

0014
M-1

	TOTAL U.S. '000	GRADUATED COLLEGE A '000	B % DOWN	C % ACROSS	D INDX	ATTENDED COLLEGE (1-3 YRS.) A '000	B % DOWN	C % ACROSS	D INDX	GRADUATED HIGH SCHOOL A '000	B % DOWN	C % ACROSS	D INDX	ATTENDED HIGH SCHOOL (1-3 YRS.) A '000	B % DOWN	C % ACROSS	D INDX
TOTAL	184117	35927	100.0	19.5	100	36617	100.0	19.9	100	71864	100.0	39.0	100	21818	100.0	11.9	100
AMERICAN BABY	2622	591	1.6	22.5	116	569	1.6	21.7	109	1143	1.6	43.6	112	*270	1.2	10.3	87
AMERICAN HEALTH	2770	744	2.1	26.9	138	669	1.8	24.2	121	1129	1.6	40.8	104	*154	0.7	5.6	47
AMERICAN WAY (AMERICAN AIR)	509	253	0.7	49.7	255	*196	0.5	38.5	194	**51	0.1	10.0	26	**5	0.0	1.0	8
ARCHITECTURAL DIGEST	2804	1256	3.5	44.8	230	957	2.6	34.1	172	475	0.7	16.9	43	**97	0.4	3.5	29
ARCHITECTURAL DIGEST/ BON APPETIT (GROSS)	6605	2581	7.2	39.1	200	2263	6.2	34.3	172	1347	1.9	20.4	52	332	1.5	5.0	42
AUDUBON	1416	562	1.6	39.7	203	485	1.3	34.3	172	315	0.4	22.2	57	**38	0.2	2.7	23
BABY TALK	1916	406	1.1	21.2	109	411	1.1	21.5	108	775	1.1	40.4	104	*281	1.3	14.7	124
BARRON'S	1083	639	1.8	59.0	302	275	0.8	25.4	128	*136	0.2	12.6	32	**33	0.2	3.0	26
BASEBALL WEEKLY	1845	353	1.0	19.1	98	438	1.2	23.7	119	765	1.1	41.5	106	*255	1.2	13.8	117
BETTER HOMES AND GARDENS	23552	5099	14.2	21.6	111	5756	15.7	24.4	123	9570	13.3	40.6	104	2193	10.1	9.3	79
BON APPETIT	3802	1325	3.7	34.9	179	1306	3.6	34.4	173	872	1.2	22.9	59	235	1.1	6.2	52
BRIDAL GUIDE	1461	*219	0.6	15.0	77	438	1.2	30.0	151	630	0.9	43.1	110	**109	0.5	7.5	63
BRIDE'S & YOUR NEW HOME	2415	270	0.8	11.2	57	832	2.3	34.5	173	998	1.4	41.3	106	*252	1.2	10.4	88
BUSINESS WEEK	6530	3282	9.1	50.3	258	1730	4.7	26.5	133	1279	1.8	19.6	50	188	0.9	2.9	24
THE CABLE GUIDE	7812	1360	3.8	17.4	89	2061	5.6	26.4	133	3330	4.6	42.6	109	860	3.9	11.0	93
THE CABLE GUIDE/TV TIME (TOTAL TV)(GROSS)	8630	1484	4.1	17.2	88	2320	6.3	26.9	135	3628	5.0	42.0	108	943	4.3	10.9	92
CAR AND DRIVER	5265	1145	3.2	21.7	111	1418	3.9	26.9	135	1974	2.7	37.5	96	664	3.0	12.6	106
CAR CRAFT	2169	*143	0.4	6.6	34	428	1.2	19.7	99	1053	1.5	48.5	124	429	2.0	19.8	167
COLONIAL HOMES	1801	465	1.3	25.8	132	499	1.4	27.7	139	695	1.0	38.6	99	**57	0.3	3.2	27
CONDE NAST SELECT (GROSS)	37826	10351	28.8	27.4	140	11653	31.8	30.8	155	12751	17.7	33.7	86	2617	12.0	6.9	58
CONDE NAST TRAVELER	1377	653	1.8	47.4	243	477	1.3	34.6	174	194	0.3	14.1	36	**31	0.1	2.3	19
CONSUMERS DIGEST	3742	1020	2.8	27.3	140	1004	2.7	26.8	135	1493	2.1	39.9	102	*175	0.8	4.7	39
COSMOPOLITAN	11702	2213	6.2	18.9	97	3328	9.1	28.4	143	4843	6.7	41.4	106	1144	5.2	9.8	82
COUNTRY HOME	3550	737	2.1	20.8	106	974	2.7	27.4	138	1499	2.1	42.2	108	*246	1.1	6.9	58
COUNTRY LIVING	8033	1966	5.5	24.5	125	2136	5.8	26.6	134	3260	4.5	40.6	104	466	2.1	5.8	49
EBONY	9749	970	2.7	9.9	51	1939	5.3	19.9	100	4523	6.3	46.4	119	1756	8.0	18.0	152
ELLE	2437	794	2.2	32.6	167	830	2.3	34.1	171	726	1.0	29.8	76	**70	0.3	2.9	24
ENTERTAINMENT WEEKLY	3244	701	2.0	21.6	111	876	2.4	27.0	136	1220	1.7	37.6	96	*364	1.7	11.2	95
ESQUIRE	2235	740	2.1	33.1	170	537	1.5	24.0	121	821	1.1	36.7	94	**101	0.5	4.5	38
ESSENCE	5020	573	1.6	11.4	58	1020	2.8	20.3	102	2491	3.5	49.6	127	698	3.2	13.9	117
FAMILY CIRCLE	17533	3103	8.6	17.7	91	4449	12.2	25.4	128	7217	10.0	41.2	105	1973	9.0	11.3	95
FAMILY CIRCLE/MCCALL'S (GRS)	30226	5096	14.2	16.9	86	7494	20.5	24.8	125	12766	17.8	42.2	108	3532	16.2	11.7	99
THE FAMILY HANDYMAN	2602	667	1.9	25.6	131	601	1.6	23.1	116	1047	1.5	40.2	103	207	0.9	8.0	67
FIELD & STREAM	9908	1376	3.8	13.9	71	2084	5.7	21.0	106	4400	6.1	44.4	114	1505	6.9	15.2	128
FIELD & STREAM/OUTDOOR LIFE (GROSS)	16812	2373	6.6	14.1	72	3406	9.3	20.3	102	7562	10.5	45.0	115	2569	11.8	15.3	129
FINANCIAL WORLD	1231	499	1.4	40.5	208	370	1.0	30.1	151	273	0.4	22.2	57	**78	0.4	6.3	53
FIRST FOR WOMEN	4402	674	1.9	15.3	78	1389	3.8	31.6	159	1812	2.5	41.2	105	406	1.9	9.2	78
FOOD & WINE	1981	769	2.1	38.8	199	410	1.1	20.7	104	626	0.9	31.6	81	*130	0.6	6.6	55
FORBES	3386	1957	5.4	57.8	296	837	2.3	24.7	124	547	0.8	16.2	41	**34	0.2	1.0	8
FORTUNE	3451	1785	5.0	51.7	265	1148	3.1	33.3	167	489	0.7	14.2	36	**27	0.1	0.8	7
GQ/GENTLEMEN'S QUARTERLY	3617	1030	2.9	28.5	146	1193	3.3	33.0	166	1116	1.6	30.9	79	*266	1.2	7.4	62
GLAMOUR	7857	1673	4.7	21.3	109	2185	6.0	27.8	140	3156	4.4	40.2	103	729	3.3	9.3	78
GOLF DIGEST	4092	1647	4.6	40.2	206	1070	2.9	26.1	131	1256	1.7	30.7	79	*106	0.5	2.6	22
GOLF DIGEST/TENNIS (GROSS)	5704	2313	6.4	40.6	208	1503	4.1	26.3	132	1633	2.3	28.6	73	*231	1.1	4.0	34
GOLF MAGAZINE	3018	1151	3.2	38.1	195	652	1.8	21.6	109	1087	1.5	36.0	92	*117	0.5	3.9	33
GOOD HOUSEKEEPING	18685	3456	9.6	18.5	95	4691	12.8	25.1	126	7674	10.7	41.1	105	1980	9.1	10.6	89
GOURMET	2782	1206	3.4	43.4	222	791	2.2	28.4	143	605	0.8	21.7	56	**109	0.5	3.9	33
GUNS & AMMO	4179	405	1.1	9.7	50	903	2.5	21.6	109	2000	2.8	47.9	123	701	3.2	16.8	142
HACHETTE MAG. NETWORK (GRS)	39430	8242	22.9	20.9	107	10479	28.6	26.6	134	15775	22.0	40.0	103	3983	18.3	10.1	85
HACHETTE MEN'S PACKAGE (GRS)	18338	4007	11.2	21.9	112	4972	13.6	27.1	136	7050	9.8	38.4	98	2008	9.2	10.9	92
HARPER'S BAZAAR	2425	623	1.7	25.7	132	790	2.2	32.6	164	732	1.0	30.2	77	*267	1.2	11.0	93
HEARST HOME BUY (GROSS)	16411	4296	12.0	26.2	134	4546	12.4	27.7	139	6078	8.5	37.0	95	977	4.5	6.0	50
HEARST WOMAN POWER (GROSS)	51374	10076	28.0	19.6	101	13575	37.1	26.4	133	21148	29.4	41.2	105	4936	22.6	9.6	81
HOME	3282	651	1.8	19.8	102	791	2.2	24.1	121	1363	1.9	41.5	106	394	1.8	12.0	101
HOME MECHANIX	2000	360	1.0	18.0	92	354	1.0	17.7	89	840	1.2	42.0	108	336	1.5	16.8	142
HOT ROD	5065	328	0.9	6.5	33	1148	3.1	22.7	114	2715	3.8	53.6	137	714	3.3	14.1	119
HG/HOUSE & GARDEN	3343	1045	2.9	31.3	160	1097	3.0	32.8	165	884	1.2	26.4	68	*220	1.0	6.6	56
HOUSE BEAUTIFUL	4132	1112	3.1	26.9	138	1152	3.1	27.9	140	1371	1.9	33.2	85	310	1.4	7.5	63
HUNTING	3327	280	0.8	8.4	43	716	2.0	21.5	108	1477	2.1	44.4	114	544	2.5	16.4	138
INC.	1155	594	1.7	51.4	264	290	0.8	25.1	126	193	0.3	16.7	43	**78	0.4	6.8	57
INSIDE SPORTS	4439	684	1.9	15.4	79	1038	2.8	23.4	118	1835	2.6	41.3	106	688	3.2	15.5	131
JET	9745	843	2.3	8.7	44	1825	5.0	18.7	94	4534	6.3	46.5	119	1973	9.0	20.2	171
KIPLINGER'S PERS FINANCE MAG	1718	888	2.5	51.7	265	520	1.4	30.3	152	223	0.3	13.0	33	**80	0.4	4.7	39
LADIES' HOME JOURNAL	14363	2648	7.4	18.4	94	3859	10.5	26.9	135	6083	8.5	42.4	109	1277	5.9	8.9	75
LIFE	11927	2913	8.1	24.4	125	2960	8.1	24.8	125	4205	5.9	35.3	90	1423	6.5	11.9	101
LOS ANGELES TIMES MAGAZINE	3775	1287	3.6	34.1	175	1248	3.4	33.1	166	1041	1.4	27.6	71	*109	0.5	2.9	24
MACWORLD	1006	568	1.6	56.5	289	287	0.8	28.5	143	*135	0.2	13.4	34	**11	0.1	1.1	9
MADEMOISELLE	5015	1234	3.4	24.6	126	1552	4.2	30.9	156	1813	2.5	36.2	93	395	1.8	7.9	66
MCCALL'S	12693	1993	5.5	15.7	80	3045	8.3	24.0	121	5549	7.7	43.7	112	1599	7.1	12.3	104
MONEY	6587	3099	8.6	47.0	241	1776	4.9	27.0	136	1524	2.1	23.1	59	*145	0.7	2.2	19
MOTOR TREND	3919	656	1.8	16.7	86	991	2.7	25.3	127	1595	2.2	40.7	104	556	2.5	14.2	120
MUSCLE & FITNESS	4070	695	1.9	17.1	88	1253	3.4	30.8	155	1796	2.5	44.1	113	293	1.3	7.2	61
NATIONAL ENQUIRER	18394	1188	3.3	6.5	33	3482	9.5	18.9	95	8850	12.3	48.1	123	3548	16.3	19.3	163
NATIONAL EXAMINER	3959	251	0.7	6.3	32	572	1.6	14.4	73	1893	2.6	47.8	123	840	3.9	21.2	179
NATIONAL GEOGRAPHIC	24403	8322	23.2	34.1	175	6078	16.6	24.9	125	7785	10.8	31.9	82	1541	7.1	6.3	53
NATIONAL GEOGRAPHIC TRAVELER	1752	722	2.0	41.2	211	446	1.2	25.5	128	498	0.7	28.4	73	**55	0.3	3.1	26
NATURAL HISTORY	1470	789	2.2	53.7	275	308	0.8	21.0	105	288	0.4	19.6	50	**47	0.2	3.2	27
NEWSWEEK	20318	7432	20.7	36.6	187	5792	15.8	28.5	143	5814	8.1	28.6	73	943	4.3	4.6	39
NEW WOMAN	3077	545	1.5	17.7	91	1076	2.9	35.0	176	1274	1.8	41.4	106	*161	0.7	5.2	44

Source: Simmons Market Research Bureau, Inc. 1992.

Use of Media Models

"A *model* is a simplified representation of reality, or in the case of media planning, a description of a process. But it is more than a simple description because it must explain logical relationships, both quantitative and qualitative, between parts of the process and the whole."[9]

FIGURE 12.6

Three Approaches to Scheduling the Media Effort

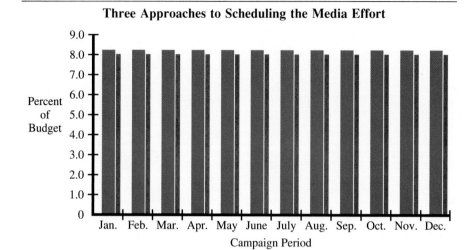

Campaign Period

(A)

Continuous Media Schedule

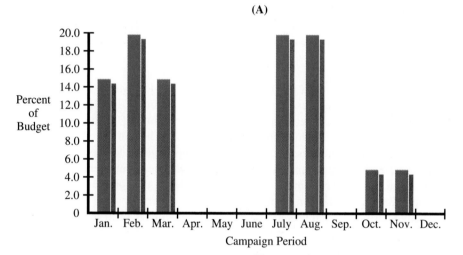

Campaign Period

(B)

Flighting Media Schedule

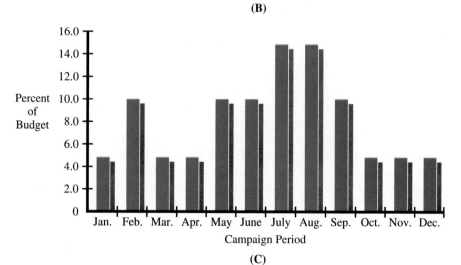

Campaign Period

(C)

Pulsed Media Schedule

Media models first were popularized over 30 years ago. Since then, various researchers have worked on improving existing ones as well as developing new approaches.

FIGURE 12.7

A Sample Media Flowchart

Flowcharts usually are for an entire campaign period, but the one shown here is limited to two quarters.

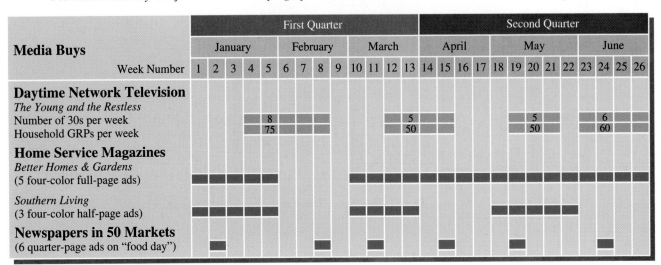

One of the earliest media planning and selection models was developed by the advertising agency of Batten, Barton, Durstine & Osborn (BBDO). Their model applied the mathematical technique of **linear programming** to the problems of media evaluation and selection. The model attempted to help media planners select and schedule media purchases so as to deliver the largest audience of prospects with the desired frequency over specified periods of time. Computers facilitate the complicated linear programming computations to select the combination of media that optimize the satisfaction of media goals.

Another early approach was the **High Assay Model** developed by the Young & Rubicam agency. The model was based on simulating the communication and behavioral process of the target consumer. A decision system uses the computer to find the lowest cost medium per prospect. It attempts also to determine whether optimum prospect exposure has been reached. The approach differs from linear programming in that it attempts to simulate the effects of specific media schedules, whereas linear programming is designed to choose the best schedule from a large number of possible advertising vehicles.

More recently, comprehensive media planning models have been developed that use decision calculus as the underlying mathematical approach. The first of these was MEDIAC; a newer model, ADMOD, involves some general improvements. Among the unique aspects of these models is that they deal analytically with a large number of marketing and advertising facets of the media problem. The models take into account such things as market segments, sales potential, the probabilities of exposure to media, marginal response rates, product seasonality, and media discounts. Several media research companies offer the use of these models in an interactive computer mode. This permits a media planner to test alternative media schedules by varying data input at a computer terminal.

Whereas the models just discussed are "comprehensive" in that several elements of the media process are involved, **exposure estimation models** deal primarily with the matter of the reach and frequency distribution of a media schedule. Thus, models of this type are more limited in their scope. The aim is simple enough: if planners are buying several different issues of several different magazines for a particular

General Media Strategy

Although current "media trends" were discussed earlier in the chapter, there also are a number of future trends that pertain to general media strategy. Among these are the following:

Combining different sources of media information Rather than a planner getting media information from several different research companies, more information will be obtained from a "single source." For example, instead of getting sales data from one source and television viewing patterns from another, the trend is to have one company provide both sets of information. The purpose is to improve the overall accuracy and dependability of information. This trend already is occurring, but will increase in the future.

"Integrated marketing communications" strategy As more and more advertisers and advertising agencies adopt an integrated marketing communications approach to strategic decisions, the way in which advertising media decisions are viewed will change. Integrated marketing communications involves the coordination of such things as media advertising, direct marketing, sales promotion, and/or public relations for a company or brand. The idea is to bring all elements of the communication process into harmony and not deal with the individual variables as if they exist in a vacuum. For example, a brand using network television and consumer magazines, that is, traditional media, needs to coordinate this strategy with such

things as events sponsorship (sponsoring a racing car in NASCAR events), public relations, and sales promotion activities (say, a sweepstakes or contest).

Data base marketing Although somewhat related to the above trend, data base marketing specifically refers to the ability to reach customers *individually* through data base-driven direct marketing. As a result of enhanced information technology, consumers can be reached in a very direct and individualized way. For example, a particular advertisement bound into a national magazine can have the subscriber's name included in the message. Direct mail, telemarketing, and videotext likewise will increasingly be used to reach what is being called a "segment-of-one."

Global advertising Global advertising is discussed in Chapter 21, yet is is important to point out here that advertising will become increasingly more international in the future. The result of this trend has notable implications for media strategy. For example, media planners must be well versed in the strategic and tactical values of the different media systems throughout the world. Further, not all media are available commercially in all countries; a media plan that works well in, say, Western Europe, may not be feasible in South America. Additionally, the amount of reliable information available about the media—considered by most to be abundant in the United States—varies greatly among countries.

plan, for example, they will want to know the percentage of their target market that is likely to be reached by the buy—and, of those reached, how many will be reached by one exposure, two exposures, three exposures, and so on. By having such knowledge, media planners objectively evaluate alternative plans.

Exposure estimation models (also known as **exposure distribution models**, because the frequency distribution of a schedule is derived) utilize various mathematical techniques to arrive at the estimates, including Boolean algebra. The aim is to use a solution that provides estimates of reach and frequency distributions that are closest to actual media delivery. The speed and capacity of the computer have facilitated experimentation with these models.[10]

It is easy to overdramatize the use of media models. Although most provide large amounts of numerical data, the planner continually must recognize the limitations of each model, as well as remain aware of the subjective component of media decision making. Ronald H. Pyszka has provided an excellent review of this situation:

> Clearly, the media selection models offer many advantages. They help to select the optimum media mix—or at least a very good one. They are capable of dealing with large numbers of options and constraints. They ensure that selection criteria are consistently applied, and they serve to point out weaknesses in the selection procedures as well as in the data. When used with computers, the models are fast and relatively inexpensive. Thus, they allow the media planner to concentrate on evaluation rather than selection.
>
> It should be recognized that the solutions generated by these models are the solutions to the problems as they are abstracted by the models. Yet, none of the models reflects all of the complexities of the real-world situation. A solution is only as good as the model and the data on which it is based. For this reason, the solutions generated by the models are best thought of as the starting point for further analysis. This is particularly important since the explicitness of the models often gives a false sense of definiteness.[11]

Media models for decision making will probably continue to evolve as newer and more sophisticated techniques are discovered and adapted. The computer will, of course, facilitate use of the models, but there is still much to be learned about the media process itself and the response of individuals to advertising messages.

Summary

The media bring the communicator and the audience together. In practice, planning media strategy is a complicated job. Certain trends—such as the increased complexity of media, changes in buying and selling methods, availability of product and media usage data, and the growth of new media technology—have made this so.

Media planning is very much a part of marketing strategy. The media analyst must be concerned with such factors as marketing objectives, the characteristics of the product being advertised, pricing strategy, the distribution of the product, and the promotion mix.

The media plan itself is formed from the marketing inputs. Planners generally are concerned with a host of decision areas, including the setting of media objectives (in terms of reach, frequency, gross rating points, and continuity); defining target markets to match them with media vehicles; selecting media types, vehicles, and units; and establishing a media schedule.

Although media decision-making involves many subjective judgments, the use of mathematical models, especially exposure estimation models, has become popular. The development of media models will continue in the future, but for such approaches to be useful, more must be learned about the media process itself.

Among the future trends in advertising that bear on media strategy are the growth of single-source research companies, the use of integrated marketing communications, greater reliance on data base marketing to reach individual consumers, and greater focus on global advertising.

Questions for
Discussion

1. In what ways might the media trends discussed in this chapter influence an advertiser's media plan?
2. To what extent is it possible to compare one medium with another on the basis of cost?
3. To what extent is media strategy related to creative strategy?

4. What types of media research are needed to make media strategy more valuable?
5. How do planners balance reach, frequency, and continuity in working out a media plan?
6. What do we mean when we say a particular media buy had a reach of 62 percent and a frequency of 3.4?
7. What influence are media models likely to have on media strategy?
8. Assess the media plan presented in the Appendix to Part 2.

Notes

1 For a more complete discussion of these changes, see Henry Assael, *Marketing Principles & Strategy,* 2d ed. (Fort Worth, TX: Dryden Press, 1993), 106–121. Also, see Louis E. Boone and David L. Kurtz, *Contemporary Marketing*, 7th ed. (Fort Worth, TX: Dryden Press, 1992), 262–278.
2 Boone and Kurtz, *Contemporary Marketing*, 269.
3 Donald W. Jugenheimer, Arnold M. Barban, and Peter B. Turk, *Advertising Media: Strategy and Tactics* (Dubuque, IA: WCB Brown & Benchmark, 1992), 415–416.
4 *Mediaweek*, February 10, 1992, 13.
5 Arnold M. Barban, Steven M. Cristol, and Frank J. Kopec, *Essentials of Media Planning: A Marketing Viewpoint*, 3d ed. (Lincolnwood, IL: NTC Business Books, 1993), 9.

6 Jugenheimer, Barban, and Turk, *Advertising Media*, Chapter 3, 10–11.
7 Barban, Cristol, and Kopec, *Essentials of Media Planning*, 54.
8 Ibid., 32.
9 Jack Z. Sissors and Lincoln Bumba, *Advertising Media Planning*, 4th ed. (Lincolnwood, IL: NTC Business Books, 1993), 360.
10 For a more complete discussion of both comprehensive and exposure distribution models, see John D. Leckenby and Kuen-Hee Ju, "Advances in Media Decision Models," *Current Issues & Research in Advertising* 12, (1990): 311–357.
11 Ronald H. Pyszka, "Media Selection Models: A Review," unpublished paper, Department of Advertising, University of Illinois, Urbana, IL.

Suggested Readings

Barban, Arnold M., Steven M. Cristol, and Frank J. Kopec. *Essentials of Media Planning: A Marketing Viewpoint*, 3d ed. Lincolnwood, IL: NTC Business Books, 1993.

Gensch, David H. *Advertising Planning: Mathematical Models in Advertising Media Planning*. Amsterdam: Elsevier, 1973.

Hall, Robert W. *Media Math: Basic Techniques of Media Evaluation*, 2d ed. Lincolnwood, IL: NTC Business Books, 1991.

Jugenheimer, Donald W., Arnold M. Barban, and Peter B. Turk. *Advertising Media: Strategy and Tactics*. Dubuque, IA: WCB Brown & Benchmark, 1992.

Kaatz, Ronald B. *Cable: An Advertiser's Guide to the New Electronic Media*. Chicago: Crain Books, 1982.

Lancaster, Kent M., and Helen E. Katz. *Strategic Media Planning*. Lincolnwood, IL: NTC Business Books, 1989.

Leckenby, John D., and Kuen-Hee Ju. "Advances in Media Decision Models." *Current Issues & Research in Advertising* 12 (1990): 311–357; and McGann, Anthony F. and J. Thomas Russell. *Advertising Media*, 2d ed. Homewood, IL: Irwin, 1988.

Rust, Roland T. *Advertising Media Models*. Lexington, MA: Lexington Books, 1986.

Sissors, Jack Z., and Lincoln Bumba. *Advertising Media Planning,* 4th ed. Lincolnwood, IL: NTC Business Books, 1993.

Appendix to Part Two

A Sample Media Plan

Following is an actual media plan developed by advertising agency Leo Burnett Company, Inc. for the John G. Shedd Aquarium in Chicago.

SHEDD AQUARIUM 1992 MEDIA PLAN

PURPOSE:

To Present 1992 Media Plan for Shedd Aquarium

AGENDA

Planning Considerations
- Review of 1991 Media Plan
- 1992 Budget
- 1992 Creative

1992 Media Objectives and Strategies
- Overall Advertising Objective
- Target
- Geography
- Seasonality
- Communication and Scheduling

Media Plan Development and Recommendation
Next Steps
Appendix

Planning Considerations

REVIEW OF 1991 MEDIA PLAN

New Oceanarium at John G. Shedd Aquarium was focus of our advertising and media plans in 1991.

- Opened to public on Saturday, April 27th

Tickets on sale Friday, March 15th through Ticketmaster

- Significant amount of public relations, press, and protest surrounding opening

Media plan needed to be sensitive to this in vehicles selected and scheduling

334

Following is a review of John G. Shedd Oceanarium 1991 media objectives and strategies . . .

TARGET

Objective
- Direct advertising to persons most likely to visit John G. Shedd Oceanarium

Strategy
- Primary focus on families in Chicago metro area
- Secondary focus on families visiting Chicago metro area
- Use Adult 25–54 buying target

Rationale
- Aquarium has established reputation as place for family
  - Special exhibits for children
  - Teacher/Educator
  - Oceanarium will continue this focus
- According to recent census, 783,292 households with children 2–18 years old in Chicago
  - Large broad-based target
  - Opportunity to increase attendance
  - While Oceanarium may not be individually strong enough to attract out-of-state visitors,
    - Want to be at top of families "to do" list
    - Reach this target when they arrive, not before
  - No specific emphasis on any ethnic group for grand opening
    - However, in fourth quarter, expanded target to reach out to more blacks and Hispanics
  - Families with children not a reported demographic in radio audience sources
    - Buying target of Adults 25–54 is most logical

GEOGRAPHY

Objective
- Provide advertising covering Chicago metro area

Strategy
- Purchase media covering the entire Chicagoland area
  - Balance between city and suburbs

Rationale
- Focus on areas with most potential visitors (close to Oceanarium)
  - Biggest opportunity for repeat visitors
  - Develop sense of community
    - Reach teachers, volunteers, new members, and contributors
  - Concentrated effort increases impact and awareness
    - Most efficient use of available dollars

COMMUNICATION AND SCHEDULING

Introductory Oceanarium advertising ran in second quarter 1991.

- In April, local radio and newspaper advertising ran prior to grand opening
  - Provided information on tickets, hours of operation, transportation, and parking

Radio stations purchased were WLUP-AM/FM, WBBM-AM and WGN-AM.

- High concentration of Adults 25–54 and news/information formats
- Live sponsorships of news, weather and traffic

- On WGN-AM, helped secure on-air promotions and live remote
- Weight scheduled Wednesday morning–Sunday morning
  – Family weekend planning

Weekend sections of *Chicago Sun-Times*, *Chicago Tribune*, *Daily Herald* and *Reader* were purchased.

- Sources of family weekend planning
- Requested and received museum/zoo adjacencies

In May and June, we purchased local magazines, Transit and Touch Chicago.

Channel 11 (WTTW), *Chicago*, *Inside Chicago*, *Chicago Parent*, *Where*, *Chicago Life* and *New Expressions* were our print vehicles.

- Sources of family weekend planning
- Requested and received museum/zoo adjacencies
- Note, *Chicago Life* was purchased when cost was reduced

Purchased interior signage on Chicago area CTA buses and trains.

- Paid for month of May but still continue to see over-rides
- Were able to heavy-up on routes surrounding the Shedd Aquarium

Purchased new Touch Chicago System.

- Located on concierge's desk and provides directions to hotel guests

Determined that majority of Touch Chicago volume was in June, July and August (see Table A).

T A B L E   A

**Shedd Aquarium/Oceanarium
Touch Chicago 1991 Tracking**

	Guest Requested Access	% of Total	Guest Printed Info	% of Total
January	203	3%	96	2%
February	308	5	143	3
March	586	9	318	8
*April**	636	9	396	10
May	359	5	177	4
June	793	12	500	13
July	954	15	615	16
August	922	14	600	15
September	490	7	272	7
October	464	7	299	8
November	517	8	311	8
December	362	6	215	6
Total	6,594	100%	3,942	100%

*Oceanarium opened on April 27, 1991

On June 4th, 10-second live read and two complimentary passes to Oceanarium were sent to 24 Chicago area radio stations.

- Requested free advertising by station's disc jockey

Total 1991 media budget of $308,300 (net) (see Exhibit A).

EXHIBIT A

Shedd Oceanarium 1991 Media Plan

© 1985–1990 MediaPlan, Inc.

In fourth quarter 1991, expanded Oceanarium message by using . . .

- Black radio station (WGCI-FM) with high concentration of Adults 25–54
- Spanish language newspaper ad in *La Raza*
  - Large circulation and highly targeted

1992 BUDGET

Current 1992 advertising budget of $296,000 (net).

- Agency waiving 15% commission

Estimate 1992 production budget will be $15,000 for radio, print and transit.

Total of $281,000 remains for 1992 media.

Client has total 1992 direct advertising commitments of $30,277.

- 52 weeks of *Key* magazine
- 12 months of *Where* magazine for $25,857

Leaves $250,723 for Leo Burnett Company, Inc. 1992 media planning.

1992 CREATIVE

Currently developing black and white non-bleed print creative.

- "Boy, 8, Walks from Red Sea to Amazon" is first ad being developed (see Exhibit B)
  - Working to finalize layout week of March 30th

EXHIBIT B

BOY, 8, WALKS FROM RED SEA TO AMAZON.

There was a time when exploring the world meant slogging through mud, braving ice-cold winds, and finding yourself face to face with big, scary bugs.

Well that was a long, long time ago, but many families still act as if it were true. So they stay home, watch TV and maybe mow the lawn or something. But the John G. Shedd Aquarium offers a better way to see the world. We've brought the world to Chicago. Made it easy to see in one day. So now, even an eight-year-old can come face to face with sleek, Amazon stingrays and, minutes later, find himself in the presence of the Red Sea's long-finned round-head. Explore the Caribbean first.

Here you'll see iguanas darting from rock to rock, witness the calm beauty of angel fish and wonder at the hypnotic grace of green moray eels.

Next, travel to the Indo-Pacific's world of miniature marine jewels and sinister lion fish, which stun unwary trespassers with their venomous fins. Patient visitors may even catch sight of tiny flashlight fish. Bright, blinking lights are all you'll see of these fast-moving creatures. And our Animals of the Cold Oceans exhibit contains exotic sea anemones and large American lobsters, which can grow up to 50 pounds! River otters, white fish and perch—they're all native to Lake Michigan, and the John G. Shedd Aquarium. See them in our Great Lakes display. Then, step over to our 90,000 gallon coral reef exhibit, where you might

observe one of our divers hand-feeding an assortment of tropical fish and other animals.

And if all that's not enough, visit our Oceanarium. It's the largest indoor marine mammal exhibit in the world, and is home to delicate sea stars, beluga whales, and everything in between. Here you'll find these magnificent creatures in a near-perfect replica of their natural environment.

Call Ticketmaster at (312) 559-0200 for reservations. There's lots of parking at Soldier Field, two restaurants, and a number of special programs, as well. So make plans to visit the John G. Shedd Aquarium. It's like a trip around the world, without all the icky stuff.

OPEN 7 DAYS 9-6

THE JOHN G. SHEDD AQUARIUM

TICKETS AT: **TICKETMASTER**   including Carson Pirie Scott, Rose Records, Bergner's Sound Warehouse, Hot Tix & Tower Records locations   CHARGE-BY-PHONE (312)559-0200

Have discussed developing other print ads.
- "70 species discovered near loop"
- "Ocean found in building"
  - Second Oceanarium ad

Also have 1991 Oceanarium ad available in English and Spanish language versions.

Radio and transit creative is being developed.
- 60-second radio spot (see Exhibit C), 10-second live read, and 5-second live tag
  - 5-second live tag will be read at end of 60-second spot
- Interior signage on CTA buses and trains
- Will consider developing Spanish language versions

 LEO BURNETT U.S.A.

35 WEST WACKER DRIVE, CHICAGO, ILLINOIS 60601
(312) 220-5959

EXHIBIT C

SHEDD AQUARIUM
60-Second Recorded Radio Announcement
"MYSTERY"
SHEDD AQUARIUM

As Recorded: 05/08/92 mlr

R-1056-ZLBA

Job #: P15530

1	PERSON 1:	They were only 'bout six inches tall I'd say.
2	PERSON 2:	We could see their mouths movin', like they were tryin' to
3		talk or somethin'.
4	PERSON 3:	And they had these gill things.
5	ANNCR:	Close encounters with bizarre, fish-like creatures.
6	PERSON 1:	It was a strange place. First it looked like the Amazon.
7		Then I turned the corner and boom! I'm 20,000 leagues under
8		the sea.
9	ANNCR:	Hyper-travel from one continent to another.
10	PERSON 2:	They took me all the way to Africa, but had me home in time
11		for dinner.
12	PERSON 3:	Me too!
13	ANNCR:	A gigantic building just south of Chicago's famed loop has
14		been the site of daily occurrences like these for more than
15		sixty years. Creating a strange attraction for people,
16		young and old alike.
17	PERSON 4:	I was a little girl when I first visited the John G. Shedd
18		Aquarium. And I have never been the same.
19	ANNCR:	If you, or anyone you know, has not been to the John G.
20		Shedd Aquarium lately, or visited their new Oceanarium, call
21		Ticketmaster at 312-559-0200. Operators are standing by to
22		help you enter this wonderous world. The John G. Shedd
23		Aquarium.
24	KID:	There's somethin' very fishy going on over there.

1992 Media Objectives and Strategies

OVERALL ADVERTISING OBJECTIVE

Provide strong incentive to visit and continue visiting Shedd Aquarium.

- Above and beyond Oceanarium
- Want Shedd to be "must see" Chicago attraction for all ages

TARGET

OBJECTIVE

- Direct advertising message to persons most likely to visit Shedd Aquarium and Oceanarium

STRATEGY

- Primary focus on families in Chicago metro area
- Secondary focus on . . .
  - Black and Hispanic families in Chicago metro area
  - Families visiting Chicago metro area
- Use Adult 25–54 buying target

RATIONALE

- Examined national MRI research data to determine targeting opportunities for Shedd Aquarium
  - Client has very little quantitative information on what type of people visit Aquarium
- First, should explain what MRI (Medimark Research, Inc.) research data is . . .
  - Roughly 20,000 people 18 years and older living in 48 contiguous states are given syndicated surveys
  - One respondent per household
  - Surveys conducted year round
  - Sample weighted to reflect census population estimates
  - Surveys gather . . .
    - Multi-media audience estimates
      - Do you read *National Geographic*?
    - Extensive product usage data
      - Do you use a Nikon camera?
- Although, surveys are truly national, feel they can be applied to large market like Chicago
- Broke out MRI targeting information based on three different questions

  1. Have you gone to a museum in past 12 months?
  2. Have you gone to a zoo in past 12 months?
  3. Have you gone to a museum or zoo in past 12 months?
     Note: Data on aquarium visitors is not available

- Targeting information is similar across all three questions, so we focused primarily on last question
  - "Fits" better with Shedd Aqarium/Oceanarium visitors
- Should also explain how to read (% and index) MRI data presented in Table B.

TABLE B

**Demographic Characteristics of
Adults Who Went to a Museum or Zoo**

	% Went to a Museum or a Zoo	Index
Base: Adults (000)	35,843	
Sex		
Men	42.70	90
Women	57.30	110
Education		
Graduated college plus	31.35	173
Attended college	24.03	130
Graduated high school	33.85	86
Less than high school	10.77	45
Age		
18–24	13.97	99
25–34	31.02	129
35–44	25.88	131
45–54	12.89	95
54–64	8.78	71
65 +	7.52	46
Employment		
Employed	74.96	118
Not employed	25.50	69
Full-time employed	63.58	116
Part-time employed	11.38	129
Household Income		
$50,000 +	36.73	148
$40,000–49,999	15.90	129
$30,000–39,999	17.73	110
$20,000–29,999	15.56	91
$0–19,999	14.09	48
Market Statistical Area (MSA)		
Central city MSA	39.84	111
Suburban MSA	44.61	108
Non MSA	15.56	68
County Size		
Size A	49.82	118
Size B	30.54	102
Size C	12.01	81
Size D	7.63	58
Marital Status		
Single	21.97	103
Married	64.31	106
Widowed/Divorced/Separated/Living Together	13.72	76
Household size		
1 Person	9.32	76
2 People	27.61	87
3–4 People	46.70	115
5 + People	16.38	107

	TABLE B	
	(*Continued*)	
	% **Went to** **a Museum** **or a Zoo**	**Index**
Race		
White	91.76	106
Black	5.88	52
Other	2.37	94
Spanish speaking	5.77	99
Occupation		
Professional	16.38	186
Executive/Administrative/Managerial	11.66	143
Clerical/Sales/Technical	23.81	121
Precision/Craftsman/Repairman	5.76	77
Other	17.33	89
Presence of Children		
Any	48.77	118
One	19.95	118
Two	18.13	121
Three +	10.69	113
Parents	42.83	125
Age of Children		
2–11 Months	4.92	104
12–23 Months	4.34	118
2–5 Yrs.	21.95	139
6–11 Yrs.	23.76	126
12–17 Yrs.	18.43	100

Source: MRI 1991 Doublebase, last 12 months

- For example, 57.3% of all adults who went to a museum or zoo in past 12 months were female
- Of the people who went to a museum or zoo in past 12 months, women are 10% (110 index) more likely to have been a visitor than the average adult
- In general, Shedd Aquarium visitors tend to be . . .
  - Relatively equally split between men (43%) and women (57%)
  - Educated
    - Attended college (130 index) and graduated college plus (173 index)
  - Primarily between ages of 25 and 54
  - Employed in professional, executive/managerial and sales positions
  - Making over $30,000 a year
  - Relatively equally split between cities (40%) and suburban areas (45%)
  - Married with children
    - Children tend to be between ages of two and eleven
  - White
    - With 99 index for Spanish speaking
      - Note that Spanish speaking index is much higher for zoos (113 index) than for museums (86 index) (see Appendix Table)

APPENDIX TABLE

Demographic Characteristics of Adults Who Went to a Museum Versus Adults Who Went to a Zoo

	% Went to a Museum	Index	% Went to a Zoo	Index
Base: Adults (000)	21,781		23,169	
Sex				
Men	41.88	88	42.89	90
Women	58.12	111	57.11	109
Education				
Graduated college plus	37.20	205	29.20	161
Attended college	23.86	129	23.82	128
Graduated high school	29.63	75	35.62	91
Less than high school	9.31	39	11.35	47
Age				
18–24	11.88	84	15.34	109
25–34	26.28	109	35.81	149
35–44	27.32	138	25.87	131
45–54	14.94	110	11.01	81
54–64	10.33	85	6.49	53
65+	9.24	57	5.49	34
Employment				
Employed	73.82	116	76.57	121
Not employed	26.17	72	23.42	64
Full-time employed	63.30	116	63.81	117
Part-time employed	10.52	119	12.76	144
Household Income				
$50,000+	41.28	167	34.97	141
$40,000–49,999	16.25	132	15.43	125
$30,000–39,999	17.07	106	18.11	113
$20,000–29,999	13.68	80	16.59	97
$0–19,999	11.72	40	14.90	50
Market Statistical Area (MSA)				
Central city MSA	38.90	109	40.82	114
Suburban MSA	46.86	113	43.29	105
Non MSA	14.24	63	15.90	70
County Size				
Size A	53.68	127	47.67	113
Size B	28.08	94	32.46	109
Size C	11.19	75	12.15	82
Size D	7.04	54	7.73	59
Marital Status				
Single	22.73	106	21.21	99
Married	63.68	105	65.36	108
W/D/S/LT	13.59	75	13.43	75
Household Size				
1 person	10.94	89	7.46	61
2 people	30.00	94	24.96	79
3–4 people	45.17	111	48.66	120
5+ people	13.89	91	18.92	123

APPENDIX TABLE

(*Continued*)

	% **Went to a Museum**	**Index**	% **Went to a Zoo**	**Index**
Race				
White	92.43	107	91.80	106
Black	5.26	47	5.84	52
Other	2.30	92	2.37	94
Spanish speaking	5.01	86	6.57	113
Occupation				
Professional	19.25	219	15.39	175
Exec./adm./mgr.	13.67	167	10.17	125
Cler./sales/tech.	21.52	110	25.84	132
Prec./crft./repair	5.02	67	5.95	80
Other	14.37	74	19.22	99
Presence of children				
Any	43.10	104	55.08	133
One	17.76	105	21.84	129
Two	16.65	112	20.40	137
Three +	8.70	92	12.84	136
Parents	37.92	111	48.35	141
Age of children				
2–11 months	3.56	75	6.12	129
12–23 months	2.90	79	5.51	150
2–5 yrs.	16.72	106	27.97	177
6–11 yrs.	21.34	113	26.89	142
12–17 yrs.	18.89	103	18.39	100

Source: MRI 1991 doublebase, last 12 months

- As part of our secondary target, want to attract . . .
  - Black and Hispanic families in Chicago metro area
  - Families visiting Chicago metro area
- Although MRI figures were not particularly strong for blacks, still represent an opportunity to increase attendance
  - 783,292 total households with children 2–18 years old in Chicago
  - Approximately 155,092 black households with children 2–18 years old in Chicago
    - Represents 19.8% of total
- MRI numbers on Spanish speaking visitors of zoos and museums were flat (99 index)
  - However, index is higher for zoos (113 index)
  - Shedd can certainly be more like a zoo with this target
    - Reading little or no information
  - Approximately 66,580 Hispanic households with children 2–18 years old in Chicago
    - Represents 8.5% of total
- Want to attract visitors outside immediate city and suburbs
  - Be at top of families ''to do'' list
  - Reach this target when they arrive, not before

- Since families with children not a reported demographic in radio audience sources
    - Buying target of Adults 25–54 is most logical

GEOGRAPHY
OBJECTIVE

- Cover Chicago metro area with our advertising message
- When Chicago metro area has been adequately covered, consider scheduling advertising in surrounding markets
    - Within short driving distance to John G. Shedd Aquarium

STRATEGY

- Purchase media covering the entire Chicagoland area
    - Balance between city and suburbs
- Secondarily consider purchasing media covering state of Illinois, northwest Indiana and southern Wisconsin

RATIONALE

- Focus on areas with most potential visitors
    - Those closest to Aquarium have priority
        - Biggest opportunity for repeat visits
- Working to develop sense of community
    - Reach teachers, volunteers, new members and contributors
- Concentrated effort increases impact and awareness
    - Most efficient use of available dollars

SEASONALITY
OBJECTIVE

- We have two major seasonality objectives for 1992 . . .
    - Introduce new Shedd Aquarium advertising
    - Advertise when attendance is lowest

STRATEGY

- As affordable, schedule weight during May and June and between September and December

RATIONALE

- Summarized 1989, 1990 and 1991 attendance figures forwarded by Client (see Table C).
    - For 1991 we broke out Aquarium and Oceanarium separately
- Discovered that July and August have historically been Shedd's strongest attendance months
    - Client has mentioned at or near capacity
        - Especially with addition of Oceanarium
    - Advertising presence is not as critical
        - Especially with limited media dollars
- Excluding January and February, September–December has historically been slowest time of year
    - Opportunity for advertising to help increase attendance
- May and June weight will introduce and ''seed'' new advertising campaign
    - Also earliest all elements of our creative will be ready

TABLE C

Attendance for 1989, 1990, and 1991

	1989 Aquarium Attendance	Index	1990 Aquarium Attendance	Index
January	55,095	64	64,006	60
February	47,685	55	59,006	55
March	105,385	122	128,743	120
April	96,751	112	125,355	117
May	98,097	114	126,971	118
June	100,750	117	126,229	118
July	141,463	164	185,228	172
August	146,830	171	182,197	170
September	59,632	69	73,361	68
October	63,093	73	69,274	64
November	62,394	72	85,027	79
December	55,934	65	63,569	59
Total	1,033,109		1,288,966	
Average	86,092		107,414	

	1991 Aquarium Attendance	Index	1991 Oceanarium Attendance	Index
January	58,624	73	—	—
February	70,822	89	—	—
March	135,642	170	—	—
April	119,160	149	—	—
May	92,647	116	167,132	110
June	80,073	100	172,060	114
July	142,499	179	181,825	120
August	131,503	165	182,343	120
September	25,863	32	126,236	83
October	33,050	41	140,517	93
November	34,252	43	127,441	84
December	33,319	42	115,113	76
Total	957,454		1,212,667	
Average	79,788		151,583	

Source: Shedd Aquarium

COMMUNICATION AND SCHEDULING

OBJECTIVE

- Increase awareness of Shedd Aquarium and Oceanarium
- Introduce new advertising campaign
- Provide information on tickets, hours, transportation and parking
- As affordable, build and sustain awareness

STRATEGY

- As affordable, schedule introductory level of media weight beginning in May
  - Also would like strong weight levels between September and December

- Schedule Shedd media weight in one–two week flights
  - Concentrate weight prior to weekend
    - Off air Sunday, Monday and Tuesday
- Consider combination of radio, newspaper, magazines and transit
  - Select sources of family weekend planning

RATIONALE

- As mentioned, introductory level of weight in May will increase awareness (off air since December 1991) and introduce new campaign
  - September–December weight levels need to be strong because of historically low attendance figures during this time of year
    - Client does have major promotion with Warner-Lambert planned for September and October
- Scheduling weight in one–two week flights allows for higher weight levels when on-air
  - Using available dollars, Shedd will be more visible
  - Scheduling weight prior to weekends also keeps advertising more concentrated
- Multi-media effort necessary to attain highest possible reach

Media Plan Development and Recommendation

Analyzed variety of media vehicles used by Shedd.

- Radio
- Newspapers
- Local magazines
- Transit
- Outdoor
- Touch Chicago

Requested not-for-profit rates.

Based on limited media dollars, had to eliminate media vehicles which are not efficient and/or do not meet our objectives and strategies.

For print vehicles, requested cost information on alternative page sizes.

- Want to reduce cost but still remain dominant item on page
  - Insure that illustrations in ad are large enough to be seen
- Smaller ad size also makes sense because we are reminding people to visit Shedd

Finalize fourth quarter media scheduling once Chicago Bears home football schedule is published.

- Avoid problems with visitor parking/traffic

RADIO

Considered radio for Shedd.

- Frequency medium
- Very efficient
  - CPM = $5.54 using $205 planning cost-per-rating point and Adult 25–54 universe of 3.7 million
- Low out-of-pocket cost
- Compatible environment
  - Select stations that specialize in news and information

- Opportunities for sponsorships, live reads and live remotes (Johnny B on WLUP-AM/FM)
- Timely delivery of advertising message
- Will reach people not reading Chicago newspapers or magazines

Recommend following dayparts.

- Wednesday–Friday AM drive
  - 6:00 am–10:00 am
  - Highest rated daypart
- Wednesday–Friday PM drive
  - 3:00 pm–7:00 pm
  - Second highest rated daypart
- Saturday day
  - 10:00 am–3:00 pm
  - Reach families while they are finalizing weekend plans

Rating point equals one percent of target audience.

- 2.8 rating on WGN-AM in AM drive represents 2.8% of all Adults 25–54 in Chicago metro area
- $.028 \times 3,662,400$ (Adults 25–54 in Chicago metro area) $= 102,547$

Word "gross" represents total of all rating points.

- 10 commercials on WGN-AM equals 28 gross rating points

Recommend minimum of 75 Adult 25–54 GRPS per week.

- Necessary to break through clutter
- Similar to minimum weight levels used for Oceanarium in 1991, Chicago Historical Society and Field Museum

Recommend following daypart mix.

- 40% of Adult 25–54 GRPS in Wednesday–Friday AM drive
- 40% of Adult 25–54 GRPS in Wednesday–Friday PM drive
- 20% of Adult 25–54 GRPS in Saturday day
- Enough weight in each daypart to have strong frequency
  - Rule of thumb is 8–12 commercials on station per daypart per week
- Mix of dayparts increases target reach

Will evaluate stations based on:

- Adult 25–54 audience ratings
- Efficiency
- Environment
- If they meet our objectives and strategies
- Promotional opportunities

Will conduct negotiations to determine final station list.

- Buy 3–4 stations total

Will send 10-second live read to all Chicago area stations

- Ask if they can read live copy at no charge

PRINT

Analyzed newspapers and local magazines based on:

- Editorial environment
- Out-of-pocket cost and Adult 25–54 CPM
- Circulation
- Positioning opportunities
- Closing dates

Print materials will be ready at end of March

CHICAGO NEWSPAPERS

Evaluated five newspapers:

- *Chicago Sun-Times*
- *Chicago Tribune*
- *Daily Herald*
- *Reader*
- *New Expressions*

Chicago Sun-Times

Second largest Chicago daily newspaper.

Offers ability to target message by using selected sections.

- News
- Commentary
- Fashion
- Arts & Show (daily, section 2)
- Business
- Weekend Plus (in Friday issue)

Tabloid size newspaper.

- Full-page measures $10^{13}/_{16}''$ × 14″ or 71 column inches
- Three-fourths page vertical measures $8^5/_8''$ × $10^1/_2''$ or 42 column inches

	Net Cost	Circ. (000)	Estimated Adult 25–54 Audience (000)	Adult 25–54 CPM
Full Page				
City & Suburbs	$6,720	531.4	975.7	$6.89
Suburbs only	3,196	333.4	612.1	5.22
Three-Fourths Page Vertical				
City & Suburbs	$4,191	531.4	975.7	$4.30
Suburbs only	2,324	333.4	612.1	3.80

- Weekly closing dates

Chicago Tribune

Largest Chicago daily newspaper.

Offers a variety of sections.

- Tempo
- Main News
- Chicagoland
- Style
- Friday
- Sunday Arts

Friday section is tabloid size.

- Full-page measures $10^{13}/_{16}''$ × 14″ or 71 column inches
- Three-fourths page vertical measures $8^5/_8''$ × $10^1/_2''$ or 42 column inches

	Net Cost	Circ. (000)	Estimated Adult 25–54 Audience (000)	Adult 25–54 CPM
Full Page				
City & Suburbs	$7,642	757.7	1,207.0	$6.33
Suburbs only	5,365	443.7	706.8	7.59
Three-Fourths Page Vertical				
City & Suburbs	$6,510	757.7	1,207.0	$5.39
Suburbs only	5,053	443.7	706.8	7.15

- Weekly closing dates

Daily Herald
Large suburban daily newspaper.
Covers all northwest suburbs

- Lake, Cook, and DuPage counties
- Libertyville to Naperville

Friday Showcase section is tabloid size.

- Full-page measures $10\frac{13}{16}'' \times 14''$ or 71 column inches
- Three-fourths page vertical measures $8\frac{5}{8}'' \times 10\frac{1}{2}''$ or 42 column inches

	Net Cost	Circ. (000)	Estimated Adult 25–54 Audience (000)	Adult 25–54 CPM
Full Page	$1,639	120.0	205.3	$7.98
Three-Fourths Page Vertical	$1,140	120.0	205.3	$5.55

- Weekly closing dates

Reader
Free, weekly publication.

- Distributed every Thursday throughout the city
- Features on urban issues, politics, arts and entertainment, film, theater, and music

Each issue contains three sections.

- Section 1: Neighborhood news, editorial features
- Section 2: Reader's guide to music scene, silver screen and theater
- Section 3: Classifieds

Slightly different size than other Chicago newspapers.

- Full-page measures $10'' \times 16''$
- Junior-page measures $8'' \times 10\frac{1}{4}''$

	Net Cost	Circ. (000)	Estimated Adult 25–54 Audience (000)	Adult 25–54 CPM
Full Page	$1,967	135.2	154.1	$12.76
Junior Page	$ 953	135.2	154.1	$ 6.18

- Weekly closing dates

New Expressions

Free local monthly publication written by Chicago high school teens.
Circulated in 85 public and private high schools.
Tabloid size newspaper.

- Full page measures $10^{13}/_{16}'' \times 14''$
- Half page vertical measures $8^5/_8'' \times 10''$

	Net Cost	Circ. (000)	Estimated Adult 25–54 Audience (000)	Adult 25–54 CPM	Overall CPM
Full Page	$1,275	80.0	N/A	N/A	$15.94
Half-Page					
Vertical	$ 637	80.0	N/A	N/A	$ 7.96

Closing Dates

Issue Date	On Sale Date	Order	Materials
May	May 5	March 14	March 21
June	June 2	May 8	May 15
September	September 1	July 10	July 17
October	October 6	August 14	August 21
November	November 3	September 11	September 18
December	December 1	October 9	October 16

Recommendation

Recommend buying three-fourths page vertical size ad.

- Dominant item on page
- More efficient CPM
- Size is equivalent to full-page magazine ad
  - Reduce production costs

Recommend buying city and suburban editions.

- Provide complete coverage of our target

Chicago Newspaper Summary

Based on newspapers full-run editions and three-fourths page vertical size ad or equivalent.

Publication	Net Cost	Circ. (000)	Estimated Adult 25–54 Audience (000)	Adult 25–54 CPM
Chicago Sun-Times	$4,191	531.4	975.7	$4.30
Chicago Tribune	6,510	757.7	1,207.0	5.39
Daily Herald	1,140	120.0	205.3	5.55
Reader	953	135.2	154.1	6.18
New Expressions	637	80.0	N/A	7.96*

* = Overall CPM

CHICAGO MAGAZINES

Evaluated five publications.

- *Channel Eleven (WTTW) Magazine*
- *Chicago Magazine*
- *Chicago Parent*
- *Key*
- *Where*

Note that *Inside Chicago* has suspended publication.

Channel Eleven (WTTW) Magazine

Monthly magazine for subscribers of Chicago's public broadcast station (WTTW)

- Articles focus on environmental and social concerns, television and film personalities, travel, automobiles and a channel 11 TV guide
- Full-page ad measures 8½″ × 11″
- Half-page vertical ad measures 4⅝″ × 7⅜″

	Net Cost	Circ. (000)	Estimated Adult 25–54 Audience (000)	Adult 25–54 CPM
Full Page	$2,842	177.0	180.5	$15.75
Half-Page Vertical	$1,550	177.0	180.5	$ 8.59

Closing Dates

Issue Date	On Sale Date	Order	Materials
May 1	April 24	March 16	March 25
June 1	May 25	April 15	April 25
September 1	August 24	July 15	September 25
October 1	September 24	August 14	October 26
November 1	October 23	September 16	November 25
December 1	November 23	October 15	December 23

Chicago Magazine
Monthly magazine for Chicago area residents interested in Chicago's quality of life

- In-depth articles deal with community issues (education, crime, health, etc.), events, films, restaurants and personalities
- Full-page ad measures 8½" × 11"
- Half-page vertical ad measures 4⅝" × 7⅜"

	Net Cost	Circ. (000)	Estimated Adult 25–54 Audience (000)	Adult 25–54 CPM
Full Page	$4,887	200.0	464.0	$10.53
Half-Page Vertical	$2,962	200.0	464.0	$ 6.38

Closing Dates

Issue Date	On Sale Date	Order	Materials
May 1	April 24	March 26	April 4
June 1	May 25	April 25	May 1
September 1	August 24	July 23	August 30
October 1	September 24	August 24	September 31
November 1	October 23	September 23	October 1
December 1	November 23	October 23	November 1

Chicago Parent
Free monthly parenting news magazine directed to families living in greater Chicago-land area.

- Distributed through day care centers, private schools, libraries, doctor and dentist offices, hospitals, activity centers, and selected retail stores.
- Features include child-related articles and a comprehensive calendar of events, programs and activities for families "on the go"
- Printed on newsprint
- Full-page ad measures 10¼" × 12⅜"
- Three-fourths page vertical ad measures 7½" × 9¼"

	Net Cost	Circ. (000)	Estimated Adult 25–54 Audience (000)	Adult 25–54 CPM
Full Page	$1,386	94.5	175.8	$7.89
Three-Fourths Page Vertical	$ 910	94.5	175.8	$5.18

Closing Dates

Issue Date	On Sale Date	Order	Materials
May	April 24	April 7	April 14
June	May 29	May 5	May 12
September	August 26	August 4	August 11
October	September 25	September 1	September 8
November	October 30	October 6	October 13
December	November 27	November 3	November 10

Key

Free monthly publication providing information about city events.

- Edited for visitors and distributed in Chicago hotels, high rises and airports
- Full page ad measures 5⅜″ × 8¼″

	Net Cost	Circ. (000)	Estimated Adult 25–54 Audience (000)	Adult 25–54 CPM
Full Page	$85/wk.	20.0/wk.	32.8	$2.59

- Weekly closing dates

Where

Free monthly publication providing information about Chicago and city events.

- Edited for visitors and distributed in Chicago hotels, high rises and airports
- Full-page ad measures 8⅜″ × 11⅛″
- Half-page vertical ad measures 4⅝″ × 7⅜″

	Net Cost	Circ. (000)	Estimated Adult 25–54 Audience (000)	Adult 25–54 CPM
Full Page	$2,155	100.0	295.8	$7.29
Half-Page Vertical	$1,742	100.0	295.8	$5.89

Closing Dates

Issue Date	On Sale Date	Order	Materials
May 1	May 1	March 26	April 9
June 1	June 1	May 23	April 25
September 1	September 1	July 23	July 30
October 1	October 1	August 20	August 27
November 1	November 1	September 24	October 1
December 1	December 1	October 22	October 29

Recommendation

Recommend buying full-page size ad . . .

- Except in *Chicago Parent* where we can use three-fourths page vertical size

Chicago Magazine Summary
Based on magazines full-page size ad except for *Chicago Parent.*

Publication	Net Cost	Circulation (000)	Estimated Adult 25–54 Audience (000)	Adult 25–54 CPM
Channel Eleven Magazine	$2,842	177.0	180.5	$15.75
Chicago	4,887	200.0	464.0	10.53
Chicago Parent	1,386	94.5	175.8	7.89
Key	85 per week	20.0 per week	32.8	2.59
Where	2,155	100.0	295.8	7.29

TRANSIT

Evaluated signage on city bus and train routes.

- Provides inexpensive impressions on a regular basis—reach and frequency
- 1.9 million Chicago Transit Authority (CTA) riders daily

		%
Buses	1.4 million	74
Trains	.5 million	26
	1.9 million	100%

- Each bus averages 18,000 riders a month.
- Each train averages 12,000 riders a month.

Certain bus and train routes offer opportunity to target message.
CTA provides interior signage on buses and trains at low cost for not-for-profit groups.

- $4 per card labor charge
- Cards or ads must be 11″ × 28″ on .015 styrene
  - Live area is 9½″ × 26½″
- Accept minimum of 200 cards, maximum of 3,000
- Guarantee signage for 30 days; will stay up as long as sign lasts
- Require 10-day lead time to insert cards

TOUCH CHICAGO

Interactive computerized city guide.
Allows hotel guests to get information on entertainment and restaurants.
Placed at concierge's desk.
In 10 hotels with total 9,889 rooms.

- Number of rooms increased by 44% versus year ago

$2,450 for 12 months.

- Updates at no additional charge
- CPM = $257.89 based on 9,500 requests (assumes 44% increase in requests versus year ago)

EXHIBIT D

Shedd Aquarium and Oceanarium 1992 Media Plan Option 1

1992 Media Vehicle	$ (000)	January	February	March	April	May	June	July	August	September	October	November	December
Local Radio													
Subtotal	$164.0												
Local Newspapers													
Chicago Sun Times	$33.5												
Chicago Tribune	$52.1												
Subtotal	$85.6												
Local Magazines													
Key	$4.0												
Where	$26.4												
Subtotal	$30.4												
Transit													
May Posting	$7.6												
Media Total	**$287.6**												

March 26, 1992

EXHIBIT E

Shedd Aquarium and Oceanarium 1992 Media Plan Option 2

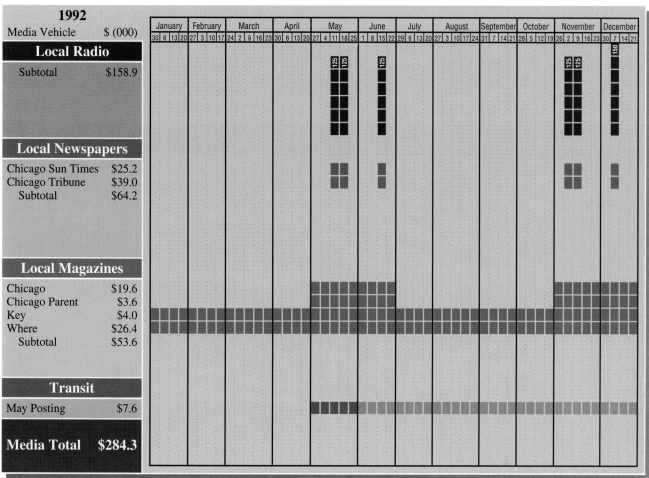

1992 Media Vehicle	$ (000)	January 30 6 13 20	February 27 3 10 17	March 24 2 9 16 23	April 30 6 13 20	May 27 4 11 18 25	June 1 8 15 22	July 29 6 13 20	August 27 3 10 17 24	September 31 7 14 21	October 28 5 12 19	November 26 2 9 16 23	December 30 7 14 21
Local Radio													
Subtotal	$158.9					125 125	125					125 125	150
Local Newspapers													
Chicago Sun Times	$25.2												
Chicago Tribune	$39.0												
Subtotal	$64.2												
Local Magazines													
Chicago	$19.6												
Chicago Parent	$3.6												
Key	$4.0												
Where	$26.4												
Subtotal	$53.6												
Transit													
May Posting	$7.6												
Media Total	**$284.3**												

March 26, 1992

RECOMMENDATION

Recommend option 2 (see Exhibits D and E) for John G. Shedd Aquarium in 1992.
- Use Warner-Lambert promotion to cover September and October
- Radio weight more concentrated
- Higher weekly radio weight levels for greater impact
- Add two strong sources of family weekend planning
  – *Chicago Magazine* and *Chicago Parent*

Currently $3.3M over budget of $281.0M
- Feel we can eliminate this overage via spot radio negotiations

Next Steps

Gain Client approval of recommended 1992 media plan.

Order media.

PART 3

Advertising Campaign Planning: Tactics

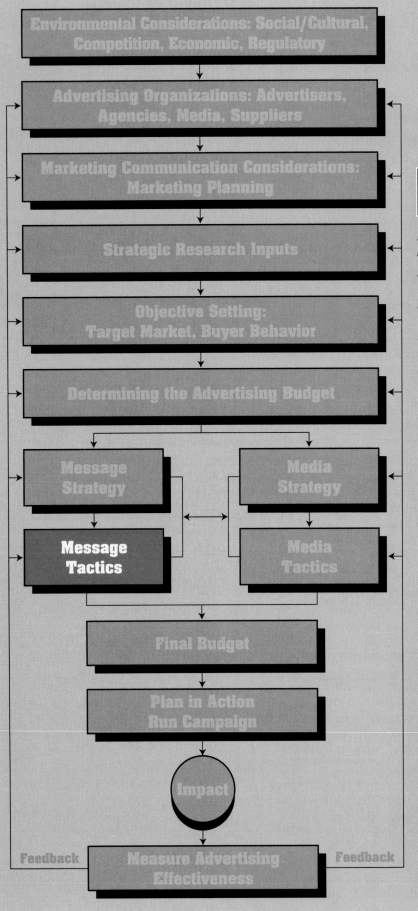

LEARNING OBJECTIVES

In your study of this chapter, you will have an opportunity to:

- Understand how the elements in print tactics work together.
- Learn the functions of headlines and what makes a good headline.
- Understand differences and guidelines for the various types of body copy.
- Learn the functions and qualities of an effective layout.
- Understand the importance and functions of different types of illustrations.

Chapter 13

Message Tactics: Print Advertising

CHAPTER TOPICS

COORDINATING THE MAJOR ELEMENTS
ATTRACTING ATTENTION THROUGH HEADLINES
Types of Headines
Subheads
BODY COPY

FUNCTIONS OF A LAYOUT
How the Layout Is Prepared
Qualities of an Effective Layout
ILLUSTRATIONS
Classifying Illustrations
Illustration Techniques and Color

Message tactics are developed to carry out or fulfill message strategy; hence, message tactics are a direct outgrowth of message strategy. Chapter 11 noted that message strategy refers to an idea statement of "what to say." Such elements as art, illustrations, text, and headlines are developed to bring message tactics to life.

This chapter will discuss the verbal and visual elements used to formulate print messages. Verbal elements include headlines and body copy. Visual elements include layout and illustrations.

Coordinating the Major Elements

In effective advertising a synergism exists among all of the elements. Separately, the headline, copy, and illustration have little effect. Together, their effect is greater than the sum of their parts. Creative advertising professionals must think both verbally and visually at the same time, whether they are copywriters or artists. Headline, body copy, and illustration are interrelated and can be thought of as indivisible.

Among the first questions creative people must face when they begin to implement their strategies in print are: "Shall I express the message idea verbally or visually? " and "Which comes first, the text or the illustration? " Many professionals believe that "it's what's up front that counts."[1] The headline and illustration work in combination to attract attention and create the crux of the message.

Advertising copy is an extension and amplification of the headline and illustration. The basic job of the **body text** usually is (1) to arouse interest in the proposition, (2) to provide believable information that is easy to understand, and (3) to impel the reader to see the product and to try it, or at least to accept the image the writer has presented.

FIGURE 13.1

An Advertisement with Both Headline and Illustration Directing
the Reader to the Copy

The headline and illustration usually "open the door" and put the reader in a receptive mood for what the text is about to say. The resulting message must be memorable and readable. For example, both the headline and the small gum illustration in Figure 13.1 invite the reader into the ad while the body copy enhances the message.

Attracting Attention through Headlines

Headlines are often considered the most important element in a print ad. In fact, studies indicate that four of five readers never get past the headline.[2] At times, the headline may serve as the whole text (see the Ad Insight "Partnership for a Drug-Free America" in Chapter 9).

Headline length is often a point of debate among creative people. Research on headline length indicates that 60 percent of magazine headlines are betrween 1–8 words. Less than two percent of the advertisments contain no headlines. While most headlines are short, advertisers realize that it is okay to use a long headline, when needed.[3]

Two primary jobs of any headline are to attract the attention of potential consumers and to offer a worthwhile reward for reading. Unusual words, expressions, or techniques are often used to gain attention. Figure 13.2 shows an advertisement that uses an unusual technique. The broken words lead the reader into the text.

Rewards are often used to attract attention. As consumers scan the advertisements in the mass media, they select ads that promise some reward. Every ad has in it a host of signs that help busy readers predict which ads offer them a reward and which do not. Ideally, the headline should flash a sign to readers that there will be a reward if they read on. Communication research shows that headlines offering a promise of reward attract more attention and achieve more impact than those that do not.

Types of Headlines

Understanding headlines is often easier if we ask oursleves, "Which type of headline seems most appropriate in this particular situation?" Although the categories often overlap and the distinctions between them appear fuzzy, they are nevertheless useful to practitioners. No one type of headline is necessarily more effective than another.

FIGURE 13.2

Unusual Headline Directs Readers into the Text

FIGURE 13.3

Advertisements Showing Different Types of Headlines

News Headline

Direct Headline

Command Headline

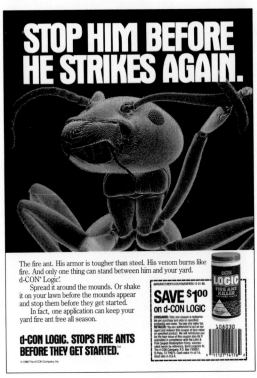

A headline's effectiveness is based on its appropriateness to the particular ad and the skill with which it is written.

In general, headlines can be classified by their manner of presentation—direct, indirect, and combination—and by their content—news, how-to, question, and command. Figure 13.3 provides examples of three types of headlines. The following briefly discusses all seven.

Manner of presentation refers to the way the headline is formed in terms of selecting the audience, Direct headlines are straightforward and informative in terms of selecting readers. They leave little doubt as to what the ad is all about.

Indirect headlines do not usually mention the product or service. For example, see Figure 13.1, "An Ounce of Prevention." Such headlines rely on curiosity value in an attempt to reach a mass audience rather than a select audience. The use of an indirect headline is usually more risky because it asks more of the reader.

Combination headlines seek to combine the straightforward approach of direct headlines with the curiosity value of indirect headlines. Thus, the combination headline loses little in terms of curiosity value, yet makes sure that readers know immediately what product has made them curious. For example, "For every 50 business travelers who try Red Lion Inns, a certain number don't come back." The reader is informed the ad is about Red Lions Inns, yet is left in doubt about customers who do not return.

Content refers to the specific format of the headline. News headlines are extremely effective when the product has something new to offer the customer. The most important prerequisite is that it reveals what is "new" to the customer. How-to headlines appeal to the reader's sense of curiosity and willingness to learn. These headlines have the ability to personalize the purchasing situation by reaching customers who want to take some form of action. Question headlines seek to lure the reader into the ad by providing the "answer" within the text and illustration. Command headlines order the reader to do something. This is a very direct approach that at times calls for immediate action. The Ad Insight "Checklist for Writing Effective Headlines" offers some tips on headline writing.

Subheads

Very often advertisements have only one headline. Some have several. One of these is usually called the main headline, and others subheads. The purpose of subheads is to enhance the headline and provide key information. Subheads reinforce the headline and copy. Although subheads can appear almost anyplace within the ad, they are often found above or below the headline. At times, subheads are also found within the body copy.

Body Copy

Body copy, sometimes called "body text," is usually the main message of the advertisement. After the headline and subhead are developed, the rest of the copy should flow naturally.[4] One of the most difficult tasks facing creative professionals is to get people to read the body copy. We know that over 80 percent of the readers never get past the headline.

It is indeed a challenge to develop persuasive body copy that actually gets read. Short body copy will attract more readers. However, the copy must be long enough to communicate the message idea. Good body copy holds the reader's interest in order to stress key ideas and benefits. The Ad Insight entitled "Guidelines for Writing Body Copy" offers some writing tips.

Body copy is often divided into the following categories or types: reason-why, humorous, descriptive, testimonial, dialogue, and narrative. These classifications help to explain different aproaches to writing body copy. Figure 13.4 illustrates reason-why and testimonial body copy types.

Checklist for Writing Effective Headlines

No universal list exists of qualities that headlines should include, because each situation is different. The following, however, can serve as a general checklist:

- If possible, some promise of reward should be included. Show how the product advertised will satisfy one or more consumer drives.
- Headlines should be specific and to the point, not general and applicable to any product or any situation.
- Headlines should be coordinated with other elements of the advertisement.

- Headlines should be understandable at a glance. Readers will not spend time trying to figure out what you are saying.
- Headlines should have words or other cues that help select prospects.
- Avoid clichés.
- Headlines should be action-impelling, making an immediate impact on the reader.

Any copy that features a reward in the headline or illustration and explains "why" it is true is called reason-why copy. This emphasizes a rational appeal to the audience. The approach is very common in print advertising because it allows readers to proceed at their own pace from headline to copy.

FIGURE 13.4

Advertisements Showing Types of Body Copy

Reason-Why

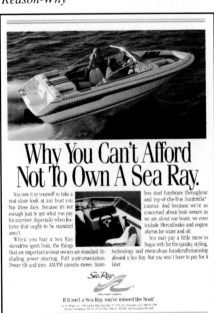

Testimonial

Guidelines for Writing Body Copy

Most creative practitioners are understandably suspicious of copywriting "formulas." Copywriters maintain that writing is a basically creative function and each communication situation is a little different. Nevertheless, certain principles distinguish effective copy from ineffective copy. Some important guidelines are summarized here.

Make it interesting Interest should be captured with the first sentence or lead-in paragraph.

Make it specific The specific word, phrase, or sentence communicates a much sharper image than does a general one.

Keep it simple Simple language communicates best. Do not overwrite.

Make it concise Get to the point quickly.

Make it believable Believability and conviction are key goals of advertising communication.

Use language that sparkles Avoid clichés and seek out language that is meaningful to the reader. Rather than relying on adverbs to define action, choose dynamic verbs.

Provide a surprise Copy that is overly predictable tends to be dull. Inject something that will keep and hold the reader's attention.

Make it persuasive Successful copy usually states the impression or action the ad seeks of the reader.

Develop rhythm throughout the copy Vary the length of your sentences and the length of words within the sentences. Use sentence fragments when appropriate.

At times humorous copy is used to gain both attention and interest. When used properly it is an effective emotional appeal that can create good feelings about the product. However, a funny idea must not leave the product and main communication idea behind.[5] Humor is not an end in itself. Additionally, it is more difficult to be universally funny in print because of the lack of both audio and movement.

Most copy includes some description of the product or service. At times the illustration and headline are not adequate to describe the main idea or key benefit. When the description becomes the major focus of the advertisement, the approach is called descriptive copy. This approach is used when the appearance of the product or the reward it promises needs strong emphasis to make it clear to prospective buyers.

Testimonial copy uses a spokesperson or third person to establish the credibility of the message. Celebrities, satisfied customers, or authority figures are all used to present the message and "represent" the product. When using such a spokesperson, a good match between the product and the individual is important. A spokesperson must be able to fit in with the message idea. For example, the Jockey advertisement in Figure 13.4 shows how the company uses Olympic Triple Gold Medalist Nancy Hogshead to endorse its product.

In narrative copy, the story is the main attraction in the ad. A good story can communicate the major message idea. Among the common forms of narrative copy are the short story, the picture and caption, and the cartoon. As a special form of narrative, dialogue copy involves conversation. Writing good dialogue is an extremely difficult task. The Myers's Rum advertisement in Figure 13.8 on page 373 is an example of how a short story with dialogue is used to create a mood for the product.

Functions of a Layout

A layout is an arrangement of elements into a meaningful message. The layout allows the planner to visualize the ad.[6] Layouts are designed to perform both mechanical and symbolic functions. Physically, the layout is the plan that indicates where the component parts of the ad (headline, subheads, illustrations, and body copy) are to be placed for most effective communication. The artist can experiment with alternative arrangements until he or she arrives at the most promising one. The layout guides the copywriter in planning copy and the lettering specialists, typographers, and other production experts in their work. Additionally, the layout provides a guide for estimating costs.

The layout also performs a symbolic function. The layout will "speak to the eyes."[7] The final layout, transformed into the finished advertisement, gives the audience its first impression of the organization sponsoring the advertisement. A very formal layout gives the impression that the advertiser is stable, conservative, and solid. A modern, informal layout gives the same audience the impression of a dynamic company. Considerable white space in an ad projects an image of exclusiveness. Conversely, a layout crowded with elements and heavy black type gives the impression of a "discount" organization and is frequently used in retail advertising.

How the Layout Is Prepared

Layout artists often work within certain space limitations. In newspapers and magazines, they are limited to certain standard sizes and shapes, typefaces, and so on, that the medium is willing to make available to advertisers. In designing most outdoor posters, for example, they are limited by standard billboard sizes.

The artist can do a better job of visualizing the ad if the copywriter has already done some visual thinking. Both should be working toward the same basic goal: expressing the message idea in the most effective form. Some writers put in very rough form the visual as they conceive it, so that the artist can have some help in arranging the elements. Many artists prefer to do the complete job themselves, with only verbal help from the writers. In the case of many retail store layouts, the writer is likely to be a jack-of-all-trades who is responsible for layout and **production** instructions, as well as for writing the headlines and copy.

Figure 13.5 shows some of the layout stages of an ad. Most artists begin by making several **thumbnail** sketches, or miniature rough sketches, of possible layouts. Ordinarily, these rough sketches are smaller than the final ad. A thumbnail sketch offers artists an opportunity to try out a variety of ideas.

The **rough layout** will be the exact size of the final advertisement. Many artists make numerous roughs, other artists only a few. Some layouts are sent to the printer or to newspapers in very rough form, depending on how much service the media provide. In a rough, headlines are often hastily lettered in and body text indicated only in pencil. These layouts, which are closer to the final form, help all concerned visualize which of several alternatives provides the greatest promise of success.

When a selection has been made among alternative roughs, the **finished layout** is composed. The artist may complete this layout or may instruct a commercial studio to do it. The illustration, lettering, and the logotype will be drawn the way they are to appear in the final advertisement. The text will be indicated by lines neatly ruled in blocks of varying lengths to simulate paragraphs. A finished layout is almost a facsimile of the finished advertisement.

When the finished layout is carried one step further, the **comprehensive** layout is the result. If, for example, the illustration is to be a painting or a drawing, the artist will probably be asked to make the final illustration for the comprehensive.

FIGURE 13.5

Various Stages in a Layout

Thumbnail sketch

Comprehensive, all elements are combined, including type

Final ad sent to magazine

The type will be set and a proof of it pasted on the layout. The comprehensive must be painstakingly put together to look like the final product.

Layouts tend to fall into certain classifications according to the format they follow. Seven basic types are suggested:[8]

1. *Standard layout*   This consists of a dominant illustration, headline, body copy, and logotype—generally in that order.
2. *Editorial layout*   The ad resembles editorial material in a publication.
3. *Poster layout*   Almost total emphasis is put on the visual.
4. *Cartoon layout*   This includes everything from the "pure" cartoon of the *New Yorker* or *Playboy* type to the long-copy advertisement with a cartoon at the beginning to attract attention.
5. *Comic-strip layout*   Cartoon drawings follow the format of the comic strip.
6. *Picture-caption layout*   Pictures and captions are used to show the many facets of the product or service advertised.
7. *Picture-cluster layout*   This uses a single dominant element made up of a set or cluster of items.

Like copywriting, layout cannot be done by formula. There are, however, certain qualities that tend to distinguish more effective layouts from the others.

Composition

Although professionals often disagree among themselves on the specifics of **composition**, they seem to have an instinctive appreciation of good composition. The following guidelines are helpful:

Qualities of an
Effective Layout

1. Ideally, the picture should occupy slightly more than one-half of the entire space. The total area of all illustrations combined should occupy that amount of space.
2. The headline usually occupies 10 to 15 percent of the total area. Headlines are usually placed below the illustration and above the copy.
3. Unless the name of the product is prominently displayed in the headline or shown in the illustration, the logotype should be emphasized and put in a prominent setting.
4. Repetition of the same themes helps unify an advertising layout.
5. **Borders** are useful to keep readers from wandering away from the ad, especially in newspaper advertisements.
6. Typographical consistency reassures readers that they are looking at one ad, not several.

Balance

An advertisement is balanced when it looks balanced. Symmetrical balance means all elements are centered around a vertical or horizontal axis. This is also termed formal balance and is used most where dignity or stability is dominant. Informal or asymmetrical balance, has the elements informally grouped around the center of the page. Informal balance usually generates eye movement and more excitement and is used in the majority of print advertisements.[9] Figure 13.6 shows examples of balance.

Movement

Every advertisement should move the eye naturally from one element to the next. Readers are likely to focus first above and to the left of center and then roam around the page. But their eye movements can be controlled by skillful manipulation of the elements. Some of the more common devices follow.

FIGURE 13.6

Types of Balance in Advertising Layouts

Formal Balance   *Informal Balance*

1. *Gaze motion*   Eyes direct other eyes. Readers follow the gaze of people or animals in illustrations.
2. *Size*   Readers are attracted by the largest and most dominant matter on the page.
3. *Pointing devices*   These include hands, arrows, rectangles, triangles, or lines of type.
4. *Cartoons or pictures with captions*   The reader must start at the beginning and follow the sequence to get the point.
5. *Gutters of white space*   These are areas between dark masses of type or illustrative material. The contrast and arrangement between these and the darker background directs eye movement.

Proportion

Two areas are more pleasing to the eye if one is slightly larger than the other. It is more appealing to have masses of space in proportions, such as three to five or two to three. These are less monotonous than equal masses.

Contrast

One way to emphasize a particular element is by contrast. Dark masses stand out against a light background, as does almost any illustration that is surrounded by a sea of white space.

White Space

At times, white space can communicate effectively. To promote a prestige product or create a high-quality image, it is wise to use plenty of white space to convey this impression.

Illustrations

Illustrations are usually the most important visual element in any print advertisement. Illustrations work to enhance the headline and body copy. They contribute to its effectiveness in one or more of the following ways: (1) they attract the attention of the desired target audience; (2) they communicate a relevant idea quickly and effectively—often one that is difficult or complicated to convey verbally; (3) they interest the audience in the headlines and copy; and (4) they help make the advertisement believable.

Some illustrations attract and select the desired audience because they say to the reader, "Here is a reward you will be interested in." In these instances the desired audience must be able to identify with the illustration. Illustrations are often used to quickly communicate a relevant idea that would be difficult to put into words.

Many illustrations attract the interest of the audience in the headline and copy. To accomplish this, the illustration should tell enough to develop a person's desire to read the headline and the text. Some creative people feel that learning is more often facilitated by a picture–word sequence than a word–picture sequence.

Unless the illustration is perceived to be fantasy, it must help make the ad believable. The illustration must reinforce the credibility of the message. Readers quickly pick out anything that is illogical. For example, during focus group tests for bulldozer parts and service items, customers quickly noted that the mechanic in the print ad "had hands that were too clean." In order to make the ad more believable the mechanic was depicted with dirty hands and wearing a dirty uniform.

FIGURE 13.7

Two Types of Illustrations

Product Itself   *Product in Use*

Classifying Illustrations

Creative professionals make specific decisions as to what will and will not be included in an illustration. At times, an illustration can be found in more than one category. The following highlights the different ways a product or service can be depicted. Figure 13.7 shows two of these classifications.

Product Itself In many instances, such as for appearance, style, or to help identify the product at the store, a picture is necessary. Generally, product pictures are rated highly in readership tests.

Part of the Product Sometimes the appeal rests with a particular part of the product rather than with the whole. In such a case a particular feature may be emphasized by close-up illustration or photography. For example, a safety feature such as an air bag in an automobile might be lost in showing the whole car.

Product Ready for Use An illustration in a setting ready for use can make the product come alive. Kitchen appliances are often placed in a setting ready for use.

Product in Use In many cases, showing use illustrates the benefits of a product.

The Product Being Tested At times, illustrations show the tests a product undergoes before it is sold.

Differentiating Features of the Product Many brands have a unique or differentiating feature that can be visualized.

Consumer Reward from Using the Product Although every product ad should offer a reward, some rewards are more visual than others. Before-and-after illustrations of weight-loss programs are an example.

Effect of Not Using the Product In a sense the illustration can be used to illustrate the results of not using the product. Usually, the results are negative, such as a continuing headache that would otherwise go away if the product were used.

Testimonials Pictures of celebrities and other spokespersons are often used to draw attention and credibility.

Most advertising illustrations are created by one or two techniques: photographs or original artwork. Color may be used by either to add impact.

Much of print advertising success depends on the skillful use of photographs and on taking advantage of the many dimensions of photography. Photographs are effective in realistically portraying the product or subject of the advertisement. Figure 13.8 shows an example of the excellent use of photography.

Although good original artwork tends to cost more than photography, it is often used successfully to create a desired mood or symbolism. The use of artwork varies in different countries. Recent research shows that French advertisers tend to use more original artwork than U.S. advertisers.[10] A skillful artist can excel if some product feature or reward is sought or some special impression of warmth, coolness, or sophistication needs to be emphasized. The diagram is another useful form of artwork, especially in illustrating complicated products or data. Figure 13.8 shows an example of original artwork that is used to create a mood.

Color is a major tool available for print tactics. Color can be used to create attention, make products appear very real, or provide symbolism by creating moods. Readership tests indicate that using color increases the attention-getting value of an ad. It is important to make sure the color obtained is the color originally sought. Magazines provide the most accurate use of color while newspapers generally do not reproduce colors as well.

The value of color is obvious for making some products look realistic. Creators of food ads strive to have very realistic photographs in order to make the products look appetizing (See the Ad Insight for Del Monte Foods). Color is also used to create certain feelings and moods. Certain hues and shades can create very warm feelings while other tones can create cool feelings.

Illustration Techniques and Color

FIGURE 13.8

Illustration Techniques

Photography

Original Artwork

Del Monte's Effective Use of Print

Del Monte Foods, a leading food marketer, made a dramatic shift in its advertising policy by moving almost all of its advertising budget into magazines. George W. Pace, Del Monte's vice president of marketing, noted several reasons for moving almost exclusively to print. "Magazines let us target existing, new, or lapsed users of our product." Mr. Pace noted that the color photography of magazines allows for a positive perception of taste. Additionally, the same graphic format allows customers to immediately know, "This is a Del Monte ad."

Graphic consistency works to build an overall brand image while promoting individual products. Note how the two advertisements here stress both continuity of message and the positive perception of taste.

Source: Magazine Publishers Association

Summary

The first step in putting creative print tactics into practice is to find the most effective combination of verbal and visual elements. Verbal elements consist of headlines and body copy. Visual elements consist of layouts and illustrations.

The verbal elements usually come into focus in the headline, which is designed to gain attention, encourage reading of the body text, and attract target prospects from a large, often heterogeneous audience. Body copy serves to amplify the headline theme or visualization in order to communicate the message idea.

Headlines may be classified on the basis of manner of presentation—direct versus indirect—or on the basis of their content—news, how-to, questions, and command.

The principal classifications of body copy are reason-why, humorous, descriptive, testimonial, dialogue, and narrative. These are seldom used individually but serve as a method for organizing one's thinking in planning the copy.

In print advertising, ideas are usually put into visual form in the layout. The print layout is both a plan indicating where the various elements are to be placed and, in the finished advertisement, a visual symbol of the product, service, or institution sponsoring the message. A layout normally starts with a thumbnail sketch, which can be made quickly to check alternative arrangements of the visual elements. Other stages can include a rough layout, a comprehensive layout, and finally the finished advertisement.

Layout artists strive for good composition, balance, movement, proportion, contrast, simplicity, clarity, and the judicious use of white space.

The major visual element in most print advertisements is the illustration. The primary purposes of illustrations are (1) to attract and select the desired audience, (2) to communicate the relevant advertising idea, (3) to interest readers in the headline and the body text, and (4) help make the ad believable.

If we classified illustrations by subject matter, we would include the following: the product itself, part of the product, the product ready for use, the product in use, the product being tested, a special feature of the product, a consumer reward from using the product, the effect of not using the product, and testimonials for the product.

Among the more important illustrative techniques available to the advertising illustrator are photographs and original artwork. The extra cost of color is usually justified on the basis of one or more of the following reasons: attention value, more exact communication of a product's qualities or rewards, and symbolic communication.

Questions for Discussion

1. What is the relationship between the headline and the body copy of an advertisement?
2. What are the principal headline types? Select an example of each.
3. How can a good advertising headline be distinguished from a bad one?
4. What are the principal types of copy? Find an example of each in current magazines or newspapers.
5. What are some of the most effective methods of making copy interesting?
6. To what extent should the layout be used to gain attention in a print advertisement?
7. What is the primary function of a thumbnail sketch?
8. What is the difference between formal and informal balance? Select an example of each.

Notes

1 W. Keith Hafer and Gordon E. White, *Advertising Writing*, 3d ed. (St. Paul, MN: West, 1989), 98.
2 Ibid.
3 David A. Wesson, "Headline Length as a Factor in Magazine Ad Readership," *Journalism Quarterly*, Summer, 1989, 466.
4 Philip Ward Burton, *Advertising Copywriting*, 6th ed. (Lincolnwood, IL: NTC Publishing Group, 1990), 12.
5 Ibid., 90.
6 A. Jerome Jewler, *Creative Strategy in Advertising*, 4th ed. (Belmont, CA: Wadsworth, 1992), 150.
7 Eleanor Seleme, "10 Steps Simplify Process of Visual Marketing Strategy," *Marketing News*, March 28, 1988, 12.
8 Hafer and White, *Advertising Writing*, 89–92.
9 Sandra E. Moriarty, *Creative Advertising Theory and Practice*, (Englewood Cliffs, NJ: Prentice Hall, 1992), 233.
10 Bob D. Cutler and Rajshekhar G. Javalgi, "A Cross-Cultural Analysis of The Visual Components of Print Advertising: The United States and The European Community," *Journal of Advertising Research*, January/February 1992, 71–80.

Suggested Readings

Albright, Jim, *Creating the Advertising Message*. Mountain View, CA: Mayfield Publishing, 1992.

Burton, Philip W. *Advertising Copywriting*, 6th ed. Lincolnwood, IL: NTC Publishing, 1990.

Hafer, W. Keith, and Gordon E. White. *Advertising Writing*, 3d ed. St. Paul, MN: West, 1989.

Howard, Daniel J., and Thomas Berry. "The Prevalence of Question Use in Print Advertising: Headline Strategies."

Journal of Advertising Research 28 (August–September 1988): 18–25.

Jewler, Jerome A. *Creative Strategy in Advertising*, 4th ed. Belmont, CA: Wadsworth, 1992.

Moriarty, Sandra E. *Creative Advertising: Theory and Practice*, 2d ed. Englewood Cliffs, NJ: Prentice-Hall, 1991.

Nelson, Roy P. *The Design of Advertising*, 6th ed. Dubuque, IA: William C. Brown, 1989. Chapters 3–7.

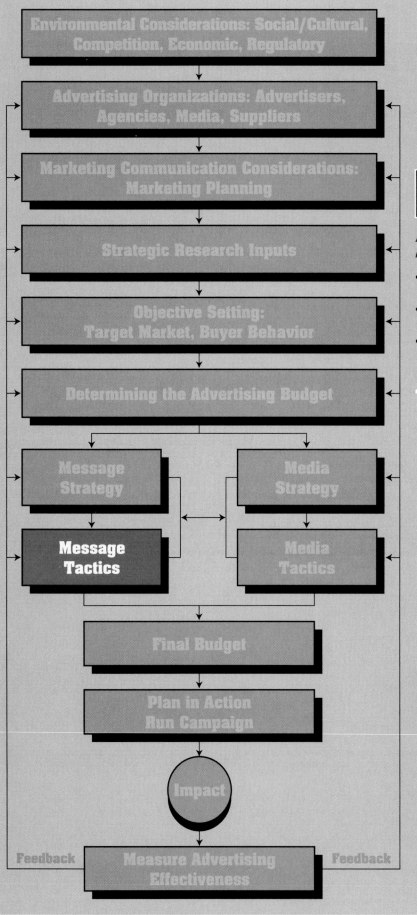

LEARNING OBJECTIVES

In your study of this chapter, you will have an opportunity to:

• Learn guidelines for creating effective radio and television commercials.
• Recognize the types of radio and television commercials.
• Examine the major methods of presentation utilized in radio and television advertising.

Chapter **14**

Electronic Message Tactics

CHAPTER TOPICS

STRUCTURE OF COMMERCIALS
AUDIENCE AND COMMERCIALS
RADIO COMMERCIALS
  Types of Radio Commercials
  Creating Effective Radio Commercials

TELEVISION COMMERCIALS
  Television Storyboards
  Types of Television Commercials
  Television Presentation Techniques
  Creating Effective Television Commercials
  Use of Color

Not long ago, television and radio advertising were simple to understand—commercials were broadcast to audiences by network-affiliated and independent television and radio stations. However, the introduction of new electronic media has altered how commercials are delivered. Today, radio and television commercials are delivered not only by broadcast stations, but also by satellite-fed cable systems, rented videocassette movies, home-delivered videocassettes, and other computer-assisted information services, including those which operate in retail stores. The one common feature of all these media delivery systems is that electronically conveyed commercials are bound and controlled by time in delivery and in reception.

This chapter focuses on the special characteristics of creating radio and television commercials. Creators of electronically conveyed commercials use most of the same principles described in Chapter 13 on print advertising tactics. But at the same time they must deal with some fundamental differences in the way radio and television commercials communicate.

Structure of Commercials

Print advertisements are structured by space, television and radio commercials by time. Given a specific amount of time, radio writers must decide how to use most effectively the words, sound effects, and music that will fit into a commercial. Television writers, who may have 10 to 30 seconds, also have sight, motion, and color to evaluate.

Because the commercial is time oriented and therefore fleeting, and because audiences often give only part of their attention to the message, good commercials are usually simple in structure. Some veteran writers suggest that the writer should be able to sum up the basic idea in one sentence. If the writer cannot achieve conciseness, chances are that the listener or viewer will find it difficult to remember what the commercial said. The discipline of putting ideas into one sentence requires that writers strip away the nonessentials and get to the heart of the message. In television writing, agency executives Kenneth Roman and Jane Maas define the heart of the commercial as the "key visual"—that one frame that sums up the point of the message.[1] In radio writing, the "rule-of-thumb" is that the commercial must grab the listener's attention in the first 3 seconds.

Audience and Commercials

Several characteristics differentiate the audience for television and radio commercials from the audience for print advertisements. In the print media, readers can start paying attention at any point in the ad they like—the signature, the headline, or the illustration. They can review points that interest them; they can skim the ad or read the copy in detail. In the electronic media, the advertiser has more control over commercials. The listener or viewer must tune in to the material provided by the copywriter, or miss the message. Only in the case of viewer-controlled devices such as videocassette recorders can the audience go back and review a commercial that has struck a responsive chord.

Audiences tend to remember combinations of words, like Pepsi's "Uh-Huh," UPS's "We Run the Tightest Ship in the Shipping Business," and Nike's "Just Do It," better in electronic form than in print. Melodic jingles that combine music and theme gain high audience recall. The sound of the human voice and the movement of people make the television message easier to remember than the printed one.

However, unlike reading, watching television or listening to the radio is not a focused event. People seldom stop whatever they are doing to listen to the radio. Even with TV, large numbers of viewers are simultaneously reading, playing, talking or, in some cases, doing household chores or office work. It is an established fact that more than 90 percent of all viewers miscomprehend some part of what they see on TV, no matter what type of content they are watching.[2] The normal range of miscomprehension is between one-fourth and one-third of any televised content—whether program or commercial. On the whole, however, viewers are slightly less likely to miscomprehend commercials than entertainment and news programs.

These medium-specific characteristics make the creation of radio and TV commercials a difficult task. Creatives understand that the unique properties of electronically conveyed messages place demands on their talents.

Radio Commercials

Creating radio commercials is far less complex than creating TV commercials, principally because radio is an aural medium. Radio speaks to the ear, and its power rests in how creatives use music, voices, and sound effects to engage the listener's imagination. This power—the ability to engage the listener's imagination—is called **audio imagery** and, if properly used, can be as powerful as visual imagery. For years, the Radio Advertising Bureau, the trade association for the medium, has used the theme "I saw it on the radio" to promote radio and its power of audio imagery.

Once a mass medium, radio is more likely these days to reach small, specialized audiences, some of whom are on roller skates, some driving their cars, some jogging, some watching a baseball game, and almost all doing something other than concentrating on radio listening. Thanks to the skills of advertising creatives, radio advertising works because[3]

1. *Radio advertising is attention getting*   People respond to voices, music, and sounds that "slap the ear." Within the first three seconds, an effective radio commercial will make the inattentive listener an attentive listener.
2. *Radio advertising builds memorability*   Radio commercials have "staying power." Radio advertising is built on repetition, and people tend to remember brands and selling points long after the ads have stopped. A good example is Budweiser. Years after Anheuser-Busch switched to "This Bud's for you," people still remember and even sing "When you say Budweiser . . ."
3. *Radio advertising builds identification*   Radio commercials cannot show brands, but they can associate them with music, jingles, and personalities. For example, the "ugly yellow building at Foushee and Broad" probably reminds Richmonders of a long-ago, defunct furniture store.
4. *Radio advertising is intimate*   People form strong attachments to radio stations and personalities. Familiar voices speak directly to listeners, giving radio advertising a "personal presence"—it is with us in the morning when we awake, it is with us going to and from work, and it is with us at spectator events, or on other occasions when we are just relaxing.
5. *Radio advertising is emotive*   Radio commercials have "feeling" power. Because radio is personal and intimate, commercials can be emotionally charged—they can make people laugh, they can make people sad, and they can make people feel threatened.

Radio commercials can be classified into five types according to format: singing, or jingle commercial; narrative commercial (one minute or less); straight commercial; personality commercial; and donut commercial. Classification is based on major emphasis, for any radio spot can be a combination of the formats.

Types of Radio Commercials

Singing Commercial

The singing commercial, or jingle, is usually based on a catchy tune—either original or borrowed from a popular song. One of the oldest forms of advertising, the singing commercial gained popularity in the early days of radio. Perhaps the first radio jingle, and certainly one of the most famous, was: "Pepsi-Cola is the drink for you; twice as much for a nickel, too; Pepsi-Cola is the drink for you. . . ." Today, we tap our feet to Ray Charles's melodic "Uh-Huh."

Narrative Commercial

Narrative commercials tell stories. Slice-of-life dramas and dialogues between individuals are examples. An example of a dialogue spot is presented in Figure 14.1

Narrative spots are widely used in spite of the difficulty of telling a story in 60 seconds or less. Many depend on humor for development of characters and plots. A classic example is the commercial created by Stan Freberg for the Radio Advertising Bureau.[4] Note the imagery power of the spot—that ability to engage your imagination.

FREBERG: Okay people, now when I give the cue, I want the 700-foot mountain of whipped cream to roll into Lake Michigan, which has been drained and filled with hot chocolate. Then the Royal Canadian Air Force will fly overhead towing a ten-ton maraschino cherry which will be dropped into the whipped cream to the cheering of 25,000 extras.
FREBERG: All right, cue the mountain.
SFX: (Creaks, groans, prolonged splash)
FREBERG: Cue the Air Force.
SFX: (Propellers roar into and past mike; wing struts whine.)
FREBERG: Cue the maraschino cherry.

FIGURE 14.1

A Humorous Dialogue Radio Spot from NYNEX's Long-Running Campaign

---

NYNEX YELLOW PAGES: 'GENEALOGIST'

Announcer: As they say, you can find anything in the Nynex Yellow Pages, and today under the heading of Genealogists we found Dr. Ian Hadley.

Dr. Hadley: Michael.

Announcer: Dr. Hadley, you trace family roots, I guess.

Dr. Hadley: Yes, as a matter of fact, we traced your family roots as far back as the Battle of Hastings.

Announcer: Well, that's interesting.

Dr. Hadley: Your ancestor Ethelred the Fleet led the retreat from the battle to the forest.

Announcer: Probably just regrouping.

Dr. Hadley: They spent the next several hundred years living as vassals and indentured servants. And they reappear, interestingly, at the time of the American Revolution. The Battle of Lexington was fought on their land.

Announcer: Minutemen, fighting for the young country.

Dr. Hadley: Well, no, they had left a week earlier to, ah, disappear into the forest.

Announcer: To fight on as guerrillas.

Dr. Hadley: That's speculation.

Announcer: I guess this is the family coat of arms?

Dr. Hadley: Yes, this is your family crest.

Announcer: Mighty oak tree, spreading its limbs.

Dr. Hadley: Yes, and if you look carefully, you'll notice a small man cowering behind the mighty oak tree.

Announcer: Well . . . If it's out there, it's in your Nynex Yellow Pages. [Aside] We can't vouch for the accuracy of all these services, of course . . .

Dr. Hadley: And the Latin inscription, *Festina ad silva . . .*

Announcer: Why would anyone need another?

Dr. Hadley: Or . . . "Make haste to the woods."

Best Radio Ad: Humorous, long-running campaign for Nynex Yellow Pages is kept fresh in this execution from Chiat/Day/Mojo and Crawford Wu Productions.

SFX:	(Screaming, whistling fall, and large plop)
FREBERG:	Okay, 25,000 cheering extras.
SFX:	(Prolonged and tumultuous ovation)
FREBERG:	Now—you want to try that on television?
SPONSOR:	Wel-l-l-l—
FREBERG:	You see, radio's a very special medium because it stretches the imagination.
SPONSOR:	Doesn't television stretch the imagination?
FREBERG:	Up to 21 inches—yes.

Straight Commercial

The straight commercial is an announcement delivered by one person. No special devices are used to disguise or enhance the presentation. A straight spot typically begins with some variation of "I want to tell you about . . ." and ends with "Try it." This type of commercial is simple to produce and adapt to almost any product or situation. Quite often, it is delivered live by an on-air announcer. An example of a popular straight commercial is shown in Figure 14.2.

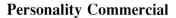
FIGURE 14.2

Example of a Straight Radio Commercial

:60 Radio — Comparison Spot

Hi. Tom Bodett here for Motel 6 with a comparison. You know, in some ways, a Motel 6 reminds me of one of those big fancy hotels. They've got beds, we've got beds. They've got sinks and showers, by golly we've got 'em too. There are differences, though. You can't get a hot facial mudpack at Motel 6 like at those fancy joints. And you won't find French-milled soap or avocado body balm. You will, however, find a clean, comfortable room, and the lowest rates nationwide. Under 21 bucks* in most places. A lot less in some, a little more in others, but always the lowest price of any national chain. And always a heck of a deal.

Motel 6 has 400 locations from coast to coast. And we operate ever' darn one of 'em, which means they're always clean and comfortable.

Oh sure, it'll be rough to survive one night without avocado body balm or French-milled soap, but maybe the money you save'll help you get over it. It always works for me. I'm Tom Bodett for Motel 6.

*Alternate Texas: Under 19 bucks.

Personality Commercial

A personality commercial features one or more celebrities who may deliver the selling message in any of the three previously described formats. People like John Madden, Ed McMahon, Reba McIntyre, William Shatner, and Richard Petty have been used successfully in personality commercials. There is danger, however, that the personality will get in the way of the message or that the copy will not be suited to the style of the featured personality. To overcome this problem, whether for a radio spot or for any other advertising form, great care must be taken to match the personality with the brand. This practice is known as the "match-up hypothesis" and it explains why some personality commercials work better than others.

Donut Commercial

The donut commercial opens with some device such as music, an announcement or a narrative is dropped in, and then the opening device is brought back up to close the spot. Often the opening and closing are prerecorded, and the message is dropped in by a local announcer. The donut commercial is especially useful for advertisers who must modify messages because of local or regional sales and distribution considerations.

These ten rules are guides for writing effective radio commercials, regardless of the type:

1. *Make the commercial stand out in clutter* Use a theme, a character, or an idea that makes the commercial memorable. For example, the city of Baltimore created a game for listeners to play. The game caught on because it was fun. The creators called it "Trash Ball" and invited people to play by throwing their trash into sidewalk wastebaskets. The idea was well suited to repetition on radio and it worked in helping keep Baltimore clean.
2. *Identify the brand and the product reward early* Both Dr Pepper and Coca-Cola have proved that mentioning the product and what it will do for the user early and often increases memorability and need not turn off listeners.

Creating Effective
Radio Commercials

3. *Spell out the product name*   If the name is at all confusing, spell it out at least once. Three times is often better. The Rolaids campaign is a good example of this rule in action.

4. *Use short words and sentences*   These add a conversational lilt to the copy and give it better emphasis. "Fine" car has more punch than "excellent" or "exceptional" car.

5. *Supply the visual*   If the product or package has a green label, promote package identification by mentioning it. You can say or sing "Watch for the green label." Write for the mind's eye.

6. *Repeat basic ideas or themes*   Repetition is the heart and the strength of today's radio. Repetition does not become boring to the average listener, especially if it is done with variations. For example, Budweiser beer has been saying the same things in many ways for years—"This Bud's for You."

7. *Tailor the message to time, place, and specific audience*   Radio is a local medium. If your commercial is targeted at Atlanta residents, include references to familiar Atlanta places and faces.

8. *Keep the message simple*   Radio is much better for building awareness of a brand or a theme than for registering lists of copy points or making complex arguments. A retail store can communicate the store image more easily than a list of its weekly specials.

9. *Consider image transfer*   Use the soundtrack of the product's television commercials on radio. Listeners hear the familiar music, voice, or theme, and they "replay" the television commercial in their minds. Chrysler commercials featuring Lee Iacocca are good examples.

10. *Use sound carefully*   Sound (and silence) are often misused. Remember that the sound of an impatient person drumming on the dinner table while waiting for dinner sounds just like hoofbeats in the distance, and the sound of rain falling in the forest sounds like bacon sizzling in a frying pan. The sound effect is effective only when the listener knows what it means or suggests. One possibility is to build the commercial around the sound effects. For example, a brokerage house created an image of financial power with the sound of kettledrums because it was made clear what the musical sounds were supposed to symbolize: power.

A checklist for creating more effective radio commercials appears in Figure 14.3.

Television Commercials

Television is an audio-visual medium. It speaks both to the ear and to the eye. However, a good TV commercial is created to produce visual impact—it should communicate the same message to the audience even if the sound is turned off. Audio devices such as voiceovers, music, and sound effects are typically used to reinforce and support visual impact.

Creating and producing effective TV commercials is difficult for three reasons. First of all, good commercials tend to be expensive, sometimes costing as much as the programming itself. Shooting on location, incorporating special effects, or featuring popular personalities may all sound like wonderful TV concepts until the production estimates come in.

Second, commercials must penetrate television clutter to communicate messages. The proliferation of cable channels has not only further fragmented the TV audience, but have increased the number of commercials on television. Obviously commercial creators must constantly search for techniques to attract attention, or in many cases, just to keep their existing share of the consumer's mind.

The third problem is potentially the most serious—**zipping, zapping, and grazing.** Viewers armed with remote controls and VCRs, are no longer captive to the television set. If they do not like commercials, they can "zap" them by switching channels.

FIGURE 14.3

How to Create More Effective Radio Commercials

1. Stretch the listener's imagination with voices and sounds.
2. Use a memorable sound to make the commercial stand out from the clutter.
3. Focus on one main sales message and repeat it.
4. Use the beginning of the commercial to flag the intended audience.
5. Mention the brand and its promise upfront in the commercial.
6. Capitalize on events and relevant tie-ins—music trends, fashion changes, interesting social topics, etc.
7. Keep the music simple and relevant.
8. Ask the listener to act.
9. Take advantage of radio personalities.
10. Keep many commercials in your pool, so that they can be rotated to avoid radio advertising's wearout factor.
11. Increase imagery transfer by using the sound elements of TV commercials.
12. Judge radio commercials in the context of program content and never in script form.

Source: Copyright © 1976 by St. Martin's Press, Inc. Adapted from *How to Advertise* by Kenneth Roman and Jane Maas, pp. 61–66. Adapted by permission of St. Martin's Press, Incorporated.

If they gave recorded commercials, they can "zip" past them by fast-forwarding. "Grazing," a general viewing pattern, refers to the tendency of viewers to flip through channels, and is particularly prevalent among male viewers of athletic events. To overcome, zipping, zapping, and grazing, commercials must be more creative than ever. One technique, pioneered in Europe, is to make television advertising a continuing story, with a plot that unfolds over time. Perhaps the most famous example of "plot" advertising on American TV is the campaign for Taster's Choice coffee. One of the Taster's Choice spots is presented in Figure 14.4.

Techniques that have been found by Ogilvy & Mather to work well on television were described in an advertisement directed to clients and prospective clients of the agency (see Figure 14.5). The ad was one of a series that ran in newspapers and magazines with heavy business readership.

Television Storyboards

The television commercial is usually put in visual form for the first time when a **storyboard** is composed. This sequence of cartoons or pictures visualizes the flow of the commercial and provides dialogue and instructions for production specialists. A typical storyboard is shown in Figure 14.6.

Like the print layout, the storyboard gives everyone connected with a particular campaign a chance to appraise the commercial. At many agencies, for example, commercials are shown to the Creative Review Board (an internal agency review group composed of experienced executives) in rough storyboard form with the audio recorded and played on tape. Prescreening gives the agency a chance to make corrections and modifications. In most agencies, the client will also review the commercial in storyboard form and approve it or suggest changes. Once the client has approved the storyboard, the agency usually sends it, along with detailed instructions, to several studios for bids. The production process is covered in some detail in Chapter 15.

FIGURE 14.4

An Example of a "Plot" Commercial

Each commercial in the popular Taster's Choice campaign builds on the relationship between the male and female characters.

Storyboards are sometimes used to pretest the reaction of the general public to a proposed commercial. If the storyboard is well done, almost anyone can, with a little practice, gain a general idea of what the final commercial will look like in spite of the fact that each picture is static and instructions on camera technique are given in a series of sometimes confusing abbreviations (for example, "CU" for **close-up** and "cut" for a quick change from one scene to another). Some agencies attempt to eliminate this confusion by videotaping the commercial, often using their own staff as actors and simplified sets from the agency as background. This technique produces what is known as an **animatic.** Another technique especially useful for pretesting commercials is to photograph the scenes on a filmstrip and then record the audio on tape. The two are then synchronized before the storyboard is reviewed by a creative board or by a test audience. This is known as producing a **photomatic.**

The more frames included in the storyboard, the easier it is for everyone to visualize the final commercial. To envision the finished commercial from a storyboard is much harder than to visualize a finished magazine advertisement from a rough layout.

Types of Television Commercials

Some television experts divide commercials into three simple categories—live, film, and tape. Some classify them on the basis of time (10-second, 30-second, and so forth). Some use the presentation format (straight-announcer or demonstration). Some talk of commercials in terms of production techniques. This confusion testifies to the dynamic nature of television. Writers should not become too closely wedded to strict categories, although some typology is helpful in organizing one's thinking. An empirically derived typology of commercial methods of presentation is shown in Figure 14.7. This section will examine some of the common formats and then some of the most common techniques used in connection with each.

FIGURE 14.5

One of a Series of Advertisements Intended to Impress the Clients and Prospective Clients of an Advertising Agency

Source: Reprinted with permission of Ogilvy & Mather Inc.

Straight Announcement

The announcement is the basic format for many TV commercials and consists primarily of someone looking at the camera and delivering a sales talk, perhaps pointing at or holding up the product. It is subject to countless variations, from the simple retail announcement by a store owner to the announcement using a celebrity.

The economy of the straight announcement is obvious when the story is a dramatic or newsworthy one. One good television salesperson and a simple set can carry the message. But to be effective, it has to compete for the viewer's attention with a host of dramatic and entertaining commercials.

FIGURE 14.6

Storyboard for a Television Commercial

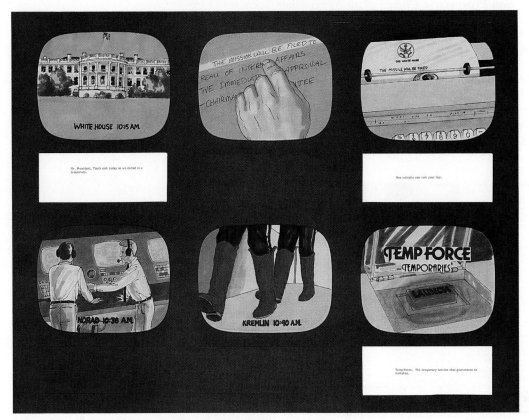

Source: Courtesy of The Joey Reiman Agency.

Demonstration

Demonstration is so important in television that it should be considered as a possibility for every commercial. Because people are interested in what products will do for them, demonstration is usually good communication. In a large percentage of commercials, demonstration of the product or service is the dominant theme. Commercials that effectively use the demonstration format are shown in Figure 14.8.

Demonstration can be used effectively for a variety of objectives. For example, Canon wanted to show amateur photographers how easy it would be to use one of its new 35mm cameras. Demonstration was used in a commercial featuring baseball star Dale Murphy talking about the camera's "green zone." The green zone is a setting on the camera that assures perfect photos even for the most unsophisticated photographer.

Demonstration commercials are usually filmed or taped because even the best of products occasionally fails to operate correctly—for example, the refrigerator door may not open. The commercial is more believable when the demonstrator is someone who might normally use the product under the circumstances depicted.

Testimonial/Celebrity

The use of famous people in advertising can draw attention to a product or idea. A commercial with a celebrity format is shown in Figure 14.9.

FIGURE 14.7

An Empirically Derived Typology of Commercial Methods of Presentation

Individual-Oriented Structures

Individual-oriented structures are those in which the primary emphasis of the commercial focuses on an individual who is: endorsing the product, acting as a spokesperson for the product, or shown in association with or consuming the advertised product. There are four categories:

Celebrity Endorser

The message is presented by an individual recognized as a celebrity for his or her accomplishments (typically athletic or entertainment). The celebrity must express a preference or liking for the product or experiences with it.

Typical Person Endorser

The focus is on an individual (but noncelebrity) who expresses a preference or liking for the product or experiences with it.

Spokesperson

An announcement-type sales message is presented by the celebrity in a manner similar to a presentation by a radio announcer or off-camera TV announcer. In contrast to the endorsement commercial, the spokesperson does not provide a testimonial per se.

Personality

The focus is on an individual (not necessarily a celebrity) who is not verbally endorsing the product nor acting as a spokesperson. Primary attention of the commercial is devoted to an individual portrayed in various roles: using the product; in association with but not using the product; or, perhaps, engaged in an activity completely unrelated to the product. Regardless of role, the individual is clearly the center of attraction throughout the commercial.

Story-Oriented Structures

Commercials in which a story is dramatized or narrated are included in this general structure. There are three specific categories:

Video Drama (off-camera sales message)

A drama portrays life or character by means of dialogue and action. In this form, a drama is performed on video, but the primary sales message is delivered by an off-camera announcer.

Video Drama (sales message by performers)

In this form, a drama is performed and the performers in the drama also deliver the primary sales message.

Narration

In this form, the commercial study is narrated, not dramatized. Quite often in TV advertising a connected succession of happenings (a story) is depicted in the video while an off-camera announcer discusses the advertised product and relates what is transpiring on camera. Frequently, the narration describes historical places or events, glamorous settings, the nostalgic past, enchanting geographic locales, and so on.

Product-Oriented Structures

The major emphasis in some TV commercials is the product rather than individuals. Specific product features or the entire product are the center of emphasis. There are two categories.

Demonstration

Most all commercials involve some type of demonstration. In some commercials, however, the dominant emphasis is the demonstration; all other aspects of the commercial are secondary.

Product Display and/or Performance

The distinguishing characteristic between this method and the demonstration is that a specific product feature is not being demonstrated, even if a product is in featured action. A product is displayed but is not demonstrated.

Technique-Oriented Structures

Many TV commercials convey the sales message through the use of a special technique that clearly stands out as the predominant aspect of the commercial. There are two types:

Fantasy

This method includes commercials that employ imaginative and unnatural plot and/or characterization. Included in this category are commercials using animated characters, talking animals, and dreams in which the product is the object of the dream.

Analogy

The advertised product is compared, by analogy, to an unrelated item. Through analogy the advertiser attempts to convey certain features of the product by relating it to attributes of an analogous object. For example, advertisements that compare the product to a beautiful woman, a fine animal, or a precious jewel are conveying the sales message by analogy.

Source: Terrence A. Shimp, "Methods of Commercial Presentation Employed by National Television Advertisers," *Journal of Advertising* 5 (Fall 1976): 30–36. Reprinted with permission.

One of the most successful users of the format in television was the American Express company. American Express first used testimonials from actual cardholders filmed in exotic cities around the world. When the successful campaign was copied by other advertisers, the agency decided a new variation was needed. Both the

FIGURE 14.8

Commercials Using a Demonstration Format

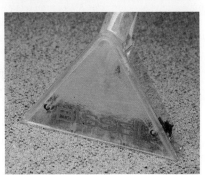

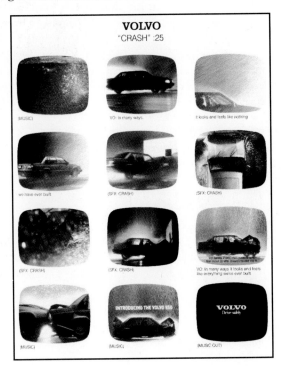

FIGURE 14.9

Commercials Using a Celebrity Format

agency and its client wanted to avoid the "pat" testimonial of the smiling star saying how much he or she liked the credit card. A decision was made to look for persons whose faces were well known but whose names were not. In the commercials, the spokespersons confessed that the whole world didn't know who they were and that they often needed the American Express card to get recognition. Always, the commercials began, "Do you know me?"

Later American Express commercials featured individuals whose names were often more familiar than their faces. One, for former U.S. Representative William Miller, began "Do you know me? I ran for the Vice President of the United States in 1964." Sometimes the very famous were placed in an unfamiliar situation (Jack Nicklaus on the tennis court, Fran Tarkenton playing rugby). According to one creative director, the campaign worked because it was ever-changing, credible, entertaining, and intelligent.[5]

Testimonial/celebrity commercials work best when the celebrity has credibility as a source. Problem celebrity endorsers and consumer skepticism are discussed in the Ad Insight entitled "The Trouble with Celebrity Endorsers."

McCollum/Spielman, a large advertising research supplier, offers the following suggestions for the use of celebrities:

1. Determine the message strategy and then find the right celebrity. Don't select a celebrity and then develop the strategy.
2. Make certain the celebrity's image and personality are congruent with the product's personality.
3. Give the celebrity a logical reason to endorse the product.
4. Make it clear that the celebrity should be viewed as an authority or credible source.
5. Get the celebrity involved with the product by featuring a demonstration or product in use.

The Trouble with Celebrity Endorsers

Advertisers spend millions on celebrity endorsers every year. Sometimes, however, their investments fail to return expected dividends for two basic reasons: (1) circumstances and (2) overexposure.

Consider, for example, the following victims of circumstances:

- Bruce Willis was dumped by The Seagram Company because of his "bad boy" image and a wife who campaigned against alcohol abuse.
- The Beef Industry Council replaced James Garner after he had quintuple-bypass heart surgery and Cybill Shepherd because she confided to a woman's magazine that she did not eat much red meat.
- Mike Tyson was dropped by Diet Pepsi after the heavyweight champ's much publicized marital problems.

Other celebrities damage their credibility by endorsing anything. Take the case of the late John Houseman, who had great success pitching Smith Barney, Harris Upham & Company ["We make money the old-fashioned way. We earn it.], but was a flop as a spokesman for McDonald's. Over the years, Ed McMahon has endorsed 44 different banks, beer, dog food, insurance, consumer contests, and numerous other products, a pace that many believe has diminished his value as a credible spokesperson.

According to Carol Colman of Inferential Focus, a consulting firm that maps trends among consumers for many Fortune 500 companies, "consumers are wising up." Today's consumers see many media and sports celebrities as opportunists who believe less in the product or service they are endorsing than in the money they are making.

How do advertisers deal with problem celebrity endorsers and consumer skepticism?

First, they drop the commercial or advertisement; then they drop the celebrity, notes marketing consultant Jack Trout.

Source: Richard Burke, Knight-Ridder Newspapers, reported in the *Athens Daily News/Athens Banner-Herald,* November 27, 1988, 8D.

The Ad Insight entitled "The Match Game: Linking Celebrities, Brands" reinforces each of the five points. Consumers have definite ideas about which endorser is right for a particular brand. Avoid using celebrities when:

1. The celebrity has lost his or her glitter.
2. The celebrity is idiosyncratic and has a controversial personality.[6]

Dramatization

In a dramatized commercial, the point is presented through a story that can be told briefly, even in 30 seconds. The theme is sometimes presented as a contrast— "before using the product" versus "after." Sometimes it is a serious story, as in the successful series for Kodak. Human interest heightened when the teacher used Kodak to shoot instant pictures of the children on their first day in class to break the ice and to make them feel a part of the new environment. Other examples of classic dramatizations include Hallmark Cards' heart-tugging commercials, Miller High Life's "Miller time" commercials, and McDonald's "You deserve a break today" spots.

The Match Game: Linking Celebrities and Brands

Advertisers have long sought to link images of celebrities to those created for brands. The working assumption is "the more consumers associate positive personality qualities with brands, the more of those brands they will buy."

Certainly, Reebok had this in mind when they contracted professional basketball star Dominique Wilkins to appear in their ad for Above the Rim Basketball Shoes and Apparel. Any serious basketball fan will tell you that the 'nique's game is above the rim.

In the early 1990s, Total Research Corporation conducted a study to determine who would be the most effective celebrity spokesperson for particular brands. Famous people and the brands that they best matched with were:

Bob Hope	Disney, Hallmark, Maxwell House
Bill Cosby	Corning Ware, Diet Pepsi, Fisher-Price
Walter Cronkite	Bayer, Cream of Wheat
George Bush	Bell, Disney, Exxon
Pope John Paul II	Hallmark, Hershey, Pepsi
Michael Jordan	Cadillac, Minute Maid, NBA basketball
Meryl Streep	Kodak, Lenox, Volvo
Jack Nicholson	CNN, Levi's, Nike
Luciano Pavarotti	Cuisinart, Wall Street Journal

Source: Total Research Corp.
Source: Melissa Turner, "Business Report: On Media and Advertising," *Atlanta Journal,* Tuesday, October 29, 1991, D2.

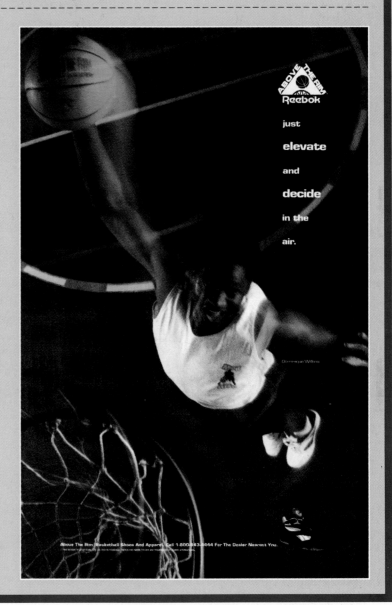

Dramatization of a product's uniqueness is often made more noticeable if a touch of humor or a bit of exaggeration is added. Years ago, Mennen commercials popularized the line "Thanks! I needed that" for its Skin Bracer. In 1984, a commercial for Wendy's introduced the catch-phrase "Where's the beef?" A dramatized commercial with a humorous touch is shown in Figure 14.10.

Because the time frame for a television spot is so short (most are now 30 seconds

FIGURE 14.10

A Dramatized Commercial with a Humorous Touch

A Jeep spot spoofs a "rival" company, which needs a helicopter to get its car to the top of a hill that a Jeep can climb.

and many are 15), the plot must be simple. If possible, all three of television's elements—sight, sound, and motion—should play an integral part in telling the story.

Dialogue

Any commercial in which two or more people are talking could be called a dialogue commercial. For that matter, a person talking to an inanimate object could fall into this category. Remember the Parkay margarine commercials in which a bemused human was regularly fooled by a margarine box that alternately retorted "butter" or "Parkay"?

A dialogue commercial might include famous, well-known actors as spokespersons or feature those whose name and face are largely unknown to their audience. Actress Mariette Hartley had little name awareness when she began doing commercials with TV-and-film star James Garner. Their series of TV commercials for Polaroid's One-Step camera was named one of the "100 best" by *Advertising Age* for three consecutive years, and according to industry estimates, was instrumental in selling two million cameras within six months of the product's introduction.

The dialogue format is also popular at the local market level, where retailers and spokespersons are often featured talking about products and services. In Atlanta, for example, long-running commercials for a retail furniture store have featured the "Wolfman" and his daughter bantering about whom customers should ask for when they come in to buy furniture.

The basic advantage of the dialogue commercial is its ability to involve viewers and to encourage them to participate in the dialogue. Research indicates that such commercials "should be more effective over a longer period of time than those which simply present a straightforward sales story."[7]

Television Presentation Techniques

Among the most common techniques used to present advertising messages on television are the following: live action, cartoon animation, stop motion, and photo animation.

Live Action

Live action is television's approximation of real life. It is designed to make characters believable and the situation real. Live action is the most frequently used technique in television advertising because it is appropriate for presenting almost every type of commercial—from straight to dialogue to testimonial.

Sometimes live action is combined with one of the other presentation techniques—cartoon animation, stop motion, photo animation—to produce a spot. One animation technique called **rotoscoping** was used in a Schick commercial to draw whiskers on a man's face. The whiskers were rotoscoped in to show a "whisker shock," a condition that resulted from not using Schick razors.

Cartoon Animation

Sometimes well-known cartoon characters are used to make a point in a commercial. These characters may be used to add warmth or humor to a sales message. Sometimes they are used to exaggerate a point—a point that is understood by the viewer and is therefore not deceptive. Baskin-Robbins has had great success with the Silver Spoon, and for years, General Mills has used the Honey Nut Cheerio bee in animated commercials (see Figure 14.11). Research has indicated that "cartoons and animation are effective with children but are below average with adults."[8]

In perhaps one of the world's most expensive commercials, Anheuser-Busch used painstaking cutout animation to produce its "Ultimate Sports Bar" commercial. The spot, shown in Figure 14.12, was produced for the 1990 Super Bowl. Additional trends on animation are provided in the Ad Insight entitled "Animation: It Stands Out on TV, and It Really Sells."

FIGURE 14.11

Use of Cartoon Animation in TV Commercials

FIGURE 14.12

A Commercial Using Cutout Animation

AD insights

Animation: It Stands Out on TV, and It Really Sells

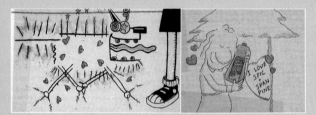

Animation is used to sell everything from eggs to cat food to mental services. Its major strength is its ability to draw strong emotions in people, ranging from fear to elation. In addition, it gives the advertiser control—animated characters don't get arrested or involved in controversial activities.

The style of animation used in a commercial depends on the client, the product, the message, and the concept. Some of the most popular animated techniques are mixing live action with animation, the Blechman loose-line, and the Disney style. The average animated spot costs $15–25,000 to produce, although costs vary due to a number of factors, including style and animation technique, whether live action is used, and the number of characters.

Source: Cyndee Miller, "Agencies Agog about Animation: Its Trendy, Stands Out on TV, and It Really Sells," *Marketing News,* 24:16 (August 6, 1990): 1–2.

Stop Motion

An ingenious technique, **stop motion,** can make products appear to walk, march, dance, sing, and do tricks. The product or trade characters are set up and photographed for the first frame of the film, then moved to the next position, photographed again, and so on. When projected, 24 successive photographs give the illusion of movement of one-second duration.

An advanced form of stop action is claymation. This technique made possible the now famous series of commercials featuring the California Raisins and that pizza villain, "The Noid" (see Figure 14.13).

An award-winning British commercial featuring claymation is shown in Figure 14.14.

Photo Animation

This low-budget technique can be quite effective. Its success depends on the ingenuity of the script writer in creating clever and interesting tricks with still photos of the products, packages, bottles, trademarks, and the like, that will present the ideas effectively.

Use of Stop-Action Technique in a TV Commercial

Creating Effective Television Commercials

As the cost of creating and producing television commercials escalates, advertisers and agencies find it expedient to spend millions of dollars to find out what works in television, what does not, and why. A useful list of ten ways to create more effective TV commercials is given in Figure 14.15. The balance of this section offers guidelines that have emerged from television research.

Visualize the Message

As earlier discussed, television is a visual medium, and many of its most successful writers have experience in motion pictures. A prime example of excellent visualization is the famous "Manhattan Landing" commercial for British Airways. Though 90 seconds long, this commercial was almost entirely visual, with only 40 words of copy. Another example of powerful visualization is Nike commercials, most of which feature strong visuals and interesting sound effects.

Speaking at an annual Advertising Age Creative Workshop, Burton Manning, a seasoned advertising executive, said that consumers "can be persuaded primarily through the visual sense with incredible effectiveness. They want to see intensity of movement and action and can grasp images with astonishing speed."[9] Even so, 15-second commercials put increasing pressure on the creative side of TV advertising. Findings about 15-second spots and guidelines for their creation are presented in the Ad Insight entitled "Update: The 15-Second Commercial."

Demonstrate If Possible

Both ASI Research and a series of studies conducted for Ogilvy & Mather mentioned demonstration as one of the qualities of high-scoring commercials. As ASI pointed out, demonstration can be done even when the product is somewhat dull. For example, Pine Sol cleaner, starting in sixth place in a highly competitive field, ran a series of "graffiti" commercials showing the product at work, making things "more than just clean." Pine Sol cleaned not just a dirty floor but D-I-R-T spelled out on

FIGURE 14.14

An Award-Winning British Commercial Featuring Claymation

Two spots for a British electric utility group in which animated 3-D tortoise and parrots extol the qualities of electric heat.

UpDate: The 15-Second Commercial: Findings and Guidelines

Summary of Findings

- Today, 15's constitute nearly two-fifths of commercials on the air. They are certainly a major presence in the medium—they have arrived.
- Five years since their inception, it's clear that 15's are here to stay, and that they are working. They are capturing attention, delivering essential communication, and persuading.
- The trend is now to create original 15's to a much greater extent than abridgements of existing 30's.
- It is, however, difficult to produce an outstanding 15″. The rate of failure for 15's is higher than for 30 second commercials.
- While fewer lifts are being produced, it is also true that fewer lifts are being copy-tested. This is based on the erroneous assumption that a good 30″ breeds a good 15″. We have no evidence to suggest that this is true and, in fact, more evidence to suggest that the rate of failure for lifts is greater than the rate of failure of independent 15's.
- The 15″ length is only minimally used to launch new products—wisely, because new products require more exposition, explanation, and pizazz to make them stand out (most new products are neither original nor unique).
- There is good reason to suspect an environmental effect, and questions still abound about how much crowding consumers will accept. There continues to be reason to suspect that adding more commercials yields an increase in negative attitudes towards programming and the medium.

GUIDELINES FOR BETTER 15-SECOND COMMERCIALS

Streamline

A 15″ has room for only one core claim or benefit—only very essential communication should be present.

Source: McCollum/Spielman, *Topline* 31, August 1989, 4.

Accentuate the Visual

The shorter length is a clear opportunity to visualize in a central, dominant image. A visual medium is especially good for demonstrable attributes and benefits: taste, beauty shots, packaging advantages.

Product Appropriateness

15's work best when the product is relatively simple, unique and easy to convey in one "punch."

Be Bold

Bold creative signatures in terms of visuals, slogans, theme music, or the big idea are needed to fight the crowd and stand out.

Explore Synergy

Many advertisers are now exploring, and there is evidence that this is working well, the use of 15's and 30's in a campaign. The campaign will begin, and establish itself, with 30's—then 15's take over with greater frequency as reminders. They support one another.

New Uses

Other intelligent uses that we're seeing are to "preview" longer commercials as supplemental advertising and the use of 15's in special promotions and pricing "specials"—especially with more local advertisers with limited ad budgets. Obviously, this has been a boon to local advertisers with limited budgets. There's no doubt that the 15″ works!

Pairs in the Pod

When advertisers use a 15/15 pod to advertise two products, compatibility is important. Two distinctly different products that go together (fragrance and eye make-up) do it better than two very similar products (shampoo and conditioner) that can become confused.

---

a white floor. It disinfected by wiping out G-E-R-M-S spelled out on a tile wall. The demonstrations helped Pine Sol climb to first place in the industry.

FIGURE 14.15

Ten Ways to Create More Effective TV Commercials

1. Let the picture tell the story. TV is a visual medium.
2. Look for that one frame—the "key visual"—that sums up the intended message.
3. Grab the viewer's attention in the first five seconds. Attention to TV commercials does not build.
4. Avoid making the viewer do a lot of mental work. The message must be uncomplicated and single-minded.
5. Use visuals and words to register the brand in the viewer's mind. Viewers often remember commercials, but not brands.
6. Have a "moment of affirmation"—show that the product has a payoff.
7. Show people, not objects. Viewers are interested in objects in relation to users and uses.
8. Reflect the personality or image of the brand.
9. Be specific and avoid talky scripts. Every word must work.
10. Think of building campaigns, not individual commercials. Successful commercials communicate with main selling points, with slight variations in execution.

Source: Copyright © 1976 by St. Martin's Press, Inc. Adapted from *How to Advertise* by Kenneth Roman and Jane Maas, pp. 14–19. Adapted by permission of St. Martin's Press, Incorporated.

Simplify

To simplify in television is always wise. The viewer, after all, is often not paying close attention to the commercial—to the backgrounds, the scenes, or to the dialogue. In general, television is less tolerant of complex wording than are print media. The simple declarative sentence is usually preferable to the rhetorical one, and often a sentence fragment or a simple, everyday word will make the meaning perfectly clear. In the interest of simplicity, every element not relevant to the objective should be dropped.

Use Action Where Possible

The eye can comprehend very quickly and it can easily drift away. However, motion on the screen makes it difficult for the viewer to leave the commercial. Commercials should be structured to grab the reviewer's attention in the first few seconds of exposure and to build on that attention until the final call to action. Action helps to make the viewer say: "What's going on here? I think I'll stay tuned to find out!"

Use Entertainment to Communicate

Entertainment in a commercial always should be a means to an end—not an end itself. If used well, television can entertain people and persuade them at the same time. As a popular text on advertising writing points out, "there is always excitement in every television venture because it is, after all, advertising and show business combined." [10]

Some writers recommend the use of music in television commercials to enhance the entertainment appeal when the promise of reward is a simple one and the appeal is emotional. However, a comprehensive series of experiments has revealed a difference in effectiveness according to whether the product was a high- or low-involvement one.[11] In the case of high-involvement products (automobiles, electronics), behavioral intention was higher when there was no music in the commercial. In the case of low-involvement products (toilet paper, chewing gum), the commercial with music was more effective than the no-music commercial.

Humor is a favorite technique of writers hoping to entertain viewers. Used well it can be very effective in gaining awareness, particularly if the humor is related to the product and not simply thrown in for attention-getting purposes. Humor is less effective in gaining recall, comprehension, source credibility, and persuasion, and can be especially dangerous as a technique when the product or service is sensitive or controversial.[12] Guidelines for the effective use of humor and other entertainment techniques are provided in Figure 14.16. Additional points on the use of humor are described in the Ad Insight entitled "McCollum/Spielman on Humor in Commercials."

Adapt Commercial to Program and Audience

Programs and stations set the mood for commercials. The audience listening to Jay Leno is receptive to the commercial he delivers during break. These same commercials would not be as appropriate during *Meet the Nation* or *Crossfire*. Commercials should be compatible with the program, but different enough so that they register as the advertiser's message.

With the growth of cable television, low-power stations, independent stations, and public television, audiences are becoming more selective in what they watch. Television is moving toward **narrowcasting**. This means that writers can know their audiences better and can write commercials aimed at more specific interests and desires. They can depend less on broad, sometimes irrelevant attention-getting gimmicks. This selectivity will force writers to provide more information and more specific benefits from advertised products.

Make Commercials Believable

Writers are faced with the problem of making commercials both interesting and believable. Sometimes this is very tricky because facts must be presented but not

---

FIGURE 14.16

Some Tips on Entertainment in TV Commercials

The sales message of a TV commercial can be overwhelmed by entertainment values. Restraint is necessary when writing TV commercials:

1. Use humor when it contributes to the sales message. Viewers remember funny incidents, but often forget the advertised object.
2. Use sex to sell "sexually relevant" products. Sex may attract attention, but it will not hold attention for "sexually irrelevant" products.
3. Use music when it reinforces the sales message.
4. Use emotion to involve the viewer in the advertising story. Don't bore the viewer.
5. Use special effects to drive home the sales message. Don't use them for the sake of the special effects themselves.

Source: Copyright © 1976 by St. Martin's Press, Inc. Adapted from *How to Advertise* by Kenneth Roman and Jane Maas, pp. 25–27. Adapted by permission of St. Martin's Press, Incorporated.

McCollum/Spielman on Humor in Commercials

Having reviewed the field of humor, here are a few guidelines which we offer to make the most effective use of this most talked-about device:

- Determine if your product is compatible with a humorous treatment.
- Keep the humor relevant and related to the message and product.
- The more subtle and true-to-life devices appear more effective because they allow the consumer to laugh *with* the commercial characters and situations, not *at* them.
- Parody or spoof also seems effective because it borrows interest from an object that is already well-liked, and familiarity with the object of spoof means that less time is needed for setup.
- Light-spirited music and jingles often heighten the impact of humor.
- Whimsy and animation have the advantage of charm, much freedom for creative experimentation, and often a long life.

In studying this field we also uncovered some pratfalls to avoid:

- It is generally inadvisable to use humor to launch new products.
- Funny children and animals should be used with care to prevent them from upstaging the product. Children should be screened for intelligibility, and should not appear too sophisticated.
- Broadly drawn, exaggerated humor in slapstick and humorous characters can be risky. In these types of executions production values can be overwhelming, and consumer identification can be inhibited. Additionally, it should be remembered that not everybody appreciates broad humor.

In sum, humor can be a very effective device for getting attention and generating good feelings towards the product that transfer to buying interest. However, as with any other advertising device, humor should be used purposefully so that all elements of the commercial contribute towards enhancing the product's sales values.

Source: McCollum/Spielman, *Topline* 17, 6.

in a manner that will bore the viewer. As noted in the Ad Insight entitled "Consumers' Love–Hate Relationship with Commercials" people's opinion about commercials vary by product and these can significantly influence their reactions to TV spots.

As odd as it sounds, sometimes the sales presentation can be "twisted" in such a way that a TV commercial becomes even more believable. A good example of using an unbelievable spokesperson to communicate the beneficial features of a product was Isuzu's "Trust Me" campaign featuring "Joe Isuzu." We knew Joe Isuzu was lying, but the product is represented in a credible manner through disclaimer subtitles and negative consequences to Joe's actions. Figure 14.17 is an example of a TV commercial that effectively builds product believability.

Use of Color

Now that virtually all television commercials are in color, most writers of television continuity must learn how to merge the elements with which they work to make the proper impression on the audience. For example, the creator must work with sets of various colors in a given series of frames and with actors moving about in colored costumes. The product may not look the same to viewers in their homes as it does to the producer in the studio.

Consumers' Love-Hate Relationship with Commercials

Results of a recent national poll showed that 91 percent of consumers enjoy at least some advertising. The commercials that Americans like most are for pet food, electronics, soft drinks, cars, packaged foods, toys, fast food, and snack food. However, the respondents surveyed felt that only commercials for electronics, packaged foods, and toys provided them with new ideas or facts to help them distinguish between brands and make purchases.

While respondents found soft drink advertising very enjoyable, they also thought it excessive, over-produced, and over-burdened by celebrities. Snack food spots were considered insufficiently entertaining, as well as uninformative. Most felt that there are too many car spots on the air that, although nice to look at, fail to provide the information that consumers need.

The affective response to advertising for the remaining categories—cosmetics, toothpaste, cereal, shampoo, skin care, household cleaner, communications and insurance—ranged from mild irritation to indignation. Nonetheless, commercials in two categories that enjoyed little affection, toothpaste and household cleaner, earned high ratings for providing useful information.

Source: McCollum/Spielman, *Topline* 36, 1.

Using color effectively is fairly easy when the product itself has strong visual appeal—for example, automobiles, foods, and fashions. A good example is the Dockers commercial in Figure 14.18. If it is skillfully integrated, color can also be used effectively to add realism to a story. As in the print media, color in television is often used for package identification and to create a certain mood for the commercial. For example, reds are warm colors and tend to be exciting; blues are cool and

FIGURE 14.17

Good Example of a TV Commercial That Effectively Uses Humor to Build Product Believability

The Nissan Sentra SE-R

FIGURE 14.18

A TV Commercial Using the Communicative Power of Color
Dockers' great background music and snappy copy are a good fit.

quieting. The danger exists, however, that the symbolic use of color will become a television cliché and will lose its power to communicate. Two other dangers in using color in television are:

1. Using too much color, changing scenes frequently, and getting a jumpy effect.
2. Making the presenter or his or her outfit so colorful that the product is lost.

Also, because some consumers see the commercial in black and white, sharp contrasts and subtle differences should be avoided, because these will be lost on the black-and-white screen.

Summary

General communication principles apply to both the print and the electronic media. However, television and radio are different from the print media in that they are time oriented, somewhat simpler in structure, emphasize showmanship and entertainment more, are more personal, achieve a high degree of recollection for simple ideas, and have a less attentive audience.

The main types of radio commercials are singing, narrative, straight, personality, and donut. For commercials, modern radio tends to be a spot announcement medium. Effective commercials are distinguished from ineffective ones in the following ways: most sound quite conversational (unless they are singing jingles), use short words and sentences, spell out product names, indicate the visual when needed, use a lot of repetition, use sound creatively, and are gauged to how people listen.

Certain distinguishable types of television commercials and certain principles of effective television writing have emerged. The common types of commercials are straight announcement, demonstration, testimonial/celebrity, dramatization, and dialogue. If we classify them by production technique, the main ones are live action, cartoon, stop motion, and photo animation.

Effective commercials capitalize strongly on visual impact; they demonstrate; they simplify the message; they use entertainment as a device rather than an end in itself; they fit the mood of the program; and, above all, they are believable.

Because most of today's television commercials are in color, creative people have to learn how to use color effectively to communicate. This may be easy in the case of products or services with strong visual appeal, but not so easy when color must be used to create a certain psychological mood.

1. How does time orientation influence the content of radio and television commercials?
2. What purpose does a jingle serve? How do you account for its continued popularity?
3. What are the principle types of television commercials? Find an example of each on a local television station and appraise its effectiveness.
4. What are the major communication advantages of radio and TV commercials?
5. For which types of products is the demonstration commercial most appropriate? The cartoon commercial?
6. Why do some writers avoid humor in radio and television commercials?

[1] Kenneth Roman and Jane Maas, *How to Advertise* (New York: St. Martin's Press, 1976), 15.

[2] Jacob Jacoby, Wayne D. Hoyer, and David A. Sheluga, *The Miscomprehension of Televised Communication* (New York: American Association of Advertising Agencies, 1980), 17.

[3] Sandra E. Moriarty, *Creative Advertising*, 2d ed. (Englewood Cliffs, NJ: Prentice-Hall, 1991), 280–286.

[4] Ibid., 283.

[5] William B. Taylor, "We Know Them Now, American Express," *Advertising Age,* August 24, 1984, 34.

[6] "Starpower: Will the Force Be With You?" *Topline,* newsletter published by McCollum/Spielman, August 1980, 8.

[7] Allan Greenberg and Charles Suttoni, "Television Commercial Wear-out," *Journal of Advertising Research* 13 (October 1973): 47.

[8] David Ogilvy and Joel Raphaelson, "Research on Television Techniques That Work—and Don't Work," *Harvard Business Review* 60 (July–August 1982): 16.

[9] Gay Jervey, "Nestlé Bar Sells with a Passion," *Advertising Age,* November 12, 1984, 2, 113.

[10] Keith Hafer and Gordon E. White, *Advertising Writing,* 3d ed. (St. Paul, MN: West, 1989), 124.

[11] C. Whan Park and S. Mark Young, *The Effects of Involvement and Executional Factors of a Television Commercial on Brand Attitude Formation* (Cambridge, MA: Marketing Science Institute, 1984), 23–32.

[12] Thomas J. Madden and Marc G. Weinberger, "Humor in Advertising: A Practitioner's View," *Journal of Advertising Research* 24 (August/September 1984): 23–29.

Albright, Jim. *Creating The Advertising Message.* Mountain View, CA: Mayfield Publishing Company, 1992

Arlen, Michael J. *Thirty Seconds.* New York: Penguin Books, 1980.

Baldwin, Huntley. *How Television Commercials Are Made.* Chicago: Crain Books, 1981.

Hafer, W. Keith, and Gordon E. White. *Advertising Writing,* 3d ed. St. Paul, MN: West, 1989.

Hall, Jim. *Mighty Minutes: An Illustrated History of Television's Best Commercials.* Chicago: Crain Books, 1983.

Jewler, A. Jerome. *Creative Strategy in Advertising,* 4th ed. Belmont, CA: Wadsworth, Inc., 1992.

Moriarty, Sandra E. *Creative Advertising: Theory and Practice,* 2d ed. Englewood Cliffs, NJ: Prentice-Hall, 1991.

Roman, Kenneth, and Jane Maas. *How to Advertise.* New York: St. Martin's Press, 1976.

Steward, David W., and David H. Furse. *Effective Television Advertising.* Lexington, MA: Lexington Books, 1986.

Ziegler, Sherilyn K., and Herbert H. Howard. *Broadcast Advertising,* 2d ed. Columbus, OH: Grid, 1984.

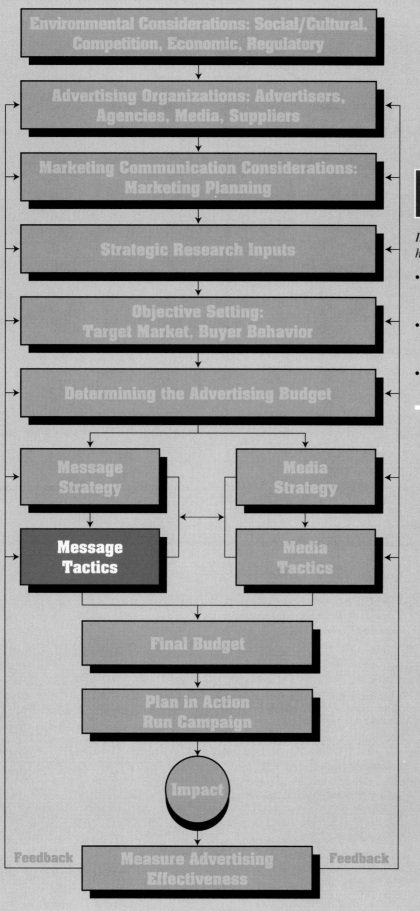

Chapter **15**

Message Production

CHAPTER TOPICS

DECISION MAKING IN ADVERTISING
   PRODUCTION
     The Creation and Production Processes
PRODUCING MESSAGES FOR THE PRINT MEDIA
     Using Technology to Create the Message
     Selecting the Type
     Specifying Type
     Reproducing the Illustrations
     Printing the Advertisement
     Duplicating the Advertisement
PRODUCING MESSAGES FOR THE ELECTRONIC
   MEDIA

PRODUCING THE TELEVISION COMMERCIAL
     Film or Videotape
     Choosing Cast and Set
     Using Modern Technology
     Editing the Commercial
     Duplicating the Original
     Control over Quality and Cost
PRODUCING THE RADIO COMMERCIAL
     Live versus Recording
     Duplicating the Original

After the ads and commercials have been created and approved, they must be produced for placement in the media. This chapter covers the major decisions involved in the production of print, television, and radio advertising.

The introduction of computers, along with other technological advances, has made decision making much more complex than a couple of decades ago when type was set by hand, TV commercials were shot without computer-assisted enhancements, and radio spots were recorded without sophisticated mixing equipment. The more you know about mechanical and technical processes—such as typesetting, printing, videotaping, recording, and computer technology—the more appreciation you will have of the ads and commercials which you encounter.

Decision Making in Advertising Production

The vocabulary used in advertising production often seems like a foreign language to those unfamiliar with this high-tech world. Terms like halftone, photon, and digital stripping are examples. The temptation for some advertising executives is to leave the decision making to specialists in the production field. However, many think this is a serious mistake and that brand managers, account executives, copywriters, and art directors should all understand the basics of the production process. Spiraling costs make it important to understand the production process. Such knowledge will keep costs in line with original cost estimates, and will help bring in the finished ads and commercials on schedule.

Advertising executives must realize that production should be viewed in two ways. First, production must be seen as providing a frame through which the reader, viewer, or listener receives the message. The less obvious the frame, the more visible the message will be. Second, production must be seen as a stage, dramatically lighted and interestingly furnished, on which the creator's ideas are played out. Production specialists, regardless of the medium in which they are working, usually try to fuse the two. They try to make the message interesting to look at, easy to read and understand, pleasant to hear, and most of all, convincing. A primary objective of all involved in the creation of advertising is *not to let production techniques overpower the advertising message.*

The Creation and Production Processes

Ad creation and production are distinct yet interrelated parts of the creative process in advertising. Figure 15.1 presents a descriptive model of the creative process, depicting creation and production as separate stages. The two stages should be distinguished from one another because:

1. Activities associated with the creation of ads and commercials typically take place within the ad agency. Whether creating a print ad, a TV spot, or a radio commercial, the creative decisions are the same.

FIGURE 15.1

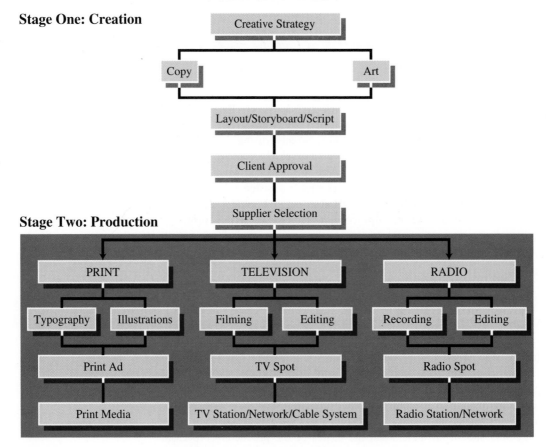

**A Model of the Two Stages of Advertising Creativity:
Creation and Production**

Source: Adapted from David A. Aaker, Rajeev Batra, and John G. Myers, *Advertising Management*, 4th ed. (Englewood Cliffs, NJ: Prentice-Hall, 1992), 441.

2. Activities associated with the production of created ads and commercials are typically performed by suppliers outside of the agency. Production activities tend to differ by medium.[1]

Note the word *typically*. Some agencies have in-house production facilities and do not always go outside for production services. An ad for an infomercial producer is shown in Figure 15.2. The ad ran in trade publications read by advertising professionals.

Producing Messages for the Print Media

One of the most rapidly developing aspects of advertising production concerns printed messages. Advertising agencies and design companies are creating more advertisements via desktop computers, thus forcing changes in the production process. The field is now a combination of both traditional and computerized production methods. However, some experts predict that in the near future virtually all print production will be computerized.[2]

Technology offers new and exciting ways of expanding their creative abilities. Scanners and computers offer artists and photographers new tools for creating pictures, logotypes, graphs, charts, and print layouts (Figure 15.3). The artist may look at the computer screen as a palette that can be modified instantly to try more variations. Computer software offers a variety of illustration and color options. Pictures, words, data, and other formats can be produced as a paper copy, sent on-line to the typesetter or sent directly to the publication in which the advertisement is to be placed.

Using Technology to Create the Message

FIGURE 15.2

An Ad for an Infomercial Producer That Ran in Advertising Trade Publications

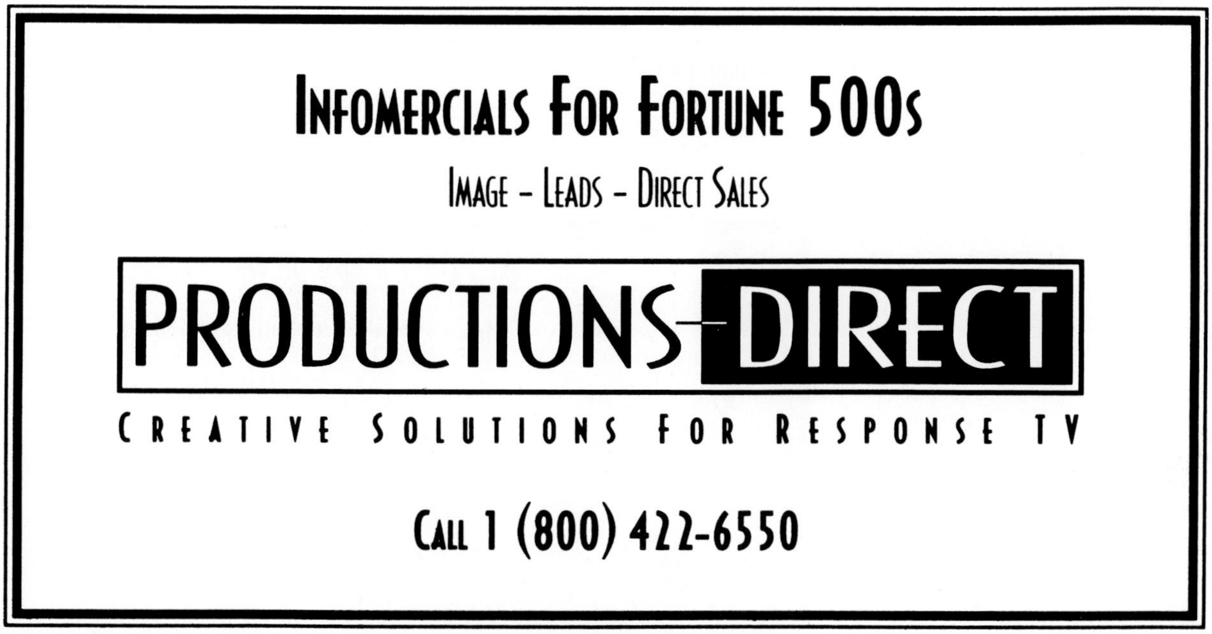

INFOMERCIALS FOR FORTUNE 500s

IMAGE – LEADS – DIRECT SALES

PRODUCTIONS DIRECT

CREATIVE SOLUTIONS FOR RESPONSE TV

CALL 1 (800) 422-6550

Graphics Software for the Personal Computer

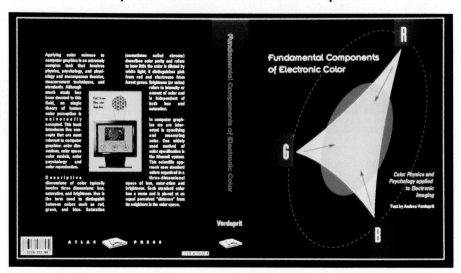

Source: This illustration was produced using the Adobe Illustrator 88™ software program. © 1990–1992 Adobe Systems, Incorporated. Design and illustration by John Ritter.

Selecting the Type

Typography is the ground upon which the advertisement is built. The correct typeface will help establish the mood and tone of the message. Noted designer and typographer Jonathan Hoefler points out the importance of typography in setting a tone and base for written material:

> Typography is to writing what a soundtrack is to a motion picture: supportive, sometimes invisible, never intrusive.[3]

Categories of Type

Dozens of typefaces are in common use today. Many are hundreds of years old, while some may have been recently introduced. The study of type and the successful use of it is a technique requiring specialization. Type is grouped into categories, according to some basic characteristics. The following are three of the major categories.

Roman letters contain heavy stemmed or light strokes with serifs, which are small hairlines at the end of each stroke (see Figure 15.4). Its subclassifications include Old Style, Traditional, Modern, and Egyptian.

FIGURE 15.4

Examples of Three Different Typeface Categories

Roman (Serif)	Sans Serif	Script
Roman	**Gothic**	*Script*
Roman	**Gothic**	Script
Roman	Gothic	Script
Roman	**Gothic**	Script
Roman	Gothic	Script

San Serifs are faces with strokes of even thickness without serifs. Faces in this group provide a clean, streamlined look, with uniform weight to each stroke of the letters. Futura, Helvetica, and Gothic are some of the major subclassifications.

Script (or cursive) faces appear linked together, giving the impression of handwriting. Script faces are difficult to read in large blocks and are used principally to convey an impression of exclusiveness.

Variations of an individual category comprise a family of type, which may include regular, condensed, extended, italic, bold, and other forms. Families of type are divided into **series**, and the series are divided into **fonts**. Fonts represent the size of the type. For example, Modern Roman is a category. Bodoni is a family in that category, Ultra Bodoni is a series within that family (a fat letter with an unusual stroke), and 24-point Ultra Bodoni would be a font in that series.[4]

It is necessary to identify type by face, size, and variation within the typeface. Type is measured on a **point** system. There are 72 points to an inch. Most typefaces are available in sizes ranging from 8 points to 72 points, which refers to the height of the letters. The widths of letters are not used in measuring type sizes because each typeface is designed differently.

Variations occur in the heights of various letters of the alphabet, of course. The type size is measured to include the ascending letters (b, d, f, h, k, l, t) and the descending letters (g, j, p, q, y). It also includes a small amount of space so that descenders in one line will not touch ascenders in the next line.

The width of lines of type is measured in **picas**. There are 6 picas to an inch. The text of this book is set on 28 picas. The typeface is Times. The configuration "10/12" indicates that the type size is 10 points with 12 points of leading. **Leading** is extra space between lines. Most printed material has some leading, because it improves readability. However, type can be set solid, that is, with no extra space between the lines.

An **agate line** is the standard unit of measuring space in most publications. Fourteen agate lines equal one column inch, regardless of whether there is type in the space.

One further dimension that distinguishes typeset copy is **justification**, which is the forced alignment of the column edges. Lines do not usually end neatly; therefore, a system is needed to make sure each line ends at the same point. Extra space that follows the last word is redistributed equally back through all of the spaces between words. As a result, the spacing between words is not uniform from line to line.

Specifying Type

Guidelines for Proper Use of Type

With practice, almost anyone can learn to distinguish an appropriate typeface from an inappropriate one and a readable face from one that is not. Here are three general guidelines:

Legibility Certain typefaces, such as Roman, tend to be more legible than others, but any one can be misused.

Appropriateness The typeface will influence the mood and objective of the advertisement. Appropriateness stems from the design of the typeface and the way it is used. A soft delicate typeface is a good choice for flowers, while a bold typeface is a good choice for machinery.

Harmony A sense of harmony should be achieved between the type and the other elements of the advertisement: the message to be conveyed, the layout, and the illustrations. For example, if the layout is tall, the type should have prevailingly perpendicular lines.

The Ad Insight entitled "Some Tips on Type" discusses some of the basics in using type.

Some Tips on Type

"In typography, there are no rules,"[1] because typography is considered to be an art. Instead of rules there are conventions that many typesetters have decided to adopt. The following are some tips:

- Solid lines of captital letters or italics are difficult to read, but both can be used effectively for emphasis.
- The background has a decided influence on legibility. Black type on a white background is much more legible, for example, than the same type on a dark background.
- Leading between lines of types generally increases legibility.
- Short paragraphs and sentences are more readable than long ones
- Use serif type for running text. Most Americans find it easier to read.

- Sizes smaller than 8 point and larger than 12 point ordinarily are not good for body text.
- Lines should not be too long or too short. About 40 characters per line is advisable.
- Spacing between words should be monitored. Words should not be isolated by white space nor placed too close together.
- Readability is improved by allowing greater space between paragraphs than between lines within the paragraph.

[1]Kathleen Tinkel, "Typographic 'Rules,'" *Aldus Magazine,* March-April 1992, 32.

Source: Many of these items are also taken from Larry Percy, "A Review of Effect of Specific Advertising Elements upon Overall Communication Response," in *Current Issues & Research in Advertising,* eds. James H. Leigh and Claude R. Martin, Jr. (Ann Arbor: University of Michigan, 1983), 97–98.

Typesetting

Printers call the setting of type *composing* and the type itself *composition.* There are several methods of setting type, ranging from frequently used computer-based electronic photosetting to infrequently used hand composition.

Computer phototypesetting prints out a **slick** on photographic paper or a film negative. It is the most common method of typesetting for newspapers and magazines. The slick, or negative, is then used to electronically etch a metal plate that is used on an offset press for printing. Rapid changes in desktop publishing—driven by the upsurge in use of personal computers—have created faster and more accurate electronic typesetting. In some cases, advertising agencies have been setting their own type rather than sending it to specialized production houses.[5] When this is done, the advertisement goes directly to the publisher.

Reproducing the Illustrations

Line art and halftones are the two major categories of art. **Line art** refers to images that are solid black lines on a white page. Pen-and-ink drawings and other illustrations composed of lines without shading are reproduced. The lower production cost of line art makes it ideal for retail advertisers. Figure 15.5 shows an example of line-art illustrations.

Photographs that require many degrees of shading are typically reproduced as **halftone.** The entire surface of the halftone is broken up by a series of minute dots. The size of each dot determines the amount of ink it will carry, and therefore the shade of gray that it will give to the paper. The dots are put on the negative by photographing the artwork through what is known as a halftone screen—a screen

FIGURE 15.5

An Example of a Line Art Illustration

placed in the camera between the lens and negative holder. When the image on the negative is printed on sensitized metal, the pattern of dots becomes part of the picture. During the etching process, the acid eats away the metal between the dots, leaving them standing as tiny blunt cones that are the only parts of the halftone that print. Small dots produce a gray effect; larger ones (with less white space surrounding) produce a much darker effect.

A halftone is identified by its screen. For example, a 50-screen halftone has 50 dots per linear inch; a 133-screen halftone has 133 dots per inch. The more dots per inch, the better the paper needed to print the halftone and the sharper the reproduction will be. Newspapers are printed at extremely high speeds, and newsprint has a comparatively poor printing surface. Consequently, screens used for printing on newsprint or other rough-surfaced papers are usually 65 lines per inch. A typical magazine press runs at about half the speed of the newspaper press and uses much finer screens, which can run from 90 to 200 lines per inch.

Color Reproduction

Printing has the ability to reproduce with fidelity all the colors that an artist can mix or a camera can see through its lens. This is accomplished by using only four colors of ink—the three primary colors (red, blue, and yellow) and black.

The work to be reproduced is photographed through filters that shut out all except the color desired. Thus, four halftone negatives are required to make a set of four-color plates: one for yellow, one for red, one for blue, and one for black. When these filters are used, all degrees of one color are collected on each negative. These values are transferred to each plate when the negative is printed (in reverse) on the sensitized metal. The black plate is known as the general plate and is used for depth of color and as an aid to the photoengraver in approaching the true color values of the original artwork.

The negatives are developed, stripped, printed on metal, etched, and finished in much the same way that halftones are, but they require considerably more time for "staging in" and reetching by the color finisher to achieve true color reproduction on the color proofs.

The engraver returns a complete set of color proofs plus a set called progressives. There are usually seven proofs in a set of progressives: (1) the yellow plate; (2) the red plate; (3) the yellow and red plates printed together; (4) the blue plate; (5) the red, yellow, and blue plates printed together; (6) the black plate; and (7) the yellow, red, blue, and black plates printed together. These proofs show printing values and the progression in which the various plates are printed.

Computerization has made color processing much faster. Advertisements designed and created on the computer, go directly to film. There is a growing trend toward computerized color. A special photo retouching technique called digital processing is described in the Ad Insight entitled "Digital Stripping Creates Special Photos for Budweiser."

*P*rinting the *Advertisement*

If the advertisement is scheduled for final printing in a newspaper or magazine, it will be reproduced by the same process as the newspaper or magazine. In such cases the production experts will make sure that the ad is adapted to the process of the medium. It may be reproduced by any of the four basic methods of printing.

Letterpress

In **letterpress**, or relief printing, the printing surface is raised above the rest of the surface, inked, and then pressed onto the paper to print. A rubber stamp works on this principle. This is the oldest form of printing and is seldom used. By the 1970s, most major printers had moved away from this method.

Offset Lithography

Most newspapers and magazines use **offset** printing, whereby a camera-ready original is photographically transferred onto an aluminum plate. There is one plate for each color. This smooth plate is attached to a cylinder that, as it revolves, comes in contact with a roller that dampens the blank areas of the plate, thus dampening the nonprinting areas. The design, which is covered with a chemical that repels water, and the ink, being oily, will not adhere to a damp surface, but will to the dry surface. As a result, when the inked printing surface comes in contact with paper, the image is transferred.

The printing surface in lithography is practically smooth; it has no ridges or depressions. **Flexography** is a similar process. However, it uses a water-based ink and there is a different press setup. It also uses a rubber blanket that makes it suitable for packaging.

Gravure

The opposite of the letterpress method is **gravure.** As Figure 15.6 indicates, the printing surface is depressed instead of raised. The ink lies between the raised surfaces rather than on top of them. The design is etched into the plate below the general level of the metal. The surface of the plate is inked and then wiped clean, leaving ink only in the depressions. When printing takes place, the hollows below the surface give up their ink and transfer the design to the paper. Because there is no wear on the surface, gravure works well for long runs and photographic reproduction. The principal advantage of gravure is the excellent reproduction of illustrations. Quality printing for magazines and many advertising inserts use this technique.

Screen Print or Serigraphy

One of the oldest and simplest methods of reproducing material is **screen printing** or serigraphy. A semiliquid ink or pigment is pressed through a fine mesh screen

Digital Stripping Creates Special Photos for Budweiser

Using a computer technique called digital stripping, Budweiser created a series of ads portraying such illusions as white-water rafters swirling through malty foam.

The technique combines color photography and electronic retouching. Transparencies and a detailed blueprint of the layout are sent to a firm specializing in digital stripping. The pieces are entered into a computer and combined into one image. Various elements are repositioned, enhanced, duplicated, or eliminated to create the finished piece. The key to the realism is the degree of refinement in all elements, from the lighting, staging, and photography to the digital retouching.

for a given design on a surface. Ordinarily, one stencil is used for each color. Serigraphy can be used on any surface—wood, paper, glass, metal, plastic, fabric—in any shape or design, of any thickness, and in any size. It is frequently used for small runs of display ads, outdoor posters, decals, banners, point-of-sale material and T-shirts. High-speed machinery recently has made screening practical for some long-run work.

FIGURE 15.6

Basic Printing Methods

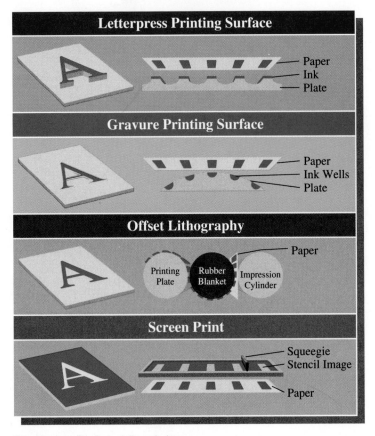

Source: Graphic Arts Technical Foundation.

Duplicating the
Advertisement

Because advertisements run in multiple publications, there needs to be a method that allows for a quality copy to be sent to each publication on the schedule. For offset printing a **proof** or "slick" is sent. These are either photoprints or photostats, which are less expensive, or veloxes, which are higher quality and more expensive. When color is used an overlay color-key is sent indicating the various colors. Also, a separate piece of film is sent for each color.

For letterpress, one of the most widely used and cheapest forms of duplication is the **matrix,** or **mat**. It is made from layers of soft paper or similar materials. When dampened, it is forced under great pressure into the interstices of the type, line plates, or halftones that make up the advertisement. When the mat is removed from the form, it duplicates the whole advertisement by preserving the raised portion of type and engravings as depressions on its surface. In addition to sending a mat the agency sends a proof to show what the advertisement is to look like. For gravure, film positives are sent to the publications.

Producing Messages for the Electronic Media

Producing advertising commercials for the electronic media is a a three-step process:

1. Preproduction—activities prior to the actual production of the commercial.

FIGURE 15.7

Three Phases of Production for Electronic Media

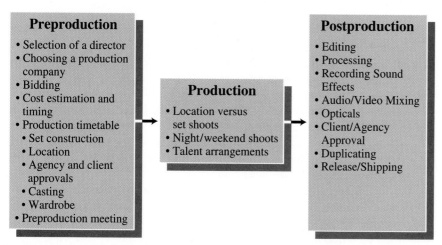

Preproduction
- Selection of a director
- Choosing a production company
- Bidding
- Cost estimation and timing
- Production timetable
- Set construction
- Location
- Agency and client approvals
- Casting
- Wardrobe
- Preproduction meeting

Production
- Location versus set shoots
- Night/weekend shoots
- Talent arrangements

Postproduction
- Editing
- Processing
- Recording Sound Effects
- Audio/Video Mixing
- Opticals
- Client/Agency Approval
- Duplicating
- Release/Shipping

Source: Adapted from *What Every Account Representative Should Know about Television Commercial Production*, 1989. Adapted by permission of the American Association of Advertising Agencies, Inc.

2. Production—the period during which the commercial is actually recorded and/or shot.
3. Postproduction—activities after the commercial has been produced.

The phases of the commercial production process and some of the activities included in each production phase are outlined in Figure 15.7

The production of a commercial is a joint project. When a commercial is produced in-house, agency people—account executives, copywriters, producers—and client representatives work together to complete the project. When a production house is brought in on a project, agency and client people work with outside production specialists. In either situation, the person most involved in the process is called the producer. A good producer must (1) know every production phase and technique, (2) have an eye for artistic detail, (3) understand and appreciate budgetary restraints, and (4) be a "handholder" and a diplomat.[6]

The remainder of this chapter will focus on the production of the two most utilized forms of electronically conveyed advertising—television and radio commercials. However, much of the discussion is relevant to any form of electronic advertising in which audiovisual elements are involved: videocassettes, videotext, satellite transmissions, or theater commercials.

Producing the Television Commercial

In earlier chapters we examined the process by which the television commercial is created and carried to the storyboard stage. The storyboard is the rough equivalent of the print layout in that it is created to serve as a guide for the production of the TV commercial. However, before a storyboard can be transformed into a finished commercial, the preproduction and postproduction decisions outlined in Figure 15.7 must be addressed. Among the more important questions are:

Should the TV commerical be recorded on film or videotape?
What cast and set props will be necessary?

Can recent production technology be used to enhance the final effect?

What editing is necessary?

What control over production quality and cost is to be exercised?

Film or Videotape

Most TV commercials are produced and sent to the medium on film or videotape. Few are delivered live, even at the local level. One obvious reason for this is that few advertisers or their agencies are willing to forgo the option of retakes, editing, or, if necessary, redoing the entire commercial. Also, the use of special effects and special sets is quite limited in live commercials.

To many advertisers, comparing film with videotape is like comparing 100 percent cotton with a cotton-polyester blend. It is a matter of taste. For example, the head of one large production firm believes the decision should be based on such factors as whether the spot will be released in tape or film, the time period needed to shoot it, and the look desired by the advertiser.

Film is a better choice than videotape if you want to achieve special or very tricky visual effects or if the commercial is a composite of sequences filmed at different times or on different locations. If the commercial requires figure animation, film is the preferred medium.

Videotape equipment allows the producer to record electronically on magnetic tape both the video and audio parts of the commercial, to check it immediately, and to make whatever editing changes are needed with minimum delay. Videotaping provides excellent reproduction in color or black and white, and it is generally less expensive than film for simple commercials that can be produced in the studio or on nearby locations. If the action is not broken up into a lot of scenes and if special effects are kept to a minimum, videotape is usually preferred to film, but it is generally less flexible. Figure 15.8 presents a more complete accounting of the advantages and disadvantages of film versus videotape.

Choosing Cast and Set

The producer is responsible for the TV commerical from the time the agency and client give final approval until it is turned over to the station or network for broadcast. Most large agencies have several producers on their staffs and a top-level executive in charge of their television production. The television producer is like the architect who designs a house. Advertisers and agencies must trust the producer to visualize the TV spot as it will appear on the viewer's screen. Producers are also available on a free-lance basis in a number of production centers around the country. The producer might send the storyboard and helpful suggestions to several studios to solicit bids, which should cover all costs indicated by the storyboard, plus provision for any overrides.

The producer will usually make a list of everything needed to produce the commercial on the basis of the script and storyboard. He or she will probably have a meeting with the director of the studio, the agency's director assigned to the commercial, a representative of the advertiser, the agency's account executive, the commercial writer, and perhaps the artist who works on the account at the agency. At this meeting, all major decisions regarding filming or taping should be made—decisions on such things as camera angles, types of models needed for the cast, and sound effects.

Possible models and actors will be auditioned and final choices made, probably by the producer or the agency's casting director. Because most professional models and actors are unionized, the payment will probably not vary much from person to person unless a celebrity is chosen.

Special sets needed for a commercial can usually be supplied by a production house. If the set is complicated or special effects are desired, a production house accustomed to filming similar commercials probably will be chosen. If the commercial is filmed on location, the producer will select a site and obtain permission for

---

FIGURE 15.8

A Comparison of Videotape and Film

Advantages of Videotape	Advantages of Film
• The director can immediately view playbacks. • Editing can begin immediately after production. • The medium is excellent for a low-cost, simple production shot in "real time" (a stand-up spokesperson pitch, for example). • The lighting task is easier. • A "live," here-and-now look results. • It is easier to achieve special effects, such as speeding up, slowing down, and reversing the action and to add zooms, wipes, and computer animation through an analog computer.	• The medium is excellent for closeups of foods, faces, and other details. • Equipment is more mobile for location shoots. • Soft, "cinematic" qualities can be achieved that can be especially effective in commercials with strong emotional appeals. • It is easier to make stop-motion or animated commercials that are shot one frame at a time. • The medium is better for complex editing jobs that use montages and complicated dissolves. • The director can often substitute 16mm for 35mm equipment without a significant loss in visual quality.

Source: Elizabeth J. Heighton and Don R. Cunningham, *Advertising in the Broadcast and Cable Media*, 2d ed. (Belmont, CA: Wadsworth, 1984), 155.

---

filming if needed. If, for example, the location were a street in midtown New York or Chicago, arrangements would be needed for handling spectators, transportation of equipment, and even security. If the location is outdoors, the possibility of bad weather must be dealt with.

Gathering even the props can become complicated. Every detail must be checked. Some product labels or packages must be "color corrected" so they will have the true color when they are filmed in color and the proper contrast when seen in black and white.

Music for the commercial can come from existing tunes or music created especially for it. Music protected by copyright cannot be used without permission and, usually, the payment of a fee. If original music is desired, writers or arrangers are commissioned to compose it. The music arranger is responsible for making sure the music and the action are coordinated.

Using Modern Technology

Almost anything a creative director imagines can be recreated in a television commercial by graphics experts using video's latest electronic developments. As Chapter 14 indicated, today's production specialists have at their disposal a wide variety of commercial presentation techniques—live action, stop-action, animation, claymation, rotoscoping, and computer graphics—that they can use to produce attention-grabbing and memorable TV commercials.

Of the recent technological developments, perhaps the most influential is computer graphics. Today's high-powered computers allow creative people to devise all sorts of special effects with the assurance that an innovative producer will probably figure out how to implement them in a commercial. An example of how computer graphics has been used to enhance automobile ads is provided in the Ad Insight entitled "Computer Graphics Enliven Car Ads." In today's media environment, many advertising experts believe such efforts are necessary to hold the interest of viewers who are generally not attentive to anything graphically mundane.

Computer Graphics Enliven Car Ads

By John P. Cortez and Cleveland Horton

Automakers are turning more than ever to special effects as a way to get noticed in the clutter of more than 30 car and truck campaigns.

Since the 1992 models started rolling out, at least three car companies—Lexus, Buick and Plymouth—have relied on computer graphics to catch the eye.

Toyota Motor Sales USA's Lexus division needed a gimmick to help introduce the ES 300 sedan, a replacement for the ES 250.

"We wanted to create a halo from the early LS 400 image," said J. Davis Illingworth, Lexus VP-general manager. "We needed to connect the LS 400 [the luxury division's top-of-the-line model] and the new ES 300."

Source: *Advertising Age* (September 16, 1991): 337.

The division borrowed a computer graphics metamorphosis technique from the feature film "Terminator 2: Judgment Day" for a 30-second spot. The commercial opens with a car under a cover outdoors. The wind picks up the cover and blows it away to reveal the LS 400. Then the skin of the car starts to flap like a cover and it, too, blows away, revealing the new ES 300.

The effect was created by Rhythm & Hues, Hollywood, Calif., for Team One, El Segundo, Lexus' agency.

"Morphing"—a means of transforming one image into another—was also used in General Motors Corp.'s Buick division spot for the new LeSabre.

A hook lifts the outer shell off a 1991 model like a giant sheet—actually an air-brushed silk of the vehicle.

Editing the Commercial

Most filmed and videotaped TV commercials are edited before they are released for telecasting. This process consists of deleting some portions, revising others, and then refilming and recording the finished commercial. Some use technology for editing selected takes of each; others are transferred to a computer-oriented device. Using a light pen, one can call up scenes, have them displayed on the monitor, and then decide which are to be used

Rough Cut

If the TV commercial has been filmed, a copy of the film rather than the original itself is used in the editing. The editor will review all the footage and splice together the most promising parts to form the rough cut. Although the sound has not yet been added, the editor can synchronize sight and sound on an editor's projector that permits him or her to adapt the film to the sound track.

Underneath, it's the 1992 LeSabre. The spot was directed by Los Angeles director David Dryer and the effects produced by Pacific Data Images.

"The LeSabre was a car with a huge reputation for quality," said John Mead, exec VP-executive creative director at Buick agency McCann-Erickson Worldwide, Troy, Mich. "We wanted to make it clear that the new car was coming out of the old one."

In another illusion at the end of the spot, a man pulls down a huge curtain with a pastoral landscape and road on it, gets in the car and drives into the image. A quick motion blur, an edit of the car on stage and insertion of the car on the road resulted in the final image.

Chrysler Corp.'s Plymouth division needed an image campaign that would also deliver the facts, said Bert Gardner, executive creative director of Bozell, Minneapolis, which created the Laser spot.

"Instead of just doing an image campaign, we wanted to do an image campaign that could be used as retail, one that the dealers would like," Mr. Gardner said. "We thought the talking cars would be the image side, and the facts they presented about themselves would satisfy retail needs."

Plymouth has four spots featuring talking cars. In the Laser spot, the car drives up and down a brick wall, telling a man in a sultry female voice, "Don't try this at home." He asks if he can go for a spin, gets in and the car begins to revolve like a top as the spot ends.

It took many takes and composite edits to produce the final version, Mr. Gardner said. The actor was alone on an empty stage for most of the shoot. The brick wall was painted on the floor and the car drove over it, with scenery reflected at appropriate angles in the windows to produce the illusion of ascension. Digital computer graphics and single-frame edits were used so the car wouldn't appear rubber as it turned to climb the wall.

"The whole notion of digitalizing everything from video to music and then just working with those digits and never going back to film has allowed us to do a tremendous amount," Mr. Gardner said. "The technology was originally invented to save time, but all it does is open up more options and make things take longer."

The commercial, which makes its network TV debut today, was directed by Lol Creme, a former member of rock groups 10cc and Godley & Creme. Mr. Creme also directed the last three Plymouth campaigns.

The lastest project took more than a month, Mr. Gardner said.

"It's not easy to make a car speak for itself," he said, "but let's hope it's worth it."

The next step is to make transitions from one scene to the other as smooth as possible by using such optical effects as a **dissolve** (one scene dissolves into another), a **fade** (one scene fades away as another appears gradually), or a **wipe** (one scene wipes the other off the screen).

Answer Print

After both the film and the voice track have been edited, audio elements are mixed with the voice track and sound effects (if needed) are added. The TV commercial is then ready to be assembled. When the film, optical effects, and sound track are all combined, we have an **answer print** (gives an "answer" as to the quality of the commercial). The answer print is usually screened by the account executive, a representative for the client, and anyone else whom the producer wants to consult before approving the commercial for distribution to stations on the media schedule.

Duplicating the Original

Copies of filmed TV commercials are normally made from the finished negative, which includes all the video and sound elements. Duplicates are called release prints. Each station usually receives two copies, one as a spare in case of difficulty with the original.

Duplicating a videotape commercial can be a bit more complicated. Because most stations now have videotape equipment, they can telecast directly from a duplicate tape, which does the best job of preserving the clarity of the original production. To save the cost of additional videotapes for all stations on the media schedule, the commercial may be converted from tape to a film called a **kinescope**. Usually, however, some quality is sacrificed when the commercial is kinescoped.

Control over Quality and Cost

A good deal of time and effort at advertising conferences is devoted to discussing how to control cost and quality in television commercials. Producing a commercial is quite costly, although the average cost varies by product category. The typical commercial for large advertisers costs over $100,000 to produce, and some cost more than a million dollars.

The first safeguard is to estimate and agree on all possible costs before production starts. A change in dialogue or in the lighting of a set is simple to make in the planning stage, but very costly after shooting or videotaping starts.

The following are factors that can increase the cost of the production of a commercial:

1. Children and animals
2. Location shooting
3. Large cast
4. Superstar talent
5. Night or weekend filming
6. Animation
7. Involved opticals, special effects, stop-motion
8. Both location and studio shooting for one commercial
9. Expensive set decoration
10. Special photographic equipment
11. A second day of shooting
12. Legal requirements
13. A simple word or sentence of dialogue
14. An extremely simple, close-up commercial[7]

All costs should be described in the bids solicited from production studios (see Figure 15.9). Although most items in the production budget are a one-time cost, talent is not. Talent contracts are complicated, but they usually allow for extra payments according to the number of times the commercial is telecast and the extent of the media schedule.

High-quality standards will, of course, normally result in higher production expenditures. But advertising managers or account executives can take these steps to improve quality control without spending more money: (1) insist on the involvement of creative specialists and (2) check the progress of the production process at logical stages, such as the assembly of the rough cut. In general, advertising managers and account executives have to tread the line between oversolicitous intervention and indifference. Control is easier if all concerned trust each other and have agreed on specific production details.

Producing the Radio Commercial

The radio commercial is much simpler to produce than the television commercial. For example, many radio commercials are still delivered live, and production problems for these tend to be minimal. But the decision as to whether the commercial should be live or recorded is always troublesome. For example, duplicating the original is no simple job if the commercial is to be sent to any sizable segment of the more than 8,000 commercial stations in the United States.

Live versus Recording

Live radio commercials are used primarily when advertisers want to use local announcers or personalities, to fit the commercials into a local program format, or to keep down production expenses. Advertisers will often send the script, plus a recording of any music or special effects to be included, to the local announcer. A common alternative is to send the station a fact sheet on the product, rather than a script. In such cases, local announcers are expected to create, often extemporaneously, their own commercial message. This approach can capitalize on the popularity and familiarity of local announcers within their community. When uniformity is important, however, a recorded commercial is probably preferable. Advertisers

FIGURE 15.9

Television Production Estimate Form Used to Write Up Job Specifications

The form is sent to studios interested in bidding on a particular job.

LEO BURNETT U.S.A.
A DIVISION OF LEO BURNETT COMPANY, INC.
ADVERTISING
PRUDENTIAL PLAZA · CHICAGO, ILLINOIS 60601
312-236-5959

Job # P –

CHECK-LIST FOR BIDDING

BIDDING AND PRE-PRODUCTION

	A	P	NA
Set design			
Character sketches			
Casting			
Preparation of special releases			
Signing of releases by performers			
Union talent paid up? Member?			
Product props			
Actual advertiser's product			
Actual advertiser's package			
Color-correction of above			
Home Economist			
Wardrobe			
Technical Advisor			
Stylist			
Stock/footage search and purchase			
Pick-up footage from com'l #			

RECORDING VOICE/MUSIC

	A	P	MP	NA
Recording V.O. track				
Paying V.O. talent				
Talent report				
Music to be recorded				
Existing music track				

Identification

Master at

	A	P	MP	NA
Mixing				
Transferring				

PRODUCTION

Talent session fees			
Talent reports, Union talent forms, W4's etc.			
First edit			

SCHEDULE INFORMATION

EDITING & POST-PRODUCTION

	A	P	PP	NA
Screening of dailies				
Title art lay-out				
Finished art				
1st trial 35				
1st trial 16				
Talent report				
Transfer film to VTR				
Dub to ¾" Sony cassette				

MUSIC OWNERSHIP & USE INFORMATION

Title

- ☐ Client owns already
- ☐ Client negotiating rights
- ☐ Being created; client will purchase on an outright ownership basis.
- ☐ Music used in com'l #

STUDIOS TO BE BID

Talent count for bidding purposes

SAG/SEG/AFTRA class	Com'l #1	#2	#3	#4	#5	#6	#7	#8
SAG/AFTRA on camera								
SAG/AFTRA voice-over								
SEG general extra								
SEG product buy-out								
Special contract talent								

A – Agency
P – Production Studio
PP – Post production company
MP – Music production company
NA – Not applicable

9-14B R-73

Source: Leo Burnett, Inc.

The Cat's Meow of Radio Advertising

Catspaw Productions is an Atlanta-based, full-service creative group specializing in the creation and production of radio commercials. The company offers clients two choices: "full-creative" service or "production-only" service.

"Full-creative" means the client says, "Here, you guys do it all." Develop the concept—write the script—create the music—cast and book talent—produce the commercial—traffic the finished spot to the media.

"Production-only" means the client says, "Here, take this finished script, cast it, direct, and produce it. We'll handle the rest."

Since opening its doors in 1985, Catspaw has produced radio spots for clients like Eastern Air Lines, Pepto-Bismol, Coca-Cola, Bunny Bread, Pet Dairy, Hardee's, and Texaco, to name a few.

Catspaw's success proves two points—(1) an organization can be successful by specializing in one facet of the advertising business and (2) you don't have to be in New York to be respected and demanded by advertising professionals.

Source: Catspaw Productions, Inc., Atlanta, GA 30305, November 17, 1988.

often use local production houses (services), either for full-creative service or for production only, to create local advertising. The Ad Insight entitled "The Cat's Meow of Radio Advertising," describes one such local production house—Catspaw Productions, an Atlanta-based production service.

Duplicating the Original

Duplicates of radio commercials are normally distributed on quarter-inch tapes or on recordings (electrical transcriptions). The electrical transcription is the most economical method for a large number of stations that are widely scattered. From a master duplicate record, over a thousand duplicate records can be made, all quite sharp and capable of being played an almost infinite number of times.

Summary

An understanding of the production of print, television, and radio can contribute significantly to making advertising more effective. In the case of print production, special attention should be devoted to using current technology for improving communication—especially type, reproduction of illustrations, printing the complete advertisement, and duplicating the advertisement. Some experts feel that the future of print production will be almost entirely computer based.

In print advertisements, type must be chosen carefully and displayed in a readable and appropriate manner. Type should serve as the groundwork for print advertising. The correct type should be supportive, sometimes invisible, never intrusive. The planner should understand certain fundamentals of typography. These fundamentals include a general understanding of type categories and some basic guidelines for the use of type.

The principal types of illustration reproduction are line art and halftones. Final reproduction of the printed advertisement will be by one of four printing methods: letterpress (printing surface is raised), lithography (printing and nonprinting surfaces on the same level), gravure (printing surface depressed), or screen printing (ink pressed through fine fabric to a flat surface). Following the production, a duplicate is sent to the different publications on the schedule.

Between the time a television storyboard is approved by the client and the completed commercial is broadcast, many production decisions are required. Among these are determining whether to use film or videotape; choosing the producer and cast; acquiring sets and props; editing the commercial; choosing the method of duplication; and controlling cost, quality, and distribution. In all of these, the producer must act as the overseer in ensuring that the commercial is completed as efficiently as possible, with maximum quality and within the budget set by the various principals. In addition, producers must keep abreast of the sweeping changes brought by the electronic media.

Radio commercials are, of course, much less complicated to produce than those for television. Two problems that must be faced are whether the commercial should be live or recorded and how the original can be duplicated for distribution to stations on the schedule.

Questions for Discussion

1. How are computer developments impacting print production?
2. How does the use of type impact print production? What are some of the basics with regard to understanding type?
3. Under what conditions would you prefer halftones to line art?
4. How has modern technology changed the way type is set for advertisements?
5. Under what conditions would you use film rather than videotape to transmit commercials?
6. Would you change the nature of your commercial message if you knew it was going to be used on cable as well as regular television?
7. Describe the role of the producer in the television production process.
8. How can the producer and the account executive control the mounting costs of producing television commercials?
9. Of the many technological developments discussed in this chapter, which is likely to have the most long-lasting impact on the writing and production of advertising messages?

Notes

1 David A. Aaker, Rajeev Batra, and John G. Myers, *Advertising Management*, 4th ed. (Englewood Cliffs, NJ: Prentice-Hall, 1992), 440.

2 Betsy Spethmann, "Print Ads Read into Computer Revolution," *Advertising Age*, May 25, 1992, 43 (opposite Spethmann).

3 "Type Designers," *Aldus Magazine*, March/April, 1992, 25.

4 Roy Paul Nelson, *The Design of Advertising* (Dubuque, IA: William C. Brown, 1989), 181.

5 Opposite Spethmann, 43.

6 Paul Schulman and Bruce E. Reid, *What Every Account Representative Should Know about Television Commercial Production* (New York: American Association of Advertising Agencies, 1979), 1.

7 Kenneth Roman and Jane Maas, *How to Advertise* (New York: St. Martin's Press, 1976), 79–81.

Suggested Readings

Guide to Quality Newspaper Reproduction. Washington, DC: American Newspaper Publishers Association and Newspaper Advertising Bureau, 1986, 19.

Heighton, Elizabeth J., and Don R. Cunningham. *Advertising in the Broadcast and Cable Media,* 2d ed. Belmont, CA: Wadsworth, 1984.

Nelson, Roy P. *The Design of Advertising,* 6th ed. Dubuque, IA: William C. Brown, 1989. Chapters 11, 12, 13.

Schulman, Paul, and Bruce E. Reid. *What Every Account Representative Should Know about Television Commercial Production.* New York: American Association of Advertising Agencies, 1979.

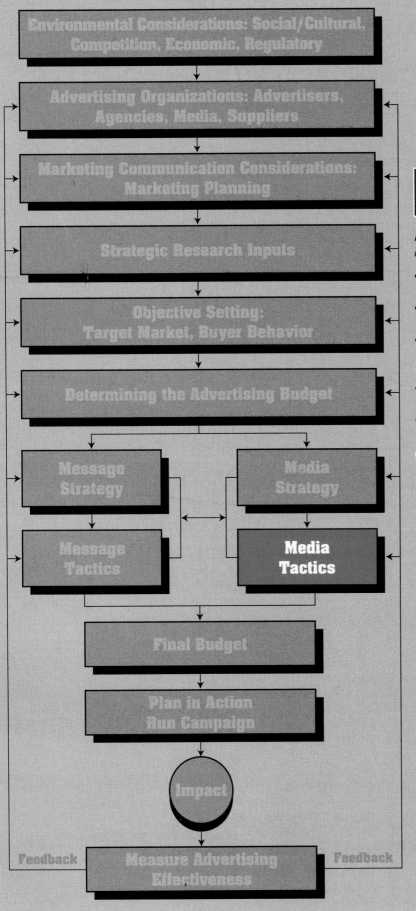

Environmental Considerations: Social/Cultural, Competition, Economic, Regulatory

Advertising Organizations: Advertisers, Agencies, Media, Suppliers

Marketing Communication Considerations: Marketing Planning

Strategic Research Inputs

Objective Setting: Target Market, Buyer Behavior

Determining the Advertising Budget

Message Strategy

Media Strategy

Message Tactics

Media Tactics

Final Budget

Plan in Action Run Campaign

Impact

Measure Advertising Effectiveness

Feedback   Feedback

LEARNING OBJECTIVES

In your study of this chapter, you will have an opportunity to:

• Learn about the classes and types of newspapers and magazines.
• Observe circulation and audience patterns of the print media.
• Understand newspaper and magazine rate structures as an element in media buying.
• Examine the factors that are considered in buying print media.
• See how cost comparisons are used in deciding alternative print vehicles.

Chapter 16

Media: Newspapers and Magazines

CHAPTER TOPICS

NEWSPAPERS
- *Advantages of Newspaper Advertising*
- *Limitations of Newspaper Advertising*
- *Readership Patterns*
- *Types of Advertising*
- *Newspaper Sizes and Shapes*
- *Rate Structure*
- *Rate Comparisons*
- *Factors to Consider in Buying Newspaper Space*
- *Newspaper Supplements*

MAGAZINES
- *Types of Magazines*
- *Advantages of Magazine Advertising*
- *Limitations of Magazine Advertising*
- *Kinds of Advertisers*
- *Circulation and Readership Patterns*
- *Magazine Sizes and Shapes*
- *Rate Structure*
- *Methods of Comparison*

Even the most elegant media strategy, poorly carried out, likely will result in an unsuccessful campaign. We now begin a three-chapter discussion dealing with the tactics of media strategy. Such tactics primarily involve the process of buying— that is, deciding which media vehicles, within a media type, should be included in a schedule, and which advertising units are appropriate for the situation. For example, an advertising planner who intends to use home service magazines in the media mix would choose from among such magazines as *Better Homes & Gardens, Southern Living*, and *House Beautiful*. After selecting each vehicle, the planner would decide such things as the size of the advertisement, whether or not to use color, and the scheduling. All tactical executions must be performed within the context of the strategic decisions and must be carefully monitored, through control techniques, to be sure that what has been ordered is received.

This chapter focuses on newspapers and magazines, which together account for almost one-third of all advertising expenditures.

Newspapers

If media were rated on the basis of total dollars spent, newspapers would be in first place. Daily and Sunday newspapers account for about one-fourth of total advertising expenditures, almost nine-tenths of which comes directly or indirectly from retailers. **Cooperative advertising** is run over the retailer's signature but the manufacturer of the merchandise featured pays part or all of the bill.

The first regularly published newspaper in the colonies, the *Boston News Letter*, had a circulation of approximately 300 copies a week and continued publication until 1776. The first regularly published daily paper did not appear until 1783. During the nineteenth century, the newspaper became truly a mass medium. Benjamin Day established the *New York Sun* in 1833, the first major newspaper to sell for a penny, and treated publishing like a business. Later in the century, publishers such as Joseph Pulitzer, James Gordon Bennett, and Horace Greeley made newspapers a dynamic force in American social and political life.

Newspapers are usually classified according to frequency of publication—either daily or weekly. In addition, a number of dailies publish a Sunday edition, and a few papers issue only on Sunday. Table 16.1 indicates the total number of daily and Sunday newspapers for selected years between 1950 and 1992. Note that the number of morning dailies and Sunday papers has increased for the period shown, whereas evening dailies have been declining in number since 1960. (Two-thirds of all dailies are published as evening newspapers.) The net result is that the total number of daily newspapers has declined from 1,772 in 1950 to 1,570 in 1992.

Figure 16.1 shows circulation trends for morning, evening, and Sunday newspapers for a sample of years between 1950 and 1992. The circulations of morning and Sunday newspapers have risen rather consistently over the period, but circulations for evening dailies peaked in 1970 and have declined since then. The 17.8 million circulation figure for evening papers in 1992 was 55 percent of the circulation in 1950.

In addition to daily and Sunday newspapers, there are approximately 7,500 weeklies in the United States. The paper with the largest circulation, *The Wall Street Journal*, sells almost 2 million copies a day; the smallest daily may have a circulation of only a few thousand. Most daily papers serve local areas. *The Wall Street Journal* and *USA Today* are notable exceptions.

Daily newspapers are often categorized on the basis of the size of the market area. Thus, national advertisers may decide to take the "first ten markets," "first fifty," and so on.

Usually, the weekly or community newspaper is published in a small, homogenous community. This may be a small town in Montana or a suburban area near New

TABLE 16.1

Number of Morning, Evening, and Sunday Newspapers for Selected Years, 1950–1992

Year	Morning	Evening	Total M & E[1]	Sunday
1950	322	1,450	1,772	549
1960	312	1,459	1,763	563
1970	334	1,429	1,748	586
1980	387	1,388	1,745	735
1985	482	1,220	1,676	798
1986	499	1,188	1,657	802
1987	511	1,166	1,645	820
1988	529	1,141	1,642	840
1989	530	1,125	1,626	847
1990	559	1,084	1,611	863
1991	571	1,042	1,586	874
1992[2]	596	994	1,570	893

Source: *Editor & Publisher*, as reported in *Facts about Newspapers '93*, published by the Newspaper Association of America.

[1] There were 20 "all-day" newspapers in 1992. They are listed in both morning and evening columns but only once in the total.

[2] Preliminary data.

FIGURE 16.1

Circulation of Morning, Evening, and Sunday Newspapers, 1950–1992

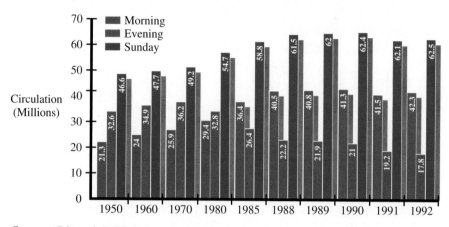

Source: *Editor & Publisher*, as reported in *Facts about Newspapers '93*, published by the Newspaper Association of America.

York City. The publisher of a weekly newspaper frequently depends heavily on job printing for revenue.

Newspapers may also be classified according to paid circulation or **controlled circulation**. The shopping newspaper, or "shopper," for example, is normally distributed free and therefore its circulation is controlled. It is usually distributed to certain parts of a town or to selected types of homes. The majority of newspapers, however, are not distributed free.

Newspapers may also be distinguished on the basis of the audience they attract. Thus, in addition to the general-interest newspapers, many cater to special groups (such as African Americans, Chinese, foreign language, labor, or trade). These papers are like magazines in many ways, although their format is similar to that of other newspapers.

Size is another criterion for classifying newspapers. Generally speaking, there are two basic sizes: the tabloid and the standard, or **broadsheet**. Tabloids typically have an advertising page 14 inches deep and 10 13/16 inches wide. There are five columns per page, with each column 2 1/16 inches wide and 1/8 inch between columns. (The five columns are for advertising space allocation; a tabloid may run editorial content in three or four columns.)

The standard, or broadsheet, advertising page is 21 inches deep and 13 inches wide. The six columns per page are each 2 1/16 inches wide, with 1/8 inch between columns. (As with tabloids, the number of editorial columns may be different.) Among the major newspapers in New York City, the *Daily News*, *Newsday*, and the *New York Post* are tabloids; *The New York Times* is standard size. New York City, however, is not typical—95 percent of all dailies are of standard size.

The newspaper is the major advertising medium for most local advertisers, including retail stores. About 50 percent of all local advertising expenditures in 1992 went to newspapers. The attraction that newspapers have for local businesses is easy to understand when one considers how well newspaper characteristics fit retail communication needs—for example, their circulation distribution in the trading area, their day-after-day appearance, their use as shopping guides by consumers, and their prestige.

Until the mid-1940s, the newspaper was also the leading medium for national advertisers. Since 1955 television has been the leader—in direct expenditures, at least. Actually, it is almost impossible to estimate how many dollars of national advertising are diverted through retailers' hands as cooperative advertising and thus

Advantages of *Newspaper Advertising*

A Profile of USA TODAY

Gannett Company, Inc. is one of the largest diversified news and information companies in the United States. The information presented here profiles Gannett's *USA TODAY* national newspaper.

FACT SHEET

First Day of Issue	September 15, 1982
Readership	The Simmons Market Research Bureau survey results for 1991 report that USA TODAY remains the most widely-read newspaper in the nation, with a daily readership of more than 6.5 million.
Circulation	The publisher's statement to the Audit Bureau of Circulations for the six months ending March 1991, subject to audit, showed an average daily paid circulation of 1,863,436, making USA TODAY the second largest daily newspaper in the USA.
Market Concentration	USA TODAY is available on the same day of publication in the USA's top 100 ADIs.
Print Sites	32 in the USA, 1 in Hong Kong, and 1 in Switzerland.
Pages	Each issue has a maximum capacity of 56 pages, with a 16-page maximum of color; 11-page maximum for color advertising. Four-color is available in all four sections. A fifth bonus section can add up to 24 pages.
Satellite	The USA TODAY domestic satellite is ASC-1 located in stationary orbit 22,300 miles above the Pacific Ocean. This ASC-1 satellite plus one Intelsat satellite (Pacific Ocean region) are used for Hong Kong transmissions. One Intelsat Atlantic region satellite is used for Switzerland transmissions.
Transmission Time	Approximately 3½ to 4 minutes for a full black-and-white page; up to 6 minutes for each of the 4-color separations for editorial color. From 5 to 15 minutes for each separation for color advertising. Transmission time varies with the content on the page.
Press Time	*First edition press start:* Midnight, Monday – Thursday; 11:30 P.M., Friday *Chase edition press start:* 1:10 A.M., Monday – Thursday; 1:40 A.M., Friday *Second edition press start:* 2:10 A.M., Monday – Thursday; 2:30 A.M., Friday
Advertising	In 1991, USA TODAY advertising pages totaled 3,370
Advertising Rates	Full-page B&W: $57,505, M–Th; $65,810, F Full-page four-color: $74,757, M–Th; $85,552 F (Weekend rates are higher, reflecting the weekend edition's larger circulation.)
International Edition	The USA TODAY International Edition is available worldwide. It has a minimum of 16 pages in two sections. USA TODAY International has been printed in Hong Kong since April 1988 for distribution in Asia and the Pacific. Since May 1986, the International Edition for Europe and the Middle East has been printed near Lucerne, Switzerland.
Staff Size	395 Editorial, 2,100 Total
Headquarters Address	1000 Wilson Blvd. Arlington, Va. 22229 (703) 276-3400
Advertising Offices	535 Madison Ave. New York, N.Y. 10022 (212) 715-5350

Source: Copyright, *USA Today*. Reprinted with permission.

HOW USA TODAY IS PRODUCED

1. Articles written and edited.
2. ATEX computer processes articles.
3. Articles are printed by high-speed computer typesetters.
4. Pages are pasted up in the composing room.
5. Completed newspaper pages are photographed.
6. A "glossy" positive print of the newspaper page is produced.
7. Laser scanner converts page to signal that can be transmitted via satellite.
8. Satellite dish transmits signal.
9. Satellite parked in stationary orbit 22,300 miles above the equator broadcasts signal back to remote printing sites.
10. Satellite dish at print site receives signal.
11. A computer at the print site converts the signal from the satellite into full-page image.
12. Lasers on facsimile recorders expose film in a darkroom.
13. Film is processed and an offset printing plate is produced.
14. High-speed offset presses print copies of USA TODAY.
15. Newspapers are trucked to distribution points.

USA TODAY SPINOFFS

USA TODAY Baseball Weekly—an all-baseball tabloid printed at 18 of USA TODAY's 33 print sites. The newspaper includes expert analysis, team-by-team reports for Major and Minor league teams, a week of box scores, television and radio schedules, and reports devoted to fans who play in fantasy leagues or collect baseball memorabilia. It publishes every Wednesday during baseball season and every other Wednesday during the off season.

USA TODAY Sky Radio—a constant program wheel of live news, financial reports, sports scores, and weather reports throughout the day delivered to airline passengers through the audio systems already installed on many commercial aircraft. Sky Radio will use a customized radio channel delivered to aircraft via satellite technology.

Additionally, Sky Radio plans to offer live professional and college sports during evenings and weekends. Broadcasts began in 1992.

USA TODAY Update—a news and information service consisting of 18 executive news summaries delivered to business environments worldwide. The decision-line reports are sent electronically to the subscriber's database beginning at 4 A.M. Of the 18 reports, 13 are targeted to a particular profession or industry, four concentrate on general news, and one report deals in-depth with the day's top issue. Also, USA TODAY Update lifestyles reports, full-text features selected from USA TODAY, cover entertainment, money, and sports. USA TODAY Update also is available on home information networks and on Minitel, the French videotex network.

USA TODAY Sports Hotline—a comprehensive two-minute report that provides late-breaking sports headlines and scoring updates from the nation's stadiums and arenas. The Hotline is updated every 10 minutes to report sports news and scores as they happen. The Hotline is available 24 hours a day, seven days a week. The number: 1-900-850-1414.

USA TODAY Books—a line of books developed from material that has appeared in USA TODAY. Among them: *Portraits of the USA*; *Tracking Tomorrow's Trends*; *The USA TODAY Crossword Puzzle Book*, Volumes I & II; *Desert Warriors: The Men and Women Who Won the Gulf War*; *The USA TODAY Cartoon Book*; *BusCapade: Plain Talk Across the USA*; *And Still We Rise: Interviews with 50 Black Role Models*; *U.S.A. Citizens Abroad: A Handbook*; *The Making of McPaper: The Inside Story of USA TODAY*; *Window on the World: Faces, Places & Plain Talk from 32 Countries*; *Profiles of Power: How the Governors Run our 50 States*; *Truly One Nation*.

USA TODAY Online Library—The Online Library allows users to research stories and information that has appeared in USA TODAY, USA WEEKEND, Gannett News Service, and The Louisville Courier Journal. The public may access this online library by calling Data-Times, Inc. in Oklahoma City, 1-800-642-2525.

USA TODAY Classline Today—This four-page lesson plan aids students and teachers in the classroom as they study with The Nation's Newspaper. Classline Today is delivered with USA TODAY to schools each Tuesday and Wednesday morning.

USA TODAY Sports Center—An on-line, comprehensive sports network with everything for the sports fan. Offers statistics, boxscores, schedules, sports and news wire services, Sports Collector Exchange, injury reports, and complete coverage of major sporting events. Includes fantasy baseball, basketball, and football as well as an electronic mail system, opinion polls, forums, a sports discount store, and classified ads exclusively for Sports Center users.

show up in retail classifications. However, newspapers have fared much better in the face of competition from television than many predicted. Their flexibility for use in test campaigns and in filling gaps in national schedules has kept them in high esteem among space buyers who represent national advertisers. The top ten newspaper advertisers in 1992 are listed in Table 16.2. Note that all of these are national retailers.

A number of the characteristics of newspapers appeal to both retail and national advertisers. Others appeal to only one.

Flexibility

Newspapers typically offer national advertisers more territorial flexibility than other media do. Whether advertisers use them for basic coverage or to fill in gaps left by network television, they are able to advertise heavily in one area and lightly in another. The market may be fertile in Kokomo, Indiana, but not in Kankakee, Illinois. One area may be having a heat wave while another is having moderate temperatures. Newspaper advertising can be placed where the potential market looks best.

Territorial flexibility has special appeal to national advertisers who want to test a new product. They can advertise it in certain test areas and save the time, trouble, and expense of a national campaign. Also, the mass coverage most newspapers provide, the chance to put the new product ad in a news context, and the opportunity of getting fairly immediate action all enhance the desirability of newspapers for introducing new products.

Retail advertisers, operating within a trading area, are not so concerned with territorial flexibility. Nevertheless, some newspapers, especially in large markets, offer retailers only a portion of their total circulation; see *zone* advertising later in this chapter. They are, however, interested in the newspaper's time flexibility (that is, the advertisement may be changed up to a few hours before the paper goes to press). Changes in the weather, in merchandise available for sale, and many other unforeseen circumstances may make last-minute revisions desirable.

The rise of **run-of-paper (ROP)** color offers advertisers still more flexibility in their use of newspapers. Almost all daily papers provided at least one color in 1994.

Community Prestige

Both retail and national advertisers like to associate themselves with the prestige most local papers enjoy in a community. One of the best indications of how people feel toward their newspaper is their behavior when they are without it. Several studies have been made in U.S. cities that have been deprived of their daily paper. All have indicated the deep impact a newspaper has on a community.

Intense Coverage

In some areas, more than 80 percent of the homes can be reached through a single newspaper. In most areas, around 62 percent of all homes read some paper. Almost every newspaper includes news of interest to all groups of the population—sports fans, homemakers, and businesspeople. Advertisers can select customers of a particular group by placing their advertisements in a special-interest section.

Reader-Controlled Exposure

Because readers can scan, skip, or plod through the paper, they need not suffer the boredom or resentment they might undergo in the broadcast media. This point is of special importance to retailers who depend on newspaper advertisements to provide shopping information for readers. Through newspapers they can tell consumers what the merchandise looks like, how much it costs, and where they can

TABLE 16.2		
Top Ten Newspaper Advertisers, 1992		
Rank	Advertiser	Dollars Spent (millions)
1	May Department Stores	$303.5
2	Circuit City Stores	186.9
3	Federated Department Stores	176.0
4	R.H. Macy & Co.	171.3
5	Sears, Roebuck & Co.	166.0
6	Dayton Hudson Corp.	120.2
7	Kmart Corp.	117.5
8	Dillard Department Stores	117.0
9	Montgomery Ward & Co.	107.6
10	Carter Hawley Hale Stores	106.4

Source: Newspaper Association of America, as reported in *Advertising Age,* April 26, 1993, S-14.

get it. Readers can take as much or as little time as they want in reading the ad and can refer to it later if they like.

Dealer–National Advertiser Coordination

Both the national advertiser and the dealer can profit from the fact that their advertisements can complement each other. The advertiser of a new biscuit mix advertises the advantages of the mix over competing products. The local supermarkets tie in with these ads and tell readers where they can get the mix and how much it costs. Sometimes the space cost is shared by the dealer and the manufacturer (cooperative advertising). Many newspapers have special staffs to help dealers and manufacturers coordinate their advertising.

Services Offered

For the national advertiser, many newspapers offer merchandising services. They can help broaden distribution in local stores, convince local retailers that they should promote the product, and assist the manufacturer's representative in analyzing the local market. Many papers send out newsletters to drugstores and grocery stores, notifying proprietors that certain brands will be advertised by the manufacturer in the newspaper during the coming week. Many offer extensive research facilities, such as readership studies and consumer surveys. Most newspapers provide help in securing local advertising funds from national advertisers (cooperative advertising).

For the retailer, the services are important but in somewhat different ways. The small store probably uses most the newspaper's free copy and art service, while the larger stores are more likely to use the paper's research facilities.

Special Techniques

Newspapers offer advertisers special techniques that improve the impact of advertising, including zone editions, total market coverage (TMC), and inserts. Through the use of zone editions, newspapers can "break out" their circulation according to the geographic area they serve and thus offer an advertiser only a portion of their total circulation. For example, the *Houston Chronicle* offers eight zone editions, allowing an advertiser to place ads in one or more of eight territories. This service has special appeal for a retailer with a limited trading area, but it can also be used by national advertisers seeking to develop segmented targets.

Total market coverage, or TMC, permits a newspaper to extend its coverage of a market to almost 100 percent. Suppose, for instance, a newspaper circulates to 65 percent of the households in its trading area. If the newspaper also publishes a weekly supplement and sends it free to everyone, it can offer advertisers the opportunity to extend their market coverage to almost 100 percent. There are many different forms of TMC, and the delivery systems vary from carrier-delivered to mailed.

Inserts permit an advertiser to produce an advertisement that is atypical of the kind printed on the newspaper's printing presses. These ads are produced by specialized printers and shipped to the newspaper for insertion into a particular issue. Inserts can be of many different forms and shapes, from a single sheet to multipage insert sections. These are discussed later in the chapter.

Limitations of Newspaper Advertising

Despite their advantages, newspapers have several limitations.

Short Life

There is nothing quite so stale as a newspaper a few days old. The chances that advertising will have any impact beyond the day of publication are therefore very low.

TABLE 16.3

Average Weekday Readership of Daily Newspapers

Category	Total Adults
By Gender	
Men	64%
Women	60
By Age	
18–24	53%
25–34	57
35–44	65
45–54	66
55–64	72
65 years or older	64
By Education	
Graduated from college	75%
Attended college	71
Graduated from high school	61
Attended high school	51
Did not attend high school	40
By Household Income	
$50,000 and over	73%
$40,000 and over	71
$30,000 and over	69
$20,000–$29,999	60
$10,000–$19,999	53
Under $10,000	45
Total	62%

Source: Simmons Market Research Bureau, 1991.

Hasty Reading

Most studies indicate that the average reader spends about 45 minutes on the paper. This means the ad must make its impression quickly, or it will fail.

Poor Reproduction

Even though reproduction has improved substantially in the past decade, the newspaper still rates well below magazines in this respect. If appearance is important in the sale of a product, the product is likely to suffer when its picture is reproduced in the newspaper. Note how often an automobile manufacturer emphasizes the beauty of the car in magazine ads, but stresses mechanical superiority or economy in newspaper advertising.

Readership Patterns

People who read the paper usually comprise a cross-section of the residents of the trading area served by each newspaper. In itself, a newspaper is not a particularly selective medium. It is read by men and women of all age, educational, and income levels. Yet some variation in readership occurs. For example, the average weekday audience is somewhat higher among older age categories. As shown in Table 16.3, around two-thirds of those over 35 read a weekday paper. This compares with a 53 percent readership level for the age category 18–24. As would be expected, the highest readership levels are among college graduates (75 percent read a daily newspaper) and those earning $50,000 and over household income (73 percent).

Readership studies show that newspaper audience size varies little over the five weekdays, with only slightly higher than average reading on Thursday and Friday. Further, newspaper reach is virtually constant throughout the year. Almost four of five pages are opened and looked at by the typical reader. Research has shown that the average page opening according to content is as follows:[1]

General news	93%
Food, cooking	74
Sports	77
Home furnishings	73
Business	73
Editorial page	78
Comics	74
Entertainment	78

In recent years, newspaper publishers and advertisers have been somewhat concerned with a trend toward lower overall readership levels. For example, whereas 72 percent of all adults read a daily newspaper in 1975, the figure stood at 67 percent in 1982, 65 percent in 1987, and had dropped to 62 percent by 1991. The drop in readership has occurred because some people have switched to television as their main source of news coverage.

Types of Advertising

Newspaper advertising can be divided into several types, generally the following:

1. Display advertising:
   a. National (general) advertisers
   b. Local (retail) advertisers
2. Classified advertising
   a. Regular classified
   b. Display classified
3. Special advertising (for example, public notices, political ads, and government reports)

Display and classified advertising account for most of a newpaper's total dollar volume. A retailer selling suits or a manufacturer selling air conditioners, for example, will be interested mainly in display advertising. Figure 16.2 shows newspaper advertising expenditures as divided among national, retail, and classified advertisers. Retail advertising accounts for over half of the total expenditures.

Display advertising has strong attention value because of the illustrations, the arrangement of headlines and body text, the white space, color, or other visual devices. Much classified, however, is published without conspicuous display. As the name implies, classified advertisements are arranged under subheads according to the product or service advertised or the want it is supposed to satisfy. A person selling a house or car would most likely use classified advertising rather than display advertising. *Classified display*, on the other hand, allows more flexibility of arrangement than regular classified in that borders, larger type, white space, photos, and occasionally color may be used (see Figure 16.3). Some newspapers have the advertising of real estate agents and builders handled under classified display, others under retail. In some newspaper markets, classified is growing faster than retail.

Newspaper Sizes and Shapes

Prior to the mid-1980s, newspapers used two quite different approaches to sell advertising space. For local advertisers, both tabloids and standard broadsheets figured space by the column inch. A newspaper measures its pages, for advertising purposes, by the number of columns wide and the number of inches deep—for example, the *Birmingham News* is 6 columns by 21 inches. Rates are figured by the column inch. Thus, if an advertisement extends 3 columns wide and 10 inches deep, the ad unit is 30 column inches (3 × 10). If the rate quoted is $70 per column inch, the cost of the space would be $2,100 (30 column inches × $70 per inch). This approach continues to be used for local rates.

For national advertisers, newspapers used the **agate line** system for many years. An agate line (usually shortened to "line") is defined as 1/14 inch in depth and one column wide (or 14 lines per column inch). To complicate matters, some newspapers used six columns per advertising page, others eight columns, and yet others, nine columns. Thus, an advertisement that was 3 columns by 10 inches deep would contain 420 agate lines (3 × 10 × 14). And, of course, a 420-line advertisement in a 6-column newspaper would be of a different size and shape than in a 9-column paper. Rates were quoted in terms of dollars per line; thus, a line rate of $3.50 would result in a cost of $1,470 for the 420-line ad ($3.50 per line × 420 lines). This system made newspaper buying a rather complicated process for national advertisers, who typically buy many newspapers in different markets throughout the country.

FIGURE 16.2

Newspaper Advertising Expenditures, by Type

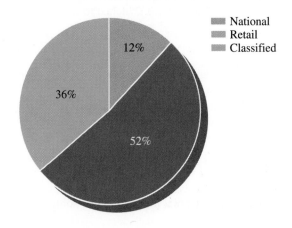

■ National
■ Retail
■ Classified

12%
36%
52%

In 1984, the newspaper industry switched to a more standardized system for national advertisers. Column widths are 2 1/16 inches, with 1/8 inch between columns. A tabloid has 5 columns per page; including space between columns, this is 10 13/16 inches. Standard broadsheets have 6 columns for a total of 13 inches. The depth of a page generally is 14 inches for tabloids and 21 inches for standards, although there still is some slight variation among different newspapers. In effect, therefore, the new system switches from agate lines to column inches and to standard page sizes.

In addition to these changes, the newspaper industry adopted the **Standard Advertising Unit (SAU)**, whereby each paper offers the national advertiser 57 standard-size units (see Figure 16.4). Thus the unit marked "2 × 14" will be 2 columns wide (4 1/4 inches) by 14 inches deep (28 column inches). One mechanical

FIGURE 16.4

The Standard Advertising Unit (SAU) System

Of the 57 SAUs, 56 fit broadsheet newspapers and 33 are possible in tabloids.

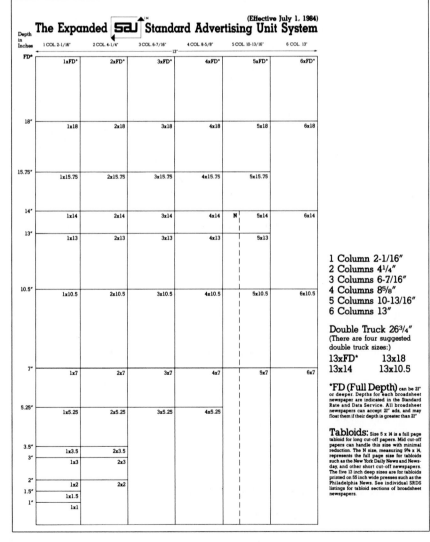

Source: American Newspaper Publishers Association. SAU® is a registered trademark of ANPA. Permission to use the SAU® was granted by ANPA.

Classified Advertising: A History...A Tradition...A Future

by Bernard F. Ott

Assistant Advertising Director, Springfield Newspapers, Springfield, Massachusetts

The "Want Ad" has the distinction of being the oldest form of advertising. Indeed, it was the forerunner of all modern day advertising. Its history traces the chronicles of civilization. The prototype of this advertisement saw its origins as a Business Service, Public Notice, Auction or Article for Sale, or people communicating a need to other people either by the oral or written word. Obviously, this communication was not via the sophisticated Classified system of "Want Ads" we recognize today; rather, it was transmitted as a single unit, a lone "Want Ad" notice.

The use of "Want Ad" advertising dates back as far as the 10th Century B.C. Early models of the "Want Ad" have been discovered on the papyri of the ancient Egyptians, and Thebes, ancient Greek messages offering rewards for runaway slaves have been discovered and preserved. These, of course, were pre-newspaper Business Announcements, Personals, and Lost and Found notices, but nevertheless, "Want Ads," using whatever means of communication that was available.

The term "Classified" did not evolve until eons later, after the printing press was invented and newspapers came into existence, when "Want Ads" were arranged in captioned categories with other "Want Ads" of similar nature.

Before the printed word, when education was the privilege of the advantaged few, advertising was by word of mouth. In these early days of commerce, tradesmen with something to sell, artisans, and professional people had to rely on strong vocal chords to publicize their wares or skills. If word was to spread to other communities, it was necessary to have some mobility, to become an itinerant tradesman.

Symbols and pictorial signs were popular forms of advertising in this era before reading and writing were within the reach of the average citizen. These symbols and signs would identify a type of business by use of some familiar drawing or emblem that might be suggestive of the business.

The next phase in the evolution of classified was the crier who would travel from area to area in his client's stead, calling out his client's sales messages wherever he trod.

After printing was invented and greater numbers learned to read, paving the way for newspapers, advertising began to flourish and become more sophisticated. "Want Ads" or "Public Notices," as they were often called, found their way into print. They were initially published as small news items on the front pages of the early newspapers. When a ship came into port laden with products from abroad, the master hurried to place such a notice in the local gazette describing the cargo that was for sale. When a shopkeeper received a shipment of goods, he would also use his local newspaper to inform the townspeople of the new items. Some of these early notices were used to locate and hire workers, thus the Help Wanted ad saw its beginnings.

The first known newspaper advertisement appeared in a German newsbook in 1591. It was an advertisement for a book, an Article for Sale. This paper is preserved in The British Museum.

The first commercial and miscellaneous advertisement was printed in a Dutch newspaper in 1629. This was set in type different than that used for news copy and was an Auction ad for such items as sugar, pepper, ivory, etc.

In England, advertisements started to appear around 1625. By 1655 ads regularly appeared in weekly newspapers such as the London News Gazette. In 1682 the City Mercury, a London newspaper, displayed a list of Articles for Sale that included coal, masks, leather, painted sticks, and quills. It was the editor of this paper, Mr. John Houghton, who first advocated that the newspaper had other functions than the mere printing of current news.

Ads went daily with the first regularly distributed paper, the Daily Courant (1702). From this time on, especially with gradually improved methods of printing, the newspaper began to be used for advertising with greater frequency.

Source: *Principles and Practices of Classified Advertising* (Danville, IL: Association of Newspaper Classified Advertising Managers, 1991), 1–2.

In 1710, Joseph Addison and Sir Richard Steele's Tatler devoted an entire issue to advertisements and a discussion of advertising giving new meaning to the word. Previously advertisement meant a notice of any sort but the Tatler redefined advertising to include business announcements.

While the first newspaper venture in the Colonies was in 1690 with the publications of the short-lived "Publick Occurences both Foreign and Domestick," the first newspaper "Want Ad" didn't appear in America until 1704 in the Boston News Letter. By 1728 the New England Weekly was carrying advertisements in every issue. In 1789 The Independent Gazette in New York ran 34 classified advertisements.

These newspaper notices replaced the town crier and were an important new chapter in the history of commerce. The early "Want Ads" were essential to the movement of goods to the consumers and were the means of communicating to a rapidly expanding populace.

The demand for these small ads grew as the power of newspapers was realized. Publishers initially ran such advertisements without charge positioned on the front page, but the proliferation of these notices caused some concern that these advertisements would push the news items off the front page.

Two occurrences in the 1830's changed the course of "Want Ads." In 1839, The New York Sun grouped all the small ads together, giving birth to the Classified section. Then around 1833, the "Penny Press" emerged upon the newspaper scene and began charging for the little ads.

Subsequently, the decision was made to classify these small ads under special headings and to relocate them from the front page to elsewhere in the newspaper. Thus the "Want Ads" were redefined as "Classified Ads."

The industrial revolution, which altered the whole complexion of civilization, gave tremendous impetus to advertising, particularly newspaper advertising. The needs, the output, the vocations and avocations of man multiplied a thousandfold in the period of half a century. Business and commerce expanded rapidly and an effective means of commercial communication was imperative. Newspaper advertising, particularly Classified advertising, met this need, tying together all commerce, from raw product supplies to employment, manufacturing, distribution and financing. Classified advertising

secured the workers, the buyers and the means to move merchandise. It told the job seeker who needed his services and also told him where to find a home for his family.

Classified advertising is a newspaper exclusive, a unique form of advertising born of human wants and developed from the Want Ad to the sophisticated system of classifying ads of like nature under a common heading that is used today. Classified advertising stands on its own. Unlike television, radio, magazine, run-of-paper newspaper advertising, etc., it doesn't require adjacent news or entertainment to attract the viewer or reader. Where other advertising seeks out the interested, the interested seek out Classified; they turn to the Classified columns to satisfy some specific need or want.

Classified has long been called "the people's marketplace." It is the only form of advertising the average individual can economically buy on a line or word basis. It requires no special knowledge of typography, layout, or illustration to create an effective ad. It does, however, require care in writing to assure the best results.

Classified advertising is a convenient form of advertising. From the comfort of one's office or home, a Classified ad can be placed easily and most likely in the next day's newspaper by simply picking up the telephone and dialing the Classified department of a newspaper.

Classified is universal. It is an advertising medium that can be found wherever newspapers are published. Whatever the newspaper, the reader can find ads from private parties intermixed with ads from the business community, a homogeneous blend of ads from heterogenous sources creating a popular marketplace with built-in reader appeal offering quick results. Classified has a tradition of satisfying the needs of both buyers and sellers.

Classified advertising is flexible. It is geared to short deadlines for immediate action. It is adaptable to growing needs and new wants, while still maintaining the orderly, reliable, consistent marketplace the reader and advertiser have come to know and expect.

The "Want Ad" has shown through history that it has a rather special malleable characteristic. It is an advertising form that can adjust yet remain basically the same. It has echoed the needs and wants of people for centuries using whatever means of communication that has been available and it will for milleniums more.

reproduction of an ad would fit every newspaper in the country that accepts SAUs. Currently, most U.S. newspapers use the SAU system. Those not offering SAUs continue with the agate-line method.

The major source of information for newspaper sizes is Standard Rate & Data Service (SRDS). SRDS also lists rates, circulations, mechanical requirements, issuance and closing dates, copy regulations, and market data for newspapers as well as other media. A sample listing is shown in Figure 16.5.

Rate Structure

ROP versus Premium Position

When a newspaper quotes a basic rate for an advertisement, it is understood that the ad is placed **ROP (run-of-paper)**. This means that the ad can appear on any page, in any position in a column—even buried among other ads. If the media buyer wants to make sure the ad is placed next to reading matter, such space can be ordered at an extra charge. This is called a premium position buy. For example, to be sure that an ad is placed at the very top of the page and next to reading matter along one vertical side (full position), the advertiser may have to pay as much as one-third more. If the advertiser specifies a particular page—for example, the back page of the sports section—the newspaper may charge a 15 percent premium. Frequently, though, advertisers can obtain these premium positions without extra charge by negotiating with the newspaper.

Retail versus National Rates

Most newspapers charge more per column inch for national (general) than for retail (local) space. This is a sore point among national advertisers and their agencies, because **local rates** (with discounts) sometimes are less than half of **national rates**.

FIGURE 16.5

Listing of Rates in Standard Rate & Data Service for Newspapers

Paso Robles

San Luis Obispo County—Map Location C-6

PRESS
Box: 427, 1050 Park St., El Paso Robles, CA 93447.
Phone 805-238-0330. Fax: 805-238-6504.

Location ID: 1 NSNL CA   **Mid 016189-000**
Member: ACB, Inc., NAA
EVENING (except Saturday & Sunday).
(Not Published Christmas, New Years, Thanksgiving, Memorial Day, July 4 and Labor Day.)
1. PERSONNEL
Pub—Ben Reddick.
Gen Mgr—R.D. Reddick.
Natl Adv Mgr—John Echeveste.
3. COMMISSION AND CASH DISCOUNT
15% to agencies; 2% 15th following month.
4. POLICY-ALL CLASSIFICATIONS
30-day notice given of any rate revision.
Alcoholic beverage advertising accepted.
ADVERTISING RATES
Effective January 1, 1992.
Received August 14, 1992.
5. BLACK/WHITE RATES
SAU flat, per inch 6.30
Inches charged full depth: col. 21.5; pg. 129.
6. GROUP COMBINATION RATES-B/W & COLOR
Also sold in combination with (Wed.) Paso Robles North County Journal, comb. flat, per col. inch 7.80.
Circulation not received since 3-31-91.
7. COLOR RATES AND DATA
Available daily.
Use b/w rate plus the following applicable costs:
                        b/w 1 c   b/w 2 c
Extra 80.00   160.00
Color of day—25.00 discount.
Closing date: 2 days before publication.
11. SPECIAL DAYS/PAGES/FEATURES
Best Food Day: Wednesday.
Agri-Business, Monday and Tuesday; Real Estate, Thursday and Friday; TV/Entertainment: Friday; Dining Guide, Thursday.
12. R.O.P. DEPTH REQUIREMENTS
Ads over 19 inches deep charged full col.
14. CLOSING TIME
Published Evening (ex. Saturday and Sunday).
Day   Time   Closes   Day   Time   Closes
Mon .... 11 am   Thu   Thu .... 11 am   Tue
Tue .... 11 am   Fri   Fri .... 11 am   Wed
Wed .... 11 am   Mon

15. MECHANICAL MEASUREMENTS
PRINTING PROCESS: Offset.
6 col; ea 2-1/8″; 1/8″ betw col.
Inches charged full depth: col. 21.5; pg. 129.
16. SPECIAL CLASSIFICATIONS/RATES
Amusement and Political—general rates apply.
Cash in advance.
17. CLASSIFIED RATES
For complete data refer to classified rate section.
20. CIRCULATION
Established: weekly 1886; daily 1952, per copy .35.
Net Paid—Sworn 3-31-92
                     Total   CZ   TrZ   Other
ExSat 5,307   3,710   1,469   128
For county, MSA & ADI data, see CIRCULATION 93.

Petaluma

Sonoma County—Map Location B-1

ARGUS-COURIER
A Scripps League Newspaper, Inc. Newspaper
Box: 1091, 830 N. Petaluma Blvd., Petaluma, CA 94953.
Phone 707-762-4541. Fax: 707-765-1707.

ABC

Location ID: 1 NSNL CA   **Mid 016190-000**
Member: NAB, Inc.; ACB, Inc.
EVENING (ex. Sat.) AND SUNDAY.
1. PERSONNEL
Pub—Gregg McConnell.
Adv Dir—Barry Blansett.
2. REPRESENTATIVES and/or BRANCH OFFICES
Newspaper Advertising Services Co.
3. COMMISSION AND CASH DISCOUNT
15% to agencies; 2% 15th following month.
4. POLICY-ALL CLASSIFICATIONS
30-day notice given of any rate revision.
Alcoholic beverage advertising accepted.
ADVERTISING RATES
Effective April 1, 1992. (Card No. 30).
Received March 15, 1992.
5. BLACK/WHITE RATES
SAU flat, per inch (ex. Wed.) 12.76
Wednesday, per inch 15.65
Inches charged full depth: col. 21.5; pg 129.
6. GROUP COMBINATION RATES-B/W & COLOR
Above Wednesday rate includes insertion in TMC.
Circulation not received since 3-31-90.

7. COLOR RATES AND DATA
Use b/w rate plus the following applicable costs:
                    b/w 1 c   b/w 2 c   b/w 3 c
Extra 125.00   195.00   250.00
8a. INSERTS
PREPRINT INSERTS
8 Pg Tab or Less   Flat   12-24 Tab   28-40 Tab
10,000 (Argus-Courier) . 550.00   600.00   650.00 ...
23,000 TMC .... 975.00   1,100.00   1,250.00 ...
Less than 10,000 or full
   combo .... 65.00   70.00   75.00 ...
11. SPECIAL DAYS/PAGES/FEATURES
Best Food Day: Wednesday.
12. R.O.P. DEPTH REQUIREMENTS
Ads exceeding 266 lines charged full column.
14. CLOSING TIME
Published Evening (ex. Sat.) and Sunday.
Day   Time Closes   Day   Time Closes
Mon .... 1 pm   Thu   Thu .... 1 pm   Tue
Tue .... 1 pm   Fri   Fri .... 1 pm   Wed
Wed .... 5 pm   Thu   Sun .... 1 pm   Thu
15. MECHANICAL MEASUREMENTS
PRINTING PROCESS: Offset.
6 col; ea 2-1/32″; 5/32″ betw col.
Inches charged full depth: col. 21.5; pg. 129.
16. SPECIAL CLASSIFICATIONS/RATES
Amusement, Political (cash with order)—general rate applies.
POSITION CHARGES
25% additional. Definite page (when available) 25% additional.
17. CLASSIFIED RATES
For complete data refer to classified rate section.
20. CIRCULATION
Established 1855. Per copy .25.
Net Paid—A.B.C. 9-30-92 (Newspaper Form)
                    Total   CZ   TrZ   Other
ExSat 8,686   6,882   1,619   185
Sun 8,890   7,069   1,636   185
A.B.C. Zip Code Analysis available from publisher.
For county, MSA & ADI data, see CIRCULATION 93.

Pinole

WEST COUNTY TIMES
Location ID: 1 NSNL CA   **Mid 016125-003**
See Contra Costa Daily Group listing at beginning of State.

Newspaper publishers and business managers defend this differential on several bases. In general, their experiments with lowering national rates to the same level as local rates have resulted in only small increases in total space from national advertisers. Newspaper executives maintain that the demand for national advertising is inelastic (will not expand as the price lowers or contract as the price increases), compared with that for local advertising. They also point to the agency commission on national but not usually granted on local sales, the payment to the national representatives for their services (for example, selling agencies and their clients on the local newspapers), the merchandising services furnished national advertisers, and the fact that the national advertiser is less likely than a retail counterpart to be a year-round user of advertising. Some newspaper executives point also to the higher readership of the retail advertisements, maintaining that these add more to the newspaper's attractiveness and reader appeal.

The national advertisers and their agencies do not generally accept these as valid reasons for the huge differential that often exists. They point to the fact that most papers maintain a large and costly staff to service the advertising of the local retail advertiser (usually at no extra charge). They hint also that newspaper managements may be somewhat more sensitive to protests from the retailers, who are, after all, their friends and neighbors, than from the more distant national advertisers.

Although efforts have been underway for many years by national advertisers and agencies to lower the so-called **rate differential** between national and retail rates, the fact is that the differences have increased systematically over the past 50 years. Whereas the rate differential was around 38 percent in 1933 (that is, national advertisers paid 38 percent more for identical space than local advertisers), it has generally risen consistently over the years. The current differential is around 75 percent.[2]

Sliding Scale

Newspapers may offer either **flat rates** (the same regardless of how much space is used by the advertiser) or **open rates** (subject to various discounts). When the newspapers think the price is elastic, they may set up a schedule of discounts (or a sliding scale) to encourage businesses to advertise more, or more often. These discounts are more frequently used at the retail level, but certain newspapers offer them to general advertisers as well. The scale of rates for national advertising in the *Baton Rouge Advocate* is shown in Table 16.4.

TABLE 16.4

Black-and-White Rates for National Advertisers Using the *Baton Rouge Advocate*, Based on Column Inches Used Per Year

Column Inches	Daily	Sunday
Open	$46.36	$50.78
135 to 269	35.11	41.46
270 to 539	33.66	39.58
540 to 1,319	32.74	38.50
1,320 to 2,639	31.27	37.17
2,640 or more	30.34	35.82

Source: Standard Rate & Data Service, *Newspaper Rates and Data*, June 1993, 245.

Rate Comparisons

The rates charged per column inch are often a poor guide to the actual cost of the space. Common sense should tell any buyer that a newspaper with a large circulation will charge more than a newspaper with a small circulation. Consequently, rates must be reduced to some sort of common denominator in order to compare them realistically. The typical method used to make such comparisons is the **cost per thousand**, or **CPM**, where "M" is the Roman numeral for 1,000. (When the agate-line method was used for national advertisers, the yardstick most frequently used for comparison was the **milline rate** [cost per line per million circulation].) The formula typically used in calculating the cost per thousand is:

$$\text{Cost per Thousand} = \frac{\text{Column inch rate} \times 1,000}{\text{Circulation}}$$

Thus, if two newspapers in a city had column-inch rates of $25 and $30—and circulations of 65,000 and 100,000, respectively—we could compare than as follows:

$$\text{Newspaper A:} \quad \frac{\$25 \times 1,000}{65,000} = \$0.385$$

$$\text{Newspaper B:} \quad \frac{\$30 \times 1,000}{100,000} = \$0.300$$

If all other decision factors were equal, Newspaper B would be the more efficient buy at 30 cents per thousand circulation (versus 38.5 cents).

An alternative way to make comparisons is to use the cost of the space—that is, a particular SAU. For example, let's say an advertiser is buying a 6-column by full-depth advertisement. This is a full page in a standard paper: 126 column inches. For Newspapers A and B above, page costs are $3,150 (126 × $25) and $3,780 (126 × $30), respectively. Thus, the cost-per-thousand circulation in each paper is as follows:

$$\text{CPM (Newspaper A):} \quad \frac{\$3,150 \times 1,000}{65,000} = \$48.46$$

$$\text{CPM (Newspaper B):} \quad \frac{\$3,780 \times 1,000}{100,000} = \$37.80$$

Regardless of the method used to make the calculation, the result is the same—Newspaper B is more efficient. The use of color in an ad incurs an additional charge, and this would have to be taken into account in the cost comparisons. On the average, a full-color, full-page ad will cost 21 percent more than a corresponding black-and-white advertisement. If only one color is used in addition to black, the extra charge would average 12 percent.

Factors to Consider in Buying Newspaper Space

A media buyer has several aspects to consider when purchasing newspaper space.

Market Considerations

Although newspapers collectively offer both the widest and the most concentrated national coverage, their number and cost make it difficult to use them on a truly national basis. For example, a media planner who bought only one daily newspaper in each market having a daily would buy more than 1,500 cities in the United States! The logistics of such a buy would be formidable, even if each of the 1,500 papers offered SAUs.

The cost of a single, full-page, black-and-white (B & W) advertisement in the top 100 markets would cost over $3 million, even though such a buy would cover around 82 percent of all U.S. households. A similar buy in the top 50 markets, which would cover 64 percent of all households, would cost $2.3 million, or $118 million annually for a once-a-week schedule (see Table 16.5).

Thus, the media buyer who thinks that newspapers should be the sole medium to support a product nationally is in trouble unless there is an unusually large advertising budget to invest. Because of the cost factor, all newspapers or even all the newspapers in any classification are rarely purchased. Sometimes an extensive newspaper list will be used for a single advertisement, such as the announcement of a new car or a special offer. But when a sustained effort is to be made, newspaper advertising is usually planned in **flights** and often in selected areas and selected markets. For example, during a calandar year an advertiser might have three flights, each of eight weeks' duration. These might be spaced uniformly throughout the year, or they might appear during a product's three best-selling seasons. They might perhaps be planned to put extra sales effort into certain territories.

Primary versus Supplementary Usage

Newspapers may be used as a primary or supplementary medium in the media mix. When they are used exclusively, coverage is usually not national. Often, they are used as the major, but not exclusive, medium for both national and regional coverage. For example, they are commonly used to highlight a campaign and are thus confined to approximately 100 markets that each have more than 480,000 in population. The media buyer might then support this primary effort with advertising in magazines or spot television.

When they are used as a supplementary medium, newspapers can put pressure on a weak sales territory or support magazines in certain areas where the coverage is weak. Newspapers are often chosen to fill in the spots not covered well by network television.

Inserts versus ROP

One area of rapid growth in newspaper advertising is the use of inserts, many of which are in color. An advertiser must consider whether to use the regular pages of the newspaper for advertising (ROP) or have the advertising message produced

---

TABLE 16.5

Circulation and Costs for Daily Newspapers, by Top Market Groups[a]

Markets	Total Circulation	Page Cost (B & W)
Top 10	19,301,000	$ 969,065
Top 20	26,995,000	1,437,792
Top 30	32,397,000	1,785,863
Top 40	36,096,000	2,033,759
Top 50	39,489,000	2,269,885
Top 60	42,396,000	2,481,480
Top 70	44,816,000	2,677,250
Top 80	46,812,000	2,831,142
Top 90	48,713,000	2,965,481
Top 100	50,358,000	3,087,820

Source: Newspaper Advertising Bureau, Inc.

[a] Daily newspapers in each market are included on the basis of circulation rank until the combined circulations exceed 50% coverage of the market.

by a specialized printer and shipped to the paper for insertion into an issue. The newspaper thus becomes a distributor of the insert material.

Multipage inserts generally are printed in a tabloid size and can be on regular newsprint or high-quality glossy paper stock. These inserts are used extensively by national retailers such as Sears, J. C. Penney, and Kmart, but also are used by local retailers and national advertisers. For example, an automobile manufacturer may introduce a new model line with an 8- or 16-page color insert. Some advertisers distribute a small catalog of their items via insert in order to get mail-order sales from newspaper readers.

Card inserts include single cards, with an advertising message on one side and a return-address order blank on the other. Some film processing labs use an envelope–order form. One advertiser, who was introducing a new paper towel, distributed a sample sheet of the new brand, with a wraparound that contained the advertising message.

A special type of insert that has grown in importance in recent years is the **free standing insert (FSI).** An FSI is a grouping of ads for several different advertisers and brands and consists mostly of advertisements that feature coupons. An independent producer puts the insert together, selling space to individual advertisers; the insert is printed and then shipped to cooperating newspapers who carry the insert. as part of their Sunday newspaper.

The advantage of using an insert rests largely in its ability to attract more attention to the advertising message through its unique appearance and often high-quality color. This advantage must be weighed against the increased costs over ROP advertising.

Audience Delivery

Until rather recently, most media buyers had only circulation data on which to base decisions about newspaper selection. Although newspaper circulations still are used in the analytical process, buyers now have available audience information as well. The Scarborough Research Corporation offers a newspaper audience service that provides readership information for the top 50 markets.

The use of audience data permits media planners and buyers to analyze newspapers as part of the media mix in ways that are more similar to the way they analyze such media as magazines and broadcast. By relating audience figures to the demographic characteristics of readers, the matching of media delivery and target markets within a plan is facilitated. Also, newspaper reach and frequency estimates can be more readily compared with those in other media than is the case when only circulation data are at hand.

Newspaper Supplements

A **supplement** is a part of most Sunday papers. There are two types—the syndicated national supplement and the locally edited supplement. Each syndicated supplement is compiled, edited, and printed by a central organization. It is then sold to newspapers at a fixed cost per thousand. Newspaper supplements often compare favorably with leading national magazines in the quality of editorial matter. Advertising space in the syndicated supplements is sold at a group rate. Advertisers may contract to use the total distribution or only selected regions—for example, *USA Weekend* offers nine regions (see Figure 16.6). Comic supplements are usually sold on a national or group basis.

Newspaper supplements offer four-color printing at rates surprisingly close to that of black and white. They are printed on paper that is heavier and better finished than newsprint. Therefore, reproduction, both in black and white and in color, is superior to anything that can be offered in the regular columns. The same mechanical advantages are found in the locally edited supplements. Advertising can be bought separately in each of them, but for greater convenience to media buyers and to

FIGURE 16.6

*USA WEEKEND Offers Advertisers Nine Regions in Which
Advertising Space Can Be Purchased*

USA WEEKEND'S 9-NATIONS

NEW NEW ENGLAND (1)
HEARTLAND (2)
ATLANTIC EXPANSE (3)
NEW SOUTH (4)
TRADITIONAL SOUTH (5)
GULF COAST (6)
MADE IN THE USA (7)
WESTERN HORIZONS (8)
MULTI-CULTURE (9)

Copyright 1992, Claritas/NPDC

compete successfully with the syndicated supplements, a number of them have been formed into cooperative selling groups. See Table 16.6 for circulation and cost data of national supplements.

TABLE 16.6

Circulation and Costs for National Supplements

Publication	Circulation	Number of Newspapers Carrying	Page Cost (B & W)	Page Cost (Four-Color)
Parade	36,070,954	351	$416,400	$514,500
Sunday	16,524,615	28	192,036	236,892
USA WEEKEND	16,392,614	382	200,490	237,165

Source: Standard Rate & Data Service, *Newspaper Rates and Data*, June 1993, 801–802.

Magazines

Although magazines rank fourth among the media in total dollar revenue, more manufacturers advertise in magazines than in any other mass medium. This is not surprising when we consider some of the special advantages magazines offer. Most products appeal to some groups and not to others. Few individuals besides camera enthusiasts are inordinately interested in zoom lenses and autowinders; few but tennis players need racquets and tennis balls; only farmers want hybrid seed corn. Special-interest magazines offer to the manufacturers of such products a unique opportunity to reach a select audience. Magazines thus make it possible for companies with small budgets to make a substantial impact on limited markets.

Although several periodicals existed during the 1700s in the United States, the magazine did not really become an important literary and advertising force until late in the nineteenth century. The Postal Act of 1879 granted second-class mailing privileges to magazines and made possible low-cost national distribution through the mails. By the end of the nineteenth century, magazines had become a major advertising medium.

During the twentieth century, American magazines have shifted more to factual material and have emphasized fiction somewhat less. During the 1980s and 1990s, more emphasis was placed on reaching special audiences not served adequately by other mass media. Thus, a magazine like *Discover* achieved a circulation of almost 1,000,000 within a few years. The magazine with the highest circulation, *Modern Maturity*, has a monthly circulation of almost 23,000,000 and reaches a total audience of more than 55,000,000 persons. The trend toward specialized audiences is likely to continue throughout the remainder of the 1990s and beyond. A selection of special-interest magazines, offered by a major magazine publisher, is shown in Figure 16.7.

FIGURE 16.7

Some Special–Interest Magazines Offer Advertisers Unique, Select Audiences

The Standard Rate & Data Service classifies magazines according to frequency of publication and the audience to which they are directed. On the basis of frequency, weeklies and monthlies are the most important types. We find, in addition, a smattering of semimonthlies, bimonthlies, and quarterlies. Monthly magazines outnumber all other types.

On the basis of the audience served, there are three principal types of magazines:

1. *Consumer magazines*   These are edited for people who buy products for their own consumption.
2. *Farm magazines*   These circulate to farmers and their families. Although there is some overlapping with the consumer classification, the farm audience is a fairly distinct one.
3. *Business magazines*   These are published for business readers. They fall into three subgroups: (1) trade papers—addressed to retailers, wholesalers, and other distributors; (2) industrial magazines—addressed to businesspeople engaged in all phases of manufacturing; and (3) professional magazines—directed at physicians, lawyers, architects, and other professional people.

Consumer Magazines

In the Standard Rate & Data listing, consumer magazines are divided into 67 subclassifications, from airline-inflight magazines at one end of the alphabetical listing to youth magazines at the other. Magazines such as *The Atlantic* and *Reader's Digest* are considered general–editorial magazines.

Consumer magazines might be distinguished also on the basis of their distribution. Among the women's service magazines, there are both circulation-distributed magazines and store-distributed magazines. *Ladies' Home Journal* is an example of the former, and *Woman's Day* (distributed primarily through grocery stores) is an example of the latter classification. The Standard Rate & Data listing for a consumer magazine is shown in Figure 16.8.

Farm Magazines

Farm magazines may be general or specialized, nationwide or regional. The advertiser wanting to reach all types of farmers might use *Successful Farming*. To reach a more specialized group, the advertiser might buy space in *Beef* or *Hoard's Dairyman*. To reach Wisconsin farmers, *Wisconsin Agriculturist* might be used.

Business Publications

In the thick Standard Rate & Data book for business magazines, about 5,400 business publications are listed and described, including such general business publications as *Fortune* and *Harvard Business Review*, which SRDS covers also in its consumer magazine edition. Although trade magazines (or papers) are edited primarily for retailers and wholesalers, many of them are read also by the sales personnel of manufacturers. Some, such as *Women's Wear Daily*, try for fairly broad coverage. Some, such as *Florist's Review*, are more specialized.

Industrial magazines may cover the field in either of two ways—horizontally or vertically. The horizontal publication is aimed at a specific function or activity within many industries, while the vertical one attempts to do a complete job of covering one industry. *Sales & Marketing Management*'s coverage is horizontal because it is edited for sales managers and their staffs, regardless of their type of business. By contrast, *Iron Age* and *Railway Age* attempt to cover entire industries.

The circulation of business magazines may be controlled or paid. The publisher of a controlled-circulation magazine concentrates on a specialized business audience and limits coverage to this one group, tailoring the editorial material to its needs.

FIGURE 16.8

Typical Page from Standard Rate & Data Service for Consumer Magazines

The publisher usually sends the magazine free to this select group in order to obtain high coverage, depending entirely on the advertising revenue for support. Some controlled-circulation magazines are sold in bulk to such firms as utilities, which then distribute them free to special classes of customers.

Advantages of Magazine Advertising

Magazines offer advertisers a number of advantages: (1) market selectivity, (2) quality of reproduction, (3) the instrument's long life, (4) inherent prestige, and (5) extra service to advertisers. The Ad Insight entitled "Some Marketing Success Stories Associated with the Use of Magazines in the Media Mix" presents some marketing success stories to demonstrate the value of magazines to specific advertisers.

Selectivity

Unless the market the advertiser is trying to reach is very small, at least one magazine is probably edited primarily for it. As soon as any group starts to grow, someone sees the chance of making a profit by publishing a magazine for this new market. This is a happy situation for most businesses, because few of them are trying to talk to everybody. Even the biggest companies are more interested in certain audiences than others, and they need channels to reach them. The small company may make a considerable impact in the limited market at which it must aim if it is able to reach it cheaply and intensively.

Sometimes, however, an advertiser of a specialized product, such as grass seed or outboard motors, uses general magazines like *Reader's Digest*. The advertiser is probably aware that much of the circulation is wasted, but may have other media objectives in mind. He or she may be trying to win new users. Or perhaps the total market reached here is greater than that reached by any of the specialized magazines, in spite of the waste. Or the advertiser may want to impress dealers with the firm's success and to get them to feature the brand as "advertised in *Reader's Digest*."

The selectivity of magazines can be translated into a low cost per thousand for reaching desired audiences. If most members of the audience are real prospects, the advertiser can divide total readership into page cost, but if only half the readers are prospects, only half the readership can logically be used in the calculation. If the advertiser can manage with half or quarter pages, the cost per thousand drops even further.

Reproduction

Most magazines are printed on good paper stock and can provide excellent reproduction in black and white or in color. In recent years, magazines have widened the variety of mechanical features offered to advertisers. Some magazines offer special attention-attracting inks. Some offer gatefolds and odd-sized pages that are likely to attract attention. Magazine advertisements can be made to "pop-up" when a page is opened, may contain a fragrance, and some even "talk."

Long Life

Magazines are kept around the home longer than other media and are often used for reference. One study, for example, showed that the average person picked up a monthly magazine on four different days and picked up a weekly or biweekly just under two days. Another study found that 76 percent of men and 78 percent of women referred to or reread something in a magazine issue that they had previously read. About three-fourths kept the magazine read on hand for future reference and, on average, a magazine is kept accesssible for over 28 weeks.

The relationship between magazine editors and readers has been described as an ongoing conversation that in time creates a bond of trust, belief, expectation, and empathy.

Inherent Prestige

Many magazine publishers claim that advertising lends prestige to the product; although it is difficult to prove just how much prestige magazines in general provide. Many studies indicate, however, that copies of such prestigious magazines as *Fortune, National Geographic*, and *The New Yorker* enjoy an exceptionally long and active life, a good part of it spent in doctors' and corporations' reception rooms. There is little doubt, however, that many advertisers buy space in such magazines for prestige purposes. On the other hand, magazines such as *True Story* probably do little to add prestige to a product, although they may be quite useful for other purposes. The number of readers per copy are much fewer than for the more prestigious magazines.

Services Offered

Some magazines offer many extra services to advertisers. Some have their merchandising staff call on retailers to inform them of the products advertised in a particular issue. Merchandising of this kind often improves an advertiser's distribution and is a welcomed service. Other magazines will create and mail to an advertiser's dealers a direct-mail advertisement that ties-in with the magazine's advertising program.

Some Marketing Success Stories Associated with the Use of Magazines in the Media Mix

WHAT HAPPENED WHEN BUICK LeSABRE INVESTED ALMOST 70% OF THE AD BUDGET IN MAGAZINES?

When J.D. Power named Buick LeSabre as the most trouble-free American car, the company acted to tell the story fast. In a bold move these auto marketers headed straight for magazines. They had impressive news to tell: the Buick LeSabre sedan had broken into the ranks of the world's top 10—the only American car to place there—in the J.D. Power and Associates 1989 Initial Quality Survey.

Results came fast. Within the five months that followed the magazine campaign launch, *sales were up 40 percent,* according to Jay Qualman, Buick's Director of Advertising.

Why did Buick, and their agency McCann-Erickson, make a U-turn against the industry's conventional media selection—and focus almost 70 percent of their media dollars in magazines.

The fast-close advantage was a key reason. "As soon as J.D. Power released the data," Qualman explains, "we sent fast-close ads to the newsweeklies. Using black & white, we could get the facts out in a matter of days— then follow up with four-color ads in a range of select publications."

Source: Courtesy of Magazine Publishers of America

"*Custom tailoring, flexibility, depth of sell*—all played a part in our decision to go heavily into magazines," says Qualman. Fact-filled ads could be adapted for specific audiences—such as fleet buyers, where the LeSabre is very popular.

"*People tore ads* out of magazines and brought them along right into dealerships," reports Qualman. "Many Buick dealers kept the magazines handy in showrooms, to flip open as a selling tool."

Good news repeats. In 1990, the LeSabre was again ranked as the most trouble-free American car. And again, Buick elected to tell the story in magazines.

The power of magazines. During the 1989 model year, magazine readers spent $128 billion on new automobiles– an increase of over 24 percent since the previous year. It's a spending trend that continues to increase.

ONCE EACH DECADE ESTEE LAUDER LAUNCHES A NEW LINE. IN MAGAZINES.

For the '90s and beyond, Lauder introduced Origins— one unique product at a time—choosing magazines to present these new experiences in sensory therapy, as well as colors and skin care which incorporate plant extracts. Origins sets the theme: "The power of nature brings beauty to its senses."

With this newest division, Estée Lauder continues the successful pattern of launching a major new cosmetics company with each new decade. Aramis. Clinique. Prescriptives. All have been characterized by advertising with distinct personality and appeal. *All have relied heavily on magazines.*

In August 1990, Origins premiered at Bergdorf Goodman and Nordstrom, advertising in magazines on both coasts.

The advertising challenge was to establish an image as unique as the concept: nature-based beauty products incorporating advanced understandings of aromatherapy.

"This is our line for the '90s," says Daria Myers, VP of Marketing. "The ads take a single bottle or tube and make it larger than life. They stop you with powerful graphics. Very clean. We virtually print our packaging copy on the ad, with an intriguing headline to announce that this product is different."

Impact on sales can be measured immediately. "Every time an ad runs in this area, Bergdorf gets an enormous number of orders over the phone—sight unseen," Myers reports. "Everything about this line has been beyond our expectations," she adds. By Fall 1991, the number of Origins doors will be expanded to America's top 30 stores.

"We'll extend our magazine advertising into additional national books as well as regional magazines," says Myers. "We'll stay with our distinctive style and single pages, possibly adding inserts such as bounce-back cards."

Again in the '90s, magazines provide Estée Lauder with the appropriate base for establishing a new product personality for a new decade—and presenting it to a select target audience, with maximum efficiency.

DEL MONTE FOODS SWITCHES TO MAGAZINES—INCREASES SALES AND SHARE.

Three years ago, this leading food marketer made a dramatic shift in its media mix, switching almost the entire budget into magazines. Surprising the competition, they have since then consistently increased sales and share in the Del Monte Foods advertised product lines.

George W. Pace, Del Monte's senior vice president of marketing, speaks frankly, "Although we now use some TV on a tactical basis, we felt that the product benefits for our ongoing business lines could be better communicated in print. We needed *more continuity* and magazines were the way to get it—if we had put twenty million dollars into television it would have been a yawn."

Wanting to maintain a presence for "more than a few weeks in any quarter," Del Monte and their agency McCann-Erickson, planned a 12-month campaign and created a series of four-color page ads featuring new recipe ideas or serving suggestions. "Magazines let us target existing, new, or lapsed users of our products," says Pace. "We also wanted to bring *younger customers* into our franchise—and found magazines to be an excellent vehicle for that."

Color photography, of course, is critical. "When you look at food presented in an appealing way, you have a *positive perception of taste* before you ever taste it," explains Pace. And all Del Monte ads carry the same graphic format so that when consumers turn the page they immediately know, "This is a Del Monte ad." The company's graphic consistency works—along with the media plan—to build an overall brand franchise while promoting individual products as different as green beans, Cajun stewed tomatoes, or a handy vanilla pudding cup.

1990 Results. All four of the Del Monte advertised categories: Vegetables, Fruits, Fruit Snack Cups, and Stewed Tomatoes were up in share last year. (Fruit Snack Cups jumped by a robust 5.9 share points!) George Pace says this about his company's decision to use magazines—"We're totally committed to it."

The power of magazines. During the past year, magazine readers spent almost $750 billion on food products—an increase of nine percent over the previous year. If you're selling food, put your product in a consumer's hands. Put it in a magazine.

Another service that appeals to many advertisers is the opportunity of testing one's advertisements through a **split run**. In split-run testing, two or more versions of the copy for an advertisement are printed in alternate copies of a given press run. In each test advertisement, some offer is made to spur replies. The assumption is that the version that prompts the most replies is superior. The split run is often used to test advertisements on a small-scale basis to see which is the best action producer; the winner is then used in large space in a national campaign.

Limitations of Magazine Advertising

Magazines are not as flexible as newspapers or spot radio and television in either area or time. Most magazines are so widely distributed that it is not possible to fit copy to local conditions. However, many publishers try to overcome this problem by offering regional editions. There are more than 300 consumer magazines offering regional editions, and the advertising volume from such editions is about a third of the medium's total. The extent of geographical flexibility varies greatly by magazine. For example, *Field & Stream* offers five regional editions covering broad areas of the United States (Northeast, Midwest, South, and so on), whereas *Time* regionals can be purchased in any of the 50 states or in 50 city markets.

The nature of magazine publishing makes it impossible to make last-minute changes in advertising. Most magazines are printed in great quantities, sometimes by several printers, and the forms often must be closed several weeks before the publication date. For example, *People Weekly* has a seven-week closing date; an advertisement in *Time* must be at the publisher at least four weeks before the publication's issue date.

Kinds of Advertisers

A large proportion of all national advertisers use some form of magazine advertising. In addition to national manufacturers, many national retailing chains—such as Sears and Kmart—invest in magazine advertising. Kmart, for example, currently spends more than $27 million in the medium, which amounts to 14 percent of its total media mix. Local retailers also are increasingly able to use the medium because of city editions of national magazines (such as *Time*) and the large number of cities with their own magazine (for example, *Atlanta*, *Boston Magazine*, *Chicago*, *D* in Dallas/Fort Worth, *Detroit Monthly*, *Houston Metropolitan*, and *San Francisco Focus*).

The top ten magazine advertisers are shown in Table 16.7.

TABLE 16.7

Top Ten Magazine Advertisers, 1991

Rank	Advertiser	Dollars Spent (millions)
1	General Motors Corp.	$250.4
2	Philip Morris Cos.	215.1
3	Ford Motor Co.	149.6
4	Procter & Gamble Co.	142.9
5	Chrysler Corp.	106.7
6	Toyota Motor Corp.	105.4
7	Grand Metropolitan	83.3
8	Unilever NV	81.0
9	Nestlé SA	77.1
10	Time Warner	66.9

Source: *Advertising Age* (September 23, 1992): 63.

TABLE 16.8

Top Fifteen Consumer Magazines by Circulation

Rank	Magazine	Circulation
1	Modern Maturity	22,879,886
2	Reader's Digest	16,258,476
3	TV Guide	14,498,341
4	National Geographic	9,708,254
5	Better Homes & Gardens	8,002,585
6	The Cable Guide	5,889,947
7	Family Circle	5,283,660
8	Good Housekeeping	5,139,355
9	Ladies' Home Journal	5,041,143
10	Woman's Day	4,810,445
11	McCall's	4,704,772
12	Time	4,203,991
13	People	3,506,816
14	Sports Illustrated	3,432,044
15	Playboy	3,402,630

Source: *Advertising Age* (February 22, 1993): 27.

Circulation and Readership Patterns

To match coverage with potential markets, most buyers of magazine space depend on both circulation and audience (readership) data. Some buyers regard newsstand sales as one criterion to evaluate the quality of a medium's circulation because purchases at a newsstand are completely voluntary. Many media analysts also watch carefully the trends in subscription sales of various magazines, especially the rate at which subscribers renew their subscriptions. Table 16.8 shows the 15 largest consumer magazines in terms of circulation.

From circulation data, analysts can compare magazines also on the basis of how the subscriptions were produced (by mail, by catalog, by field selling staff), duration of subscription, percentage sold in combination, percentage in arrears, percentage sold at regular price, and percentage with special offers.

During recent years, the general circulation trend has been up, but single-copy sales have decreased. Circulation of the more selective magazines has been increasing at the most rapid rate among all magazines. From several audience studies that have been done in recent years, we can note the following highlights of magazine readership:

Magazine Readership in the United States

- 156.3 million adults, or 88 percent of the U.S. population 18 years of age and older, read one or more magazines during an average month. They read an average of 10.0 different magazine issues during the month.
- Each reader spends an average of 51 minutes reading a magazine copy.
- Magazine reading is heaviest among college-educated people and those with household incomes exceeding $50,000.
- Each reader is exposed an average of 1.7 times to the average page in a magazine.

Source: Magazine Publishers of America.

Media analysts are often confused by the fact that a particular magazine seems to have audiences of different sizes, depending on which researcher made the study. When such differences occur, there usually are many reasonable explanations: varying dates of measurement, different sample sizes, and contrasting methods of measuring readership. Nevertheless, the user of such information often finds large differences difficult to reconcile.

Magazine Sizes and Shapes

The largest regular unit of space in a magazine is the double-page spread. This usually consists of two pages that face each other. In magazines that are saddle-stitched (that is, pages are held together by staples, which are pushed through the center of the magazine when it is open), it may be the center spread. For example, *Time* is saddle-stitched.

Other shapes of advertisements may be made by full, half, and quarter pages. The full page is, of course, a common size in all magazines. A few advertisers like the full page plus either a half or a quarter page facing it. These ads may be designed as a complete unit or as two separate facing advertisements.

Most magazines offer **bleed** pages, which permit the dark or colored background of the advertising to extend to the edge of the page (or to "bleed" off the page). The printing space is a little greater than on ordinary pages, and the artist has more leeway in expressing an idea (see Figure 16.9).

Layout artists and media buyers often wonder which size is most efficient. Should a given amount of money be used to buy a large number of smaller advertisements

FIGURE 16.9

A Bleed Advertisement for Hearst Magazines Seeking Advertisers for Its Publications

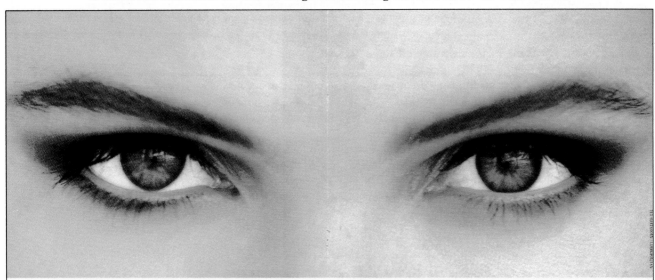

Hearst puts you eyeball to eyeball

with the women you want most.

No one gets you closer to your customers than Hearst Magazines—because we do more than inform and entertain them. We help them live their lives.

The lives of millions of young women are shaped each month by *Cosmopolitan*. *Redbook* influences a new generation of young working mothers. Certainly no one speaks to the concerns of today's New Traditionalists more believably than *Good Housekeeping*. And the *Victoria* woman's favorite magazine reflects her uniquely romantic outlook. Each of these magazines deals with the personal things that women care about most—their careers, their looks, their health, their loves.

When it comes to contemporary style in the home, who can speak with more authority than *House Beautiful*?

For devotees of classic American living, *Colonial Homes* is the bible. And *Country Living* has set its own stamp on American family life. Hearst takes women to the forefront of high fashion through the pages of *Harper's Bazaar* and inside the lives of affluent Americans in the pages of *Town & Country*.

Each Hearst magazine plays an important role in the lives of its readers. The editorial environment creates an emotional bond between the audience and the magazine that no other medium can match. Your advertisement becomes part of that unique bond. We get you closer to the people you want to reach most.

Hearst Magazines is a division of The Hearst Corporation. © 1992 The Hearst Corporation.

Hearst Magazines

Some Guidelines to Effective Magazine Advertisements

WHAT MAKES A MAGAZINE AD EFFECTIVE?

The Pretesting Company for the past six years has tested ads and commercials in a controlled "real world" simulation. Patented systems allow comparisons between TV, Print, Radio, Outdoor and FSI advertising.

Beyond ad recall, tests also measure involvement, competitive imagery and impulse change in purchase selection.

Based on tests of between 4,000–5,000 magazine ads over a six-year period, The Pretesting Company has uncovered some interesting and perhaps startling findings about magazine advertising.

- Up to 40 percent of readers do not start from the front-of-the-book. Many "fan" a magazine with their left hand and will look at ads and articles starting from the back-of-the-book. In fact, according to a report from Time Marketing, 67 percent of magazine readers start reading a publication from some other place than the front-of-the-book.
- With 18,000 products currently available in a typical supermarket (versus 10,000 only four years ago), *print advertising has been found to be the strongest medium in terms of helping a respondent be aware of a new variety of product or what the product looks like on the shelf.*
- Few 15-second television commercials have been able to communicate competitive imagery. *The use of print and television has been found to be a far better solution to the problem of poor communication* (if the print ad is a good one).
- What fails to hold reader attention and gain a high level of communication:

  Metallic paint
  White copy on white background
  Black copy on black background
  Copy that is too large
  Copy that is too small
  Little space between the words

- Print ads that are used as "billboard" ads, simple reminders of television commercials, are an ineffective and inefficient use of magazines, and usually do not increase communication. Print ads *must* stand on their own, communicate the advertiser's objectives, and support the marketing strategy to be effective.
- Descending order of magazine advertising size impact:

  1. Three single-page ads following each other on the right side.
  2. Two single-page ads in different sections of the same magazine on the right side.
  3. Double-page spread.
  4. Single-page ads on right.
  5. Single-page ads on left with strip on right.
  6. Single-page ads on left.
  7. Checkerboard ads on right.
  8. Checkerboard ads on left.
  9. Half-page ad, upper right.
  10. Half-page ad, lower right.
  11. Strip on both right and left sides.
  12. Half-page ad, upper left.
  13. Half-page ad, lower left.
  14. Third-page block, lower right.
  15. Strip (one-column), extreme right.
  16. Strip, extreme left.

- An exceptionally strong ad will usually perform well no matter where it is placed in a magazine.

Source: Courtesy of Magazine Publishers of America.

or a smaller number of larger advertisements? Much depends on the purpose of the campaign outlined by the marketing plan, although the buyer generally can find research that provides some insight into the situation.

Rate Structure

Although magazine space is quoted in column inches as well as in larger segments, it is actually sold primarily on the basis of pages, half pages, quarter pages, and so forth. For example, SRDS gives the following scale for black-and-white space in *Time*:

1 page	$85,000
2 columns	63,800
1/2 page	51,000
1 column	34,000
1/2 column	21,300

These are standard space units in *Time*; other publications may have different sizes of space listed as standard units. Each page of *Time* is three columns wide. The fourth (back) *Time* cover costs $164,000. *Time*, like many magazines, charges an extra 15 percent for bleed pages. Some periodicals, however, require no extra charge for bleeds, and some charge only 10 percent.

The rates quoted so far have been for single insertions. Most publishers offer discounts to encourage the purchase of more space or more frequent advertising. These practices may be combined, however, in a single-rate schedule. Thus, discounts increase as more space is used—and they increase even faster if the ads are spread out throughout the year.

Methods of Comparison

Every media buyer knows that no magazine page is exactly the same as another, so it is important to keep an eye on the **cost per thousand** (**CPM**). For magazines, the CPM is computed as follows:

$$\text{Cost per thousand (CPM)} = \frac{\text{Page Rate} \times 1,000}{\text{Circulation (or Audience)}}$$

Usually the audience of a publication is used instead of circulation. Ideally, the media planner attempts to use the target audience in the formula.

The cost-per-thousand figures for a four-color page in three leading magazines are as follows:

Magazine	Circulation CPM	Adult Audience CPM
Reader's Digest	$ 8.06	$ 3.69
The New Yorker	58.68	13.90
Business Week	70.84	10.18

Note how much lower the cost per thousand is for reaching *Reader's Digest* readers than it is for the other two magazines. The differential here may be due to the much larger circulation and audience of *Reader's Digest*, as well as the fact that it reaches a much broader type of audience than the other two magazines. Generally the cost is higher, on a relative basis, to reach a selective audience.

Summary

Almost one-fourth of all advertising dollars go to newspapers. The newspaper's strength among retail and national advertisers is based on its flexibility; its acceptance in a community; its intense coverage; the fact that readers can scan, skip, or concentrate on it as they like; the coordination of advertising between dealer and national advertiser; and the services—usually free—offered buyers.

Future Trends: Newspapers and Magazines

A few key trends likely to affect newspapers and magazines in the future include the following:

- *Negotiation of rates* Until rather recently, print advertising rates generally have not been negotiable. However, during the economic recession in the early 1990s, several magazines began to negotiate their published space rates with buyers in much the same way as the broadcast media. The trend toward negotiated rates, involving newspapers as well as magazines, likely will continue for the foreseeable future.[3]
- *Customized publications and advertising* With the advancement of printing technology, coupled with the use of computers, publications will be able to provide individual subscribers information of a customized nature. For example, a subscriber to *Newsweek* will be able to purchase a special editorial section of the magazine, say, on "Books in the News." This ability to target readers with special editorial content can easily be transferred to advertising uses. Currently some publications can print individual advertisements with a subscriber's name included in the ad; the ability to do this will become more widespread. With the advancement of database marketing, an advertiser will not be limited to the names on a magazine's subscription list—the advertiser will be able to provide their own list.
- *Limits on increased circulation* In the past, most print media have attempted to increase their circulation at all costs; they have felt it essential to do this in order to attract advertisers to their pages. As media decision making becomes more sophis-

ticated, many publications will likely focus more on the *quality* of their circulation rather than on quantity itself. Advertisers will look more carefully at *how* circulations are obtained—most newspapers and magazines can increase circulation by offering low prices. The advertiser in the future will be more interested in how committed a reader is to a particular publication.
- *Satellite transmission of advertisements* A company—AD/SAT—already exists that transmits newspaper advertisements from an advertiser (or agency) via satellite directly to a host of newspapers throughout the United States. This type of technology will continue to advance, especially in terms of "digital delivery." Under this system, a special piece of equipment is installed in newspapers that provides PostScript broadcast communications via satellite. The advertisement sent in this manner would never appear on paper prior to its appearance in the newspaper.
- *Distribution of product samples and coupon books* Currently, print publications, especially newspapers, are experimenting with using the medium to distribute product samples, coupon books, and similar items along with the publication. "Newspac" is a program whereby a container with a product sample is mechanically inserted into newspapers for delivery. In a test of the method, Procter & Gamble distributed 50,000 samples of Bounce fabric softener to a Chicago suburb via the *Chicago Tribune*.

People who read a newspaper usually comprise a cross-section of those living in a particular area, thus making the newspaper a broad-based medium.

The buying and selling of newspaper space has undergone significant changes in recent years, with the result that national advertisers can use the medium more easily than in the past. However, the national advertiser is likely to pay substantially more than a local retailer for the same amount of space. An important part of the newspaper business is the Sunday supplement, which is part newspaper and part magazine, offering advertisers some of the advantages of both.

The term magazine covers a multitude of publications in three main fields—consumer, farm, and business. Of these, consumer magazines account for the greatest dollar expenditures, business magazines for the largest number of magazines.

The main advantages of magazine advertising are its selectivity, high quality of reproduction, long life, inherent prestige, and services offered. Its lack of flexibility is its main disadvantage.

Magazines have been studied extensively both on a circulation and readership basis. Circulation studies often focus attention on the quality of the circulation. As a result of readership studies, it is possible to delineate certain patterns of magazine usage by age, income, and other demographic factors. Unfortunately, the audience studies are often contradictory.

Rates are most frequently based on circulation and audience, and comparisons are made on a cost-per-thousand (CPM) basis. Usually, magazines that cater to a highly selective audience charge more per thousand than others.

A few key trends likely to affect print media include the negotiation of rates, the customization of publications and their advertising, focusing more on the *quality* rather than the *quantity* of circulation, delivering ads from creator to publication via satellite, and using print publications to distribute more than their normal contents.

Questions for Discussion

1. How do you explain the fact that newspapers account for more advertising dollars than any other advertising medium?
2. Newspaper A has a column inch rate of $25.63 and a circulation of 124,215, whereas Newspaper B has a column inch rate of $32.75 and a circulation of 154,027. Assume that you are buying an SAU that is 2 columns wide by 7 inches deep. Compare the two newspapers on a cost-per-thousand circulation for this space unit and indicate which is the better buy. What other factors would you consider in choosing between A and B?
3. Make a list of all the newspapers and magazines you have seen during the past week. What approximate percentage of time did you devote to each?
4. On what basis are newspaper and magazine rates established? To what extent do they follow pricing policies you have learned in your economics or marketing courses?
5. What is the primary function of newspaper supplements?
6. Under what conditions will an advertiser devote the major portion of the budget to newspapers? To magazines?
7. Compare the cost of full-page, four-color advertisements in *Time, Newsweek,* and *U.S. News & World Report.* (Check your school library for a copy of Standard Rate & Data.)
8. If you were planning to use consumer magazines in a media schedule, what kind of information would you like to have to help you select specific magazines?
9. Assume you are a space salesperson for your local daily or weekly newspaper. What sales approach would you take in calling on local advertisers, such as a bank and a clothing store?

Notes

1 "Selling with Research," *Newspaper Advertising Bureau,* 1992, 50.
2 "Newspapers Could Get More National Ads If Publishers Rethought Rate Disparity," *Mediaweek* (May 18, 1992): 6.
3 See, for example, "Ogilvy & Mather Media Executive Tom Bell Presents Some Views on Magazine Negotiation," in Donald W. Jugenheimer, Arnold M. Barban, and Peter B. Turk, *Advertising Media: Strategy and Tactics* (Dubuque, IA: WCB Brown & Benchmark, 1992), 318–319.

Bovée, Courtland L., and William F. Arens. *Contemporary Advertising,* 4th ed. Homewood, IL: Irwin, 1992. Chapter 13.

Jugenheimer, Donald W., Arnold M. Barban, and Peter B. Turk. *Advertising Media: Strategy and Tactics.* Dubuque, IA: WCB Brown & Benchmark, 1992. Chapter 15.

McGann, Anthony F., and J. Thomas Russell. *Advertising Media,* 2d ed. Homewood, IL: Irwin, 1988. Chapters 8, 9.

Russell, J. Thomas, and W. Ronald Lane. *Kleppner's Advertising Procedure,* 11th ed. Englewood Cliffs, NJ: Prentice-Hall, 1990. Chapters 10, 11.

Shimp, Terence A. *Promotion Management and Marketing Communications,* 3d ed. Fort Worth, TX: Dryden Press, 1993, Chapter 13.

Sissors, Jack Z., and Lincoln Bumba. *Advertising Media Planning,* 4th ed. Lincolnwood, IL: NTC Business Books, 1993. Chapters 12, 15.

Suggested Readings

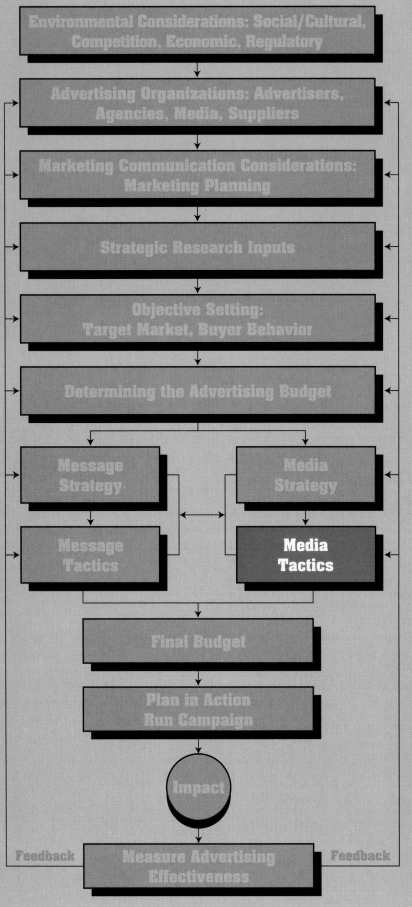

Environmental Considerations: Social/Cultural, Competition, Economic, Regulatory

Advertising Organizations: Advertisers, Agencies, Media, Suppliers

Marketing Communication Considerations: Marketing Planning

Strategic Research Inputs

Objective Setting: Target Market, Buyer Behavior

Determining the Advertising Budget

Message Strategy

Media Strategy

Message Tactics

Media Tactics

Final Budget

Plan in Action Run Campaign

Impact

Measure Advertising Effectiveness

Feedback

Feedback

Chapter 17

Media: Television and Radio

CHAPTER TOPICS

TELEVISION
  Types of Advertising
  Advantages of Television Advertising
  Limitations of Television Advertising
  Kinds of Users
  How Television Is Used
  Measuring Broadcasting Audiences
  Audience Trends
  Rate Structure
  Cost Comparisons

RADIO
  Types of Advertising
  Types of Stations
  Advantages of Radio Advertising
  Limitations of Radio Advertising
  Kinds of Users
  Programming Trends
  Audience Measurement and Trends
  Rate Structure

Television and radio have much in common as media of communication. Unlike newspapers and magazines, which are space-oriented, television and radio are time-oriented. Both media market time in segments, generally ranging from 10 to 60 seconds (television has been experimenting with "infomercials" of up to one hour in length). Both have similar general classes of time to sell—network, spot (time bought by a national advertiser in one or more markets), and local. (Television also is classified according to national and local **cable**, as well as **syndication**.) Both use similar methods of measuring their audiences. Both use the public airwaves and can operate only under a license from the Federal Communications Commission. Among national media companies, many own both radio and television stations. For example, each of the major network television companies—ABC, CBS, and NBC—owns radio stations in several cities.

Television

For some advertisers, television seems to be the ideal medium. The combination of sight and sound, along with a diverse range of graphics technology, provides advertisers with an opportunity to create dramatic and effective messages. Yet, other advertisers believe that the cost of producing commercials and buying time is not efficient for their needs. This chapter analyzes the status of television and its place in the media program.

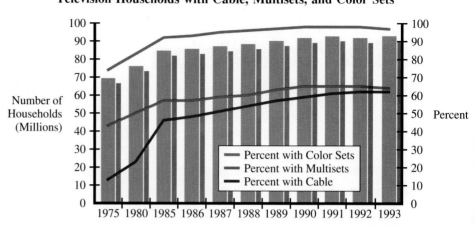

FIGURE 17.1

Television Households with Cable, Multisets, and Color Sets

Source: Courtesy of Nielsen Media Research; cable television information from *Cable TV Facts,* 1992.

Television has grown faster than any advertising medium in history. The growth in television households is shown graphically in Figure 17.1. Presently, the medium is almost at a saturation point; the 93.1 million television households in 1993 out of a total household population of 94.7 million represents a penetration of 98.3 percent. Only 9 percent of the households owned TVs in 1950. This had grown to around 90 percent by the early 1960s. In 1980 the percentage of households with television was 97.9 percent, and this level, of around 98 percent, has remained constant throughout the 1980s and early 1990s. Multiset ownership has also continued to grow—from 22 percent of all TV households in 1965, to 50 percent in 1980, and 64 percent in 1993. Of all TV households, 98 percent have at least one color set. The number of homes equipped to receive cable television increased from 23 percent of all TV households in 1980 to the current level of 62 percent.

Within 20 years, total estimated expenditures in the medium rose from just over $4 billion (18 percent of total advertising investment) to $29.4 billion (22 percent of total advertising expenditures), making television second only to newspapers in terms of total dollar investment. Because all except $8.6 billion of the total is spent by national advertisers, television is the leading national medium.

The increase in television stations is almost as spectacular. The first commercial station began operating in New York City in 1941. By 1954 the number had risen to 402, and currently there are over 1,300 commercial stations in the United States. In addition, almost 11,000 cable systems serve over 56 million homes.

Types of Advertising

Television advertising can broadly be designated as network, spot, or local. Network and local can further be divided into over-the-air transmission and cable system delivery. In addition, a small but growing amount of television advertising now is classified as **syndication**. A syndicated program is a television program developed by an independent firm that attempts to place it on as many television stations throughout the United States as possible. The program can be sold to a station, which in turn sells advertising commercials to local and/or national advertisers. Or, in the case of barter syndication, the show may be offered to a station free, with presold national spots. Syndicated programs include *Wheel of Fortune, The Oprah Winfrey Show,* and *Jeopardy.* Figure 17.2 shows the relative amounts of total television expenditures according to the various types. Over-the-air network television advertising accounts for the largest amount—almost 33 percent. National and local spot advertisers combined account for 53 percent of total television expenditures.

FIGURE 17.2

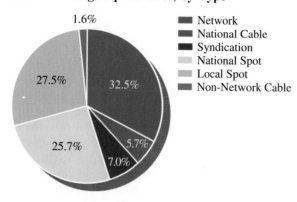

Total Television Advertising Expenditures, by Type

- Network
- National Cable
- Syndication
- National Spot
- Local Spot
- Non-Network Cable

1.6%

27.5%

32.5%

25.7%

5.7%

7.0%

Source: Compiled from *Advertising Age* (May 3, 1993): 4.

Network

The three major national over-the-air television networks are Columbia Broadcasting System (CBS), National Broadcasting Company (NBC), and American Broadcasting Company (ABC). (Each of them also operates a radio network.) Fox Broadcasting Company is the newest network, covering somewhat less of the total United States than the other three. Public television is represented by the Public Broadcasting System (PBS), and although they do not air brand "commercials" in the usual sense of the term, program sponsorship (such as on *Masterpiece Theater* and *Mystery*) provides a means of company recognition. A sizable number of cable television networks also send their programming by satellite transmission to cable systems in local communities. These include ESPN, Cable News Network (CNN), Nickelodeon, The Discovery Channel, and Black Entertainment Television. Figure 17.3 is a trade advertisement for The Discovery Channel.

Network telecasting involves tying together stations primarily by means of satellite transmission. The use of satellites involves a network broadcaster sending a signal to an orbiting satellite, with stations in local areas picking up the signal through a receiving antenna. The programs received by a local station can then be transmitted to local viewers either by (1) broadcasting an over-the-air signal or (2) sending it by coaxial cable to subscriber homes. These two methods distinguish the differences between "network television" on the one hand, and "national (or network) cable" on the other.

The main advantages of network broadcasting (compared with spot) are (1) wide and simultaneous coverage through a single telecast, (2) low cost-per-thousand coverage of the country, and (3) the prestige of using first-rate talent.

National Spot

In broadcasting circles, the term **spot advertising** is used in both a geographical and a time sense. National spot advertising is any non-network broadcasting paid for by a national (or regional) advertiser; the advertiser buys commercials on different television stations in specific markets. In this context, spot refers to pinpointing geographic markets within the United States. The term spot is also used in a time sense—for example, a "spot" announcement is a broadcast advertisement of short duration.

The big advantage of spot advertising for national advertisers is its flexibility. An advertiser can buy on a market-by-market basis and put the pressure on where it is more likely to pay off. Differences in sales potential, in dealers, or in some

FIGURE 17.3

Trade Advertisement for
The Discovery Channel,
a Cable Television Network

local condition may make it advisable to advertise in one area and not in another. Through spot advertising a new product can be introduced one area at a time. Also, it is often advisable to vary the programs or the times from one area to another, depending on local conditions.

Local

Local advertising is primarily advertising by retailers and other local organizations, such as banks. Sometimes it consists of programs developed locally and sponsored by one or more local firms; an example would be a station's six o'clock news program. Often *local* means that a local firm has bought a syndicated program, which it has decided to sponsor in its own particular market. If a local television station is affiliated with a network, such as CBS, a local advertiser can purchase commercials adjacent to a network show, such as *Murphy Brown*. Local television advertising can be bought from an over-the-air station or a local cable system; in the latter instance, for example, an advertiser might buy a commercial during a break in an ESPN sports broadcast. As in newspapers, a great deal of the advertising classified as local is cooperative advertising placed by the retailer and paid for, at least partially, by the manufacturer.

Advantages of *Television Advertising*

All media planners have to decide whether to include television in a particular media schedule. If the decision is affirmative, the planner must then tackle the vast number of additional decisions involved in using it correctly. In this section, we discuss two types of users—national and local—and three broad types of television—network, spot, and local.

Impact

Used wisely, television has almost unbelievable impact. Many brands have been introduced to the American public via television, and the success stories probably outweigh the failures. But it is of course always difficult to prove that the same time and money put into another medium might not have produced as well.

Television brings into the viewer's home a combination of moving picture and the speaking voice. It is thus almost the equivalent of a door-to-door sales staff who can make visits at less than one cent a call. When the person presenting the sales pitch is a noted personality, such as Candice Bergen or Michael Jackson, the advertising can be very effective indeed. The advancement in video technology, especially developments in computer-generated graphics, has allowed television commercials to be extraordinarily dramatic and exciting.

Mass Coverage

Theoretically, advertisers can reach almost everyone with a combination of newspapers, or even of magazines. But television reaches with considerable impact a large number of persons not effectively reached by the print media, in addition to the many who are reached by print. A large number of theoretically literate Americans (some say from 30 to 50 percent) find reading so arduous that they do very little of it. Yet these people spend several hours a day watching television programs.

Repetition

Repetition helps to explain the success of such campaigns as those of McDonald's and Coca-Cola. Constant reiteration of the sales message helps make people feel that they know the product, whether or not they like it. Television makes it possible to repeat a message as often as the advertiser can afford.

Flexibility

There are few directions in which television advertisers cannot move. Whether they want to demonstrate their product, create a mood, use abstract symbols, make a blockbusting announcement about the product, or try it out in certain areas, they can usually find some combination of television presentations that will communicate the desired impression. A retail store can change its commercials from dresses to coats if a spring day turns chilly, or it can capitalize on a sudden snowstorm by changing from footballs to sleds.

Prestige

Not all television has prestige, but some of it has a great deal. There is little doubt, for example, that Hallmark improved its prestige through its *Hall of Fame* dramatic presentations or that Xerox has gained prestige through its program sponsorships. Some national advertisers choose television because they can buy a section of an outstanding program or one with a name they can merchandise to their dealers. When Ed McMahon was the main announcer of *The Tonight Show With Johnny Carson*, Budweiser gained prestige with distributors, especially when McMahon visited them or they met him at a sales get-together.

Television advertising involves several unique problems.

Limitations of Television Advertising

Fleeting Messages

On television, advertising messages come and go quickly. If people have their sets on—but are not watching or listening—they cannot return later (unless of course they have a videocassette recorder). And when commercials are bunched together (say, at the station break), a viewer might use the time to get a snack. Additionally, there is the problem of commercials being zipped (fast-forwarded) when programs are recorded on a VCR.

Costs

Although some network shows reach viewers for a surprisingly low cost per thousand, certain minimum cost considerations can sometimes price the medium-sized advertiser out of the television field. In addition to the charges for air time, advertisers incur heavy costs for artwork and art material, talent, music, sound effects, licenses and fees, direction, supervision, scripting, camera, rehearsal, and so forth. A 30-second filmed or taped commercial is costly, and it becomes less expensive only if it can be used many times and can reach a sizable audience.

As an example of network costs, a single 30-second commercial run in prime time costs about $150,000. If the commercial is scheduled once a week for 20 weeks, the expenditure is $3 million. The cost per thousand, though, for such a buy may be quite efficient, probably in the range of $10 to $14 per thousand homes.

Mortality Rate

The sheer impact of television causes both programs and commercials to wear out at a rate unparalleled in other media. Public tastes in entertainers, program formats, and commercial approaches are ephemeral and require constant checking.

Lack of Selectivity

Mass coverage can be a handicap as well as an advantage. As the last chapter pointed out, many advertisers need a special audience. This limitation, though, is

Study Shows Advertising Executives Think Network TV Still Works, but Consider Cable and Radio More Efficient

by Richard Brunelli

Despite its well-documented erosion, network TV still is the name of the game in audience reach and power to convince consumers to buy products, says a survey by Myers Marketing Research.

Among Myers' Worldwide Marketing Leadership Panel—a group of 3,500 advertising/marketing execs—88 percent of respondents rated network TV very effective in audience reach potential. General-interest magazines scored 42 percent and FSIs 41 percent.

Network TV also ranked tops in influencing consumer motivation. Fifty-seven percent of the respondents said it was very effective; 53 percent said cable TV was; and direct mail/marketing communications scored 51 percent.

Ranking by price efficiency, cable scored a 59 percent "very effective" rating; radio was second (57 percent); network TV was third (35 percent).

Some media directors questioned the survey results. "Cable's rated way too high," said Rick Hosfield, director of media for General Mills. "People are infatuated with it now, but in reaching an audience it's lacking somewhat."

Ken Pool, senior vp/director of marketing and media at Y&R/Detroit, said the study "tries to assign the media inherent value above and beyond the message. Different media take on different value depending on what you're trying to accomplish."

Source: Courtesy of *Mediaweek*, (February 10, 1992): 33.

Price Efficiency	Mean	Rating Very/ Extremely Effective
Cable Network Television	3.65	59%
Radio	3.64	57
Special Interest Magazines	3.10	31
Broadcast Network Television	3.02	35
Free Standing Inserts	2.91	29
Direct Mail/Marketing Communications	2.86	30
General Interest Magazines	2.86	21
In-Store Media	2.78	29
Newspapers	2.52	12

becoming less pronounced. Mass audiences are becoming more fragmented because of multiple sets in a home and access to more channels through cable television and public television.

Clutter

Clutter in television involves (1) the total amount of nonprogram time within a program and (2) the total number of commercials shown within a given commercial break. Both aspects have increased in recent years, and the concern is the likely impact this has on viewer retention of commercial content. In a recent study it was shown that the prime time commercial load has grown by as much as 14 percent since 1983.[1] There also has been a trend toward shorter length commercials which adds to the clutter problem. For example, the percent of network television commercials by length across a ten-year period, 1980 versus 1990, is shown at right:[2]

Total Audience Reach Potential	Mean	Rating Very/ Extremely Effective	Ability to Influence Consumer Motivations	Mean	Rating Very/ Extremely Effective
Broadcast Network Television	4.46	88%	Broadcast Network Television	3.62	57%
General Interest Magazines	3.27	42	Cable Network Television	3.48	53
Free Standing Inserts	3.22	41	Direct Mail/Marketing Communications	3.44	51
Radio	3.22	37	Special Interest Magazines	3.31	45
Newspapers	3.14	39	In-Store Media	3.14	40
Cable Network Television	3.11	31	Radio	3.03	30
Direct Mail/Marketing Communications	3.06	35	Free Standing Inserts	2.89	25
Special Interest Magazines	2.81	22	General Interest Magazines	2.76	15
In-Store Media	2.74	27	Newspapers	2.48	14

Length of Commercials (in seconds)	Percent of Commercials	
	1980	1990
10	0.7%	0.1%
15	0	35.4
20	0	1.4
30	94.6	60.1
45	2.7	1.0
60	1.9	1.7
90 and longer	0.1	0.3
Total	100.0%	100.0%

Almost 95 percent of all commercials in 1980 were 30 seconds long, whereas ten years later only 60 percent were of this length. Most importantly, over a third (35.4 percent) in 1990 were only 15 seconds long.

Kinds of Users

Package goods advertisers account for a substantial portion of television expenditures, as Table 17.1 shows. Package goods are widely distributed mass-consumption brands sold, for the most part, in supermarkets and pharmaceutical outlets. Consequently, the advertisers depend heavily on the mass media to reach a mass audience and presell them on the brand. Television also is well suited for demonstrating how products can be used, and this may account for the amount of automobile advertising in this medium.

Cable television networks and local cable systems do not rely on advertiser support to the same degree that over-the-air networks and stations do. Yet, advertising revenue in cable is growing rapidly and is estimated to be over $5 billion in 1995. Table 17.1 shows the top ten cable advertisers, several of whom also appear in the top ten in the other television categories.

Procter & Gamble spends more on television advertising than any other advertiser—almost a *billion* dollars ($978 million) a year. Another big spender, General Motors Corporation, bought over $818 million worth of television time. The Philip

---

TABLE 17.1

Top Ten National Television Advertisers, 1992

Rank	Advertiser	Network Expenditures (Millions)	Rank	Advertiser	National Spot Expenditures (Millions)
1	Procter & Gamble	$499.9	1	General Motors	$344.5
2	General Motors	431.9	2	Ford Motor	250.5
3	Philip Morris	373.6	3	Procter & Gamble	236.8
4	PepsiCo	243.3	4	Toyota Motor	220.4
5	Ford Motor	239.9	5	General Mills	202.4
6	Kellogg	239.8	6	Philip Morris	182.3
7	Chrysler	206.2	7	Chrysler	181.0
8	McDonald's	200.0	8	Nissan Motor	149.7
9	Johnson & Johnson	199.6	9	Mazda Motors	90.0
10	Sears	191.8	10	Kellogg	83.0

Rank	Advertiser	Syndicated Expenditures (Millions)	Rank	Advertiser	Cable Expenditures (Millions)
1	Philip Morris	$159.1	1	Procter & Gamble	$112.0
2	Procter & Gamble	129.4	2	General Motors	41.9
3	Kellogg	66.8	3	Anheuser-Busch	37.7
4	Warner Lambert	55.8	4	Philip Morris	34.9
5	Unilever NV	44.6	5	General Mills	33.5
6	PepsiCo	44.4	6	Hasbro	29.7
7	Hasbro	40.2	7	American Home Products	25.4
8	Johnson & Johnson	38.7	8	AT&T	25.0
9	Mattel	38.3	9	Mars Inc.	21.9
10	McDonald's	37.2	10	Eastman Kodak	21.4

Source: *Mediaweek* (February 22, 1993): 7.

Morris Companies—which advertise such brands as Miller beer, Kraft cheeses, Jell-O gelatin, Oscar Mayer meats, and Maxwell House coffee—spent almost $750 million advertising in the four television categories.

Like any medium, television may be used in a wide variety of ways. However, the choices available to the advertiser in television are probably more numerous and more complicated technically than in the other media. For example, the time buyer for a national advertiser has to decide among regularly scheduled network shows, special network shows, spot announcements, spot programming, and the various other classes of time. Even the local advertiser has to decide among stations, announcements and programs, kinds of program sponsorship, and classes of time. It would be far beyond the scope of this book to explore the possibilities in detail.[3] The various copy treatments have already been considered in Chapter 14, and the pros and cons of network and spot programming were discussed earlier in this chapter. Let us look briefly at two additional problems involved in television usage: the choice between programs and spot announcements and the choice of stations.

*H*ow Television *Is Used*

Programs versus Spot Announcements

When a firm sponsors a program, it gains at least two important advantages. The first is sponsor prestige if the program is popular and the firm sponsors all or a major portion of it. The public may then identify the product, the firm, or the retail store with the program. The second is the control the firm has over the placement and content of its commercials. For example, the firm may wish to integrate its commercials into the show. Or it may want to concentrate them in two or three strategic positions. Sponsors are, of course, limited in the amount of total program time they may use for commercials (generally, about 11 percent of the total time at night and 16 percent in the daytime).

The spot announcement provides much greater flexibility. Advertisers can, if they like, spread their available money over a wide variety of time slots or market areas. Or they can concentrate their energy and money in a saturation campaign. They may want to introduce a new product with a strong spot-announcement campaign, then later switch to a less concentrated campaign or a program that will sustain interest week after week.

An advertiser who is the sole sponsor of a program will obviously capitalize more on the program's prestige than advertisers who share sponsorship. Many advertisers, however, are not willing to sacrifice flexibility by committing themselves to sole sponsorship. They prefer to share sponsorship with other advertisers. By participating in sponsorship, an advertiser can often save enough money to use spot announcements in addition to program sponsorship. With the high cost of today's television, it is difficult for even the big advertiser to buy heavily in both program and spot campaigns. At present, only a very few network programs are sold on a sponsorship basis, and these are mostly specials; for example, companies such as IBM, Hallmark, and Xerox will on occasion sponsor a noted dramatic presentation.

Thus, most television advertising today is bought on participating programs. An advertiser (usually through an advertising agency) goes to a particular network, ascertains which programs the network will be airing during a certain time period, what the costs are for various program commercials, and then decides what to buy. For example, during a three-month period, the advertiser might contract for forty 30-second commercials on CBS programs as follows:

- *Murphy Brown*—13 commercials
- *Northern Exposure*—12 commercials
- *60 Minutes*—9 commercials
- *CBS Evening News*—6 commercials

The total time cost for these 40 commercials might be $7,000,000.

As mentioned earlier, around 60 percent of all network television advertising today is for 30-second spots. The trend has been toward the 15-second commercial, which currently accounts for over a third of all network units. However, there is some indication that the trend toward 15-second commercials has peaked.[4]

Station Selection

Even when network time is bought, some choice in stations is available—beyond the basic network buy, that is. The only advertiser who does not have to worry about station selection is the retailer in a one-station market.

In general, the agency time buyer will decide on the market before selecting the station. If the market is desirable, he or she looks over the available stations. Similarly, the retailer evaluates the stations that cover the market.

Stations are almost always evaluated on a coverage and audience delivery basis. In determining this, buyers are likely to depend partly on such mechanical factors as power, frequency, antenna height, type (UHF or VHF), the degree of the local cable system's penetration, and partly on evidence from research. For example, the research methods discussed later in this chapter are used in appraising stations as well as programs. Data from the Nielsen Station Index Service and Arbitron indicate the degree of viewing by station. Many buyers will be influenced by the network affiliation of a station and by the extra merchandising it offers. And, of course, they will consider the cost of the stations.

Measuring Broadcasting Audiences

Television research methods evolved from the study of radio audiences. Several organizations have been established primarily to measure television audiences, but the methods are similar to those used for radio. Radio was a medium for almost 20 years before research became an important part of the business, whereas extensive television research was begun while the medium itself was still in its infancy.

Early Efforts

In the early days of radio, great stress was laid on listener mail as an indication of audience size and distribution. Later, it was determined that more accurate measurements could be obtained if interviewers asked people about their listening habits or telephoned them to find out what they were listening to at a given moment.

Broad-scale, public-opinion-type surveys are still used. Among the most common are penetration studies, used to estimate the extent of ownership and the distribution of sets; coverage surveys, used to measure the geographic area in which people view or listen to a particular station; and program popularity studies, designed to measure viewer preference of specific programs or types of programs.

Modern Rating Services

Four techniques have been used to measure broadcast audiences.

Telephone Coincidental One of the oldest methods, telephone coincidental, was widely used in radio before television became a major medium. An interviewer calls a household chosen at random and asks the person who answers which program he or she is watching at the moment. The great advantage of the coincidental is its rapid reporting of ratings (usually the next morning). The main disadvantage is its lack of complete coverage—only the homes with listed telephones are covered.

Roster Recall Method The **roster recall method** involves interviewers who ring doorbells and ask the person who answers which programs he or she saw or heard the day before. Each interviewer carries a roster of programs broadcast the day before and lets the householder look at the roster while answering. At the end of the interview, the interviewer asks questions about age, education, and so forth.

The advantage of this method is that it is relatively inexpensive considering the large block of time covered and the detailed audience information it provides. The main limitation is the danger that the lengthy roster may discourage careful response, because people may exaggerate the amount of listening or point to prestige programs. A further limitation is the difficulty in getting interviewers to go into certain parts of a city.

Electronic Recorder An electronic measurement device, the **Audimeter**, was perfected by the A. C. Nielsen Company to measure objectively the tuning of television sets. The Audimeter is an outgrowth of an earlier mechanical measuring device Nielsen used to monitor radio programming. Currently meters are used by both of the major companies that measure broadcast audiences: Nielsen Media Research and The Arbitron Company.

Electronic meters are attached to the television set or sets in a sample home and automatically measure (1) when a set is on, (2) the channel to which it is tuned, and (3) how long the set is tuned to a specific channel. This information is stored in another electronic device, which is connected by special telephone lines to the central computers of Nielsen or Arbitron. The stored information is retrieved daily by the central computers through telephone dialing. The entire process is automatic and requires no work on the part of the sample household.

At the start of the fall 1987 television season, the A. C. Nielsen Company, along with two other companies, began use of **people meters** to measure network television audiences. The people meter is an electronic device placed on or near a TV set (with an accompanying hand-held remote device) with numbers on it for each member of the household as well as possible guests (see Figure 17.4).

A person entering a room where a TV is playing punches in his or her number. The meter knows by that number the demographic characteristics (for example, sex, age, and income) of the viewer. Thus, data on viewing habits can be fed immediately into company computers, making the information readily available for analysis. Currently, over 4,000 households are measured by Nielsen Media Research in this manner. Prior to the use of people meters, individual television viewing was obtained from *diaries* kept by members within a selected household.

Several companies, including Nielsen and Arbitron, are experimenting with "passive" people meters, which use sensing devices (such as light sensors) to determine the number of people in a room where a TV is on, thus eliminating the need for an individual to punch in a number on the meter. The ultimate goal of any people measuring device is to determine exactly who is potentially viewing a program at the precise time a commercial is delivered.

The A. C. Nielsen Company provides audience data for two situations: network and local market viewing. Network information is presented through the Nielsen Television Index (NTI) and is based on the electronic meters. To measure viewing patterns in approximately 200 local television markets, Nielsen offers its Nielsen Station Index (NSI). Meters are used for several of the largest markets in the country, with diaries used in all other areas. Thus, to learn the national audience of *Murphy Brown* or *60 Minutes*, the media planner simply consults an NTI report. To determine how these programs were viewed in a specific city (for example, Dallas/Ft. Worth), along with the viewing of such local programs as the 10 o'clock news, an NSI report is checked.

The Arbitron Company provides local audience measurement similar to Nielsen. Local market reports are available for over 200 television markets. Of the 200 markets, the two dozen largest are measured by meters. The remainder are measured primarily through diaries, but Arbitron also uses telephone coincidentals and recall surveys.

FIGURE 17.4

The Nielsen People Meter Measures Which Specific Individuals Are in a Room When a Television Is On

FIGURE 17.5

Arbitron Diary Page Explaining the Details TV Viewers Are to Record

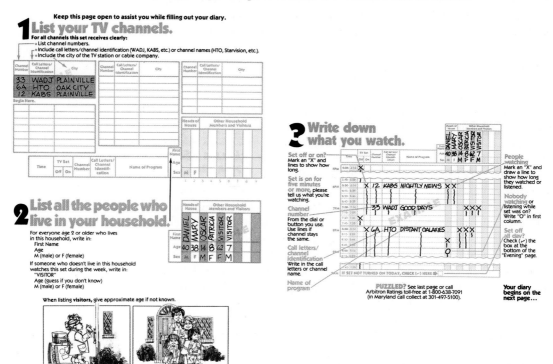

Diary Method As already mentioned, both Nielsen and Arbitron use diaries to record local market television viewing. Preselected homes are given listener diaries, in which each person is asked to write down the stations and programs watched. The method has the advantage of being less expensive than using electronic meters, yet requires a great deal of cooperation on the part of viewers. Figure 17.5 shows the "explanation page" from an Arbitron diary. Note the amount of information that must be completed by the members of a sample household.

Sample pages from an Arbitron television report, with instructions on how to read the information included, are shown in Figure 17.6.

How Audience Research Data Are Used

Broadcast ratings have been the target of both satire and extensive, serious criticism. Congressional investigations have been suggested. All the hullabaloo must seem strange to people who take for granted the right of communicators to collect as much information as possible. The trouble comes in the misuse of the research data. A salesperson who is promoting a moderately successful program can usually find some audience-measurement rating to indicate that the program is outstandingly successful; a competitor, through other research, may "prove" that the rating is untrue and offer a superior one.

In general, buyers of television time are most interested in the following types of audience data: **program rating** (percentage of homes in the sample tuned in to the program); **sets in use** (percentage of homes in the sample where the set was turned on); **share of audience** (percentage of sets in use tuned in to a particular program); **total audience** (total number of homes reached by some portion of the program as projected from the sample); and **audience composition** (distribution of the audience by demographic factors).

Although television research is more accurate than many critics both in and out of the industry believe, it is still subject to sampling error. It means little when one program receives a rating of 14.8 and another one of 14.2. For all practical purposes, the programs can be considered to have the same number of viewers, because the difference is insignificant. But if one program receives a rating of 22.1 and another one of 13.0, the former is most probably attracting a significantly larger audience than the latter.

Significant gaps still exist in audience data. In the early years of television, most viewing was done on a family basis, with one television set per household. This viewing situation influenced how data were gathered. Today, with around 65 percent of homes having more than one set, viewing is much more individualized. Measuring services have of course taken these trends into account, but methodological problems still remain. The measurement of viewing in cable and VCR homes is especially complicated. Whereas a noncable home may have 4 or 5 channels from which to choose, cable systems typically offer 25 to 30, or even more, viewing channels. This wide choice affects the sample sizes needed to obtain accurate information about television viewing. VCR homes provide the added complication of measuring what was recorded and whether or not this was later viewed (with yet another complication of determining the degree to which commercial segments were skipped over).

Users of television data also must deal with the variation between national viewing patterns and those in specific local markets. In general, much more detail is available for network programming patterns than for local patterns. The media planner must take such differences into account.

Even the buyers of media often concentrate too strongly on the program ratings (some regard them as types of batting averages) and lose sight of the wealth of extra data that help to clarify them and make them meaningful in a given marketing situation.

FIGURE 17.6

Sample Pages from an Arbitron Television Report

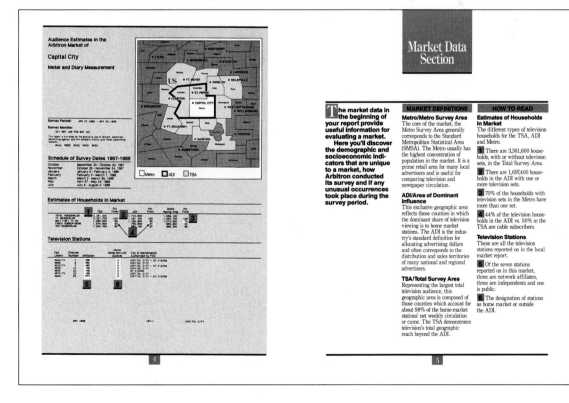

Many agencies buy television time on the basis of **gross rating points:** the sum of the ratings for the individual commercials bought. For example, if a media buyer purchases ten television commercials, each of which averages a 15 rating, the buyer has purchased 150 gross rating points. A rating point means an audience of 1 percent of the coverage base; hence 150 gross rating points mean 1.5 messages per average home. One source, for example, listed the spot television cost per gross rating point per home in 1992 as follows:[5]

| Markets | Cost per Gross Rating Point (30-second commercial) | |
	Daytime	Prime Time
Top 10	$1,506	$ 5,670
Top 20	2,179	7,942
Top 30	2,728	9,543
Top 50	3,285	11,188
Top 100	4,138	13,479

Thus, for example, the cost of 100 gross rating points for a 30-second prime time commercial in the top 50 markets would be $1,118,800. Rates vary, of course, by time of day and length of commercial.

Audience Trends

From the wealth of audience data have come many indications of how people are using television.[6]

1. Television viewing increases throughout the day as more and more people have time available for viewing. A peak is reached between 8:00 and 10:00 P.M., when over 60 percent of all households have their sets on. After that, usage levels decrease as people go to bed.
2. Television usage can vary considerably from winter to summer. The greatest differences occur during late afternoon and early evening; the smallest differences occur during early morning and late night.
3. At present, daily television usage averages slightly over seven hours (7 hours, 4 minutes). In recent years, usage was slightly higher, but a trend toward less time spent with television is unlikely.
4. Household characteristics can influence viewing habits. For example, households of three or more persons view 61 hours, 49 minutes a week; two-person households view 49 hours, 54 minutes; and one-person homes, 40 hours, 19 minutes. Viewing is greater in cable households (especially those subscribing to pay cable channels) than in noncable homes.
5. As a general rule, women view more television than men, and older men and women view more than younger adult age groups. Younger children view more than older children and teenagers.
6. Sunday evenings attract the largest audiences (an average of over 110 million people). Monday is the next most popular night, with 101 million viewers.
7. Program preferences vary from group to group. For example, in a recent year, feature films attracted the largest total audiences, but situation comedies were first among children and teens (see Figure 17.7).
8. Individual television programs vary in their appeal to demographic groups. For example, in a recent year the following were the top five programs for their respective categories:

Rank	Men 18 and Over	Women 18 and Over	Teens 12–17	Children 2–11
1	60 Minutes	60 Minutes	Fresh Prince of Bel Air	Full House
2	NFL Monday Night Football	Murder, She Wrote	Blossom	Dinosaurs
3	Roseanne	Roseanne	Roseanne	Step By Step
4	Home Improvement	Murphy Brown	Simpsons	Simpsons
5	Coach	CBS Sunday Movie	Beverly Hills, 90210	Family Matters

9. Television audiences can be sizable. For example, *Roseanne* typically is seen in almost 20 million homes. Special events, such as an Olympics broadcast, deliver almost 200 million persons over a 16- to 17-day period. Popular miniseries often reach as many as 150 million persons. Super Bowl XXVII, broadcast in January 1993, had an audience of over 133 million people.

FIGURE 17.7

Audience Composition by Selected Network Program Types
Regularly Scheduled Network Programs 7–11 P.M. (Average Minute Audiences)

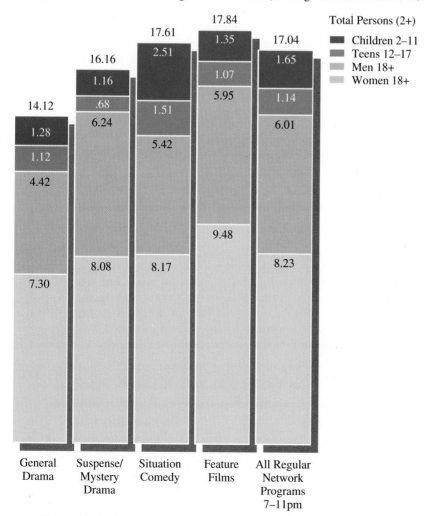

Total Persons (2+)
- Children 2–11
- Teens 12–17
- Men 18+
- Women 18+

Source: Nielsen Media Research.

Rate Structure

The typical time periods used in television are as follows for the Eastern or Pacific time zones; times in the Central and Mountain zones are generally an hour earlier.

Early morning	6:00 A.M. to 9:00 A.M.
Daytime	9:00 A.M. to 4:00 P.M.
Early fringe	4:00 P.M. to 7:00 P.M.
Prime access	7:00 P.M. to 8:00 P.M. (6:00 P.M. to 7:00 P.M. on Sundays)
Prime time	8:00 P.M. to 11:00 P.M.
Late fringe	11:00 P.M. to 1:00 A.M.

Saturday and Sunday mornings also are especially designated because of children's programs; weekend afternoons are predominantly filled with sports broadcasts. Advertising rates vary according to the particular time period (daypart), as well as according to the program being broadcast. These rate variations are based primarily on the size of audience delivered.

Many stations price their spot announcements on what is called a grid basis. Each time period for each day is given a grid number, the number being based on the station's rating for that particular time. Thus 7:00 to 7:30 P.M. on Monday may be priced at a higher rate than 7:00 to 7:30 P.M. on Tuesday.

When issuing a contract for a unit of spot television time, a media buyer wants to know, as nearly as possible, how long the rate will be in effect. The rates of television stations are subject to change at any time. Under certain circumstances, however, it is possible to protect the rate in effect at the time of purchase for a period; for example, time ordered prior to an effective date of increase often receives rate protection for three months. Spot television rates are subject to a variety of discounts, based primarily on the quantity and frequency of advertising. Like newspapers (and radio), many stations have both national and retail rates.

Rates for television time, although based on the size and type of audience delivered, typically are determined through negotiation. The advertising agency television buyer, representing a particular advertiser, works with a television salesperson to determine such things as program availability, guarantees of audience size and composition, cancellation rights, and the like. The price to be paid for a particular buy is part of the total negotiating process.

Following are some current average network television costs, as estimated by the Leo Burnett media department:[7]

Daypart	Cost Range of a 30-Second Commercial
Prime time (ABC, CBS, NBC)	$70,100–$132,600
Daytime	$ 6,900–$ 18,500
Evening news	$13,200–$ 36,100
Late evening	$ 7,600–$ 28,700
Saturday morning (children's shows)	$ 6,500–$ 23,000

Marketer's Guide to Media estimated spot television costs (30-second commercial), on a cost per television home rating point basis, as follows:[8]

Markets	Daytime	Early and Late News (average)	Prime Time	Early and Late Fringe (average)
Top 10	$1,506	$3,041	$ 5,670	$1,995
Top 20	2,179	4,346	7,942	2,846
Top 30	2,728	5,327	9,543	3,584
Top 50	3,285	6,398	11,188	4,372
Top 100	4,138	8,010	13,479	5,511

Thus, to buy 50 gross rating points in prime time each week in the top 50 markets of the country—for a 20-week schedule—the total cost would be $11,188,000 ($11,188 per rating point × 50 GRPs × 20 weeks).

Cost Comparisons

Two methods are used to compare the costs of programs or stations in the broadcast media. The first is the cost per thousand (CPM), which is computed as follows:

$$\text{Cost per Thousand (CPM)} = \frac{\text{Cost of a Commercial} \times 1{,}000}{\text{Audience of Program or Station}}$$

For example, if a firm placed a 30-second commercial on a network program for $195,000 and it delivered an audience of 13,500,000 homes, the CPM (homes) would be calculated as follows:

$$\text{CPM (homes)} = \frac{\$195{,}000 \times 1{,}000}{13{,}500{,}000} = \$14.44$$

The $14.44 would be compared with the CPMs of other alternative programs. All other things being equal (which probably never is the case!), a media buyer would select the lowest CPM because this would be the most efficient buy.

A second method of comparison is quite similar to the CPM computation, but uses program or station ratings. It is known as the cost per rating point (CPRP) and is computed as follows:

$$\text{Cost per Rating Point (CPRP)} = \frac{\text{Cost of a Commercial}}{\text{Rating of Program or Station}}$$

If the network program purchased for $195,000 had a homes rating of 14.7, the CPRP would be:

$$\text{CPRP (homes)} = \frac{\$195{,}000}{14.7} = \$13{,}265$$

For information on network audiences and ratings, media buyers consult a Nielsen Television Index (NTI) report. The cost of commercials would be based on the particular buy negotiated with the networks. For spot or local television, station audiences and ratings would probably come from Nielsen Station Index (NSI) or Arbitron ratings. Costs may be available in a Standard Rate & Data Service listing, but are more likely to come from the cost negotiated with the station.

Care must be taken to use comparable figures in making the computations. Audience and rating data must be either in homes or persons for each vehicle you are comparing. Where possible, the media buyer usually tries to compute CPMs and CPRPs based on the target audience, for example, adults 18–24. Costs should reflect the actual price the buyer would pay for each vehicle. For example, in comparing two television stations in a particular market, one station may have a better discount structure for frequency of advertising—and such information should be used in the cost comparisons.

Radio

When commercial television came onto the scene at the close of World War II, some thought radio was finished as a major advertising medium. Experience has proved these prophets much too rash. Radio has had its troubles and has undergone basic changes, but it is a major and healthy medium.

After radio became established as an advertising medium in the early 1920s, expenditures rose through the 1920s, 1930s, and 1940s. By 1952 expenditures had risen to $624,000,000. Then expenditures started to drop off and did not rise again until 1956. By 1958 expenditures had passed the previous high.

In terms of total potential audience, radio can be considered the number-one medium. Ninety-nine percent of the nation's homes have at least one usable radio. According to the Radio Advertising Bureau, there are approximately 576,500,000 working radio sets in the United States. Ninety-five percent of all cars have radios. Table 17.2 shows the distribution of listening by time of day. Thus, 88.0 percent of men age 18 and older—and 88.7 percent of women 18+—are reached by radio during the 6 A.M. to 10 A.M. time period during an average work week.

Types of Advertising

As in television, radio advertisers are normally classified into network, spot, and local advertisers. However, the relative importance of these three classifications is quite different in radio. Notice, in Figure 17.8, how important local radio is compared with the other two classifications—over four times the expenditure for spot and almost 16 times that for network. This is a reversal from the early days of radio, when network was the most important type. For example, in 1935 network radio accounted for $62,600,000 of the total $112,600,000 spent for radio—well over half. The decline of network radio has taken place since 1949, when network television came into its own, although total radio expenditures kept rising until 1952.

We can also classify radio advertising as live or taped. In the days when network radio was king, many programs were broadcast live. As radio has shifted more and more to the local level, there has been a decided increase in taped shows, with little but the news and on-the-spot broadcasts coming in live. Through recorded material that is used repeatedly, the advertiser can minimize costs for each commercial and control quality.

Types of Stations

Radio stations can be classified according to method of transmission, power and range, and programming format. Station classification is important in radio time buying because so much advertising—even by nationwide advertisers—is placed on a market-by-market basis.

TABLE 17.2

Percent of Various Demographic Groups Listening to Radio, by Daypart

| Group | Weekly Reach, Monday–Friday, by Daypart | | | |
	6 AM–10 AM	10 AM–3 PM	3 PM–7 PM	7 PM–Midnight
Men 18+	88.0%	77.7%	85.1%	57.3%
18–34	87.1	78.7	87.0	65.9
25–54	89.6	75.8	87.6	58.1
35–64	89.8	74.9	86.2	53.6
Women 18+	88.7	80.9	83.8	55.3
18–34	88.3	81.9	88.4	64.9
25–54	90.3	79.0	86.6	55.3
35–64	90.4	78.5	84.3	51.2
Teens 12–17	78.5	42.3	78.4	73.8

Source: Fall 1992 Arbitron National Data Base, as reported in *Radio Marketing Guide and Fact Book for Advertisers*, 1993–94, 20

Method of Transmission

A slight majority of commercial radio stations transmit their message through amplitude modulation (AM); the other method is frequency modulation (FM), which came into widespread use in the 1940s. One difference between the two is the distance covered. FM waves go in a straight line and are not usually received effectively more than 75 miles from the transmitter. By contrast, AM radio can be heard far beyond the horizon because a ceiling of electrical particles high above the earth (the Kennelly-Heaviside layer) bounces them back to earth, particularly at night. At night listeners can often hear stations located hundreds of miles away from their receivers. If the radio signal reaches the set directly, it is called a ground wave; if it is reflected back by the Kennelly-Heaviside layer, it is called a sky wave. Musical content is transmitted better through an FM station because of the availability of FM *stereo*. Stereo is available for AM stations but has not been used as widely.

Power and Range

The coverage of an AM station is influenced by its power, by the height of its transmitter, and by its frequency. The estimated daytime range of a 250-watt station is approximately 15 miles, compared with more than 100 miles for a 50,000-watt station. Obviously, a higher transmitter will add to the area (and the quality) of reception of a station.

Broadcast channels are divided into local, regional, and clear. The local channel covers only a small area, usually around a small city, and has from 100 to 250 watts of power. Consequently, several local stations around the country may operate on the same frequency. Often these stations will be restricted to daytime operation or will be required to cut down their power at sundown, because signals travel farther after dark.

A regional channel is usually operated with from 1,000 to 5,000 watts of power. It is expected to cover more territory than the local station and must be farther away from other stations that operate on the same frequency.

The clear-channel station is usually located in one of the larger cities and can operate with 50,000 watts. Each clear channel in the United States is reserved for one clear-channel station, with perhaps a distant regional station allowed to use the same frequency.

Programming Format

From an advertiser's standpoint, classifying stations according to the type of programming they use is probably the most useful method. This is so because a station's programming format usually defines the kind of audience attracted to a particular radio station. Buyers of radio air time refer to programming format as a station's "sound." Table 17.3 shows the percent of radio stations according to their programming format. Presently, the most popular radio sound is country and western, with 26.4 percent of all stations using this format. The adult contemporary sound is used by 16.6 percent of all stations.

Immediacy

Surveys show that listeners expect to find the latest news on radio. Many radio stations broadcast national, state, and local news at least once each hour. Quite a few have news broadcasts every half hour.

Low Cost

Most cost-per-thousand studies show radio delivering audiences at an extremely low cost. Thirty-second network costs range from a low of $200 (the CBN Radio

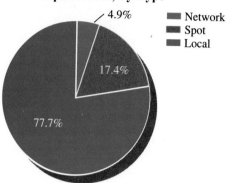

FIGURE 17.8

Total Radio Advertising Expenditures, by Type

- Network
- Spot
- Local

4.9%
17.4%
77.7%

Source: Compiled from data in *Advertising Age* (May 3, 1993): 4.

Advantages of
Radio Advertising

TABLE 17.3

Percent of Radio Stations Using a Particular Programming Format

Format	Percent of Stations
Country	26.4%
Adult Contemporary	16.6
Religious	8.7
Oldies	7.5
News/Talk/Sports	7.1
Contemporary Hit Radio (CHR)/Top 40	5.5
Middle of the Road/Standards	4.3
Album-Oriented Rock (AOR)	4.1
Spanish	3.5
Soft Rock	3.3
Urban/Black	3.2
Classic Rock	2.1
Easy Listening	1.6
Jazz/Alternative Rock	0.5
Classical	0.5
Variety/All Other	5.1

Source: *Radio Marketing Guide and Fact Book for Advertisers,* 1993–94, 2.

network of 392 stations) to around $9,000 (ABC Prime network, with 1,640 stations). Average cost-per-thousand figures are between $3.50 and $5.50 for a minute commercial. A spot buy in the top ten markets will average around $2,100 per rating point for a target of adults ages 18 and over.

Flexibility

Any communication that can be adapted to sound can be used on radio. Whether the message involves speaking, music, or some other type of sound, whether it takes three seconds or three minutes, the advertiser can use radio. Advertisers have in recent years devised some ingenious ways of communicating through radio. Also, they can change their message or its tone or even the entire commercial up to the time it goes on the air. They can, if they like, reach listeners several times a day, picking the times when they are most likely to reach potential consumers of the product.

Consider the flexibility of radio as far as geography is concerned. An advertiser may want the company's message heard in Denver but not necessarily in Dubuque, in San Antonio but not San Francisco. Advertisers can pick areas where dealers need the most support or where they think the potential is greatest.

Audience Selection

Unlike much television, radio provides a practical, low-cost vehicle for reaching a specialized audience. If the advertiser wants to reach sports fans or college students or any particular group, there is sure to be a variety of stations around the country and programming formats that make a special appeal to that group (see Figure 17.9). Like magazines, most radio stations concentrate on special market segments (for example, Hispanics); a few try for a larger, mass market.

Mobility

Radio is extremely mobile. It follows the listener from room to room, goes to the beach, rides in the car. There are few places it cannot go. It can even follow workers to their place of business—over 60 percent of adults have radios available at work.

At least four factors limit radio's effectiveness.

Fragmentation

There are few parts of the country where the listener is limited to fewer than ten stations. Radio must fight for its audiences, and in general radio is known as a media type that provides relatively small audiences. In New York City, for example, there are almost 50 stations listed in the Standard Rate & Data Service from which advertisers can choose. Even in the much smaller market—Knoxville, Tennessee—SRDS lists over 30 different stations.

Transient Quality

Radio, like any time medium, is fleeting. The message is not available for reference or for rereading.

Extent of Research Data

Although several audience survey methods are in common use, there is not the concerted attempt to find information that there is in television. The local advertiser is not so willing to sponsor research as is the national advertiser; therefore, a great deal more money is being spent on television research where national advertisers have a big stake.

L *imitations of Radio Advertising*

FIGURE 17.9

Trade Advertisement for CBS Radio Sports

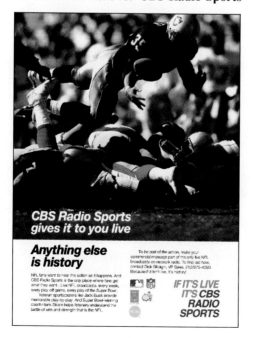

TABLE 17.4

Radio Expenditures by Product Categories

Rank	Product Category	Percent of Total Gross Expenditures		
		Spot	Network	Combined
1	Food Products	19.1%	9.8%	17.1%
2	Automotive	12.5	13.9	12.8
3	Consumer Services (financial)	6.3	14.9	8.1
4	Travel & Shipping	8.0	5.5	7.5
5	Beer, Ale, Wine	7.5	0.7	6.0
6	Retail Stores (national)	3.2	13.2	5.3
7	Drugs & Health Care	4.6	7.0	5.1
8	Gasoline & Oil	4.3	0.2	3.5
9	Publishing & Media	3.8	2.3	3.5
10	Government	3.1	2.0	2.8
11	Soft Drinks & Water	2.9	0.4	2.4
12	Apparel	2.8	0.5	2.3
13	Computers & Office Products	1.7	2.6	1.9
14	Agricultural & Garden	1.9	1.4	1.8
15	Entertainment & Amusement	1.6	1.9	1.6
16	Cosmetics & Toiletries	1.3	2.2	1.5
17	Home Furnishings/Appliances	1.6	0.3	1.3
18	Building/Hardware/Paint	1.3	1.0	1.3
19	Confections	0.6	3.4	1.2
20	Consumer Electronics	0.6	2.5	1.0
21	Soaps & Cleaners	1.1	—	0.9
22	Optical & Photo	1.1	—	0.9
23	Sporting Goods & Toys	0.9	0.1	0.7
24	Jewelry	0.8	0.5	0.7
25	All Others	7.4%	13.7%	8.8%
		100.0%	100.0%	100.0%

Source: *Radio Marketing Guide and Fact Book for Advertisers,* 1992, 31.

Cost to Deliver Extensive Reach

Whereas radio is an especially effective medium in delivering high levels of frequency, it generally requires substantial dollar outlays to deliver high reach. Since most stations deliver only a small segment of the total audience available, it requires a fairly large investment to reach a high percentage of a market's total population.

Kinds of Users

The Radio Advertising Bureau reports that food products receive the highest total expenditures of any product category, with automotive ranking second. Table 17.4 lists the 25 categories according to their share of expenditures in spot and network radio, as well as their combined expenditures. The order of products varies between spot and network. Thus, whereas food products are ranked number one for spot radio—with 19.1 percent of total expenditures—consumer services (financial) lead network radio expenditures (14.9 percent of total).

The largest spender in spot radio recently was Philip Morris's Kraft, General Foods, and Miller Beer divisions, with $21.6 million, as shown in Table 17.5. In network radio, Sears, Roebuck and Co. spent $59.2 million, followed by American Home Products, 28.1 million.

TABLE 17.5

Top Ten Spot and Network Radio Advertisers, 1992

Spot		Network	
Advertiser	**Expenditures (Thousands)**	**Advertiser**	**Expenditures (Thousands)**
Philip Morris (Kraft, General Foods, Miller)	$21,566	Sears, Roebuck	$59,221
Chrysler	20,332	American Home Products	28,154
General Motors	18,958	AT&T	26,649
Anheuser-Busch	18,655	Himmel Group	17,895
News Corp. (Fox TV)	15,844	Accor SA (Motel 6)	14,873
Kmart	14,885	Procter & Gamble	13,555
Southland (7–11)	14,836	U.S. Government	13,376
PepsiCo	13,938	Warner-Lambert	13,072
American Stores	11,608	Gateway (Hooked on Phonics)	12,979
Ford Motor	11,250	Dow Jones	12,809

Source: *Radio Marketing Guide and Fact Book for Advertisers,* 1993–94, 35.

Programming Trends

As television changed listening habits, radio programming content changed also. Radio tried to offer types of programs not found on television and avoided competing in areas in which television had a distinct advantage. In addition to offering a standard fare of musical programming—ranging from country and western to classical—radio programs include in-depth news analysis, news features, informational content (for example, a five-minute program on gardening or cooking or social advice), ethnic appeal, foreign language broadcasts, call-in talk shows, religious programming, sports, and public affairs broadcasting (such as a city council meeting).

In recent years, AM radio has been declining in popularity on a market-to-market basis. Compared to FM, sound reproduction on AM is noticeably poorer; this is especially noticeable when music is being broadcast. This situation has caused a number of AM stations to move their programming format from music to more informational forms: news, talk, sports, and the like.

Stereophonic FM radio has continued to build audiences since it was made available in the 1960s. The high-quality FM stereo sound became more and more appreciated by audiences as stations added stereo broadcasting capability and stereo reception became more widespread on receivers, including automobile radios. FM listenership is estimated to be three to four times greater than AM. Almost the reverse was the situation in many markets in the mid-1970s.

Audience Measurement and Trends

The most typical method of collecting audience information for radio is the diary, and the Arbitron Ratings Company is the main supplier of this syndicated research. A sample of individuals in a particular market is selected and asked to record their listening for a seven-day period (see Figure 17.10 for a sample diary). Audience estimates for a market are reported in a ratings book ("Arbitron Radio Market Report") and provide a broad assortment of information about the delivery of specific radio stations. Figure 17.11 shows a sample page from an Arbitron report.

To provide general information on radio listenership and audience trends, the broadcasting industry has undertaken a number of significant studies. For example,

Radio: Bridging the Programming-Technology Gap

by Rick Sklar

Radio is moving into the twenty-first century with the promise of unsurpassed technological capabilities.

Building on what has gone before, each technology discovery finds its way into the scientific journals, then into the textbooks and the classrooms and finally into the marketplace. Here forces of competition and regulation determine how it will affect the radio listener.

Result: Digital broadcasting, from the transmitter to the receiver, will provide a signal free of all interference including multipath. Stereo sound with the widest frequency range possible, enhanced to simulate any environment from the stadium to the intimate studio, will surround the listener.

At the radio station, tapeless control rooms and production facilities, using sound stored as computer data that can be shrunk, expanded and intermixed from multiple tracks, will give unsurpassed flexibility and freedom to programmers and the audio engineers. New recording techniques that give spatial three-dimensional qualities to sound promise still more surprises.

Consumers with esoteric tastes, unable to find what they want on the broadcast frequencies, will be able to turn to cable radio, delivering its brands of specialized formats compressed, sent via fiber optic cable and reassembled into sound in the home.

But radio programming has not followed the same growth curve as radio technology. Despite new technological capabilities, radio programming sounds very much the same from city to city and daypart to daypart. Not very much imagination or creativity seems to be at work. It is a world of positioning statements, music

sweeps and industry jargon like "MIX" and "ten in a row" that seem to produce ever-diminishing shares as more stations come on line.

Unlike technology, programming is not a formal discipline. Most radio programmers don't go to classes in the universities studying how radio programming evolved. Those who do, read textbooks that deal mostly with today's format clocks, relegating much of radio's earlier creative age to a few paragraphs that give no sense of the sounds of radio programming in those years. Many of today's radio programmers went from the mailroom to the music library to the PD chair. Their knowledge of radio programming and its capabilities is limited to what they have heard in the markets they have worked in and on tapes.

One key to harnessing this new technology may lie not in science but in programming's past, when technology was limited to AM frequencies, 5,000 cycles of sound and huge, boxy microphones.

Today's programmers have little or no notion of what radio sounded like in the 1930s, when it was the *only* electronic medium. They never heard the "Lux Radio Theatre" or Orson Welles Mercury players creating an incredible world in the imagination of the mind with actors, sound effects, a narrator and music. Most never heard radio versions of soap operas (where soaps began) or the great coast-to-coast network radio comedy variety shows that entertained the nation, much the way TV does today, before and during the second World War. Some have no idea that after school let out at 3 PM, a whole generation of kids listened to one 15-minute cliffhanger

Source: Courtesy of The Arbitron Company.

the Radio Advertising Bureau and the National Association of Broadcasters sponsored the All-Radio Methodology Study (ARMS) in an attempt to measure the relative accuracy of 11 different research techniques commonly used in radio-audience measurement. A second study was the Cumulative Radio Audience Method (CRAM), which was designed to overcome the cooperation bias usually found in surveys (the bias represented by the fact that heavy listeners are more likely to cooperate than light listeners). This was done by tracking down the noncooperators

after another featuring Dick Tracy, Superman and other comic-strip characters. They never heard of "Doc, Jack and Reggie," the adventurers on "I Love a Mystery." While they may have watched "Jeopardy!," they are unaware of the "$64,000 Question"—and have no notion that radio quiz shows ever existed. They cannot imagine what it would be like to walk down "Allen's Alley," the fictitious street that millions of Americans strolled on with comedian Fred Allen every Sunday night for a decade. The thought of live bands and vocalists in the studios would be hard for them to imagine.

So carefully were radio programs put together in the 1930s and 1940s that studios were designed with the ability to change the acoustics and move the walls for each program, every day. Floors, ceilings and walls were floated, suspended in air from the buildings in which they were constructed, to eliminate extraneous sound. Announcers and studio audiences entered through hallowed double sound locks. Program directors working behind sound-insulated control room booth windows used imagination to create entertainment in the listener's mind. When the director cued a sound effects man to twist a metal cover off a glass jar, the sound was heard by millions of listeners as the airlock of a spaceship from Mars, turning and opening to reveal the tentacles of Martians to a gasping crowd of onlookers in a New Jersey field (actually a group of actors standing around a microphone in a CBS studio).

The 8 o'clock news started at 8 o'clock, not three minutes before eight one morning and two minutes after, the next.

Many of today's radio programmers don't even know what the first format radio sounded like with its five minutes of news and 25 minutes of music every half-hour. They were never exposed to Martin Block's "Make-Believe Ballroom," D.J. pioneer Alan Freed or the incredibly complex sound that was WABC Radio, where each record, preproduced on its own cartridge like a scene from a movie, with opening stagers and closing jingles, was placed in its own planetary time rotation orbit and presented by all-day personality D.J.'s using a library of 400 jingles, that produced audiences of six million listeners in one market. They never heard early Todd Storz Radio or stations by Gordon McClendon or John Box. The incredible news presentations on WIL St. Louis, or KBOX, that may sound corny today electrified audiences and rolled up double-digit market shares in their time. Today's programmers can't imagine a Top 40 WINS, where there was a standing rule to start a record before a news bulletin went on for the added excitement of having the bulletin announcement (accompanied by a submarine crash dive alarm) override the record. Nor can they conceive of having the size rating shares and cumes that these stations had.

It might be a good idea to get some of our most promising young radio program directors, isolate them for a week from the world of 1991 radio, and immerse them in the sounds of radio programming from the beginning. We might really see some stretching of the minds occur. They might begin to sense the potential of sound as a creative medium. Then, when they get back to their stations, they might have some more imaginative ways to use the technology as an audio launching pad, to give us entertainment.

and then building these groups back in at the weight they should have in the final figures.

Perhaps the most ambitious radio-audience research project to date has been RADAR (Radio's All-Dimension Audience Research). Begun during 1967 and 1968, the RADAR study annually surveys a large national sample of homes to collect audience data on a quarter-hour basis by program and demographic groups and to find out product and brand usage of these listeners.

FIGURE 17.10

Arbitron Radio Diary

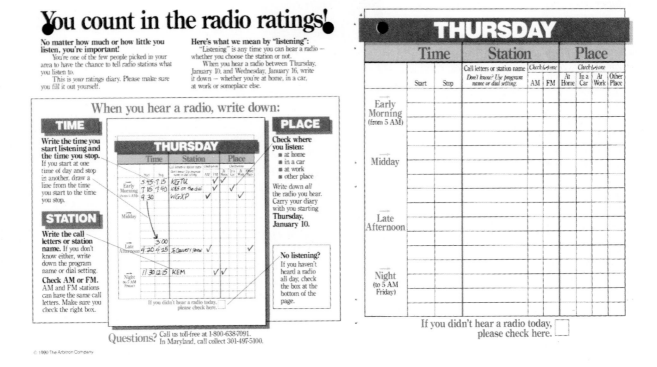

RADAR studies, as well as other research, have provided some interesting information about how radio is used:

1. There are now 5.6 radios per American family. Of these, 356 million operate in homes and around 180 million are in automobiles. Ninety-five percent of all automobiles have radios.
2. During the average week, 95.7 percent of all Americans 12 years or older listen to radio (see Figure 17.12). On the average day, almost four out of five adults listen to radio.
3. The average adult listening time is 3 hours and 20 minutes a day.
4. Sixty-one percent of all adults have a radio at work.
5. Three out of four adults are reached weekly by radio in their cars.
6. Radio can often reach demographic groups not easily reached by other media. For example, radio reaches 95.7 percent of all teenagers, 95.6 percent of all adult African-Americans, and 95.6 percent of all adult Hispanics in an average week.
7. Radio listening varies according to the time of day, with the largest percent of listening occurring during the day and early evening (see Figure 17.13).
8. Based on average quarter hour ratings, radio listening is greater than television viewing from 5 A.M. until 5 P.M. After 5 P.M., more people view television than listen to radio.

Rate Structure

Present radio rate structures reflect the degree of audience delivery. The highest rates typically apply at times when people drive to and from work. Evening rates generally are the lowest. However, a particular station in a specific market must examine its own unique situation in deciding on a rate schedule.

AQH stands for "average quarter hour"; Arbitron counts the number of persons listening to a radio station for at least five minutes during a particular quarter hour. "Cume" is the number of different people listening to a station during a specified time period for at least five minutes. RTG is the abbreviation for "rating," which is the number of people listening to a station compared to the total number of people in a market. SHR is "share"—the number of people listening to a station compared to all people listening to radio at a specific time. "Metro" and "TSA" (Total Survey Area) indicate which geographic area in a surveyed city is being measured; Arbitron defines these areas for each city studied.

FIGURE 17.11

Pages from an Arbitron Radio Market Report Showing How a Particular Target Audience (Women 18–34) Is Delivered by Different Radio Stations

Target Audience
WOMEN 18-34

	MONDAY-FRIDAY 6AM-10AM				MONDAY-FRIDAY 10AM-3PM				MONDAY-FRIDAY 3PM-7PM				MONDAY-FRIDAY 7PM-MID				WEEKEND 10AM-7PM			
	AQH (00)	CUME (00)	AQH RTG	AQH SHR	AQH (00)	CUME (00)	AQH RTG	AQH SHR	AQH (00)	CUME (00)	AQH RTG	AQH SHR	AQH (00)	CUME (00)	AQH RTG	AQH SHR	AQH (00)	CUME (00)	AQH RTG	AQH SHR
WABT METRO	21	133	.2	.7	29	116	.3	1.0	28	195	.2	1.1	4	63		.3	12	95	.1	.6
TSA	21	133			29	116			28	195			4	63			12	95		
WAIT METRO	*				1	15			*											
TSA					1	15														
WBBM METRO	69	524	.6	2.3	17	259	.2	.6	27	340	.2	1.1	9	174	.1	.7	17	162	.2	.8
TSA	93	721			31	352			35	400			17	273			28	257		
WBBM-FM METRO	331	1749	2.9	11.0	331	1827	2.9	11.6	290	2132	2.6	11.5	147	1728	1.3	11.6	248	1598	2.2	11.9
TSA	333	1769			331	1843			292	2169			148	1749			249	1619		
WBEE METRO	6	20	.1	.2	16	20	.1	.6	14	20	.1	.6	12	20	.1	.9				
TSA	6	20			16	20			14	20			12	20						
WBUS METRO	8	135	.1	.3	29	207	.3	1.0	17	168	.2	.7	7	173	.1	.6	23	148	.2	1.1
TSA	10	180			31	244			22	244			14	218			34	261		
WCKG METRO	103	890	.9	3.4	135	1197	1.2	4.7	170	1465	1.5	6.7	50	652	.4	4.0	105	1100	.9	5.1
TSA	104	916			138	1270			175	1511			51	696			107	1121		
WFMT METRO	11	115	.1	.4	9	76	.1	.3	14	132	.1	.6	12	114	.1	.9	8	48	.1	.4
TSA	11	115			9	76			14	132			12	114			8	48		
WFYR METRO	24	395	.2	.8	30	402	.3	1.0	39	532	.3	1.5	41	436	.4	3.2	26	316	.2	1.3
TSA	28	404			37	411			42	542			41	443			26	316		
WGCI METRO	1	18			3	68	.1	.4	4	88		.2	5	69		.4	4	38		.2
TSA	1	18			3	68			4	88			5	69			4	38		
WGCI-FM METRO	364	1744	3.2	12.1	274	1582	2.4	9.6	268	1597	2.4	10.6	204	1307	1.8	16.1	233	1381	2.1	11.2
TSA	365	1753			275	1591			268	1597			208	1317			233	1381		
WGN METRO	55	225	.5	1.8	48	236	.4	1.7	41	237	.4	1.6	5	101		.4	18	173	.2	.9
TSA	91	390			73	378			56	390			11	180			32	277		
WIND METRO	58	201	.5	1.9	52	184	.5	1.8	30	150	.3	1.2	13	104	.1	.8	58	136	.5	2.8
TSA	58	201			52	184			30	150			13	104			58	136		
WJJD METRO	7	43	.1	.2	18	43	.2	.6	13	43	.1	.5	2	43		.2	5	72		.2
TSA	26	106			34	87			15	67			2	43			5	72		
WJMK METRO	68	361	.6	2.3	108	446	1.0	3.8	77	657	.7	3.1	26	443	.2	2.1	41	463	.4	2.0
TSA	70	386			110	472			81	683			27	469			42	479		
WJPC METRO	8	58	.1	.3	3	59		.1	7	115	.1	.3	3	96		.2	2	20		.1
TSA	8	58			3	59			7	115			3	96			2	20		
WLNR METRO	27	269	.2	.9	17	239	.2	.6	31	369	.3	1.2	28	406	.2	2.2	41	274	.4	2.0
A/F TOT TSA	27	269			17	239			31	369			28	406			41	274		
WKQX METRO	35	307	.3	1.2	20	259	.2	.7	38	428	.3	1.5	31	444	.3	2.5				
TSA	35	307			20	259			38	428			31	444						
WKQX METRO	174	1323	1.5	5.8	136	1068	1.2	4.7	110	1368	1.0	4.4	56	840	.5	4.4	79	1006	.7	3.8
TSA	181	1351			165	1140			125	1413			57	886			81	1026		
WLIT METRO	127	678	1.1	4.2	148	521	1.3	5.2	134	694	1.2	5.3	42	358	.4	3.3	36	326	.3	1.7
TSA	127	685			153	554			139	746			42	358			36	326		
WLS METRO	20	182	.2	.7	3	121		.1	8	97	.1	.3	1	72		.1	8	101	.1	.4
TSA	22	251			14	225			21	252			2	80			17	278		
WLTH METRO	8	50	.1	.3	14	32	.1	.5	7	68	.1	.3		18			6	36	.1	.3
TSA	8	50			14	32			7	68				18			6	36		
WLUP METRO	31	199	.3	1.0	27	216	.2	.9	39	350	.3	1.5	8	109	.1	.6	22	186	.2	1.1
TSA	42	241			39	299			45	401			8	116			25	262		
WLUP-FM METRO	250	1336	2.2	8.3	89	894	.8	3.1	105	1227	.9	4.2	59	804	.5	4.7	76	926	.7	3.7
A/F TOT TSA	255	1391			95	957			107	1282			64	858			78	990		
WMAQ METRO	281	1449	2.5	9.4																
TSA	297	1546																		
WNIB METRO	68	614	.6	2.3	85	424	.8	3.0	53	555	.5	2.1	7	185	.1	.6	36	323	.3	1.7
TSA	83	707			87	520			62	649			8	200			38	357		
WNIZ METRO	7	106	.1	.2	21	215	.2	.7	9	154	.1	.4	11	113	.1	.9	14	137	.1	.7
TSA	7	106			21	215			9	154			11	113			14	137		
METRO	1	9				18			1	27			1	18	.1					
TSA	1	9				18			1	27			1	18						

ARBITRON
120

CHICAGO   WINTER 1991

Target Audience
WOMEN 18-34

	MONDAY-FRIDAY 6AM-10AM				MONDAY-FRIDAY 10AM-3PM				MONDAY-FRIDAY 3PM-7PM				MONDAY-FRIDAY 7PM-MID				WEEKEND 10AM-7PM			
	AQH (00)	CUME (00)	AQH RTG	AQH SHR	AQH (00)	CUME (00)	AQH RTG	AQH SHR	AQH (00)	CUME (00)	AQH RTG	AQH SHR	AQH (00)	CUME (00)	AQH RTG	AQH SHR	AQH (00)	CUME (00)	AQH RTG	AQH SHR
F/F TOT METRO	8	115	.1	.3	22	232	.2	.8	10	181	.1	.4	12	130	.1	.9				
TSA	8	115			22	232			10	181			12	130						
WNUA METRO	54	405	.5	1.8	54	388	.5	1.9	58	543	.5	2.3	36	398	.3	2.8	30	325	.3	1.4
TSA	54	405			54	388			58	543			36	398			32	395		
WOJO METRO	78	345	.7	2.6	78	294	.7	2.7	45	238	.4	1.8	26	263	.2	2.1	74	361	.7	3.6
TSA	78	345			78	294			45	238			26	263			74	361		
WPNT-FM METRO	71	430	.6	2.4	107	402	.9	3.7	78	597	.7	3.1	31	516	.3	2.5	42	387	.4	2.0
TSA	71	430			108	429			78	597			31	516			44	414		
WTAQ METRO	15	45	.1	.5	17	86	.2	.6	24	97	.2	1.0	6	38	.1	.3	12	69	.1	.6
TSA	15	45			17	86			24	97			6	38			12	69		
WTMX METRO	122	767	1.1	4.1	245	880	2.2	8.6	119	964	1.1	4.7	26	511	.2	2.1	73	627	.6	3.5
TSA	123	782			248	902			120	979			26	511			73	627		
WUSN METRO	50	392	.4	1.7	38	314	.3	1.3	44	478	.4	1.7	16	256	.1	1.3	56	465	.5	2.7
TSA	53	413			43	395			49	524			17	282			65	527		
WVAZ METRO	159	1017	1.4	5.3	135	923	1.2	4.7	143	1123	1.3	5.7	153	885	1.4	12.1	206	1145	1.8	9.9
TSA	159	1017			135	930			143	1123			153	885			206	1145		
WVON METRO	17	74	.2	.6	*	10	38	.1						7	20	.1	.6			
TSA	17	74			10	38							7	20						
WVVX METRO	6	19	.1	.2	10	50	.1	.3	1	19			11	99	.1	.9				
TSA	6	19			10	50			1	19			11	99						
WXRT METRO	192	1005	1.7	6.4	119	790	1.1	4.2	112	1002	1.0	4.4	47	738	.4	3.7	107	1025	.9	5.1
TSA	192	1005			119	790			112	1002			47	738			109	1046		
WYCA METRO	10	97	.1	.3	15	72	.1	.4	10	79	.1	.4	5	36		.4	6	72	.1	.3
TSA	10	97			15	72			10	79			5	36			6	72		
WYLL METRO	15	93	.1	.5	9	123	.1	.3	10	116	.1	.4	9	98	.1	.7	7	53	.1	.3
TSA	15	100			9	123			10	116			11	132			9	69		
WYSY-FM METRO	23	159	.2	.8	44	130	.4	1.5	17	129	.2	.7	4	100		.3	10	80	.1	.5
TSA	34	240			46	175			27	230			6	180			11	125		
A/F TOT METRO	23	159	.2	.8	44	130	.4	1.5	17	129	.2	.7	4	100		.3				
TSA	34	240			46	175			27	230			6	180						
WYTZ METRO	63	791	.6	2.1	79	857	.7	2.8	65	982	.6	2.6	29	645	.3	2.3	80	884	.7	3.8
TSA	79	887			83	959			68	1076			52	746			81	903		
METRO TOTALS	2999	9590	26.6		2864	8753	25.4		2523	9942	22.4		1264	7809	11.2		2079	9123	18.4	

ARBITRON
121

CHICAGO   WINTER 1991

Target Audience - Women

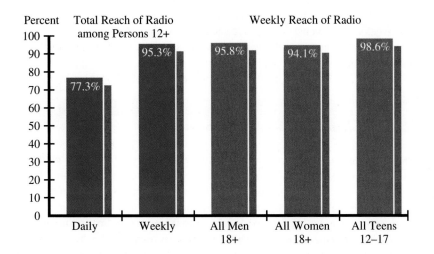

Percent
Total Reach of Radio among Persons 12+   Weekly Reach of Radio

FIGURE 17.12

Percentage of U.S. Population Reached by Radio

	Daily	Weekly	All Men 18+	All Women 18+	All Teens 12–17
Percent	77.3%	95.3%	95.8%	94.1%	98.6%

Source: *Radio Marketing Guide and Fact Book for Advertisers, 1993–94, 13, 15.*

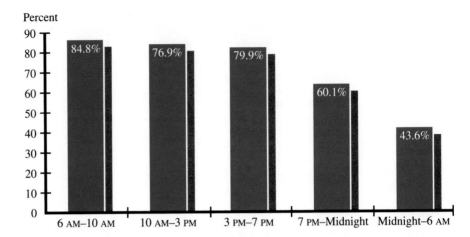

FIGURE 17.13

Weekly Radio Reach by Daypart, Among Persons 12 Years or Older

Source: *Radio Marketing Guide and Fact Book for Advertisers,* 1993–94, 14.

Spot radio rates were estimated, on a cost-per-rating-point basis, by a major advertising agency as follows:[9]

| | Cost per Rating Point for Specific Groups | | |
Markets	Men 18–34	Women 18–34	Teens 12–17
Top 10	$1,190	$1,168	$ 767
Top 20	1,665	1,635	1,090
Top 30	2,045	2,004	1,377
Top 50	2,547	2,499	1,753
Top 100	3,204	3,124	2,245

Thus, the cost per rating point to reach 18–34-year-old women in the top 50 markets would be $2,499. A schedule aimed at adult women calling for 75 GRPs a week, for 13 weeks, would cost $2,436,525 ($2,499 × 75 × 13).

To make cost comparisons, media planners use the CPM and/or CPRP methods discussed earlier.

Summary

Both television and radio are media with vast reach potential. An estimated 98 percent of American homes currently have at least one television set and 99 percent have at least one radio. Television has become the leading medium for national advertisers, although it is exceeded by newspapers in total expenditures.

The principal types of advertising in television and radio are network, spot, and local. In television, network advertising accounts for the largest portion of expenditures, but in radio, local advertising is most important. We can also make

Future Trends

Television and Radio

A few key trends likely to affect the broadcast media in the future include the following:

- *New technology* The continued advancement of technology in broadcasting probably is the most significant of future trends. Changes in electronic technology have been occurring at an increased pace for the past few years and will readily continue. The use of satellites to transmit television programming, including cable and cable-like systems, will continue to permit greater diversity of programs and systems of delivery. In radio, digital audio broadcast (DAB) will dramatically improve the quality of radio reception.
- *Audience fragmentation* Many of the advancements in broadcast technology will cause audience sizes to decrease and thus the medium will become fragmented. In some ways this will be advantageous to advertisers wanting to reach rather narrow market segments, but at the same time it will probably cost more per person reached.

- *Integration of media formats* Many of the new media technologies will cause a further blurring of different media formats. For example, whereas today we tend to think of the television set and personal computer as different entities, they are likely to become integrated in the future. By the same token, the telephone will be used in many of the same ways a computer and television set are today.
- *Changes in audience measurement* Companies measuring television and radio are experimenting with techniques that likely will improve the quality and accuracy of audience information. For example, the use of a passive meter to measure television viewing by individuals already has been mentioned. Another device currently being considered is a wristwatch that can detect what television programs its wearer is watching as well as the radio stations he or she listens to. It may even be possible for the device to determine which magazines are read, thus permitting intermedia comparisons that presently are not possible.

a meaningful distinction between AM and FM transmission in radio, and over-the-air and cable delivery in television.

Television and radio both have the advantages of a very personal approach and of extreme flexibility. Both, if carefully used, may deliver audiences at a low cost per thousand. Radio can be very selective, whereas television is more of a mass medium. Both have the innate limitations of the time media—a transient quality. The huge initial cost for even a modest television campaign often limits television advertising to the large national advertiser.

In general, makers of widely distributed, mass-consumption products are the heaviest users of both media.

Research data are fairly plentiful in the broadcast field. In both television and radio, there are four basic methods of finding out who is listening: electronic recorder, telephone coincidental, diary, and roster recall. Each has its advantages and limitations, and many advertisers use data from several sources.

Rates are usually compared on a cost-per-thousand or cost-per-rating-point basis, but such comparisons should be made with extreme care.

Key trends likely to affect television and radio include the continued advancement of new broadcast technology, which in turn may cause more audience fragmentation, the integration of media formats, and advancements in audience measurement techniques.

Questions for Discussion

1. What are the advantages of spot compared with network television?
2. For which types of products is television best adapted?
3. On what basis are the rates for radio and television set?
4. What effect does the number of television sets in a home have on audience size?
5. Which audience rating method do you consider the best? Why?
6. Do you feel that people meters are better than diaries for measuring television viewing? Explain your reasoning.
7. What would the following schedules cost?
   a. Ten 30-second network television commercials on the early evening news.
   b. Eighty GRPs in the top 30 markets for daytime television.
   c. Fifty GRPs in the top 100 markets for spot radio aimed at teenagers.
8. Compare the two television programs in terms of cost efficiency:

	Audience Size	Rating (homes)	Cost of 30-Second Commercial
Program A	11,172,000 homes	12	$175,000
Program B	13,965,000 homes	15	$210,000

Notes

1. Joanne Lipman, "Prime-Time Commercial Loads Grow," *Wall Street Journal* (February 10, 1992): 19.
2. "Trends in Television," TVB Research Department (New York: Television Bureau of Advertising, Inc., 1991).
3. For additional detail, see Donald W. Jugenheimer, Arnold M. Barban, and Peter B. Turk, *Advertising Media: Strategy and Tactics* (Dubuque, IA: WCB Brown & Benchmark, 1992), 324–341.
4. Stuart Elliott, "The Long and Short of Increasingly Infrequent 15-second Spots," *The New York Times*, January 27, 1993, D-18.
5. *Marketer's Guide to Media*, Fall/Winter 1992–1993, 27–31.
6. A. C. Nielsen Company, *Nielsen 1991–92 Report on Television.*
7. Leo Burnett, *1992 Media Costs & Coverage.*
8. *Marketer's Guide to Media*, Fall/Winter 1992–1993, 27–31.
9. Leo Burnett, *1992 Media Costs & Coverage.*

Bovée, Courtland L., and William F. Arens. *Contemporary Advertising*, 4th ed. Homewood, IL: Irwin, 1992. Chapter 14.

Jugenheimer, Donald W., Arnold M. Barban, and Peter B. Turk. *Advertising Media: Strategy and Tactics*. Dubuque, IA: WCB Brown & Benchmark, 1992. Chapter 16.

Kaatz, Ronald B. *Cable: An Advertiser's Guide to the New Electronic Media*. Chicago: Crain Books, 1982.

McGann, Anthony F., and J. Thomas Russell. *Advertising Media*, 2d ed. Homewood, IL: Irwin, 1988. Chapters 6, 9.

Russell, J. Thomas, and W. Ronald Lane. *Kleppner's Advertising Procedure*, 11th ed. Englewood Cliffs, NJ: Prentice-Hall, 1990. Chapters 8, 9.

Shimp, Terence A. *Promotion Management and Marketing Communications*, 3d ed. Fort Worth, TX: Dryden Press, 1993. Chapter 13.

Sissors, Jack Z., and Lincoln Bumba. *Advertising Media Planning*. 4th ed. Lincolnwood, IL: NTC Business Books, 1993. Chapters 12, 15.

"Special Report: Cable TV." *Advertising Age*, issued yearly as supplement to *Advertising Age*.

Suggested Readings

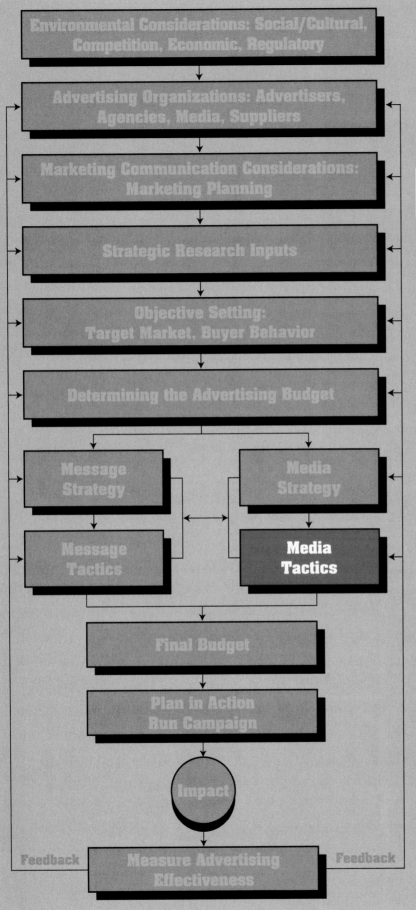

LEARNING OBJECTIVES

In your study of this chapter, you will have an opportunity to:

- Understand the types of direct mail and out-of-home media.
- Examine the factors that are considered in buying direct mail and out-of-home media.
- See how and why advertisers use direct mail and out-of-home media.
- Note the types and characteristics of directory, specialty, and in-store media.
- Know of the existence of other, miscellaneous forms of advertising media.

Chapter **18**

Media: Direct Mail, Out-of-Home, and Other Media

CHAPTER TOPICS

DIRECT MAIL
Related Concepts
Types of Direct Mail
Advantages of Direct Mail
Limitations of Direct Mail
Buying Direct Mail
Preparation of Direct Mail

OUTDOOR ADVERTISING
Types of Outdoor Advertising
Advantages of Outdoor Media
Limitations of Outdoor Media
Kinds of Users
How Outdoor Advertising Is Bought

TRANSIT ADVERTISING
Types of Transit Advertising
Advantages of Transit Advertising
How Transit Advertising Is Bought

OTHER MEDIA
Directory Advertising
Specialty Advertising
In-Store Media
Miscellaneous Media

The print and broadcast media discussed in the two preceding chapters collectively account for 60 percent of all measured media expenditures. This chapter focuses on several additional media—direct mail, outdoor, transit, directories, specialties, in-store, and miscellaneous. Outdoor and transit are generally called out-of-home media.

Print and broadcast media involve a combination of editorial and entertainment materials along with advertising content. Advertisements in newspapers and magazines, as well as commercials in the broadcast media, are in effect adjacent to the content the medium is intended to carry. Several of the types of media covered in this chapter consist only of the advertising itself.

Direct Mail

Whether used to reach a general population of consumers, or directed to business prospects, direct mail is an important medium. It would be hard to find a business firm that did not at some time use direct-mail advertising. Since 1947, direct mail has ranked second or third among the measured media in dollars spent. Direct-mail advertising currently accounts for almost 20 percent of all advertising expenditures, placing it third behind newspapers and television.

Like many other forms of advertising, direct mail owes a debt to Benjamin Franklin, who, in 1775, headed the first post office in this country. The big growth of the postal service and of direct-mail advertising came in the nineteenth century. Penny postage after 1850 encouraged use of the mails for delivery of advertising materials. After the Civil War, not only notices and circulars but almanacs became very popular. Catalogs started to appear toward the end of the century, as improvements in printing enabled advertisers to illustrate clearly the products being offered.

The first Montgomery Ward catalog, consisting of 100 pages, was distributed in 1872 and offered several hundred articles for sale through mail order. Early catalogs brought to rural and small-town communities information about items that people wanted but could not buy at the few general stores available to them. Today, catalogs are sent to people in virtually every type of community—rural, small towns, suburban, and urban markets—and offer the ease of shopping by mail or through calling an 800 number to place a credit-card order. In a recent year, the U.S. Postal Service delivered 14 billion copies of catalogs through the mails. Some catalog companies even use videocassettes as their form of catalog.

■ **R**elated Concepts

FIGURE 18.1

Use by Direct-Response Advertisers of Various Media, in Percentages

- ▨ Direct Mail
- ▨ Yellow Pages
- ▨ Free-Standing Inserts
- ▨ Telemarketing
- ▨ Magazines
- ▨ Newspapers
- ■ Radio
- ▨ Television
- ■ Catalogs

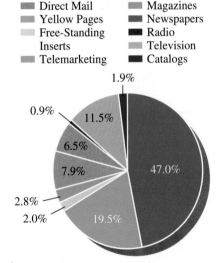

1.9%
0.9%
11.5%
6.5%
7.9%
2.8%
2.0%
47.0%
19.5%

Source: *Advertising Age* (March 30, 1988):45.

Direct mail is related to mail-order advertising, direct response, and direct marketing. Each will be described briefly here, although only direct mail is an advertising medium. Business-to-business direct mail is discussed in Chapter 20.

Mail-order advertising involves any method of selling in which the product is promoted through advertising and ordered by customers through the mail (or by telephone). No personal selling is involved. It is a way of doing business; and, consequently, the term "mail order" does not refer to an advertising medium, but to the use of any of the media that might be appropriate. Mail-order sales in the United States account for somewhat less than 10 percent of all retail sales.

Direct response is an advertising technique. The advertising, regardless of the medium used, seeks an immediate action or response, such as an order, an inquiry about the product or service, or a visit to the retail store. Various media used by direct-response advertisers are shown in Figure 18.1. Direct-mail advertising is the major medium used, with 47 percent of the total. Yellow-page directory advertising is second, with 19.5 percent of the total.

"**Direct marketing** is an interactive system of marketing that uses one or more advertising media to effect a measurable response and/or transaction at any location."[1] Direct marketing is thus a broad term that can include both mail order and direct-response advertising, as well as direct mail.

Direct mail is an advertising medium that involves distributing the advertising message through the Postal Service or other direct delivery service. The message can have any number of objectives—from direct action, such as a sale (direct response), to intermediate goals, such as providing information or changing attitudes. With postage accounting for as much as 20 percent of a direct mailer's costs—and likely continued increases by the U.S. Postal Service—advertisers presently are experimenting with private delivery services.

■ **T**ypes of Direct Mail

The term direct mail can pertain to anything from a postcard to a catalog containing hundreds of pages. The letter of application you send to a prospective employer is also direct mail, which you can prepare yourself. However, if you take a communication problem to a specialized direct-mail agency, you find that varieties of forms are almost infinite—limited mainly by your ability to pay. The following are among the more common forms.

Sales Letter

This is one of the most frequently used forms of direct mail—normally the first form any business firm will use. It can be individually typed or reproduced by a duplicating process. Computer-printed letters are used extensively (see Figure 18.2).

Postcard

Cards may be sent either third or first class, depending upon when an advertiser wants them delivered. Reply cards are often used to encourage a direct reply from the receiver of a mailing piece.

FIGURE 18.2

A Personalized Sales Letter Printed by Computer

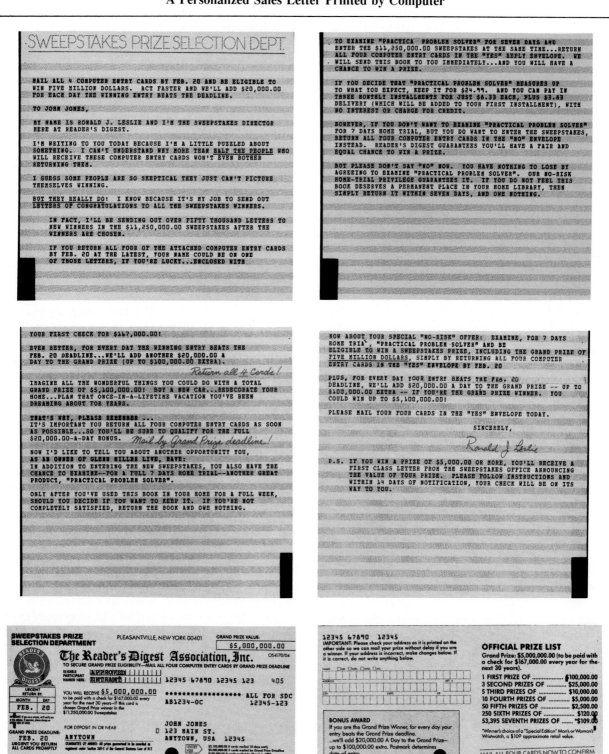

Leaflet

A leaflet is usually a single printed sheet. It is often used in conjunction with a letter to explain an offer or idea more fully.

Folder

A folder is larger than a leaflet and is usually printed on heavier stock. The larger size holds more of the sales story and permits use of more visual material. Folders can often be handled economically as self-mailers with the name and address stenciled on an open area of the cover.

Broadside

A broadside, as the term implies, is even larger than a folder. It should be large enough so that its size helps to impress the receiver with the importance of the offer. Some broadsides are sent to dealers for display in the store as posters or point-of-sale promotion pieces. Others are designed for the ultimate reader.

Booklet

A leaflet that contains several pages is more properly called a booklet. If the sales story is complicated and considerable information is needed, a single printed sheet is not enough. A booklet rather than a leaflet should be used. Most automobile companies produce such booklets. Gasoline companies produce booklets that deal with safe driving or car care.

Catalog

Like a booklet, a catalog has many pages. But its main function is to serve as a reference book. Most consumers are familiar with the big catalogs of the general mail-order houses. These are buying guides, designed to be used over a period of time. In the more specialized fields, catalogs may be more technical, but their purpose is essentially the same. L.L. Bean issues a number of catalogs each year, one of which is shown in Figure 18.3.

Advantages of Direct Mail

Direct mail offers advertisers many advantages. Probably the outstanding advantage to direct-mail advertising is its extreme selectivity. The coverage of a mass medium will seldom correspond exactly with the audience that the advertiser is trying to reach; so a "mix" is worked out. In the case of direct mail, theoretically at least, the advertiser can build any circulation he or she wants. Whether the advertiser is trying for a small audience or one of millions, whether high or low income, white collar or blue collar, a coverage pattern can be worked out.

Suppose you want to reach all your dealers once every few days for several weeks. Through direct mail, you can make the coverage as intensive as you like.

Because direct mail can be moved quickly, it can take advantage of timely or seasonal appeals. For example, the advertiser can have a mailing ready to go when the first snow arrives, and within a few days can reach all the people on the mailing list.

The previous section discussed some of the possible formats that can be used. Direct mail's format is flexible. Unlike the mass media, where the advertiser is bound by certain physical rules, direct mail involves no physical limitations—except, of course, the budget.

If the product or the situation demands it, direct mail can furnish a great deal of information. Long copy, illustrations, diagrams, or any other device that will provide useful stimulus to the sale can be included.

FIGURE 18.3

Cover and Inside Pages from an L.L. Bean Catalog

Each mailing piece can be as individualized as necessary. Many sales letters and cards are highly personalized, and such personalization has been greatly facilitated by the computer. Catalog mailers, for example, can have customers' names and addresses preprinted on the order blank and even mention the customer's last purchase.

Limitations of Direct Mail

Direct mail is expensive. Even the cheapest mailing piece has a high cost per reader. For example, a **self-mailer** averages around 40 cents for each piece mailed. When the audience is highly selective, the high cost can be justified, because there may be much less waste circulation than in the alternative way of reaching an audience—the mass media.

Much of the success of any direct-mail campaign depends on the quality of the mailing list. In some instances, obtaining a high-quality list may be excessively expensive or difficult.

Ordinarily direct-mail ads contain no editorial or entertainment material to soften the impact of the advertising message. Consequently, direct-mail advertising must evoke its own attention, arouse its own interest in what is said.

Postal regulations are often cumbersome and complicated. An advertiser using the U.S Postal Service to distribute direct-mail advertising must be knowledgeable about these regulations and aware of the procedures that make the mailing as economical as allowable.

Buying Direct Mail

Buyers of print space or broadcast time deal with a specific media vehicle, such as the *Chicago Tribune, Time,* CBS, or KRLD-TV. The space or time is allotted precisely—say, 40 column inches or 30 seconds. In return for the expenditure, the medium delivers an audience that the buyer hopes will attend to the advertisement or commercial.

Direct mail works a bit differently. To understand the distinction, we must think of the costs involved for a direct-mail advertisement. There are three basic costs: (1) production, (2) distribution, and (3) mailing list.

Production

Production costs include everything involved in preparing a product and readying it for mailing at a particular time, whether it be a postcard or a 100-page catalog. The advertiser may create a mail piece or may hire an outside specialist (such as an advertising agency); in any case, there will be costs associated with developing the concept and its design.

Other costs associated with producing the material include artwork, models, photographers, retouchers, and the like. Further costs are incurred in the printing of the direct-mail piece (materials as well as labor). Some production charges, of course, also occur for newspaper and magazine advertising. However, these media include paper and printing costs as part of the basic space charge for ROP advertising.

Finally, there may be some expenses associated with the handling of the direct mailer, such as computer programming charges, sealing envelopes, labeling, sorting, and bundling (often by zip code).

Distribution

Although direct-mail advertising can be distributed by a number of methods, including United Parcel Service, Federal Express, and private delivery services (see Figure 18.4), the U.S. Postal Service is the primary distributor. It accounts for around 97 percent of the total.

The direct-mail advertiser generally sends material by either first-class or third-class mail. Third-class mail rates are significantly below those for first-class, often as much as one-eighth. Because of the complexities associated with mailing charges and the extensive regulations for mailing, the direct-mail advertiser should confer with the local postmaster.

FIGURE 18.4

Advertisement for a Service That Offers an Alternative to Using the U.S. Postal Service

Mailing List

Perhaps the most critical element of a direct-mail campaign is the mailing list. Advertisers can develop their own mailing list or secure one from someone else.

A number of possible sources for developing a mailing list include the following:

- Automobile registrations
- Building permits
- Business directories
- Cash customers (for example, some stores have a policy of writing a customer's name and address on the receipt when a sales transaction is made)
- Charge account holders
- City directories
- Clipping bureaus (a good source of births, deaths, and new businesses)
- Coupons (some firms run a coupon in newspapers or magazines that interested people return to ask for additional information)
- Government directories
- Property tax lists
- Yellow Pages in the telephone directory

Once the list is built, it must be maintained diligently and kept up to date. People move, marry, change jobs, get divorced, remarry, have babies, and die. Businesses are begun; some fail. Others may be taken over or experience a change in name or location. All of these occurrences require mailing-list alterations.

Companies called **list houses** compile and maintain various mailing lists for sale or rental. They may publish a catalog that describes their lists and indicates the number of names available and the cost for using a list. Rates typically are quoted per thousand names and can range from a low of around $15 per thousand to as much as $300 to $400 per thousand. Rental lists average around $40 to $50 per thousand. Figure 18.5 shows a catalog from a list house.

Standard Rate & Data Service (SRDS) publishes *Direct Mail List Rates and Data,* which provides thousands of business, consumer, and farm lists.

FIGURE 18.5

Cover and Inside Page from the American Consumer Lists Catalog of Direct-Mail Lists

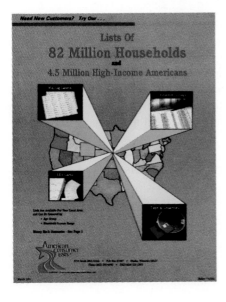
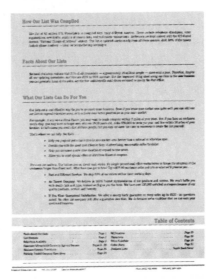

Preparation of Direct Mail

Traditionally the advertiser has taken on the job of planning, manufacturing, and mailing direct-mail pieces and has left the agency free to concentrate on the mass, commissionable media such as television or newspapers. About fifteen years ago, however, several large agencies became seriously interested in direct mail (as well as direct response advertising), and some set up or bought subsidiaries that concentrated in this medium. This trend has continued and accelerated and will likely continue in the future. Many of the larger mailing houses providing lists also handle printing and mailing and allow the agency a commission on all these charges.

Regardless of who carries out direct-mail plans, the task can be complicated. There are several major steps involved in preparing a direct-mail piece:

1. Decide on the type of direct mail and develop the basic format.
2. Write copy and select artwork.
3. Decide on printing methods, select paper, and set up schedules with the printer.
4. Develop or secure mailing lists.
5. Work out mailing costs and schedules (perhaps with the help of the local post office).
6. Address and mail.

Many of these steps involve technical knowledge, and it is essential that the planner draw on the knowledge of a specialist. For example, paper comes in a wide variety of finishes, weights, and sizes, and only an expert will be able to predict which is best for a particular job.

It is wise to have the mailing checked by the post office for size, weight, postage, and general mailability. For example, the mailer may not know about recent postal rate increases and may be underestimating the total costs of the mailing.

In the future, we are likely to see even greater use of the computer in direct mail, because it can improve direct mail in terms of selectivity, measurement of advertising impact, and personalization. Database marketing has become especially valuable in recent years (see the Future Trends box at the end of Chapter 12). The use of highly specific data bases, accessible via computers, provides marketers with unlimited combinations of audience selection criteria and enables them to direct their promotions at sharply defined market segments.

Outdoor Advertising

Today's outdoor poster is really a distant cousin of our first advertising medium—a sign identifying a place of business. Signs were followed in the nineteenth century by circus and show posters, which were widely used to publicize show business. Currently, outdoor advertising expenditures total over $1 billion, 59 percent of it placed by national advertisers and 41 percent by local firms. In certain foreign countries, where the number of media is limited or where the rate of literacy is low, outdoor advertising is among the most important of all media.

Types of Outdoor Advertising

The three major types of outdoor advertising are posters, painted bulletins, and electric spectaculars.

Posters

In poster advertising, the advertising message is printed (usually by lithography) on sheets that are then pasted on a structure. Various standard-sized posters are used in the United States, but the most common are the 30-sheet and the bleed

FIGURE 18.6

Common Advertisement Sizes for Posters and Painted Bulletins

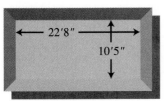

Bleed Poster

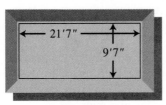

30-Sheet Poster

Painted Bulletin

poster. The term 30-sheet does not mean that the posters are made up of that many individual pieces of paper, although they were many years ago. Today, posters are usually printed in 10 to 14 sections.

The 30-sheet poster measures 9 feet, 7 inches by 21 feet, 7 inches. The bleed poster extends the artwork right to the frame of the panel. Each of these posters is mounted on a standard poster structure that is approximately 12 feet high and 25 feet long (see Figure 18.6).

Painted Bulletins

Painted bulletins are more custom-made than the poster. Each advertisement can be painted to order from a design furnished by the advertiser or the agency. The standard painted bulletin is 14 feet high and 48 feet long. Some are three-dimensional with an embellished cutout that extends beyond the frame, usually to emphasize the product or some feature of it (see Figure 18.7).

FIGURE 18.7

**Two Painted Bulletins—One with Illustrative Matter Extending
Above and to the Side of the Structure's Frame**

A great deal of experimentation in producing bulletins is currently being done. For example, fiber optics are being used to produce dramatic effects, especially at night. Fiber optics provide greater flexibility than the traditional outdoor mediums of paint and poster because the fiber optics board can create virtually any colors, change them in sequence, and provide the illusion of motion. Some painted bulletins are being produced by using reflectorized sheets to make copy sparkle or shimmer so as to create an illusion of motion and texture. Other new techniques include the following:

- A "video billboard," which involves a $7\frac{1}{2}$- by $9\frac{1}{2}$-foot TV screen that is mounted on a painted bulletin. The screen beams 45-second full color ads to motorists from sundown to midnight.
- Computerized painting systems that utilize a color scanner, much like that on a color copier, to print a life-size color image on canvas, vinyl, or acetate. This permits a greater uniformity and detail than can be obtained from painting bulletins by hand.
- Rotating faces ("Tri-Vision"), whereby the panels of a painted bulletin either slide or rotate to display two or three different messages.
- Solar-powered signs that illuminate outdoor structures with stored electricity generated by photoelectric cells, very much like the ones that power space satellites.
- Nonelectric lights that use a fluorescent light tube similar to conventional fluorescent light that requires no external power source. These new lights are expected to cost no more than conventional fluorescent lights and have a useful lifetime upwards of six months.
- Inflatables, whereby the 14- by 48-foot bulletin structure is used to mount a special display that is made of fabric or plastic and is three-dimensional as a result of being filled with gas.

Spectaculars

The large, illuminated, often animated signs located typically in and around big cities are called **spectaculars.** In New York City, for example, spectaculars dot Broadway's Great White Way. Custom-made to fit high-traffic locations, spectaculars are a common sight in industrial areas and along the expressways linking Chicago and its suburbs. They usually are extremely expensive to produce and maintain and are bought on a long-term contract, usually for at least several years. Although highly dramatic, spectaculars are only a small part of total expenditures in outdoor advertising.

Advantages of Outdoor Media

Certain advertisers, such as restaurants and motels, like outdoor advertising because it reaches potential customers close to the point where their services are on sale. Communication must be quick and simple in outdoor advertising. This quality has both virtue and limitation. The simplicity of the message makes it easy to comprehend. Through color, art, and short copy, advertisers hope to generate a quick feeling or association that will contribute to their brand image. But some messages are too complicated to be told in a manner that a driver going 55 to 65 mph can comprehend.

Repetition is another quality that appeals to many advertisers. If the product or service is advertised at a busy crossroads, audiences will see the ad again and again. Retention of an idea is essential to induce action. The more often the idea is repeated, the more likely it is to be retained. Even though the audience is limited to a specific area, the sheer weight of constant repetition is likely to produce results.

The Ad Insight about Cheerios illustrates some of the advantages associated with outdoor advertising.

Case History on the Use of Outdoor Advertising

Outdoor Advertising: It broadens your horizons for success. Here's how Outdoor Network, USA proved it for General Mills.

BACKGROUND/OBJECTIVE

- General Mills is a dominant presence in the highly competitive cold cereal market.
- To maintain its strong position, General Mills and its Agency viewed Outdoor as a potential substitute medium for spot television.

STRATEGY

- Cheerios, a leading all-family brand, was singled out for an Outdoor test.
- Cheerios' famous ability to "float" made it an ideal candidate for the high-impact instant communication unique to Outdoor posters.

TEST METHODOLOGY

- Four markets were selected for a three month test.
  Test Markets: *Phoenix, AZ and Kansas City, MO. 50 Daily Outdoor GRP's on top of regular Spot TV buy.*
  Control Markets: *Memphis, TN and Philadelphia, PA. Spot TV; dayparts reflected normal spot advertising buys.*

Source: Courtesy of Gannett Outdoor Group.

- Existing Network Television buy overlay in all markets.

ACTION STANDARD

- Sole measurement: Increased brand share in test markets after three months of Outdoor. Sales evaluated by standard measure (SAMI).

RESULTS

- Sales increased incrementally in each test market, in each month of the test, for a combined average of +3%.
- Remarkably, Outdoor also created a residual effect, with sales surging in the test markets during the fourth month—one month after the posters had been taken down.

Cheerios Outdoor Test—Sales Results

Fiscal Month	*Change in Volume* Phoenix	Kansas City	Combined
February	+0.4%	+0.2%	+0.3%
March	+0.9	+3.4	+1.9
April	+2.3	+6.6	+4.4
May	**+5.6**	**+12.4**	+9.0
Total	+1.7	+4.5	**+3.0**

Limitations of Outdoor Media

Outdoor advertising also has certain built-in limitations. One obvious limitation is brevity. How much can an advertiser tell consumers about a product on a poster or bulletin? Consumers have no chance to browse leisurely, as they do with the newspaper or magazine, or to see the product demonstrated, as they do on television.

Another limitation is the public's fear that outdoor advertisers are spoiling the landscape. This feeling came to focus in the Highway Beautification Act of 1965, in which Congress regulated the placement of outdoor advertising near interstate highways. Among other things, this act specified a penalty of 10 percent of the federal highway funds usually provided for a state in the case of failure to effect control of outdoor advertising within 660 feet of the nearest edge of the highway.

By the early 1990s more than 100,000 outdoor signs had been removed from along Interstate and primary highways. However, approximately another 100,000 were scheduled to be removed by the mid-1990s, and the U.S. Congress appropriated over $400 million to accomplish the task.[2] In addition to these limitations by federal statute, many cities have enacted legislation that limits the number and format of outdoor structures. For example, the city of Austin, Texas, passed a 1983 ordinance prohibiting the construction of new or replacement of old outdoor structures.

Kinds of Users

The top ten categories in terms of outdoor advertising expenditures are listed in Table 18.1. Cigarette and tobacco products account for around 12 percent of total outdoor expenditures, with business and consumer services advertising at 8.1 percent. The ten categories shown in the table account for 57 percent of the total spent in the outdoor medium.

How Outdoor Advertising Is Bought

Originally, the basic insertion unit for outdoor posters was the *showing*. A 100 showing theoretically meant that a specified number of poster panels were so distributed that, in a 30-day period, virtually every mobile person in the community passed one or more of them on the way to work, while shopping, or while out driving for recreation. A 50 showing, theoretically, should deliver 50 percent of the mobile population during the 30-day posting.

TABLE 18.1

Top Ten Categories of Outdoor Advertising Expenditures, 1992

Rank	Category	Expenditures (Millions)	Share of Total Outdoor
1	Cigarettes, tobacco & accessories	$123	11.9%
2	Business & consumer services	84	8.1
3	Retail	82	8.0
4	Entertainment & amusements	64	6.2
5	Miscellaneous/general retail	50	4.9
6	Automotive, auto accessories	47	4.6
7	Travel—hotels & resorts	39	3.8
8	Beer & wine	36	3.5
9	Publishing & media	34	3.3
10	Insurance & real estate	23	2.2

Source: Leading National Advertisers Outdoor Advertising Service.

Studies of outdoor audiences showed that a 100 showing in fact reached 85 percent of the adult population an average of 24.7 times a month. A 50 showing reached 79 percent of adults, with a frequency of 13 times.

In 1973 the Outdoor Advertising Association of America (OAAA) adopted as the basic unit of sales the term *100 gross rating points daily (GRPs)*. This means that the basic standardized unit is the number of poster panels required in each market to produce a daily effective circulation equal to the population of the market. The advertiser can purchase any number of units, such as 75 gross rating points daily, or 50, or 25. The standard length of purchase is still the 30-day period. Generally, there is a close correlation between a showing and a gross rating point. Although some outdoor companies still use the showing as their basic unit, most have converted to gross rating points.

The number of posters required for 100 gross rating points, of course, varies from city to city and is based on traffic surveys. For example, Table 18.2 provides information for the Birmingham, Alabama, metropolitan market. A 100 GRP poster buy consists of 68 panels located throughout the market and costs $26,860 a month. Such a buy likely will reach almost 90 percent of the Birmingham population, with an average frequency of exposure of around 35 times in a 30-day period. As the number of GRPs bought decreases, the reach will go down only slightly, but the average frequency will drop noticeably. Figure 18.8 is a map of the 320 locations of posters in the New Jersey metro area for a 100-GRP buy.

Painted bulletins are bought on an individual basis, usually for one-, two-, or three-year periods. Bulletins are either hand painted in an outdoor company's studio and put up in sections on location, or painted directly at the location. As indicated earlier, though, many methods other than hand painting are being tested for future use.

A permanent painted bulletin will remain at the same location for the entire contract period, whereas a rotary bulletin is moved every 60 or 90 days to different locations to assure market coverage.

Information about outdoor costs for markets throughout the United States, such as that shown in Table 18.2 for Birmingham, is published in the *Buyers Guide to Outdoor Advertising,* a publication of Leading National Advertisers. Standard Rate & Data Service (SRDS) also publishes out-of-home rates in *Advertising OptionsPlus.*

FIGURE 18.8

Poster Locations for a 100-GRP Showing in the New Jersey Metro Area

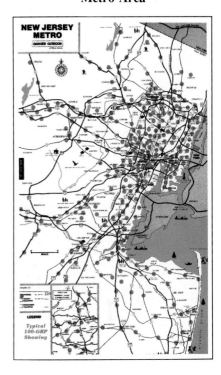

Transit Advertising

Audiences encounter **transit advertising,** like outdoor advertising, away from home—hence the term out-of-home media used for the two. In terms of advertising

TABLE 18.2

Monthly Outdoor Advertising Poster Costs in Birmingham, Alabama

GRPs	Number of Posters	Monthly Cost
100	68	$26,860
75	51	20,145
50	34	14,430
25	17	6,715

Source: *Buyers Guide to Outdoor Advertising.*

investment, transit advertising is considered a minor medium. About $250 million per year currently is spent in this medium. More than 75,000 vehicles—buses, subways, rapid transit, and commuter trains—carry transit advertising in 380 urban markets.

Local advertisers were among the first users of transit advertising. As early as 1850, the dry goods firm of Lord & Taylor used car cards as part of its advertising program. By 1895, transit advertising was available in 54 cities and 9,000 vehicles, with annual expenditures estimated at $2 million. By 1900, 93 cities and 14,000 transit vehicles were available to advertisers.[3] By then, national advertisers were noted users of the medium, including a successful campaign for Sapolio soap.

During this same era, two of the most well-known transit advertising campaigns were introduced. In 1899, the famous "Campbell's Kids" promoted Campbell's Soup through ads inside transit vehicles. The company bought a year's showing in New York for $4,200.[4] The makers of Wrigley's Gum conducted an advertising test in Buffalo, New York, for their soon-to-be-famous "spear men," used to introduce a new spearmint flavor. The firm continued to use transit advertising for many years as a major part of its media strategy.

Types of Transit Advertising

The three major types of transit advertising are (1) inside-of-vehicle ads, or car cards; (2) outside displays; and (3) station posters. Other forms of transit advertising exist—such as taxi tops, bus-shelter displays, and telephone enclosure panels—although these are not discussed here.[5]

Car Cards

The standard inside-of-vehicle rack above the windows holds a car card 11 inches high and 28 inches wide. In addition, widths of 42 and 56 inches generally are available. In some cities, card spaces that are larger and shaped differently can be bought. These are usually placed at each end of the vehicle and in the middle, adjacent to the exit door. One fairly common size for these units is 22 by 21 inches and is known as a hi-light square (see Figure 18.9).

FIGURE 18.9

Examples of Inside-of-Vehicle Transit Advertisements

FIGURE 18.10

Types of Outside Transit Displays

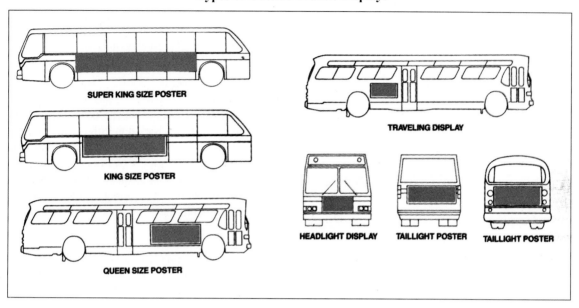

Outside Displays

The outside display is somewhat like an outdoor poster in that it is seen by pedestrians and people in automobiles. There are a number of types and sizes, and those generally available are shown in Figure 18.10. Actual outside displays are pictured in Figure 18.11. In some markets it is possible to have an entire bus repainted to a firm's specifications. For example, a bread manufacturer could have a bus painted to resemble the bread's package design.

FIGURE 18.11

Outside Transit Displays Are Seen by Pedestrians as Well as Persons in Automobiles

Station Posters

Station posters are available in only a very few of the largest U.S. markets, where there is an extensive rapid-transit system and/or commuter trains. The standard station posters are one-sheet (30 inches wide by 46 inches high), two-sheet (60 by 46 inches), and three-sheet (42 by 84 inches). In New York and Philadelphia, for example, all three sizes are available in commuter rail terminals and rapid-transit stations.

Advantages of *Transit Advertising*

Studies have shown that a transit rider averages 44 rides a month, 61 minutes per day. Thus, car card advertising can achieve both a high level of repetition and in-depth reading. A king-size outside bus display is estimated to reach about 85 percent of the total adults in a city in a month.

In addition to this kind of audience delivery, transit advertising offers high-quality color, so the advertiser can effectively show the product rewards. Inside car cards can be used to communicate an in-depth message, although outside displays have much the same copy limitations as outdoor advertising.

Transit is considered to be a flexible advertising medium in that it offers a fairly wide choice of types and sizes, permitting versatility in the creative treatment used. Additionally, transit advertising can be tailored to an advertiser's geographic segmentation.

Transit advertising (especially the use of car cards) is a good way to reach specific markets. For example, certain transit routes may have a high percentage of high school or college students; another may serve blue-collar workers who go to and from their factories; and yet another may transport white-collar employees into the central business district. Station posters and inside-vehicle ads bought from commuter train companies may effectively reach professionals. This ability to pinpoint targets makes transit useful to both national and local advertisers.

Transit can be a very efficient medium, averaging less than 25 cents per thousand exposures for inside-of-vehicle ads and 75 cents per thousand for outside displays.

How Transit *Advertising Is Bought*

Car cards are bought on the basis of full, half, or quarter showings (or service)—that is, all, half, or a quarter of the vehicles in a fleet. Rates are generally quoted for a month, with discounts granted for longer-term contracts. For example, an 11-by 28-inch car card bought on buses in the five boroughs of New York has the following rates:

Showing	1 Month	2–5 Months	6–11 Months	12 Months
Full	$36,216	$34,416	$32,616	$28,980
Half	18,108	17,208	16,308	14,490
Quarter	9,054	8,604	8,154	7,245

If the advertiser contracted a full showing for six months, the total cost would be $195,696 (6 × $32,616).

Outside displays also are bought on the basis of showings, usually given as 100, 75, 50, or 25. The gross rating points (reach × frequency) for a 100 showing typically are twice that of a 50 showing. Each level of showing is related to the number of display units bought. Discounts are available for purchasing over time. For example, a 100 showing of a 30- by 144-inch king-sized display for several different markets has the following costs:

Case History on the Use of Transit Advertising

Subway advertising is an effective way to promote a product, business, or service. Thousands of potential customers utilize public transportation everyday and as most commuters are aware, there is little else to do but read the advertising displays.

American Vision Centers of New York took advantage of the benefits of subway advertising to achieve two goals: maintain name awareness and increase store traffic. The company created a promotional campaign built around what most New Yorkers have in their pockets: a subway token.

Harve Ganz, Vice President/Sales for Gannett Transit, New York, suggested an initial five month program. When the consumer response was so positive, American Vision Centers extended the program for an additional four months.

The program took a twist on the coupon redemption idea but was far more effective. When a customer presented a token, they received $35 off their purchase of eyewear.

Source: Courtesy of Gannett Transit.

"We found that if a shopper knows a coupon is available, but doesn't have one on them, they won't walk into the store," says Don Baasch, Director of Advertising for American Vision Centers. "But nearly everyone has a token."

The idea was a success! *During the nine-month campaign, their overall business increased 20 percent.*

"We had never used subway advertising before, but were very pleased with the outcome. This was an effective campaign and helped us achieve the results we were looking for."

The subway advertising worked so well for American Vision Centers, they are planning a 12-month program next year.

Whatever your advertising goals are, Gannett Outdoor Group and Gannett Transit can help you realize them. Contact your local representative to get more information about subway, transit and shelter advertising.

Market	Number of Vehicles	Monthly Costs
New York (all counties)	4,000	$239,590
Chicago	2,200	185,625
Dallas	900	107,800
Columbus, OH	320	23,520
New Orleans	487	17,300
Knoxville, TN	75	5,160

In the few markets in which station posters are available, rates are quoted on the basis of showings—full, half, quarter, and so on. For example, a two-sheet poster (60 inches wide by 46 inches high) bought full showing in available markets has the following rates:

Market	Number of Posters	Monthly Costs
Atlanta	60	$ 7,780
Buffalo	16	1,616
Chicago	220	19,455
New York	600	86,886
Philadelphia	160	13,730
San Francisco	60	8,294
Washington, DC	100	17,500

Other Media

So far we have examined those media types that typically are considered for use in most media schedules. Yet, these media do not exhaust all possible choices. We now discuss a number of these "other" media types, including directories, specialties, in-store media, as well as enumerate and discuss briefly a few miscellaneous media. Some of these other media have been available to advertisers for many years, while others have been developed only recently.

Directory Advertising

Although most people associate directory advertising with the Yellow Pages in the telephone book, an estimated 7,500 to 8,500 classified directories of various sorts are published annually in the United States. Of these, around 6,000 are Yellow Pages directories. Directories are used by people in business as well as by consumers seeking information about products and services.

The first telephone directory was published in 1878, after the opening of the world's first commercial telephone exchange in New Haven, Connecticut. Several years later, publishers began using yellow paper to distinguish business listings from the alphabetical listing of phone customers, hence the basis of the term *Yellow Pages*.

Although it is difficult to estimate how much money is spent for all directory advertising, we have accurate expenditure figures for Yellow Pages. Presently, over $9 billion is spent for Yellow Pages advertising, with over 87 percent of that placed by local advertisers.

Types of Directory Advertising

Directory advertising can be of varied sizes and shapes. The more common types are listed below.

Regular Listings A large number of the advertisements you see in a Yellow Pages directory are of this type. The listing includes a name, address, and telephone number. In addition to using regular type, a listing may include semi-bold or bold type faces. Such listings can be noted in Figure 18.12.

Space Listings Space listings appear in the listing column and allow for various amounts of information to supplement the business listing of firm name, address, and telephone number (see Figure 18.12).

FIGURE 18.12

Common Types of Yellow Pages Advertising

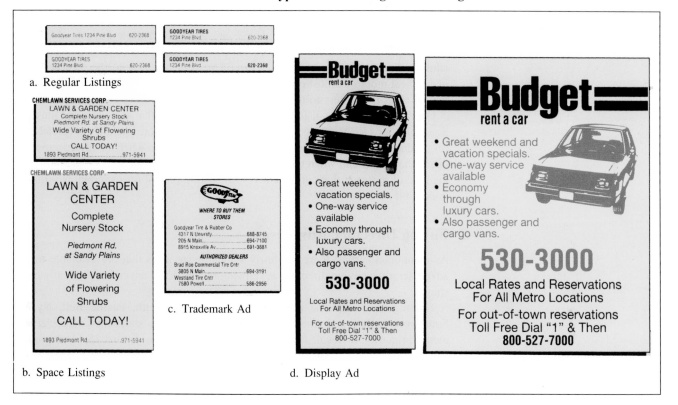

a. Regular Listings

b. Space Listings

c. Trademark Ad

d. Display Ad

Trademark Items These appear under the Yellow Pages classified heading desired (for example, "automobile tires"), and are used to identify the brand name, trademark, and local outlets. Thus, a national firm would use such advertisements to identify where its brand or service can be purchased locally (see Figure 18.12).

Display Advertisements Display advertisements provide the greatest flexibility within Yellow Pages. Sizes can range from one-eighth page to full page and include at least one illustration. The advertisement can be black printing on yellow paper, or some or all of the print can be in color, typically red (see Figure 18.12). A new process called Markolor gives the appearance of full-color printing but uses only two colors printed on yellow paper. Note the advertisement for Markolor in Figure 18.13.

In addition to the typical types of directory advertising, a number of companies are using "talking Yellow Pages," in which information is transmitted electronically via telephone lines. As more homes acquire personal computers, this technique will become more commonplace.

Characteristics

Directory advertising, like all media, has both advantages and limitations. The directory gives advertisers an opportunity to call attention to their products or services at the time the prospective customer is in the mood to buy. Directories are particularly well adapted to the needs of certain types of advertisers. For example, if your car will not start, you want help as soon as possible; you will probably look in the Yellow Pages for the name of a nearby service station or wrecker service. If you are interested in shopping for a new bicycle or stereo equipment, you may, through calls to various stores, find out which stores have what you want and what the prices are.

FIGURE 18.13

Markolor Is a Patented Process That Gives Full-Color Appearance to Yellow Pages Advertisements

The messages are usually of the reminder type and often tie-in with other advertising on television or in the newspapers. When a national advertiser uses a directory to list the names of local dealers, the goal often is to lessen brand switching at the local level after interest has been aroused by a persuasive message in another medium.

Studies have shown that most people are aware of Yellow Pages and use the source fairly often. For example, a recent study revealed that over 98 percent of all adults indicated familiarity, with almost 78 percent referring to the Yellow Pages in a typical month. Almost one in five adults used a directory on a typical day. The typical adult user refers to the Yellow Pages over three times each week.

One key problem in using directory advertising is that the message must be acceptable for a long time, usually one year. In addition, there is a fairly long lead time for production. It may be several months between the time when an advertisement is due at the printer and when the directory is issued. These limitations notably restrict the type of message that can be conveyed—listing prices, for example, is virtually impossible.

Buying Directory Advertising

As mentioned earlier, there are fairly standard-size units that are available to the advertiser, thus buying directory advertising by a national advertiser is usually quite simple.

The regional telephone companies—such as BellSouth, Pacific Bell, Nynex, Southwestern Bell, and Ameritech—have their own sales staffs that sell advertisements primarily to local, but also, national advertisers. Figure 18.14 shows an advertisement for BellSouth's Yellow Pages directories. In addition to these sales

FIGURE 18.14

Trade Advertisement For BellSouth's Yellow Pages Directories

staffs, there are a number of firms that are authorized sales representatives (ASRs) of the various directories. ASRs work with national and regional advertisers and their advertising agencies. As such, they consolidate the work of buying from a host of individual directories, thus making national buys simpler.

Each directory issues a rate card that provides prices for various units as well as necessary information for producing the advertisement. In addition, the industry's trade association—Yellow Pages Publishers Association (YPPA)—issues a national *Rates & Data* directory which provides essential price and production information for a national or regional advertiser.

Specialty Advertising

The terms **specialty advertising** and advertising specialties are catchall classifications that include a variety of items carrying the advertiser's name and address and often a short sales message. The industry's trade association—Specialty Advertising Association International—defines the medium as follows:

> Specialty advertising is an advertising, sales promotion, and motivational communications medium which employs useful articles of merchandise imprinted with an advertiser's name, message, or logo. Unlike premiums, with which they are sometimes confused, these articles (called advertising specialties) are always distributed free— recipients don't have to earn the specialty by making a purchase or contribution.[6]

The specialty is usually inexpensive and is presented to a preselected audience. The donating company hopes that if the key ring or letter opener or coffee mug is useful, the recipient will be reminded of the donor many times a year and will feel kindly toward the firm and its product. It is estimated that current expenditures for specialty advertising are about $5 billion yearly, about half as much as that spent on Yellow Pages.

Types of Advertising Specialties

Since there are more than 15,000 different types of items used as advertising specialties, it is difficult to fit them all into neat categories. Generally, though, the medium consists of five major types: (1) calendars, (2) wearable items, (3) writing instruments, (4) desk/office/business accessories, and (5) glassware/ceramics. As noted in Figure 18.15, these five categories account for about two-thirds of specialty distributor sales.

Business gifts often are mentioned as a separate category, but they are not true advertising specialties since they are seldom imprinted with an advertising message. Business gifts are, however, often sold to companies by specialty advertising counselors, and this fact probably accounts for their being included.

Regardless of the type of specialty chosen, users of the medium are advised to consider three criteria in selecting an item: (1) the specialty should be of good quality, (2) it should be familiar to the audience and easy to use, and (3) it should be useful. A recent study showed that recipients look for the following characteristics in receiving specialty advertising:[7]

- Usefulness   98.2%
- Quality   71.8
- Attractiveness   61.5
- Tastefulness   59.8

Characteristics

One of the most important attributes of specialty advertising is its long life and extended exposure opportunity. Every time you look at a firm's calendar or wear an imprinted T-shirt, you are reminded of its name and perhaps of some slogan attached to it. Many specialty items are kept, and used, for long periods of time. A

FIGURE 18.15

Relative Amount Spent on Advertising Specialties

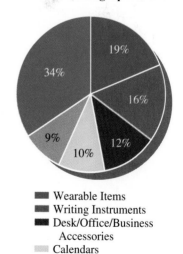

34%
19%
16%
12%
10%
9%

- ■ Wearable Items
- ■ Writing Instruments
- ■ Desk/Office/Business Accessories
- Calendars
- Glassware/Ceramics
- ■ Other

Source: Dan S. Bagley, III, *Understanding Specialty Advertising* (Irving, TX: Specialty Advertising Association International, 1991), 2.

calendar, of course, can be used for an entire year; studies have shown that people receiving specialties are still using them six months later.

Another important characteristic is the ability to preselect the targeted audience. Like direct mail, specialty advertising distribution is under the control of the advertiser. Waste circulation can thus be kept to a minimum, which is especially important if the unit cost of the specialty is relatively high.

The creative impact of a well-selected specialty item can be high. Because of their utility value, most advertising specialties naturally create involvement. For example, a specialty you may receive from your bank—say, a coffee mug, ball-point pen, calculator, or stadium seat—would be of value and usefulness.

Advertising specialties often provide goodwill to the advertiser. Receiving a gift usually is a desirable thing—the word "free" is a potent word in copywriting. We are inclined to be favorable toward firms that provide us with something of value at no cost to us.

Given that there are 15,000 specialty items available to choose from, flexibility is a key attribute. Specialties can be issued just about anytime and can be tied to a special promotion, such as a store's anniversary. The price range of specialties is broad, and the advertiser can choose from items costing only a few cents to several dollars. The advertiser can choose to provide the advertising specialty to all prospective customers, only current customers, or even to just a few select ones.

Among the limiting characteristics is the brevity of the specialty's message. Many items permit only the name, address, and telephone number, with no opportunity for additional copy points. This limitation makes the choice of the specialty most important to the advertiser. If it's important to convey a message in addition to name and address, a pencil or pen probably will not work—but other items likely will work, say, for example, a pocket planner or a calendar or perhaps a mug insulator.

Buying Specialties

Buying specialties is similar to buying direct mail in that the advertiser, or a specialist hired by the advertiser, has primary responsibility for making the purchase. There are three main business categories that make up the specialty-advertising industry through which buying takes place: (1) suppliers, (2) distributors or "counselors," and (3) direct-selling houses.

Suppliers make up the production end of the business. They manufacture, import, imprint, or otherwise produce the thousands of advertising specialty items. Distributors or counselors are the sales companies that represent industry suppliers. Not only do they call on advertisers to sell them specialties, but they also provide counseling on how the medium can fit into an overall advertising program. The typical company using advertising specialties will deal only with a counselor firm, since they can provide all necessary advice on how to effectively select a specialty, design the message, and distribute the item.

Direct-selling houses are a combination of supplier and distributor. They manufacture many of their own products and sell them to advertisers through their own sales force. They also buy specialty items from other suppliers and sell them, along with providing advice on the effective use of specialties, to their advertiser clients.

In-Store Media

Take a stroll through a retail store, say, a supermarket, or a mass-merchandise store such as Kmart or Wal-Mart. You are certain to see at least one type of in-store media, perhaps several. Supermarkets in particular have become a major testing place for several new and innovative types of media. The potential communication value of advertising messages in retail stores can hardly be overestimated. We discuss below in-store media in three categories: (1) point-of-purchase displays, (2) shopping carts, and (3) in-store television and radio.

AD insights

Two Case Histories on the Use of Specialty Advertising

Objective: A radio station wished to encourage listener participation.

Strategy & Execution: Mark and Brian, the morning broadcast team for the Los Angeles station, encouraged listeners to call in and discuss various subjects. Ad specialties, referred to as "parting gifts," were used to thank callers for their patience in getting through on the busy telephone lines. Most of the specialties were humorously renamed to complement the team's sometimes outrageous behavior. A plastic slinky became a "coil of pleasure," a corn butterer was referred to as a "cob lubricating wand," and soaps were known as "pit pals." Other gifts included lunch boxes, snow domes, cookie cutters, pedicure files, earrings, and custom gift wrap. All items were imprinted with the morning team logo and station call letters.

Results: Said the station promotion director: "These items have been an important part of each Mark and Brian show. The listeners made such an effort trying to get through the telephone lines just so they can win a Mark and Brian consolation prize."

Objective: To increase awareness and participation in programs offered by a student association.

Strategy & Execution: "Experience the Difference" was chosen as the campaign theme targeted to 9,000 new and continuing students at three campuses to get them excited about Student Association programs. The campaign kicked off with 2,000 theme-imprinted T-shirts distributed as a premium at an on-campus pub with admission ticket purchase. At this and other pubs, key-chains bearing the "Driving Impaired Can Kill" message were distributed. At the same time, 1,000 write-on/wipe-off memo boards imprinted with various student services were distributed at events and locations throughout the school system. To complement these activities, 2,500 fortune cookies with custom messages promoting the general Student Association meeting, pub nights, and various association-sponsored events were distributed at a "Chinese barbeque" held at each campus. The campaign was supplemented with flyers, bulletin board messages, announcements, and promotion within the student handbook.

Results: The Student Association president reported a 40 percent increase in pub night attendance and a 30 percent increase in student services participation. He also cited a decrease in drinking-and-driving incidents.

Source: Courtesy of Specialty Advertising Association International.

Point-of-Purchase Displays

One might classify *all* in-store media as "point-of-purchase," but the term is used here to describe the more traditional kinds of advertising found within a store. **Point-of-purchase (P-O-P) advertising** displays are the "signs and displays located in, on, or adjacent to the place where an advertised product or service is available for purchase."[8] P-O-P displays are developed by brand manufacturers who hope to deliver an advertising message to consumers at the time of purchase. Current expenditures for P-O-P displays are estimated at over $15 billion.

The extensive use of self-service in retail outlets means that advertisers must depend heavily on displays to communicate the merits of the product. P-O-P displays often are designed to reinforce a basic advertising theme carried out in other media, yet in many instances such promotional units tell the whole product story. Several award-winning P-O-P displays are shown in Figure 18.16.

Displays are also useful in attracting the attention of consumers who have not specifically planned their purchases. Studies of supermarket shoppers have shown that, on the average, 66 percent of purchase decisions are made in the store, ranging from 49 percent for baby food and baby needs to 85 percent for candy and gum and 88 percent for magazines and newspapers.[9]

Because the retailer is the final link in the chain of communication with the consumer, retail display can be extremely effective if the material is well planned. For the manufacturer, the problem is two-fold: first, to design a display that will meet the needs of the retailer; and second, to induce retailers to take advantage of it. The retailers' biggest problem is to decide how much to use of the material they receive—they cannot possibly use it all without making their store a jungle. Retailers themselves, of course, design some of the display material they use.

Fortunately, many studies have shown that retailers believe that the use of P-O-P advertising increases sales and attracts consumer attention in their stores. Research conducted by the industry's trade association, the Point-of-Purchase Adver-

FIGURE 18.16

Several Award-Winning Point-of-Purchase Displays

Source: Courtesy of Point-of-Purchase Advertising Institute.

TABLE 18.3

How Store Managers Feel about Point-of-Purchase Advertising Displays

Managers	Percent Stating That P-O-P Is Very or Extremely Effective in Attracting Customer Attention	Percent Stating That P-O-P Is Very or Extremely Effective in Increasing Sales
Automotive Stores	48%	45%
Chain Drug Stores	54	46
Convenience Stores	58	56
Home Improvement Stores	58	50
Liquor Stores	50	42
Mass Merchandisers	48	40
Supermarkets	58	48

Source: Courtesy of Point-of-Purchase Advertising Institute.

tising Institute (POPAI), is detailed in Table 18.3. As noted in the table, almost half or more of store managers felt that P-O-P advertising is very or extremely effective in attracting customer attention. A slightly smaller percentage—close to 50 percent on average—believe that such advertising increases sales.

Of the many types of P-O-P advertising displays, the most popular among retailers include the following:

	Percent of Retailers Using Displays
• Window and door signs	74%
• Counter/shelf units	70
• Floorstands	68
• Shelf-talkers	65
• Mobiles/banners	65

Shopping Carts

The use of shopping carts to carry an advertising message has been available to advertisers for many years. A frame is attached to the part of the cart facing the user or to the front of the cart. Advertisements are inserted into the frame. A number of companies specialize in this type of business; they sell space to national and regional advertisers by getting retail outlets to permit them to place frames on their carts. Figure 18.17 is a trade advertisement for ActMedia.

A new innovation in shopping-cart advertising is the use of *video monitors* mounted on a cart. The monitor involves use of a solar- or battery-powered computer that can provide a customer pushing a cart through the store with varied information, for example, where a brand is located in the store, whether a coupon is available for a brand, price information, and so on. Messages can even be triggered automatically according to the aisle in which the cart is located at a particular time. Studies have shown that sales gains of 33 percent have been achieved for brands using video carts. Figure 18.18 is an advertisement for VideOcart, the leading company in this field.

FIGURE 18.17

Trade Advertisement for ActMedia Shopping Carts

FIGURE 18.18

Shopping Cart Advertising That Uses a Computerized Video Monitor on the Cart

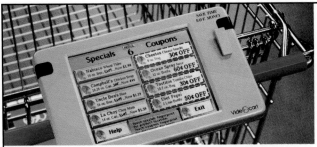

Several major retailers have been experimenting with the use of video carts in the last few years. For example, Toys "Я" Us has been using VideOcart's computerized screen at one of its New Jersey stores. Shoppers can enter into the computer a child's age, sex, and a price range to get gift ideas. Presently, video carts are available in only a relatively few retail outlets in large metropolitan areas. If the technique is to succeed, and it appears likely that it will, expansion will accelerate in the latter part of the 1990s.

In-Store Television and Radio

One of the newest types of in-store media involves television monitors that carry brand advertising, often in the checkout area of the store. As consumers stand in line, they have the opportunity to see news, weather, sports, business, and consumer programming—along with advertising. Companies such as Apple Computer, Inc. have developed in-store video media.

Another video form is to show animated computer-generated commercials on television monitors that are placed strategically throughout supermarket aisles. Shoppers' Video and Nynex Computer Services Company have developed this type of system. Shoppers' Video permits advertisers to show 15-second commercials that can be changed to promote price specials or that can be tied-in to other in-store events.

In-store radio has been available for many years, yet has recently undergone somewhat of a rebirth. Companies typically provide programming to a store in the form of prerecorded taped music and commercials, but ActMedia is a company that provides live in-store radio through its "POP Radio" network. Kmart recently introduced an in-store radio network for its own stores.[10] Programming includes music and news along with commercials and promotions for products sold in Kmart stores. Broadcasts are beamed by satellite from Kmart's headquarters in Troy, Michigan. For the past several years, Kmart has been experimenting with a variety of in-store media—including electronic shelf-talkers, instant coupon dispensers, informational kiosks, and in-store circulars—and the in-store radio service expands this trend.

Miscellaneous Media

Although there are a myriad of additional media types an advertiser can consider— from airplane banners, to blimps, to on-line information services such as Prodigy, to public restroom advertisements, to trade show display booths—we conclude our discussion of media tactics by enumerating and briefly discussing four miscellaneous types.

Motion Picture Advertising

Motion picture or "cinema" advertising in the United States dates back to 1897. Presently, there are around 24,000 theater screens in this country and most accept advertising. Cinema advertising has long been a mainstay in Europe, where there are approximately 26,000 screens; about three of every four cinemas show commercials.

Among the major companies selling commercials in motion picture theaters in the United States are Screenvision Cinema Network and Cineplex Odeon. Screenvision provides advertisers more than 6,000 screens in over 200 markets; Cineplex Odeon operates 1,100 movie screens. Most companies selling cinema advertising limit the number of commercials that are shown prior to the start of a movie, usually between three and five.

One clear advantage of motion picture advertising is that there is a captive audience, although this feature can yield negative results if the commercial is not entertaining and/or informational. Most astute advertisers using this medium tailor their advertising to the circumstances; simply using the same commercial shown on television generally has proven to be ineffective. With only a few commercials shown, there is considerably less clutter than on television. However, there also is little opportunity for message repetition. Motion picture advertising can have dramatic impact, given the size of most movie screens and use of powerful sound systems. Perhaps the biggest problem with cinema advertising is the possibility of alienating viewers who have paid to see a movie. A number of research studies have addressed this issue, but the results are somewhat inconclusive.

Videocassette Commercials

Several years ago Diet Pepsi bought a 60-second commercial in the videotape of *Top Gun*. Since then a number of other advertisers have used this medium, including Diet Coke in the initial *Batman* video and Procter & Gamble's "Downy" brand of fabric softener in *The Wizard of Oz*.

The ownership of VCRs has increased dramatically in recent years, with now around eight of ten homes having at least one unit. Many of these VCR owners, of course, rent and/or buy tapes, making the videocassette a logical advertising medium. Some of the same characteristics of cinema advertising apply here—captive audience (although perhaps somewhat less so), minimal number of commercials shown, and possibility of alienating viewers who have paid for the video. With videocassette commercials there is the added opportunity for the viewer to fast-forward through the advertising.

Channel One

Channel One is a 12-minute television news and feature-program segment that is broadcast daily to middle (junior) and high school students in the classroom. Each 12-minute segment includes two minutes for advertising (four 30-second units). It was launched in 1990 by Whittle Communications, a multimedia company.

Whittle Communications provides a participating school a satellite dish to receive the *Channel One* broadcasts, VCRs and color televisions for most classrooms, and wires the school for cable television reception. In addition, teachers are given each month a *Teachers' Guide* which provides the schedule of daily broadcasts and additional material about the subjects to be covered. Currently, *Channel One* is aired in approximately 350,000 classrooms in over 12,500 schools in 47 states.

Channel One has met opposition from a number of groups, especially educational bodies which feel that commercials should not be shown to students in school classrooms. Nevertheless, the medium presently is in around one-third of all eligible classrooms and is projected to reach almost 40 percent in the next few years. Whittle Communications also recently started a similar program for doctors' offices—*Medical News Network.*

Sports and Theater Events

Although the media types mentioned here probably could be classified elsewhere—as regular print or out-of-home advertising—they are sufficiently distinct to warrant special treatment. The three main categories of sports and theater events include: (1) *programs* sold or given free at sporting or theatrical events, (2) stadium *scoreboards*, and (3) *posters* in sports stadiums and theater lobbies.

College and professional sporting events typically sell a program that contains information about the event, the players, and so on, as well as advertising. The organization sponsoring the event either has its own sales staff to sell the advertising, or may use the services of a media sales representative (see Chapter 6 for a discussion of media reps).

Stadium scoreboards range from the simple to the elaborate. Those located in college and professional sports arenas usually are quite intricate, permitting dramatic commercial messages through the use of fiber-optics and computer-generated imagery. These scoreboards also usually have fixed advertising display units on their frames; such units look like outdoor poster signs. Advertising on scoreboards typically is sold by the sponsoring organization, such as college athletic departments and companies owning professional teams.

Sports arenas also usually have a host of other locations where poster-type advertising can be placed, for example, in the entrance area and places where food is sold. These posters, as well as those in the lobbies of theaters, are similar in appearance to those found in mass transit stations. They consist of the advertising material printed on paper and glued to the poster frame. Fences in baseball stadiums, car racing tracks, and the walls around an ice skating rink are also often painted with an advertiser's logotype and message. This type of advertising can have an added advantage of exposure to television audiences if the sporting event is broadcast.

Summary

Direct mail, outdoor, transit, and several types of other media differ from the print and broadcast media in that advertising is the only material that is communicated.

Direct mail takes many forms, the most common being sales letters, postcards, leaflets, folders, broadsides, booklets, and catalogs. Its principal advantages are its selectivity, intensive coverage, speed, flexibility, long copy, and personal approach. The main limitations of direct mail are the high cost per reader, the problems in obtaining a quality mailing list, and possible consumer resistance. The cost of a direct mailing is derived from three sources: production, distribution, and mailing lists charges.

Outdoor advertising comes in three major forms: posters, painted bulletins, and electric spectaculars. The main advantages are its simplicity, repetition, and nearness to the point of sale. Its brevity and stimulation of public ill will are disadvantages. Growth of the medium has been limited by federal and local statutes.

Transit advertising includes the ads inside and outside public carriers and at stations where people wait for them. Its main advantages are that it can reach great numbers of people cheaply and with great frequency, and it can provide color and copy to communicate product information.

A host of other media can be used by an advertiser as part of a total media mix or can be used alone. They include a broad array of options: directories, specialties,

Future Trends

Direct Mail, Out-of-Home, and Other Media

Some trends likely to affect the media discussed in this chapter include the following:

• *Unique types of direct mail* Currently, substantial experimentation in the use of direct mail likely will affect the future of this medium. For example, we will have advertisements that "talk" rather than have to be read; technology for this already is available. The increased and varied use of the computer for individualizing direct mail will occur in the future, as will the availability of improved printing inks and paper.

• *Merging of direct mail and direct marketing* It will become increasingly difficult to distinguish direct mail and direct marketing, at least in the sense that advertisers using direct marketing will continue to take a broad, "integrated" view of their media decisions. Related to this is the trend mentioned in Chapter 12—namely, the growth of "data base marketing"—whereby communication to existing and prospective customers will become more individualized and directed.

• *New types and technology in out-of-home media* In order to remain competitive, out-of-home media (that is, outdoor and transit advertising) will develop new forms of advertising as well as new technologies. Computer-generated messages, with advanced use of fiber optics, will add drama to this type of communication. Less reliance will be placed on the "standard" types of out-of-home media, resulting in new forms that will be easier to buy and schedule.

• *Attention to new and atypical types of media* In general, advertisers will be more willing to use different and nontraditional types of advertising media, such as *Channel One*, in-store television, and the like. With an accelerated focus on brand competition, advertisers no longer will be satisfied with the *status quo*. This attitude on the part of advertisers will stimulate the development of new and varied forms of media.

---

in-store media, as well as many miscellaneous types. Directory advertising primarily is in the Yellow Pages of telephone directories, although there are many other directories as well.

Advertising specialties include a variety of items imprinted with the advertiser's name and address and often a short sales message. Among the 15,000 specialties available, calendars, wearable items, writing instruments, desk/office/business accessories, and glassware/ceramic items account for around two-thirds of all sales.

In-store media include point-of-purchase displays, shopping cart advertising, and in-store television and radio. Studies have shown that a high percentage of retail store managers believe P-O-P displays increase sales and attract the attention of store customers. A new form of shopping cart advertising is the use of a video monitor that provides a shopper messages as the cart is pushed through the store. Similarly, television monitors mounted at checkout counters and near aisles in a store broadcast program content and commercials. In-store radio is used to present music, news, and advertising to shoppers.

Among other, miscellaneous media are motion picture advertising, videocassette commercials, *Channel One* in school classrooms, and a variety of types in sports arenas and theaters.

A few key trends likely to affect the other media are the development of new types and technologies in direct mail and out-of-home media, the merging of direct mail and direct marketing, and more advertiser attention given to nontraditional media types.

Questions for
Discussion

1. How does direct mail advertising differ from other advertising media, especially printed media?
2. The U.S. Postal Service proposed a significant increase in the cost of third-class mail; the increase would be much higher, as a percentage, than a proposed increase for first class. Assume you are a representative of the trade association of direct-mail advertisers. What arguments would you make to the Postal Commission against increasing third-class charges?
3. Under what conditions might an advertiser use outdoor advertising as a primary medium?
4. Assume that your local community is considering a ban on additional outdoor advertising within the city limits. What arguments would you make against such a ban? For the ban?
5. Develop a list of products that you feel would benefit from using transit advertising. Why would they benefit? Are certain kinds of products more logical users of transit than others?
6. How is transit advertising similar to the outdoor medium? How is it different?
7. Look in a Yellow Pages directory and assess several different types of advertising, especially trademark and display advertisements. What characteristics of the advertisements do you feel are most effective and why?
8. Why is specialty advertising so popular with certain advertisers?
9. Visit a local supermarket and mass merchandise store. Make a list of all the different types of in-store media. Which types do you feel are most effective and why?
10. What arguments can you present *for* advertising in motion picture theaters, within videocassettes, on *Channel One*, and in sports arenas and theaters? What are arguments *against* such advertising? Take the point of view of the advertiser on one hand, and the general public on the other.

Notes

1. Bob Stone, *Successful Direct Marketing Methods*, 4th ed. (Lincolnwood, IL: NTC Business Books, 1988), 3b.
2. Steven W. Colford, "Feds Set Fund to Ax Outdoor Boards," *Advertising Age* (March 16, 1992): 1, 50.
3. George T. Clarke, *Transit Advertising* (New York: Transit Advertising Association, 1970), 12.
4. *Ibid.*, 14.
5. For a discussion of these types of transit, see Donald W. Jugenheimer, Arnold M. Barban, and Peter B. Turk, *Advertising Media: Strategy and Tactics* (Dubuque, IA: WCB Brown & Benchmark, 1992), 404–407.
6. "Specialty Advertising Fact Sheet" (Irving, TX: Specialty Advertising Association International, not dated).
7. Dan S. Bagley, III, *Understanding Specialty Advertising* (Irving, TX: Specialty Advertising Association International, 1991), 16.
8. *The Point-of-Purchase Advertising Industry Fact Book* (Englewood, NJ: Point-of-Purchase Advertising Institute, 1992), 6.
9. *Ibid.*, 43.
10. John P. Cortez, "Kmart Tunes Up In-Store Radio," *Advertising Age* (March 16, 1992): 3, 50.

Bagley, Dan S. *Understanding Specialty Advertising.* Irving, TX: Specialty Advertising Association International, 1991.

Bovée, Courtland L., and William F. Arens. *Contemporary Advertising*, 4th ed. Homewood, IL: Irwin, 1992. Chapters 15, 16.

Clarke, George T. *Transit Advertising.* New York: Transit Advertising Association, 1970.

Fletcher, Alan D. *Target Marketing Through the Yellow Pages.* Troy, MI: Yellow Pages Publishers Association, 1991.

Jugenheimer, Donald W., Arnold M. Barban, and Peter B. Turk. *Advertising Media: Strategy and Tactics.* Dubuque, IA: WCB Brown & Benchmark, 1992. Chapters 17, 18.

McGann, Anthony F., and J. Thomas Russell. *Advertising Media*, 2d ed. Homewood, IL: Irwin, 1988. Chapters 10, 11.

Russell, J. Thomas, and W. Ronald Lane. *Kleppner's Advertising Procedure*, 11th ed. Englewood Cliffs, NJ: Prentice-Hall, 1990. Chapters 12, 13.

Sissors, Jack Z., and Lincoln Bumba. *Advertising Media Planning*, 4th ed. Lincolnwood, IL: NTC Business Books, 1993. Chapters 12, 15.

Stone, Bob. *Successful Direct Marketing Methods*, 4th ed. Lincolnwood, IL: NTC Business Books, 1988.

Suggested Readings

Appendix to Part Three

Advertising Campaign

The purpose of the appendix is to provide a current case that illustrates many of the concepts discussed throughout the text. We are fortunate to present the award-winning Longhorn Steaks campaign. In 1992, Longhorn won ''Best of Show'' for television at the national Addy awards. Longhorn advertising demonstrates many of the principles found in Part 2 of the text, Campaign Planning: Strategy and Part 3, Campaign Planning: Tactics. Additionally, the case takes on many of the characteristics of retail advertising (Chapter 19). We urge you to refer back to the appropriate chapters when reading the case.

Background

Longhorn Steaks represents a success story in the very competitive restaurant market. In 1982, George McKerrow Jr., opened the first Longhorn restaurant in Atlanta, Georgia. By 1992, Longhorn had a successful public stock offering and generated the capital for expansion. By early 1993, Longhorn grew to 45 locations in the Southeastern United States.

McKerrow's idea was to be the leader in high-quality, moderately-priced steaks, served in a casual western atmosphere. He visited several Texas steak restaurants to learn about food preparation and the overall atmosphere necessary to create a true Texas road house eating experience.

From 1982 to 1989, Longhorn used no advertising. In 1990, Longhorn hired Scharbo and Company headed by Ron Scharbo. Prior to that, Ron had owned and was president of Burton-Campbell, a successful national advertising agency located in Atlanta. Upon selling Burton-Campbell to Earle Palmer Brown, Ron wanted to direct his efforts on a smaller agency, where he could focus on high impact creative.

Brand Development and Positioning

Both McKerrow and Scharbo and Company felt it was essential to develop a strong brand image for Longhorn. Brand image was seen as a major differentiating factor in the highly competitive restaurant market. The stronger the brand, the less there is a need for discounts and other forms of price cutting, which lower profit margins.

In markets where a Longhorn steakhouse is established, the brand name is always one of the strongest in the restaurant category. A key element in Longhorn's positioning is the philosophy that brand equity is perishable and must be replenished on a regular basis through advertising.

The Longhorn brand was created and enhanced to communicate a specific position. The brand name was developed to be synonymous with a Texas Style steak dinner, not associated with discounting. Longhorn's positioning statement is:

> Position Longhorn steaks as the best restaurant choice for high-quality, moderately-priced steaks in a casual, western atmosphere.

Research

Longhorn conducts both on-site surveys and advertising-tracking studies (many of the findings are associated with the research concepts in Chapter 8). Research revealed a number of key issues:

1. Longhorn is perceived as a very satisfactory dining experience. The major element of success is to provide a quality product that will generate repeat business.

2. While food is the major reason for choosing Longhorn, service and atmosphere are also very strong reasons. Return visits are based on product quality and an enjoyable dining experience.
3. Customer return rate is extremely high. Of all visits, 87 percent are repeat customers.
4. The typical Longhorn customer visits 2.3 times per month.
5. Customer loyalty is important. A heavy visit customer returns at least 4 times per month. Heavy visit customers comprise 29 percent of all customers and 49 percent of all visits.
6. Heavy visit customers are primarily male (82 percent) and are between 25 to 49 years of age (79 percent).
7. Tracking studies for Longhorn show that advertising creates awareness and trial.
8. In well-established markets, such as Atlanta, awareness of Longhorn Steaks advertising is 76 percent among the target audience of 25- to 49-year-old men.
9. In markets where a location is well established, Longhorn Steaks has a 91 percent brand awareness.

Advertising is considered to be a major factor in developing and maintaining Longhorn's position and image. As noted above, advertising is an important factor in both awareness and trial.

The Role of
Longhorn Advertising

Advertising Objectives

Overall, the advertising objectives are comprehensive. The objectives follow many of the characteristics found in Chapter 9, because they focus on awareness, attitude and action. The following are key advertising objectives:

1. To maintain top-of-mind awareness.
2. To reinforce favorable customer and potential customer attitudes concerning Longhorn.
3. To secure the specific position of Longhorn being the best choice for high-quality, moderately-priced steaks in a casual, western atmosphere.
4. To stimulate trial and retrial.
5. To stimulate enthusiasm among employees at Longhorn restaurants.

Creative Strategy

Longhorn used many of the principles found in Message Strategy (Chapter 11). The major message idea is to capture the feeling of dining at Longhorn—high quality food in a fun, zany, western atmosphere (see Figure A.1). The philosophy behind Longhorn's creative strategy is that advertising must be entertaining in order to effectively convey the Texas road house experience. The Longhorn Franchisee Advertising and Promotions Manual states:

> In all of our advertising to current and prospective customers, the skillful use of humor enables us to get attention, create awareness, and develop a favorable attitude.

Broadcast

Radio has become a foundation and primary medium. Radio has effectively served to establish a fun and entertaining tone (see Figure A.2).

Television was first used in the spring of 1992 on both cable and broadcast stations. Television commercials carry forth the image of Longhorn (see Figure A.3). Longhorn television has become an instant creative success.

Print and Outdoor

Newspapers and magazines use large headlines and short copy to extend Longhorn's messages to print. The Longhorn logo was designed to appear on an angle to stimulate a "branding" effect, which is highly conducive to print. Note how all of the print conveys the Longhorn theme (see Figure A.4).

Longhorn uses outdoor designs that are bold, simple and unique. Print and outdoor are coordinated to establish the same image (see Figure A.5).

Awards

Longhorn has received 26 creative awards for its advertising. It has received awards in both print and broadcast on both the local and national level. In 1992, Longhorn received the most prestigious National Addy Award, "Best of Show" for its television commercial titled "Big Haired Lady." Also, in 1992 Longhorn received two National Addy Citations for Local Radio.

FIGURE A.1

Longhorn Uses Humor to Introduce Salmon

FIGURE A.2

Longhorn Radio Script
(60-Second Commercial)

SCHARBO & COMPANY
Longhorn Steaks-Talkin' 'Bout Longhorn Radio Lyrics

MUSIC: EASY PICKIN' AND STRUMMIN' IN "G"

GEORGE: Hi, this is George McKerrow of Longhorn Steaks
I'm in the studio checkin' out my new jingle
Play it boys

LYRICS: Talkin' 'bout Longhorn
And their Pan-Fried Steaks
Come on out and eat one
No matter what it takes

They got big bowls of peanuts, Texas Taters
And ice cold brew
And some animal heads on the walls
Starin' back at you

GEORGE: Oh, brother!

LYRICS: You can bring people here and they'll prob'ly say
Thanks for bringin' me here
Cause this is one place that's just
Eat up with atmosphere

GEORGE: Uhhh

LYRICS: So if you got friends who like a good time
In a place that's neat
Come on in to Longhorn Steaks
And eat some meat

TOMMY: Is that 60 seconds yet?

GEORGE: I just don't believe this folks

LYRICS: Talkin' 'bout Longhorn
Longhorn Steaks
Talkin' 'bout Longhorn
Longhorn Steaks...

GEORGE: Trust me folks,
Our steaks are a whole lot better than our jingles

TOMMY: Where's that lady with the big hair?
She got our money?

GEORGE: Uhhh

MUSIC: FADE OUT

©Copyright, 1992. Catspaw Productions, Inc., All Rights Reserved.

Credits

CLIENT: Longhorn Steaks, Inc.
George McKerrow, Owner
AGENCY: Scharbo & Company
CREATIVE DIRECTOR: Ron Scharbo
COPYWRITERS: Stuart Hill
Sarah Cotton Scharbo
SINGERS: Stuart Hill
Tommy Dean

FIGURE A.3

Storyboard.
"Best of Show" for Television
1992 National Addy Awards.
(30-Second Commercial)

MUSIC: EASY GUITAR PICKING

LYRICS: Talkin' 'bout Longhorn and their pan-fried steaks, come on out and eat one no matter what it takes

They got big bowls of peanuts, Texas taters and ice cold brew, and some animal heads on the walls staring back at you

So if you got friends who like a good time in a place that's neat, come on into Longhorn Steaks and eat some meat

Longhorn . . . Longhorn Steaks (fades out)

BEST OF SHOW
TELEVISION

Title:	*"Big Haired Lady"*
Agency:	Scharbo & Company
	Atlanta, GA
Client:	Longhorn Steaks, Inc.
	Atlanta, GA
Credits:	Ron Scharbo – Creative Director
	Susan Haynes – Art Director/ Producer/Director
	Sarah Cotton Scharbo, Stuart Hill – Writers

Cowboy Cuisine.

The steaks are gourmet all the way. But the atmosphere is a kick. Plain and simple, that's why people fancy us over any other steak place.

Go With The Flo.

Find out why our regulars love our incredibly tender, thick and juicy Flo's Filet. In the 7- or 9-ounce size, it's pan-fried perfection.

Even Our Fish Are Steaks.

Big, fresh salmon steaks flown in from British Columbia and marinated our special way. Choose between great steaks. Or a great steak.

FIGURE A.5

Outdoor

1. How did Longhorn define their market?
2. Discuss the role of advertising in attracting and maintaining customers.
3. Review Longhorns advertising objectives. How well do the objectives follow criteria in, The Basics of Writing an Advertising Objective (Ad Insight, Chapter 9, p. 237).
4. What is the message idea behind Longhorn advertising?

Questions for
Discussion

PART 4

Special Purpose
Advertising

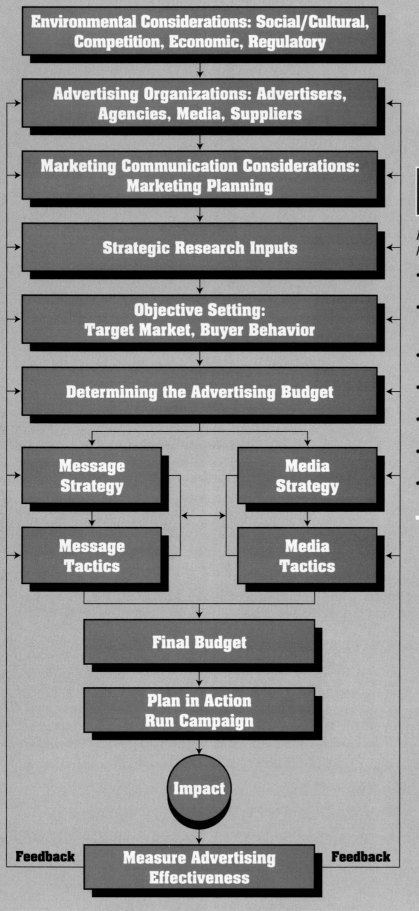

Chapter **19**

Sales Promotion and Public Relations

CHAPTER TOPICS

SALES PROMOTION
> *Differences between Advertising and Sales*
> > *Promotion*
> *Consumer Promotions*
> *Trade Sales Promotion*

PUBLIC RELATIONS
> *Differences between Advertising and Public*
> > *Relations*
> *Size and Organization of Public Relations*
> *Activities and Planning*
> *General Public Relations Techniques*
> *Institutional Advertising as a Public Relations*
> > *Technique*

Throughout this textbook we have noted that advertising decisions should be made in conjunction with other marketing and communication decisions. Figure 19.1 shows what we learned in Chapter 7—that advertising works best when it is integrated with all other forms of communication. Two major decision areas—sales promotion and public relations—are discussed in this chapter. Each area represents an important aspect of marketing communications that requires a more in-depth discussion because it has a separate and unique relationship to advertising. In most cases sales promotion and public relations are planned in conjunction with advertising.

Sales Promotion

Sales promotion can be defined as "short-term incentives to encourage purchase or sale of a product or service."[1] The use of sales promotion has risen steadily from the 1980s to the 1990s. Companies now spend close to 70 percent of their marketing budgets on all forms of promotion and 30 percent on media advertising.[2] The major reason for the growth of sales promotion is that companies are interested in quick results.

While most advertising is oriented toward building market share and sales through image and long-run consumer loyalty, sales promotion is oriented toward obtaining market share and sales by immediate action. In sales promotion, the inducement is the major reason for action and long-term customer loyalty is not usually a goal. Many times the two elements are coordinated to take advantage of advertising's

FIGURE 19.1

All Forms of Communication Are Integrated to Present Clear and Consistent Marketing Efforts That Speak in One Voice

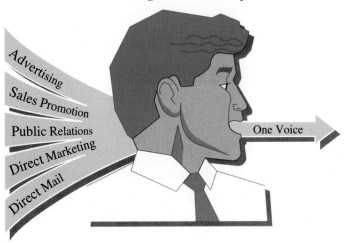

Advertising
Sales Promotion
Public Relations
Direct Marketing
Direct Mail

One Voice

ability to develop image and customer loyalty and sales promotion's ability to produce short-term action. Figure 19.2 shows the major differences between advertising and sales promotion.

Sales promotion tools are aimed at quickly moving the product toward the final purchaser. All sales promotions directed at consumers are called **consumer promotions**. Sales promotions directed at resellers, such as distributors, wholesalers, retailers, or salespersons, are referred to as **trade promotions**. Figure 19.3 shows the different forms of consumer and trade sales promotion. The next sections will discuss many of the major consumer and trade sales promotions.

Differences in Advertising and Sales Promotion

Consumer Promotions

Sales promotions aimed at consumers can directly influence behavior. A study by the Promotion Marketing Association indicates that 76 percent of consumers participate in using some form of promotion. People who are most apt to change their purchase behavior because of a promotion are middle-aged college graduates

FIGURE 19.2

Differences between Advertising and Sales Promotion

Advertising

Creates brand awareness, attitudes, and/or image over time.
Conveys brand position information
Contributes to brand share and sales by creating loyalty.
Oriented to long-term image and sales.

Sales Promotion

Creates brand awareness and immediate impact.
Conveys less brand position information
Contributes to brand share and sales by creating special inducement or contribution.
Oriented to short-term sales rather than long-term loyalty.

FIGURE 19.3

Overview of Consumer and Trade Sales Promotion

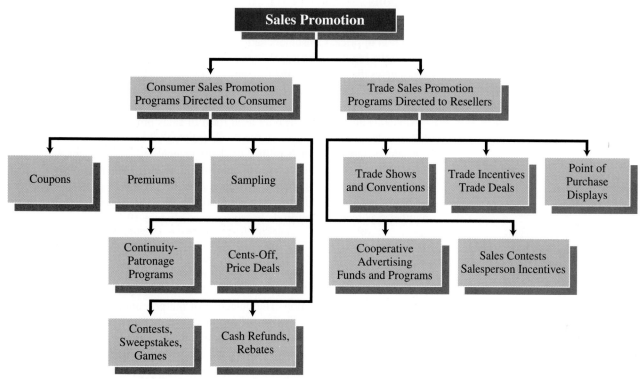

Source: Patricia J. Daugherty, Richard J. Fox, and Frederick J. Stephenson, Jr. "Frequency Marketing Programs: A Clarification with Strategic Marketing Implications," *Journal of Promotion Management*, 1993.

FIGURE 19.4

Can Promotions Change Behavior? The Percent of Consumers Using Coupons, Rebates, Sweepstakes, and Premiums in Different Buying Situations

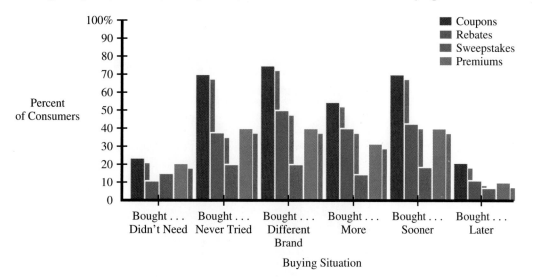

Source: "Study: Some Promotions Change Consumer Behavior," *Marketing News*, October 15, 1990, 12.

with annual incomes of more than $45,000.[3] Figure 19.4 shows the percentage of consumers using coupons, rebates, sweepstakes, and premiums in different buying situations.

Coupons

Coupons used as a sales promotion device are, in effect, offering consumers a reduction in price. Consumers take these to the retail store, where they can buy the item at the regular price less the amount specified on the coupon. The manufacturer reimburses the retailer for the face amount of the coupon, plus an additional amount for handling. One of the prime objectives of coupons is to attract consumers to a brand by offering them a reduced price for a limited time.

Coupons are the most heavily used form of sales promotion. Over 75 percent of all households use coupons. Marketers distribute 300 billion cents-off coupons and consumers redeem over 8 billion of them annually.[4] The total consumer annual savings from coupons is reported to be 4 billion dollars. Manufacturers pay retailers almost $600 million in fees for coupon handling. Currently, 80 percent of the coupons are distributed in free-standing inserts (FSI) in Sunday newspapers, with another 5 percent placed in daily newspapers.[5] Figure 19.5 shows a coupon offer.

Premiums

A premium is a tangible reward offered for free or at a reduced price in return for performing some task. Premiums are earned by making a purchase, deposit, financial contribution or other action. The objective of the premium is to give the customer an immediate reason for buying the product. The premium may be free, or it may be self-liquidating (the customer pays enough to cover the marketer's out-of-pocket costs). The use of premiums has grown from $5 billion per year in the late 1970s to over $17 billion per year in the 1990s.[6] Seventy-four percent of marketers report they use some form of premiums.

Direct premiums come at the time of purchase, such as free blades attached to a shaving razor or a toy placed inside a box of cereal. Such premiums work best when they have a direct tie-in with the market. For example, White Castle restaurants offered a Kids's Castle Meal containing hamburger, fries, drink, and a premium:

FIGURE 19.5

Coupon Offer Is Used as a Form of Price Reduction

FIGURE 19.6

Premium Used to Generate Product Interest

The Real Ghostbusters Slimer Mint or Slimer Bubblegum toothpaste, a Ghostbuster hairbrush or soap, or a neon-colored toothbrush. The promotion was held in conjunction with the American Dental Association's National Children's Dental Health Month.

Mail premiums are offered after a consumer purchase or action has taken place. For example, during fund-raising drives most public television stations offer viewers a variety of premiums depending on the level of donation made to the station. Figure 19.6 shows how a premium is used to generate interest in a business-to-business product.

Some premiums are designed to work over a period of time which lasts longer than one purchase. For example, a supermarket might give (or sell at a self-liquidating cost) one volume of an encyclopedia for every $10 purchase. Once a customer has one encyclopedia, he or she has a vested interest in continuing to patronize the store to complete the set.

Sampling

This technique allows consumers to try the product free of charge or for a small fee. It is often used to have consumers experience a new or modified product. When a product's features or benefits—for example, flavor or aroma—cannot be fully conveyed in advertising, sampling can be most effective.

Normally, sampling is coordinated with other marketing tools, such as advertising and in-store promotions. For example, Aramis introduced Tuscany Per Donna, the women's version of its Tuscany men's fragrance, with 78 million samples delivered through magazines, direct mail, and in stores. Sharon Levan, vice president of marketing for the fragrance company, points out the role of advertising for image development and sampling for trial:

> Advertising will still be needed to establish an image, but we've found the most important thing we can do is to get the product into the hands of the consumer.[7]

While sampling is often thought of for consumer package goods, it can—on special occasion—be used to have consumers experience more expensive products and services. For example, American Airlines gave away 500 tickets to business and community leaders from Chicago to destinations in England in an effort to introduce its new European service. The samples were incorporated into an advertising campaign designed to increase name recognition and travel for American's new service to England.[8]

Sampling is carried out by mail, in stores, and through delivery to the consumer at home. There are many companies in the sampling field that provide a variety of services for an advertiser. One of the largest is the Reuben H. Donnelley Corporation, which typically distributes samples by "occupant" mass mailings, door-drops, or handouts. A number of companies, including Donnelley, limit samples to people with special characteristics (such as demographic traits). Gift Pax Inc. distributes samples to expectant mothers, servicemen, and college students.

Effective as sampling is, when properly used, it does bring up certain problems. One of these is cost. Not only is the sample itself costly to produce, but also the sampler must pay for getting it into the hands of the consumer. A related problem is deciding on the size and form of the sample. Consumers should be given enough of the product to enable them to give it a fair trial but not enough to keep them so well supplied that they will be out of the market for a long time.

Continuity–Patronage Programs

The objective of continuity and patronage programs is to promote extended product use. These programs require customers to use the product or service on a continuous basis in order to obtain a gift or reward. Customers are rewarded for their continued use of the product or service. For example, all of the major airlines have frequent flier clubs that reward continued use by giving patrons special rewards, based on the number of miles they have flown. These rewards can include a seat upgraded to first class, discounted airline tickets, or free airline tickets. Hotels, credit cards, and auto rental companies also offer patronage reward programs. Figure 19.7 shows an offer where customers get a free upgrade to a larger car when they use their American Express card to rent a car from Budget. This type of cooperation between two companies is often termed a **cross-promotion**.

Trading stamps, which were extremely popular in the 1960s and 1970s, are used on a limited basis. Customers receive stamps based on the amount of purchase from grocery or other retail stores; these stamps are then redeemed for gifts.

Cents-Off Deals and Price Deals

By offering a price reduction for a limited time only, the manufacturer gives a reason for immediate action, but avoids regular price reductions. A **cents-off** promotion is a reduction in the regular price. These deals are often advertised in both media and point-of-purchase displays.

Price deals can take different forms. In a **bonus pack** customers are provided with "more" of the product for the regular price. For example, Ivory shampoo ran a promotion where the customer was offered 25 percent more shampoo for the regular price. In a banded pack two or more of the units are physically banded together at a price that is less than the two units sold separately. In many cases, this is a two-for-one deal.

Contests, Sweepstakes, and Games

The objective of these promotions is to generate enthusiasm among customers or potential customers. They often add excitement or interest. The popularity of these techniques grew in the 1980s but has declined in the 1990s.

FIGURE 19.7

A Patronage Program Offering an Upgrade in Rental Cars

FIGURE 19.8

Contest Held by Lands' End Is Used to Promote Interest in Ties

A contest involves participants competing for prizes based on a person's skill, ability, or other characteristics. The use of contests is mostly on a local level. For example, the *Atlanta Journal and Constitution* sponsors a contest that allows fans to match wits with sportswriters in picking football winners and losers. The fan with the highest winning percentage wins a T-shirt and mug. The promotion generates enthusiasm for the newspaper. Figure 19.8 shows a contest held by Lands' End.

A **sweepstakes** only requires participants to submit their name to a drawing or other selection process that involves chance, not skill. For example, Goody's headache remedy sponsors the Goody's Home Run Jackpot Inning during Atlanta Braves' baseball games. A fan's name is drawn during the seventh inning; if a home run is hit during that inning, the individual wins the cash jackpot.

A game is a form of sweepstakes that provides continuity by lasting a long time. For example, in Super Cash Bingo games customers return to the store to acquire additional bingo cards or other pieces that improve their chances of winning.

Cash Refunds (Rebates)

In some situations the manufacturer offers to return a certain amount of money directly to the consumers after the purchase. The customer sends in a coupon or proof of purchase and is mailed a check by the manufacturer. Figure 19.9 shows an example of a refund used in conjunction with a coupon.

In recent years, automobile manufacturers have relied on a number of rebate techniques. Initially, these rebate programs were used on a limited basis to stimulate sales of certain models or to sell cars at the end of the model year. However, the programs have become so widely used that many customers expect a rebate or wait

FIGURE 19.9

Refund and Coupon Offer Are Used to Stimulate Sales

for rebate offers to be advertised. When this happens the automobile rebates become a regular form of price-cutting and lose their promotional value. Some marketing experts feel the automobile rebate money would be better spent on advertising to build a strong image.[9]

Trade Sales Promotion

Programs directed to resellers, including distributors, wholesalers, retailers, and salespersons working for the manufacturer, are an important form of sales promotion. Manufacturers spend 50 percent of their total budgets on programs.[10] Manufacturers use trade promotions tools for several reasons:

1. To persuade retailers or wholesalers to carry the brand or carry more of the brand
2. To induce retailers to promote the brand by featuring the brand, displaying the brand, or through price reductions
3. To stimulate retailers to sell the product
4. To stimulate enthusiasm among the sales force

Trade Shows and Conventions

While some shows and exhibits, such as automobile and boat shows, are directed to the ultimate consumer, most are directed to the trade; thus, related industries and trade organizations organize trade shows, exhibits, and conventions. Trade shows and exhibits provide excellent opportunities for marketers to promote their products or services through display and demonstration. Distributors, wholesalers, retailers, and other industry professionals are able to examine the products and can often make comparisons with competing brands. Exhibitors increase their dealer contacts and distribute literature and samples.

Trade shows are particularly useful in promoting new products or innovations in existing products or services. They are especially important in fields in which technical innovations are appearing at a rapid rate.

A great deal of professional skill is required to design effective trade shows and exhibits. Many major companies have a department set up to coordinate and develop trade shows and exhibits. Some companies hire specialists to design and build their exhibits. In most cases company personnel work at the booth, showing the product, answering questions, handing out sales literature, and, on occasion, taking orders.

Trade Incentives and Trade Deals

These programs are usually directed to retailers in order to increase sales volume. Trade incentives are offered to retailers who perform certain tasks. One form termed a *buying loader* awards gifts for buying a certain number of products. Another form, termed a *display loader* allows the retailer to keep the special display after the promotion.

In a similar fashion, trade deals are oriented to retail performance. Retailers are given special allowances, discounts, or direct payment for providing a special promotional effort. For example, a display allowance is a direct payment from the manufacturer to the retailer when the retailer agrees to set up a specified display.

Salesperson Contests and Salesperson Incentives

Many programs are developed to increase the performance of the sales staff. Usually these contests are held for a specified time period and have prizes. The prizes often include vacations, trips, cash rewards, or gifts. They serve as an incentive to sell the product or some other aspect of the company. Sales contests are often held annually.

Many companies offer incentives for sales training. Sales personnel for GMC and Chevrolet were offered a program to sharpen their skills with regard to selling truck engines. Participants received training lessons in both written and audio form. Sales personnel who scored 90 percent on the lesson were offered a number of gifts. Sales personnel who scored 100 percent on all three areas advanced to a second level of competition. Prizes at the second level included a notebook computer and other valuable items. The grand prize was a vacation to Nassau and Freeport on the Carnival cruise line. Figure 19.10 shows a display poster used to create interest in the sales training program.

Another form of incentive is called **push money**, sometimes termed *spiffs*, which offer salespersons a cash reward for selling a certain number or kind of product. For example, an appliance manufacturer might offer a bonus for selling a particular model or a tire manufacturer may offer a bonus for selling a particular line of tires.

Point-of-Purchase Advertising

Point-of-purchase advertising consists of displays and other promotions developed by the manufacturer and used by the retailer to promote a product at the point of purchase or sales. These displays can be considered a form of trade promotion because retailers are often offered incentives to use the displays, which in turn generate retailer interest. However, point-of-purchase advertising is primarily a media type and is covered extensively in Chapter 18.

Cooperative Advertising (Co-op)

Co-op advertising is a financial agreement whereby a manufacturer offers to pay part, or all, of a retailer's advertising when the retailer features the manufacturer's product in its advertising. Approximately 18 billion dollars is spent per year on such programs. Co-op advertising is covered extensively in Chapter 20.

FIGURE 19.10

Incentive Program Uses Prizes to Sharpen Personal Selling Skills

Good luck and
good selling!!

Public Relations

Public relations, like advertising, is responsible for communicating an image. However, the role of public relations is much broader. Public relations is often defined as the firm's communication and relationship with various publics, including employees, prospective recruits, industry partners, prospective and current customers, suppliers, the financial and investment community, government officials, and the society in which it operates.

The following sections will examine the difference between advertising and public relations, the organization and size of public relations, activities and planning, and the major public relations techniques, including a special form termed institutional advertising.

Differences between
*Advertising
and Public Relations*

In most organizations, advertising and public relations functions tend to overlap and, as a result, must be carefully coordinated. In corporate planning, advertising often is used as a communication tool in a public relations program; in marketing planning, public relations often is used to support an advertising campaign. While there is a great deal of overlap, there are four clear distinctions between advertising and public relations:[11]

1. Advertising focuses on selling goods and services; public relations focuses on generating public understanding and fostering goodwill for an organization, which may indirectly contribute to sales.
2. Advertising works through the mass media; public relations relies on a broad range of communication channels—brochures, slide presentations, special events, speeches, news releases, feature stories, and the like.

3. Advertising is addressed primarily to external audiences—consumers and the trade for marketed goods and services; public relations is addressed usually to both internal (employees) and external audiences (stockholders, vendors, community leaders, and so on).
4. Advertising is a more narrowly defined communication form; public relations is broader in scope—dealing with the policies and activities of the entire organization, from relations with stockholders to the way receptionists respond to telephone calls.

As a public relations tool, advertising has the advantage of control over message content, message placement, and message repetition. On the other hand, it has the disadvantages of sponsor-paid credibility and media costs.

Size and Organization of Public Relations

Public relations is a growing industry with revenues increasing by 20 percent a year. Estimates indicate that the public relations industry employs 160,000 people and that almost 2,000 public relations firms operate in the United States. Some of the largest firms are Shandwick-Kaufman Public Relations, Hill & Knowlton, Burson-Marsteller, Ogilvy & Mather Public Affairs, Fleishman-Hillard, and Rowland Worldwide. Additionally, there are thousands of smaller firms and many one-person shops.[12]

One major reason for the growth in public relations is the need for corporations to communicate in a rapidly changing environment. Environmental concerns, the rise of multinational firms in a global economy, concerns with the ethical conduct of business, and regulatory pressures are all major factors in the need for professional public relations staffs.

In some organizations, public relations is combined with advertising under the umbrella "corporate communications" or "public affairs"; in others, they function as separate but coordinated departments. In most firms the public relations function is located at corporate headquarters. It is useful to recognize the complexity of public relations and the many functions it includes. The diagram in Figure 19.11 shows the relationship between public relations functions and formalized communication programs in an organization. Note that the communicative function of public relations is to manage the relations between external and internal publics and the organization's managerial system. In any situation, the basic role of public relations is to build goodwill between management and its publics.

FIGURE 19.11

A Model of the Public Relations Function in an Organization

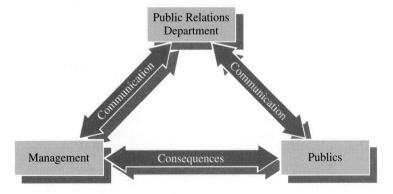

Source: James E. Grunig and Todd Hunt, *Managing Public Relations* (New York: Holt, Rinehart & Winston, 1984), 10.

Activities and Planning

Public relations departments typically perform the following five activities. These activities go beyond the scope of direct product support.[13]

- *Press relations* Places information in the news media to attract favorable attention to corporation, person, product, or service.
- *Corporate communication* Covers internal and external communication and promotes understanding of the organization.
- *Product publicity* Involves various efforts to publicize specific products and services.
- *Counseling* Advises management about public issues, company philosophy, and image.
- *Lobbying* Deals with government officials with regard to laws and regulations that impact the company.

Marketing management expert Phillip Kotler points out three ways that public relations can specifically support the marketing effort: (1) building awareness and credibility for the product or company through news media story placement and communicating in an editorial context, (2) boosting sales force and dealer enthusiasm, and (3) creating favorable articles about the product or company, thus helping the sales force sell the product.[14]

General Public Relations Techniques

A variety of methods are available for the dissemination of public relations material. This section briefly discusses some of the major techniques that do not use advertising media space that is paid for and controlled. These techniques are publications, news releases, press conferences, events and exhibits, open houses and tours, speakers, and videotapes and photographs.

Publications

Public relations workers prepare a variety of publications, including employee newsletters, annual reports, bulletins (for distributors), pamphlets, and a host of other printed material.

News Releases

The news release is written to convey information to various media, editors, and reporters. Each news release should be specifically geared to a particular medium. The goal of the news release is to have the medium run the story as news or information.

Press Conferences

A press conference involves a gathering of media reporters with the objective of announcing new information, such as product development, to state a company's position on an issue, or to make a policy statement.

Events and Exhibits

Special events are sponsored to gain attention for either the company or a specific product. These events can include sporting events, concerts, museum tours and exhibits, and trade show exhibits. Corporate sponsors are now major supporters of almost all professional sporting events and many concert tours. All major professional arenas offer promotional packages to attract corporate sponsors. These packages can include signs in front of and throughout the stadium; special promotionals, such as drinking cups with the sponsors' names; and an assortment of other items identifying the sponsor.

Open Houses and Tours

The purpose is to show the public how the company operates. Many major companies provide scheduled tours that give the public a first hand view of what takes place inside the company.

Speakers

Many companies have a bureau or list of speakers who are made available to present information to group meetings. For example, Apple Computer, Inc. conducts seminars at various universities and schools. The seminars consist of a presentation and discussion that allow the speaker to demonstrate the capabilities of Apple products.

Videotapes and Photographs

Many companies supply a videotape that discusses their products, services, or corporate policies. They can be very effective product demonstrations. For example, Nordic Track uses a videotape to show prospective customers how their exercise equipment works. Companies commonly receive requests for photographs of people, products, or events. Many companies keep large picture files to honor such requests.

Institutional advertising involves the use of nonpersonal, mass-mediated communication by an identified sponsor to accomplish goals that are not related directly to the sale of products or commercial services. As a tool of public relations, it can be used to help accomplish a variety of public relations functions, including the following:

- Improving relations with the organization's employees and recruiting prospective employees (Figure 19.12)
- Publicizing a plant opening, expansion, or improvement
- Improving market value of corporate stock prior to a merger or takeover
- Promoting a public service such as adult education
- Stating the firm's position on a controversial, legislative, or administrative issue
- Offsetting unfavorable news coverage or editorial treatment
- Publicizing organizational accomplishments, awards, or public contributions

Institutional advertising covers a wide variety of objectives, audiences, and communication tools. It has been used by management to communicate its corporate philosophy or what management thinks about a legislative issue. During strikes, it has been used by both management and labor to explain to the public their respective points of view on an issue. Trade associations, such as the American Association of Advertising Agencies, have utilized it to build good will for their members or to fight ideas considered opposite to the interests of their constituency. Churches, schools, hospitals, professional societies, voluntary organizations, governments—local and federal—and even private citizens have employed institutional advertising to promote favorable attitudes and actions toward the institution as well as toward its policies and activities.

Institutional advertising can be commercial or noncommercial in nature. Commercial institutional advertising involves paid messages in the media that seek to promote a favorable climate for the sponsor's financial gain. Such messages do not seek to directly sell products or services; instead, they seek to indirectly affect sales by presenting the sponsor as a responsible corporate citizen.

Noncommercial institutional advertising, in contrast, involves either paid or donated mass media messages that seek to promote the nonfinancial interests of sponsors. An example of a noncommercial institutional advertiser is the Advertising Council, an industry organization, which was discussed in Chapter 3. See Figures

Institutional Advertising as a Public Relations Technique

FIGURE 19.12

Institutional Ad Aimed at Recruiting College Students

3.15 and 3.16. As one of the major public relations arms of the advertising industry, the Ad Council produces public service messages, covering a wide range of social issues, which are disseminated in time and space donated by the mass media.

Obviously the distinction between commerical and noncommercial institutional advertising is blurred when profit-seeking organizations are involved. Profit-seeking companies often sponsor public service advertising to promote the public's social well-being. Although their sponsorship might be motivated by social consciousness, such messages surely have some indirect impact on corporate financial well-being as well as the long-term social good. Even nonprofit organizations reap the same indirect benefit from institutional advertising, although the messages would not be considered commercial in the strictest sense of the term—that is, for financial gain. However, nonprofit organizations must be financed through contributions, grants, or donations; and sponsored messages, whether paid for or donated by the media, undoubtedly result in support.

Types of Institutional Advertising

Institutional advertising can be classified into two major types: image and advocacy. Most forms of institutional advertising fall into these two categories.

Image Advertising   Image advertising seeks to show that the corporation has a human side. Carole Cole, a leading public relations consultant in the area of institutional advertising stated, "What's happened is that leading-edge companies are believing that they have to have a corporate soul."[15] Image advertising is designed to create a favorable climate of opinion for an organization by building name recognition, associating the sponsor with positive values, and producing favorable public awareness of the organization's interests and activities.[16]

Most organizations, whether profit oriented or nonprofit oriented, use this form of institutional advertising to communicate values and activities that might otherwise go unreported through other media channels. A corporation, trade association, or a professional society, for example, may use image advertising to inform the public of its research and development contributions, its fair hiring practices, or its active role as a corporate citizen. The Ad Insight entitled "Food for Thought" shows an institutional image campaign for Del Monte.

Advocacy Advertising   In form, advocacy advertising resembles image advertising, but not in content.[17] Unlike image advertising, it is generally argumentative, deals with controversial issues, and is directed at either specific or general targets and opponents—political activists, the media, competitors, consumer groups, or government agencies. Its sole purpose is to promote the sponsor's viewpoint on social, political, or economic issues in an effort to gain attitudinal and behavioral support for the sponsor's interests. An advocacy ad on the value of nuclear energy is shown in Figure 19.13.

Summary

While a great deal of advertising is oriented to long-term brand share and sales by creating loyalty, sales promotions are mostly oriented to short-term sales. Most sales promotions help create sales by offering a special inducement to purchase the product. Sales promotions directed at consumers are termed consumer promotions. Coupons, premiums, sampling, continuity-patronage programs, cents-off and price deals, contests, sweepstakes, and games are commonly used consumer promotions. Over three-fourths of U.S. homes participate in using some form of consumer promotion. The most heavily used consumer promotion is coupons. Sales promotions directed toward resellers (retailers, distributors, wholesalers, and salespersons) are

Food for Thought—Del Monte Uses Institutional Image Advertising

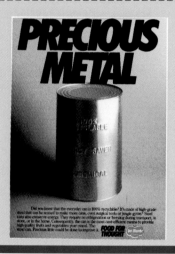

Del Monte Foods launched a $3 million corporate environmental print campaign entitled, "Food for Thought." The ads show a steel can with copy that praises recyclability, energy conservation, and the ability to seal in nutrients without preservatives.*

The campaign typifies the use of advertising as a public relations technique, more specifically referred to as institutional image advertising. The campaign creates a favorable climate of opinion by associating Del Monte with the positive values of recycling, energy conservation, and freshness without preservatives.

*"Newswatch," *Advertising Age* (September 17, 1990): 12.

FIGURE 19.13

Advocacy Ad by U.S. Council for Energy Awareness Communicates the Value of Nuclear Energy

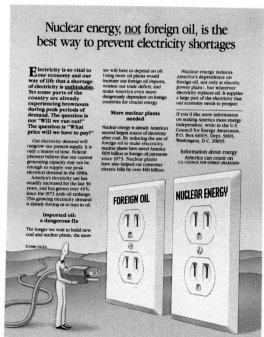

termed trade promotions. Major forms of trade promotion include trade shows, trade incentives and trade deals, salesperson contests, and point-of-purchase and cooperative advertising.

Advertising and public relations overlap in many organizations. Both are concerned with image. While advertising focuses on selling goods and services, public relations is more broadly oriented and focuses on generating understanding and goodwill in a number of both internal and external groups. Public relations activities include press relations, corporate communications, product publicity, counseling, and lobbying.

There are a variety of general public relations techniques. Some of the major techniques include publications, news releases, press conferences, videotapes, and photographs. Institutional advertising is a specialized public relations technique used to create a favorable corporate image or to advocate a particular corporate viewpoint.

Questions for Discussion

1. Distinguish between advertising and sales promotion. How are they related?
2. Why would the manufacturer of a branded product use sales promotion?
3. Under what conditions might you prefer to use a coupon rather than a sample?
4. Look through current magazines and newspapers and find examples of coupons and premiums.
5. Distinguish between advertising and public relations. How are they related?
6. Distinguish between image-oriented and advocacy-oriented institutional advertising. Find examples of each type.

Notes

1. Philip Kotler, *Marketing Management*, 7th ed. (Englewood Cliffs, NJ: Prentice-Hall, 1991), 567.
2. Don E. Schultz, William A. Robinson, and Lisa A. Petrison, *Sales Promotion Essentials*, 2d ed. (Lincolnwood, IL: NTC Business Books, 1993): 1–2.
3. "Study: Some Promotions Change Consumer Behavior," *Marketing News* (October 15, 1990): 12.
4. Scott Hume, "Coupon Use Jumps 10% as Distribution Soars," *Advertising Age* (October 5, 1992): 3.
5. Scott Hume, "Couponing Reaches Record Clip," *Advertising Age* (March 3, 1992): 1.
6. Howard Schlossberg, "Growth of Their Business Follows General Trend," *Marketing News* (March 18, 1991): 9.
7. Pat Sloan and Scott Donaton, "Sampling Smells Sweet for Scent Biz," *Advertising Age* (August 3, 1992): 17.
8. Kevin Kelly, "Europe Won't Be a Joy Ride for the Yanks," *Business Week* (September 15, 1992): 36.
9. Kotler, *Marketing Management*, 634.
10. "Category Management: Marketing for the '90s," *Marketing News* (September 14, 1992): 12.
11. Dennis L. Wilcox, Phillip H. Ault, and Warren K. Agee, *Public Relations: Strategies and Tactics*, 3d ed. (New York: Harper & Row, 1992), 13–15.
12. Louis E. Boone and David L. Kurtz, *Contemporary Marketing*, 7th ed. (Ft. Worth, TX: Dryden Press, 1992), 582.
13. Kotler, *Marketing Management*, 641.
14. Ibid., 643.
15. Don Oldenburg, *Washington Post* (as reprinted in *Athens Banner Herald*), June 28, 1992, C–1.
16. Herbert Waltzer, "Corporate Advocacy Advertising and Political Influence," *Public Relations Review* 14 (Spring 1988): 43.
17. Ibid., 44.

Bowman, Russell D. *Profit on the Dotted Line: Coupons and Rebates*, 2d ed. Chicago: Commerce Communications, 1985.

Daugherty, Patricia J., Richard J. Fox, and Frederick J. Stephenson, Jr., "Frequency Marketing Programs: A Clarification with Strategic Marketing Implications," *Journal of Promotion Management*, 1993.

Kotler, Phillip. *Marketing Management*, 7th ed. Englewood Cliffs, NJ: Prentice-Hall, 1991, Chapter 23.

Robinson, William A. and Christine Hauri, *Promotional Marketing*, Lincolnwood, IL: NTC Business Books, 1991.

Shimp, Terrence A. *Promotion Management and Marketing Communications*, 2d ed. Hinsdale, IL: Dryden Press, 1989, Chapters 15–20.

Schultz, Don E., William A. Robinson, and Lisa A. Petrison, *Sales Promotion Essentials*, 2d ed. Lincolnwood, IL: NTC Business Books, 1993.

Wilcox, Dennis L., Phillip H. Ault, and Warren K. Agee. *Public Relations*. 3d ed. New York: Harper & Row, 1992.

S*uggested Readings*

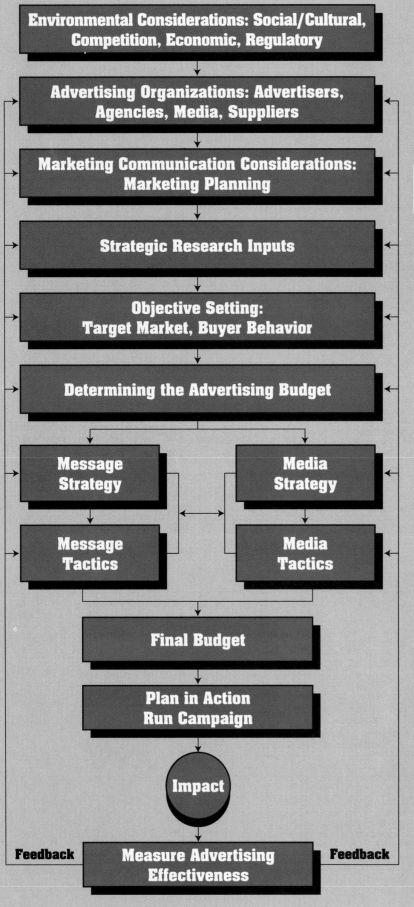

Environmental Considerations: Social/Cultural, Competition, Economic, Regulatory

Advertising Organizations: Advertisers, Agencies, Media, Suppliers

Marketing Communication Considerations: Marketing Planning

Strategic Research Inputs

Objective Setting: Target Market, Buyer Behavior

Determining the Advertising Budget

Message Strategy

Media Strategy

Message Tactics

Media Tactics

Final Budget

Plan in Action Run Campaign

Impact

Feedback   Measure Advertising Effectiveness   Feedback

LEARNING OBJECTIVES

In your study of this chapter, you will have an opportunity to:

- Appreciate how retail advertising is different from general (national) advertising.
- Understand how various types of retailers advertise.
- Understand the retail communication mix.
- Learn the advantages and disadvantages of co-op advertising for both retailers and manufacturers.
- Learn about the different kinds of business-to-business advertisers and the characteristics of business markets.
- Focus on the role of advertising for business-to-business marketers.
- Understand the business-to-business media mix.

Chapter **20**

Retail and Business-to-Business Advertising

CHAPTER TOPICS

RETAIL VERSUS NATIONAL ADVERTISING

DEVELOPMENTS IN RETAILING

Promotional, Semipromotional, and Nonpromotional
Stores
The Retailer's Media Mix
Assistance to the Retail Advertiser
Cooperative Advertising

BUSINESS-TO-BUSINESS ADVERTISING
Business Advertising Objectives
Organizing for Business Advertising
The Business-to-Business Media Mix
The Business Advertisement

Throughout this textbook we have discussed and used examples of consumer, retail, and business-to-business advertising. However, retail and business-to-business advertising require some additional attention because they represent two areas that can require specialized expertise.

Initially, this chapter discusses retail advertising by looking at the differences between retail and national advertising, developments in retailing, the retailer's media mix, and special decision areas. This is followed by a separate section on business-to-business advertising that includes objectives, organization, the media mix, and the business-to-business advertisement.

Retail versus National Advertising

Retail advertising accounts for 43 percent of all advertising expenditures. Compared to national advertising expenditures, retail expenditures usually follow sales much more closely. This is largely due to the fact that retailers expect to see immediate action from their advertising. Limited sales growth of the late 1980s caused a slowdown in retail advertising expenditures. This slowdown has been reversed and retail advertising expenditures are expected to rise throughout the 1990s, as retail sales grow.[1]

Retailing typically is defined to include "all of the activities involved in the sale of products and services to the ultimate consumer."[2] Advertising and promotion by retailers not only includes stores that sell goods—department stores, supermarkets, drugstores, and discount fashion outlets, for example—but also the myriad of service establishments, such as video rental stores, health spas, travel agencies, and financial institutions. Although the retail marketing of goods and services is primarily done in stores, there are also important nonstore retailers, such as telephone and mail-order catalogue sales, vending machines, and at-home sales.

When people walk into a store, they may be seeking a specific product or service or they may just be looking around to see if anything appeals to them. The store that persuades people to enter has already succeeded in one retail advertising objective—building store traffic. The volume of a store's traffic has an important effect on its total sales. This is one reason why retailers in malls and other shopping areas are always concerned with the overall traffic pattern of the surrounding stores. Successful stores tend to build the traffic of adjoining stores.

National advertisers are eager to build a favorable image of their products and to persuade consumers to ask for their products, rather than for competing brands. In most cases national advertisers are willing to leave the choice of store up to the consumer. By comparison, retail advertising is usually action oriented. The store management must promote the belief that the nationally advertised product—which is identical in all stores—can be purchased more advantageously in their store. To persuade successfully, a store must add something of its own to the nationally advertised product. It must promise customers something other stores do not offer or do not offer as well. For example, the retailer may advertise lower price, larger selection, special credit, delivery, easy exchange, or return policies that guarantee satisfaction.

National campaigns are usually developed by individuals who specialize in advertising and sales promotion. In many cases, retail advertising is developed or managed by individuals who are responsible for many other duties. This can lead to advertising that does not always live up to its potential.

National advertisers would like dealers to give special emphasis and attention to their brands. A retailer invests inventory money in several competing brands, however, and is committed to selling all of them. The stock of items of each brand represents working capital that is tied up until the stock is sold.

The retail advertisement is more likely than the national one to have a directed audience. People often get in the habit of looking for and paying attention to the advertisements of certain local stores. This is particularly true for special inserts and ads in Sunday newspapers that often contain coupons and indicate weekly sales. Many retail ads are packed with specific information—not only about prices but about such things as size, color, and weight. The ad often informs consumers where in the store they can expect to find the merchandise.

Developments in Retailing

The relative importance of advertising varies from one type of store to another. Furniture, consumer electronics, and video stores spend substantially more of each sales dollar for advertising than do drug and proprietary or grocery stores, as shown in Table 20.1.

The hectic pace of retailing at times makes it very difficult to establish a coordinated advertising program. Retailing is often thought of as dynamic and demanding in terms of understanding trends. Many factors influence the relationship between retailers and customers. Fashion seasons, weather, staff, inventory controls, and general economic conditions are apt to change. Many retailers are experimenting with new hours to accommodate changing shopping habits. Harold Rowen, chief executive officer of Kinney Shoe Corporation notes, "Being open from noon to 10 P.M. daily would tie-in better from the standpoint of the working women. Like it or not, Sunday is getting bigger and bigger every year."[3]

One of the most ambitious retail projects has been built in Bloomington, Minnesota. The Mall of America opened in 1992, is 78 acres, and features 4.2 million

---

TABLE 20.1	
Advertising as a Percentage of Sales for Selected Retail Businesses	
Furniture Stores	6.5%
Video Rental Stores	4.2
Radio, TV, and Consumer Electronic Stores	4.1
Eating Places	3.4
Motion Picture Theatres	3.2
Jewelry Stores	3.2
Department Stores	2.5
Apparel and Accessory Stores	2.4
Drug and Proprietary Stores	1.5
Auto and Home Stores	1.4
Grocery Stores	1.2

Source: "Advertising-to-Sales Ratios," *Advertising Age* (July 26, 1993), 27.

---

square feet of floor space. It may also be a glimpse of the future of retailing. The mall combines the drawing power of a regional shopping center with the excitement of an amusement park. The mall contains 350 specialty stores, 14 movie theaters, 5 nightclubs, and at least 12 restaurants or eating areas. In the center of the mall is a 7-acre Knotts Berry Farm theme park. It is the nation's largest shopping complex.[4]

The nature of retailing has shifted in recent years to include a wide range of new stores. These stores are examined in the Ad Insight entitled "Trends in Retail Stores."

In deciding on the ingredients in the marketing mix, the retailer should be guided by store objectives, the attitudes and habits of potential customers, the general attitude of the trade, characteristics of the products or services to be sold, and the activities of the competition. The factors are easier to analyze in the retailer's marketing program if we look at them in terms of store types. A useful classification is one based on promotion policy—promotional, semipromotional, and nonpromotional.

Promotional Stores

The typical promotional store receives only part of its business from regular customers. It depends heavily on consumers who come in to the store in response to advertised promotions. The promotional store emphasizes its low prices. Customers are accustomed to waiting for reduced-price promotions, which in some promotional stores are almost continuous. Figure 20.1 shows an advertisement for a promotional store.

Promotional stores typically spend higher percentages of their marketing dollars on advertising than do the other types of promotional stores. Higher advertising costs are necessary in order to call attention to the continuous sales and to generate store traffic. These stores generally offer less customer service, fewer floor personnel, and depend on high sales volume.

A major variation of the promotional store was introduced by the late Sam Walton. Mr. Walton, founder of Wal-Mart stores, was named *Advertising Age*'s Adman of the Year in 1992 because of his innovative approaches in retailing. The major difference between Wal-Mart and major rivals is everyday low price (see Figure

Promotional,
Semipromotional, and
Nonpromotional Stores

FIGURE 20.1

**Advertisement for a
Promotional Store**

Trends in Retail Stores

Showcase Store (Nike Town)

Drive–Through (Burger King)

Recent years have seen a number of changes in retail stores. The following highlights some of the new stores that have developed and are expected to maintain fast growth:

Warehouse Clubs

Stores such as Sam's Price Club, Costco, and Pace offer no frills, low prices, and accept cash only. Club stores generally offer only top-selling brands and have limited product assortment. The key is high turnover. The core of the club concept is membership. There are over 500 club stores generating $28 billion in sales. Advertising and promotion for these stores is very limited.[1]

Discount Mall Outlets

Factory outlet malls and value retail centers are growing in size and popularity. Outlet malls have sales of over $6 billion. The number of mall outlets increased from 115 in 1987 to almost 300 in 1992. Even traditional, nonpromotional, upscale stores such as Saks Fifth Avenue are opening stores in outlet malls. Experts feel this trend is apt to continue.[2]

Showcase Stores

These stores take heavily advertised products and give them their own "showcase" to promote and push their fast growing product lines. Reebok, Nike, and Sony have used this concept to bring special attention to their offerings by devoting a whole store to selling the product. This devotion helps reinforce the product's image. Mark Karros, general manager of Reebok's retail division, notes, "Our stores function like a living billboard to show customers what we make and to show our retailers the latest methods for displaying merchandise."[3]

Drive-Throughs

Several fast-food chains are developing more drive-through restaurants. These retail outlets only serve products to go. By offering lower start-up, less labor costs, limited menus, and more streamlined operations, these stores are proving to be the most rapidly growing aspect of the fast-food business.

[1] James M. Degen, "Warehouse Clubs Move from Revolution to Evaluation." *Marketing News* (August 3, 1992): 8.
[2] Adrienne Ward, "New Breed of Mall Knows: Everybody Loves a Bargain." *Advertising Age* (January 27, 1992): S–5.
[3] Kate Fitzgerald, "Marketers Learn to 'Just do It,'" *Advertising Age* (January 27, 1992): S–7.

20.2). Wal-Mart is the nation's top-volume retailer and continuously searches for ways to reduce costs and undercut competitors on branded products.

Semipromotional Stores

Many of the large department and specialty chain stores fall within the classification of semipromotional. This type of store advertises regularly but devotes less of its sales dollar to advertising than does the promotional store. Its advertising usually emphasizes something other than prices, such as service, guarantees, warranties, fashion, and selection. Its prices tend to be higher than those of the promotional store. An advertisement for a semipromotional store is shown in Figure 20.3.

Many semipromotional stores depend on regularly scheduled sales events—such as an August back-to-school sale, pre-Christmas sale or post-Christmas clearance, and Washington's Birthday sale—rather than on a barrage of reduced-price promotions in rapid succession.

Nonpromotional Stores

The nonpromotional store usually has a loyal clientele that depends on it for the latest fashions or the finest merchandise. Advertising reflects a specific image. The basic appeal is status or quality, not price. The advertisement in Figure 20.4 reflects the nonpromotional character of the store.

The nonpromotional store is ordinarily a regular advertiser, but it depends more on a long-range, prestige-building strategy. It is likely to spend a higher percentage of its sales dollar on rent, window and store display, personal selling, and service of all kinds than do other types of stores. Its expenditure for advertising is usually lower than that of semipromotional and promotional stores.

FIGURE 20.2

Wal-Mart Advertisement Stating the Store's Key Benefit, "Always the Low Price"

FIGURE 20.3

Advertisement for a Semipromotional Store

The Retailer's
Media Mix

Media use by a retailer depends largely on the extent of the store's trading area, the store's goals, and its financial resources. Retailers rely on a range of media types. Table 20.2 shows retail advertising spending in various media.

Newspapers dominate the retailer's media picture. They account for about 50 percent of all local advertising expenditures. Their dominance is not too surprising when we consider the major role the newspaper plays in helping shoppers make purchase decisions. Consumers often scan retail ads when deciding which products to buy. In the newspaper, shoppers find essential information that they can read at their own speed and reread. They can clip out information or coupons. One other characteristic with special appeal to retailers is the flexibility of newspapers. Changes can often be made in the advertisement up to a few hours before press time.

In recent years, retailers have increased their use of the broadcast media. Although both local radio and television have much less retail advertising than newspapers, the growth rate has been increasing faster than newspapers.

National retailers such as Sears and J.C. Penney have used television advertising on a national and regional basis. The use of television for national and regional chain stores is usually more image oriented. However, local retailers are becoming increasingly more sophisticated in the use of television to reach their special markets. Television accounts for 14 percent of retail advertising. Local cable television advertising has doubled in the last few years and accounts for almost a billion dollars in retail advertising. At times, a local cable station can target more effectively than a local newspaper. One media expert gives the following example, "If you're an auto dealer in the northeast part of a city and can get on two or three cable systems, you can target more effectively than by advertising in a big newspaper."[5]

Projections indicate that radio will continue to enjoy very strong growth in retail advertising dollars. Experts are predicting that retail advertising on radio will grow at over 6 percent a year through 1996.[6] Radio offers a great deal of flexibility with regard to changing ads quickly for special sales or other factors.

FIGURE 20.4

Advertisement for a Nonpromotional Store

TIFFANY & CO.

Most retailers use in-store communication devices termed point-of-purchase. These include in-store displays, signs, and new electronic media. The Point of Purchase Advertising Institute (POPAI) reported that 15 billion dollars per year are spent on all forms of in-store promotions. A POPAI supermarket study indicated that customers make 66 percent of their supermarket decisions in-store.

The Yellow Pages directories list all area businesses with a phone number. Retailers can also purchase additional advertising space to draw attention to their

TABLE 20.2

Retail Advertising Spending

	Expenditures (millions)	Percent of Total Ad Budget
Newspapers	$27,925	50%
Yellow Pages	8,165	15
Television	8,095	14
Radio	6,370	11
Other Local Media (in-store, point-of-purchase displays, shoppers)	5,345	10
Total	$56,260	100%

Source: Robert Coen, "Insiders Report," McCann-Erickson, June, 1992.

businesses. Yellow Page advertising can be an important part of many retailer's media mix. Retailers believe that customers who take the time to seek out an area business in the Yellow Pages are in a frame of mind to buy.

Many retailers use in-store radio that includes both entertainment and advertising. Also, the major networks and other programmers have developed programming and advertising that can be seen only in certain stores. This is termed **place-based media**. For example, NBC has developed On-Site, a system that delivers programming to food stores, drug stores, and fast food chains.[7] Customers watch the monitors as they shop, eat, or stand in line.

Supermarkets are also using VideOcart developed by Information Resources Inc. A screen, providing both entertainment and advertising information, is attached to a shopping cart. As shoppers push the VideOcart down the aisles, ads for the brands on the shelves appear.

Assistance to the *Retail Advertiser*

Although many large retailers, such as department stores, have advertising and promotion departments, quite a few must rely extensively on others to assist them in planning and executing their advertising. Such help typically comes from the media, advertising agencies, and national manufacturers.

Almost all retailers, including those with their own advertising staff, use the services of the media. Newspaper, radio, and television salespeople, for example, can help retailers plan advertising and assist in writing and producing advertisements or commercials.

A number of newspapers provide store managers with research, and most provide free copy and layout services. Newspapers also subscribe to services, which provide standard types of artwork that can be inserted into a layout. Newspapers also offer planning guides to help retailers spend their money during the months when potential sales are greatest.

Many retailers hire an advertising agency. The agency can provide expert advice on all phases of the advertising program—from planning to producing commercials. The use of agencies for retailing has grown in recent years. This is due to increases in the use of television (which requires professional production expertise) and changes in the fee structure which make it easier for retailers to work with agencies. Some retailers—for example, banks—have always relied on agencies to develop and enhance their image.

A third source of help to the retailer is the manufacturer. Manufacturers often provide their retail dealers with a host of advertising assistance—from planning guides to seminars on advertising to prepared advertisements and commercials. The retailer merely adds the store's logotype to the prepared material. Much of the manufacturer's assistance is in the form of **cooperative advertising**.

Cooperative *Advertising*

Cooperative advertising (co-op) is a financial agreement whereby a manufacturer offers to pay part, or all, of a retailer's advertising when the retailer features the manufacturer's product in the advertising. Retailers are usually reimbursed anywhere from 50 to 100 percent for featuring the manufacturer's product. It is estimated that 24 billion dollars are made available annually by manufacturers and that 18 billion dollars are actually invested in co-op by manufacturers and retailers. Over 6,000 manufacturers sponsored co-op are available to retailers.[8] Co-op dollars as a percentage of total budget for select retail stores are listed in Table 20.3.

Local media also view co-op as a major source of revenues. Therefore, local media are active in helping retailers obtain these funds. Although a majority of co-op spending is in newspapers, there has been a trend toward other media. The percentage of co-op spending in each medium is shown in Table 20.4.

TABLE 20.3

Co-op Dollars as a Percentage of Total Ad Budgets for Selected Retail Stores

Appliance Dealers	80%
Food Stores	75
Drugstores	70
Shoe Stores	50
Department Stores	50
Specialty Stores	50
Clothing Stores	35
Jewelers	30
Furniture Stores	30
Household-Goods Stores	30
Discount Houses	20

Advantages and Disadvantages for Manufacturers

Co-op offers a number of advantages to manufacturers. The key to having effective co-op advertising is to develop programs that are flexible and easily comprehended by retailers.[9] It gains the retailer's endorsement of the product. Such an endorsement improves relations between manufacturers and retailers, assists the manufacturer in getting more products into the store, and creates a more enthusiastic selling environment for the product. For example, television ads in a recent co-op campaign between Valvoline oil and Wal-Mart stores featured the quality of Valvoline oil at the low price of Wal-Mart. Valvoline's Vice President of International Marketing, Dennis Doggett, noted the co-op program, "Reinforces Valvoline's quality and tells the consumer where they can buy it at a fair price. This signals more partnership with retailers."[10]

Co-op often allows the manufacturer to utilize the retailer's knowledge of the local market in terms of the best way to reach and appeal to customers. Manufacturers know that effective co-op helps sell the product to consumers. Finally, co-op allows the manufacturer to buy more advertising space for less money. Cost savings are achieved because (1) manufacturers usually split the cost with retailers rather than pay the total cost and (2) retailers purchase media space at the less expensive local rate rather than the national rate (Chapter 16 noted the differences in these two rates).

TABLE 20.4

Percentage of Co-op Dollars Spent, by Media Type

Newspapers	65.0%
Direct Mail	11.0
Television	10.0
Radio	8.0
Magazines	3.5
Other	2.5

Co-op has some disadvantages from the manufacturer's point of view. The most important disadvantage is lack of control over both the final creative and the timing of media placement. Although the manufacturer has guidelines, ultimately the retailer decides how the ad should look and when the ad will be run. Retailers are likely to complain if a manufacturer imposes too much control, thus causing disagreements. Also, a co-op program can take away funds from the national effort. Finally, legal difficulties represent a problem. Some retailers ask for special promotional deals, including extra cooperative funding. If manufacturers go along with them, they violate the **Robinson-Patman Act**, which notes that all promotional allowances be available to distributors and retailers on proportionately equal terms. Therefore, if a retailer in an area is given co-op advertising dollars, other similar retailers must be given the same opportunity to use co-op funds.

Advantages and Disadvantages for Retailers

The main advantage to retailers is that co-op advertising offers the chance to do more advertising than they would do otherwise. Money from the outside helps them do what they know they should do anyway—advertise regularly. Co-op also allows retailers to benefit from the marketing knowledge of the manufacturer.

Yet co-op can have disadvantages. Some large retailers chafe at the restrictions that go along with co-op money. Some retailers think they can decide better than the manufacturer what copy and media they should use. They think that the manufacturer should allow them more flexibility in their use of the co-op allowance.

Business-to-Business Advertising

Business-to-business advertising represents a unique form of promotion that is deserving of special attention. As opposed to consumer advertising, which focuses on selling to individuals, business-to-business advertising is directed to organizations that purchase goods or services to be used in the maintenance of those organizations, in the creation of their products or services, or for redistribution to the ultimate consumer.

Business-to-business advertising can take a number of forms. As used here, the term encompasses four distinct types: industrial, trade, professional, and agricultural.

Industrial advertising involves the advertising of goods and services that are used in the production of further goods and services. Industrial products can become part of an end product, can be used in the manufacturing process, or can be part of the normal operation and maintenance of the firm. An ad for an industrial product aimed at operation and maintenance is shown in Figure 20.5.

Trade advertising involves the advertising of goods or services to wholesalers and retailers who buy these goods and services for resale. A majority of retailers feel that trade publication advertising is a highly effective way to influence purchasing decisions for both existing and new products.

Professional advertising is directed to professional people, such as doctors, lawyers, university professors, architects, and other individuals who are in the position to either prescribe products, influence the buying process, or use the product in their occupations. An example of professional advertising is shown in Figure 20.6. Note how the advertisement points out the value of using a particular magazine in order to reach potential customers. The objective is to get marketing professionals to advertise their product in the magazine.

Agricultural advertising addresses the farmer as a business consumer. The farmer serves as a market for a host of grower, raiser, and producer commodities. The size of the farm market for petroleum, fertilizer, machinery, equipment, chemicals, feed, and seed warrant a distinct category of advertising.

FIGURE 20.5

Industrial Ad Aimed at Operations and Maintenance

FIGURE 20.6

Ad Directed to Marketing Professionals Points Out the Benefits of Advertising in a Specific Magazine

Characteristics of the Business Market

Business markets have unique traits that are different from consumer markets. The following are some key traits that need to be considered:

- Market size is more condensed; fewer purchasers, each buying in great quantity.
- In many instances the purchases involve large expenditures.
- The purchase process usually involves a longer lead time and is not made as quickly as the majority of consumer purchases.
- Purchases are usually made by professional buyers who, in many instances, possess specific technical expertise.
- Many purchase decisions are made by more than one individual; for example, industrial purchases are often made by committee and trade decisions by a team of retail buyers.
- Business purchasers often select more than one source in order to protect their supplies.
- Many of the products are more technical in nature than consumer products, and purchases are often made on clear specifications.

Many of these characteristics fit the accompanying jet ad. Certainly the product is aimed at a limited market and involves a major expenditure. Additionally, in most cases purchase involves a long lead time, the purchase decision is made by more than one individual in the company, and it utilizes both professional and technical expertise.

At small airports, it is better to appear conspicuous, than not to appear at all.

The incomparable Learjet 31A gets down to business, wherever business leads you.

Fully loaded, the Learjet 31A can operate routinely from runways of less than 3,000 feet and fly 1,500 miles nonstop while capitalizing on its unique combination of time-saving speed and low operating costs. Characteristics that make the Learjet 31A stand out from the crowd — like the companies that operate them.

To take advantage of more opportunities, fly the business jet that reaches more places. The Learjet 31A. See where it can take you and your business. For details call Ted Farid, Vice President Domestic Marketing, at (316) 946-2450.

Learjet
Nothing else comes close.

As noted in the Ad Insight entitled "Characteristics of the Business Market" there are many factors that make the business market unique.

Business Advertising Objectives

Business-to-business marketers generally spend a smaller percentage of sales for advertising than do retailers or consumer marketers. This is because business-to-business marketers tend to focus on personal selling as their primary promotional tool. However, advertising still plays an integral role in the sales process. Studies have noted that the average cost of a business-to-business personal sales call is $230.[11] Given the high cost of a personal contact, marketers use advertising to familiarize potential customers with the product or service and create a favorable impression. Table 20.5 shows that most of the business advertising objectives are

TABLE 20.5

Percent of Time Advertising Objectives Are Used by Business-to-Business Advertisers

Advertising Objective	Percent of Time Used
Awareness	35%
Knowledge	35
Liking	9
Preference	1
Conviction	3
Purchase	10
Other	7
	100%

Source: Adapted from Steven W. Hartley and Charles Patti, "Evaluating Business-to-Business Advertising," *Journal of Advertising Research,* April/May, 1988.

related to creating awareness and knowledge. Creating both awareness and knowledge no doubt makes the salesperson's job easier.

By developing awareness and knowledge and creating a positive image, advertising can cut lead time for purchases. A study conducted by the Advertising Research Foundation indicated that business publication advertising can cut the lead time of a sale four to six months.[12]

A Laboratory of Advertising Performance (LAP) study indicates that advertising plays an important role in generating qualified leads for salespeople.[13] Many business publications offer "bingo" cards at the end of the magazines. Readers can circle an advertiser's name if they desire more information. The cards are sent to the business publication, which in turn forwards them to the advertiser for follow-up. Additionally, many business-to-business marketers use 800 numbers for direct contact or specific mail-back coupons in the ad.

Finally, business-to-business advertising is used to reach prospective buyers that are either unknown or inaccessible to salespeople. In many companies, salespeople may call only on certain individuals—usually purchasing agents. Yet several other individuals may influence the purchase decision. Advertising may be the only way of reaching such inaccessible decision makers. In other cases, the salesperson simply does not know all of the decision influences in a company, and to rely solely on personal selling would not be feasible. Advertising serves to broaden promotional reach.

The organization of the advertising function among business-to-business advertisers is basically similar to the organization within consumer goods companies. Yet there are a few differences that should be noted.

For one thing, the advertising department in business-to-business firms often is not as high in the organizational hierarchy as in consumer goods companies, a fact that reflects the greater emphasis given to personal selling. In many companies the advertising manager reports to the sales manager rather than shares equal status.

Second, advertising people who work for business-to-business companies are more apt to be involved in the actual construction of advertising than their consumer goods counterparts, because of the technical nature of much business advertising. Although a company may use an advertising agency to prepare the advertising and to select media, the company advertising department may need to screen copy carefully to be sure it is technically correct. Many advertisements are directed to

Organizing for
Business Advertising

people with specialized and technical backgrounds—doctors, engineers, scientists—and advertising copy must reflect this situation. People with technical educations are often found on the advertising staff of a business advertiser.

The trend is toward greater use of the advertising agency by business-to-business advertisers. Much can be gained from using objective and professional communicators for the advertising task. Many advertising agencies specialize in business advertising and can offer the services of skilled professionals who are competent in technical areas.

The Business-to-Business Media Mix

Just as television is the national advertiser's main medium and newspapers are the major retail medium, the business publication receives the greatest share of the business-to-business advertiser's budget. As Table 20.6 shows, 35 percent of the average business-to-business budget is spent on business publications. Business publications, catalogs, trade shows, and direct mail account for 71 percent of the total budget.

Business and Farm Publications

Business and farm publications are aimed at a number of business types and specializations. There are over 600 business publications and 300 farm publications. Almost every major industry has a publication directed to its members. Three billion dollars are spent each year on business publication advertising.[14]

Business publications can be classified as either **vertical** or **horizontal**. Vertical publications, such as *Beverage World, Electronic Engineering Times,* and *Pet Age* deal with a specific industry. Horizontal publications are directed toward specific job functions that cut across many industries, for example, *Purchasing World, Public Relations Journal,* or even *Forbes,* which has a general management appeal.

In deciding which business publications to use in the media plan, the advertiser applies the general principles of media selection. Thus, media buyers will choose vehicles that best deliver the audience they seek to reach and consider the relative efficiency of alternative publications.

Catalogs

The catalog is a special type of direct advertising and is distributed either directly to prospective customers, usually by the salesperson or dealer, or through direct mail. At times, catalogs serve as a showcase for the company. One great advantage of catalogs as a business medium is that they can be used over a long period of time. Thus, they can serve as a reference for ordering and to remind customers of products and services between personal sales calls. Some catalogs are placed in loose-leaf binders that can be updated by sending additional sheets for inclusion or notices of product cancellation.

Although the specific reasons for using a catalog vary from industry to industry as well as among specific companies, the most common reasons are (1) to produce orders; (2) to develop recognition and remind buyers; (3) to generate requests for information; (4) to supplement the salesperson between calls; (5) to assist in group decision making; (6) to reach multiple people in an organization; (7) to stimulate invitations to bid; and (8) in technical areas, assist in helping the buyer specify the order.

Catalog preparation requires great attention to detail. If products are to be shown, care must be taken in drawing or photographing each item. The copy must be technically accurate; often performance data and servicing requirements are detailed.

Trade Shows and Exhibits

Trade shows and exhibits are one of the major sales promotion media available to business-to-business advertisers. The use of trade shows has increased in the past

---

TABLE 20.6

Allocation of Advertising Budget for Business-to-Business Marketers

Item	Percent of Total Budget
Business Publications (including production costs)	35%
Catalogs	16
Trade Shows	12
Direct Mail	8
Other General Media (such as general magazines, radio, television)	8
Advertising Department Administrative Expenses	6
Dealer and Distributor Aids	4
Videocassettes and Other Audiovisuals	4
Telemarketing	1
All Other Budget Items (including publicity)	6
	100%

---

few years from 8 percent to 12 percent of the advertising budget. Exhibiting at a trade show can accomplish several goals: (1) meet potential customers; (2) explain a new product to existing customers; (3) develop a list of prospective buyers; (4) demonstrate equipment or services that could not be taken on a sales call; (5) build goodwill among present customers; (6) introduce new products and services and estimate their possible success in the marketplace; and (7) observe the efforts of competitors. (Chapter 19 also discusses trade shows and exhibits.)

Direct Mail

The importance of direct mail to business advertisers is illustrated in Table 20.6, which shows that 8 percent of the advertising budget is spent on it. (Chapter 18 fully discusses the general use of direct mail.) Direct mail offers the business advertiser several advantages. For one thing, direct mail can be a highly personal medium, in which a message can be tailored to specific individuals. Because many business markets are very narrow, consisting of relatively few individuals, such personalization is feasible. For example, dealers of heavy earth-moving equipment send different direct-mail pieces according to customer size. The dealers know that smaller customers have different equipment needs than larger customers.

The fact that much business advertising is very technical and detailed accounts for the popularity of direct mail. Direct mail can specifically target certain customers and point out product features that are most desirable. Also, direct mail can effectively be used as follow-up to the sales call after the salesperson has explained the product.

Direct-mail advertising is most flexible in terms of format. Advertisers can send postcard reminders, sales letters, bulletins, brochures, price lists, and even samples of the product. Notices can range from mimeographed material to full-color illustrations on high-quality stock.

Perhaps most important for the successful use of direct-mail advertising is the quality of the mailing list. Although some advertisers develop and maintain their own lists, most rely on companies that are in the business of selling or leasing mailing lists (as discussed in Chapter 18). Many mailing lists for business advertisers are developed by publishers of specialized business publications and farm papers.

FIGURE 20.7

Advertisement Telling Marketers How Interactive Computer Disks Can Be Used as Promotional Material

General Media

Several general media often thought of as exclusively for consumer markets are also used by business advertisers. General magazines, newspapers, radio, and television account for approximately 8 percent of the budget. Usually, these media provide a large amount of waste circulation for a business advertiser, but they can be very effective under certain circumstances.

Specialized cable programs such as CNN MoneyLine target business people. The rise in such channels provides a business-oriented audience and has less wasted coverage. Caterpillar Inc. ran a series of ads for electrical generator sets on the morning Cable News Network (CNN). The ads were aimed at creating awareness and developing inquiries.

Some business advertisers do find that such media can be fairly efficient. For example, they may be useful in reaching business people when they are not performing their occupational roles. Many consumer media have specialized sections or broadcasts that appeal especially to certain vocational groups. Some radio and television stations direct a portion of their programming to farmers—weathercasts, grain and livestock marketing reports, and the like.

Outdoor, to a limited extent, is being used successfully to reach business people. For example, Semi-Alloys Packaging featured outdoor advertising that displayed its packaging material, and Belcrest-Bentz Interiors used outdoor advertising that generated interest in business interior designs.

Business advertisers are especially likely to use general media when they wish to make an impact or create primary demand. Sometimes business advertisers use institutional advertising in consumer magazines or newspapers to communicate aspects of their public relations program (as discussed in Chapter 19). They may, for example, want to discuss problems of impending government regulation or their labor regulations. A company may seek to show how it is fulfilling its role as a socially responsible corporation.

New Media and Computer Disks

Videocassettes and other forms of audiovisual material are being utilized by marketers. The videocassette enables business marketers to reach customers with a specialized message. This provides an excellent opportunity for technical messages to specifically demonstrate a product. Cassettes may assist the salesperson in presenting product or company features, or they can be used to demonstrate or discuss the product when the salesperson is not present. In some instances, cassettes are used when a prospect is hard to reach or does not warrant the attention of a personal sales call.

The proliferation of personal computers has led to the distribution of promotional material via floppy disks. The business marketer provides a current or prospective customer with software containing company or product information. The material provides an interactive base that can answer specific questions regarding a company's product or service. The advertisement in Figure 20.7 announces a form of computer disk distribution from Forbes. The 5¼ computer disks are actually bound inside a copy of *Forbes* magazine and will run on most IBM compatible PCs. In one instance the Forbes' disk contained information from such marketers as American Express, Chevrolet Corvette, Chicago Board of Trade, Jaguar, and Merrill Lynch. Computer disks offer selectivity and the ability to provide a great deal of information to an interested audience.

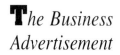

The Business Advertisement

Obviously, the principles of good writing, layout, and illustration apply to business advertising. Here we will look briefly at some of the unique aspects of the business advertisement.

Most business-to-business copy is written for individuals who have some kind of professional expertise in their field. It is critical that individuals who create

**Business-to-Business Ad That Emphasizes
Straightforward Factual Copy**

business advertising and write the copy have acquired the technical expertise needed to understand the product.

Most successful business advertising is factual and offers a hard-hitting message.[15] One suggestion is to avoid any hint of exaggeration. As noted, most business people, farmers, and professionals are experts in their field. Exaggeration will be easily detected, and the whole communication will suffer.

Copy should avoid being flamboyant. The approach should generally be kept as straightforward and rational as possible. Even though this no-nonsense approach appeals to the more serious nature of the business reader, it does not mean that messages must be dull and boring. Excitement and interest can be generated through crisp writing and attractive illustrations (see Figure 20.8). Much successful business copy is directed so that the reader feels that the special problems of his or her particular business are understood by the advertiser. Of special importance for business advertising is to present news and information in easily understood language.

A case history often makes a good business advertisement. This is in essence a type of endorsement or testimonial, and business people like to read about successful cases that may apply to their situation. Through the case history, the reader can be given facts and figures that come alive because they are based on real-life performance.

Although differences exist between consumer and business advertisements, communication principles are valid across all types of advertising. Many experts in the field agree that business advertising has become more like consumer advertising in recent years. Greater attention to the creative process and improvements in the reproduction of business advertisements, especially full-color ads, have contributed to this trend.

Summary

Retail advertising is an important part of the total advertising picture, representing over 43 percent of the total volume. It includes all the advertising done by institutions selling goods or services directly to the public.

The promotional store uses the highest percentage of sales for advertising, the nonpromotional store the lowest. In addition to promotional, semi-promotional, and nonpromotional stores, there are several retail trends, including warehouse clubs, discount mall outlets, showcase stores, and drive-through restaurants.

Newspapers account for the largest portion of retail expenditures. However, radio and television are increasing their share of retailers' media expenditures. Cable television is now offering a great deal of selectivity. Also in use are in-store media, such as radio and place-based media, which shows in-store television programming and advertising.

Co-op advertising provides an agreement between manufacturers and retailers whereby a manufacturer offers to pay a portion of the ad costs when a retailer features the manufacturer's product. At least $18 billion is spent annually in this area.

Business-to-business advertising involves communicating with industrial marketers, middlemen, professionals—such as doctors and architects, and farmers. The business market is often more condensed, with larger sales to fewer prospects. Buyer characteristics of business people are also different.

Among many business advertisers, the amount of advertising is lower as a percentage of sales than it is among retailers or consumer advertisers. Nevertheless, advertising is important in the marketing mix of industrial, trade, professional, and agricultural marketers. Such advertising can create a favorable climate for the salesperson, cut sales time, and help produce sales leads. It also can be used to create primary demand for a company's customers and to reach buyers that are either unknown or inaccessible to salespeople.

The major media used by business advertisers are business and farm publications, catalogs, trade shows, and direct mail; these account for 71 percent of the advertising budget. VCR cassettes and computer disks are developing as important promotional tools.

Business advertisements are aimed at people who are experts in their field, and the copy should therefore be technically correct and avoid any hint of exaggeration.

Questions
for Discussion

1. Why is retailing viewed as dynamic? What do you think retail stores will be like by the year 2000?
2. Why has the newspaper traditionally been the major medium of retailers? Is it likely that any other medium will become dominant in the retail field in the near future?
3. What are the advantages and disadvantages of cooperative advertising to the manufacturer? To the retailer?
4. What are the principal differences between retail and national advertising copy?
5. Distinguish between industrial, trade, professional, and agricultural advertising. Try to bring to class an example of each.
6. Why is personal selling generally a more important promotional tool than advertising for a business marketer?
7. What are the major objectives of advertising for business marketers?
8. Why have business publications traditionally been the major medium of the business advertiser? Do you think they will remain dominant in the future? What other media are growing among business-to-business advertisers?

[1] Robert Coen, "Insider's Report," McCann-Erickson, June, 1992, 7.

[2] Louis E. Boone and David L. Kurtz, *Contemporary Marketing,* 7th ed. (Ft. Worth, TX: Dryden Press, 1992), 458.

[3] Steve Kerch, "New Shopping Habits Reshape Retail Trade," *Chicago Tribune,* June 11, 1991, Section 3; 1, 6.

[4] "78-acre Mall of America Nears Debut," *Atlanta Journal and Constitution,* Sunday, August 6, 1992, C6.

[5] Walt Potter, "Cable TV Nips at the Ankles of Advertising," *Presstime,* July 1992, 6.

[6] Carrie Goerne, "Communications Spending Expected to Grow 7.1% over Next Five Years," *Marketing News* (April 3, 1992): 5.

[7] Joe Mandese, "Big 3 TV Nets Take Video from Home to Retail Outlets." *Advertising Age* (August 17, 1992): 28.

[8] Laura Dalton, "Co-op Advertising: Everybody Benefits," *Gannetter* (May 1993): 6.

[9] Vicki Clift, "Co-op Relationships Need a Little Romance," *Marketing News* (August 17, 1992): 15.

[10] Jennifer Lawrence and Christy Fisher, "Wal-Mart Links Up with Valvoline Oil for Co-op Ad Effort," *Advertising Age* (June 1, 1992): 4.

[11] Steven W. Hartley and Charles Patti, "Evaluating Business-to-Business Advertising," *Journal of Advertising Research,* April/May, 1988, 21–27.

[12] "Study Shows Frequent Four-Color Ads Attract More Attention in Trade Press," *Marketing News* (March 14, 1988): 13.

[13] "Business Marketers Can Take 10 Steps to Building Strong Marketing Ad Programs," *Marketing News* (March 14, 1988): 18–19.

[14] Robert Coen, McCann-Erickson Inc., "Estimated Annual U.S. Advertising Expenditures," Prepared for *Advertising Age,* June 1992.

[15] Sandra E. Moriarty, *Creative Advertising,* 2d ed. (Engelwood Cliffs, NJ: Prentice-Hall, 1991), 382–383.

Notes

Boone, Louis E., and David L. Kurtz. *Contemporary Marketing*, 7th ed. Ft. Worth, TX: Dryden Press, 1992. Chapter 14.

Hutt, Michael D., and Thomas W. Speh. *Business Marketing Management*, 4th ed. Hinsdale, IL: Dryden Press, 1992.

Kotler, Philip. *Marketing Management*, 7th ed. Englewood Cliffs, NJ: Prentice-Hall, 1991. Chapter 20.

Patti, Charles H., Steven W. Hartley, and Susan L. Kennedy, *Business To Business Advertising.* Lincolnwood, IL: NTC Business Books, 1993.

Rogers, Dorothy S., and Mercia M. T. Grassi. *Retailing: New Perspectives.* Hinsdale, IL: Dryden Press, 1988.

Sandra E. Moriarty, *Creative Advertising,* 2d ed. Engelwood Cliffs, NJ: Prentice-Hall, 1991, 380–385.

Suggested *Readings*

```
┌─────────────────────────────────────────────┐
│ Environmental Considerations: Social/Cultural, │
│     Competition, Economic, Regulatory         │
└─────────────────────────────────────────────┘
                      ↓
┌─────────────────────────────────────────────┐
│    Advertising Organizations: Advertisers,    │
│        Agencies, Media, Suppliers             │
└─────────────────────────────────────────────┘
                      ↓
┌─────────────────────────────────────────────┐
│  Marketing Communication Considerations:      │
│            Marketing Planning                 │
└─────────────────────────────────────────────┘
                      ↓
┌─────────────────────────────────────────────┐
│         Strategic Research Inputs             │
└─────────────────────────────────────────────┘
                      ↓
┌─────────────────────────────────────────────┐
│            Objective Setting:                 │
│       Target Market, Buyer Behavior           │
└─────────────────────────────────────────────┘
                      ↓
┌─────────────────────────────────────────────┐
│      Determining the Advertising Budget       │
└─────────────────────────────────────────────┘
              ↓               ↓
┌──────────────────┐   ┌──────────────────┐
│     Message      │   │      Media       │
│     Strategy     │   │     Strategy     │
└──────────────────┘   └──────────────────┘
         ↓         ←→          ↓
┌──────────────────┐   ┌──────────────────┐
│     Message      │   │      Media        │
│     Tactics      │   │      Tactics      │
└──────────────────┘   └──────────────────┘
                      ↓
┌─────────────────────────────────────────────┐
│              Final Budget                     │
└─────────────────────────────────────────────┘
                      ↓
┌─────────────────────────────────────────────┐
│             Plan in Action                    │
│             Run Campaign                      │
└─────────────────────────────────────────────┘
                      ↓
                  ( Impact )
                      ↓
Feedback  ┌──────────────────────────┐  Feedback
          │   Measure Advertising     │
          │      Effectiveness        │
          └──────────────────────────┘
```

LEARNING OBJECTIVES

In your study of this chapter, you will have an opportunity to:

- Understand the reasons for the growth of global advertising.
- Appreciate the difference between planning and executing advertising campaigns in a foreign market as compared to the domestic market.
- Comprehend the unique problems of organizing for effective operation in foreign matters.
- Understand the role of advertising as compared with other promotional elements in the global marketing mix.
- Understand the interrelationship of advertising and politics in the global marketplace.

Chapter 21

Global Advertising

CHAPTER TOPICS

WHAT IS GLOBAL ADVERTISING?
WHY HAS GLOBAL ADVERTISING GROWN?
    Rise of the Multinational Corporation
    Increase in Global Brands
    Increase in Global Media
    New Trade Agreements
    Increased Trade in Goods and Services
    Worldwide Improvement in Living Standards
    Political Changes
    Improvements in Communication and
      Transportation
THE INTERNATIONAL LANGUAGE OF
  ADVERTISING

ORGANIZATION OF GLOBAL ADVERTISING
REGULATION OF GLOBAL ADVERTISING
GLOBAL PLANNING AND STRATEGY
    Marketing Mix
    Creative Strategy
    Research
    Media Strategy
POLITICAL AND ECONOMIC CONSIDERATIONS
GLOBAL ADVERTISING AND PUBLIC POLICY
FUTURE OF GLOBAL ADVERTISING

When Coca-Cola—one of the pioneers in global advertising—wanted a global campaign to cover 50 countries, it used 15 different market adaptations. The company used the same commercial all over the world but included some element peculiar to each market in each of the 15 versions. On the other hand, Revlon covers the global marketplace with basically the same advertisement in each market. Major advertisers and their agencies, as they move toward an international focus, are becoming more sophisticated in adapting advertising strategy to global markets. After all, advertising by U.S. marketers has increased faster *outside* the United States during the 1980s and 1990s than in the domestic market.

The largest U.S. agency, Young & Rubicam, received in 1992 an estimated 50.8 percent of gross income from advertising placed in markets outside the United States. In 1992 it was serving clients in 54 markets around the world. The top American—as well as worldwide—advertiser, Procter & Gamble, had in 1992 approximately 46.9 percent of its $29.4 sales outside the United States. The world's largest food company, Nestlé S.A., based in Switzerland, had over 95 percent of its sales outside its home country. The Anglo-Dutch conglomerate Unilever was the top advertiser outside the United States, spending $1.6 billion in 1991.

Many advertisers, agencies, and media have long had thriving international operations. Cockerill of Belgium built its first foreign manufacturing plant (textile machinery) in Prussia in 1815, well before U.S. factories had been built abroad. American-made Singer sewing machines and International Harvester farm machinery were sold in many foreign markets by the mid-nineteenth century. The first U.S. agency to establish an office abroad was J. Walter Thompson in London in 1899, although the major expansion of U.S. agencies has occurred since World War II.

By 1992 British-based WPP Group and Saatchi & Saatchi had bought large U.S. agencies and were the two largest agency groups in the world. *Reader's Digest* and *Cosmopolitan* (see Figure 21.1) with home offices in the United States and the *Economist* based in Great Britain are available in many foreign markets. Some are surprised to learn that well-known U.S. firms, such as Lever Brothers, Saks Fifth Avenue, and Miles (Alka-Seltzer), are subsidiaries of foreign corporations.

Although overseas advertising expansion has exceeded the U.S. pace for nearly a decade, economist Robert Coen of McCann-Erickson predicted foreign advertising growth of 4.0 percent in 1993 to $169.6 billion. Total worldwide advertising expenditures were projected to $308.9 billion in 1993 for a gain of 4.8 percent over 1992.

In a study for the International Advertising Association, Starch INRA Hooper estimated that the United States spent about $128.6 billion in advertising in 1990, with Japan second with $38.4 billion (see Table 21.1). Switzerland ranked highest in per capita advertising expenditures with the United States in second place. Advertising as a percentage of gross national product varied from 2.4 percent in the United States and Spain to a fraction of one percent in Lebanon, Morocco, Nigeria, Qatar, and the United Arab Emirates.

What Is Global Advertising?

Such terms as global, international, multinational, and export sometimes cause confusion when applied to advertising. Part of this confusion stems from the fact that some business firms have wholly or partly owned subsidiaries in a variety of countries through which they manufacture and market their products. Some concen-

FIGURE 21.1

Business Magazine Advertisement Emphasizing the Global Scope of *Cosmopolitan*

TABLE 21.1

Advertising Expenditures in Leading Countries

Country	Total Reported 1990 Advertising Expenditures (millions)	1990 Expenditures per capita	Percent of GNP
United States	$128,640	$613	2.4
Japan	38,433	311	1.2
United Kingdom	15,816	295	1.7
France	12,891	225	1.2
Spain	10,350	263	2.4
Australia	3,847	226	1.3
Israel	587	127	1.2

Source: *World Advertising Expenditures*, 22d ed. (Mamaroneck, NY: Starch INRA Hooper, Inc., 1992) Reprinted with permission.

trate primarily on export from their home country or from another manufacturing country; some conduct their marketing abroad primarily through licensees or franchisees; and some engage in all these forms of marketing. Thus, we find Procter & Gamble advertising Ivory soap in Italy but exporting to other smaller markets where its local distributor may do most of the advertising. Long before it started manufacturing automobiles in the United States, German-based BMW was a major advertiser that exported to the U.S. market.

What is now the **International Advertising Association** was until the 1950s the Export Advertising Association. The name change recognized that advertising was becoming truly international—less advertising by exporters and more by advertisers, agencies, and media that operated in more than one country. Increasingly, professionals have moved to the term global, partly because they are seeking more and more to find themes or creative strategy that will apply to several countries and partly because they are putting more emphasis on **global brands.** For example, Eastman Kodak introduced and marketed blank tapes for videocassette recorders as a world brand with a worldwide agency handling advertising in each country. However, much of Eastman's worldwide business is decentralized, with companies in each country retaining considerable control over activities in that country.

Global advertising can be defined as the advertising activities of any profit or nonprofit organization in more than one country. It is similar to domestic advertising, but, as Figure 21.2 illustrates, must penetrate some special communication

FIGURE 21.2

The Process of Global or International Advertising Communication, Including Constraints That May Cause Communication Problems

constraints or barriers. Global advertising includes the overseas advertising of U.S.-based firms such as Coca-Cola and General Motors and also non-U.S. based companies like Sony and Unilever.

Global advertising includes advertising campaigns that have messages changed only slightly from one country to the next (Coca-Cola is an example). In other countries, ads are adapted to the characteristics of each market (see Figure 21.3). Global advertising includes the activities of advertising agencies, media, research firms, radio/television production houses and many other firms that serve clients in some way and also function internationally.

The special characteristics of global advertising become easier to understand if we examine the reasons for its growth and then how global advertising strategy is put into practice.

FIGURE 21.3

Print Advertisements for Colgate in Japan, Taiwan, Spain, Russia and Uruguay

Note how the same visual and Colgate brand name recur in each advertisement.

Why Has Global Advertising Grown?

A major influence on the growth of international advertising has been the rise of the multinational corporation. Many are based in the United States, but an increasing number are based in other countries, particularly in Western Europe and Japan. Although definitions vary, the multinational corporation is usually defined as one that has its major headquarters in one country but manufactures and markets in a variety of others. Thus it can take advantage of opportunities for manufacturing, marketing, raising of necessary funds, packaging, and distribution in those countries where operations are likely to be most efficient.

The multinational corporation has often been the cause célèbre of international politics and economics. It has been subjected to widespread scrutiny and considerable public vilification both in individual countries and in supranational bodies like the United Nations and the European Community (formerly the European Economic Community). Attention has focused on the rapid growth of multinationals and the suspicion that they have too much political and economic power. For example, we hear of the "selling of America" as foreign concerns buy out U.S. corporations.

Critics of multinationals have tried to pressure both host and home governments to regulate them more strictly. Criticism has been fueled by rising nationalism, questionable payoffs to government officials, rising unemployment in many countries, and a spate of critical books. However, both critics and defenders agree that the growth of multinationals has spurred the growth of advertising and that international advertising has in turn solidified the gains of these multinationals.

Rise of the
Multinational
Corporation

Although multinationals have long used global brands, they made special effort in the 1980s and 1990s to promote them. **Global brands** tend to be manufactured, packaged, and positioned the same in every country regardless of culture, economics, or distribution. For example, Canadian Club uses the same brand and virtually the same message in 46 markets around the world. Even Japan, which has had few brands, has expanded its branding policy during the 1990s. Traditionally the company name has been the only brand in Japan, but now—as more companies move into multiple branding—there is less and less identification of products and services associated with the companies.[1] Toyota is a good example.

In Europe, Germany, and the United Kingdom, marketers are most likely to favor standardized branding, according to a Eurocom (international agency) study. The use of the same product and brand name across Europe was favored most by the Germans (96 percent) and British (95 percent) compared to about 77 percent for U.S. respondents and 69 percent for French.[2]

In addition to central control by advertisers, the increase in global brands has led to centralization of agencies. Multinational clients often like to use the same agency for the same brand in as many foreign markets as possible.

Increase in
Global Brands

Most major U.S. media have expanded globally during the 1980s and 1990s. *Reader's Digest* had the largest circulation of all magazines in 1990 (28.2 million worldwide, including 17.9 million in North America). *Time* announced in 1990 a five-year plan to raise its Atlantic edition (Europe) rate base to 750,000 by 1995. Like *The Wall Street Journal,* it added United Kingdom printing plants in the early 1990s to expedite publication and distribution of its international editions. Global advertisers are increasingly using television satellite services to reach several countries simultaneously—especially in Europe.

Increase in
Global Media

New Trade Agreements

Trade agreements between two or more nations tend to lower tariffs, eliminate quotas on imports, and attempt to stimulate competition among the signatory nations. As any good marketer knows, these are important ingredients of a healthy mass market.

For example, the Maastricht agreement (European Community) if approved will remove physical, fiscal, and technical barriers to trade among the 12 nations of the European Community, the most prosperous and important markets in Europe. Naturally advertisers, agencies, and media hope to take advantage of this market, which would then be larger than the United States. Included in the new plan are uniform standards for television commercials, which would make it possible for a foreign advertiser to use the same TV spot across Europe. Although the spots might use different voice-overs in each local language, the savings in planning and production costs would be huge.

The leaders of the United States, Canada, and Mexico hope to achieve approval by 1993 or 1994 of a trade agreement among the three North American countries. In contrast 96 countries have signed the General Agreement of Tariffs and Trade (GATT). Whether trading blocks are large or small they tend to encourage mass markets and thus the growth of advertising.

Increased Trade in Goods and Services

Although much publicity has been devoted to the U.S. deficit, the fact is that U.S. trade with foreign countries increased consistently during the 1980s and early 1990s. And at the same time advertising in foreign countries increased. One reason for this: A decrease in the value of the dollar—as compared to important foreign currencies—made the purchase of advertising space and time cheaper in the United States for a foreign advertiser and the purchase of foreign media more expensive for U.S. firms.

A study of U.S. business firms confirmed that advertising has contributed favorably to the U.S. balance of trade in that the sales of services to foreign firms exceeded purchases.[3]

Worldwide Improvement in Living Standards

Although there is still much want and hunger around the world, living standards have generally improved during the past two decades. This improvement has increased both the ability and the desire of people to own what they had previously considered luxuries. Per-capita income (or gross national product) of several leading countries is shown in Table 21.2.

Political Changes

The most spectacular change of the early 1990s was the dissolution of the USSR and the movement of its satellite nations toward capitalism. Thus we saw a movement of Western firms toward joint ventures with Eastern European businesses and the establishment of new advertising agencies to service these new ventures. At the same time rules governing the establishment of foreign firms in such countries as China and Mexico also relaxed, which resulted in heightened interest in integrating these countries into the global market.

Improvements in Communication and Transportation

Alfred Sloan and his associates at General Motors traveled by boat to Germany in March 1929 to consummate that company's first real overseas venture—the purchase of Adam Opel A. G. The round-trip crossing took approximately two weeks, and they spent several weeks on the continent. Communication to the home office was limited to telegraphic cable. Today, by contrast, supersonic travel makes it possible for an executive to cross the Atlantic in a matter of hours to attend a single meeting. With vastly improved communication, such as computer networks to most countries of the world, large amounts of data can be quickly and inexpensively transmitted

---

TABLE 21.2

Per-Capita Income or GNP and Population for Selected Countries

Country	Per-Capita Income or GNP	Population (Thousands)
Israel	$ 9,460	4,371
China	360	1,130,065
India	350	844,000
Russia	3,000	147,400
USA	16,444	248,709
Japan	15,030*	123,776
United Kingdom	14,535*	57,121
France	17,830*	56,184
Switzerland	30,270*	6,628

Source: *World Almanac and Book of Facts*, 1992 (New York: Pharos Books (200 Park Avenue, NY, 10166, 1991), 734–821.
*Per-capita GNP (per capita income not available).

---

from overseas to the head office. There they may be digested by digital computers, and critical operating data can be channeled to executives.

Organizations like today's multinational corporation could not have operated effectively before these developments. Worldwide, centrally controlled business firms represent major capital investments and their success acts as a force to encourage other businesses to expand abroad.

The International Language of Advertising

As every field develops, it spawns its own special language. In baseball it includes terms like *foul ball* and *strike;* in data processing, *modem* and *byte;* and in marketing, *promotional mix.* Global advertising has become an international language in that international marketers can communicate the same message in several countries regardless of local language, local cultures, or local media. Note the example of Coca-Cola, the world's No. 1 soft drink marketer. In the early 1990s it was using a package of television commercials that stressed the uniqueness and heritage of Coca-Cola Classic with a blend of new and old film footage harkening back to its "real thing" positioning. The commercials tried to take advantage of the wide international acceptance of motion pictures and the longtime acceptance of Coca-Cola around the world.

The international language of advertising consists of symbols, part of which are primarily visual (for example, a Mercedes-Benz hood emblem), part of which are verbal (for example, brand names like Gillette and Crest). The best global communicators know when to use these symbols without change and when to use them with local modifications.

Organization of Global Advertising

At first glance the international advertising industry appears to be organized much the same as domestic advertising. It is carried out primarily by agencies, advertisers, and media just as it is within the boundaries of most countries. A significant portion of U.S. advertising abroad is planned and executed by foreign branches of U.S. agencies. However, British agencies with U.S. branches, such as Saatchi & Saatchi and WPP, solicit accounts from both their host and home countries at the same time as they serve many multinational clients. U.S.-based Young & Rubicam in 1992 handled Colgate-Palmolive advertising in 44 foreign markets and Xerox in 23. However, it also handled noncompeting local accounts in each of these markets. All major U.S. agencies and most large agencies around the world have at least one foreign office.

Ownership and control vary from country to country. In France, for example, certain agencies are owned in part by the central government. In some countries, agencies and media have joint ownership—a practice considered highly suspect by many countries because of possible conflict of interest.

By the end of 1992, New York had surpassed Tokyo as the top city in agency billings. According to *Advertising Age,* New York agencies billed $25.5 billion in 1992 as compared with $24.1 billion by Tokyo agencies.[4]

The manager of a large U.S. agency who wanted to expand internationally would have several alternatives. One would be to establish a wholly-owned branch in London or Buenos Aires. Another would be to locate an established agency in the country and purchase all or part of the stock. Another alternative is to set up a new agency jointly owned by the U.S. agency and a local agency (for example, Dentsu–Young & Rubicam in Japan). This joint venture taps the talents and knowledge of the local agency and also the prestige and experience of the foreign agency.

Yet another alternative would be to join an agency network system. There are several networks in Europe that have formed integrated groups to offer local services, talents, and ideas on an organized exchange basis.

Then again, the agency may choose to work through affiliate agencies abroad. This method seems to work fairly well where the domestic agency has an international department with good media files and some specialized personnel to keep tab on the operations.

A final alternative would be to select another agency that specializes in international accounts. This international agency would assume the job of choosing appropriate associate or affiliate agencies throughout the world. Such an agency functions much like the international department of a large domestic agency. See Table 21.3 for leading worldwide agencies.

Like the agencies, internationally minded companies and media have been divided on just how their international advertising and promotion operation can best be organized. Companies like International Business Machines and National Cash Register have worked toward an international identity by emphasizing their acronym-nicknames (IBM and NCR) rather than their full, American-sounding names.

The exact form of an international firm's advertising organization depends on a wide variety of factors (nature of product, market characteristics, management philosophy, laws, and so on). The corporate executive's dilemma in organizing an efficient overseas operation has been explained as follows:

> The goal in organizing for international marketing is to find a structure that enables the company to respond to relevant differences in international market environments and, at the same time, enables the company to extend valuable corporate knowledge, experience, and know-how from national markets to the entire corporate system. It is this pull between the value of centralized knowledge and coordination and the need for individualized response to the local situation that creates a constant tension in the international marketing organization.[5]

French-based L'Oreal, which many consider "the most global marketer in the world," decided in late 1992 to spend $15 million on an international campaign in Europe for its Biotherm skincare line. Plans call for later expansion to Latin America

TABLE 21.3

Top Ten Agencies Worldwide

1992 Rank	Agency	Worldwide Gross Income (millions)	Percentage Change from 1991
1	Dentsu Inc.	$1,356.2	−4.2%
2	McCann-Erickson Worldwide	922.3	11.7
3	Euro RSCG	876.7	−7.2
4	Young & Rubicam	822.7	−0.2
5	J. Walter Thompson Co.	774.8	12.4
6	Saatchi & Saatchi Advertising	685.6	3.0
7	BBDO Worldwide	681.5	5.9
8	Hakuhodo	661.1	0.8
9	Leo Burnett Co.	643.8	11.7
10	Ogilvy & Mather Worldwide	642.3	3.9

Source: *Advertising Age* (April 14, 1993):8.

and Asia. Like other L'Oreal lines, Biotherm will have the same agency, ad campaign, packaging, and positioning everywhere in the world.[6]

The leader in non-U.S. spending, Unilever, must coordinate its worldwide advertising from two administrative centers—Rotterdam and London. It has a joint committee composed of top executives from both headquarters to coordinate all business activities. In 1992 it was advertising in 26 countries around the world.

The principal worldwide organization for the advertising industry, the International Advertising Association, is headquartered in New York but has members and chapters throughout the world (see the Ad Insight entitled "International Advertising Association Head"). It serves as a medium for exchange of information, ideas, and techniques and as a representative for the industry on the international scene. The European Advertising Agency Association headquartered in Brussels represents agencies throughout Europe.

Regulation of Global Advertising

International advertisers, agencies, and media are understandably concerned about the increase in restrictions on advertising in certain countries and trading blocks. Some restrictions are already in place, and pressure to further regulate advertising is on the rise in most countries based on the belief that consumers need extra protection. Some laws are vague, such as Hungary's relatively new law banning ads that would "enhance the consumption of tobacco." In early 1993 a French law abolished agency commissions, decreeing that media must pay any commissions directly to advertisers.

There is increasing pressure on supranational organizations such as UNESCO (United Nations Educational, Scientific and Cultural Organization) to regulate at the international level so that international advertisers cannot avoid the more heavily regulated countries and increase advertising in the less regulated ones. Exceptions to the trend toward more regulation do exist however. For example, television in France has increased the time allowed for commercial (as opposed to noncommercial) telecasts. A major part of the effort of such organizations as the International

AD insights

International Advertising Association Head

Norman Vale is the first Director General of the International Advertising Association, the principal organization representing agencies, advertisers, media, and supporting firms in 86 countries around the world. Previous heads have been called Executive Secretary or Executive Director.

The multilingual Mr. Vale is fluent in Spanish and has a working knowledge of Portuguese and German. As a world citizen he spends much of his time traveling to corporate and individual members around the world, although the IAA is based in New York.

Mr. Vale joined the IAA in 1990 after a career in international advertising and management. He joined the Grey Agency in 1954 for a period of six years and then worked in the international operations of three U.S. based agencies, living in Puerto Rico, Germany, and Spain. He returned to Grey in 1974 as Senior Vice President and Grey's first area director in Europe.

During the 13 years he held this post, Grey Europe grew from 7 offices with billings of $100 million a year to a network of 31 advertising offices and 37 specialized communications offices in 13 countries with billings of nearly one billion dollars. In 1987 he became Managing Director, Grey International, a post he held until 1990 when Grey's international billings had reached two billion dollars.

He lectures on international advertising and marketing at universities and colleges in both the United States and Europe. Along with his IAA work, meetings, and lecturing, he maintains a fitness routine of cycling, swim-

Norman Vale

ming, and running each morning and tennis at least once a week.

Advertising runs in Mr. Vale's family. His wife has her own antique jewelry business, but she once worked in TV production at Ogilvy & Mather. Daughter Maggi is an account director at FCB/Leber Katz Partners and daughter Jennifer is a senior account executive at Grey Direct.

Advertising Association is devoted to keeping members up-to-date on the status of advertising regulation in various countries.

As in the United States, regulation of advertising worldwide can be either through government (laws or administrative decisions) or through voluntary efforts by the industry itself. In some countries where self-regulation does not run into problems of antitrust regulation, as it did for many years in the United States, voluntary or self-regulation plays an important role.

In general, global regulatory efforts cover the following areas:

1. Content of the advertising message—for example, sexism and decency
2. Type of product—for example, liquor or cigarettes

3. Media to be used (Television cannot be used for commercial purposes in some countries.)
4. Amount of advertising a single firm may use
5. Use of advertising materials prepared outside the country—for example, Australia
6. Use of local as compared with foreign-owned agencies
7. Restrictions on who may work in the local branch of a foreign agency
8. Taxes imposed on advertising expenditures
9. Transmission of research data on consumers or media outside the country
10. Use of foreign terms or brand names in ads

Global Planning and Strategy

What works at home will not necessarily be successful in a foreign market. Unilever, based in the United Kingdom and the Netherlands, has created a pool of European commercials for its fabric softener (Snuggle) produced in New York from European creative work. Previously each country created its own spots featuring the teddy bear used successfully in the U.S. Snuggle campaign. Procter & Gamble found that the fluoride appeal of Crest, so successful in the United States, meant much less to English consumers. However, U.S. trade characters such as Kentucky Fried Chicken's Colonel Sanders and the Marlboro cowboy transferred successfully from the U.S. to most foreign markets, although Marlboro sales went up especially fast in Hong Kong when the Marlboro cowboy rode a white horse in the commercials. The Ad Insight provides guidelines for globalizing advertising strategy. The print ad promoting the international brand, SONY, is especially well suited to the German market, as shown in Figure 21.4.

FIGURE 21.4

German Print Ad for Sony Stereo Equipment, an International Brand

Headline says "Scenario. Design for well-defined relations." Couple argues whether technical and sound superiority or the look of the building block-like stereo is a more important feature.

Guidelines for Transferring Advertising Strategy to a Foreign Market

1. Study the environment in which the advertising is to be run. Every market is different, if not on the surface at least beneath it. Are cultural barriers such as language or religion or ethics important in acceptance of the product and in understanding the consumer? Are there legal or economic barriers that will cause difficulty in advertising the product or service?

2. Check the role of advertising as compared with other promotional variables. It does not perform the same function in all countries even when it is applied to the same product. In the United States, advertising is used more often to build brand awareness or awareness of certain features; sales promotion in all its many forms is often used to add immediacy to the impact of advertising; and public relations performs a broad spectrum of services. In many countries the role of advertising, sales promotion, public relations, and even personal selling is quite different from that in the United States.

3. Study the media to be used. Some media are not available for advertising in certain countries (for example, television). In some countries, although not the United States, cinema is a major medium. Even when all media are available, they may perform different functions from country to country. Newspapers in England or Japan are normally national media, and newspaper advertising will be addressed to a large audience. In Italy newspapers are more local; in some cases they are politically suspect. In countries where television is allowed to present only blocks of commercials at a few limited times, the medium is different than in countries where television advertising is spread throughout the programming day.

4. Check the product positioning. Most soft drinks are positioned as refreshers or as part of the good life in the United States. In many countries they are positioned as desirable drinks to have at dinner instead

of wine or beer. Food is especially difficult to position in a foreign culture. For example, soup is something Americans have at lunch with their sandwich or salad. In many countries it is the first course in a major meal. Often a brand is positioned differently from country to country because it is in a different stage of the product life cycle. Polaroid was already an established product in the United States when it was in the introductory stage in France. The U.S. campaign was transferred with only minor changes to the French market, and the results were disappointing.

5. If pattern, or prototype, ads are used in foreign markets, look for local touches that can be included. When Johnson & Johnson tested its U.S. ads for Affinity Shampoo, it found that British women did not identify with the "Nancy Reagan" type featured in the ads—even though the product was in both markets aimed at women over 40. A more independent-looking, more British model worked better.

6. Keep in mind that primarily visual messages are easier to transfer than those that depend on the verbal. Coca-Cola is a good example of successful dependence on the visual. When television is used, it is always easy to add voice-over in the local language or patois to the visual message.

7. Expect that a global approach is most likely to be successful when the message is aimed at an upscale consumer or an industrial audience. IBM and Westinghouse are good examples of this approach.

8. Consider the people factor when working with foreign nationals on transferability. Some are likely to emphasize the N.I.H. (Not Invented Here) factor and maintain that the market is really different. Successful international advertisers make sure that the foreign office as well as the home office knows the rationale for transferring the advertising approach. If people in a foreign market do not want the transferred campaign to work, it probably will not work.

In planning international campaigns, special care must be given to the marketing mix, creation of the advertising message, research, and media strategy. McCann-Erickson's landing of the Puma USA (U.S. subsidiary of a German parent) account was attributed to the agency's emphasis on global advertising.[7] However, McCann-Erickson has pointed out that use of a worldwide marketing strategy does not imply that it also uses global execution.

A study of 27 leading multinational corporations found several unsuccessful and costly attempts by leading American marketers to standardize their marketing mix.[8] On the basis that there was "no need to rediscover Rome," headquarters executives often said, "Let's standardize and save money." Three major U.S. food companies decided to invade Europe with products and marketing programs quite similar to those in the United States. All three found the going rough, even in England, and had to cut back substantially on their proposed expansion abroad. They simply did not take into consideration differences between markets. The main argument given for standardizing marketing programs is to reduce costs, but there is no hard evidence that standardizing does produce savings. During the 1990s there has been a pronounced increase in globalization of advertising.

Advertising is one of the most difficult marketing elements to standardize, sometimes because of legal restrictions that require changes in the copy or make certain media unavailable, but more often because of differences in language, **culture,** economics, or distribution systems. According to one study of multinational marketing, advertising was more difficult to transfer than sales promotion, at least partly because it is more influenced by cultural differences.[9]

One large U.S. corporation marketed two major food products in France and put in effect two quite different promotional mixes. The first product was a high-quality biscuit (cracker) promoted through advertising, which met with some, but far from satisfactory, success. The company tried to build consumer loyalty for the brand as it had in the United States, but found it impossible. It experimented then with various mixes and decided to drop media advertising completely. Instead, it concentrated on contests, color films, and regional meetings where the retailers were wined and dined. During the same period, the company introduced a second biscuit that had been highly successful in the United States. The company decided to use advertising here, but to design each advertisement specifically for the French market and to remove a seal identifying the package as American. This campaign was relatively successful.

If an international campaign is to be successful input must be obtained from the various national markets as well as the firm's top management. It must be determined which elements of the marketing mix can be globalized and which probably cannot. Professor John Quelch of the Harvard Business School identified nine elements in the move toward globalization. He grouped these as follows in terms of the extent to which they may be globalized:

1. Most readily globalized
   Marketing strategy
   Product characteristics
   Product positioning
2. May or may not be globalized
   Branding
   Packaging
   Advertising
3. Almost always localized
   Consumer promotion
   Distribution
   Trade promotion[10]

After analyzing a wide variety of theoretical and empirical studies on standardization of advertising, Sak Onkvisit and John J. Shaw concluded that the key to applying standardization was to look for a "limited degree of homogeneity" at some level.

Marketing Mix

Creative Strategy

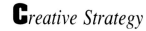

Without this, global standardization is "nothing more than a quixotic effort in search of an 'impossible dream.'"

Some creative approaches are easier to adapt than others. Pepsi-Cola found that its theme "Come alive, you're in the Pepsi generation" in some countries was translated as "Pepsi brings you back from the dead." On the other hand, some products are not well adapted to the U.S. market. A Japanese soft drink called Calpiss and a German dumpling mix called Pfanni ran into difficulties in the U.S. market. See Figure 21.5 for a successful Brazilian ad showing a couple wearing only Artex towels.

Mars Inc. successfully ran a global television ad staged on a desert island for its Bounty candy bar, but the company changed some of its European brand names to conform with their corresponding American brand names in order to make future worldwide campaigns easier. American Express found that many restaurants, stores, and other outlets in Europe were reluctant to accept AmEx cards because the company charges higher fees than its competitors. Young & Rubicam won the assignment in 1992 to develop a creative strategy that would help overcome this resistance. The print campaign that resulted was called "Acceptance." In one of their ads the first page shows a restaurant entrance in black and white with only the big, blue AmEx decal in color on the door. The second page featured a big plate with the names and addresses of eight select European restaurants that display the AmEx decal.

In working out creative strategy it is wise to emphasize the visual wherever possible. Television is particularly well suited to visual communication, although the print media also may profit from a visual emphasis. Good examples are Coca-

FIGURE 21.5

Brazilian Advertisement for a Well-Known Brand of Towels

Headline translates, "Artex Towels: For people who are sensitive inside and out."

Toalhas Artex. Para pessoas sensíveis por dentro e por fora.

ARTEX
Viver com arte.

Cada gotinha do seu corpo é absorvida com carinho pelas Toalhas Artex. Macias, 100% algodão. Nos modelos clássicos, românticos ou contemporâneos para você escolher aquela que mais combina com você. Nova coleção Artex. Venha correndo se enxugar nela.

FIGURE 21.6

**Part of a Mexican Print Campaign for Coppertone Waterproof
Tanning Lotion**

*Note the series of computerized pictures of a surfer riding a large wave. The
waterproof tanning formula is a new concept in Mexico, and the creative is
designed to illustrate the product benefit.*

Cola and McDonald's, which are marketed worldwide with only minor changes in the
visuals. Both are marketed as "quintessential American," while Chanel is marketed
internationally as a quintessential French product. See Figure 21.6 for a Mexican
ad emphasizing the new technology used in the product.

John O'Toole, former chief executive officer of Foote, Cone and Belding and
later president of the American Association of Advertising Agencies, believes understanding cultural differences is "essential to advertising effectively abroad" and at
the same time "a fascinating and rewarding pursuit." He warns international advertisers not to show the woman preceding the man in a commercial in Japan or Germany.
The wedding ring should be shown on the right hand rather than the left in Spain,
Denmark, and Holland. Further, Denmark is a good market to promote cigars to
women since 15 percent of them smoke cigars. O'Toole's former agency relies
heavily on the local staff in each overseas office so that creative strategy can be
attuned to the folkways and mores of the country. An example of an advertisement
for an international client prepared by the French partner of an American agency
is shown in Figure 21.7.

The Japanese market has presented a special creative challenge to many foreign
advertisers since their culture is so different from ours in the United States. Although
most U.S. agencies have branches in Japan, they tend to rely heavily on the Japanese
creative experts in their Tokyo offices. A typical advertisement for a successful
international advertiser is shown in Figure 21.8. Note the combination of English
and Japanese languages in the ad.

An approach that seems to work for some international advertisers is the development of a prototype or pattern campaign. For example, Goodyear International has
long directed worldwide advertising from its headquarters in Akron, Ohio.[11] The

FIGURE 21.7

**French Poster Advertisement for a
Volkswagen Polo Peppermint**

*Note the emphasis on price of this
German automobile. Translation:
"43,600 F [French francs] ... it is
good because I did not give you
anything for Christmas!"*

FIGURE 21.8

Spot Announcement for Sharp Corporation on Japanese Television

Note the demonstration for a 100-inch Liquid Crystal Vision TV screen. A young boy looks at a small TV set and remarks that "The sumo wrestler I see on the 14-inch screen is always smaller than I am." Moving up, the boy looks at a 37-inch screen with the image of the wrestler still smaller than he. Then comes "the 100-inch shock" from the giant screen, and the boy is overpowered by the sheer size of the wrestler.

pattern ads are based on common denominators drawn from consumer research in representative markets around the world. Finished ads are not prepared in the United States but prototype ads point the way for localization. The more developed markets, such as Brazil, Mexico, and South Africa, have more discretion as to what part of the pattern campaign they will adopt than do the firm's less developed markets. Goodyear believes that the pattern helps assure high-quality advertising—especially in the lesser developed markets.

Some researchers have found that brand awareness does not cross borders as easily as some marketing managers like to think. It does not always pay to feature the brand in the ad. In general it is more advisable to feature the brand if you are advertising luxury items, cars, services, and video/stereo equipment (see Figure 21.9). On the other hand it may be dangerous to feature brands when you are promoting food or confections.

One of the most dangerous assumptions in global creative strategy is that humor is universal. The fact is that what is humorous in one country can well be offensive in another. It is important to check through research the adaptability of a successful humorous ad in another market. See Figure 21.10 for an example of wry humor used successfully in the European market. See Figure 21.11 for a successful bridging of several potentially dangerous creative barriers.

Research

Because most global marketers do not have firsthand experience with a large number of foreign markets, they need accurate information on foreign markets. Fortunately both the amount and quality of information on foreign markets has increased in recent years. For example, A. C. Nielsen, the world's largest research firm, had 59 percent of its international revenue from non-U.S. operations, and second-ranked

FIGURE 21.9

Featuring the Brand is Advisable

The headline for this print ad for Matsushita's Panasonic car stereo in Saudi Arabia reads "Mood music on the move." The North African instrument in the ad resembling a mandolin is known as an oud.

IMS International had 67.8 percent from non-U.S. operations in 1991. According to a survey by *Advertising Age,* international operations accounted for 38.8 percent of the $3.4 billion in worldwide revenues from 84 companies, up 37.9 percent from 1990.[12]

The lack of research data is a special problem in the case of media. Media research is more likely than most other types of research to need adaptation to each country. An analysis of international advertising literature published in U.S. journals since 1980 revealed the following problems: (1) the literature has remarkably few multi-country empirical studies; (2) the vast majority of studies are fragmented, "one-shot" efforts; (3) a large number of studies fail to borrow, develop, or build from supporting fields, such as sociology, psychology, or anthropology; (4) we have not been very creative in use and development of research methodologies appropriate for international and cross-cultural studies; and (5) researchers have failed to take advantage of integrative review pieces that can serve as stepping stones for further international research.[13]

FIGURE 21.10

A 60-Second Pan-European Spot Announcement for Levi's Jeans

The spot was produced in London to depict a reverse Cinderella story. . . . A woman searches for the owner of a pair of jeans that fell from his motorbike when he defended her against a stranger one night. She wanders all over asking men to try on the pants to the song "Another Piece of My Heart," made famous by Janis Joplin. At a gym she recognizes his motorbike in front of a garage and finds the owner of the jeans inside.

Media Strategy

According to a study of international advertisers by one of the authors, the major headache facing U.S. companies advertising overseas is the problem of media strategy. Over half the firms queried said that "lack of intensive media coverage" was the major problem, while almost as many complained of "poor media data" and "media costs." These reflect the frustration almost all international media strategists face when they try to devise an international media plan. For example, many U.S. advertisers who depend heavily on television as an advertising medium find they have to forego it in important markets like Sweden (where commercial television does not exist), or "wait in line" for the limited amount of time they can buy in some other countries. By contrast, they find that advertising in cinemas—a relatively minor medium in the United States—is important in many countries and often attracts the best creative talent in that country. For example, in France cinemas reach an annual circulation of about 150 million, and each shows about five to ten commercials during intermissions.

In England, to reach the whole country with a print advertising campaign, the obvious choice would be national newspapers. But advertisers who wanted to concentrate on special groups would be likely to choose magazines. In Italy, however, the

FIGURE 21.11

Sample Ad from Newspaper Campaign in Malaysia for SmithKline Beecham's Badedas Shower Gel

Creatives had to surmount several obstacles in this Islamic country, such as not being able to show a person in a bath and only showing the model's face. The model was of mixed race to appeal to the country's varied ethnicity.

situation is almost the reverse. Newspapers are primarily local media and are read much more by men than by women. To achieve more print coverage of the whole country, the advertiser would need to use a combination of magazines that cover the whole country and are read by both sexes.

In countries like Denmark, where television is just becoming available for advertising, print expenditures are high. In many other countries, television would be much more widely used if the state did not control it so tightly (see Table 21.4).

One of the problems in international media selection is obtaining reliable information on media rates and audiences to work out efficient coverage of the target market. Young & Rubicam uses the computer to match media and markets in various countries. Whenever there is a reliable and valid survey available for purchase, the agency buys it and feeds it into the computer. According to the worldwide media coordinator, "We can evaluate the media in any country where there is a survey we think is reliable. Where there is none, we will try to get some kind of data and make it conform to our standards of media planning." A common source of information on media rates in various countries is **Media Guide International.** During the late 1980s several leading international agencies hoped to improve the efficiency of their media buying by forming joint ventures that would buy space and time in various foreign markets on behalf of the clients of the participating agencies.

Such common yardsticks as milline rates and cost per thousand are often of limited benefit in international media purchases. We commonly think of rates as

TABLE 21.4

1990 Advertising Expenditures in Various Media

Country	Print	Television	Radio
Argentina	$ 262.3	$ 250.9	$ 72.4
Australia	1,869.7	1,357.4	335.2
Austria	566.0	264.7	119.3
Belgium	527.4	321.4	21.5
Brazil	1,121.8	1,825.9	153.0
China, People's Republic	159.7	117.4	19.1
Denmark	897.1	129.3	22.6
Finland	1,167.3	210.3	62.5
France	3,627.0	2,523.3	619.8
Germany, Federal Republic	8,429.8	1,708.2	550.8
Greece	232.8	221.1	35.6
Hong Kong	363.0	421.9	37.9
India	599.9	177.1	22.9
Indonesia	172.2	26.1	53.5
Ireland	168.8	84.9	35.2
Israel	415.3	20.0	30.1
Italy	2,466.9	2,908.1	91.7
Japan	11,971.1	11,164.4	1,612.7
Korea, South	1,370.0	845.2	134.7
Malaysia	321.7	153.5	130.7
Mexico	314.4	1,649.1	235.8
Netherlands	2,232.4	331.7	59.9
New Zealand	281.2	210.1	83.6
Norway	730.4	20.0	8.0
Portugal	154.9	181.7	32.6
Singapore	200.3	95.4	6.6
Spain	4,051.8	2,393.8	784.9
Sweden	1,706.8	39.9	—
Switzerland	1,895.3	162.7	41.0
Taiwan	710.4	458.1	84.7
United Kingdom	9,055.6	4,149.4	290.9
United States	42,174.0	28,400.0	8,726.0
Venezuela	136.5	285.7	8.5
Zimbabwe	17.3	4.6	3.0

Source: *World Advertising Expenditures,* 23d ed. (Mamaroneck, NY: Starch INRA Hooper, Inc., 1991). Reprinted with permission.

Note: Amounts shown are in millions of U.S. dollars.

based on costs and demand for space and time in a free market. However, in some countries rates are set or heavily influenced by government policy, by monopolies, and by density of population.

Advertising rates are firm and nonnegotiable in some countries; in others they are merely a point from which one starts to bargain. Rates may well be higher for foreigners than for nationals. Most developed countries have at least one organization that audits the circulation of media much as the **Audit Bureau of Circulations** does in the United States. Many have a cooperatively supported research organization similar to the U.S.-based **Advertising Research Foundation.**

International media are much less important than national media in international advertising, but they are increasing in importance. For example, an Australian-turned-American, Rupert Murdoch, had by late 1988 acquired ownership of media in every major market of the English-speaking world, and Germany-based Bertelsman was the world's largest media company, with annual revenues of over $6.5 billion from publications in Western Europe and the United States. The weakness of the U.S. dollar makes media properties especially attractive to buyers from Europe and the Far East. Composite circulation for 15 international newspapers and magazines monitored by *Advertising Age* grew 2.5 percent in circulation in 1988 as compared with 1987. A 1992 survey of the most influential Europeans indicated that 34.1 percent read regularly at least one international publication (vs. 32.9 percent in 1988).

Magazines such as *Reader's Digest, Time, Newsweek,* and *Cosmopolitan* have special editions to serve foreign markets, many of which are produced in the local market under license from the U.S. patent office. *The Wall Street Journal* has both Asian and European daily editions. The *International Herald-Tribune,* edited in Paris, covers the international market. Most international publications are in English, but *Reader's Digest* publishes in 17 languages and *Newsweek* provides both a Japanese and an English edition for its readers. Many professional and trade magazines provide international editions. In general, the international media are aimed at an affluent, decision-making, or specialized market whereas the local media concentrate more on the mass markets in each country.[14] In the broadcast field, certain radio stations such as Radio Luxembourg try for international coverage, and satellites are making telecasts available to audiences in several countries of Europe where cable facilities are accessible.

Direct marketing has not developed as rapidly in Europe and the Far East as it has in the United States. However, expansion in Europe is likely to be helped by the elimination in 1993 or later of physical, fiscal, and technical barriers to trade among the 12 EC countries. Another possible help is the expansion of satellite TV, which is a major medium for direct marketing. However, inclusion of direct response telephone numbers in TV spots is complicated by the fact that some EC countries forbid it.

Political and Economic Considerations

Because Karl Marx contended that capital invested in "trade" was part of the "dead expense of the capitalistic economic system," one might assume that socialist planners would avoid advertising. Such is not the case. For example, advertising was recognized in the 1960s for the first time as economically worthwhile. In the 1970s Russia consented to have Pepsi-Cola bottled and later advertised on a barter basis (see Figure 21.12). Pepsi-Cola was bartered for Russian vodka (Stolichnaya) to be sold in the West. The government thus avoided having to convert any profits from the sale of Pepsi into dollars. In fact, marketers were still worried in 1992 about the convertibility of the ruble although a date had been set for the official debut of the convertible ruble. Consequently many foreign marketers are still reluctant to take the plunge into the Russian market.

Although some foreign marketers saw Eastern Europe as a potential disaster zone, others were intrigued by the potential of this market. For example, Gillette was running corporate advertising messages on Soviet television with ads promoting specific products to follow. And while some marketers emphasized the relatively high education level of Eastern Europeans, others saw it as a European market that was "European but not Western" where "cheating customers is as pleasant a pastime as it is in any non-Western country."[15] A study commissioned by the United States Information Agency in 1992 indicated that Russians chose technical expertise, food, and medical supplies as the principal sources of help from Westerners. Only 11 percent chose investment by foreign companies.

FIGURE 21.12

**Russian Magazine Advertisement for Pepsi-Cola,
a Well-Known Brand in Russia**

In both Eastern Europe and in China, the world's most populous market, the government has encouraged joint ventures with Western agencies and media. For example, a joint venture was consummated between Young & Rubicam and Vnesh-torgreklama, the government agency responsible for foreign advertising in Russia.

Isvestia, the former Soviet government's official newspaper, has since 1988 accepted advertising and in 1992 started publishing *We/My,* an English and Russian-language title that is a joint venture with U.S.-based Hearst Corporation.

Agencies are also moving into China in force. Dentsu Young & Rubicam has been in China since 1986; it opened a small office in Guangdon province and upgraded its now full-service Shanghai office to be similar to the one it has in Beijing. DDB Needham opened a Beijing office in a joint venture with Beijing Advertising Corp., a large government ad unit with DDB holding the majority interest. With the opening of the various socialist markets, increasing emphasis has been put on competition. The result has been a need for more sophisticated advertising. Domestic agencies in these and other burgeoning markets have copied the foreign marketers by using long-range planning. However, planning is often difficult because of the lack of detailed market research, audience ratings, and readership profiles. Other problems are the shortage of trained advertising professionals, a critical paper shortage that restricts print advertising space, the use of old-fashioned printing technology, and the wide differential between rates charged for foreign and domestic advertising.

Global Advertising and Public Policy

Although advertising professionals do not normally become involved in public policy, their actions in the international field often influence a country's relations with other foreign countries. The advertisements for foreign products and services often constitute the primary face of foreign business in a country. How many Americans are influenced in their attitudes toward Japan by the ads they see or hear for Toyota or Sony? How many Japanese or Italians are influenced by the ads for McDonald's or IBM? Non-U.S. audiences are in fact more likely to see or hear an advertising message for a U.S. product than to see or hear a message from the United States Information Agency or some other arm of the U.S. government.

Sometimes the influence of advertising on international relations is positive, sometimes negative. For example, the United States and certain other developed countries are respected for their expertise in advertising, and students wanting to study advertising are likely to head for the United States. Advertising contributes to a favorable balance of trade. International advertising tends to reflect the most favorable aspects of capitalism (for example, free competition, lowered prices, and consequent higher living standards) to many countries trying to decide which form of government to adopt. Also, in most countries advertising is a major source of revenue for the media. As foreign advertisers invest more money in local media, the media tend to become stronger, better managed and more independent of local political pressures. In some countries the role of advertising is viewed more favorably as the country moved from socialism toward capitalism. The advertisement in Figure 21.13 represents an attempt to counter racism in Germany.

Advertising is influenced by a country's adoption of a market economy where the government acts as a peace officer to make sure that competition is fair. The United States and such U.S. laws as the Federal Trade Commission Act are examples. On the other hand, some capitalistic countries such as Japan lean more toward an "industrial policy" where the government encourages certain industries or firms and discourages others.

The negative aspects of international advertising are also worth noting. Advertising messages are sometimes insensitive to local customs and cultures, especially when they promote overly materialistic concepts. Advertising can raise unrealistically the economic aspirations of a country's poor and cause disappointment when the country cannot fulfill the expectations. Foreign advertising may hurt a country's image when the messages seem naive or patronizing to local consumers. Antagonism toward the country of origin may well result.

FIGURE 21.13

German Poster Ad Designed to Affect Public Policy and Attitudes

This poster featuring the German flag is headlined "Stop the Mob." It supports the government's anti-racism campaign.

Creative Strategy for USAir in France

The following is a creative strategy statement and sample of print advertising for a campaign prepared by a French agency for a U.S. client.

1992 program

a/ The target

➡ General public

— business men/women
— managers, top executives in Paris and Paris area

➡ travel trade professionals

— travel agents, tour operators in Paris and Paris area

b/ Communication objectives

To create USAir awareness in France of USAir brand image

➡ through

— USAir worldwide brand image
— USAir new route Paris/Philadelphia
— USAir Philadelphia hub

c/ Brand positioning

USAir, with the new Paris/Philadelphia route, is the alternative for travellers to reach key markets in the USA through the Philadelphia hub.

d/ The reason why

➡ Paris/Philadelphia

— place & schedule
—> the earliest departure time from Paris
—> the early arrival at Philadelphia for connections

➡ Philadelphia hub

— fast entry into the United States
—> less travellers
—> customs facilities
—> fast & easy access to USAir connection flights
—> about 40 connections within 3 hours
—> 147 USAir jets + 116 USAir express flights per day from Philadelphia

e/ Target benefits

— travel agents + tours operators:
➡ to sell trips and/or tickets to their business (& leisure) customers by offering a highly attractive alternative route to NYC, Washington or Boston airports.
— business travellers:
➡ to reach US destinations fast and easy via Philadelphia (airport departure + schedule)
➡ to travel with a leading company providing high quality service (Department of Transportation 1991 survey: USAir, first for the fewest consumers complaints and second for on-time arrivals)

Source: CIA—Ketchum, Paris.

Future of Global Advertising

It is always risky to predict the future in such a rapidly changing area of advertising, but certain trends are already at work. If we project these into the future we find the following likely developments in the 1990s:

1. Full satellite deployment and the increase in technology will bring new media options for global advertisers.
2. Some of the largest nations, such as China and India, are slowly but steadily increasing the buying power of their people and providing a viable market for foreign products.
3. Advertising professionals will do more business away from their home countries as they build confidence and expertise in global advertising.
4. Technological improvements, such as high-definition television, computer interfacing, and electronic mail will provide new creative challenges.
5. Elimination of trade barriers in Europe and North America will heighten all forms of competition.
6. Advertisers, agencies, and media will put a premium on people who have both U.S. and international experience.
7. Competition in all forms will increase as business firms in Europe, the Pacific Rim, and Latin America generate new, attractive products and services.
8. It is likely that worldwide advertising expenditures will be close to one trillion dollars by the year 2000 and that 60 percent of that will be invested outside the United States.

Summary

Agencies, advertisers, media, and the firms that serve them have expanded rapidly into the international field, advertising and promoting products of a firm's foreign subsidiaries, its exports to other markets, and products and services produced under licensing or franchising arrangements in foreign markets. Reasons for the growth are many but the main ones seem to be (1) the rise of the multinational corporation, (2) increase in global brands, (3) increase in global media, (4) trade agreements, (5) increased trade in goods and services, (6) worldwide improvement in living standards, (7) political changes, and (8) improved communication and transportation. The increase in global advertising has fostered an international language of advertising—partly visual, partly verbal.

Agencies, advertisers, and media continue to experiment with various organizational patterns as they try to achieve a balance between country-by-country flexibility and control from headquarters. Legal requirements and cultural traditions are likely to influence the type of organization that emerges.

Regulation of advertising varies from country to country but public pressure and international organizations are making an important effort to standardize it. Regulations influence content of the advertisement, type of product allowed, use of the media, amount of advertising, materials and personnel used, taxes, transmission of data outside the country, and use of foreign terms or brand names.

Planning and strategy are basically similar from country to country but there are differences that require special attention. The marketing mix may vary because some of its elements do not fit in well with foreign markets. Creative efforts and media strategy must be adapted to the cultural, marketing, and legal characteristics of the country. Research is a problem but credible data are becoming somewhat more available. Media strategy is a special problem area since both media and media vehicles vary substantially in efficiency from one country to another.

Advertising has been making inroads in such formerly anti-advertising countries as Russia and China and in Eastern Europe. In many countries and in some supranational organizations, it is an important consideration in public policy. In developing countries, advertising is gaining recognition as an essential organ of economic growth. Even governments are recognizing the importance of advertising as a communication tool.

Questions for Discussion

1. What are the principal reasons for growth of international advertising and promotion during the past 20 years? What are the prospects for growth during the next decade?
2. Distinguish between international, multinational, global, and export advertising.
3. Why are television and radio limited as advertising media in certain countries? Do you think U.S. television should be noncommercial?
4. What guidelines might an advertiser follow in deciding whether to use a campaign in a foreign market that has proven successful in the domestic market?
5. To what extent is the advertising system of a country related to the political system?
6. Is it usually better for an agency that is expanding abroad to buy all or part of an existing agency in each country or to start a new agency?
7. How does the increase in global brands affect international advertising? What are the pros and cons of global advertising?
8. To what extent is the advertising system of a country related to the cultural, political, and economic system?
9. Should government leaders look upon international advertising as an aid or deterrent to international relations? If you think it is an aid, what steps would you recommend that government leaders take to maximize its help?

Notes

1 Laurel Wentz, "Japan Rethinks Branding in Europe," *Advertising Age* (July 13, 1992).
2 Bruce Crumley, "Who Favors Branding with 'Euro' Approach?" *Advertising Age* (May 28, 1992): I–16.
3 *United States Department of Commerce News,* September 29, 1988.
4 "New York Regains Agency Crown," *Advertising Age* (April 14, 1993):1.
5 Warren J. Keegan, *Multinational Marketing Management,* 3d ed. (Englewood Cliffs, NJ: Prentice-Hall, 1984), 567–568.
6 Laurel Wentz, "How L'Oreal Plans to Get Biotherm Line Back on Track," *Advertising Age* (September 28, 1992): I–1, I–30.
7 Alan Radding, "Puma Thinks Globally," *Advertising Age* (November 21, 1988): 24.
8 Ralph Z. Sorenson and Ulrich F. Wiechmann, "How Multinationals View Standardization," *Harvard Business Review* (May–June 1975): 38ff.
9 S. Watson Dunn, "Effect of National Identity on Multinational Promotional

Strategy in Europe," *Journal of Marketing* 40 (October 1976): 50–57.
10 Quoted by Norman Vale in "Global Marketing in Hungary—Myth or Reality?" Speech to Hungarian chapter of the I.A.A., February 1992.
11 Dean M. Peebles and John K. Ryans, Jr., *Management of International Advertising* (Boston: Allyn & Bacon, 1984), 79–81.
12 H. Craig Endicott, "Plenty of Room in Europe, 'Ripe' Asia," *Advertising Age* (June 22, 1992): S–4.
13 Roberto Friedman, "Research Opportunities in International Advertising," Proceedings of the 1990 Annual Conference of the American Academy of Advertising, Austin, TX. American Academy of Advertising, 1990, RST 193.
14 Deborah Halverson, "Internationals Aim for Top of the Market," *Advertising World,* (September 1984):10–13, 16.
15 Cyndee Miller, "Eastern Europe Bleak Now, but Long-term Potential 'very good'," *Marketing News* (June 8, 1992): 17.

Baudot, Barbara Sundberg. *International Advertising Handbook.* Lexington, MA: Lexington Books, 1989.

Boddewyn, J. J. *Sexism and Decency in Advertising.* New York: International Advertising Association, 1989.

DeMente, Boye. *How to Do Business with the Japanese.* Binghampton, NY: Haworth Press, 1990.

deMooy, Marieke, and Warren Keegan. *Advertising Worldwide.* Englewood Cliffs, NJ: Prentice Hall, 1991.

Dunn, S. Watson, and E. S. Lorimor, eds. *International Advertising and Marketing.* Columbus, OH: Grid, 1979.

Miracle, Gordon E., and Terence Nevitt. *Vountary Regulation of Advertising.* Lexington, MA: Lexington Books, 1987.

Peebles, Dean M., and John K. Ryans, Jr. *Management of International Advertising.* Boston: Allyn and Bacon, 1984.

Rijkens, Rein. *European Advertising Strategies.* Rutherford, NJ: Cassell, 1992.

Root, Franklin R. *Entry Strategies for International Markets.* Lexington, MA: Lexington Books, 1991.

World Advertising Expenditures, 23d ed. Mamaroneck, NY: Starch INRA Hooper, 1991.

Yi, Xu Bai. *Marketing to China: One Billion New Customers.* Chicago: American Marketing Association, 1991.

Suggested *Readings*

Sources of Information about Advertising

Many industry organizations will provide information about the advertising business. You can write to any of the following organizations for information on a specific topic.

ADVERTISING AND MARKETING ASSOCIATIONS

The Advertising Council
261 Madison Avenue
New York, NY 10016-2303
(212) 922-1500

Advertising Educational Foundation
666 Third Avenue
New York, NY 10017
(212) 986-8060

Advertising Research Foundation
641 Lexington Avenue
New York, NY 10022
(212) 751-5656

American Academy of Advertising
Robert L. King, Executive Secretary
University of Richmond
School of Business
Richmond, VA 23173
(804) 289-8902

American Advertising Federation
1101 Vermont Avenue, NW
5th Floor
Washington, DC 20005
(202) 898-0089

American Association of Advertising
  Agencies
666 Third Avenue
13th Floor
New York, NY 10017
(212) 682-2500

American Marketing Association
250 S. Wacker Drive
Suite 200
Chicago, IL 60606-5819
(312) 648-0536

Association of National
  Advertisers, Inc.
155 E. 44th Street
New York, NY 10017
(212) 697-5950

Business/Professional Advertising
  Association
901 N. Washington Street
Suite 206
Alexandria, VA 22314
(703) 683-2722

International Advertising Association
342 Madison Avenue
Suite 2000
New York, NY 10173
(212) 557-1133

National Advertising Division
Council of Better Business Bureaus
4200 Wilson Boulevard
Suite 800
Arlington, VA 22203
(703) 276-0100

National Advertising Review Board
845 Third Avenue
New York, NY 10022
(212) 832-1320

MEDIA ASSOCIATIONS

American Business Press, Inc.
675 Third Avenue
Suite 400
New York, NY 10017
(212) 661-6360

Cabletelevision Advertising Bureau
757 Third Avenue
New York, NY 10017
(212) 751-7770

Direct Marketing Association
11 W. 42nd Street
New York, NY 10036-8096
(212) 768-7277

Institute of Outdoor Advertising
342 Madison Avenue
New York, NY 10173
(212) 986-5920

International Newspaper Advertising
and Marketing Executives, Inc.
P.O. Box 17210
Washington, DC 20041
(703) 648-1168

Magazine Publishers Association
575 Lexington Avenue
New York, NY 10022
(212) 752-0055

National Association of Broadcasters
1771 N. Street NW
Washington, DC 20036
(202) 429-5350

National Yellow Pages Service
340 E. Big Beaver Road
5th Floor
Troy, MI 48084
(313) 362-3300

Newspaper Advertising Bureau, Inc.
1180 Avenue of the Americas
New York, NY 10036
(212) 704-4547

Outdoor Advertising Association of
America
1212 New York Avenue
Suite 1210
Washington, DC 20005
(202) 371-5566

Point-of-Purchase Advertising
Institute, Inc.
66 N. Van Brunt Street
Englewood, NJ 07631
(201) 894-8899

Radio Advertising Bureau, Inc.
304 Park Avenue South
New York, NY 10010
(212) 254-4800

Specialty Advertising Association
International
3125 Skyway Circle North
Irving, TX 75038
(214) 252-0404

Television Bureau of Advertising, Inc.
477 Madison Avenue
New York, NY 10022
(212) 486-1111

Trade Show Bureau
1660 Lincoln Street
Suite 2080
Denver, CO 80264
(303) 860-7626

DIRECTORIES AND TRADE MAGAZINES

Advertising Age
740 Rush Street
Chicago, IL 60611-2590
(312) 675-4380

Adweek
49 East 21st Street
New York, NY 10010-6213
(212) 529-5500

Business Marketing
740 N. Rush Street
Chicago, IL 60611-2525
(312) 649-5260

Editor and Publisher Market Guide
11 W. 19th Street
New York, NY 10011-4234
(212) 675-4380

*Gale Directory of Publications and
Broadcast Media*
835 Penobscot Bldg.
Detroit, MI 48226-4094
800-877-GALE

Madison Avenue Handbook
17 E. 48th Street
New York, NY 10017
(212) 688-7940

Marketing Communications Report
P.O. Box 570217
Miami, FL 33257-0217
(305) 252-7757

Media Market Guide
Bethlehem Publishing
Box 119
Bethlehem, NH 03574
(603) 869-3135

Media Week
49 E. 21st Street
New York, NY 10010
(212) 529-5500

Standard Directory of Advertisers
121 Chanlon Road
New Providence, NJ 07974
(800) 521-8110

*Standard Directory of Advertising
   Agencies*
121 Chanlon Road
New Providence, NJ 07974
(800) 521-8110

Standard Rate & Data Service
3004 Glenview Road
Wilmette, IL 60091
(800) 323-4588

OTHER ADVERTISING DATA SOURCES

A.C. Nielsen Company
1290 Avenue of the Americas
New York, NY 10104
(212) 708-7500

The Arbitron Company
142 W. 57th Street
New York, NY 10019
(212) 887-1300

Audit Bureau of Circulations, Inc.
900 North Meacham Road
Schaumburg, IL 60173-4968
(708) 605-0909

Broadcast Advertisers Reports, Inc.
142 W. 57th Street
New York, NY 10019
(212) 887-1300

Business Publications Audit of
   Circulation, Inc.
360 Park Avenue South
New York, NY 10010
(212) 532-6880

The Gallup Organization
100 Palmer Street
Princeton, NJ 08542
(609) 924-9600

Leading National Advertisers, Inc.
11 W. 42nd Street
New York, NY 10036
(212) 789-1400

Marketing Science Institute
1000 Massachusetts Avenue
Cambridge, MA 02138
(617) 491-2060

MediaMark Research, Inc.
708 Third Avenue
New York, NY 10017
(212) 599-0444

National Retail Federation
100 W. 31st Street
New York, NY 10001
(212) 244-8780

Public Relations Society of America
33 Irving Place
New York, NY 10003-2376
(212) 995-2230

Simmons Market Research Bureau
380 Madison Avenue
New York, NY 10017
(212) 916-8900

Starch INRA Hooper, Inc.
566 E. Boston Post Road
Mamaronech, NY 10543
(914) 698-0485

The Survey of Buying Power–Market
   Statistics
633 Third Avenue
New York, NY 10164-0700
(212) 986-4800

Account executive Person in an advertising agency responsible for overall administration of one or more accounts

Advertising Paid, nonpersonal communication through various media by business firms, nonprofit organizations, and individuals who are in some way identified in the advertising message and who hope to inform or persuade members of a particular audience

Advertising Council Nonprofit organization supported by the advertising industry to organize and carry out public service advertising campaigns

Advertising Research Foundation Association of advertisers, agencies, media, and research firms concerned with improving research practices

Advocacy advertising Advertising used to espouse a controversial viewpoint

Agricultural advertising Advertising directed to farmers

Agate line Unit of measuring advertising space, one column wide and 1/14 inch deep, regardless of column width

Aided recall Research method of checking readership, viewership, or listenership in which respondents are shown the advertisement or given other aids to help them remember it

American Advertising Federation (AAF) Association of clubs and other advertising groups

American Association of Advertising Agencies (AAAA) Association of leading U.S. agencies

Animatic Technique for pretesting commercials in the agency or studio with the help of live actors

Animation Drawings with movement (e.g., filmed cartoons); also displays with moving parts

Announcement Spot ad one minute or less in length

Answer print First cut, spliced, and edited print of a filmed program or commercial for customer approval

Appropriation When applied to advertising, the total amount of money allocated to a project or campaign

Arbitron One of several national firms engaged in television and radio audience research

Audience Total number of persons reached by an ad or medium

Audience composition Distribution of audience by demographic factors

Audimeter Device used by A. C. Nielsen Company to record audience tuning of television sets

Audio imagery Ability to engage the radio listener's imagination

Audiotex Leasing of telephone lines to deliver advertising messages

Audit Bureau of Circulations (ABC) Agency that verifies circulation figures claimed by publishers of print media

Background music Live or recorded music used to establish the mood and tempo of a program or announcement

Bait-and-switch advertising Offering a product at an unusually low price to entice buyers to the store, where they may find it difficult or impossible to buy the product at the advertised price

Ben Day (also benday) A method of laying tints (dots, lines, or other textures) on negatives or metal plates. Ben Day plates are copper or zinc

Better Business Bureau (BBB) Organization supported by business contributions to find and aid in prosecution of commercial and financial frauds and to correct misleading advertising

Billing Total of bills charged clients by an agency, including media costs, production costs, and agency charges

Bleed The area of a plate or print that extends beyond the trim mark of the printed page, allowing the background to extend to the edge of the page

Block Wood or metal base on which a printing plate is mounted. A mounted plate is "blocked"

Body text Main copy block of an advertisement

Bold A heavy-faced type, usually used with lighter faced type to show emphasis or to attract attention. Also called boldface

Bonus pack Promotion providing customers with more of the product for the regular price

Border Finishing line or design around the edge of a plate; also, a metal rule or design around the edge of a printed ad

Brand equity Value that a brand can add to the product independent of other production and marketing factors

Brand manager Person in an advertiser's firm responsible for marketing a particular brand

Broadcast Advertisers Report (BAR) Commercial broadcast monitoring service available on a network and market-by-market basis

Broadsheet Standard size of the newspaper

Budget When applied to advertising, a specific itemization of each cost associated with a project or campaign

Bureau of Alcohol, Tobacco, and Firearms Division of Treasury Department involved in advertising regulation

Buyer behavior The area of research and investigation that seeks to understand why and how people purchase and consume products

Buying service *See* **Media buying service**

Cable television System whereby television signals are disseminated to subscriber homes by cable and paid for by subscription

Campaign Series of ads with a similar theme placed in one or more media over a particular period

Caption Text accompanying an illustration

Category management system System whereby each brand within a category has an advertising and brand manager

Cents-off promotion Promotion through reduction in price

Channel One Television news and feature program prepared by Whittle Communications for the classroom

Circulation Number of copies of a publication that are distributed

Classified Advertising arranged according to the product or service promoted

Client Advertiser served by an agency or medium

Close-up (CU) Close-range camera shot to show a single object or part of a person (usually the head and shoulders)

Column inch Unit of space one column wide, one inch deep

Communication Exchange of meaning between sender and audience

Competitive spending Budgeting approach based on expenditures of competitors

Composition Setting of type for printing

Comprehensive Layout of a printed advertisement indicating elements to be included, how they are arranged, and what the headlines and body text will say

Computer graphics Devising of special effects in TV commercials through use of computers

Connotative meaning Subjective or evaluative interpretation of what a sign, symbol, or message means

Consumer behavior *See* **Buyer behavior**

Consumer franchise The portion of the market loyal to a particular brand. Such loyalty usually translates to repeat purchases

Consumerism The focusing of social pressure on business to dramatize the rights of those who buy goods and services

Contextual meaning The interpretation evoked by the surroundings in which the message is read, listened to, or seen

Continuity Sequence within an outline or script; also the group of name cards that make up the completed slide film. In measurement, the period of availability for exposure to media. In media scheduling, the general pattern of message deliveries over a specified period of time

Controlled circulation Distribution of publications, usually free, to selected individuals

Cooperative (co-op) advertising Retail advertising partly or fully paid for by a manufacturer; also, a single campaign sponsored by two or more manufacturers or retailers

Copy Original material—photographs, paintings, drawings, text, etc.—to be put into form for printing; also used to denote the body text

Copyright Exclusive right granted by an act of Congress to an author or artist to protect an original work for a limited time from being printed, reprinted, plagiarized, used, or sold by another without express consent

Corrective advertising Messages that correct earlier claims a company has made in advertising

Cost per thousand Cost to the advertiser of delivery by media of 1,000 circulation readers, viewers, or listeners. The figure is computed by dividing the ad cost (times 1,000) by the total audience

Creative boutique Advertising agency limited to the creative function

Cross promotion Cooperative promotion between two or more marketers

Cue Visual or auditory indication of the proper time for action, speech, music, etc.

Culture Learned attitudes and behavior of a society; often a major barrier in international advertising

DAGMAR A system for setting and measuring the effectiveness of advertising, based on various elements of the communication process. Acronym for Defining Advertising Goals for Measured Advertising Results

Day After Recall (DAR) Test to determine how many persons recall an ad's message the day after exposure

Demographic segmentation Dividing market by such characteristics as age and sex

Digital stripping Computerized technique which combines color photography and electronic retouching

Direct broadcast satellite system (DBS) Relaying a broadcast signal via satellite directly to home of subscriber who has a small receiver dish

Direct mail Advertising medium involving distributing the advertising message through the mail or other delivery service

Direct marketing Sending ad messages direct to target market to produce immediate response by mail, telephone, or other means

Directories Advertising medium consisting of locators, buying guides, and mailing lists, which carry advertising aimed at specialized audiences

Display advertisement Ad using physical incentives such as size, color, and illustration to attract readers and present the product advantageously; contrasted with classified advertising

Dissolve (DISS) Blending the beginning of a TV scene over the end of the previous scene (sometimes called "cross-dissolve" or "lap dissolve")

Drummers Salesmen who solicited business for wholesalers

Electronic recorder Device attached to television set to measure when set is on and channel to which it is tuned

Electrotype Plate made by depositing metal electrolytically on a mold of wax or metal pressed from the original plate

Encoding Transfer of message to words, visuals, motion for transmission

Expense When applied to advertising, a cost or investment that is necessary for marketing a product or service. Expenses are usually considered short-run and justified on an annual basis

Exposure estimation model Media planning model dealing with reach and frequency in media schedules

Face That part of type that makes contact and does the printing

Fade Disappearance of an image as another gradually appears, or a decrease in sound volume

Federal Communications Commission (FCC) Commission regulating television (including cable television), radio, telephone, and telegraphy in the interests of public "interest, convenience, and necessity"

Federal Trade Commission (FTC) Federal agency empowered to take action against any company using unfair trade practices (including deceptive advertising)

Feedback Communication term describing transmission of audience reaction through a specific message from audience to communicator

Field of experience Total of a person's life experience

Flat rate Advertising rate not subject to discount

Flexography Printing process similar to lithography but using water-based ink

Flight (flight saturation) Concentrating advertising within a short time period. Also an advertising campaign that runs for a specified number of weeks, followed by a period of inactivity (called a hiatus), after which the campaign resumes

Focus group Type of market research involving indepth interviewing of two or more people to elicit qualitative information

Font Part of a type series

Food, Drug, and Cosmetics Act Legislation that forbids interstate commerce of adulterated or misbranded foods, drugs, devices, and cosmetics. The act is enforced by the Food and Drug Administration

Form An assemblage of type and plates that constitutes the complete unit to be printed

Free-standing insert Unbound advertisement distributed with a newspaper or magazine

Frequency The number of times a person or family is exposed to a medium within a given period of time. Also, the number of times an ad message is presented within a given period of time

General advertising *See* **National advertising**

Global advertising   Advertising by profit or nonprofit organizations in more than one country

Global brand   A brand of products or services used by a multinational advertiser in several foreign markets

Gravure   Printing process in which the printing surface is depressed, not raised; also called "intaglio"

Grazing   Tendency of many TV viewers to flip through channels

Gross rating points (GRP)   The total weight of advertising that derives from a particular media buy; reach times average frequency

Halftone   Relief plate whose negative has been made by photographing copy through a halftone screen. Also a print made from such a plate. Halftones consist of a series of dots, the groupings and densities of which determine darkness

Hierarchy of effects   Structuring of the effects of advertising from the lowest impact (awareness) to the highest impact (changes in behavior)

High assay model   Media planning model based on simulation of consumer behavior

Horizontal publication   Publication directed to a specific job classification that cuts across many industries

House agency   Advertising agency owned or controlled by an advertiser. Also called "in-house agency"

Independent station   Broadcast station that is not affiliated with a network

Industrial advertising   Advertising directed to process users

Infomercial   Commercial which combines selling and information and is longer than typical commercials

Inquiry test   Method of comparing advertisements or media according to the number of inquiries sent in by readers

Insert   Separately printed page or pages to be added to or bound into a publication

Institutional advertising   Advertising that promotes the name, image, personnel, or reputation of a company or organization, instead of the actual products or services it markets

Integrated marketing communications   Coordination of communication tools used for a brand

International Advertising Association   Organization of advertisers, agencies, media, and supporting organizations from many countries that join together to exchange information, collect data, and work on behalf of international advertising

Investment   When applied to advertising, an appropriation that will return profits in the future. Investments are usually considered long-run and justified over more than one year

Italic   In typography, the slanted version of a typeface. *These words are in italics*

Jobber   Merchant wholesalers that take title to the merchandise they handle. Also called "distributors" or "mill supply houses," depending on the trade

Justification   Forced alignment of the column edges

Kinescope   Copy of the original program or commercial sent to the station in lieu of a videotape

LNA/BAR Multi-Media Report Service   Syndicated service that provides advertiser expenditure information for seven different media

Lanham Act   Federal statute governing registration of trademarks, trade names, service marks, and other identifying symbols used in interstate commerce. This legislation is enforced by the U.S. Patent Office

Leading   Inserting of leads (blank strips of metal) between lines of type to widen space and improve readability. Unleaded type is "set solid"

Leading National Advertisers (LNA)   Syndicated service that provides information on advertising expenditures by brand in specific magazines and outdoor advertising

Letterpress   Process in which the printing surface is raised above the rest of the surface

Line copy   Copy suitable for line plate reproduction

Line cut   Relief plate made without use of a screen

Linear programming   Mathematical technique used for media evaluation and selection

Listener diary   Method of television and radio research in which the audience keeps a continuing record of viewing or listening

List house   Company that rents or sells mailing lists

Local advertising   Advertising paid for by a local dealer; advertising that sells to the ultimate consumer

Local rate   Advertising rate offered by media to a local advertiser that is lower than the rate offered to a national advertiser

Logotype   Signature or standard nameplate of an advertiser, usually cast in one unit

Loss leader   Retail product sold at or below cost, designed to attract additional store traffic

Ludlow composition   Handset type later cast into a slug

Mail order   Product or service promoted through advertising and ordered by mail or telephone

Market analysis   Research that helps locate markets for a particular brand

Market segmentation   Process of dividing up the market for purposes of allocating advertising resources on the basis of demographic, psychological, or social criteria

Market share   Portion of a market controlled by a firm or its brands

Marketing   Planning and executing the conception, pricing, promotion, and distribution of ideas, goods, and services to create exchanges

Marketing concept   A firm's emphasis on the wants and needs of target markets as a basis for the marketing plan

Marketing mix   Combination of ingredients a marketer chooses in presenting products or services to consumers

Marketing opportunity   Area of marketing activity in which a company enjoys a differential advantage

Marketing plan   Written document that analyzes, summarizes, and directs the actions of the firm's total marketing effort

Mass communication   Communication to a large number of individuals at approximately the same time

Mat (matrix)   Papier-mâché or composition molds pressed from plate or type forms. Used for plate making

Meaning   Sharing of signs by both communicator and audience

Media buying service   Agency that focuses on one or more aspects of the media selection function

Media Guide International   Source of information on rates and related information regarding media in markets around the world

Media schedule   List of media selected for a campaign and the times and dates the advertisements will be run

Medium   Channel through which the advertising message is carried to the audience

Milline rate   Rate computed by multiplying a publication's line rate by one million, then dividing by the circulation. Used for comparing rates

Model A simplified representation of reality used to describe advertising practices and to make decisions

Multinational corporation Firm that operates in two or more countries outside its home base and maintains control over business activities from the home office

Multi-point distribution system Distribution of broadcast signal by microwave within 20–25 mile radius

Narrowcasting Broadcasting to a narrowly defined market group as opposed to a broad, undifferentiated one

National advertising Advertising purchased by a firm that attempts to reach a broad audience across the country. Also called "general advertising"

National Advertising Review Board Group consisting of members from advertisers, agencies, media, and the general public that serves as the principal self-regulatory body for advertising in the United States

National Association of Broadcasters Trade association of radio and television station owners

National rate Rate charged by local media to advertisers who do not qualify for the lower, retail rate

Negative Reversal of tone values. Black looks white and vice versa as in a photo negative

Network Series of interconnected television or radio stations

A.C. Nielsen Company World's largest market research firm, providing much audience, media, and market data to the advertising industry

Objective (task) approach A common method of budgeting for advertising in which decisions are made by setting an objective and calculating the cost of reaching it

Offset (offset lithography) Printing process in which the image is transferred to a rubber roller and printed onto the printing surface

Open rate The highest advertising rate before discounts are earned. Also called "basic rate" and "one-time rate"

Optical effects Laboratory produced transition effects (e.g. wipes, dissolves)

Package inserts Advertising literature packed into a box with a product to advertise a different product

Participating program Show sponsored by more than one advertiser

Percent-of-sales method Budgeting approach which utilizes a fixed percentage of either past or anticipated sales

People meter Electronic device used to measure how individuals view TV programs and commercials

Personal selling Selling through personal representatives as compared with selling through the mass media

Photomatic Pretesting technique utilizing photographs of scenes and recorded audio on tape

Pica In typography, a unit of linear measurement equaling 12 points or $\frac{1}{6}$ of an inch

Place-based media In-store media providing special programming and advertising

Point Standard vertical type size measurement—$\frac{1}{12}$ of a pica or $\frac{1}{72}$ of an inch

Point-of-purchase display Display prepared by a manufacturer for use by dealers

Positioning Creative strategy in which an attempt is made to place the product or service in the consumer's mind and differentiate it from competitors' products

Primary advertising Advertising promoting generic products or services

Primary research Information collected specifically for the current investigation

Prime time Hours when viewing is at its peak on television, usually the evening hours

Production Conversion of an advertising idea into a print or broadcast advertisement. Also used to denote the department of an agency or other organization responsible for broadcast production problems and handling, printing, and engraving

Product life cycle Concept that suggests products pass through various stages of development during their life (e.g. introduction, growth, maturity, and decline)

Professional advertising Advertising directed to professionals such as doctors and lawyers

Program rating (delivery) Percentage of the sample tuned to a program or station at a particular time

Projective technique Research method using indirect approaches for gaining information

Proof Photoprint or photostat of the completed print ad

Prototype campaign Also called pattern campaigns. Used internationally as the basis for localization in various countries

Psychographics Method of defining markets on the basis of psychological factors

Publicity News about a company or organization prepared for media use

Public relations The many communication practices used to build rapport with various sectors of the public

Puffery Description of a product or service that exaggerates its good qualities

Pull-push strategy Pulling or pushing a product through distribution channels by stimulating demand for it by consumers or by convincing distributors to handle it

Push money Money offered salespeople for selling a certain number or kind of product

Rate Charge for a unit of media space or time

Rate differential The difference between local and national (general) advertising rates

Rating *See* **Program rating**

Reach The number of different persons or households exposed to a particular media vehicle or media schedule at least once during a specified time period

Readership Percentage of the audience who recall an advertisement, with or without aid; also total audience of a publication

Reason-why copy Features a reward in headline and backup in the body copy

Re-etching Additional etching to highlight the tone values of certain areas of a plate

Reference group A group of people an individual respects, identifies with, or aspires to join

Rep A media representative. Also slang for a national sales representative

Retail advertiser *See* **Local advertiser**

Robinson-Patman Act Legislation that forbids price and payment (including payment for advertising) discrimination among customers. Enforced by the FTC.

Roman Type face containing heavy stemmed or light strokes with serifs

Roster recall Research method in which a list of radio or TV programs or stations is submitted to respondents for recall

Rotoscoping Pretesting technique utilizing live action combined with other presentation techniques

Rough layout Rough form of a print ad the exact size of the final advertisement

Run-of-paper (ROP) Placement in any position or any page of the publication

Sales promotion Promotional activities that support advertising, public relations, and personal selling

Sample A small representation of a larger universe or market that is used to study that universe

Sans serif Type group also called *block*, *gothic*, or *contemporary*. Has no serifs and uniform thickness of strokes

Satellite television station A special type of station that may originate programming but primarily duplicates broadcasts and relays by satellite

Screen The glass plates used in halftone reproduction (e.g., 110-line screen); also, printing process in which stenciled designs are applied to a screen. A squeegee forces paint or ink through the screen to the paper

Script Type face with letters linked together giving the impression of handwriting (also cursive)

Secondary research Information already available from previously existing studies

Selective advertising Advertising promoting a particular brand

Self-mailer A direct-mail piece that is mailed without an envelope

Series Part of a family of type

Serifs Short marks at the top and bottom strokes of some typefaces

Set Locale in which a scene takes place (room, street, etc.)

Sets in use Percentage of homes in a sample where the set is turned on

Share of audience (share) Percent of sets in use that are tuned to a particular station, network, or program

Showing Measure of audience coverage used in outdoor and transportation advertising

Sign Visual, verbal, or audio elements that stand for something in the minds of both communicator and audience

Signature Single printing sheet that, when folded, will form four or a multiple of four pages

Simmons Market Research Bureau (SMRB) A syndicated that provides product usage data and information on media audiences

Single source service Research firm that provides a range of marketing information

Slick Negative on photographic paper printed by computer phototypesetting

Slug Cast line of type

Specialty advertising Medium which offers articles of merchandise with advertiser's name, message, or logo

Spectacular A large, illuminated sign, often animated, that is custom-made to fit a special high-traffic location

Split run Two or more different ads from the same advertiser running simultaneously and in similar positions in different copies of the same publication, used to test and compare response

Split screen Means of showing images from two cameras at the same time on one frame

Spot advertising Practice of purchasing broadcast advertising time on a market-by-market basis

Spot announcement Commercial that lasts one minute or less

Spot television (also **spot radio**) Market-by-market purchase of broadcast time

Spread Two facing pages, usually in the center of a publication

Standard Advertising Unit (SAU) System whereby newspapers offer national advertisers 57 standard size space units

Standard Rate & Data Service (SRDS) Major source of information on media

Stop motion Photo process used in television in which inanimate objects appear to move

Storyboard Visual units in sequence drawn to portray copy, dialogue, and action planned for a TV commercial

Subliminal advertising Advertising that operates below the threshold of consciousness.

Subscription television (STV) Television signal sent over the air to subscribers whose TVs can receive the signal through a special decoding device; different from cable television, which uses a coaxial cable to deliver the signal into a home

Supplement Newspaper feature section in magazine format

Sweepstakes Promotion involving drawing of names of winners, depends on chance rather than skill

Syndicated program Program sold to two or more local stations by an independent firm

Target market A group of people defined by certain characteristics and focused on as the intended receivers of the advertising message

Teletext One-way communication system in which pages or frames of text are broadcast and displayed on a television screen

Testimonial Statement by a user endorsing an advertised product or service

Thumbnail Miniature rough layout used to experiment with various arrangements of the elements to be included in a print advertisement

Total audience Total homes reached by some portion of the program

Trade advertising Advertising directed at retailers or wholesalers

Trademark Brand name, mark, or symbol used to identify a product or service. Regulated by U.S. Patent Office

Transit advertising Advertising messages carried on the inside or outside of public transportation vehicles or stations where people board them

Type high Same height as normal type: .918 of an inch. A plate is type high when mounted to this height for printing

Unaided recall Research method used to determine without aid whether people saw or heard advertising messages

Unit of sale Budgeting approach based on past or anticipated physical volume of sales

Values and lifestyles (VALS) Use of psychological and sociological characteristics to identify groups of consumers

Vehicle An advertising-media outlet, such as a certain magazine or a specific station

Vertical publication Business publication dealing with one industry

Videocassette recorder (VCR) Device used to record and play back over-the-air television programs. Programmed cassettes, such as movies, can be purchased or rented and viewed in the home

Videodisc player (VDP) Device similar to VCR but limited to playing back discs that have been professionally produced

Videotape Simultaneous recording of sound and image on tape. Allows immediate playback and rapid editing

Videotex Interactive electronic system in which data and graphics are transmitted from a computer network over telephone or cable lines and displayed on a television or computer terminal screen

Voice-over Voice or sound heard without its source being seen

Waste circulation Media circulation in an area in which the advertiser has no sales potential or distribution

Wheeler-Lea Amendments Amendments to the FTC Act for-bidding unfair competition in interstate commerce, especially false or misleading advertising. Enforced by the FTC

Wholesaler Person who buys from manufacturers and sells to retailers

Window strip Narrow advertising poster gummed for attaching to a dealer's store window

Wipe Fast-transition shot wiping one picture off the TV screen and simultaneously replacing it with another

Wireless cable television Transmission of broadcast by satel-lite to ground-based transmitter which sends signal to receiv-ing homes

Zapping The practice of using remote control devices to switch channels or avoid commercials

Zipping The practice of fast forwarding on a videocassette recorder to avoid the advertising messages in recorded television programs

Absolut campaign, 50
Accessibility, 240
Account executive (AE), 178
A. C. Nielsen Company, 467, 584, 603
Actionability, 240
Action for Children's Television (ACT), 83
Action-effect tests, 221–223
Action emphasis slogans, 304
ActMedia, 513, 514
Acura Legend campaign, 114
Added value, 111–115
ADMOD, 330
AD/SAT, 453
Advertisers
　account executive as liaison to, 178
　agency charges to, 181–182
　agency choice by, 168–173
　client-agency conflicts, 183
　client-agency relationship, 192
　corporate manager functions, 164–166
　early professional organizations listed, 25
　functions of, 17–18
　local (retail), 172–174
　NAD/NARB self-regulation, 146–149
　national, 163–164
　outdoor advertising, 500
　radio, 474
　ten top magazine, 448–449
　ten top newspaper, 429
　ten top radio, 478–479
　ten top television, 464–465
Advertising
　advocacy, 31, 544–545
　bad taste in, 72–73, 78–80
　bait-and-switch, 145
　brag, 30
　budgeting for, 259–271
　business-to-business, 558–565
　campaign planning overview, 199–210
　classifying, 13–17
　clearance issues, 150–157
　communication functions of, 62–64
　comparative, 77–78
　constructive vs. combative, 106–109
　consumer, 13
　continuity, 320–321
　cooperative (co-op), 423–424, 539, 556–558
　corrective, 143–144
　current volume of, 312–313
　deceptive, 139–142
　defining, 12, 3–19, 105–109
　directory, 506–509
　economic issues, 103–123
　emergence of national, 23–33
　evolution of, 19–23
　facilitating marketing goals through, 248–251
　global, 569–595
　image, 544
　informational, 281
　institutional (nonproduct), 15, 543–545
　institutional role of, 6
　in-store, 510–514

　as instrument of marketing, 37–38
　major issues facing, 157
　message production, 403–421
　message strategy of, 273–306
　motion picture, 515
　objectives of, 235–255
　outdoor, 153–154, 190, 496–506
　planning decisions, 47–48
　point-of-purchase, 512–513, 539, 555
　political, 89–91
　prices and, 109–111
　as promotion mix element, 44
　regulatory issues, 127–157
　research process, 213–232
　role during sales process, 45–46
　shift to promotion from, 268
　social and ethical issues, 69–98
　specialty, 509–511
　sports and theater events, 516
　structure described, 18
　subliminal, 78
　trade, 13, 203
　transformational, 281
　transit, 501–506
　See also Communication; Marketing; Media
Advertising Age (magazine), 156, 585, 589, 602
Advertising agencies
　account planning, 180–181
　advertiser's choice of, 168–173
　compensation to, 181–183
　described, 18
　Doyle Dane Bernbach agency, 290
　essential agency service issue, 25
　ethical issues confronting, 74–75
　evaluating performance of, 166–167
　functions of modern, 176–180
　future trends and suggestions, 193
　global ad organization by, 575–577
　global centralization of, 573
　global focus of, 569–570
　handling competing accounts, 183
　in-house vs. independent, 170–171
　internal monitoring mechanisms, 154
　Leo Burnett agency, 32
　management and financial services, 180
　1992 income for U.S., 175–176
　no competing accounts policy, 25
　N. W. Ayer & Son, 23, 27
　origins of the, 21–23
　running political campaigns, 91
　specialized services by, 18–19, 174–177, 191–192, 556
　top ten global, 577
　Trout & Reis agency, 290
　U.S. locations for, 174–175
　world's top 25, 184–185
Advertising in America (Bauer and Greyser), 72
Advertising associations, 154, 601
Advertising audiences. *See* Audiences
Advertising campaigns
　added values derived from, 112–113

　adjusting, 209–210
　client-pitch ads, 178
　corrective advertising during, 142–144
　defining, 199–200
　determining advertising budget, 208–209
　determining message and media strategy, 209
　direct mail, 489–496
　elements of successful, 8–10
　geographic segmentation, 245
　hierarchy of effects during, 64
　implementing plan, 209
　integrated marketing communications, 204–206
　Longhorn case history, 520–527
　marketing mix planning, 200–204
　measuring success of, 109
　message strategy of, 273–306
　objectives of, 208, 235–255, 521
　outdoor, 499
　planning framework, 207
　Seagram's subliminal, 78
　strategic research inputs, 207–208
　successful global, 581
　targeted to singles, 244
　tobacco, 134–135
　transit, 505
Advertising Club of New York (1906), 25–26
Advertising Council
　address listed, 601
　creation of, 31, 95
　functions of, 95–97
Advertising Educational Foundation, 601
Advertising-equals-information school, 107–109
Advertising-equals-market-power school, 107–109
Advertising objectives
　advertising campaigns, 208, 235–255, 521
　business advertising, 560–561
　characteristics of, 237
　described, 235–236
　doing (conative), 252
　feeling (affective), 252
　function of, 236–237
　key inputs to, 237–238
　learning (cognitive), 251–252
　media, 319–321
　models of buyer behavior, 252–255
　sample of advertising, 340, 344–347
　to facilitate marketing goals, 248–251
Advertising OptionsPlus, 501
Advertising Research Foundation, 588, 601
Advertising and Selling (1909), 25, 28
Advertising Substantiation Program (1971), 144
Advertising-to-sales (A/S) ratio, 262, 266
Advocacy advertising, 31, 544–545
Advocacy Institute, 135
Adweek (magazine), 602
AE, 178
Affective strategy, 284
Affirmative disclosures, 142

African-American Marketing & Media Association, 244
African Americans
market, 244–245, 311
stereotypes, 87–89
Agate Club (1894), 25
Agate line, 407, 432
Age composition, 310
Age target groups, 241–242
Aggregate consumption, 118–119
Agricultural advertising, 13, 558
AHF Marketing Research, 194
Airport Channel, 32
Albion, Mark S., 104, 116, 118–119
Alcohol-free designations, 133
Alcohol products, 80–82, 133
All-Radio Methodology Study (ARMS), 480
Ally, Carl, 71–72
American Academy of Advertising, 601
American Advertising Federation (AAF), 154, 601
American Association of Advertising Agencies, 25, 601
American Association of Advertising Agencies (AAAA), 154, 156, 175, 183, 262
American Biscuit and Manufacturing, 23
American Broadcasting Company (ABC), 459
American Business Press, Inc., 601
American Express campaign, 387–388
American Marketing Association (AMA), 38, 601
American Newspaper Directory (1869), 22
American Vision Centers campaign, 505
Amplitude modulation (AM) transmission, 475, 479
Andersen Consulting campaign, 202
Animation techniques, 384, 392
Appeals, rational and emotional, 56
Applied Science Laboratories (ASL), 225
Appropriation, 260
Arbitron Company, The, 230, 466–468, 603
Arbitron Radio Market Report, 479, 483
Art directors, 179
Artistic expression, 295
Art studios, 19, 191
Artwork, 373
ASI Market Research, 222, 224
ASI Market Research Print Plus, 222
ASI Research, 394
Associated Advertising Clubs of the World (1905), 25–26
Association of National Advertisers (ANA), Inc., 25, 154, 601
Audi of America campaign, 205
Audiences
adaption of commercial to, 397
broadcasting, 466–471
broading, 466–471
clearance issues and, 153
of commercials, 378
composition of, 468
data on global, 587
data on newspaper, 440
described, 13–14, 60
feedback, 25–27, 54, 58
future trends in TV/radio, 485
media, 309

messages to specific, 382
newspaper, 428–429, 431
penetration studies, 466
radio, 476–477, 479–482
research, 57–58
selectivity of magazine, 444–445
total, 468
transit advertising, 504
of TV advertising, 460–463
Audimeter, 467
Audio imagery, 378
Audiotex, 318
Audit Bureau of Circulations, Inc., 588, 603
Authorized sales representatives (ASRs), 509
Average quarter hour (AQH), 483
Awareness
and attitude posttesting, 228–229
creating brand, 293–295
Ayer agency, *See* N. W. Ayer & Son

Baasch, Don, 505
"Baby FTC" acts, 139
Bacal, Griffin, 169
Bad taste advertising, 72–73, 78–80
Bain de Soleil ads, 91–92
Bait-and-switch advertising, 145
Balance, layout, 370
Basic cable networks, 316
Batten, Barton, Durstine & Osborn (BBDO), 330
Bauer, Raymond, 72
Bedell, Clyde, 285
Benefits
key, 279
segmentation by, 246–248
Benetton campaign, 69–70
Bennett, James Gordon, 424
Benson, John, 29
Bernbach, Doyle Dane, 287
Bernbach, William, 286–287, 290, 293
Bernbach Award, 287
Better Business Bureaus, 25, 146
Black Entertainment Television, 459
Bleed pages, 450
Body copy, 365–368
Body text, 361
Bogart, Leo, 5, 218
Bonus pack, 536
Borden, Neil H., 104–105, 288
Boston News Letter (newspaper), 424
"Brag" advertising, 30
Brand equity, 113
Brand image strategy approach
Longhorn campaign, 520
radio commercial, 381
used by Ogilvy, 289–290
Brand management system, 166–167
Brand products
added values and, 112–113
conviction of, 296
creating awareness of, 293–295
creative leverage for second-tier, 294–295
global, 571, 573
identifying symbols of, 301–304
image development for, 250
investment in building, 262
loyalty to, 123

name recognition of, 202
Broadcast Advertisers Reports, Inc. (BAR), 219, 603
Broadcast media, 57
See also Radio stations; Television
Broading audiences
future trends of, 470–471
measuring, 466–468
research data on, 468–470
See also Audiences
Broadsheet newspaper size, 425
Broadside, 492
Brobeck, Steve, 130
Budget
checklist of considerations, 268–270
determining, 259
impact on profits, 260–262
influences on, 267
methods listed, 262–267
Shedd Oceanarium sample, 337–338
vs. appropriation, 260
See also Expenditures
Buick LeSabre campaign, 446
Bureau of Alcohol, Tobacco and Firearms (BATF), 132–133
Burnett, Leo
on advertising message, 273
on client loyalty, 169
on creativity, 300
estimating TV commercial costs, 472
hierarchy of creative objectives, 293
inherent drama approach, 282, 284–285
lasting influence of, 286–288
view of advertising, 5
Burson-Marsteller, 541
Burton-Campbell, 520
Business cycle, 116–118
See also Economics
Business gifts, 509
Business Marketing (magazine), 602
Business/Professional Advertising Association, 601
Business publications, 443–444, 562
Business Publications Audit of Circulation, Inc., 603
Business-to-business advertising
described, 558–559, 561–562
media mix, 562–564
objectives of, 560–561
successful copy, 564–566
Buyer behavior
advertising cause-effect on, 7–8, 71
advertising's role in, 252–255
creation objective and, 297
described, 248
doing (conative) objectives and, 252
objectives based on consumer, 208, 238
Buyers Guide to Outdoor Advertising, 501
Buying loader awards, 539

Cable News Network (CNN), 459, 564
Cable television
impact of, 316–317
national and local, 457
types listed, 316
See also Television
Cabletelevision Advertising Bureau, 601

Calkins, Earnest Elmo, 285
Campaigns. *See* Advertising campaigns
Caples, John, 26, 285
Captions, 371
Car cards, 502
Card inserts, 440
Carey, James, 6
Cartoons, 371
    animation technique, 392
    layout, 369
    programs, 136
Cash refunds, 537–538
Catalogs, 492, 562
Category management system, 167–168
Catspaw Productions, 420
Caveat emptor (let the buyer beware), 128
Caveat venditor (let the seller beware), 128
Celebrity endorsements, 386–390
    See also Testimonials
Cents-off promotions, 536
Chamberlin, Edward, 104
Channel, 54
Channel One, 515–516
Channels of distribution, 319
"Chicago School of Advertising," 5
Children
    advertising impact on, 83–84
    cartoon program advertising to, 136
    FTC regulations regarding, 144–145
    NAD/NARB Children's Advertising Unit,
        146
    tobacco campaigns influence on, 135
Cinemas, 515, 586
Cipollone, Rose, 135
Circulation, media, 309
Clam Plate Orgy, The (Key), 78
Class advertising audience, 13–14
Classified advertising, 186, 431–435
Claymation technique, 393
Clear radio channel, 475
Close-up (CU), 384
Clow, Lee, 285, 292
Coalition on Smoking or Health, 134, 135
Coca-Cola's global campaign, 569, 572
Coen, Robert, 570
Cole, Carole, 544
Colley, Russell, 253
Colman, Carol, 389
Color
    message through, 373
    print media reproduction, 409
    run-of-paper (ROP), 428
    used in TV commercials, 398–400
Columbia Broadcasting System (CBS), 459
Combative advertising, 106–109
Comic (Book) Code Authority, 150
Comic-strip layout, 369
Commercial camouflage, 295
Commercial speech, 128
Commercials (radio)
    described, 378–382
    duplicating the original, 420
    expenditures, 475–476, 478–479
    in-store, 514
    live vs. recording, 419–420
    Longhorn campaign, 521, 523
    national advertising on, 554

rate structure, 482–484
    See also Radio stations
Commercials (television)
    audiences of, 378, 397
    believable of, 397–398
    choosing cast and set, 414–415
    cost comparisons, 473
    creative strategy/tactics, 56, 381–383
    demonstration during, 394–395
    duplicating the original, 418
    editing the, 416–417
    effective use of color, 398–400
    film vs. videotape, 414
    French regulations, 577
    humor in, 397–398
    in-store, 514
    Longhorn campaign, 522, 524
    love-hate consumer relationship, 399
    message visualization, 394
    modern technology used, 415
    mortality rate of, 461
    national advertising on, 554
    with "plots," 383
    presentation methods listed, 384–391
    production estimate form, 419
    production services, 191
    programs vs. spot announcements, 465–466
    quality and cost control, 418
    rate structure of, 472–473
    simplifying TV, 396
    structure of, 377–378
    television storyboards, 383–384
    TV clutter and, 462, 464
    using entertainment in, 396–397
    VCR "zipping" through, 311, 318, 382–383,
        461
    videotape, 515
    within videocassette, 317
    See also Satellite transmission; Television
Committee on Public Information, 27–28
Communication
    advertising and, 37–39, 62–64
    advertising setting, 60–61
    barriers to, 59–60
    basic concepts, 52–54
    concept, 48–49
    defining, 11–12, 52
    hierarchy of effects, 7
    improved global, 574–575
    integrated marketing, 204–206, 326–327
    international symbols of, 575
    media scheduling and, 335–337, 346–347
    planning environment, 50–51
    power types listed, 8
    pretesting and posttesting effects of, 221–
        231
    process elements listed, 54–59
    through color, 373, 400
    using entertainment as, 396–397
    visual, 582–583
    within house agencies, 170
    See also Public relations
Communication-effect tests, 221–223
Comparative advertising claims, 77–78
Competition
    between media reps, 190
    brand-management system of, 166–167

handling competing ad accounts, 183
    impact of increased, 25
    regulation to protect, 129
    research on, 218–219
Competitive advertising environment, 9, 11
Competitive spending budgeting, 265
Composition, 369–370
Comprehension, 295–296
Comprehensive layout, 368
Computer technology
    database marketing, 496
    digital stripping, 411
    global media matches with, 587
    illustration and color options, 405, 410
    painting systems, 498
    personalized sales letter by, 491
    phototypesetting, 408
    promotional material sent via, 564
    video in-store commercials, 514
    See also Technology
ConAgra, 311
Concentration strategy, 240–241
Condoms, 82
Consent order, 140
Constructive advertising, 106–109
Consumer advertising, 13
Consumer advocates, 130
Consumer information processing (CIP), 58
Consumerism, 130–131
Consumer magazines, 443
Consumer organizations, 131
Consumer promotions
    cash refunds, 537–538
    cents-off deals and price deals, 536
    contests and games, 536–537
    continuity-patronage programs, 536
    coupons, 534
    defining, 532–533
    premiums, 534–535
    sampling, 535–536
    See also Sales promotion
Consumers
    advertising and behavior of, 9, 11
    advertising duration on, 122–123
    behavior of, 7, 71, 208, 216–217, 297
    buyer behavior models, 252–255
    coupons redeemed by, 534
    creative leverage with, 294–295
    demographic factors, 241–245, 341–345
    direct marketing to, 203–205
    geographic factors, 245
    influencing choices of, 113–114
    learning hierarchies of, 64
    love-hate relationship with commercials, 399
    protection of children/elderly, 129
    psychographics and lifestyle of, 245–246
    rise of consumer movement, 30
    sales promotion impact on, 533
    understanding behavior of, 238
    use of retail ads, 554
    See also Marketers; Research; Target market
Consumption, 118–119
Contests, 536–537
Continuity, campaign strategy, 320–321
Continuity programs, 536
Contrast, layout, 371
Controlled circulation, 424

Controversial products, 80–82
Conventions, 538–539
Conviction, 296
Cooperative (co-op) advertising, 423–424, 539, 556–558
Copy
  advertising decisions on, 48
  as agency creative service, 178–179
  as artistic expression, 295
  business advertisement, 564–565
  copy platform described, 279, 281–282
  creative objectives of, 292–297
  differential-copy advantage, 278–279
  during postwar years, 32
  magazine, 190
  multistage encoding process of, 60
  origins of, 22–23
  Shedd Oceanarium sample, 338–339
  significance of using, 57
  types of body, 365–368
  use of "free" concept, 510
  See also Message strategy; Print advertising
Copy platform, 279, 281–282
Copyright Act of 1978, 137
Corporate advertising, 15
Corrective advertising, 143–144
Cost per Rating Point (CPRP), 473
Cost per thousand (CPM), 309, 452, 473
Council of the Better Business Bureaus, 83
Coupons, 534
CPM (homes), 473
Creative boutiques, 18–19, 174, 191
Creative Code (AAAA), 154, 156
Creative director, 179
Creative leverage, 294–295
Creative mix, 283
Creative objectives
  awareness, 293–295
  comprehension, 295–296
  consumer action, 297
  copy, 292–297
  copy platform statement of, 279
Creative Review Board, 383
Creative services, 178–179
Creative strategy
  commercial, 56
  global advertising, 581–584
  Longhorn campaign, 521–522
  summary of, 284
  USAir in France, 592
Creative tactics, 56
Creative work plan, 280
Creativity
  brainstorming technique, 301
  judgement criteria listed, 297–298
  message strategy and, 298–301
  production process, 404–405
  research on, 300–301
  specialty item, 510
Credibility, 397–398
Crichton, John, 288
Crisis in control of consumption, 23
Crossley, Arch, 28
Cross-promotions, 536
CU (close-up), 384
Cultural values
  advertising influence on, 17

global advertising and, 580–584
global media strategy and, 586–589
research on, 230
  See also Social/cultural environment
Cume, 483
Cummings, Barton, 286
Cumulative Radio Audience Method (CRAM), 480
Cut technique, 384
Cutting, Richard, 152

DAGMAR model, 253–254
D'Arcy Masius Benton & Bowles (DMB & B), 246
Database marketing, 496
Data collection, 215
  See also Research
Day, Benjamin, 424
Day After Recall (DAR), 224
DDB Needham, 590
Dealers, 429
Deceptive advertising
  agencies control over, 154
  association control over, 154
  described, 139–140
  FTC remedies to, 140–142
  media clearance policies and, 151–154
  trade associations control over, 154–155
Decoding, 54, 58
Defining Advertising Goals for Measured Advertising Results (DAGMAR), 253–254
Del Monte Foods campaign, 447
Delta Air Lines advertising campaign, 89–90
Demographic factors
  radio audience, 474
  sample case, 341–345
  sampling according to, 536
  target market, 241–245
  See also Geographic segmentation
Demonstration commercial, 386
Department of Agriculture, 132
Department of Transportation, 137
Dervin, Brenda, 107
Descriptive copy, 367
Dialogue commercials, 391
Diary method, 468
Differential-copy advantage, 278–279, 291
Differentiation strategy, 241
Diffusion strategy, 55–56
Digital broadcasting, 480
Digital stripping, 411
Direct-action advertising, 16–17
Direct broadcast satellite system (DBS), 316–317
Direct mail
  advantages of, 492–493
  business-to-business, 563
  buying, 493–495
  described, 489–490
  DMMA control over, 153
  future trends, 517
  limitations of, 493
  preparation of, 496
  related advertising concepts, 490
  types listed, 490–492
Direct Mail List Rates and Data, 495

Direct Mail Marketing Association (DMMA), 153
Direct marketing
  communication through, 204–205
  described, 490
  distribution through, 203
  future trends in, 517
Direct Marketing Association, 602
Directory advertising, 506–509
Direct premiums, 534–535
Direct response, 490
Direct-selling houses, 510
Discount mall outlets, 552
Discovery Channel, The, 459
Display loader, 539
Displays
  advertising, 431–432, 507
  point-of-purchase (P-O-P), 512–513, 539, 555
Disposable income, 118
Dissonance-attribution hierarchy, 64
Dissonance-attribution model, 254–255
Distribution
  choosing channels of, 203
  direct mail, 494
  strategy, 43
Distributors, 510
Do-feel-learn hierarchy, 64
Do-feel-learn model, 254–255
Doggett, Dennis, 557
Doing (conative) advertising objectives, 252
Dominick, Joseph, 60
Donut commercial, 381–382
Doyle Dane Bernbach agency, 290
Dramatization commercials, 389–391
Drive-throughs, 552
Drummers, 21
Dummy advertising vehicles, 223
Duplication methods, 412
Durability, 297
Dusenberry, Philip, 285, 292
Dzodin, Harvey, 152

Ebony (magazine), 311
Economic Effects of Advertising, The (Borden), 104
Economic environment
  defining advertising, 11
  during 1920s, 27–28
  during Great Depression, 28–30
  World War II, 30–31
Economics
  advertising impact on, 5–6
  advertising in terms of, 105–109
  business cycle, 116–118
  consumer choice, 113–114
  duration effects of advertising, 122–123
  factors affecting prices, 109–116
  improving advertising, 122
  Rolling Stone's case study, 119–120
  theories of, 103–109
Economists, 103–105
Editorial layout, 369
Editor and Publisher Market Guide (magazine), 602
Education target groups, 243
Elderly stereotypes, 86–87

Electronic measurement techniques, 231
Electronic media, 412–413
  See also Television
Emotional appeals, 56
Encoding, 54
Entertainment
  need for, 294–295
  using, 396–397
Environment
  advertising and urban, 20–21
  creativity and, 301
  defining advertising, 9, 11
  opportunities, 41–42
  regulatory, 11, 129–137
  See also Social/cultural environment
Environmental noise, 58
Environmental opportunities, 41–42
Environmental Protection Agency, 137
ESPN, 459, 564
Essential agency services, 25
Estée Lauder campaign, 446–447
Ethics
  advertisement systems of, 73–74
  advertising associations code of, 154
  agency compensation issues, 182–183
  comparative advertising, 77–78
  controversial products, 80–82
  deceptive advertising practices, 75–77
  major advertising issues, 157
  offensive advertising, 78–80
  political advertising, 89–91
  subliminal advertising, 78
Exchange, 38
Executional-impact approach, 292
Execution emphasis approach, 290
Exhibits, 542, 562–563
Expenditures
  agency media, 183, 186
  business-to-business advertising, 560–561, 563
  changing media, 311–312
  direct mail, 493–495
  directory advertising, 508–509
  during sales process, 46
  global advertising, 571, 576
  global media, 588
  national supplements, 441
  outdoor advertising, 500–501
  point-of-purchase (P-O-P) displays, 512
  radio advertising, 475–476, 478–479, 484
  retail advertising, 555
  sales promotion, 204, 260–261
  savings with house agency, 170
  for selected retail businesses, 551
  setting advertising budgets, 208–209
  specialty advertising, 509–510
  of top 20 U.S. advertisers, 164
  transit advertising, 504–506
  TV advertising, 461, 472–473
  World advertising, 570
  See also Budget; Revenues
Export Advertising Association, 571
Exposure distribution media models, 331
Exposure estimation media models, 330–331

Families
  changing composition of, 310

life cycle, 243–244
  of type, 407
Farm publications, 443, 562
Farris, Paul W., 104, 116, 118–119
Fast-close advantage, 446
FCB (Foote, Cone & Belding's) Strategy Planning Model, 291–292, 293
Federal Communications Commission (FCC), 83, 132–137
  See also Regulations
Federal Energy Regulatory Commission, 137
Federal Trade Commission Act (1914), 132
Federal Trade Commission Act (1938), 30, 591
Federal Trade Commission (FTC)
  affirmative disclosure orders, 142
  "Baby FTC" acts, 137–139
  corrective advertising orders, 143–144
  deceptive advertising control by, 139–142
  Federal Practice Rules issued by, 155
  function of, 132
  guidelines regarding children, 83
  information intent of, 78
  political advertising regulations, 128
  puffery and, 76
Federation of Women's Advertising Clubs of the World, 26
Feedback
  described, 54, 58
  origins of technologies, 25–27
Feeling (affective) advertising objectives, 252
Feeling power, 8
Feel-learn-do model, 254
Field of experience, 53
"Finally Somebody Has to Get Out an Ad" (speech by Leo Burnett), 273
Finished layout, 368
First Amendment rights
  advertising and, 93–94
  advertising to children and, 83
  clearance policies and, 153
  commercial speech protection, 128
  political advertising and, 89
  tobacco and alcohol advertisers and, 81
Flat newspaper rates, 437
Fleishman-Hillard, 541
Flexography, 410
Flights, 439
Focus groups, 277
Focus pretesting groups, 223–224
Folder, 492
Food, Drug, and Cosmetic Act (1938), 30
Food and Drug Administration (FDA), 132–133
Fox, Stephen, 5, 32, 72
Franklin, Benjamin, 490
Frazer, Charles, 282, 284
Freberg, Stan, 379
Frederick, Christine, 26
"Free" concept, 510
Freedom of speech. *See* First Amendment rights
Free standing insert (FSI), 440, 534
Frequency, media, 320
Frequency modulation (FM) transmission, 475, 479
FTC Improvements Act (1980), 132

FTC Trade Improvements Act (1975), 132
Full-creative service, 420
Functional advertising classifications, 14

Galbraith, John Kenneth, 115, 118
Gale, Harlow, 25
Gale Directory of Publications and Broadcast Media (magazine), 602
Gallup & Robinson Inc., 222
Gallup, George, 28
Gallup Organization, The, 603
Galvanic skin response (GSR), 225
Games, 536–537
Ganz, Harve, 505
Gaze motion, 371
Gender target groups, 242, 310
General advertising
  described, 14
  newspaper, 186, 188, 429, 431–432
  See also National advertising
General Agreement on Tariffs and Trade (GATT), 574
Generic creative strategy, 284
Geographic segmentation, 245, 324–325
  media plan consideration, 335, 345
  100-GRP buy, 501
  radio measurements of, 483
  radio station, 475, 476
  spot advertising to, 459–460
  See also Demographic factors
Georgescu, Peter, 115
Getchell, J. Sterling, 285
Gift Pax Inc., 536
Global advertising
  described, 570–572
  future trends, 593
  growth of, 573–575
  international language of, 575
  marketing mix, 581
  media strategy, 586–589
  1990 expenditures, 571
  organization of, 575–577
  planning and strategy of, 579–581
  political and economic issues, 574, 589–590
  public policy, 590–591
  regulations of, 577–579
  research on, 584–585
  stereotyping in, 85
Global brands, 571, 573
Global living standards, 574
Global politics, 574, 589–590
Global transportation, 574–575
Goodyear Certified Auto Service campaign, 239
Gossage, Howard, 285
Goughenur, Bob, 245
Government
  federal authorities listed, 137
  federal regulation agencies, 132
  influence over media by, 93
  Library of Congress, 137
  major regulation laws listed, 132
  Patent Office, 136–137
  Postal Service, 137
  public disapproval and regulations by, 30
  regulatory environment created by, 11, 129–137

state and municipal, 145
See also Federal Communications Commission (FCC); Regulations
Gravure, 410
Grazing, 382–383
Great Depression, The, 28–30
Greeley, Horace, 424
Green Giant peas campaign, 284
Greyser, Stephen, 72
Gross rating points, 320, 504
Ground wave, 475
Gutters of white space, 371

Halftone, 408–409
Halftone screen, 408–409
Harvey Research Organizations Inc., 222
Headlines
    attention through, 362–363
    checklist for effective, 366
    subheads, 365
    types of, 363–365
Health focus, 311
Hierarchy of effects, 7, 64
High Assay Media Model, 330
"High involvement" model, 253–254
Hill & Knowlton, 541
Hispanic Business (magazine), 311
Hispanic market, 244, 311
Hispanic stereotypes, 86
Hopkins, Claude C., 22–23, 285–286
Horizontal publications, 562
Hosfield, Rick, 462
House agencies, 170–171
Hower, Ralph, 22, 30
Human needs and wants, 38
Humor
    in commercials, 397–398
    in copy, 367
    global differences in, 584
Hunt, Shelby, 107

Ideas
    encoding, 56
    illumination step, 300
    managing, 299
    verification of, 300
    See also Creativity; Information
Identifying symbols
    guidelines for using, 305
    licensed names, 302
    protection for, 304–305
    slogans, 303–304
    trade characters, 303
    types of, 301–302
Illustrations
    classifying, 372
    functions of, 371
    print media reproduction, 408–410
    techniques and color, 373
Image, 56, 289
    See also Products
Image advertising, 544
Image consistency, 297
Image transfer, 382
Income
    disposable, 118
    global, 575

Income target groups, 242–243
Independent program producers, 189
Indirect-action advertising, 16–17
Industrial advertising, 13
Industrial magazines, 443
Industry concentration, 114–116
Inferential Focus, 389
Inflatables, 498
Infomercials, 133–134, 312
Information
    awareness of, 293–295
    comprehension of, 295–296
    conviction of, 296
    creative process and, 300
    on global audiences, 587
    impact on consumers, 295
    product and media usage, 315
    public relation speakers, 543
    using audience data, 468–470
    See also Ideas; Research
Information research, 26–27
    See also Research
Information Resources Inc., 230
Information school. *See* Market competition school
Informational advertising, 281
Inherent drama approach, 282, 284–285
Inquiry/direct response pretesting, 25–26, 229
Inquiry testing, 25–26
Inserts
    FSI (free standing), 440
    newspaper, 429
    tabloid vs. card, 440
    vs. ROP, 439–440
Inside-of-vehicle ads, 502
Institute of Outdoor Advertising, 602
Institutional (nonproduct) advertising, 15, 543–545
Institutional roles (advertising), 6
In-store media, 510, 512–514
In-store radio, 514
In-store television, 514
Integrated marketing communication, 204–206, 326–327
International advertising. *See* Global advertising
International Advertising Association (IAA), 571, 577–578, 601
International Business Machines (IBM), 576
International Newspaper Advertising and Marketing Executives, Inc., 602
Interpersonal communication setting, 60–61
Interpersonal communicators, 55–56
Interpersonal influence, 123

Jaffe, Daniel, 157
Jobbers, 21
Johnnie Walker campaign, 85
Judicious Advertising (1903), 25
Justification, typeset copy, 407
J. Walter Thompson agency, 16–17, 178, 244, 569

Kaatz, Ron, 326–327
Kaldor, Nicholas, 104
Kellogg's campaign, 206

Kennedy, John E., 6, 23, 285
Kennelly-Heaviside layer, 475
Key, Wilson Bryan, 78
Key benefits, 279
Keynes, John Maynard, 104
Kinescope, 418
Kirkpatrick, Miles, 138
Krone, Helmut, 287
Krugman, Herbert, 254
Kummel, Eugene, 287
Kurnit, Paul, 169

Laband, David N., 107
Laboratory of Advertising Performance (LAP) study, 561
Landsdowne, Helen, 285
Lanham Act (1947), 132, 136–137
Lanham Trade-Mark Act (1946), 301
Lasker, Albert D., 23, 57
Lawrence, R. Quigg, 169
Layouts, 368–371
Leading, 407
Leading National Advertisers (LNA), Inc., 219, 603
Leaflet, 492
League of Advertising Women of New York, The, 25–26
Learn-feel-do hierarchy, 64
Learn-feel-do model, 253–254
Learning (cognitive) advertising objective, 251–252
Learning hierarchy, 64
L'eggs pantyhose packaging, 201–202
Leo Burnett agency, 32
Let the buyer beware concept, 128
Let the seller beware concept, 128
Letterpress, 410
Levan, Sharon, 535
Leverage, 297
Levitt, Theodore, 39
Lewis, Richard, 50
Library of Congress, 132, 137
Licensed names, 302
Lifestyle, consumer, 245–247
Lighting, bulletin, 498
Linear programming media model, 330
Line art illustration, 408–409
Lippert, Barbara, 85
Listerine campaign, 144
List houses, 495
Litigated cease and desist order, 140
Live action technique, 392
Living standards, 574
LNA/Arbitron Multi-Media Report Service, 219
Lobbying, 542
Local advertising, 14
Local cable system programs, 316
Local display, 186
Local newspaper rates, 436–437
Local radio channel, 475
Locking power, 8
Logotype, 302
Longhorn advertising campaign, 520–527
Longman, Kenneth, 278
Lord & Thomas agency, 23
L'Oreal, 576–577

Low-involvement learning hierarchy, 64
"Low involvement" model, 254
Lynch, William, 169

Maas, Jane, 378
Maastricht agreement, 574
McCaffrey, James, 288
McCann-Erickson, 225
McCollum Spielman Worldwide, 194
McGruff, The Crime Dog campaign, 96–97
Machine-assisted interpersonal communication
  setting, 60–61
McKerrow, George, Jr., 520
McLaughlin, Robin, 275
McManus, Theodore, 285
Madison Avenue, U.S.A. (Mayer), 7
Madison Avenue Handbook (magazine), 602
Magazine Publishers Association, 602
Magazines
  advantages of, 444–447
  advertising departments within, 189–190
  advertising subsidy myth, 119–121
  advertising trade, 156
  circulation/readership patterns, 449–450
  clearance policies, 151, 153
  cost per thousand (CPM), 452
  coverage sold in, 312
  described, 57
  effective advertisements in, 451
  future trends, 453
  kinds of advertisers, 448–449
  limitations of, 448
  media plan development, 352–355, 358
  rate structure, 452
  readership by education level, 328
  services to advertisers, 445
  sizes and shapes of, 450–451
  specialized, 311
  split run testing, 448
  types of, 443–444
Magnuson-Moss Warranty Act/FTC Trade Improvements Act (1975), 132
Mailing list, 495, 563
Mail-order advertising, 490
Mail premiums, 535
Male-female roles, 310
Malls, 550–552
Manhattan Landing commercial, 394
Manning, Burton, 394
Manufacturers
  emergence of advertising by, 23–25
  product reassignment by, 202
  retail advertisers and, 173
  urbanization of, 19–21
Market competition school
  described, 107–109
  on prices and advertising, 110
Marketers
  advertising cause-effect on, 7
  awareness of subliminal techniques, 78
  coupons distributed by, 534
  influence of, 93
  international focus of U.S., 569
  L'Oreal, 576–577
  rise of public disapproval of, 30, 72–73
  use of audiovisual material, 564
  See also Consumers

Marketer's Guide to Media, 472
Marketing
  ad agency services in, 179
  advertising as function of, 165–166
  advertising objectives and, 235–255
  Coca-Cola's global, 569, 572
  concept vs. selling concept, 38–40
  database, 496
  defining, 11, 38
  direct, 203–205
  facilitated through advertising, 248–251
  identifying opportunities, 41
  industry concentration, 115–116
  inquiry testing, 25–26
  objectives, 42
  packaging, 201–202
  plan, 40–48
  rise of feedback technologies, 25–27
  rise of information research, 26–27
  See also Market competition school; Market
    power school
Marketing associations, 601
Marketing Communications Report, 602
Marketing mix
  campaign planning of, 200–204
  decisions listed, 43
  defining, 11
  global, 581
  promotion in, 203–204
  selecting distributions, 203
  setting prices, 202–203
Marketing plan
  advertising objectives, 47–50
  basic components of, 41–42
  determining strategy, 43
  global advertising, 579–581
  objectives and media, 318–319
  promotional strategies, 46–47
  promotion mix, 43–46
  setting objectives, 42–43
  See also Communication
Marketing Science Institute, 603
Marketing strategy
  determining, 43
  global advertising, 579–581
  media planning as part of, 318–319
Market power school, 107–110
Market tests, 229
Markets
  business, 560
  changes in structure of, 310–311
  defining, 38
  magazine coverage of, 312
  monitoring, 230–231
  newspaper advertising and, 438–439
  newspaper coverage of, 429–430
  radio coverage of, 478, 483–
    484
  segmentation decision, 43
  strategic research on, 218
  target, 238–248
  television coverage, 471
Marlboro man image, 289–290
Marshal, Alfred, 104, 106
Marsteller, William, 6, 301
Mass advertising audiences, 13–14
Mass communication

advertising as form of, 52
  setting, 60–61
Mass communicators, 55
Mass media, 19
Mass production, 19–20
Mat, 412
Matrix, 412
Maybelline campaign, 251
Mayer, Martin, 7, 193
Maynes, E. Scott, 130
Meaning (communication), 54
Measurability, 240
Mechanical noise, 59
Media
  ad agency department of, 179
  ad agency expenditures for, 183, 186
  ad allocation by type of, 314
  advertising decisions regarding, 48–49
  advertising departments within, 186–190
  advertising impact on, 91–93
  advertising as subsidy of, 104, 119–121
  available data on, 309–310
  budget and selecting, 323–325
  business-to-business ad use of, 564
  cable television/delivery systems, 316–317
  changes in buying/selling methods, 312, 315
  Channel One, 515–516
  clearance policies by, 150–154
  compensation commissions from, 181
  determining strategy for, 209
  direct, 489–496, 517
  directory advertising, 506–509
  early advertising through, 21–23
  global expenditures, 588
  global strategy, 586–589
  government influence over, 93
  increase in global, 573
  increasing advertising volume, 312
  increasing complexity of, 311–312
  information research regarding, 26–27
  in-store, 510, 512–514
  marketing strategy using, 318–319
  market structure changes, 310–311
  mass, 19
  models listed, 328–331
  motion picture advertising, 515
  objectives listed, 319–321
  outdoor, 190, 153–154, 496–506
  out-of-home, 517
  place-based, 556
  plan considerations, 334–339
  plan development, 319–327
  postwar advertising and, 32
  product and media usage data, 315
  public service advertising, 95–97
  representatives, 190
  retailer's mix of, 554–556
  scheduling, 325–327, 329, 346–347
  selecting vehicle and units, 325
  specialty advertising, 509–511
  sports and theater events, 516
  target market and, 321–322
  trend of format integration, 485
  VCRs/videodisc players, 311, 317
  vehicle types, 57–58
  videocassette commercials, 515
  videotex and audiotex, 317–318

work with retail advertisers, 173
  See also Print media; Radio stations; Television
Media associations, 601–602
Media buying services, 18–19, 191, 315
Media Guide International, 587
Media Market Guide (magazine), 603
MEDIAC, 330
Mediamark Research (MRI), Inc., 218, 315, 603
Media mix
  business-to-business advertising, 558–559, 561–562
  retailers, 554–556
Media Records, 219
Media Sexploitation (Key), 78
Media vehicles, 119
Media Week (magazine), 603
Medical News Network, 516
Medium advertising classification, 14
Medium. *See* Media
Men, Messages and Media (Schramm), 120
Merchandising services, newspaper, 429
Message-matrix approach, 291
Message production
  creation/production processes, 404–405
  for electronic media, 412–413
  print media, 405–412
  technology of, 405
  understanding process of, 403–404
Messages
  appeal, 56
  business advertisement, 565
  codes, 56–57
  described, 56–57
  directory advertising, 508
  dominance, 297
  fleeting radio, 477
  fleeting TV, 461
  global visual, 580
  idea statement, 279
  shopping carts, 513
  specialty advertising, 510
  structure, 56
Message strategy
  approaches of industry "greats," 285
  copy platform, 279, 281–282
  creative mix evolution, 283
  creative objectives, 292–297
  creative strategy alternatives listed, 284
  creative work plan, 280
  creativity and, 298–301
  described, 273–274
  determining message idea, 274–279
  electronic (television/radio), 377–401
  Execution emphasis approach, 290
  FCB Strategy Planning Model, 291–292
  Inherent drama approach, 282, 284–285
  judgement criteria, 297–298
  making tactical decisions, 282
  positioning approach, 290–291
  print advertising, 361–375
  unique selling proposition (USP), 288–289
  visualizing TV commercial, 394
  vs. message tactics, 274
Method of presentation, 56
"Me-too" products, 46

Metro, 483
Miller, James C., III, 81, 144
Minorities, 244–245, 311
Mirror Makers, The (Fox), 72
Modern Maturity (magazine), 310, 442
Montgomery Ward catalog, 490
Moore, William, 78
Morris the Cat/9-Lives campaign, 209
Morton Salt Company's campaign, 142
Motion picture advertising, 515, 586
Motion Picture Association of America (MPAA), 154
Movement, layout, 370–371
Moving power, 8
MPAA's rating system, 155
MTV global market analysis, 218–219
Multinational corporation, 573
Multi-point distribution system (MDS), 317
Murdock, Rupert, 589
Music, 379, 475
Myers, Matthew, 134
Myers Marketing Research, 462

Nader, Ralph, 130, 138
Narrative commercial, 379–380
Narrative copy, 367
Narrowcasting, 397
National advertising
  described, 14
  inserts used in, 440
  media reps selling, 190
  newspaper, 186, 188, 429, 431–432
  newspaper rates for, 436–437
  newspaper supplements, 440–441
  spot advertising, 459–460
  television, 554
  transit advertising used in, 502
  vs. retail, 110–111, 549–550
National Advertising Division (NAD), 146–149, 601
National Advertising Review Board (NARB), 146–149, 601
National Association of Attorneys General (NAAG), 145
National Association of Broadcasters
  address/telephone, 602
  antitrust violations in 1982, 155
  guidelines for children's advertising, 83
  history of advertising codes, 150–151
  sponsor of All-Radio Methodology Study (ARMS), 480
National Biscuit Company, 23–25
National Broadcasting Company (NBC), 459
National Cash Register (NCR), 576
National Organization for Women (NOW), 84
National Retail Federation, 603
National Vigilance Committee (1912), 25
National Yellow Pages Service, 602
Neilson vs. Harriscope, 135
Nestlé S.A., 569
Networks
  media, 188–189, 459
  telecasting, 459
New Industrial State, The (Galbraith), 118
Newspac, 453
Newspaper Advertising Bureau, Inc., 602
Newspapers

advantages of advertising in, 425, 428–430
advertising department within, 186, 188
audiences, 440
circulation trends, 424–425
clearance policies, 151
controlled circulation classification, 425
cooperative advertising, 423–424
future trends, 453
inserts vs. ROP, 439–440
Isvestia advertisements, 590
limitations of, 430–432
market considerations, 438–439
media described, 57
media plan development, 348–351
merchandising services, 429
primary vs. supplementary usage, 439
rate comparisons, 438
rate structures listed, 436–437
readership patterns, 431
retailer use of, 554–556
sizes and shapes of, 432–433, 436
special techniques available, 429–430
Standard Advertising Units (SAUs) sold in, 312
supplements, 440–441
ten top advertisers, 429
types of advertising, 431–432
USA Today, 426–427
News releases, 542
Newsweek, 589
New York Biscuit, 23
New York Sun (newspaper), 424
Ney, Edward, 286–287
Nickelodeon, 459
Nielsen, A. C., 28
Nielsen Media Research, 230, 467
Nielsen Retail Index, 231
Nielsen Station Index Service, 466
Nielsen Television Index (NTI), 467, 473
9-Lives/Morris the Cat campaign, 209
No competing accounts policy, 25
Noise
  barriers to communication, 59–60
  classifications of, 58–59
Nonalcoholic designations, 133
Nonproduct advertising, 15
Nonpromotional stores, 553
Nonverbal codes, 57
Norris, Vincent, 6, 106, 121
Novello, Antonia, 81
N. W. Ayer & Son
  conducts first research project, 27
  National Biscuit Company campaign, 23–25, 57
NYNEX's radio campaign, 380

Objective-and-task budgeting, 264
Objectives. *See* Advertising objectives
Objects
  communication, 54
  marketing, 38
Obsession perfume campaign, 108–109
Occupation target groups, 243
Ocean Spray campaign, 143
"Offensive" ads, 72–73, 78–80
Offset lithography, 410
Ogilvy & Mather Public Affairs, 541

Ogilvy, David
 on brand image, 6, 32, 289
 on creativity, 300
 hierarchy of creative objectives, 293
 on lasting influence of, 286–288
 on reflective nature of advertising, 71–72
Ogilvy Center for Research and Development, 262
100 gross rating points daily (GRPs), 501
Onkvisit, Sak, 581
On-the-Air pretesting techniques, 224–225
Open houses, 543
Open newspaper rates, 437
Opportunities (marketing), 41–42
Organizational opportunities, 41–42
Osborne, Alex, 285
O'Toole, John, 274, 286, 583
Outdoor advertising
 advantages of, 498
 advertisers, 500
 buying, 500–501
 Cheerios' campaign, 499
 limitations of, 500
 local plant operators, 190
 Longhorn campaign, 526
 self-regulation of, 153–154
 types listed, 496–498
Outdoor Advertising Association of America (OAAA), 153–154, 501, 602
Outside displays, 503

Pace, George W., 447
Packaging, 201–202
Painted bulletins, 497–498
Palmer, Volney, 21
Parrish, Steven, 135
Passive people meters, 467
Patent Office, 132, 136–137
Patronage programs, 536
Pattern campaign, 583–584
Pease, Otis, 37
Penetration studies, 466
People-metered television, 230
People meters, 467
Pepsi-Cola global campaign, 582, 589
Percent-of-sales budgeting, 264–265
Perdue, Frank, 295
"Permissible lies," 76
Personal computers (PCs), 315
 See also Computer technology
Personality commercial, 381
Personal selling
 defining, 12
 marketing mix role of, 203–204
 promotion mix element, 44
Person-to-person communicators, 55–56
Persuasion advertising role, 62
Pertschuk, Michael, 135
Pharmaceutical Manufacturers Association, 154
Photo animation technique, 393
Photoengravers, 191
Photography
 digital stripping, 411
 in layouts, 373
 photo animation technique, 393
 public relation, 543

stop motion technique, 393
 using, 191
Photomatic technique, 384
Photoprints, 412
Photostats, 412
Physiological pretesting methods, 225
Picas, 407
Picture-caption layout, 369
Picture-cluster layout, 369
Pine Sol "graffiti" commercials, 394–395
Place-based media, 556
Planning process, 4, 10
Plastic Pig awards, 84
Plummer, Joseph T., 246
Pointing devices, 371
Point-of-Purchase Advertising Institute, Inc., 602
Point-of-purchase displays (P-O-P), 512–513, 539, 555
Point-of-Research Purchase Advertising Institute (POPAI), 513, 555
Point system, typeface, 407
Political advertising, 89–91, 128
Political considerations, 574, 589–590
Pollay, Richard W., 72
Pollet, Richard, 152
Pool, Ken, 462
POP Radio network, 514
Positioning creative strategy, 284
Positioning message approach, 290–291
Postal regulations, 493
Postal Service, 132
Postcard, 491
Poster advertising, 496–497, 527
Posttesting
 awareness and attitude tests, 228–229
 defining, 221
 market tests/monitoring, 230–231
 measures of past sales, 231
 readership tests, 227–228
 recall tests, 228
Postwar advertising, 32
Potter, David, 6
Power, J. D., 446
Powers, John E., 285
Precipitation advertising role, 62
Preemptive creative strategy, 284
Premium position buy, 436
Premiums, 534–535
Press conferences, 542
Press relations, 542
Preston, Ivan, 76
Pretesting
 defining, 221
 dummy advertising vehicles, 223
 focus groups, 223–224
 inquiry/direct response, 229
 market tests, 229
 on-the-air techniques, 224–225
 physiological methods, 225
 projective techniques, 225–226
 single source services, 229–230
 theater-type tests, 224
Pretesting Company, 451
Prices
 advertising and, 109–111
 advertising and added value, 111–115

impact on media planning, 318–319
 marketing impact of setting, 202–203
 promotions, 536
 strategy, 43
Primary advertising, 15–16
Primary medium, 439
Primary research, 215
Principles of Economics (Marshal), 104
Print advertising
 body text/copy, 361, 365–367
 Colgate international, 572
 duplicating advertisement, 412
 headlines, 362–366
 illustrations, 371–373
 layout, 368–371
 Longhorn campaign, 525
 printing the, 410–412
 See also Copy
Printers' Ink (1888), 22, 25–26, 139, 156
Printers' Ink Statute (1911), 25
Printing methods, 410–412
Print media
 advertisement duplication, 412
 illustration reproduction, 408–410
 media plan development, 348–358
 printing the advertisement, 410–411
 specifying type, 407
 type categories listed, 406–407
 typesetting, 408
 types listed, 57
 use of technology in, 405
 See also Magazines; Newspapers
Procter & Gamble, 569, 579
Production
 direct mail, 494
 instructions, 368
Production houses, 19, 191, 420
Production-only service, 420
Product life cycle (PLC), 45–46, 321, 326
Product positioning, 218
Products
 advertising clearance issues and, 153
 benefit segmentation, 247–248
 brand identification, 381
 brand management system, 166–167
 category management system, 167–168
 checklist of budgeting consideration, 268–270
 classifying illustrations of, 372–373
 commercial camouflage of, 295
 comparative advertisements of, 77–78
 competing ad accounts, 183
 controversial, 80–82
 criticism of advertising, 71
 factors determining prices, 109–115
 global strategy for, 580
 handling publicity about, 542
 house agency familiarity with, 170
 as marketing mix ingredient, 201–202
 "me-too," 46
 personality of, 289, 318
 prestige of magazine ad, 445
 pricing strategy for, 318–319
 radio expenditures by, 478
 regulations regarding, 129
 repurchase cycle, 321
 spelling out name of, 382

strategic research on, 217–218
strategy, 43
usage data, 315
Professional advertising, 13, 558–559
Profile Bread campaign, 143
Programming format
radio, 475–476
technology and radio, 480–481
Program rating, 468
Progressive set, 410
Projective pretesting techniques, 225–226
Promotion
defining, 12
determining mix, 43–46
determining strategies, 46–47
in marketing mix, 203–204
media planning and, 319
personal selling as, 12
shift from advertising to, 268
strategy, 43
targeting individuals through, 33
via floppy disks, 564
within magazines, 190
See also Sales promotion
Promotional stores, 551, 553
Proof, 412
Proportion, layout, 371
Prototype campaign, 583–584
Psychographics, 245–246
Psychological noise, 59
Publications
business and farm, 562
consumer, 443
directories and trade magazines listed, 602–603
international editions of, 589
public relation, 542
Public Broadcasting System (PBS), 459
Publicity, 12
Public policy (global), 590–591
Public relations
agencies, 19
defining, 12, 204
functions, 542
institutional advertising as, 543–544
as promotion mix element, 44
size and organizations, 541
study on impact of, 116–118
techniques listed, 542–543
vs. advertising, 540–541
See also Communication
Public Relations Group, 541
Public Relations Society of America, 603
Public. *See* Marketers
Public service advertising, 97
Puffery, 76
Pulitzer, Joseph, 424
Pull strategy, 46–47
Push money, 539
Push strategy, 46–47
Pyszka, Ronald H., 331

Qualman, Jay, 446
Quantitative/experimental budgeting, 265–266
Quelch, John, 581

Race target market, 244–245

RADAR (Radio's All-Dimension Audience Research), 481–482
Radio Advertising Bureau, Inc., 378–480, 602
Radio Expenditure Report (RER), 219
Radio Luxembourg, 589
Radio stations
advertising advantages, 475–477
advertising department within, 188
audiences, 476–477, 479–482
commercial classifications, 378–381
creating effective commercials, 381–383
international coverage of, 589
limitations of radio, 477–478
media plan development, 347–348
message tactics, 377–401
networks, 188–189
postwar advertising and, 32, 474–475
programming trends, 479
rate structure, 482–484
technology and programming of, 480–481
ten top advertisers, 478–479
types of advertisers, 474
types described, 474–478
See also Commercials (radio)
Range Rover campaign, 200
Rates & Data directory (Yellow Pages), 509
Rates
magazines, 452
media, 309
national vs. retail, 436–437
newspapers, 436–438
radio, 482–484
television, 472–473
Rational appeals, 56
Ray, Michael, 254, 279, 293
Reach, media, 319–320
Reader's Digest, 449, 573, 589
Readership posttesting, 227–228
Readex Readership Research, 222
Reason-why copy, 22–23, 366
Rebates, 537–538
Recall Plus, 224–225
Recall posttesting, 228–229
Receivers, 58
Recessions
advertising during, 116–118
client loyalty during, 169
Reeves, Rosser
hierarchy of creative objectives, 293
lasting influence of, 287
Unique Selling Proposition (USP) approach, 288–289
Regional radio channel, 475
Regular directory listings, 506
Regulations
advertising, 127–129
advertising industry self-, 145–157
areas controlled by, 129
deceptive advertising, 139–144
environment created by, 11, 129–137
major laws/agencies affecting, 132–133
political advertising, 90–91, 128
state and municipal, 145
tobacco products, 134–135
trademark infringement, 136–137
See also Federal Communications Commis-

sion (FCC); Federal Trade Commission (FTC)
Reilly, James C., 206
Reinforcement advertising role, 62
Reinhard, Keith, 287
Reis, Al, 290
Relief printing, 410
Religious target market, 244–245
Reminder advertising role, 62, 64
Reproduction
magazine, 445
print media color, 409
Research
on advertising and business cycle, 116–118
advertising data sources listed, 603
on advertising duration, 122–123
on advertising media subsidy, 119–121
on advertising and prices, 109–111
on advertising and teen drinking, 81
on advertising-to-sales (A/S) ratio, 262
on audiences, 57–58, 477, 468–482
on business-to-business ads, 561
on children's advertising, 83–84
on client loyalty to agencies, 169
companies which provide, 218–219
comparative claims effectiveness, 77–78
on creativity, 300–301
on cultural values, 7, 230
directory advertising, 508
on effective magazine ads, 451
establishing information needs, 214–215
on facilitation of marketing goals, 248–251
on global market, 584–585
on magazine readership patterns, 449–450
MTV market analysis, 218–219
on newspaper readership, 431
on personality profiles, 245–246
on point-of-purchase (P-O-P) displays, 512–513
pretesting/posttesting, 219–231
primary, 215
process steps in, 213–214
provided by ad agency, 179
secondary sources of, 215
on sexy advertising, 79–80
on singles market, 244
on stereotyping, 89
strategic, 207–208, 215–220
on television commercials, 394–400
on TV effectiveness, 462–463
on TV stations, 466
on using original artwork, 373
See also Information
Research companies, 19, 192, 194
Resistance to counterattack, 297
Resonance strategy, 284
Resor, Helen, 285
Retail advertising
assistance in, 556
business-to-business, 558–565
cooperative (co-op), 423–424, 539, 556–558
described, 172–174
local TV, 460
newspaper, 186
newspaper rates for, 436–437
transit advertising for, 502
vs. national, 110–111, 549–550

Retailers
  advertising by, 21
  increased competition among, 25
  media mix, 554–556
  nonpromotional stores, 553
  promotional stores, 551, 553
  semipromotional stores, 553–554
  trends, 550–552
Reuben H. Donnelley Corporation, 536
Revenues
  ad agency compensation, 181–183
  media reps, 190–191
  percentage by media type, 187
  for U.S. ad agencies (1992), 175–176
  See also Expenditures
Revlon's global advertising, 569
Reward emphasis slogans, 304
Riney, Hal, 285, 292
Robinson-Patman Act, 558
Rogers, Everett, 55
Rolling Stone advertising campaign, 119–120
Roman, Kenneth, 298–299, 378
Roman typeface, 406
ROP (run-of-paper) rate schedule, 436, 439–440
Rossiter, Donovan, 248
Rossiter, Percy, 248
Roster recall method, 466–467
Rotating faces, 498
Rotoscoping technique, 392
Rough layout, 368
Rowell, George P., 21–22
Rowen, Harold, 550
Rowland Worldwide, 541
RTG, 483
Rubicam, Raymond, 285
Run-of-paper (ROP) color, 428
Ryder Trucks campaign, 205

Saatchi & Saatchi, 570, 576
Sales
  advertising role in, 45–46
  advertising-to-sales (A/S) ratio, 262, 266
  measures of past, 231
  pretesting and posttesting, 229–231
Sales letter, 490
Salesperson contests, 539
Sales promotion
  ad agency services in, 179
  budgeting for, 260–261
  consumer, 532–538
  described, 12, 204, 531–532
  as promotion mix element, 44
  trade, 538–539
  See also Promotion
SAMI/Burke, 230
Sample design, 215
Sampling, 535–536
Samuelson, Paul, 115
Sandage, Charles, 6
San Serifs typeface, 407
Satellite transmission
  AD/SAT, 453
  global advertisers use of, 573, 589, 593
  types listed, 316–317
  See also Commercials (television); Television

ScanTrack, 231
Scarborough Research Corporation, 440
Scharbo, Ron, 520
Scheduling (media)
  communication and, 335–337
  selecting, 325–327, 329
Schramm, Wilbur, 120
Schudson, Michael, 6
Scientific Advertising (Hopkins), 286
Scott, Walter Dill, 25
Screen print, 410–411
Script typeface, 407
Seagram advertising campaign, 78
Seasonality, 345
Secondary research sources, 215
Second-tier brands, 294–295
Securities and Exchange Commission, 132, 137
Segmentation
  benefit, 246–248
  psychographics and lifestyle, 245–246
  See also Demographic factors; Geographic segmentation
Selective advertising, 15–16
Self-mailer, 493
Self-regulation
  advertising industry, 145–157
  by advertising associations, 154
  by advertising press, 156
  by agencies, 154
  by trade associations, 154–155
  NAD/NARB, 146–149
  outdoor advertising, 153–154
  through media clearance, 150–154
  See also Regulations
Selling concept, 39–40
Semantic noise, 59
Semipromotional stores, 553
Serigraphy, 410–411
Service, 268–270
Sets in use, 468
Sex
  innovation of using, 57
  research on using, 79–80
Shandwick-Kaufman Public Relations, 541
Share of audience, 468
  See also Audiences
Share-of-voice, 51
Shaver, Thomas W., 244
Shaw, John J., 581
Shedd Aquarium/Oceanarium, 334–339
Shoppers' Video and Nynex Computer Services Company, 514
Shopping cart advertising, 513–514
Shopping newspaper, 425
Showcase stores, 552
SHR, 483
Sign manipulation, 52–53
Simmons Market Research Bureau (SMRB), 190, 218, 245, 315, 603
Singing commercial, 379
Single-mindedness, 297
Single source services, 229–230
Size, movement and, 371
Sky wave, 475
Slick, 408, 412
Sliding scale, newspaper, 437

Slogans
  action emphasis, 304
  described, 303–304
  reward emphasis, 304
Smikle, Ken, 244
Smokey the Bear campaign, 96–97
Social communication, 37–38
  See also Communication
Social/cultural environment
  criticism of advertising within, 71–73
  current changes in, 310–311
  defining advertising, 9
  impact on advertising, 69–70
  See also Cultural values
Social issues
  advertising to children, 83–84
  controversial products, 80–82
  impact of advertising, 91
  negative beliefs regarding ads, 74
  public service advertising, 95–97
  See also Ethics
Solanot, Ruben, 235, 259
Solar-powered signs, 498
Sound
  music, 475
  singing commercial, 379
  use of, 382
Source identification, 54, 55
Space directory listings, 506
Speakers, public relation, 543
Special events, 542
Special newspaper advertising, 431
Specialty advertising, 509–511
Specialty Advertising Association International, 602
Specificity, 297
Spectaculars, 498
Spiffs, 539
Split run testing, 448
Sport events advertising, 516
Spot advertising, 459–460
Spot announcements
  described, 459–460
  for international television, 584, 586
  political, 89
  vs. programs, 465
Stadium scoreboards, 516
Standard Advertising Unit (SAU), 312, 433, 436
Standard Directory of Advertisers, 603
Standard Directory of Advertising Agencies, 603
Standard layout, 369
Standard of living, 5
Standard of Practice (AAAA), 154
Standard Rate & Data Service (SRDS), 218, 436, 443–444
  address/telephone, 603
  mailing lists available from, 495
  outdoor advertising rates, 501
  radio stations listed, 477
Starch, Daniel, 28
Starch INRA Hooper, Inc., 222, 570, 603
Starkist tuna campaign, 284–285
Station posters, 504
Stereotypes
  advertising challenges, 89

of African Americans, 87–89
of the elderly, 86–87
of Hispanics, 86
of women, 84–87
Stereophonic FM radio, 475, 479
Stop motion technique, 393
Stopping power, 8
Storyboard, 60
Straight announcement commercials, 385
Straight commercial, 380–381
Strategic Planning Institute, 262
Strategic research
    competitive situation, 218–219
    consumer, 216–217
    defining, 215–216
    market analysis, 218
    product, 217–218
    sources for, 220
    See also Research
Strategy adherence, 297
Strategy fit, 297
Strategy process
    sample of media, 340–347
    summery of, 4
Strickland, D. E., 81
Subculture markets, 311
Subheads, 365
Subliminal advertising, 78
Subliminal Seduction (Key), 78
Subscription television (STV), 316
Subsidy (advertising as), 104
Substantiality, 240
Sullivan, Louis, 81
Superstations, 316
Supplementary medium, 439
Supplements, newspaper, 440–441
Suppliers, 510
Survey of Buying Power-Market Statistics,
    The, 603
Sweepstakes, 536–537
Symbols. *See* Identifying symbols
Syndicated art services, 173–174
Syndicated market research services, 315
Syndicated national supplement, 440
Syndicated television, 189, 457, 458
    See also Television
Tabloid inserts, 440
Tabloid size, 425
Tachistoscope, 225
Target markets
    advantages of, 239–240
    basis for, 240
    benefit segmentation, 246–247
    defining the, 43, 321–322
    determining, 238, 241–245
    geographic factors, 245
    media plan consideration, 335
    part of copy platform, 279
    psychographics/consumer lifestyle, 245–246,
        341–345
    religious, 244–245
    TV rates and, 473
    types of strategies for, 240–241
    See also Consumers
Target segment fit, 297
Taster's Choice coffee commercials, 383
Technology

digital stripping, 411
future trends in radio/TV, 485
global advertising and, 593
illustration/color options, 405, 410
newspaper/magazine future trends, 453
radio and programming, 480–481
used in message production, 405
See also Computer technology
Telephone coincidental method, 466
Television
    ABC clearance guidelines, 152
    advantages of, 460–461
    advertising department within, 188
    advertising to children on, 83–84
    audience, 466–471
    audiotex, 318
    business-to-business ad use of, 564
    cable, 316–317, 457
    cartoon program advertising, 136
    changes in, 311
    clearance procedures, 151
    cost comparisons, 473
    effectiveness of, 462–463
    global spot announcements, 584
    impact of cable, 316–317
    independent program producers, 189
    infomercials, 133–134
    irritating commercials on, 78–80
    limitations of, 461–464
    local advertising on, 460
    message tactics, 377–401
    narrowcasting, 397
    national spot advertising, 459–460
    networks, 188–189, 459
    people-metered, 230
    political spot announcements, 89
    postwar advertising and, 32
    presentation techniques listed, 392–393
    program vs. spot announcements, 465–466
    rate structure, 472–473
    station selection, 466
    storyboards, 383–384
    syndicated, 189, 457, 458
    ten top advertisers, 464–465
    time-units sold, 312
    videodisc players (VDPs), 317
    videotex, 317
    See also Commercials (television); Media;
        Videocassette recorders (VCRs)
Television Bureau of Advertising, Inc.,
    602
Testimonials
    celebrity commercials, 386–390
    copy, 67, 565
    illustrations which are, 373
Theater advertising, 516
Theater-type pretesting, 224
Theme, 56, 381, 382
Thompson, J. Walter, 16, 27
Threat appeal, 281
Thumbnail sketches, 368
Tie-in advertising, 30
Time, 573, 589
Time frame, 391
Time-units, 312
Tobacco products, 80–82, 133–135
Tone

competitive, 281
copy, 279
Total audience, 468
    See also Audiences
Total market coverage (TMC), 429–430
Total promotion mix fit, 297
Total Survey Area (TSA), 483
Tours, 543
Toy Manufacturers Association, 154
Trade advertising, 13, 203, 558
Trade agreements, 574
Trade associations, 154–155, 174
Trade characters, 303, 579
Trade deals, 539
Trade incentives, 539
Trademark infringement, 136–137
Trademark items, 507
Trade name, 302
Trade sales promotions
    cooperative advertising (Co-op), 423–424,
        539, 556–558
    described, 532, 538
    point-of-purchase advertising, 539
    salesperson contests and incentives, 539
    trade incentives and deals, 539
    trade shows/conventions, 538–539
Trade Show Bureau, 602
Trade shows, 538–539, 562–563
Trading stamps, 536
Traffic department (agency), 179
Transformational advertising, 281
Transit advertising
    advantages of, 504
    buying, 504–506
    car cards, 502
    described, 501–502
    example of, 505
    outside displays, 503
    station posters, 504
Tribe, Laurence H., 134
Tri-vision, 498
Trout & Reis agency, 290
Trout, Jack, 290, 389
TV Answer, 317
Typographers, 191
Typography
    described, 406
    specifying type, 407
    type categories listed, 406–407
    typesetting, 408

Undifferentiation strategy, 241
Uneeda biscuit campaign, 23–25
UNESCO (United Nations Educational, Scien-
    tific and Cultural Organization), 577
Unilever, 569, 577, 579
Unique selling proposition (USP), 56, 284,
    287, 288–289
"United Colors of Benetton" campaign, 69–70
United State Baking Company, 23
United States
    advertising expenditures in 1992, 570
    advertising growth vs. overseas, 314
    global transfer of trade characters, 579
    increased international trade, 574
    international focus of marketers, 569

Postal Service, 137
    trade agreements, 574, 591
United States Information Agency, 589
Unit of sale budgeting, 265
Urbanization
    impact on advertising, 22–23
    impact on manufacturers, 19–21
Usage rates, consumer, 246–247
USAir, 592
U.S. Army recruiting campaign, 274, 277
USA Today, 426–427
USA Weekend, 441
U.S. Brewers Association, 154
USSR, 574

Vale, Norman, 578
Values
    added, 111–113
    perceived, 114–115
    research on cultural, 17, 230
    See also Cultural values
Values and lifestyles (VALS), 245–247
Vaughn, Richard, 253, 291, 293
Veloxes, 412
Verbal codes, 57
Vertical publications, 562
Video billboard, 498
Videocassette recorders (VCRs)

impact of, 311, 317
    public relation videotapes, 543
    used by marketers, 564
    videotape commercials, 515
    zapping and grazing with, 382–383
    See also Zipping
Videodisc players (VDPs), 317
VideoOcart, 513–514
Videotex, 317
Voice-overs, 85
Volkswagen campaign, 290

Wall Street Journal, 573, 589
Wal-Mart, 551, 553
Walton, Sam, 551
Wanamaker, John, 8
Want ads. *See* Classified advertising
War Advertising Council, 31
Warehouse clubs, 552
Warner-Lamert's Listerine campaign, 144
Watson, John B., 27
Wax, Ed, 169
Weinberger, Casper, 138
Weithas, William, 287–288
Wells, Mary, 285
Wells, William, 293
Wheeler-Lea Amendments (1938), 30, 132,
    137

See also Federal Trade Commission (FTC)
White, Gordon E., 273
"White-coat" prohibition, 152
White space, 371
Whittle Communications, 515–516
Wholesalers, 21
Wilkie, William, 55, 59–60
Wine Institute, 154
Wireless cable television, 317
Women
    advertising stereotypes of, 84–87
    League of Advertising Women of New
        York, The, 25–26
    proportion of working, 310
Women Against Pornography, 84
Wood, James Playsted, 30
World War II advertising, 30–31
WPP Group, 570

Yellow Pages advertising, 506–509, 555–556
Yellow Pages Publishers Association (YPPA),
    509
Young & Rubicam agency, 330, 569, 576, 587
Young, James Webb, 285, 300–301

Zapping, 382–383
Zipping, 311, 318, 382–383, 461
Zone editions, 429

CREDITS

Figure 18.17 ActMedia, Inc.
Figure 18.18 VideOcart, Inc.

Figure 19.5 Tyson Foods, Inc.
Figure 19.6 Caterpillar, Inc.
Figure 19.7 American Express/Budget.
Figure 19.8 Reprinted courtesy of Land's End Catalog.
Figure 19.9 Miles Inc./Warner Bros., Inc.
Figure 19.10 Caterpillar Engine Division at Mossville.
Figure 19.12 The Kroger Co.
Box, p. 545 Del Monte Foods
Figure 19.13 U.S. Council for Energy Awareness.

Figure 20.1 Kmart Corporation.
Box, p. 552 (left) Courtesy of Nike, Inc.
Box, p. 552 (right) Courtesy of Burger King Corporation
Figure 20.2 Wal-Mart
Figure 20.3 Radio Shack/Tandy Corporation
Figure 20.4 Tiffany & Co.
Figure 20.5 Canon U.S.A., Inc.
Figure 20.6 Magazine Publishers of America/Times Mirror.
Box, p. 560 Learjet, Inc.
Figure 20.7 Forbes Magazine.
Figure 20.8 Caterpillar, Inc.

Figure 21.1 The Hearst Corporation.
Figure 21.3 Colgate Palmolive Company
Box, p. 578 Courtesy of International Advertising Association.
Figure 21.4 Sony/Ernst & Partners.
Figure 21.5 D.P.Z. Propaganda.
Figure 21.6 Coppertone Tanning Division of Schering Plouth Corp./Teran Publicidad.
Figure 21.7 Volkswagen.
Figure 21.8 Sharp Electronics Corp. Dentsu, Inc. Tokyo.
Figure 21.9 Panasonic/Saatchi & Saatchi Advertising.
Figure 21.10 Levi Strauss & Co.
Figure 21.11 Smithkline Beecham.
Figure 21.12 Pepsi-Cola International.
Figure 21.13 Young & Rubicam and Hessischer Rundfunk.
Box, p. 592 Courtesy of USAir and CIA-Ketchum, Paris.

SOURCE LIST

Figure 1.3 Reproduced from *Advertising in Contemporary Society: Perspectives Toward Understanding* with the permission of South-Western Publishing Co. Copyright © 1986 by South-Western Publishing Co. All rights reserved.
Figure 1.9 From article, "Corporate Advocacy Advertising and Political Influence" by Robert Waltzer from *Public Relations.* Spring 1988, Volume 14. Reprinted by permission of JAI Press, Inc.
Box, p. 45 From article, "Seeing is Believing" by Elinor U. Biggs from *The Advertiser,* Spring 1992. Reprinted with permission from The Advertiser, a publication of the Association of National Advertisers, Inc., 120 E. 38th St., NY, NY 10016. © 1992.
Figure 2.3 & 2.4 Adapted from *Marketing.* Third Edition by Louis E. Boone and David L. Kurtz. Copyright © 1987 by Louis E. Boone and David L. Kurtz. Reprinted by permission of the authors.
Figure 2.5 Figure from *Contemporary Marketing* by Louis E. Boone and David L. Kurtz, copyright © 1986 by The Dryden Press, reproduced by the permission of the publisher.

Figure 2.6 Figure from *Contemporary Marketing,* Seventh Edition by Louis E. Boone and L. Kurtz, copyright © 1992 by The Dryden Press, reproduced by permission of the publisher.
Figure 2.13 From *The Dynamics of Mass Communication* by Joseph R. Dominick. Copyright © 1990 by Joseph R. Dominick. Reprinted with the permission of McGraw-Hill Book Company.
Figure 2.17 From *The Dynamics of Mass Communication* by Joseph R. Dominick. Copyright © 1990 by Joseph R. Dominick. Reprinted with the permission of McGraw-Hill Book Company.
Box, p. 81 From article, "Don't Blame Advertising for Teenage Drinking" by James C. Sanders from *USA Today.* Copyright © 1991, *USA Today.* Reprinted with permission.
Box, p. 85 AI Excerpt from article, "The Sexism Watch" from *U.S. News & World Report.* Copyright © March 27, 1989, U.S. News & World Report. Reprinted by permission of U.S. News & World Report.
Box, p. 87 Adapted from article, "She's Come a Long Way Baby" from *Time.* Copyright © 1990 Time, Inc. Reprinted by permission.
Box, p. 88 Excerpt from article, "Going for the Gold" by Melinda Beck, from *Newsweek,* April 23, 1990. Copyright © 1990, Newsweek, Inc. All rights reserved. Reprinted by permission.
Box, p. 114 From article, "Value-added Ads: The Problem, Not the Solution" by Lawrence H. Wortzel from *Advertising Age.* Reprinted with permission from the November 6, 1989 issue of Advertising Age. Copyright © 1989 by Crain Communication Inc.
Box, p. 128 From article, "Regulate Political Ads? They Give Us a Bad Image" by John O'Toole from *Advertising Age.* Reprinted with permission from the November 28, 1988 issue of Advertising Age. Copyright © 1988 by Crain Communication Inc.
Box, p. 130 Reprinted from Volume II, Number 1, April 1990 issue of *At Home With Computers* published by the Direct Selling Education Foundation. DSEF is a 501 c (3) not-for-profit public education institution.
Box, p. 134 Excerpt from article, "Tobacco Marketers Claim Ruling Spares Them From Changing Ads" by Joanne Lipman from *The Wall Street Journal.* Reprinted by permission of The Wall Street Journal, Copyright © 1992 Dow Jones & Company, Inc. All Rights Reserved Worldwide.
Box, p. 152 From article, "ABC Seeks to Relax Advertising Guidelines" by Skip Wallenberg from *Marketing News,* October 14, 1991. Reprinted by permission of American Marketing Association.
Box, p. 166 Excerpt from article, "The Value of Evaluating Agency Performance" by Stephen W. Rutledge from *The Advertiser.* Fall, 1991. Reprinted with the permission from the Advertiser, a publication of the Association of National Advertisers, Inc., 120 East 38th Street, NY, NY 10016, © 1992.
Box, p. 169 From article, "Study Shows Clients Jump Quickly" by Joanne Lipman from *The Wall Street Journal.* Reprinted by permission of The Wall Street Journal, Copyright © 1992 Dow Jones & Company, Inc. All Rights Reserved Worldwide.
Table 6.1 Reprinted with permission from

the January 6, 1992 issue of *Advertising Age.* Copyright © 1992 by Crain Communications, Inc.
Tables 6.2, 6.3, 6.4, and 6.5 Reprinted with permission from the April 13, 1992 issue of *Advertising Age.* Copyright © 1992 by Crain Communications, Inc.
Table 6.6 Reprinted with permission from the January 6, 1992 issue of *Advertising Age.* Copyright © 1992 by Crain Communications, Inc.
Box, p. 193 Adapted from article, "Martin Mayer Returns," reprinted with permission from the March 25, 1991 issue of *Advertising Age.* Copyright © 1991 by Crain Communications, Inc.
Figure 8.1 Figure from *Marketing Research: Methodological Foundations.* Fifth Edition by Gilbert A. Churchill, copyright © 1991 by the Dryden Press, reproduced by permission of the publisher.
Table 8.1 Reprinted with permission from the November 18, 1991 issue of *Advertising Age.* Copyright © 1991 by Crain Communications, Inc.
Box, p. 220 & 222 From *Fundamentals of Advertising Research* by A. D. Fletcher and T. A. Bowers. Copyright © 1991 by A. D. Fletcher and T. A. Bowers. Reprinted by permission of Wadsworth Publishing Company.
Figure 9.5 From article, "Home Alone-With $660 Billion" by Laura Zinn from *Business Week.* Reprinted from July 29, 1991 issue of Business Week by special permission, copyright © 1991 by McGraw-Hill, Inc.
Figure 9.7 From article, "A Modernized Family Life Cycle" by Patrick E. Murphy and William A. Staples from *Journal of Consumer Research,* June 1979. Reprinted with the permission of The University of Chicago Press.
Figure 9.13 From *Defining Advertising Goals for Measured Advertising Results* by Russell H. Colley. Copyright © 1961 by Russell H. Colley. Reprinted by permission of The Association of National Advertisers, Inc.
Figure 10.2 Reprinted with permission from the September 23, 1992 issue of *Advertising Age.* Copyright © 1992 by Crain Communications, Inc.
Table 10.4 Reprinted with permission from the January 6, 1992 issue of *Advertising Age.* Copyright © 1992 by Crain Communications, Inc.
Table 10.5 Reprinted by permission from the July 13, 1992 issue of Advertising Age. Copyright © 1992 by Crain Communications, Inc.
Box, p. 275 Adapted from article, "The Moment of Creation" by Paula Champa from *Agency.* Copyright © May/June 1991 by Agency Magazine. Reprinted by permission.
Box, p. 286 "Heroes: Advertising's Creative Greats" from *Agency.* Copyright © Spring 1992 by Agency Magazine. Reprinted by permission.
Box, p. 294 Adapted from article, "That's Entertainment: Creative Leverage Uses Art" by David N. Martin from *Marketing News,* November 6, 1989, Volume 23, Number 3. Reprinted by permission of American Marketing Association.
Box, p. 298 Adapted from article, "Do You Have It?" by Emanuel H. Demby from *Marketing News,* November 8, 1985. Reprinted by permission of American Marketing Association.
Box, p. 322 Courtesy of Tony Nacinordi, Senior VP Associate Media Director, and

Ogilvy & Mather Advertising, New York.
Box, p. 326 "Towards Better Media Comparisons" by Professor Ron Kaatz. Copyright © by and reprinted by permission of the author.
Figure 12.5 Copyright © 1992 by Sammoms Market Research Bureau, Inc. Reprinted by permission.
Figure 12.2 Reprinted with permission from the May 3, 1993 issue of *Advertising Age.* Copyright © 1993 by Crain Communications, Inc.
Table 12.1 Reprinted with permission from the May 4, 1992 issue of *Advertising Age.* Copyright © 1992 by Crain Communications, Inc.
Box, p. 390 Chart of "The Match Game" reprinted by permission of The Total Research Corporation.
Box, p. 395 Adapted from article, "The 15-Second Commercial: Findings & Guidelines" by Paula Kay Pierce from *Topline Newsletter.* Copyright © 1989 by McCollum Spielman Worldwide. Reprinted by permission.
Box, p. 398 Adapted from article, "McCollum Spielman on Humor in Commercials" by Paula Kay Pierce from *Topline Newsletter.* Copyright © 1982 by McCollum Spielman Worldwide. Reprinted by permission.
Box, p. 399 Adapted from article, "Consumers' Love-Hate Relationship With Commercials" by Paula Kay Pierce from *Topline Newsletter.* Copyright © 1992 by McCollum Spielman Worldwide. Reprinted by permission.
Figure 15.1 David A. Aaker/Rajeev Barta/John G. Meyers, *Advertising Management,* 4e, © 1992, p. 441. Adapted by permission of Prentice Hall, Englewood, Cliffs, New Jersey.
Box, p. 416 From article, "Computer Graphics Enliven Car Ads" by John P. Cortez and Cleveland Horton from *Advertising Age.* Reprinted with permission from the September 16, 1991 issue of *Advertising Age.* Copyright © 1991 by Crain Communications, Inc.
Figure 15.7 Adapted from What Every Account Executive Should Know About Television Commercial Production, 1989. Reprinted by permission of the American Association of Advertising Agencies, Inc.
Box, p. 426 "A Profile of *USA Today,*" copyright ©, USA Today. Reprinted with permission.
Box, p. 434 Excerpt from *Principles and Practices of Classified Advertising* (Reston, VA: Newspaper Association of America, 1991), pp. 1-2. Reprinted with permission by the Newspaper Association of America.
Box, p. 451 Reprinted with permission from Magazine Publishers of America, Inc.
Table 16.1 From *Facts About Newspapers,* 1992 Edition. Copyright © 1992 and reprinted by permission of Newspaper Association of America.
Table 16.2 Reprinted with permission from the April 26, 1993 issue of *Advertising Age.* Copyright © 1993 by Crain Communications, Inc.
Table 16.3 Copyright © 1991 by Simmons Market Research Bureau, Inc. Reprinted by permission.
Table 16.4 From *Newspaper Rates & Data,* June 1993. Copyright by Standard Rate & Data Service. Reprinted by permission.
Table 16.5 From *Facts About Newspapers,*